THE LIFE OF

MAYAKOVSKY

Wiktor Woroszylski

Translated from the Polish by Boleslaw Taborski

The Orion Press　　New York　　1970

☙ Preface ☙

Mayakovsky's life was violent and dramatic. To present it, one need only quote contemporary sources, without any additions or comments.

Contemporary accounts have their value, even when they are uncertain or contradictory. The legend born in a poet's lifetime, in his circle, is part of his life. Sometimes people kill themselves in order not to kill their legend.

I have written a book about another writer, the nineteenth-century utopian, Saltykov Shchedrin, who wanted to change the world. He was a committed writer and his Maximalism was at the root of his personal suffering and literary achievement. In that book, entitled *Dreams Under the Snow*, I allowed myself the experiment of impersonating the hero and speaking in the first person, as if I myself were Saltykov.

This time I am choosing a less audacious, and altogether opposite, method of reconstruction. I want to look at Vladimir Mayakovsky from the outside, excluding conjecture, hypotheses, and my own emotions. Only records of various kinds will be allowed to speak. But this does not mean that I renounce the authorship of this biography. I have gathered the "case records" and arranged them in a certain sequence, in accordance with my understanding of the importance and connection of events. My vision has been shaped by events, and the result of the task I have undertaken could not possibly have been foreseen at the start. I do not, however, delude myself that by accepting the discipline of fact searching I have arrived at an absolutely objective view of the poet and his time. I believe that the picture of Mayakovsky I am presenting is a true one; but it is not a truth read by an impersonal computer. All things considered, it is still "my" Mayakovsky.

Is it my duty to define the genre to which, as I see it, this book belongs? It is closest, perhaps, not so much to literature as to a film chronicle, made up of old shots and captions. Or it may be seen as a play, in which the various characters come on stage not only to relate the story of the hero but to influence it. The course of the play does not, of course, depend on the person who stages it, but he can direct the lighting.

Having been fascinated with Mayakovsky's personality since my earliest youth, I collected and studied material concerning him for many years. However, I would not have been able to publish this book but for the help of many persons, above all in the U.S.S.R., but also in Poland, France, and the United States. I would like to express my most sincere thanks to all those I cannot mention here—symbolically—via the persons who were nearest to Vladimir Mayakovsky: Mme Lila Brik of Moscow and Mr. David Burliuk of Hampton Bays, New York.

W. W.

❦ Contents ❦

Contents

⚜ List of Illustrations ⚜

✤ 1 ✤

Childhood

✤

There is no poet yet; no man, rebel, gypsy, revolutionary, mocker, friend, voyager, lover. There is a child, who one day will be all that; will be Vladimir Mayakovsky, poet.

ALEXANDRA MAYAKOVSKAYA:

. . . At that time we lived in Georgia, in the Bagdadi settlement, in the Bagdadi forestry area. . . . My husband, Vladimir Konstantinovich, was the forester.

The Bagdadi Forest occupied an extensive area. All around us were high mountains, covered with woods. There were many animals in the forest: stags, bears, foxes, boars, hares, squirrels—and a variety of birds.

Gamekeepers occasionally used to bring small animals and birds. Volodya was very fond of animals. He preserved that fondness for living creatures all through his life.

At that time Bagdadi was a remote village. There were no schools, teachers, or doctors. . . . We had great difficulty with the children's education. We sent our eldest daughter, Ludmila, to Tiflis.

There was no real winter in Bagdadi. There were rains and wet snow; strong winds blew. The nights were dark.

Houses in Bagdadi are surrounded by orchards, vineyards, gardens. Beyond them are mountains and forests.

The forest was very near, while the houses stood at great distances from one another. We had no close neighbors.

Jackals used to creep right up to the house. They moved in large packs and howled terribly. Their howling was most unpleasant and frightening.

It was there that I first heard those wild piercing howls. The children could not sleep for fright and I used to reassure them, "Don't be afraid, we have good dogs, they won't let them come near."

. . . Volodya was born on July 7 (or July 19, according to the new calendar), 1893, the same day as his father; for this reason he was named Vladimir. His birthday and that of his father were celebrated on the same day.

We had visits from relatives and friends. We had friends of various nationalities: Georgians, Armenians, Poles . . .

In 1899 we moved to a brick house. The place where the house stood was called "the fortress," but the only remnants of an old fortress were the wall surrounding the house and a trench overgrown with bushes.

We lived upstairs, and below us was the landlord's cellar in which wine was made and kept. We used to be treated to the fresh grape juice, which was called *madjari* in Georgian.

In the courtyard stood empty wine jars—called *tchuri*—so big that the man who washed and cleaned them could get inside them quite comfortably.

When the *tchuri* were lying sideways on the ground, Volodya used to get into one of them and tell his sister, "Go some distance, Olga, and listen to how my voice sounds." He recited the poem "Don Pedro was a cruel king . . ." His voice sounded loud and clear. Volodya was then six years old.

. . . In the fall of 1899, Olga went with Ludmila to Tiflis and entered the same boarding school as her sister. Volodya missed her a great deal. It was the first time he was without Olga.

. . . Nobody taught Volodya to read from the primer. To everybody's great surprise, when he was about six years old he taught himself, almost unnoticed, to read. But his own way of reading seemed too slow to him and he used to ask the grownups to read aloud to him.

Neither his writing nor his arithmetic was good. We had to think seriously about preparing him for school. There were no teachers in Bagdadi and I had to move with my son to Kutais. Vladimir Konstantinovich remained in Bagdadi with my mother, Volodya's grandmother.

We stayed with our good friend, Mme Julia Glushkovsky. She was a teacher and also tended to Volodya's schooling.

But there was no freedom or space in Kutais. The yard was small and enclosed by a high wall. The gate was locked even in the daytime. The children could not run into the street. The landlord kept a watchful eye on his possessions. He feared that someone might find his way into the yard and steal the things lying there. There was a bell attached to the gate which one had to ring, and then the landlord, or someone from his family, opened it.

The rooms had polished waxed floors and one had to walk on very narrow strips of carpet spread all over the house. The landlord, an old veterinary surgeon, was a harsh man. He always picked on Volodya and shouted at him, "Why do you have to walk on the floor. Can't you see the carpets! You're not in the forest now!"

In the window of the room where Volodya sat over his books there hung a cage with a canary. Volodya looked at it with sadness, for until that time he had only seen birds flying freely and singing in the forest.

. . . In May 1902, Volodya took the entrance examination for school.

I made him a pair of long navy blue pants, a white sailor's tunic with an anchor on the sleeve, and bought him a sailor's cap with a ribbon and the word "Sailor" on it. Volodya was very fond of that suit.

On the last day of his examination, Volodya contracted a high temperature: he had typhoid fever. I stayed with him in Kutais, while Ludmila and Olga went to Bagdadi to stay with their father.

The illness was really bad and lasted a long time. We were very worried . . . But he finally recovered. The doctor came and gave him permission to go to Bagdadi. "But please be careful not to drink unboiled water," he said. Volodya remembered those words all his life . . .

Volodya spent the summer in Bagdadi and got much stronger. In the fall, the entire family, except Father, moved to Kutais.

On September 1, Volodya, dressed in his school uniform, went to the same school his father and uncle had attended.

. . . In January 1904, the Russo-Japanese war began. The general mood was one of restlessness. Aunt Anyuta used to come to us from the hospital and talk a lot about the wounded and about the mobilization.

For the summer we went to the forest again and stayed at Nergiyeti, a village adjoining Bagdadi.

The mail was brought to Bagdadi at noon by stagecoach. The distance between Nergiyeti and Bagdadi is four kilometers. Volodya walked to Bagdadi every day to get the mail. On his way back he would read the newspapers. One could walk quite safely on the road. Only occasionally did a cart or a rider on horseback pass by. The newspapers and journals Volodya brought were then read aloud. He listened too. Volodya was very keen on reading all he could get hold of. He used to take the magazines and books, whistle for the dogs, fill his pockets with fruit for himself and bread for the dogs, and then go into the thick of the orchard and lie down under a tree. The dogs, Vega and Boston, lay in the grass nearby and "watched" over him. He spent a great deal of time there reading, undisturbed.

In August 1904, Ludmila went to study in Moscow . . . Volodya entered second grade, Olga fourth. After Ludmila's departure they began to feel grown up. They corresponded with their sister, read a lot, took an interest in social affairs . . .

On January 9, 1905, the first Russian revolution began. In Kutais, as in the rest of the country, there were disturbances among the workers, soldiers, and students.

Volodya, together with his schoolmates, sang "La Varsovienne," "Boldly, Comrades," and other revolutionary songs, in Georgian.

In the spring of 1905, on the banks of the Rion, the revolutionary soldiers and schoolboys held mass meetings at which fiery speeches were made. Volodya used to go there too.

Early in June 1905, Ludmila came home on vacation and we went to Bagdadi together. She brought with her political books and pamphlets, both legal and illegal, and gave them to Volodya to read when she realized that he had grown up intellectually and took an interest in political matters. He was twelve then . . .

Many persons in our circle were of the opinion that we gave the boy too much freedom and independence for his age. But I could see that he was developing in accordance with the needs of the time, so I encouraged Volodya in his interests.

. . . On February 19, 1906, a great misfortune befell our family: quite unexpectedly Volodya's father died of blood poisoning . . .

Three days after the funeral Ludmila arrived. We suffered together. We discussed the situation and decided to move to Moscow.

We were left without a means of livelihood. We never had any savings and my husband died one year before he was due to get his retirement pension. We were given only ten rubles a month as a grant. I applied to the Department of Forestry in St. Petersburg for a full pension. In the meantime we maintained ourselves by selling our furniture. When it was all sold, we borrowed two hundred rubles from a good friend to pay for our journey and set out for Moscow. Our friend told us, "You will pay me back when your children have been educated."

. . . So, on August 1, 1906, we came to settle permanently in Moscow. We found lodgings on the second floor of Jelchinski's house at the corner of Kozichinski Alley and Little Bronna Street. The apartment was empty. We had to borrow money in order to buy the necessary furniture. We managed to get something from friends.

It was difficult to make a start. The big city had its own life. Alone among a million people we decided to fight for our existence, for our future.

I went to St. Petersburg to try to get my pension increased. I was helped in that—through the Ministry of National Estates—by my husband's brother, Mikhail Konstantinovich Mayakovsky. He had been transferred from Tiflis as forester to the Bialowieza Forest and lived in Pruzana. He notified me that I must go to St. Petersburg. After protracted and difficult negotiations, meetings, and applications I was given, for myself and the children, a pension of fifty rubles a month.

On my way back from St. Petersburg I caught pneumonia and was ill for a long time. While I was ill a telegram came from Poland with the news that Mikhail Konstantinovich had died suddenly. I said to Volodya, "Now you are the heir to the Mayakovsky name."

. . . The apartment was expensive. We were advised to sublet one of our three rooms. A Georgian whom Ludmila knew came to live with us. He soon left, but his place was taken by a friend, also Georgian, a second year university student and a Social Democrat.

Ludmila entered her third year at Stroganov College. Olga was placed in the private Jezhova School, thanks to the help of our friends, the Medvyedyevs. Volodya was admitted to the fourth year at School Number Five, where the emphasis was on classical education. The school was situated at the corner of Povarska (now Worovsky) Street and the Great Molchanovka.

In those days electric streetcars ran in the center of the city and horse cars in other districts. The droshky was still a most popular conveyance. Volodya used to walk around Tverska, Sadova, and other streets and alleys, looking at Moscow's monuments, but above all at people and the way they lived in the big city.

On our arrival in Moscow, Volodya and Olga befriended Medvyedyev, the brother of Ludmila's college friend, a native Muscovite, and he used to show them around the city. Medvyedyev was a pupil at School Number Three, two years ahead of Volodya. They used to go to the movies together. Volodya was very interested in and fascinated by the cinema but, for lack of money, he could not go very often. There were few movie houses in Moscow at that time, and the silent films shown there were not very good.

Volodya and Olga also used to attend the evening drawing classes at Stroganov College. Ludmila used to get small jobs, such as firing and coloring wooden objects of all kinds: boxes, caskets, Easter eggs. Volodya was good at drawing and at Kutais he had acquired a knowledge of firing. He helped his sister and in the morning took the finished objects to the store, as Ludmila had to hurry to class. They were paid badly for their work, but it was better than nothing.

Winter came, everything was deep in snow. It was cold and frosty, sleds appeared in the streets. The children enjoyed the winter, skating, skiing, sledding. There had been no real winter in the Caucasus and no winter sports. Here, in the North, everything was new and thrilling. But Volodya was interested above all in his new friends and acquaintances and in the lives of our student tenants. He often looked into their rooms, borrowed books, listened to conversations and discussions.

At thirteen, Volodya was not only physically well developed and looked several years older but he had also developed intellectually: he was widely read, serious, and could mix with the best pupils of more advanced classes and with college students.

Other members of the family, and myself, treated Volodya like an adult, even though he was the youngest child . . .

☙ 2 ☙

Politics

☙

It began in his childhood, at the school in Kutais. The poet mentions this in his autobiography, and his elder sister, Ludmila, quotes the letters which the twelve-year-old Volodya used to write to her. In the reminiscences of the Moscow Bolsheviks—Medvyedyev, Karakhan, and Weger—as well as those of an active member of the Socialist Revolutionary party, Isidore Morchadze, we see Volodya as a thirteen-, fourteen-, and fifteen-year-old conspirator. We see him also through the eyes of the agents shadowing him. From police protocols, transcripts of interrogations, correspondence of the Security Department, and other documents, one can reconstruct the story of the three arrests of a boy who wanted to be a professional revolutionary.

FROM MAYAKOVSKY'S AUTOBIOGRAPHY:

Sister has come from Moscow. Very enthusiastic. Secretly gave me some long sheets of paper. Liked it: big risk. I still remember the first:

> Come to your senses, comrade, come to your senses,
> quickly throw your rifle to the ground . . .

That was revolution. That was verse. Verse and revolution somehow mingled in my head . . .

Demonstrations and mass meetings began. I went too. Pretty. I reacted to colors: the anarchists in black, the Socialist Revolutionaries in red, the Social Democrats in blue, the Federalists in other colors . . .

I began to regard myself as a Social Democrat. I took Father's guns to the Social Democratic committee.

I liked Lassalle, from his appearance. Maybe because he had no beard; looked younger. I got Lassalle mixed up with Demosthenes; used to go to the river Rion and make speeches with stones in my mouth.

FROM A LETTER FROM MAYAKOVSKY TO HIS SISTER, OCTOBER 1905:

Dear Ludmila!

Please forgive my long silence. How are you? Do you have lectures? We had a five-day strike, then the school was closed for four days because we sang "La Marseillaise" in church . . .

FROM A LETTER TO HIS SISTER, NOVEMBER 1905:

. . . So far nothing terrible has happened in Kutais, though both secondary schools went on strike. And with good reason; big guns were pointed at our school; at the other school they went even further: guns were put in the school yard and they said that if there was as much as one shout they would leave no stone unturned . . .

MOSCOW, 1906–1908. FROM THE REMINISCENCES OF SERGEI MEDVYEDYEV:

I cannot say that we were very close to each other: I was a pupil at another school, two years ahead of him; still we were friendly and had common interests. Volodya liked being in my company and that of my schoolmates; he took part in our meetings and conversations. He had no special friend, was rather withdrawn, reserved, and, as we thought then, gloomy. He never talked about personal matters, even with those he knew best, like myself and my school friend, Volodya Gzovsky . . .

There was a Social Democratic circle at our school. Mayakovsky was its only outside member . . . All members of the circle were older than Volodya, but they treated him like an equal . . .

Early in the school year 1907–1908, some time in September or October, I was, with a few others, expelled from the school . . . Shortly afterwards Gzovsky and I got to know a certain comrade, Natasha, and through her devoted ourselves to party activities. We were used for the purpose of liaison between cells and also concerned ourselves with propaganda among workers. I think it was through us that Mayakovsky started this kind of activity . . . Volodya treated his activities and duties as a propagandist most seriously, unlike his school duties which he found more and more onerous . . .

After six months in the fifth year, Volodya decided, early in 1908, to give up school in order to devote himself to professional revolutionary activities. We still saw each other quite often. He used to come to me as before, even though the circle of Volodya's acquaintances widened considerably; he already had friends older than himself among the student revolutionaries who lived with the Mayakovskys as tenants. Whenever he came to me, we talked only in my room. As for the general conversations at the family table, Volodya remained ostentatiously reserved, never took part in them, and was gloomily silent. With people much older than himself he was very independent, free and easy, and did not attempt to be polite. In those days Volodya revealed a somewhat scornful attitude toward people; he never tried to hide the fact if someone did not interest him in the least or he did not care about him. Prone to making jokes, he was sometimes very sharp or even brutal in his remarks, which at that time estranged many people from him.

FROM THE REMINISCENCES OF IVAN KARAKHAN:

Our meetings began with my helping him with his homework. He was very bad at mathematics. He was still a schoolboy and I was a law student in my third year, some ten years older than he. It began with my tutoring . . . When I got to know him better, I started talking to him about various things, to give him illegal publications: *The Spark*, leaflets, proclamations, the writings of Lenin and Plekhanov. Doubtless his first lessons in politics were from me, and it was with me that he took his first steps . . . First he worked with me: made contacts with people and hid illegal publications. He liked working with adults and was annoyed if treated like a child. I observed that trait of his as soon as I met him.

I was then a member of the city committee of the Bolshevik party . . . In the fall of 1907, Mayakovsky, sufficiently prepared, became a full member of the Party and from then on worked on his own.

FROM THE REPORT OF THE MOSCOW SECURITY DEPARTMENT, MARCH 29, 1908:

Acting on the strength of evidence provided by an informer to the effect that a secret printing press had just been installed in Konoplin's house at Chukhnin Alley, on the night of March 29 a search was conducted in the said house, as the result of which the active printing press of the Moscow committee of the Russian Social Democratic Workers party was seized.

THE DEPOSITION OF POLICE OFFICER SOLOVYOV:

. . . I was sent with officer Ryabko to guard the sealed room in Konoplin's house, in the apartment of a tailor, whose name I do not recall . . . At two o'clock in the afternoon a young man called at the tailor's apartment with a bundle under his arm. Later at the police station he said his name was Mayakovsky. Asked to whom he had come, he replied, "To the tailor's." But when the tailor's apprentices were asked about him, they said . . . that the man we had apprehended used to come, not to the tailor, but to the lodgers whose apartment I was guarding . . . On the apprehended man were found the same proclamations as those you are now showing me (exhibit produced) . . .

FROM THE POLICE PROTOCOL:

On March 29, 1908, Vladimir Vladimirovich Mayakovsky, when interrogated, declared that he had brought proclamations for an unknown man, whom he had met under the Pushkin monument in Tverska Street on March 20 and who on that occasion had handed him those proclamations, asking him to take them to Konoplin's house, Apartment No. 7. He had known the man since May 1907 but did not know where he lived at the time. His first name was Alexander.

THE REPLY OF THE HEADMASTER OF SCHOOL NUMBER FIVE TO THE COMMUNICATION OF THE EXAMINING MAGISTRATE:

To your inquiry of May 2, ref. no. 648, I have the honor to inform you that the photograph you enclosed is indeed the likeness of a former fifth-year pupil at my school, Vladimir Mayakovsky, who entered the Moscow Secondary School No. 5 in August 1906 and was, on the decision of the teaching body, stricken from the register as of March 1, 1908, for nonpayment of school fees for the first half of the year 1908. Apart from that, the pupil's mother asked that his documents be returned and a school certificate issued, since "due to illness he cannot continue his education." All documents were returned to the mother, a receipt was given. According to an extract from his birth certificate, Mayakovsky was born on July 7, 1893.

MEDICAL REPORT:

On May 27, 1908, the medical officer of the Moscow city prison, Stepan Stepanovich Khoroshevsky, on orders from the examining officer in cases of special importance at the Moscow District Court, Roudnyev, conducted an examination of the accused minors, Vladimir Mayakovsky and Sergei Ivanov, in order to establish whether the physical and mental development of the accused was normal, with the following results:

Vladimir Vladimirovich Mayakovsky is of strong build and stature, seems older than he really is. He does not suffer from any ailments, though he stated that a year ago he had lung trouble. An objective examination established his lungs to be normal, the heart somewhat enlarged, which can be explained by Mayakovsky's accelerated growth. His pulse is 108 beats per minute . . .

THE EXAMINING MAGISTRATE'S DECISION:

Taking into account the state of health of the accused, his age (14 years), and the fact that his deposition seems trustworthy, I deem it possible to be satisfied with one of the less stringent preventive measures and . . . have decided to put the said Mayakovsky under special police surveillance in his place of residence.

FROM THE LOG BOOK KEPT DURING MAYAKOVSKY'S SURVEILLANCE BY POLICE AGENTS:

August 5, 1908. The "tall" one is residing at Boutyugina's house at 47 Dolgoroukovska Street. At eight in the morning he left the house and proceeded to the upper commerical passageway, where he was lost. At 7:50 in the evening he left the house again, walked up and down Dolgoroukovska Street several times, and returned home . . .

August 7, 1908. At 11:20 in the morning he left the house and proceeded to the City Hotel on Nikolska Street, where he stayed for 35 minutes and returned home. He was not seen leaving the house again . . .

August 9, 1908. At 9:15 in the morning he left the house and proceeded to Filipov's bakery . . . bought some rolls, returned home; he left the house again at eleven in the morning and proceeded to the City Hotel on Nikolska Street, where he stayed 30 minutes; on leaving there he proceeded to Birkel's house . . . where the "Oak" resides, and stayed there for two hours; he then went to Sadova-Soukharevska Street, met an unknown young man, talked to him for a while, then they both went to Kvnetny Boulevard, where they sat on a bench for twenty minutes and then took leave of each other . . .

On August 30, 1908, Mayakovsky was admitted to the preparatory class at the Stroganov School of Industrial Arts. Toward the end of that year the police surveillance was dropped; but it was resumed again on January 16, 1909, when it had been established that he had contacts with members of the Socialist Revolutionary party suspected of participation in expropriation activities.

IN NEW REPORTS MAYAKOVSKY IS DESCRIBED UNDER THE PSEUDONYM "SWIFT," AND MORCHADZE, ONE OF THE MAYAKOVSKYS' TENANTS, ALSO KNOWN AS KORIDZE, A SOCIALIST REVOLUTIONARY, AS "PANCAKE."

January 16, 1909. "Swift" and "Pancake" reside in Boutyugina's house at 47 Dolgoroukovska Street. The arrival of "Pot" had not been noticed. At 11:30 in the morning all three—i.e., "Swift," "Pancake," and "Pot"—left the house . . .

January 17, 1909. "Cauldron" residing in Kashtanov's house on Sivtsev Wrazhek Street. At 11:20 in the morning "Swift" left Kashtanov's house with a package wrapped in a gray scarf . . .

January 18, 1909. At eleven in the morning "Swift" left the house; when he reached Sadova, he was arrested.

MAYAKOVSKY'S DEPOSITION IN THE COURSE OF THE
INTERROGATION ON JANUARY 21, 1909:

The Browning pistol found when our apartment was searched was probably brought by an acquaintance visiting me. But I do not know specifi-
cally who brought it . . . I do not belong to any political party.

A NOTE FROM THE SECURITY DEPARTMENT FOR THE CHIEF
OF THE MOSCOW POLICE:

Confidential. Vladimir Mayakovsky was arrested on January 18 as a result
of his contacts with the anarchist-robbers. He is being held at the Sush-
chev detention center. Altogether six persons have been detained in this
connection and are being held in custody pending the clearing up of the
circumstances which caused their arrest. February 17, 1909.

*On February 27, 1909, Mayakovsky, together with the other
detainees, was set free.*

FROM THE REMINISCENCES OF ISIDORE MORCHADZE:

Although I was nineteen and he only fifteen, the difference in our ages
could hardly be felt. When we were alone we always talked in Georgian.
He often came to my room, and we often talked and recalled the city of
Kutais . . .

Soon I had to leave the Mayakovskys and go to the Western Provinces,
to Vilna, Verbolovo, and Vilkaviski. In those towns I was organizing tran-
sit magazines for arms smuggled from Germany . . . The funds for this
originated from the expropriation of the Merchants Mutual Credit Society, a Moscow bank.

The Mayakovsky family, little Volodya included, was a family of true
revolutionaries . . . Here is a small example to confirm this. The entire
Mayakovsky family knew that I took part in the expropriation, knew that
large sums of money passed through my hands, but even though they
lived in poverty and were often short, neither they nor I would ever think
of spending as much as one kopeck for our personal needs.

Toward the end of the year 1906 I was arrested . . . After my return
from deportation I could find refuge only with the Mayakovsky family
. . . That was early in 1908. They lived at the time on Dolgoroukovska

Street. I rented a room from them, but I could not register because I had no identity card. Two weeks later I managed to get a passport in the name of Sergei Koridze.

I have to explain that at that time, when reactionary forces were rampant, I was preparing a mass escape from the Taganski prison . . . When I returned home with my comrade late at night, Volodya was never asleep but waited up for us; he was always the first to greet us and open the door. His first question invariably was: "Was it all right? How far were you able to dig?" Ludmila and Olga followed suit, and their mother, Alexandra Alexeyevna, with truly maternal concern, warmed our supper and made tea for us. The entire family were let in on the secret of the underground tunnel and all of them, including the mother, took great interest in the progress of the affair.

The Taganski tunnel did not come off, we were not able to bring it to a conclusion . . . In 1909 I undertook to organize another mass escape of political prisoners from the Novinski penal servitude prison for women on Novinski Boulevard . . . In those days, for reasons of conspiratorial secrecy, I did not live with the Mayakovskys, but all the family knew of my plans and all of them, Volodya included, helped me. Volodya was dying to help me, implored me to use him for whatever purposes I needed. Of course I did use him and gave him all kinds of tasks which he carried out conscientiously. On the night of the escape, however, I could not use him to guide the escaped women, because his exceptional height might have attracted attention, which would have been risky and against the rules of conspiracy. Even so, the Mayakovsky family gave me invaluable assistance by sewing, day and night, high school uniforms for the escapees . . .

The escape was most successful. On the next day, having read in the newspapers about it, and the news that the police offered a reward of five thousand rubles for the capture of any of the escapees, or for showing the place in which she was hiding, Volodya . . . rushed to my wife's apartment to find out from her about the course of events. Volodya knew well that I was not living with my wife, and was not registered there, but he wanted to find out from her if any help was needed. Just in case, he went there with a complete set of painting utensils. Volodya rang the bell, entered the apartment, and realized at once that he had fallen into a police trap. He behaved arrogantly, mocked, jeered, and laughed at the police . . .

THE REPORT OF HIS THIRD ARREST:

On July 2, 1909, the deputy chief of the 3rd station in the Meshchansky District, Lieutenant Jakubovsky, waiting in ambush on orders of the Security Department, apprehended in Loktyev's house at 1 Meshchansky Street, Apt. No. 9, at 1:20 in the afternoon, a certain Vladimir Mayakovsky, gentleman, aged fifteen, student at the Imperial Stroganov School, living with his mother in Boutyugina's house, No. 47 Dolgoroukovska Street, Apt. 38 . . .

MAYAKOVSKY'S DEPOSITION:

On July 2 at about 1:20 P.M., I came to Helena Alexeyevna Tikhomirova in order to ask for a commission to do some drawings, as I knew I could get it there. I know Sergei Koridze, who lives at Mme Tikhomirova's; I met him at the dentist's, Mme Sievers . . . Of the escape from the Moscow women's prison I know from the newspapers, I have no other information about that . . .

SECURITY DEPARTMENT TO THE GOVERNOR OF THE
MYASNIK PRISON, JULY 27, 1909:

Confidential. With reference to the request of Vladimir Vladimirovich Mayakovsky, held in the prison administered by you, the Department informs Your Honor that there is no objection on the Department's part to the said Mayakovsky's having access to drawing utensils.

THE REPORT OF THE PRISON GOVERNOR, AUGUST 17, 1909:

Confidential. Vladimir Vladimirovich Mayakovsky, held under guard in the prison under my administration, by his behavior incites other prisoners to disobedience with regard to prison officers, insistently demands of guards free access to all cells, purporting to be the prisoners' leader; whenever he is let out of his cell to go to the lavatory or washroom, he stays out of his cell for half an hour, parading up and down the corridor. Mayakovsky does not pay attention to any of my requests concerning order . . . On August 16, when permitted to go to the lavatory at 7:00 P.M., he began to walk up and down the corridor, going up to other cells and demanding that the guard open them; when asked by the guard to go back to his cell, he refused. In order to be able to let others go to the lavatory one by one, the guard began to ask him categorically to go into his cell. Mayakovsky called the guard a lackey and began to shout in the corridor so that he could be heard by all prisoners, "Comrades, a lackey is driving your leader to his cell." In this way he incited all the prisoners, who in their turn became noisy. I arrived there with the officer on duty and restored order.

I wish to inform the Security Department of this incident and humbly beg for an order authorizing the transfer of Mayakovsky to another prison . . .

ANNOTATION ON THE REPORT:

August 17. Transfer to district prison, to a solitary cell, report when accomplished.

FROM THE REMINISCENCES OF LUDMILA MAYAKOVSKAYA:

. . . On August 7 my brother received a summons, in connection with the discovery of a secret printing press of the Moscow Committee of the Socialist Revolutionary party, to appear as a defendant at the Moscow Court on September 9, 1909.

I turned to an attorney who specialized in political cases, lawyer Lidov, who put my mind at rest, saying, "Please don't worry, we'll get him off as a minor."

On the eve of the trial, when Mother visited Volodya in prison, he persuaded her not to come to the trial and bade me and my sister not to let her. He was afraid that Mother's nerves were not up to it and that she would be very depressed by the atmosphere of the courtroom.

Volodya was led in under guard. He looked pale and thin in his black shirt. During the trial he was calm and only his fiery eyes betrayed his feelings. He kept smiling to me and to those of his friends who were present at the trial.

NOTE IN THE NEWSPAPER "MOSKOVSKYE VEDOMOSTI,"
SEPTEMBER 10, 1909:

On September 9, in a special session, the Moscow Court Chamber heard in camera the case of townsman Ivanov, peasant Trifonov, and a fourteen-year-old gentleman, Mayakovsky, charged with being members of the Social Democratic party and having installed, for party purposes, a secret printing press in which they printed revolutionary material.

. . . All three accused were declared guilty. Trifonov was sentenced to six years of penal servitude, while minors Ivanov and Mayakovsky were committed to the care of their parents for correction.

LETTER OF THE PROSECUTOR, DATED NOVEMBER 20, 1909:

With reference to your letter of October 28, ref. no. 233662, I have the honor to inform the Court Chamber that the sentence passed on September 9, 1909, on the strength of which Vladimir Vladimirovich Mayakovsky is to be committed to the responsible care of his parents, cannot be executed, as the said Mayakovsky, according to the evidence of the Governor of the Moscow district prison, remains under guard, on the strength of the decision of the Moscow Security Department, dated July 26, 1909, in accordance with note to section 33 of the State Security law, and is liable to three years' deportation to Narimski Province under open police supervision.

LUDMILA MAYOKOVSKAYA:.

Without Volodya's knowledge Mother went to St. Petersburg, in order to secure his release as a minor . . . Fortunately she succeeded this time too . . .

On January 9, 1910 . . . he was released as a minor.

He came in the evening. I remember how, while he was washing his hands, he kept embracing us with soapy hands, kissing us and saying, "How happy, how very happy I am to be with you, at home." And then, as he had no overcoat, he rushed out to see his friends, dressed only in his Stroganov school jacket.

✠ 3 ✠

The Dilemma

This fragment of his autobiography was entitled by Maya-kovsky "the so-called dilemma." But the irony came later; at the time the dilemma was a real and serious one. It was also surely a later perspective that made it necessary to justify the fact that the dilemma—clandestine political activity versus literary activities—was solved by him in favor of the latter. The sixteen-year-old revolutionary, just released from Butyrki prison, did not know yet which art was his proper vocation: painting tempted him to the same extent as poetry. But the fact remains that he felt an irresistible urge to creative activity and followed it. Mayakovsky's first steps in art, his views and aspirations, are recounted by his colleagues—Medvyedyev, Yevreinova, Zhegin—and by his teacher, Pyotr Kyelin. This period is also mentioned by the poet's sister, by the poet him-self, and—with references to his own words—by Burliuk and Asyeyev.

FROM MAYAKOVSKY'S AUTOBIOGRAPHY:

Eleven months in Butyrki. A most important period for me. After three years of theory and practice—I threw myself into belles-lettres.

I read all the newest things. The symbolists—Bely, Balmont. I was fascinated by new forms. But the subjects were alien to me, depicting life which was not the one I knew. I had a try at writing as well, but about something else. It turned out that one could not write *in the same way about something else.* The result was pretentious and sentimental . . . I filled a whole notebook with that stuff. I am grateful to the wardens, who took it away from me when I left prison . . . Having read the moderns, I embarked on the classics. Byron, Shakespeare, Tolstoy. The last book was —*Anna Karenina.* I did not finish it. During the night I was called "with my things to go downtown" . . .

The so-called dilemma. I was quite excited on my way out . . . If I remain in the Party, I have to live in hiding. It seemed to me that living a clandestine existence I would not learn anything. The perspective was—to spend all my life writing leaflets, interpret thoughts taken from books that were right but not composed by myself. Stripped of what I have read, what would I have left? . . . After all, I cannot write better than Bely. Whereas he writes gaily, "threw a pineapple up to heaven," I whine, "hundreds of tiresome days" . . . I went to Medvyedyev—then still my party comrade—and told him: I want to create socialist art. Sergei laughed and laughed: you're too big for your boots . . . I gave up party work and sat down to my studies.

Beginnings of apprenticeship. I thought to myself: I can't write poetry; my attempts have been pitiful. I turned to painting. I studied with Zhukovsky. Along with some ladies I painted miniature silver services. After a year I suddenly realized: what I am learning is no more than a handicraft. I went to Kyelin. A realist. Very good at drawing. The best of teachers. Powers of decision. Changeable. Demanding—craft, Holbein. Hating prettiness.

FROM THE REMINISCENCES OF SERGEI MEDVYEDYEV:

I remember we once spent two days in a place called Podsolnechnoe on the lake of Sinesh . . . Another of my friends was with us, a passionate lover of nature and lakes, like myself.

Volodya tried all the time to convince us that he hated nature, and his views horrified us. He was sullen, had a toothache. He would often fill his mouth with water and spit it into the lake. My friend and I were awfully irritated by this. The conversation turned to Turgenev. Volodya took a most ironical view of him, declaring with ostentatious brutality not only that Turgenev's love of nature did not appeal to him but that he was ready to spit on it . . .

At that time Volodya talked to me mostly about art and painting . . . He really had a considerable talent for drawing. He did a lot of drawing, constantly doing sketches in pencil. I recall that not only myself and my family but all my friends admired his drawings greatly. Perhaps, under the influence of that constant praise showered on him, he was driven to think that painting could become his main interest in life.

I do not clearly remember the talk we had after Mayakovsky's release from Butyrki, which he writes about in his autobiography . . . It is quite probable that I really had a somewhat skeptical attitude toward his assertions and thought he was overreaching himself. It then seemed to me that, like any man wishing to acquire solid knowledge, he should study at a university.

REMINISCENCE OF PYOTR KYELIN:

I clearly remember the time, in 1910–1911, when Mayakovsky was training at my studio. The majority of pupils were Muscovites, but there were some from the provinces too. I used to prepare them for the School of Painting, Sculpture, and Architecture and for the Academy of Fine Arts . . .

One day a young man came in. He was tall, with a bass voice. "You should become a Chaliapin," I said, amused . . .

I liked him very much. I did not even give him the customary two weeks' "probation." He was ill prepared, but I took to him at once on account of his open expression and his shyness. What was most important, one could see that he was not just a clever young man who thought that art could bring him money. He did not even ask: am I going to be any good or not? . . .

Before his first examination at the School of Painting he had worked with me for three or four months. I advised him against taking that examination . . .

On that occasion he failed the examination, but he was not discouraged. Others came back sad and depressed at not getting in (there were few of these; on the whole only two or three out of my twenty-five pupils failed), but he came full of the joy of life and said, "I want to stay another year with you and do some solid work."

One day he said to me, "Pyotr Ivanovich, you are a good portrait painter, but please give up those portraits. No one can improve on Velásquez as far as portraits are concerned. You should do something else."

I replied that I lacked culture, I had never been abroad. "If only you young people could overthrow all that tsarist filth, frontiers would melt away and we could go together to Madrid, to the Prado."

"All right, we'll do it, Pyotr Ivanovich. We'll surely do it in the near future." . . .

I was a student of Serov and I often talked about him to my pupils . . . Mayakovsky came to like Serov a great deal. When Serov died, in 1911, Mayakovsky went to his funeral and made a speech there.

I remember telling him after the funeral, "I am very grateful to you for having treated Serov so sympathetically."

And he replied, "Just you wait, Pyotr Ivanovich, we'll bury you even more beautifully." . . .

In the fall of 1911, Mayakovsky took another examination and was admitted to the School of Painting, to the class in figure painting, and so he did not lose the year.

FROM THE REMINISCENCES OF LIDIA YEVREINOVA, WHO
ATTENDED KYELIN'S CLASS AT THE SAME TIME AS MAYAKOVSKY:

One spring a very young and pretty model posed for us . . . When Pyotr Ivanovich began to inspect the drawings on the following day, a "loud" conversation took place between him and Mayakovsky.

Pyotr Ivanovich, sitting on a very low bench and clutching his knees with his hands, looked at Mayakovsky's drawing for a long time. Then he dropped his hand, which held a piece of charcoal, and said angrily, "I don't understand a thing here! What are these twisted strings and knots supposed to mean? . . . And then he says, 'Mayakovsky will astound the world!' Is it with drawings like these that you propose to astound the world, my pet?"

Mayakovsky remained silent. Pyotr Ivanovich cast a glance at his sullen pupil and asked him more calmly, "Tell me the truth. Perhaps you didn't like the model?"

"What was there to like"—Mayakovsky shrugged his shoulders—"the face of a doll like those on candy and toilet soap wrappers?"

"Eh, Mayakovsky!" sighed Pyotr Ivanovich, rising from the bench. "You can play the wise man, little father, when you become a great artist one day." Anger was again audible in Pyotr Ivanovich's voice. "And now, will you please begin from the beginning, neatly this time."

MAYAKOVSKY TOLD ASYEYEV ABOUT SOME DETAILS OF HIS EXISTENCE AT THAT TIME:

. . . He also told me how, not wishing to be a burden to his mother (as his family was living on a modest pension from his father), he decided to be "independent" and moved to the outskirts, to the Pyotrovsko-Razumovsky settlement . . . At that time he tried to live on his own earnings, as he had done from the time he was thirteen years old. He undertook various kinds of artistic jobs; he sometimes also painted rooms. In order not to starve to death in between those uncertain earnings, he had a kind of reserve: credit to the amount of ten rubles a month in a little grocery where his mother was a customer. The store was situated near his mother's lodgings in Presnya, while he himself lived in Pyotrovsko-Razumovsky. He did not have small change for a streetcar, so he walked the very long distance to Presnya in order to provide himself with dry *bubliki* and a strange "stony" sausage, whose consumption was then severely regulated by his reluctance to use up his meager credit and in that way increase the burden on his family.

"And I was so hungry, Kola. But I had to mark the sausage: half an inch for breakfast, an inch for lunch, half an inch for dinner. If I was not careful, I could eat all my breakfasts and lunches for a week at one sitting. I had to count the *bubliki* as well."

FROM MAYAKOVSKY'S AUTOBIOGRAPHY:

I entered the School of Painting, Sculpture, and Architecture, the only establishment where one could be admitted without the certificate of loyalty. I worked well there.

I was surprised at the fact that imitators were favored and the independent ones persecuted. Those like Larionov, or Mashkov. With my revolutionary instinct I associated myself with the persecuted.

LEV ZHEGIN (SHEKHTEL):

I knew Mayakovsky during the period when he was attending the School of Painting, Sculpture, and Architecture. Many years have passed, but I still clearly remember the class in figure painting: the depressingly official walls, the forest of easels, and the many—alas!—banal sketches done from a model, clothed or nude.

Among the rather dull mass of students, two vivid individuals distinguished themselves: Tchekhrygin and Mayakovsky. They were connected by a kind of friendship. At any rate, Mayakovsky's relationship to Tchekhrygin was quite affectionate. Sometimes, though the elder of the two, he forgave Tchekhrygin's aggressive and somewhat impertinent remarks, like: "You, Volodya, would do better at bending hoops in the Tambov Province than painting pictures."

As a matter of fact, Mayakovsky had in him a great deal of friendliness for people but was ashamed to show it and hid it under a mask of supposed coolness and even brutality.

Mayakovsky himself probably realized that painting was not his proper calling. He painted in oils, gaudily coloring his canvas and getting a rather cheap superficial effect.

Later, when he was a poet, in the period of his friendship with Larionov, Mayakovsky did not abandon painting. I remember his painting, especially for Larionov's exhibition, a "radial" study—chance dissonances of greens, blues, and reds, cutting across each other, with chaotic strokes of the brush. It was clear to everybody that this was not serious, and the radial picture was not destined to see the light of day.

LUDMILA MAYAKOVSKAYA:

I saw his work at the school exhibition and I can confirm that his results were good. In a year's time he could obtain the title of painter-artist.

His situation was complicated, however, by his public appearances, together with the futurists, in discussions on art. Students were categorically forbidden to do this.

4

David Burliuk

David Burliuk is by now a legendary figure: Mayakovsky's first impresario. He was the most enterprising and resourceful of the powerful Burliuk clan (father, mother, three brothers, three sisters) who engaged in painting, writing, collecting Scythian armor and provincial barbers' plaques, fostering new trends in art, publishing books, and organizing art exhibitions. The father was the only one of them who did not take part in this manifold activity. But he—an administrator of large estates in the Ukraine—provided the money. A first encounter with Burliuk has been described by Benedict Lyvshits, poet, soon to be a member of the Russian futurist movement. He is also observed, with admiration or dislike, by: Victor Shklovsky, Velimir Khlebnikov, Pyotr Kyelin, Ludmila Mayakovskaya, and—Vladimir Mayakovsky. Meanwhile David Burliuk and his wife Maria observe the young Mayakovsky.

One evening, when I was about to go to bed, suddenly Alexandra Ekster knocked on my door. She was not alone. Following her into the room was a tall, stout man, draped in a then fashionable loose overcoat. At first glance he looked thirty, but his heavy figure and the seemingly deliberate clumsiness of his movements immediately put all suppositions as to his age in doubt. Extending his disproportionately small hand with too short fingers, he introduced himself: "David Burliuk."

In getting him to come and meet me, Ekster not only fulfilled my long-standing wish but also her own. She wanted me to meet a group of her fellow fighters with whom she occupied the extreme left wing in the struggle against academic canons, waged for three years by then.

. . . During those feverish years, French painting—to which our Russian school was oriented—changed direction with dazzling speed, and the work of Van Dongen, Derain, Gleizes, La Fauconnière, brought to Russia in 1910 by Izdebski, left far behind the naïve searches for innovation conducted by members of the "Link" group.

Izdebski's exhibition played a decisive part in forming my artistic tastes and views; it taught me not only to *see* painting—all painting, including classical which, like the overwhelming majority of art consumers, I regarded superficially—but introduced me to painting, so to speak, "from within," by way of tasks that had to be performed by the contemporary artist.

. . . I knew David Burliuk not only from his paintings. In 1910 a small volume of poetry and prose was published in St. Petersburg. In it, besides Khlebnikov's "Bestiary," "Marquise Dezes," and "Crane," apart from the first poems of Kamensky, were nineteen poems by David Burliuk. Their heavy archaisms, their very roughness of form, appealed to me through their opposition to all I had done before, to my whole image of myself as a poet, the disciple of Corbière and Rimbaud. I had come to know these poems by heart, and I now looked at their author with the greatest interest.

He was sitting there in his big coat, looking like a heap of thick hairy cloth, thrown on the counter by the clerk. Holding an old-fashioned lorgnon to his nose—once the property of Maréchal Davout, he explained with a faint smile—Burliuk glanced around the walls and rested his eyes on a painting by Ekster. It was an unfinished tempera, *Intérieur,* painted in early impressionist style, long since discarded by her. From her slight blush of embarrassment and a fleeting shadow of displeasure which passed across her face, I could see what importance Ekster—who spent many months every year in Paris, an absolute "Frenchwoman" in her art— attributed to the opinion of this provincial boor.

🖎

Burliuk invited Lyvshits—like Khlebnikov before him and Mayakovsky after him—to his family citadel: the mansion in Tchernyanka, in the Kherson district.

LYVSHITS:

There was no one but us in the third-class railway carriage and we could chat freely without attracting anybody's attention. We began to talk about poetry. Burliuk did not know French poetry at all and had only vaguely heard of Baudelaire, Verlaine, perhaps also Mallarmé.

I took a little volume of Rimbaud, which I always carried with me, out of my suitcase and began to read Burliuk my favorite pieces . . .

He was astounded. He never even suspected what riches were contained in that little book. Admittedly in those days few people had read Rimbaud in the original French. Annyenski, Bryusov, and myself were the only Russian poets who were actually translating him. We agreed with David then and there that in Tchernyanka I would endeavor to make him familiar, insofar as possible, with the treasures of French poetry. Fortunately, besides Rimbaud, I had also taken with me some works of Mallarmé and Laforgue.

Every now and then Burliuk would get up, rush to the window opposite us, and hurriedly write something in a notebook he took out of his pocket. Then he would put the notebook away and return to his seat.

That activity of his aroused my interest. For a long time he did not want to explain it to me, but he finally satisfied my curiosity and gave me the sheet from his notebook. It was a poem. Written in big letters, almost printed, though not very legible because of the jerks of the train, three four-verse stanzas were sketched.

I found it difficult to consider those rhymed scribblings as poetry. A shapeless mass, a soup in which, like unmelted lumps, fragments of Rimbaud's images were floating, deformed beyond recognition.

So that was why Burliuk kept rushing to the window and anxiously jotted something down in his little notebook. It must have been his usual way of preserving impressions, assimilating material, perhaps even of expressing admiration.

"Like the devout juggler before the Gothic Madonna," David juggled fragments of his own poems before Rimbaud. This was not a sacrilege, but quite the contrary, a kind of totemism. Burliuk was devouring his god, his actual idol, before my very eyes . . .

🖤

In Nikolaev, the two travelers were joined by Burliuk's younger brother, Vladimir. David showed his brother the photograph of Picasso's latest picture which he had received from Alexandra Ekster.

LYVSHITS:

The brothers are leaning over the precious photograph like conspirators over the map of an enemy fortress.

They put their hands flat against their eyes; examining the composition, they divide the picture into segments in their minds.

A woman's skull cut open, with the occiput shining through, reveals dazzling vistas . . .

"This is good," exclaims Vladimir. "Larionov and Goncharova have had it."

From the clouds I am returned to earth. In a month's time "The Knave of Diamonds" will have another exhibition. The Burliuks will not fail.

Picasso will meet the same fate as Rimbaud . . .

If Tchernyanka's role is to be examined after the fact, it has to be described as the meeting place of the coordinates from which the movement known as futurism was born in Russian poetry and art . . .

We took the line of least resistance, of course, when—still full of school memories and giving way to the temptations of mythology surrounding us—we called the community born in Tchernyanka by the dreamy name of "Hilea" . . .

There were four of us. The shadow of Khlebnikov did not even hover

over the pile of his manuscripts; they lived their own lives, independent of his personal fortunes. Nevertheless, none of us could imagine the new association without Khlebnikov's participation.

We hardly even noticed how we became Hileans . . . And yet, on leaving Tchernyanka, we had no doubt about having originated not only a lasting friendship but also a new movement in Russian art which was to point the way of its development for years to come.

SHKLOVSKY'S EXPLANATION:

The circle was called "Hilea" after an ancient Greek colony on the Dnieper. Hilea had long since disappeared from the surface of the earth, but the Burliuks turned out to be good neighbors and preserved its name.

The group itself was only in the process of formation. Later it took the name "Budyetlan" (from the word "budu"—I shall be) . . . ·

※

In the fall of the same year, 1911, Burliuk met a student at the School of Painting, Sculpture, and Architecture—Vladimir Mayakovsky.

FROM MAYAKOVSKY'S AUTOBIOGRAPHY:

Burliuk appeared at the school. An insolent look. Lorgnon. Frock coat. Walks humming. I began to provoke him. It almost came to blows.

FROM BURLIUK'S REMINISCENCES:

I first met Mayakovsky early in September 1911 . . . An unkempt, unwashed, tall young fellow with the attractive, handsome face of an Apache began to persecute me with his jokes, taunting me with being a "cubist." Finally I was ready to fight him with my fists, particularly as I was quite an athlete and my chances of beating that long-limbed youth with fiery ironical eyes, dressed in a dusty velvet coat, were good . . . But if this happened, I, a cubist, who had had such difficulty getting into the Moscow School, would have had to leave it, the penalty for fights being expulsion. So we just gave each other looks, then we made peace, and soon we became friends and allies in the coming struggle . . . between the old and the new in art.

SHKLOVSKY:

Mayakovsky's close friend was Vassili Tchekhrygin, young and very handsome . . . Tchekhrygin was always with young Lev Shekhtel. At just that time David Burliuk arrived, stout, one-eyed, and considerably older. Burliuk had studied first in Kazan, then in Odessa. He had been abroad. He was a good painter, knew anatomy very well . . . He had read a great deal, knew much, and stopped caring how one should paint. Having acquired the craft, he lost all respect for academic painting. He could paint a picture better than any professor, but he had lost heart for academic painting . . . He was sensible and wanted to get along. In order to get a better diploma, he wanted to graduate quickly from the School of Painting, Sculpture, and Architecture . . .

Mayakovsky was homeless, had nowhere to wash his hands when he was a student at the School of Painting and Sculpture. All kinds of people were studying there: rich people who could afford the buffet, and others who had to avoid looking at the buffet; people in greatcoats, people in capes, and those who had nothing to wear . . .

The handsome tormented young man with nowhere to wash his hands befriended David Burliuk.

David came to love Mayakovsky, as an adventurer sometimes loves a homeless genius, the monarch of an undiscovered kingdom . . .

FROM MAYAKOVSKY'S AUTOBIOGRAPHY:

Civic club. Concert. Rachmaninov. The isle of the dead. I escaped from unbearable melodious boredom. So did Burliuk after a while. We both laughed on seeing each other. Then we went for a stroll together.

A memorable night. Talk. From Rachmaninovian boredom we passed on to our school boredom, and from there—to the entire classical boredom. David was angry like a master who had got ahead of his contemporaries; I was angry—being a socialist who knew that the old garbage was bound to be destroyed. Russian futurism was born.

The next night. Today I wrote a poem. Or to be exact: fragments of one. Not good. Unprintable. "Night." Sretenski Boulevard. I read the poem to Burliuk. I added: written by a friend. David stopped and looked at me. "You wrote it yourself!" he exclaimed. "You're a genius!" I was happy at this marvelous and undeserved praise. And so I steeped myself in poetry. That evening, quite unexpectedly, I became a poet.

Burliuk's oddities. The very next morning Burliuk, introducing me to someone, said in his characteristic bass, "You don't know him? My friend, a genius. The noted poet Mayakovsky." I motioned him to stop. But Burliuk went relentlessly on. Even when taking leave of me he said, "And now you go and write. Otherwise you'll be putting me in a most stupid situation."

And so every day. I had to write. I wrote the first (I mean, the first professional, printable) poem, "Scarlet and White," and others.

NIGHT
by Vladimir Mayakovsky

Scarlet and blue—pushed out and crumpled,
ducats in handfuls were thrown on the green,
in the black arms of windows crowded,
bright yellow cards were eagerly put in.

Boulevards and squares enjoyed the navy blue,
from which the buildings had their togas cut.
In the hoops of light, like in yellow wound,
hastily walked the passer-by's foot.

Flowing to the door, temptingly pushed,
the crowd—motley tom-cat—arched in the hall;
to nip off a small piece everyone wished
of the immense, laughter-cast ball.

I, in the claws of clothes at me aiming,
thrust laughter simply in their eyes—
a blow in fluttering tin plate—Negroes neighing,
till a parrot's wing blossomed o'er their face.

LUDMILA MAYAKOVSKAYA:

At about this time Volodya brought with him to our home David Burliuk, the latter's brother, and someone else, I do not recall whom. We were surprised at Burliuk's appearance: his long tailcoat, red velvet waistcoat over a prominent stomach, his lorgnon and top hat; and at his brother, who looked like a member of a student fraternity. We had not had such friends before. The impression was made deeper by their stoutness and nonchalant behavior.

Burliuk was introduced to my sister, a girl of twenty-two, in the doorway. He kept looking at her through his lorgnon at such close quarters that she began to draw back along the wall. Burliuk, not at all put out by her embarrassment, kept paying her compliments. My sister stepped back that way along the entire wall, sat in the open window, and nearly fell out.

All this made a strong and unpleasant impression which left no room for any other impression.

. . . Burliuk warmly approved of Volodya's first attempts at poetry. He even called him a genius (one must not forget, though, that all the futurists called one another "geniuses").

KYELIN:

One day, when Mayakovsky was already a poet and a friend of Burliuk's, he took me to the Burliuks' (I think it must have been in the Leontyev Alley). Burliuk, with a lorgnon in his hand, strolled around a small room (furnished only with a modest table made of rough boards and two stools) and recited poetry. Mayakovsky too recited poems.

I did not like Burliuk; he seemed conceited and arrogant. "What are those professors of painting? If I want to become a Pasternak, or a Serov, I shall be one. I can paint you a picture like any painter you name, so that you won't notice the difference."

I did not like that kind of talk.

from BURLIUK
by Velimir Khlebnikov

With a wide brush in your hand
In a red shirt you ran
Detonating the streets of Munich.
The teacher of painting
Called you
"An exuberant mare
From Russia's black soil."
And your belly shook with the exuberant joy

Of Russia's black soil.
With a resounding ho-ho-ho!
You responded to all, you knew your strength,
The one-eyed artist,
Wiping your glass dark water eye
With a handkerchief and saying: Ye-es!—
Covering with glass
In a tortoise grip.
And like a drill
From behind a glass armor
You pierced the man you were talking to.
Suddenly you were gloomy and distrustful.
Your giant strength came from the
Lonely eye.
And without revealing your secret
That the dead glass ball
Was your life's companion, you divined.
Your opponent was under the spell of your will,
Enchanted by the black, blear abyss.

.   .   .

You fat giant, your laughter resounded all over Russia.
And the stem of the Dnieper's mouth was clenched in your fist.

MARUSSIA BURLIUK:

Vladimir Mayakovsky, who even in those days called Burliuk "Dodya," used to stroll with us quite often in the evenings around the boulevards, through Trubny Square to Tverska Street, where he kept fixing his serious black eyes on the window where evening bulletins were displayed, with their silent shouts about floods, snowdrifts, and the miserable news from abroad, shining through the dull glass of those tsarist times . . .

In those remote years Mayakovsky was already a most colorful person. He used to wear a black velvet coat with a turned-down collar. At his neck was a black foulard scarf, a crumpled ribbon was visible, and Volodya's pockets were bulging with cigarette and match boxes.

Mayakovsky was tall, his chest was a bit sunken, his arms long and big, his hands red from the cold. His youthful head was crowned with thick dark hair, which much later he began to cut short. His cheeks were yellow;

his mouth was large, hungry for kisses, sweets, and tobacco. His lips were big too; the lower one twitched to the left when he was talking, which gave him the appearance of condescension and arrogance. Even then his boyish mouth was not adorned by the "charm of youth"—the white teeth. When he was talking or smiling, one could see only brown, decayed stumps, bent like nails. Mayakovsky always pressed his lips together firmly . . .

Our walks were long under the flickering lights of Moscow's Asiatic boulevards, shaded with strokes of rain or downy snowflakes.

Mayakovsky listened intently to the gay exclamations and statements on art to which we were lavishly treated by Burliuk.

In the first months Mayakovsky never contradicted him. From under the hat squashed down to his demonic brows, he looked inquisitively at the passers-by and their adverse reactions seemed to amuse the youth. What were the young, arrogant eyes of the young Apache looking for? . . . And Mayakovsky would turn around to look at the shapes disappearing in the dark.

The young Mayakovsky loved people more than they loved him.

Mayakovsky was even able to feel compassion for people, in his way.

Burliuk wrote of his friendship with Mayakovsky to Vassili Kamensky, a poet (who participated in their first anthology), painter, and . . . airplane pilot, one of the first in the Russian Empire.

FROM KAMENSKY'S REMINISCENCES:

The Mokotow airfield in Warsaw was quiet and deserted early on a spring morning. Only in a group of pilots one could hear gay shouts of "bravo" and young wholesome laughter.

That was I, one of five pilots who at that time were training in Warsaw, reading my new poems to my colleagues while putting on my chamois gloves before the flight. We already had on our flight suits and leather helmets . . .

We put out our cigarettes and climbed into our machines.

The mechanic set the propeller in motion.

The noise of the engine immediately transformed the poet into a pilot. The experienced ear listened to the sound of the cylinders . . .

Under our wings—the roofs of factories and houses, the squares of streets, gardens, and the turquoise ribbon of the Vistula.

And I myself, alone in the rays of the rising sun . . .

I thought: tomorrow is April 12, my name day.

Flying and literature had both captivated me so completely that, without peace of mind, I rushed from the airplane to poems, from poetry to flights . . .

On April 12, 1912, among various telegrams from relatives and friends received on my name day, there was one from David Burliuk in Moscow.

With his congratulations Burliuk enclosed the news that he had discovered a new genius (Volodya Mayakovsky). The first man we had considered a genius was Khlebnikov, whom I had discovered in 1907 in St. Petersburg.

I had known Burliuk since 1908, liked him, valued him highly, and I trusted his instinct.

And because Burliuk (at that time already known as an avant-garde painter) was just then studying at the Moscow School of Painting and Sculpture, I came to the conclusion that Mayakovsky must surely be a "genius" at painting.

The following fall, 1912, the Burliuks came to live at the student hostel on Little Bronna Street, in the so-called Romanovka section.

FROM THE REMINISCENCES OF DAVID AND MARUSSIA BURLIUK:

Our rooms were on the third floor. Marussia lived in Room 104. I was situated in a room on the same hall. All the meetings of young poets and painters took place in Marussia's room which was bigger and smarter . . . Vladimir Mayakovsky used to come every evening after his lectures . . . The entire building, its wide halls, resounded with music from nine in the morning till eleven at night: all kinds of instruments and music could be heard . . . Practically all the students at the Moscow conservatory were living there . . . they were, most of them, very poor . . .

Burliuk, being a Ukrainian, was fond of singing, and I began to teach

him with the help of Professor Alexandrova-Kochetova's method . . .
Having noticed the progress made by David Davidovich, Mayakovsky
soon expressed in his deep bass the desire to take a couple of lessons. My
new pupil, however, was absolutely devoid of a musical ear, and was not
willing to overcome the difficulties with hard work. Nevertheless, it
transpired that he knew a couple of bars of an aria from the opera *Sadko*
. . . From then on the two of us went through the aria every evening
and he was finally able to sing it clearly, with accompaniment.

Mayakovsky sang with gusto, never tired of the tune, and the word
"sea" always resounded with inspiration, accompanied by a smile of triumph, the way he sang it . . .

Those musical evenings in Romanovka, with Maria Nikiforovna ac-
companying Mayakovsky on the piano, were not useless. Apart from letting
him in on the art of the opera and some of its secrets, Maria Nikiforovna
helped him to use his voice properly, which the future tribune found useful when it came to making fiery speeches . . .

Many of Mayakovsky's early appearances as a reader of poetry took
place in the half-dark rooms of Romanovka, their walls covered with
cheap red damask, darkened with dirt. The witnesses and listeners to
those readings were usually his closest friends . . . Mayakovsky would sit
on a sofa, near a round table, on which, towering above heaps of all kinds
of snacks and sweetmeats, was placed the traditional samovar, with its
pleasant smell of coals. On the table also stood an oil lamp, with solid
yellow glass . . . When Mayakovsky stood up, the inevitable cigarette in
his hand, his youthful face was lit from below. It was orange-green, his
eyes were dark violet, his hair—very dark blue . . . He went to the
middle of the room and stood in such a way that he could see himself in a
dull, narrow mirror. Mayakovsky straightened up, his face remained calm,
the hand holding the cigarette would drop against his tall body, the other
he would put in the pocket of his velvet coat. Without throwing his head
back, but fixing his eyes inquiringly on the other pair of eyes in the mirror,
the poet began to read his new poems, declaim, almost chant, without
corrections, or pauses, without hesitations dictated by modesty . . .

From the poet's lips verses flowed freely, in which both the curses of
the streets preparing an uprising against the tsar and the nightmarish
echoes of drunken Moscow's night debauch could be heard . . .

With an elder brother's love, Burliuk admired that immense gift, those infinite possibilities, in a friendly manner, patting Mayakovsky on the shoulder when he finished reading; on the young, stooping shoulders, bony from undernourishment . . . Also that second spring of our friendship Mayakovsky was poorly dressed, and meanwhile the cold weather had arrived . . .

Burliuk had seen that Mayakovsky had no overcoat, so one night in Romanovka, toward the end of September 1912, when the poet was about to go home after midnight, he put on him the well-padded winter coat he had inherited from his father . . .

FROM MAYAKOVSKY'S AUTOBIOGRAPHY

I always think about David with affection. A magnificent friend. Burliuk was my true teacher. He made me a poet. He read the French and the Germans to me. Gave me books. Walked and talked all the time. Would not let me go for a moment. Paid me 50 kopecks every day. So that I could write without starving. For Christmas he took me home, to Novaya Mayachka. I brought back *Port* and others . . .

We came back from Mayachka—if not with definite views, then certainly with sharpened temperaments. In Moscow, Khlebnikov. His quiet genius was at that time overshadowed, as far as I was concerned, by the exuberant David. Here, too, arrived the futurist Jesuit of the word— Kruchenykh.

After a few nights of poetry we produced a common manifesto. David got it together, rewrote the thing, the two of us gave it a name and issued the *Slap to the Public's Taste* . . .

♯ 5 ♯

Futurism

✦

In the years 1909–1913 the manifestoes of F. T. Marinetti were published in Milan. He proclaimed futurism as a movement in general and futurist literature in particular. Together with the manifestoes of Boccioni, Pratella, and other authors, who formulated the principles of futurism for the visual arts and for music, Marinetti's manifestoes were translated into Russian and published in Moscow in 1914 by Vadim Shershenyevich. From 1911 onward there appeared in Russia artistic groups which identified themselves with futurism (such as the ego-futurists, headed by Igor Syevyeryanin, and others)—but Burliuk's group initially dissociated itself from this movement. Benedict Lyvshits tells about the period of ferment from which the Russian "cubo-futurism" gradually emerged. Lyvshits, Kruchenykh, and Shklovsky recall the Slap to the Public's Taste *manifesto, the first under which Mayakovsky put his signature, and the almanac under the same title. In 1913, Burliuk and his protégés declared themselves, in one of the group's publications, as "the world's only futurists."*

FROM MARINETTI'S MANIFESTOES:

1. We want to extol the love of danger, the habit of energy and valor.

2. The main elements of our poetry will be: courage, audacity, and rebellion.

3. Hitherto literature has dealt with meditative immobility, ecstasy, and sleep; whereas we praise the forward motion, the feverish sleeplessness, the sporting step, the somersault, the slap and the blow of a fist.

4. We proclaim that the world's grandeur has been enriched by a new beauty: that of speed. The racing car, with its body adorned by huge pipes, with its exploding exhaust . . . the roaring motorcar, which seems to speed like a ball, is more beautiful than the Winged Victory of Samothrace . . .

7. There is no beauty apart from conflict. There are no masterpieces without aggression. Poetry ought to be a cruel attack against unknown forces in order to compel them to humble themselves before man . . .

9. We want to extol war—the world's only hygiene—militarism, patriotism, the anarchists' destructive gesture, the glorious, death-giving ideas and—contempt for women.

10. We want to extinguish museums and libraries, to combat moralizing, feminism, and all opportunist and utilitarian baseness.

11. We will extol immense crowds, moved by work, pleasure, or rebellion; the multicolored and polyphonic fits of revolutions in all modern capitals; the nightly vibrations of arsenals and shipyards beneath their powerful electric moons; the voracious railway stations devouring the steaming snakes; the factories, attached to the clouds by ropes of smoke . . . the gliding flight of airplanes whose propellers flow like the flutter of flags; and the applause of a crowd of enthusiasts.

From Italy we throw this subversive and explosive manifesto, with which today we are laying the foundations of *Futurism*. From Italy, because we want to liberate her from the gangrene of the professors, archeologists, guides, and antiquarians. Far too long has Italy been a gigantic

market for dealers in old rags. We want to liberate her from the innumerable museums which have covered the country like innumerable grave-
yards.

1. Syntax must be abolished . . .

4. The adverb, that old iron cramp of words, must be abolished . . .

6. From now on punctuation marks do not exist . . .

7. Poetry must be a continuous succession of new images, or else it
will be no more than anemia and leukemia.

8. There are no such categories as noble and common, elegant and
base, eccentric and natural images. The images are assimilated by intuition, which knows neither privilege nor premeditation . . .

10. Since all order is a fatal product of insidious reason, analogies must
be concerted and arranged according to the principle of maximum disorder.

11. To extinguish the "I" in literature means to annihilate all psychology. Man has been ultimately corrupted by libraries and museums, made
subservient to a terrible logic and wisdom, and so there is absolutely nothing of interest in him any more. He has to be extinguished in literature and
substituted at last by material whose substance must be experienced intui-
tively, which is something that physicists and chemists will never be able
to do . . .

Cinematography gives us the dance of an object, which disintegrates
and is integrated again without man's intervention. It shows us a swim-
mer's jump in reverse so that his feet emerge from the sea and jump onto
the diving board again. It shows us a man running at a speed of two
hundred miles an hour. There are just as many movements in matter oc-
curring outside the laws of reason and resulting from more weighty
causes . . .

We will invent together what I call wireless imagination. We will
achieve a still greater art when we have the courage to abolish all the first
segments of our analogies in order to arrive at a continuous succession of
the second segments. For this purpose one must give up intelligibility. It is
not necessary—to be understood.

One must spit daily at the *Altar of art*. We are entering the limitless
regions of free intuition. After free verse—we shall at last have free
words . . .

Words liberated from punctuation will radiate one upon the other, will cross their various magnetisms, following the continuous dynamism of thought . . .

8. The denigration of love (feelings or senses), caused through the ever growing emancipation of woman and her erotic freedom . . .

14. A new feeling of well-being, created through tourism, transatlantic ships, and big hotels (the yearly synthesis of various races). Worship of the big city, the abolition of distances and dull isolation. Derision of the divinity of the (*unattainable*) landscape . . .

The need for laconism is in accord not only with the laws of speed which govern us but also with the perennial relations between the poet and his reader. Those relations are very much like those of old friends, who can understand each other by one word or look. That is how and why the poet's imagination should connect the most remote objects, *without a guiding hand,* by means of essential words, which are at the same time absolutely free . . .

🎴

On February 25, 1912, a discussion on modern art took place at the Moscow Polytechnic Museum, organized by "The Knave of Diamonds" group of painters. Talks were given by Maximilian Voloshin (who spoke on "Cézanne, Van Gogh, and Gauguin as precursors of cubism") and by David Burliuk.

REMINISCENCES OF BENEDICT LYVSHITS:

An invitation extended to Voloshin, a man remote from extremist tendencies in art but distinguished for his fairly broad views . . . would have been unthinkable toward the end of the same year 1912, when divisions among the various artistic groups were clearly marked.

In the spring of 1912, however, they still mixed with one another. Tomorrow's enemies coexisted peacefully. I myself, for instance, continued to contribute to *Apollon* even after I had founded "Hilea" . . . and Nicholas Burliuk intended to join Gumilev's "Poets' Guild" . . .

Having found himself in his element, Voloshin became so engrossed in the biographies of the three great Frenchmen that he forgot about the principal aim of his talk, which was to establish the genealogy of cubism . . .

David Burliuk, too, began his two-hour lecture with a remote question: he tried to define the essential canons of the visual arts. But having considered them in historical sequence, he passed on to an analysis of new views on art . . .

Burliuk first defined cubism as the synonym of modern painting and then criticized the simplified view of cubism as a movement which allegedly aims at representing the visible world by means of cubes.

"The essential aim of cubism," said Burliuk, referring to Gleizes and Metzinger, "is to render the specific plastic space, which is different from Euclidean space (which denied the deformation of bodies in movement) as well as from visual space.

"How remote from this are the aims proclaimed by the Italian futurists," he exclaimed with pathos. The fact that the movement is led not by a painter but by a poet has prejudged its character, as it were.

In Burliuk's eyes, literary qualities in a painting were, of course, a mortal sin; I do not know, however, how he substantiated his charge, since he did not know the futurists' paintings, not even from reproductions, and at best he had read only the manifesto, issued in April 1910. Even so, I wish to record the fact that when speaking for the first time publicly about futurism, David thought it proper to deprecate it as a negative phenomenon . . .

The very term "futurism" did not appeal to us at that time. It was adopted in November 1911 by Igor Syevyeryanin, who added to it the word "ego" and made it the banner of a group of St. Petersburg poets. Even later, when the ego-futurists had to formulate their program somehow, they were unable to do so. With the best intentions, in all the woolly declarations, "tables," "charts," "letters," "prologues," and "epilogues," one could not find one clear, thoroughly developed idea. Among ego-futurists were poets not devoid of ability, quite apart from the undoubted talent of Syevyeryanin; but their theoretical pronouncements were characterized by such helplessness and such a random joining of quite incongruous ideas (not even ideas but simply fashionable words) that even with maximum concentration it was difficult to understand what they were getting at, with whom and in the name of what they intended to wage war. Usurping the name "futurists," they immediately imbued this term with a pejorative meaning, which caused us to reject that label when the newspapers began to pin it on us, against our will.

Unlike Larionov and Goncharova, who opened their arms to the Italian futurists, the future "father of Russian futurism," in the spring of 1912, emphatically rejected the movement under whose banners the Hileans were eventually to enter the history of Russian art.

BENEDICT LYVSHITS GOES ON TO DESCRIBE THE TWO RIVAL AVANT-GARDE GROUPS OF PAINTERS: "THE KNAVE OF DIAMONDS" (BURLIUK, KONCHALOVSKY, MASHKOV, LENTULOV, FALK) AND "THE ASS'S TAIL" (LARIONOV, GONCHAROVA):

For both of them Italian futurism was an "invention," a seasonal novelty, which came after Parisian cubism. On this point they simply differed, in that the former agreed to pay homage to fashion while the latter did not want to. That is why at "The Ass's Tail" exhibition, canvases tinged with urbanism and pretending to be related to futurist paintings coexisted peacefully with puristic canvases of the previous period: the decorative *panneau* à la Matisse, still lifes à la Cézanne, and the female nudes and religious compositions rejected by futurists.

This juxtaposition did not mean mutual exclusion. Everything here blended into a wild wind of disintegrating solar spectra, into the virgin chaos of colors, which gave back to the human eye a barbarian sharpness of vision and with it an inexhaustible source of forgotten joys. I think mainly of Goncharova's pictures: on seeing them one did not want to think what school they belonged to, what manner they were painted in, what theoretical views the artist adhered to when she was painting them; all this was an unnecessary encumbrance . . . remained quite external in relation to the pictures themselves and could no more explain them than a Marinetti manifesto could explain the writing of Khlebnikov.

THOUGH HE CONDEMNED FUTURIST PAINTINGS, BURLIUK WAS NOT AGAINST ACCEPTING MARINETTI'S METHODS IN THE STRUGGLE FOR NEW LITERATURE. HERE IS AN EXCERPT FROM THE REMINIS-CENCES OF LYVSHITS, WHO AT THAT TIME WAS SERVING IN THE ARMY IN THE TOWN OF MEDVYED:

. . . Burliuk began to flood me with letters, asking for material—poems and prose—for the forthcoming almanac. He particularly insisted on my writing a "manifesto," which would introduce the book and set out the essential points of our program. I refused categorically. I had imagined our first public literary appearance in quite a different manner. To begin by proclaiming lightheartedly some principles not yet quite clear to ourselves, with a manifesto unwarranted by the poetry printed there, meant, to my mind, condemning ourselves to an inevitable fiasco . . .

Burliuk took a different view, did not want to wait, and in fact began to act quite energetically in Moscow. When "The Knave of Diamonds" refused to finance the almanac, David found other publishers—G. L. Kuzmin and S. D. Dolinsky—tempting them with Khlebnikov and with the Renaissance of Russian Literature (all in capital letters, of course!), whose participants were to be assured of the gratitude of posterity. Not content with that, simultaneously with the *Slap*, he arranged for another anthology, making contact with the Matyushin and Helena Guro group in St. Petersburg, and also negotiated with the "Youth Association" concerning a literary evening shared by them and by us.

Rejecting all my arguments, with the stubbornness of a born organizer he flooded me with his messages, persuading, exhorting, demanding a "manifesto," if not for the *Slap* then for the other anthology which was to be published in February at the latest. "You have to send me an article at once, in any form you like. Be our Marinetti. If you are afraid to sign it—I will sign myself: the idea is above everything else! . . ."

IT WAS AT ABOUT THAT TIME, IN THE FALL OF 1912, THAT
LYVSHITS BECAME ACQUAINTED WITH MAYAKOVSKY, WHO CAME
WITH BURLIUK FROM MOSCOW TO ST. PETERSBURG:

Dressed lightly, quite unsuitably for this season of the year, in a black navy cape buckled at the chest, with a black broad-rimmed hat pushed right down to his eyebrows, he looked like a member of the Sicilian mafia, through some strange chance transported to St. Petersburg.

His sweeping movements, abounding in a certain affected impetuosity; his bass voice, traditionally associated with operatic villains; his protruding lower jaw, which even in spite of missing front teeth did not give his mouth a look of flaccidity but one of strong will—all this made Mayakovsky look even more like a member of a bandit troop, or an anarchist bomb thrower . . . It was enough, however, to look into the wise, mocking eyes, to discern that the outward appearance was distinct from the inner man, that all this was a "theater for its own sake," which Mayakovsky had somewhat tired of already, whose value he knew and which he would renounce as soon as he found more suitable forms through which to express his place in the world.

It was, of course, a youthfully naïve protest against social convention, an individualist protest, taking the line of least resistance. But though I reacted to this walking *grand guignol* with an involuntary smile . . . I was ready to agree with Burliuk: in my new acquaintance lay an uncommon inner strength.

He talked about Moscow affairs, almost exclusively about the painting circles with which he rubbed shoulders (he had not yet made his choice of calling), about scandals ripening at the School of Painting, Sculpture, and Architecture, where Mayakovsky and Burliuk were white crows. Through his conceited "we," tinged with the *pluralis majestatis*, an anarchic "I," which would reject all group discipline, was already coming through.

He was to see and make contact with Mme D., who arranged fashionable exhibitions and salons, so he proposed that we all join him and go together. The three of us went: himself, Kola Burliuk—as the unflinching guardian of Hilean orthodoxy—and myself.

Upon our arrival at Mme D.'s apartment—later transformed into a veritable museum of avant-garde paintings—we found a few nondescript young men and some dolled-up young ladies whom Mayakovsky—goodness knows by what right, since he was seeing them for the first time in his life—treated as if they were his odalisques. At the table he was abundantly sarcastic with regard to the hostess, abused her husband (a silent man, who suffered these abuses with humility), and defiantly grasped the cake with his fingers. When Mme D. lost her patience and made some remark about his dirty fingernails, he replied with monstrous impertinence, for which I thought we would all be thrown out at once.

Nothing like that happened. Apparently Mme D., who used to treat the artistic Olympus of both capitals as her own domestic bestiary, was also greatly impressed by the young man with nothing but nerve to his credit.

We left rather late (without Kola, who disappeared immediately after tea had been served) the streetcars had stopped running and Mayakovsky suggested we walk. I wanted to get a closer look at our new comrade-

in-arms and he too showed some interest in my person. We talked freely
and frankly; that was the first time I saw Mayakovsky without his mask.

He was thoughtful, full of modest reticence, choosing his words carefully because of his extreme honesty; in short—he had nothing in common
with the man I had just seen at the table.

I decided to "examine" him thoroughly: I asked him about his past,
about the reasons why he had joined us Hileans. He tried to satisfy my
curiosity as best he could, occasionally thinking for quite a long time
about the answer he should give. I remember that, among other things, he
told me, with a certain pride, that he had already spent some time "behind
bars," for political activities, of course.

My desire to look into his poetic activity and to estimate the weight of
the baggage with which he joined our group seemed to cause him the
greatest embarrassment. I do not know what year Mayakovsky later considered to have been the start of his literary career, but in the winter of
1912 he stubbornly refused to acknowledge any of the pieces he had written up to then, except two poems: "Night" and "Morning," which were
soon to be published in the *Slap to the Public's Taste.*

He must have wished to enter literature without the ballast of the past;
to rid himself of all responsibility for it; to annihilate it without regrets.
That ruthless attitude toward himself is the best proof of how sure of
himself the young Mayakovsky was. Since everything was before him, was
it worthwhile to decide on a compromise with yesterday?

. . . He read both poems to me and waited, it seemed to me, for my
words of approbation.

I saw no reason to stand on ceremony with Mayakovsky and gave him
clearly to understand that his poems did not appeal to me. Their naïve
"urbanism," continuing the tradition of Bryusov, and their no less naïve
anthropomorphism, utterly trivialized by Leonid Andreyev, were not redeemed by two or three unexpected images, or by the "inverted" rhyme,
which Volodya Mayakovsky was inclined to declare the Archimedes
screw, capable of raising the entire world of poetry from its foundations.
All this was very loosely related to his boastful declaration about "spitting
out the past, stuck like a bone in our throats." By printing these poems in
the *Slap to the Public's Taste,* Mayakovsky committed the same mistake I
did when I put into our fighting almanac pieces from which the old sym-

bolist influence had not yet evaporated. Our slogans were more advanced than our practice.

Mayakovsky did not want to agree with me and defended his early poetic attempts from my attacks. He insisted—with an obduracy worthy of a better cause—that, after all, they were first attempts. In his treatment of urban themes he dreamed of an approach to new lexical and semantic possibilities, to a renovation of the vocabulary, a rejuvenation of imagery. Wider aims did not seem to interest him at all. He used different words, of course, but translated into the terms current today this is how it would sound.

In the heat of discussion we did not notice that we had walked to the other end of the city, somewhere near Pokrov. Somehow we managed to trudge back. At four in the morning, shivering with cold, and hungry, we met a sausage vendor at the Mytninski quai. I had not even known that such a trade existed, but Volodya was very familiar with the nocturnal customs of metropolitan suburbs. Courageously dipping his hand in the now cold tin samovar, he fished for the lethal sausages with his fingers, contrary to his normal mistrust and abhorrence. Following an instinct no less imperative than friendly solidarity, I took the risk and did the same. Our friendship began under an auspicious star. We got nothing more than an upset stomach . . .

At Christmas I came to St. Petersburg again. The *Slap to the Public's Taste* had by then been printed in Moscow and was to be on sale any day. The gray and brown paper, anticipating that of the newspapers of the nineteen-twenties, the coarse cover, and the very title of the book, whose purpose was to shock the bourgeoisie, all this hit the mark.

The main trump, though, was the manifesto . . .

THE MANIFESTO "SLAP TO THE PUBLIC'S TASTE"

To those who read—our New First Unexpected.

We alone are the *image of our* Time. The horn of time blows on us in the art of words.

The past is narrow. The Academy and Pushkin—less intelligible than hieroglyphics.

Pushkin, Dostoyevsky, Tolstoy, etc., etc., must be thrown overboard from the steamer of the Present Time.

He who does not forget his *first* love will not experience his last.

Who will be so credulous as to turn his last Love to the perfumed lechery of Balmont? Will he find a reflection of the brave soul of today there?

Who will be so cowardly as not to dare to tear the paper buckler off warrior Bryusov's black tailcoat? Will he find the dawn of unknown beauty there?

Wash your hands which have touched the filthy slime of the books written by countless Leonid Andreyevs.

All those Maxim Gorkis, Kuprins, Bloks, Sologubs, Remizovs, Averchenkos, Tchornys, Kuzmins, Bunins, etc., etc.—need only villas on a river bank. Thus fate rewards tailors.

From the height of skyscrapers we look at their littleness! . . .

We *demand* that the following *rights* of poets be respected:

1. To enlarge the *volume* of the poet's vocabulary by words arbitrary and derivative.

2. To reject the invincible hate for the language that existed before them.

3. To wrest with horror from their proud foreheads the wreath of penny glory woven out of bath birch twigs.

4. To stand on the rock of the word "we" in the midst of the sea of catcalls and outrage.

And if *for the time being* too the filthy marks of your "common sense" and "good taste" have remained in our lines, nevertheless, *for the first time*, the Lightning of the New Future Beauty of the Self-sufficient Word is already flashing on them.

D. Burliuk, Alexander Kruchenykh

Moscow, December 1912.   V. Mayakovsky, Victor Khlebnikov

LYVSHITS:

From among the seven participants in the almanac, the manifesto was signed by only four: David Burliuk, Kruchenykh, Mayakovsky, and Khlebnikov. Kandinsky was not a regular member of our group, and as for Nikolai Burliuk and myself, we were not in Moscow at the time . . .

I was particularly revolted by the style of the manifesto, or to be exact, by the lack of style: side by side with the extreme "industrial" semantics of the "steamer of the Present Time" and "the heights of skyscrapers" (it would seem that the only thing missing was "our age of steam and electricity") were the deeply provincial "dawn of unknown beauty" and "lightning of the New Future Beauty."

I could never find out from David who composed the notorious manifesto. I know only that Khlebnikov did not take part in it (he may have been away from Moscow at the time). It was with surprise that I found in this concoction the phrase about "the paper buckler of the warrior Bryusov" which I had said in a night's conversation with Mayakovsky and which for some reason he remembered. He was the only one who could put it next to expressions which were unmistakably his such as "the perfumed lechery of Balmont," "the filthy slime of the books written by countless Leonid Andreyevs," "the wreath of penny glory woven out of bath birch twigs," and that for him most typical appeal "to stand on the rock of the word 'we' in the midst of the sea of catcalls and outrage."

With all those reservations about the manifesto itself, the almanac had to be regarded as an event, if only because exactly half of the space in it was occupied by Khlebnikov. And how good those pieces by Khlebnikov were! . . . Compared with Khlebnikov, who widened the scope of words to the limits which before him had seemed incredible, everything else in the book seemed of little importance, through it also contained two poems by Mayakovsky, composed by means of "inverted" rhyme, and the enchanting—undervalued to this day—prose of Nikolai Burliuk, as well as his article on cubism, which brought into sharp relief the most crucial problems of modern painting.

I had imagined our first sortie somewhat differently, when we had discussed it in November, but—what is done is done, and then Khlebnikov redeemed all sins and reconciled me to all David's shortcomings.

KRUCHENYKH:

I remember only one instance when Khlebnikov, Mayakovsky, Burliuk, and myself were all writing a piece together—it was the manifesto for the book *Slap to the Public's Taste*. The writing took a long time; we discussed every sentence, word, letter.

I remember that when I proposed: "to throw Pushkin, Dostoyevsky, Tolstoy" . . . Mayakovsky added: "overboard from the steamer of the Present Time."

I remember my phrase: "perfumed lechery of Balmont." Khlebnikov's amendment, *"aromatic* lechery of Balmont," was not accepted . . .

"To stand on the rock of the word 'we'" and "From the heights of skyscrapers we look at their littleness" (Andreyev's, Kuprin's, Kuzmin's, and others) are Khlebnikov's expressions.

It was he who, on completion of the manifesto, declared, "I will not sign this . . . Kuzmin must be crossed out—he is sensitive." It was decided that Khlebnikov would sign for the time being and later would send a letter to the editors about his *votum separatum.* Of course the world never saw this letter.

When the manifesto was written, we dispersed. I went to dinner and ate two beefsteaks—so exhausted was I by this collaboration with the giants.

SHKLOVSKY:

In this book Khlebnikov's dates were printed for the first time. They were placed in blocks: it was assumed that dates differed by the number 317 or its multiple. The last line was: "Someone 1917."

I met the fair-haired, quiet Khlebnikov, dressed in a black coat buttoned up to his neck, at some occasion or other.

"The dates in the book," I said, "are the year when great empires fell. Do you think that our empire will fall in the year 1917?" (*Slap* was published in 1912.)

Khlebnikov replied almost without moving his lips, "You are the first man to understand what I meant."

FROM THE PREFACE TO THE "HATCHERY OF THE JUDGES II":

In the name of freedom from personal hazard, we negate orthography.

We qualify nouns not only through adjectives (as has mostly been done before us) but also through other parts of speech, and through particular letters and numbers . . .

We have annihilated punctuation marks . . .

We have crushed rhythms . . . We have ceased to search for dimensions in textbooks; all movement begets a new free rhythm for the poet . . .

The richness of the poet's vocabulary—is his justification.

We regard the word as the creator of myth; the word, dying, gives birth to myth, and the other way around . . .

We have contempt for glory: we know feelings which did not exist before us.

We are the new people of a new life.

> David Burliuk, Helena Guro, Nikolai Burliuk,
> Vladimir Mayakovsky, Katarina Nizen, Victor
> Khlebnikov, Benedict Lyvshits, A. Kruchenykh.

In March 1913 a second almanac was published, containing, among other things, several poems and drawings by Mayakovsky. In May of the same year, his first individual volume appeared, entitled I!, *with illustrations by Tchekhrygin and Zhegin.*

A POEM FROM THE VOLUME I!:

A FEW WORDS ABOUT MYSELF
by Vladimir Mayakovsky

I like watching children die.
And you will you find rising laughter's misty crest
behind ink sorrow?
And I—
in the reading room of streets—
have so often looked through the volumes of coffins.
Midnight
in me and in the fence is sticking
the finger's
wet bone
and with rain drops on its bald dome
the mad church is rushing.
Christ runaway from the icon popped his head,
rain kissed

the limb of Passion.
I am warning the brick,
I am thrusting the dagger of words possessed
into the swollen softness of the skies:
"Sun!
My Father!
Be merciful, do not strike!
It is through you the threads of my blood drip.
It is through the soul's torn shreds
my soul
in the burnt-out heaven
on the rusty cross of the belfry!
Time!
You crooked dauber,
paint my cheeks
for the misshapen chapel of the age!
I'm lonely like the last pupil in the eye
of a man who goes to the blind!"

IN AUGUST 1913 THE ALMANAC ENTITLED "THE DEAD MOON"
WAS PUBLISHED. BENEDICT LYVSHITS:

. . . I've come to stay with Nicholas Burliuk . . .

The strangest thing about it was that the only futurists in the world were resting on the narrow iron beds where we used to lie every morning.

How did this come about?

How did it happen that we, who six months earlier used the word "futurism" only as a term of abuse, not only applied it to ourselves but refused everybody else the right to use this label?

Did an article by Bryusov in *Russian Thought* play a part here—an article in which he, with his usual methodicalness and talent for classification, segregated the as yet not too plentiful material contained in our books and, our declarations notwithstanding, proclaimed us the Moscow variety of futurism, as distinct from the St. Petersburg brand, headed by Igor Syevyeryanin?

Did the gutter press influence this—the press . . . that could no longer refrain from using the colloquial name to describe the new Huns, who threatened to occupy a lasting place in their mercenary columns?

Or was it the sensible David who, having surveyed the situation, decided that it was no use swimming against the stream, that to go on refusing to accept the name forced on us would mean to cause too much chaos in the minds of the general public, and perhaps to estrange it from us?

Be that as it may, our new name received the sanction of "the father of Russian futurism," perhaps with Mayakovsky's approbation, and when I came from Medvyed I was faced with an accomplished fact: *The Dead Moon*, already gone to print and opening with my article setting out our program, had the following subtitle:

ALMANAC
OF THE WORLD'S ONLY FUTURISTS!!—
THE POETS
"HILEA"

. . . David deprecates this, saying that "newsboys have stuck a label on us," but it is quite clear that this could not have happened without Burliuk's direct participation, since our publications were at his all-powerful disposal. Taking on the label already made popular, Burliuk acted with careful premeditation, and his calculations proved right: the new term, in its scope, was eminently suited to decribe the growing movement; and as for the rest, David, who never treated terminology seriously, simply ignored it.

♯ 6 ♯

The Yellow Tunic

♯

It has been written about more than Vladimir Mayakovsky's poetry. Even then it was less important than the poetry, but to say that it had no importance at all seems wrong to me. How it came about, and what purpose it served, is told by Vassili Kamensky, Benedict Lyvshits, and Ludmila Mayakovskaya, though their accounts do not always agree. Victor Shklovsky and Boris Pasternak interpret the meaning of the yellow tunic. The events connected with it are recalled by Kornel Chukovsky. The picture is completed by the manifesto of Laryonov and Zdanyevich, notes in the journal of Alexander Blok, and by the press of the period. Vladimir Mayakovsky mounts the platform dressed in the yellow tunic and recites poetry. One of the poems is called "The Fop's Tunic."

FROM DAVID BURLIUK'S LETTER TO KAMENSKY:

Come quickly . . . It's time. New fighters have come to join us—Volodya Mayakovsky and A. Kruchenykh. These two can be depended on. Particularly Mayakovsky, who is my fellow student at the School of Painting. A wild youth, and a swashbuckler, but quite witty, sometimes too much so. A child of nature, like you and all of us. You will see. He longs to meet you and chat about flying, poetry, and all that futurism. Mayakovsky is always near me and is beginning to write good poems. He's got a savage natural talent and is very sure of himself . . . he is bursting with the desire to fight for futurism. We must act quickly . . .

ACCORDING TO KAMENSKY'S ACCOUNT, WHEN HE CAME TO MOSCOW AT BURLIUK'S REQUEST AND MET MAYAKOVSKY AT THE APARTMENT OF "THE FATHER OF RUSSIAN FUTURISM," THE FOLLOWING PLAN OF ACTION WAS WORKED OUT AND PUT ON PAPER:

1. In exactly three days, at noon, all three poets—Mayakovsky, Kamensky, Burliuk—gaudily dressed, wearing top hats, their faces painted, will go onto the Kuznetsky Bridge and, walking there, will take turns reciting their poems, aloud and with complete seriousness.

2. Do not pay attention to the possible sneers of fools or to bourgeois derision.

3. To the question: who are you?—reply seriously: the geniuses of our time—Mayakovsky, Burliuk, Kamensky.

4. To all other questions: this is how futurists live. Do not interrupt us in our work. Listen.

5. To provide Mayakovsky with a yellow tunic . . .

FROM MIKHAIL LARIONOV AND ILYA ZDANYEVICH'S MANIFESTO
"WHY DO WE PAINT OURSELVES?":

. . . We have related art to life. After a long period of separation on the part of the masters, we have loudly recalled life, and life has invaded art; it is time for art to invade life. The painting of faces—is the start of this invasion . . .

We are not concerned with aesthetics alone . . . We value print and information. A synthesis of decorativeness and illustrativeness—is the principle of our painting. We beautify life and we show things to come— that is why we paint ourselves . . .

We paint ourelves for a passing moment and the change in experience causes the change in color; as image devours image, as shop windows flicker and mingle with each other, seen from a moving car—so it is with our faces . . .

KAMENSKY:

Sitting in Burliuk's den at ten in the morning exactly three days later, according to the "timetable," as Mayakovsky called the sheet of paper we had signed, we began to prepare for our first foray into the streets.

Mayakovsky tried on a new orange tunic, made by his mother, Alexandra Alexeyevna, and by his two sisters, Ludmila and Olga.

Burliuk had on a coat with a collar on which multicolored patches had been sewn, a yellow waistcoat with silver buttons, and a top hat.

My Parisian suit, the color of cocoa, had been lined with gold brocade. I too had a top hat.

With a crayon Mayakovsky drew an airplane on my forehead. On Burliuk's cheek he drew a dog with an upturned tail . . .

At the last moment Mayakovsky gave up the idea of painting his face. He wanted to make himself up to look like a Negro but we were against it.

Our unusual excitement could be explained by the fact that on the previous day I had received a permit from the governor for this public appearance.

Exactly at noon we put wooden spoons into our lapels and went to the Kuznetsky Bridge.

We took turns reciting poems while we walked, slowly and majestically.

We walked with serious, stern expressions, without even smiling.

I noticed that all the people we passed turned back to follow us, and some ran in front of us asking anxious questions: "Who are they? Madmen? Savages from the islands? Circus clowns? Wild animal tamers? Fakirs? Wrestlers? Indians? Yogi? Americans?" . . .

Some woman with a little daughter got so frightened that she crossed herself. "God almighty!"

Her daughter ran up to us: "How beautiful!"

The woman pulled her by the sleeve: "Come away, Tanya, come away. They can harm you. We must call the police."

An officer strolling with a lady exclaimed with anger, "The scoundrels. Who gave them permission to do this?"

The lady came to our rescue: "They are variety artists. I know them very well. It's their benefit performance. Bravo!" . . .

The crowd grew bigger and bigger.

The street was so full that cabs could not go past.

Burliuk roared, "You have before you the poets of genius, innovators, futurists: Mayakovsky, Kamensky, Burliuk. We are discovering the America of new art. I congratulate you!"

The crowd was applauding, whistling, shouting, protesting.

Suddenly a long police whistle was heard.

We went back up the street.

The policemen went on whistling, trying to disperse the crowd and shouting, "Go away!"

A little girl handed Mayakovsky an orange.

He thanked her and began to eat it.

"He's eating it! He's eating it!" murmured the crowd . . .

Some clenched their fists and quite clearly wanted a fight.

We were defended, however, by some young people, particularly students, who bravely pushed off the attackers . . .

We continued our march the next day, and the day after, and on the fourth and fifth day . . .

We did not limit ourselves to the Kuznetsky Bridge and to Tverska Street but appeared everywhere: in restaurants, canteens, cafés, theaters, railway stations, beer halls, tea houses, inns. Wherever there were people.

LYVSHITS:

One October morning . . . the door opened slowly and in the doorway stood Mayakovsky, having come straight from the railway station.

I did not recognize him at first. He was quite unlike the Volodya Mayakovsky I had known before.

His green overcoat, which must have been bought the day before, and his glistening top hat changed his appearance completely. In contrast to this foppish attire was his bare neck and light orange tunic which looked particularly strange.

With childish pride Mayakovsky showed off his altered appearance, but it was quite evident that he was not yet accustomed either to his new clothes or to the new role which they were to serve.

As a matter of fact, all this was very modest indeed: the cheap top hat, the too narrow overcoat of old-fashioned cut—bought, I suppose, at a third-rate store which carried ready-made suits—the frail stick, and the undertakers' gloves. But to Volodya the outfit seemed the pinnacle of elegance—particularly his orange tunic, with which he stressed his independence from vulgar fashion . . .

Mayakovsky stunned me with his very first words. He informed me that David had ordered him to bring me to Moscow, dead or alive. I am to go with him today, at once, because on the thirteenth the "first evening of speechmakers in Russia" is to take place and my participation is absolutely essential.

There can be no excuses now that my military service has ended. Money? There is money enough; we are going first class. In fact all futurists are assured of a carefree life from now on . . .

In Moscow chaos and confusion began at once . . .

We went for a stroll, assisted by a gaping crowd, shocked by the orange tunic and by the sight of a top hat and bare neck.

Mayakovsky took to it like a fish to water.

I was delighted at the coldbloodedness with which he reacted to the looks directed at him.

Not even the shadow of a smile.

On the contrary, the sullen concentration of a man whom, for no reason, they disturb with their bothersome attention.

This looked so much like the truth that I did not know how to treat him.

I feared lest, because of an improper intonation, I should spoil the course of a perfect game.

Though Larionov had already, a month before shocked the Muscovites by appearing with a painted face on the Kuznetsky Bridge, Moscow still was not used to such shows and the crowd around us grew.

In order to avoid the police we had to turn into a less crowded side street.

We went to see some friends of Volodya's and then a number of others, all those whom Volodya deemed fit to see him in his futurist splendor. At the School of Painting, Sculpture, and Architecture, where his name was still on the roll, a triumph awaited him: his orange tunic against the background of official walls was an unheard-of challenge to the school's bar-rack-like discipline. Mayakovsky was greeted and taken leave of amidst applause.

That still was not enough for him.

Having come to the conclusion that people had now got used to his apparel, he took me to stores where astonished assistants laid out the gaudiest fabrics they could find on their shelves.

Mayakovsky was not satisfied with anything he saw.

After a long search he found a black and yellow striped fabric of unknown origin, and he decided to buy it.

Happy at last, he suggested magnanimously that I too "brighten up my clothes, even if with a spot." I got myself some motley fabric which I thought would be enough to provide a garish tie and handkerchief. That was all I had the courage for.

Volodya's mother made him the striped tunic.

He took me home. I found the fact that Volodya had a home, mother, sisters, a family life, more strange than the ugly wallpaper which contrasted, in color and other respects, with his new attire—something halfway between a jockey's jacket and a Jewish prayer coat.

Mayakovsky the affectionate son and brother—this was something that did not fit into the image of a noisy rebel, an image which he fostered himself. His mother was clearly unhappy about Volodya's new idea: she was embarrassed by the growing notoriety of her son, which as yet bore little resemblance to real fame . . .

But Mayakovsky was his family's darling: his caprices were irresistible not only to his mother, but also to his sisters, nice modest girls who worked at a post office.

One of them, at her brother's request, made me a tie, which looked unusually like the *lanhuti* from Dahomey, while his mother cut and fitted Volodya for his striped tunic.

LUDMILA MAYAKOVSKAYA:

One day, after six o'clock, upon my return from the factory I came into the room where, next to the dressing table, Mama was fitting Volodya for a fustian tunic of wide yellow and black stripes. I was about to reproach Volodya for this new idea of his, but when I saw how becoming it was . . . I desisted. Volodya asked her to hurry.

Mama and my sister were just putting the finishing touches on the tunic. Also present was Vassili Kamensky. He and Volodya were cracking jokes about the effect the Yellow Tunic would have on the audience at the literary evening. We then sat down to tea. Volodya recited fragments of poems—his own and those of others—in preparation for his public appearance. After tea we gaily bade Volodya goodbye and he went off to his literary evening.

Who would have thought that such a happy day would have such a sad ending?

I asked Mama, "How come you made that tunic?"

Mama replied, "Volodya brought the fustian to me in the morning. I was surprised at the color, asked him what it was for, and at first refused to make it. But Volodya insisted: 'But Mama, I must have this tunic. I need it for our meeting tonight. If you don't do it, I will take it to a tailor. But I have no money, so I shall have to look for money and for a tailor. I can't go in my black tunic: I wouldn't be let in by the ushers. But once this tunic catches their eye, they will lose their heads and let me through. I must appear today.'"

Mama knew that Volodya had no money, she also knew that he would do as he had said. His words seemed convincing to her. She decided to comply with his request and sat down to make him his tunic.

This is how the famous Yellow Tunic was born.

But "polite" society did not forgive him the challenge. There were noise and uproar. The newspapers were full of attacks and abuse.

"I can't understand, Alexandra Alexeyevna, how you can bear all your Volodya's pranks quietly," a certain woman she knew told Mama. "If he were my son, I would break a couple of sticks over his head and he would stop meddling in such affairs."

Mama replied, "I can tell you one thing. It is very good that Volodya is not your son. I trust Volodya. He will never do anything dishonest or bad; if he made himself such a tunic, that means he needed it."

Nikolai Khardzhiyev quotes a notice by S. Dolinsky, co-editor of several futurist volumes, to the effect that the model for Mayakovsky's tunic was worn by a jockey he knew, Synyegubkin.

He made speeches in which he talked about black cats. Dry black cats emit electricity when one strokes them . . . The purpose of his cats argument was something like this: electricity can be got even from a cat. The Egyptians had done this. It is more convenient, however, to provide electricity by industrial methods and leave the cats alone. The old art, we then thought, had achieved its effect in the way in which the Egyptians produced electricity whereas we wanted to obtain pure electricity, pure art.

Such were the theses on which talks and lectures were based. There was no possibility of printing one's works, but one could appear in public with them. For such appearances labels were needed. Nikolai Kulbin taught us how to formulate theses: as strongly as if the Turks had occupied the city and were proclaiming this by beating their drums.

LYVSHITS ON NIKOLAI KULBIN, THE STRANGE INSTIGATOR
OF RUSSIAN FUTURISM:

Tall, thin, stooping, with a skull like Socrates' and Mongolian cheekbones, above which deep-set dark brown expressive eyes looked out from under half-closed eyelids (more expressive, I suppose than the thoughts he spoke), Kulbin more than anyone else in our group was able to impress an audience. The moment he appeared on the platform, their hostile suspiciousness receded.

Of course, some of this was due to his age (he was forty-four years old at the time), his title of councilor of state, and the fact that he was a doctor by profession, as well as to his seriousness, dictated by his age and position in society but tormenting him like an incurable disease. (What lengths he went to in order to rid himself of his respectability, which consumed him like a cancer: he would stand on a chair while lecturing and shout the most paradoxical aphorisms, even maligning himself—all of this to make people believe he was young at heart.) None of this, however, really explained the rapt attention with which his words were received.

He was a peddler, on every occasion bringing his listeners some latest novelty of Western European thought, the newest fashion, not only in the spheres of visual art, music, or literature, but also in the spheres of science, politics, social ideas, philosophy. It was a pile of raw material, entirely undigested and unassimilated, from which anyone present could choose anything that appealed to him.

THEMES OF MAYAKOVSKY'S TALK ENTITLED "THE GLOVE," 1913:

1. Current taste and levers of speech.
2. Images of cities in the eyes of speechmakers.
3. A berceuse is an orchestra of gutters.
4. Egyptians and Greeks stroking dry black cats.
5. Layers of fat in easy chairs.
6. Gaudy rags of our souls.

SHKLOVSKY:

It was then that Mayakovsky put on his yellow tunic . . . Yellow was regarded as the color of futurism. The lower part of the tunic was broad, it had a turned-down collar, and the fabric was not very thick, so that through the yellow tunic—which was fairly long—black trousers were visible . . .

The tunic appealed to them more than the cats. It was easy to write about. In those days a journalist had to be given an uncomplicated door to open. He did not penetrate farther than the door.

"RUSSKIE VEDOMOSTI," OCTOBER 15, 1913:

The room was overflowing with people, the seats were sold out, and a troop of policemen divided those without tickets from those on whom fate had smiled and given tickets. The heroes of the evening kept appearing here and there, thus stimulating the excitement of the already excited public. The most heroic of them was dressed in a curious tunic of yellow and black stripes, without a belt . . . Not wishing to postpone events until the future, albeit a near one, the young striped futurist went into action at once:

"We are demolishing your old world . . . You hate us . . ."

THE NEWSPAPER "RUL," OCTOBER 21, 1913:

Mayakovsky began to recite his poems which said how "after the cabaret the crowd will take away its fat bodies along the dark alley." "You will trample me, my heart, with your dirty galoshes?" he shouted.

The air became heavy with impending scandal.

YOU HAVE IT!
by Vladimir Mayakovsky

An hour from now in the pure alley
your swollen fat (man's left-over) will flow,
and to think I've opened caskets of verse for you,
I—squanderer of priceless mines of words.

Eh you, mister, there's cabbage in your moustache
from cabbage soups you must have eaten somewhere;
eh you, lady, with the thick lipstick on your mouth,
from the shell of things you view the world like an oyster.

All of you, dirty, in galoshes and without them,
want to trample on poets' butterfly hearts.
The mob will beast-like spawn,
the hundred-headed louse will bristle up its legs.

And if today I, the brutal Hun,
won't clown for you—what will you do,
if I laugh and spit with joy,
spit in your face I will,
I—squanderer of priceless mines of words.

LYVSHITS:

All tickets sold out, mounted police, scrambles at the entrance, over-crowded room, all this changed from chance occurrences into permanent features of our appearances. On that particular evening the program had been planned on a grander scale than usual. Three talks—Mayakovsky's "Glove," David Burliuk's "Those Who Milk Emaciated Frogs," and Kruchenykh's "Word"—promised to show the Muscovites three sets of stunning truths . . .

According to the poster, six people were to take part in the evening—that is to say, the entire "Hilea" group. The announcement stated also that "speeches will be made by painters: David Burliuk, Lev Zhegin, Casimir Malevich, Vladimir Mayakovsky, and Vassili Tchekhrygin." This was to mean, not that the painters would draw us, but that we would appear against the background of specially painted screens, symbolically separating the futurists from the rest of the world.

But Khlebnikov was in Astrakhan. Besides, he could not be allowed to mount the platform because of his weak voice and the hopeless "and so on" with which he broke up his recital after the first few lines, as if stressing the continuity of his verbal emanation.

David was not in Moscow either: he had to go to St. Petersburg suddenly on some business, so he asked his brother Nikolai to read his talk. In order to remedy the situation somehow, I undertook to read, besides my own poems, Khlebnikov's texts as well.

The success of the evening was in fact Mayakovsky's success. His relaxed manner on the platform, his excellent voice, expressive intonation and gestures, made him immediately outstanding among the participants . . .

It was when Mayakovsky began to talk about layers of fat sitting in the audience that a sound not unlike the rattling of a worn-out engine was heard in the first row, which was occupied entirely by the military. The glittering cavalry officers, with their pomaded and parted hair, had taken the speaker's words as an offensive allusion to themselves and were angrily knocking their sabers against the floor . . .

Only the title of madman (which gradually changed from metaphor to reality) made it possible for Kruchenykh—without the risk of being cut to pieces—to splash a glass of hot tea into the first row of seats, with a cry that "our tails are colored yellow" and that he, "unlike the unrecognized pink moribund, flies to the Americas, because he forgot to hang himself." The public could no longer understand where irrational poetry ended and madness began . . .

Mayakovsky was reading his last poems . . .

I remember, his poem "You Have It" had a particular effect when, pointing his finger at a bearded man in the audience, he roared:

> Eh you, mister, there's cabbage in your moustache,
> from cabbage soups you must have eaten somewhere!

and right after caused great embarrassment to a girl student, who never used cosmetics, when he turned to her with:

> Eh you, lady, with the thick lipstick on your mouth,
> from the shell of things you view the world like an oyster!

But the dragoons in the first row no longer knocked their sabers when, transfixing them with his eyes, he ended:

> spit in your face I will,
> I—squanderer of priceless mines of words.

Even that least perceptive part of the audience seemed to have adapted itself to the tone of the evening within an hour.

Everybody was in a good mood. We were greeted and taken leave of with applause, in spite of Kruchenykh's declaration that he passionately desired to be booed. We were not offended by the applause, though we did not have any illusions either about its real character.

FROM THE JOURNALS OF ALEXANDER BLOK:

March 25, 1913.

. . . In recent days—discussions of the futurists—scandalous. I decided not to go. The Burliuk's, whom I have not seen yet, frighten me away. I am afraid there is more boorishness here than anything else (in D. Burliuk).

The futurists as a whole are probably a more outstanding phenomenon than the acmeists . . .

Above all, the futurists have already produced Igor Syevyeryanin. I suspect that Khlebnikov is an important phenomenon. Helena Guro deserves attention. Burliuk has a fist. All this—more earthy and lively than acmeism . . .

Pyast called, told me about the futurists. On yesterday's poster was written: the liberation of literature from the mud into which it was pushed by Andreyev, Sologub, Blok, etc. . . .

April 29.

. . . The Bayans, Kotlarevskys, Nyevyedomskys, Batyushkovs, Yablonovskys, as if they arranged this among themselves, explain the success of the futurists by saying that "we" ("symbolists" or whatever—are rotten, senile . . .

FROM THE REMINISCENCES OF KORNEL CHUKOVSKY:

. . . Although the futurists officially attacked me on the platform and in their public appearances, although in many of their manifestoes they vituperated against me . . . in real life, behind the scenes, so to speak, our relations were good . . .

Even then, in 1913, I gave a talk about the futurists at the Polytechnic Museum (and somewhere else). It was then a fashionable subject. The talk had to be repeated about three times. "All Moscow" used to come: Chaliapin, Count Olsufyev, Ivan Bunin, Muromtsev, Tolstoy's son Ilya, Savva Mamontov, and even—I do not know why—Rodzyanko with one of the grand dukes. I remember how, just as I was speaking against futurism, Mayakovsky appeared in his yellow tunic and interrupted my paper, shouting offensive remarks directed against me. Noise and catcalls could be heard among the audience.

I had smuggled his yellow tunic into the Polytechnic Museum myself. The police forbade Mayakovsky to appear publicly in the yellow tunic. The policeman at the entrance let Mayakovsky in only when he saw him dressed in a coat. I had the yellow tunic under my arm, wrapped in a newspaper. On the stairs I gave it to Vladimir Vladimirovich, who secretly put it on and impressively appeared among the audience where he hurled his thunderclaps at me.

CHUKOVSKY ALSO REMEMBERS ANOTHER EPISODE CONNECTED
WITH THE YELLOW TUNIC:

The almighty Vlas Doroshevich, chief editor of the *Russkoe Slovo*, a most influential journalist whom Vladimir Vladimirovich wanted to meet, sent me the following telegram (which I have kept to this day): "If you bring me your yellow tunic I will call a policeman, cordial greetings" . . .

LUDMILA MAYAKOVSKAYA:

As time passed, futurism became more and more inflated; this was done by the participants themselves and by the press.

One Sunday, when we were all at home, the morning papers arrived. While Volodya shaved by the dressing table I read the newspapers aloud. We used to buy nearly all the papers, because they were all writing about the futurists. I said to Volodya, "Just listen to what they are writing about you: 'His poor old mother cries her heart out for having brought up such a son of a bitch.'" (I cannot vouch for the exact words but that was their sense.)

Volodya, without stopping his shaving, said quietly, "I know that critic; he has a wife and two mistresses and has to pay for them somehow."

ALEXANDRA MAYAKOVSKAYA:

I did not go to those evening meetings. His sisters did.

Volodya used to say, "Mama, I don't want you to go to those evening meetings where they call me names and attack me. They would only depress you and get on your nerves.

BORIS PASTERNAK:

Behind his way of life one could discern something like a decision, which had already been made, so that its effects could not be avoided. Such a decision was his genius: his encounter with it had impressed him so deeply that it became for him a standing order, to whose fulfillment he devoted himself entirely, without regret or hesitation.

But he was still young, and the forms which this theme would take were still in the future. But the theme was an urgent one and did not brook delay. For this reason, in the initial period, to satisfy it he had to anticipate his future, and the anticipation realized in the first person is affectation, a pose.

From these poses, that were just as natural in the world of lofty self-expression as rules of good manners are in life, he took the pose of outward uniformity, the most difficult one for an artist and the most generous in relation to friends and those close to him. He kept that pose with such perfection that now it is almost impossible to analyze its underlying reality.

And yet, the springboard of his boldness was a wild shyness, while under the appearances of will there hid a phenomenal sensitivity, prone to unjustified gloom—lack of will. Equally deceptive also was the mechanism of his yellow tunic. He used it as a means, not to fight the bourgeois coats, but that black velvet of talent in himself, whose mawkish black-browed forms had began to irritate him at an earlier stage than it happens with less gifted people.

THE FOP'S TUNIC
by Vladimir Mayakovsky

I will make myself black trousers
of the velvet of my voice.
Yellow tunic of three yards of sunset sky.
Through the world's Nevsky Prospect I will walk
the fop's and Don Juan's step on its slippery stones.

Let earth, effeminate through peace, cry:
"You want to ravish spring's green!"
I will shout at the sun, baring my white teeth:
"I like parading on smooth asphalt!"

Is it not because the sky has a blue edge,
and my mistress is earth, with washerwoman's looks,
I will give you verses, gay like bee-bah-boh,
sharp and indispensable like toothpicks!

To women in love with my flesh I speak,
and to the girl who looks at me like a brother:
shower the poet with smiles—
I'll sew them on the fop's tunic, it will be as if in flowers!

1. Baghdadi. The house in which Mayakovsky was born.

2. The Mayakovsky family.

3. Report of the secret police agents who watched Mayakovsky, August 1908.

4. Cover of Mayakovsky's file at the Moscow secret police headquarters, 1908.

5. Mayakovsky's registration
card at the Okhrana in
Moscow, 1908.

6. Sonia Shamardina.

7. Mayakovsky as a student in
the School of Painting.

8. Mayakovsky's drawing
   of Vassili Kamensky.

9. A group photograph of
the Futurists, taken in 1913.

10. "Yellow Blouse," 1913.

11. Mayakovsky's drawing
of Velimir Khlebnikov, 1916.

The Name of Tragedy

*Maria Burliuk speaks about the eighteen-year-old Mayakov-
sky watching* Hamlet, *produced by the English stage innovator, Gordon Craig, at the Moscow Art Theater. Others tell
how Mayakovsky wrote, directed, and acted his own* Hamlet
*—his first great work—a tragedy, whose title was the author's
name.*

MARIA BURLIUK:

On the gray poster of the Moscow Art Theater shines *Hamlet*. It is the
production of Gordon Craig and K. S. Stanislavsky. Three years were
spent preparing this play for the stage, and the theater lovers grumbled,
"How is it that the English genius is not able to cope with *Hamlet,* and
that the rehearsals are taking such a long time?" There were rumors that
Craig wanted to do away not only with the footlights but with the scenery
and even the actors as well. He thought of replacing the players with
marionettes, which he hoped would give him perfect rhythm. In December 1911, I went with Burliuk and Mayakovsky to see this production of
Hamlet. We now always bought three tickets, as we got one for our friend,

the eighteen-year-old Mayakovsky. At that time he had no opportunity to attend the theater unless he (accidentally) obtained a free pass at the Moscow Academy where he was in his second year as an art student.

The performance of *Hamlet* began at 7:30 P.M. The music was furnished by the composer Satz. Instead of decorations, movable screens of various sizes, and cubes, were used. To portray the beauty and the richness of the palace Craig had some of the cubes covered with gold paper. In other scenes they appeared only gray. On the stage there were no doors, windows, or furniture. Everything depended on the imagination of the onlooker . . .

The makeup and costume of Ophelia, who was played by Gsowskaja, are splendid. She seems exceedingly thin and transparent. She sings in a weak voice as she plucks the petals from her bouquet, and the public is surprised to notice that the flowers are real . . . We had seats in the first row which cost 25 dollars for the three. Mayakovsky was very silent and attentive to the proceedings on stage.

Only two years later in St. Petersburg, on the second and fourth of December, 1913, he was all ready to put on the stage his own tragedy in two acts *Vladimir Mayakovsky* . . . The first act has twelve pages of text, and the second act has eight pages. From this minimal number of words it is possible to judge how short the performance was, and how laconic and unusual. But this conspectus of contemporaneous tragedy has so much motion, and is imbued with a multitude of scenic events . . .

And when Mayakovsky saw *Hamlet* with us, even then the plan of his own production began to grow in his mind. The tragedy, *V. Mayakovsky,* includes many facets or particles, every one of which can become a scenario in itself. [*]

LUDMILA MAYAKOVSKAYA:

The tragedy *Vladimir Mayakovsky* . . . was written in Kuntsev at Bogrovnikov's summer place, where we stayed from May 18 to the end of August, 1913.

My least pleasant recollections are connected with trips to the country: I used to go to Moscow at half-past six in the morning and come back some time between eight and nine in the evening. At that time my sister

[*] The above fragment has been taken from the original English by D. and M. Burliuk, *Color and Rhyme*, No. 31, 1956.

worked at the main post office, sometimes had late duty there and came back at midnight. Friends visited us very seldom. Only Mama and Volodya remained at home. We were used to having people often and the house seemed empty. Volodya felt lonely and we were short of money, which made things even worse.

Volodya spent whole days walking around the park in Kuntsev, also at Krylatski and Rublov, and wrote his "tragedy."

Volodya's room was in the mezzanine. Sometimes he would put down rhymes, words, lines of verse on cigarette boxes and scraps of paper. He asked Mama not to throw anything away.

That summer he frequently went to Moscow and did not come back. Mama asked him where he spent the night. "With a friend," he would say. Later it transpired that sometimes he spent whole nights out on the boulevards.

FROM THE LETTER OF CASIMIR MALEVICH TO
MIKHAIL MATYUSHIN, END OF JULY 1913:

. . . Mayakovsky is completing a drama that will be widely acclaimed. He is doing extremely well, as far as we are concerned. Our meeting, particularly the portion concerning the theater in Moscow, aroused considerable interest. The newspapers continuously write about this. Today the correspondent of *Utro Rossiyi* came to see me and, of course, received the right kind of information. I think it will be the same in St. Petersburg when we begin our activities there. Mayakovsky and I are putting forward our proposition to you; I hope you and Kruchenykh will join us. We are asking you to apply in writing to the "Youth Association" on behalf of our Theatrical Society for their support when we open with our first production . . .

MAYAKOVSKY'S STATEMENT OF NOVEMBER 16, 1913:

I, the undersigned, herewith give the painters' group, the "Youth Association," my tragedy, *Vladimir Mayakovsky*, for purposes of production in St. Petersburg during the 1913–1914 season. The production will be carried out according to my direction and under my personal artistic supervision. (The length of time of my management and the rate of my remuneration for it will be fixed by arrangement with the "Youth Association.") The fee for performances will amount to 50 (fifty) rubles per night.

LEVKI ZHEVYERZHEYEV, CHAIRMAN OF THE
"YOUTH ASSOCIATION," RELATES:

The "Youth Association" was constituted in the winter of 1909–1910 as an organization of "young" painters . . .

We wanted to reach beyond our narrow circle. We wanted to find points of contact between our own avant-garde tendencies in the sphere of painting and "modern" trends in other spheres of art.

Hence our desire for contact with young artists of the word, above all poets, a desire all the more natural because we already knew about the attempts on the part of poets to relate and justify their avant-garde intentions through the new painting.

KHARDZIYEV SAYS:

In the unpublished declaration of 1912, Khlebnikov wrote, "We want the word boldly to follow painting" . . .

In Mayakovsky's first lecture "On the Most Recent Russian Poetry," delivered at a discussion meeting of the "Youth Association" in St. Petersburg (on November 20, 1912), the following themes were significant:

3. Analogous ways of constructing artistic truth in painting and poetry.

4. Color, line, space—the independent aim of painting—the plastic concept; word, its diagram, its sound, myth, symbol—the poetic concept.

In the next paper, "Come Alone" (March 24, 1913), we find a most exact statement: "Cubism in words. Futurism in words" . . .

In the cubo-futurist group Mayakovsky was the chief representative of urbanism. From the inception of Russian cubism, critics often directed attention to the divergence between the theory of the new urban aesthetics proclaimed in manifestoes and the poetic practice of the "Hilea" group (Khlebnikov's archaism, Guro's intimism, Kamensky's folkloristics).

However, even in Mayakovsky's early work we see urbanist landscapes, in which the elements of cubism in painting are transposed to a system of poetic images . . .

ZHEVYERZHEYEV:

. . . The close contact established early in the year with the "Hilea" group of poets resulted in our association's organizing performances based on dramatic and musical material provided by members of that group . . .

The direction of the tragedy, *Vladimir Mayakovsky,* was undertaken by the author himself. His assistant was Victor Rappaport, who also undertook to engage the actors, mostly students.

We found it difficult to get a place to perform. We finally succeeded in persuading an entrepreneur who was the manager of the operetta at the theater on Ofitserskyi Street . . . The theater was called the "Amusement Park."

Due to the bad state of the theater's finances we got the place for four days, from December 2 to 5.

LYVSHITS:

Toward the end of November all the newspapers in St. Petersburg carried the announcement that on December 2, 3, 4, and 5 at the "Amusement Park" the "Four world premiere performances of the futurists of the theater will take place: on even days, the tragedy *Vladimir Mayakovsky;* on odd days, Matyushin's opera *Victory over the Sun* . . .

Prices were exorbitantly high; nevertheless on the next day all seats in the amphitheater and balcony were sold out. The newspapers published a lot of notices, whose avowed purpose was to protect the people from new attempts by the futurists to steal from their pockets, but in fact they only helped to stimulate general curiosity. Fuel was added to the fire by a letter of some repentant student published in one of the dailies two days before the first night, under the title, "The Confession of an Actor-Futurist."

The fact was, of course, that the futurists did not have and could not have a troupe of actors, either for the play or for the opera. The performers had to be recruited from among students, for whom that unexpected profit was manna from heaven. They were well paid and for every part there were a number of candidates. But at one point, the conscience of a future participant was aroused: he came to the conclusion that speaking "such nonsensical trash as Mayakovsky's verses" from the stage was beneath the dignity of an honest intellectual. So he decided to make a public confession and used this occasion to relate in detail all the preparations for the performance. The result was, as one would expect, quite the opposite from the one intended: the public was so intrigued that the last remaining tickets were quickly sold.

The focus of the performance was, of course, its author, who had written a one-man play. This was apparent not only from the literary conception of the tragedy but also from the form in which it was embodied on the stage: the only character who really acted in it was Mayakovsky. The remaining characters—the old man with cats, the man without an eye and leg, the man without an ear, the man with two kisses—were paper inventions; not because they were hidden behind papier-mâché props and seemed two-dimensional, but because—in accordance with the author's intention—they were no more than intonations of his own voice acquiring visual shape . . . With this kind of approach no conflict was possible. It was a continuous monologue, artificially split up into speeches not much different from one another with shades of intonation. If Mayakovsky had shown a greater understanding of dramatic performance, or had been more talented as a director, he would have endeavored to make his paper characters more individual, instead of presenting them as faceless figments of his imagination. But his naïve egotism cut across his poetic intentions. The only being moving, dancing, and reciting on the stage was Mayakovsky, who did not wish to give up one impressive gesture or to tone down one tiny note of his exquisite voice. Like Cronos he devoured his anemic children.

In this, however, consisted the futuristic quality of the performance, which obliterated—even though unconsciously!—the borderline between lyric poetry and drama, leaving far behind the timid avant-garde qualities of *The Fairground Booth* and *The Stranger*. Acting himself—hanging his overcoat on the wall, smoothing out his striped tunic, lighting a cigarette, reading his poems—Mayakovsky was building a bridge from one kind of art to another and he did it in the only possible way, in full sight of the unsuspecting public.

The theater was full: many people were crowded into the boxes, hallways, and wings. Writers, painters, actors, journalists, lawyers, deputies to the Duma—everyone tried to get to the opening. I remember the concentrated expression on Blok's face: he watched the stage continuously and in the interval talked excitedly to Kulbin . . .

"Utterly booed," remarked Mayakovsky later in his laconic autobiography. This is an exaggeration, dictated not by modesty, perhaps, but by his changed views on the essence and outward signs of artistic success: the way in which that first futurist play was received by the audience in its time gave no reason to call it a flop.

SHKLOVSKY:

I remember people walking around him on the stage holding cardboard shields in front of them which had strange images drawn on them. They said their lines popping up from behind those shields . . .

They were:

A girl he knew . . . Her characteristics: 2–3 fathoms. Does not speak.

An old man with dry black cats (he is several thousand years old). The others are Mayakovskys.

The man without an eye and leg, the man without an ear, the man without a head, the man with a stretched face, the man with two kisses, and the ordinary young man who loves his family. Also women, all in tears. They bring the poet their tears . . .

Mayakovsky has nowhere to stay. Around him are his own unfortunate Mayakovskys and kisses . . .

And with the principal woman it was like this:

Mayakovsky tore off a slipcover; under it was a marionette—a gigantic woman—which was later taken away.

There had been Blok's piece called *The Fairground Booth.*

Pierrot and Harlequin are in love with the same woman . . . The Columbine is made of cardboard . . . The fact that the heroine was made of cardboard was stressed in all the stage directions. The horizon was painted. Cranberry juice flows down people and down Pierrot himself.

The world of the poem *Vladimir Mayakovsky,* in spite of having things in common with the world of *The Fairground Booth,* is quite different.

In Blok, who was still a symbolist, people—that is to say, the characters in the play—were chess figures, conventional contours of parts, flickering.

They acquire, then lose reality. The play in essence is about the world shining through, being dematerialized, about everything being repeated: the girl becomes death, the death's scythe becomes the girl's pigtail; but in Mayakovsky's drama he, Mayakovsky, is most real. He has shoes with holes in them. Mayakovsky wanted to have a real laurel wreath on his head.

MATYUSHIN:

The first act began. Laughter and whistles were heard from the audience. Then everything was quiet. One heard only Mayakovsky's voice.

I appear in the next act. Mayakovsky has already entered, dressed in a long toga, a laurel wreath on his head.

—Poet!
You have been proclaimed prince.
The humble ones
throng to your door . . .

Now I am to come on. I suddenly wish to escape somewhere, leave it all. I am standing, cannot walk a step. Then someone pushes me and I not so much walk but run onto the brightly lit stage . . .

Mayakovsky is sitting on a high chair, with his legs crossed, calm and majestic. I bow to his leg and speak loud and clear:

—And now a tear.
On your slipper perhaps.
It will make a beautiful buckle.

Just then I notice a hole in the "prince's" worn slipper. I nearly burst out laughing . . .

Having finished my speech I withdraw almost to the footlights. Terrified, I look at the audience shaking with derisive laughter, echoing with catcalls. But Mayakovsky is standing calm and proud, in his toga and laurel wreath.

ZHEVYERZHEYEV:

The enormous success of the performances of the tragedy *Vladimir Mayakovsky* was due to a large extent to the impression its author made on the stage. Even the whistling front rows of the orchestra were still during Mayakovsky's soliloquies. One must note, too, that the protests and catcalls, noted by the reviewers, were mainly due to the fact that the performance, which according to the poster was to have started at eight, in fact commenced at half-past eight and ended at half-past ten, and part of the audience thought that wasn't the end.

Matyushin's opera was received with less enthusiasm than *Vladimir Mayakovsky* . . .

The painters from the "Youth Association" who had the honor to provide stage designs for both performances—I. Shkolnik and Paul Filonov for *Vladimir Mayakovsky,* and Casimir Malevich for *Victory over the Sun* —to my mind did not quite succeed in the task they were faced with.

The three-dimensional sets (with numerous ladders, bridges, and passages) originally intended by Shkolnik were not feasible in those days, so the designer went to the other extreme and contented himself with two picturesque backdrops on which were painted two excellent urbanistic landscapes, in form and content little connected with the text of the tragedy.

The most complicated (in composition, that is) "flat" costumes were provided by Filonov, who painted them personally on canvas, without preliminary sketches, and then stretched them on figure frames (corresponding to the contours of the drawing) which the actors pushed in front of them. These costumes, too, were barely connected with Mayakovsky's text.

FROM THE REMINISCENCES OF ALEXANDER MGYEBROV,
ACTOR AND DIRECTOR:

I am shown the sets. I don't understand. Various people approach me: some who like them—it means they are friends; others who laugh—they are enemies. The first are calm, the others burst out laughing, quote the text, and make the most vulgar jokes; even though they are participants too. "Why are you taking part in this?" They reply, "Why? One has to live."

The lights went out and the curtain was raised. The performance began . . . From behind the wings the play's characters—living cardboard marionettes—emerged slowly and paraded across the stage. The audience tried to laugh but their laughter stopped short. Why? Because this was not funny; it was uncanny. Not many people in the audience could explain what was happening. Suppose I came demanding a funny show, to laugh at a clown, and the clown suddenly spoke in all seriousness on a subject concerning myself? Laughter freezes on my lips. And when from the very first moment the laughter died down, one could immediately sense the audience's watchfulness, an unpleasant watchfulness . . .

Mayakovsky appeared. He mounted a rostrum without makeup, in his own clothes. He was standing above the crowd, as it were, above the city. After all, he is the son of the city and the city has erected his monument.

Why? If only because he is a poet. "Torture me now!" Mayakovsky seemed to say. "I am standing among you like a monument. Laugh, I am a poet. I am a beggar and a prince, all at once. I am—a knight for the moment. My wealth and consolation are love. My joy is that I am a poet . . . I am now glorious because you are pitiful. You are a herd, I am a leader. But I love you. I am lonely, hungry, miserable . . . Why? Just because I am a poet, because I feel and suffer. Here are my dreams—take them, if you can. Here is my tragedy—you are unable to take it . . ."

Mayakovsky did not say all this, of course, but it seemed to me that he did . . .

In reality, however, he was saying, "You are rats . . ." And the audience reacted with laughter, but their laughter recalled the fearful scratching of rats against an open door. "Mr. Mayakovsky, don't go away," shouted the public sneeringly when, troubled and excited, he was collecting in a big sack—tears, shreds of newspaper, his cardboard toys, and the audience's sneers . . .

After the first performance I realized that the futurists had suffered a fiasco. They had not passed their test before a contemporary audience. The spectators left disappointed. There were faint applause and faint hisses. The audience was calling the author out, but more for a laugh . . . Perhaps the worst thing was that there was neither a big scandal nor much laughter . . . But almost imperceptibly, inaudibly, a word passed through the house: "Mediocrity." The reviewers felt relieved. Who said this? No one knows. The futurists in the end lacked self-confidence. They were still shy and that was fatal; they did not have enough experience. Who cares about problems? The crowd did not accept them, did not understand them. And so the reviewers felt free to deal calmly, patronizingly, with slight fillips in maligning the enemy who had already been crushed and annihilated. They are not really such awful rebels, those futurists, it's just that they are somewhat lacking in scruples where other people's money is concerned, that's all . . .

The police were no less satisfied. There were very many of them. They did not understand anything, of course, but they were on guard, just in case. After the performance, the officer in charge, smiling understandingly, like a good nanny, at the protesting crowd, persuaded them to go home. The people were not satisfied, still waiting for something. Then they dispersed, and that was that.

CHUKOVSKY:

I was very happy when I succeeded at that time in publishing in *Russkoye Slovo*—then the most popular newspaper—a review of that play, in spite of the editor's serious reservations . . .

"RUSSKOYE SLOVO," NO. 279, DECEMBER 4, 1913;
K. CHUKOVSKY ON "THE FUTURIST SHOW":

It was a pity. After all, this was an imitation of L. Andreyev: the same "bom-bom," the same inflated, swollen characters—shouts, howls, the simulation of madness, the simulation of a trance, Pythian nonsense, the same manner, and in essence the same eager amassing of illusionist images to which we have been accustomed by Sergeyev-Censky, or even O. Dimov.

Naïve, provincial impressionism.

There were good points in the play. There is no doubt that the author has talent; unfortunately, though, there was no novelty, no revolt in it. Everything was commonplace and polite, as if seven years had not passed and we were again witnessing the rehearsal of *Black Masks.*

After all, in the very same theater, the late Komissarjevskaya and Meyerhold produced *The Fairground Booth, Man's Life,* etc.

It is nice that the author tries to speak poetically in the guise of an Apache standing on the verge of desperation and madness; but this is, unfortunately, the only string on which he can play. He plays well, but monotonously, and so we can feel the presence of boredom.

FROM THE FIRST ACT OF THE TRAGEDY:
The old man with cats:

Leave it!
Wise men don't need the consolation of a rattle.
I am a fossil one thousand years old.
And I see—in you the shout of torment
Crucified with laughter.

.   .   .

The softness of the moons does not rule us any more—
The glow of street lights cripples more glaringly.
In the land of cities
soulless objects have declared themselves masters

and are crawling to wipe us out.
And on the howls of the human horde
God, frenzied, looks from heaven,
and in the rags of God's beard
the hands of dust-bitten roads are fumbling.
God, and yet
he's not now talking of grace,
but promises torments to frighten little souls.
Leave him!
Better go and stroke—
stroke dry black cats!

.   .   .

We will put suns in our lovers' clothes,
we will forge silver toys out of stars.
Leave your homes!
Go and stroke—
stroke dry black cats!

                    The man without an ear:
This is the truth!
Over the city,
where there are little wooden flags—
a woman—
the eyelids of black caverns—
throws herself about,
spits on the pavement, angry,
and from her spittle giant cripples grow.

.   .   .

Gentlemen!
Stop!
One can't go on like this!
The alleys have rolled up their sleeves for the brawl.
And my longing is growing,
fearful, incomprehensible,
like a tear on the muzzle of a bleary bitch.

                    The old man with cats:
The things have to be cut to pieces.

Have you understood this at least?
Not for nothing have I foreseen you'll be smothered with caresses!

The man with a stretched face:
But maybe things have to be loved?
Maybe they have a different soul,
but still a soul?

The man without an ear:
Many things have inadvertently been sewn together.
The heart
does not listen to anger.

The man with a stretched face:
And where man has his mouth—look—
many things have the seam of the ear!

V. Mayakovsky:
Do not let hate pierce your hearts!
For you,
my children,
the lesson is hard and relentless.
People, you're all
little bells
on God's fur cap.

FROM ACT TWO:

The man with two kisses:

A big dirty man
was given two kisses.
The man was helpless,
did not know
what to do with them,
where to put them.
The city,
all feasting,
churches roared with hosannah.
People came out, their bodies handsomely dressed.
But the man was cold

and there were holes in his soles.
He chose the bigger kiss,
and put on his foot like a galosh.
But the frost was bad,
bit his fingers
on left foot and right foot.
"Eh"—
the man was angry—
"I don't need these kisses, will throw them on the road."
He did.
Suddenly
ears grew on the kiss,
He began to fidget and cry,
In a small little voice he peeped,
"I want Mama!"
The man was terrified.
With the rags of his soul he covered the trembling little body,
took it home with him,
to put in a very blue frame.
A long time he searched in the dust of suitcases
(searched for the frame).
He looked around—
the kiss was lying on a couch,
big,
fat,
has grown,
got strong,
happy!
The man cried,
"Lord!
I never thought I'd get so tired.
Now I will hang myself!"
And as long as he was hanging,
paltry,
foul—
women in their boudoirs—
factories not needing smoke and noise—

were producing kisses by the millions—
various,
large,
small—
with the fleshy levers of their smacking lips.

V. Mayakovsky:
. . . Sometimes it seems to me
that I am a Dutch cock
or
a king of Pskov.
And sometimes
I like most
my own name,
Vladimir Mayakovsky.

BORIS PASTERNAK:

I was listening intently, with all my contracted heart, holding my breath. I had never before heard anything like it . . . We all remember that close, mysterious, hot text . . . There was in it that impenetrable spirituality without which there is no originality, the infinity opening from any point of life in any direction, without which poetry is only a momentarily unexplained misunderstanding.

And how simple it all was! The art was called a tragedy. And so it should have been. The tragedy was called *Vladimir Mayakovsky*. The title contained the discovery (there was genius in its simplicity) that the poet is not the author but the object of lyric poetry, addressing the world in the first person. The title was not the author's name but the description of contents.

☗ 8 ☗

Alliances and Skirmishes

☗

*The poetic movement called "Russian futurism" grew in
strength; more and more persons and groups came to participate in it. In this chapter we shall talk about attempts to
unite the movement, about Mayakovsky's new associations
and friendships—sometimes short-lived and casual, like those
with Syevyeryanin or Shershenyevich, at other times full of
substance and fruitful, like the ones with Boris Pasternak and
Nicholas Asyeyev. All this happened toward the end of 1913
and in the early months of 1914. Other events of that period
were: a grand tour of the futurists around the provincial
cities, the arrival of Marinetti in Russia, the publication of*
The First Journal of the Russian Futurists, *and—last but not
least—Mayakovsky's expulsion from his school. In addition to
the authors whose accounts have already been quoted, Mayakovsky's alliances and skirmishes, as well as those of his*

friends, are recalled here by Boris Lavrenyev, Sergei Spasski, Ilya Ehrenburg, and others.

BORIS LAVRENYEV:

In the fall of 1913 and in 1914, the hottest period of futurism, I had several meetings with Mayakovsky.

On one occasion, in 1913, a meeting of the Moscow groups of ego- and cubo-futurists took place in my apartment. It was called on the initiative of Vadim Shershenyevich "in order to coordinate the activities" of both groups. The meeting was attended by the two Burliuks, Shershyenyevich, Kruchenykh, Bolshakov, Sergei Tretyakov, the painter and poet Khrisanf (Zak), who was the ideologist of the ego-futurists, and a few other people. The conversation was apathetic and did not make sense.

David Burliuk maintained that no contact and no ideological union of the two groups was possible because the ego-futurists were really not futurists at all and had no right to usurp that name . . . By the very prefix "ego," the ego-futurists underlined their narrow individualist horizon, while at the root of the cubo-futurists was the cube, a spacious, expansive, three-dimensional concept.

"You are egoists, while we Khlebnikovians, we Hileans are universalists," David said.

They attacked him bitterly and nonsensically. They were quarreling in a most complicated manner, their voices raised; and, of course, no conclusion could be reached.

Throughout all that verbal struggle Mayakovsky sat silent on the sofa, playing with the cat sitting on his knees. Only one or twice did he make a short remark. At the culminating point of the discussion, David jumped to his feet and, pointing at Mayakovsky, shouted, "Here is a true Hilean and cubo-futurist!"

Mayakovsky went on stroking the cat and spoke calmly, with full conviction, casting an astonished glance at all those present: "That is beside the point. I am neither cubo- nor ego-. I am a prophet of mankind of the future!"

The people in the room received this statement with an outburst of laughter. But Mayakovsky suddenly got up and gave such a thunderous look that they grew silent. His face at once became sullen and withdrawn.

He was about to say something, it seemed, but unexpectedly he waved his hand and left quickly.

. . . Who knows if the best proof of the Budyetlans' standing was not . . . our rapprochement with the ego-futurists, or more exactly—with Igor Syevyeryanin.

At that time Syevyeryanin had already severed connections with the *Petersburg Herald* group, led by Ivan Ignatiev. But to all the ego-futurists, the "northern bard" remained the recognized leader and the only trump card in their struggle with us.

The ego-futurists were our opponents on the right, while "The Ass's Tail" group made attempts to occupy our left flank in their struggle with us . . .

The fact that futurism was being threatened "from the left" did not disturb us any more than the flippant attacks of the *Herald* and *Poetry Mezonin.* The Budyetlans had a strong position and Syevyeryanin was very well aware of this when he suggested an alliance with us through Kulbin.

Kulbin, who managed to remain on friendly terms with representatives of totally opposed groups, embarked on this task with fervor. Since Mayakovsky and I were the two most stubborn people in our group, he decided on a frontal approach, so as to tackle us directly. He invited Mayakovsky and myself to his apartment and introduced us to Syevyeryanin, whom I had never seen before . . .

Syevyeryanin stood apart from all that fascinated us, as well as from everything we were waging our complex battle against. He stood apart from French painting, from symbolism. Those problems did not exist for him . . . The twenty years that divided us from the first publication of Russian symbolists were to Syevyeryanin of no account: he dissociated himself from Nadson just as we dissociated ourselves from Bryusov . . .

No neologisms, no "crème-de-mandarins" . . . could deceive me, or Mayakovsky . . . The advantages of that alliance seemed too meager to us. We employed delaying tactics, because there was no reason to hurry. Kulbin then suggested we go to "Vienna," knowing from experience that in places of that kind the most sober views must soon totter. Indeed, toward the end of the dinner there was no trace left of our prudent reserve.

Kulbin exulted. Melting with emotion, he finally said that in the shape of us three, from now on closely united in spite of all differences, he saw . . . Pushkin. I alone felt offended for Pushkin: Syevyeryanin and Mayakovsky were clearly offended each for himself.

A week later we appeared together at a gathering in some women's school.

Later that day Mayakovsky came to see me and suggested that we go to Syevyeryanin and then the three of us might spend the evening together somewhere . . .

Our visit was untimely. Syevyeryanin, true to his schedule—which he had already publicized on the covers of his first booklets—was just then receiving his female admirers. He informed us about it apologetically, but not without satisfaction.

Indeed, ten minutes were hardly up when a young lady clad in a fur coat burst into the room . . . Fifteen minutes later—another admirer came . . . Mayakovsky looked inquiringly at both girls and in his eyes I could see the same kind of curiosity with which he approached the folders with newspaper cuttings piled on the floor . . .

Mayakovsky touched the piles of dust-covered folders, and looked at both girls, in a matter-of-fact way as a prospective heir would do, impatient to count his future profits even though the devisor may still be alive. Syevyeryanin's popularity, exemplified by the newspaper cuttings and his success with women, did not arouse envy in Mayakovsky but rather—impatience.

His nervous euphoria did not leave Mayakovsky during the literary evening, which turned into a tournament between him and Syevyeryanin. They both read their best pieces, trying to outbid each other in the presence of their audience, which consisted exclusively of women. The evening had been arranged, if I am not mistaken, on Syevyeryanin's initiative. The adult school for women was one of the places where he enjoyed unfailing popularity . . . However, notwithstanding the fact that he employed his usual means of conquering simple hearts, Mayakovsky's success on this occasion was just as big . . .

Apart from common public appearances, the alliance with Syevyerya-

nin led to the publication of the *Roaring Parnassus,* in which Syevyeryanin's poems were printed as well as ours. Painters were represented in that
almanac by the two Burliuks, Puni, Rozanova, and Filonov.

THE MANIFESTO "GO TO THE DEVIL!" FROM THE ALMANAC
"ROARING PARNASSUS," PUBLISHED IN JANUARY 1914 AND CON-
FISCATED BY THE CENSOR:

Your year has passed since the publication of our first books: *Slap, The
Thunderboiling Cup, Hatchery of the Judges,* etc.

The appearance of new poetry has had the effect on the crawling
dodderers of Russian literature of a white-marbled Pushkin dancing the
tango.

The commercial dodderers had dully guessed the value of the new
earlier than the public they stupefied, and—as they were wont to
do—looked at us with their pockets.

K. Chukovsky (not a sucker either!) distributed around all market
cities the popular goods: the names of Kruchenykh, the Burliuks, Khlebnikov . . .

F. Sologub got hold of I. Syevyeryanin's cap in order to cover his bald-
ish little talent.

Vassili Bryusov, as usual, brooded over Mayakovsky's and Lyvshits'
poetry on the pages of *Russian Thought.*

Stop it, Vassya, that isn't the way! . . .

Didn't the dodderers stroke our heads in order to make themselves an
electric girdle for contacting the muses out of the sparks of our challeng-
ing poetry? . . .

Those individuals have given a pretext for a horde of young men, previously without definite occupation, to throw themselves into literature
and exhibit their grimacing faces in *Poetry Mezonin,* the *Petersburg Herald,* and others, catcalled by the winds.

While next to them a pack of "Adams with parted hair" appeared:
Gumilev, S. Makovsky, S. Gorodetsky, Pyast. They endeavored to stick
the labels of acmeism and apollonianism on dull songs about Thule samo-
vars and toy lions and then joined the motley procession around the established position of the futurists . . .

Today we spit out the past which sticks like a bone in our throats, declaring:

1. *All futurists are united solely in our group.*
2. *We have abandoned our chance prefixes ego- and cubo- and are joined in one literary company of futurists.*

David Burliuk, Alexei Kruchenykh,
Benedict Lyvshits, Vladimir Mayakovsky,
Igor Syevyeryanin, Victor Khlebnikov

LYVSHITS:

The six of us composed the manifesto in the apartment of the Punis, who financed the almanac's publication. Nicholas Burliuk refused to sign, declaring, not without reason, that one could not send to the devil, even metaphorically, people whose hands one would be shaking in an hour. Indeed, none of our declarations caused more indignation in the literary circles than this our common creative effort. Every word here sounded as if it had been calculated to offend somebody.

Vassili Bryusov—that was not a mistake but a design: the poet was fond of his name Valeri, mentioned it in his poetry, used its resonance to excess . . . Very well then—we are going to call him Vassili!

THE PUNI COUPLE NOT ONLY FINANCED THE NEW ALMANAC
BUT ALSO INSPIRED IT TO SOME DEGREE. LYVSHITS:

. . . The Budyetlans had their "salon," although one can only mention this word with quotation marks. I am thinking of the apartment of the Punis, who in 1913 returned from Paris and transferred to their attic in Gatchinski Street the atmosphere of Montmartre, full of the joy of life and freedom . . . Ksana Puni—witty, energetic, with great personal charm, quickly became a center of gravity for the Budyetlans, whose daily existence was far from comfortable.

By financing *Roaring Parnassus*, Ksana Puni contributed to the final consolidation of the Hilean bloc with Syevyeryanin. It was also she who, sitting with her legs up on the divan, incited the authors of the *Go to the Devil!* manifesto not so much by her jeering remarks as by her very presence. The authors competed with one another in their attempts to satisfy their charming publisher. It was to her that Syevyeryanin sacrificed Sologub, and Mayakovsky and I—Bryusov.

FROM DECEMBER 1913 TO MARCH 1914, MAYAKOVSKY, BURLIUK,
AND KAMENSKY WENT ON A TOUR AROUND PROVINCIAL RUSSIAN

The appearance of Mayakovsky, D. Burliuk, Igor Syevyeryanin, and his imitator, Vadim Bayan, in Simferopol took place on March 7, 1914, in the Tauridian Nobility Theater. On that occasion, called "the futurist Olympiad," apart from Mayakovsky, the leader of the Petersburg futurists, Ivan Ignatiev was to talk on the subject of "The Great Futurnalia," but he did not come (he was soon to commit suicide) . . .

On March 9, the "futurist Olympiad" was repeated in Sevastopol . . . On their arrival, in Kerch, a conflict broke out between Mayakovsky and Syevyeryanin, and as a result Igor Syevyeryanin withdrew from the cubofuturists' tour and undertook a tour of Russian cities on his own.

It is from this period that Syevyeryanin's polemical poems, directed against Mayakovsky and Burliuk, date: "The Crimean Tragicomedy" and "The Poetry of Destruction" . . .

In an interview with a correspondent of an Odessa daily, Syevyeryanin declared himself in very harsh words opposed to the use of eccentricity and the poetic practice of the Hileans and said "there is no common ground between ego-futurists and cubo-futurists."

Mayakovsky's reply was given in numerous polemical remarks concerning Syevyeryanin, contained in articles, speeches, and poems dating from 1914–1915. In all his pronouncements Mayakovsky jeers at the boudoir-perfume-gastronomic themes of Syevyeryanin's writings . . .

AFTER THEIR BREAK WITH SYEVYERYANIN, BURLIUK AND MAYA-
KOVSKY WERE JOINED AGAIN BY KAMENSKY. THE THREE POETS
VISITED JOINTLY SEVENTEEN TOWNS, IN SOME OF THEM APPEAR-
ING SEVERAL TIMES. DAVID BURLIUK RECALLS:

Some of these early lectures brought us money; later on we collected hundreds and thousands of dollars. Every evening the profits were divided among the participants, Burliuk, Mayakovsky, and Kamensky; but if the reader will look at a map of Russia, he will soon see that considering the distances from one town to another, the cost of the railroad fares, hotel bills, restaurants, and many other different expenses, the lecturers sometimes returned with a comparatively small amount of money.

MARUSSIA BURLIUK:

But even so, in February 1914, Burliuk was able to pay $1,000 to cover the cost of printing the *First Futurist Magazine,* and approximately $300 for the printing of the poem "Vladimir Mayakovsky." Burliuk proudly paid an additional $200 to his great friend, the author. This was the first money Mayakovsky received for his literary work.

DAVID BURLIUK:

Mayakovsky used to play cards. Very often he was able to double and even triple the amount he earned from lecturing, and he was now able to support his mother and his sisters . . . But I remember also a time in Minsk, or Odessa, when he lost all his money and I helped him return home . . .*

FROM DAVID BURLIUK'S LETTER TO LYVSHITS, MARCH 16, 1914:

The last lectures incurred financial losses. The press is treating us awfully: with silence . . . A great pity you don't live in Moscow. I had to entrust the printing of the *Magazine* to Shershenyevich and . . . No. 1–2 has come out trashy! . . .

REMINISCENCES OF SERGEI SPASSKY, THE POET, RELATING TO THE TIME WHEN, AS A FIFTEEN-YEAR-OLD HIGH-SCHOOL PUPIL IN TIFLIS, HE FIRST CAME ACROSS MAYAKOVSKY'S POETRY AND MET THE FUTURISTS WHEN THEY CAME THERE IN THE COURSE OF THEIR TOUR:

Early in the spring of 1914, I happened to get hold of the *Futurist Magazine.* Almost at the same time posters were stuck up in the town announcing the literary evening of Mayakovsky, Kamensky, and Burliuk.

. . . Mayakovsky's poems totally captivated me. "I will make myself black trousers of the velvet of my voice." "Please listen, if stars are being lit—it means someone needs it." Everything else in that rather chaotic book was less important.

SPASSKY VISITED THE FUTURISTS IN THEIR HOTEL:

Mayakovsky was walking around the room in his waistcoat. It was a black

* The preceding three fragments have been taken from the original English by D. and M. Burliuk, *Color and Rhyme,* No. 31, 1956.

velvet waistcoat, embroidered with red flowers. He received my visit with indifference and did not ask me any questions . . . David Burliuk shook my hand, was polite and charming. He was dressed in a raspberry-colored coat with pearl buttons. He had a small opera glass which he kept raising to his face . . . Kamensky entered . . . He had a black velvet overcoat with silver galloons, thrown over an ordinary suit. I felt I was among circus performers ready to come out into the arena.

THE TIME OF THE POETS' PUBLIC APPEARANCE CAME:
Mayakovsky rushed onto the stage in a cocked tarboosh.

"He's a tiger. Our tiger!" exclaimed Burliuk, enraptured.

I took my place in a small box, just above the stage, behind the curtain. The curtain went up, quite noisily. The futurists were seated behind a table. Burliuk paused for quite a while. Then he lifted from the table an enormous bell, got from goodness knows where, and having filled the place with its church-like sound, invited Mayakovsky to speak.

Mayakovsky threw his tarboosh on the table. Without smoothing out his disheveled hair, which fell to one side, he took a step forward and stopped in front of the reading stand. He talked, swaying his entire body as he did so. His voice resounded around the hall.

"Ladies and gentlemen. You have come here for the sake of scandal. I warn you there will be no scandal."

His hand pressed and pushed the stand. The contents of his speech were fairly simple and comprehensible. He has said the same things in several manifestos and there is no need to repeat them here. He proclaimed urban art, enriched by the sense of speed. In passing he thundered at the classics. At those points timid laughter could be heard from the audience which I could not see. Mayakovsky presented the poets Khlebnikov, Burliuk, and Syevyeryanin to the audience.

"You may not notice me in the street, you will pass each one of us by, but when you hear an airplane roaring over the town, you will stop and raise your heads."

That was the way he was talking about Kamensky, presenting him as a pilot . . .

Introducing his listeners to modern poetry, he gave them examples . . . On that evening he recited Syevyeryanin's "Tyana," interpreting that trifling poem in a tragic manner. One could clearly feel tragedy pervading Mayakovsky himself, though it was a feeling unexplained, unjustified, inconsistent with his youth, his boldness. It was a quality that separated him from us all; a quality that fascinated us . . .

Vassili Kamensky was the next to read his poems . . . Burliuk read his poetry too.

The second part of the evening was devoted to Burliuk's lecture on new trends in painting. It was an exact and brilliant account, an analysis of the art of Cézanne, Gauguin, Matisse, and Picasso. The lights were switched off on the stage and reproductions of pictures were projected on canvas by means of the magic lantern. In order to irritate the audience, Burliuk intentionally mixed up a Raphael Madonna with a newspaper publicity photograph. Apart from this, it was a thorough and conscientious lecture.

LYVSHITS:

At the end of January, Kulbin, who had a regular correspondence with those abroad, informed me that Marinetti would be coming to Russia . . .

None of the futurists were in Moscow at the time. David Burliuk, Kamensky, and Mayakovsky were in the South on the famous tour in which Syevyeryanin also took part and which ended with his quarrel with Mayakovsky.

Some three days before Marinetti's arrival a Moscow newspaper published an interview with Larionov in which the leader of the rayonists maintained that the leader of the futurists should be bombarded with rotten eggs, because he had betrayed his own avowed principles.

Malevich came to the visitor's defense and hastened to dissociate himself from Larionov's bellicose intentions; so did Shershenyevich, who used the unfortunate interview as the pretext for a flood of letters to the editor . . .

It so happened that Marinetti did not meet any of the Russian futurists while he was in Moscow . . .

On the day before Marinetti's arrival in Petersburg, Kulbin called a kind of conference in his apartment . . .

I considered it essential to issue a manifesto in which the Budyetlans would dissociate themselves from Marinetti's group.

That view was shared by Khlebnikov. All the others—Nicholas Burliuk, Matyushin, Lurie—agreed with Kulbin, who, foaming at the mouth,
argued against such a declaration . . .

The next day Khlebnikov came to me early in the morning and within
a quarter of an hour we drafted a proclamation which he immediately
took to the printer's so that we might distribute it in the evening at Marinetti's lecture.

The hall of the Kalashnikov Exchange was already filled, but Khlebnikov, whom we were to meet half an hour before the lecture began, was
still not there. Kulbin had learned somewhere about our manifesto and,
like myself, kept looking in the direction of the door.

At last, when Marinetti had already mounted the rostrum, Khlebnikov,
pale and out of breath, burst into the hall, clasping a pile of leaflets to his
chest. He handed me half of them and began to walk quickly around the
rows of seats, handing out the leaflets left and right . . .

I had hardly had a chance to hand out a dozen copies when Kulbin ran
up to me. With an adroitness one would not expect from a man no longer
young, he snatched the pile from me and, fervently tearing his booty to
pieces, ran up to Khlebnikov, already active in the back rows . . .

FROM THE APPEAL BY KHLEBNIKOV AND LYVSHITS:

Some natives and the Italian colony at the Neva are, for personal reasons,
bowing today at Marinetti's feet, thus retracting the first step of Russian
art on the road of freedom and honor, and bending the noble neck of Asia
under Europe's yoke . . .

The men with a will of their own have remained aloof. They are mind-
ful of the laws of hospitality, but their bow is taut and their forehead
frowning with anger.

You visitor from a foreign land, remember where you are.

The laces of flunkyism on the sheepskin of hospitality.

MATYUSHIN'S REMINISCENCE:

. . . Khlebnikov as a rule did not speak at other people's lectures and sat
silent on the rostrum, but at Marinetti's evening he was so angry that he
nearly threw himself on Kulbin to beat him up, and then he left at once.

THE DAILY NEWSPAPER "NOV," FEBRUARY 5, 1914:

On the Occasion of Marinetti's Arrival

While on tour in the provinces, we witnessed from afar the tragicomic "conquest" of Moscow by Mr. Marinetti . . . We now feel obliged to communicate that as far back as two years ago, in the second *Hatchery of the Judges* almanac, we stressed the fact that we had nothing in common with Italian futurism, except the name, because the miserable state of painting in Italy is disproportionate to the high, strongly beating pulse of the Russian plastic arts in the last half decade. While in poetry: our ways, the ways of young Russian literature, are set by the separate historical development of the Russian language, taking place quite independently from any Gallic channels. There can be no question of our imitating the Italians (or the other way around, for that matter), for our pieces were written earlier (the first *Hatchery of the Judges* in 1907).

As far as the "temperaments" of sympathy or antipathy to our guest (Marinetti) are concerned, everyone is free, of course, to follow his inclinations ("railway platform bunch of flowers" or "rotten eggs"); this is unimportant.

The basic message of this letter has on a number of occasions been undersigned by the names (see the second *Hatchery of the Judges*):

Burliuk, V. Kamensky, Mayakovsky, Matyushin, Kruchenykh, Lyvshits, Nizen, Velimir Khlebnikov.

"NOV," FEBRUARY 15, 1914:

Letter to the Editor

The name "Russian futurists" is used by a group, united by a hatred of the past but composed of people with differing temperaments and characters. Apart from elephantine verbal play with phrases like "rotten eggs," "railway platform bunch of flowers," we wish to state our opinion of the reception accorded to F. Marinetti and our literary attitude toward him. While we deny any debt to the Italian futurists, we want to stress a certain parallelism: futurism is a social trend, born in and because of the big city which annihilates all national differences. The poetry of the future is cosmopolitan.

This is all the truth there is in the tale about the teacher and his disciples.

The authors of the letter of February 5 were Messrs. D. Burliuk and V. Kamensky, who must have used the signatures of the other persons by way of quotation. To what extent this is permissible remains a matter for the authors' consciences.

Constantin Bolshakov,
Vladimir Mayakovsky,
Vadim Shershenyevich.

ON FEBRUARY 13, IN AN INTERVAL BETWEEN THEIR APPEAR-
ANCES IN MINSK AND KAZAN, MAYAKOVSKY AND BURLIUK WERE
PRESENT AT MARINETTI'S FAREWELL LECTURE AT THE MOSCOW
SOCIETY FOR EMANCIPATED AESTHETICS. THE EVENING WAS DE-
SCRIBED IN THE "MOSKOVSKAYA GAZIETA":

. . . On the wall hung two big portraits: of Byron and Shakespeare.

Under the Shakespeare portrait stood Burliuk in a cantor's coat, hold-ing his lorgnon. His face had been painted with black ink: on his left cheek there was a camel painted by Saryan, on the right—some unknown cabalistic signs, not unlike a centipede.

Under the Byron portrait stood the towering figure of Mayakovsky. His face had no embellishments, but he was dressed in a bright red dinner jacket with black lapels . . .

Marinetti was shooting out a thousand words a minute, like a high-speed machine gun.

Zdanyevich appeared at the table and read a manifesto in very bad French. The manifesto proclaimed that the group of Moscow futurists felt solidarity with Marinetti and regarded him as their excellent leader. Mari-netti shook Zdanyevich's hand in a friendly manner . . .

Zdanyevich, however, was speaking only on behalf of a part of the Moscow futurists. Behind Marinetti stood his opponents and inveterate enemies: Burliuk and Mayakovsky . . . They wanted to speak, but the leader of "emancipated aesthetics" did not allow them to speak in Russian, proposing a discussion in French only.

Marinetti then made his last speech about Russian futurism, calling it not futurism but savage-ism, and its followers not futurists but savage-ists, primitivists . . .

THE "SAVAGE-ISTS" CONTINUED THEIR PROVINCIAL TOUR. IN
POLTAVA THE NEWS REACHED MAYAKOVSKY AND BURLIUK THAT

THEY HAD BEEN FORMALLY DISMISSED FROM THE SCHOOL OF
PAINTING, SCULPTURE, AND ARCHITECTURE. BURLIUK:

When I went to the head of the police in P. to request permission to give a
lecture there, he took out the "futurist file" and there, among clippings
about myself and other futurists, he showed me one entitled: "Burliuk
Dismissed from School." "You are a student? You think of yourself as a
student? You have been dismissed, you know. The entire press has such an
opinion of you that I cannot grant permission for your lecture," etc., etc.

A NOTE IN "NOV," FEBRUARY 25, 1914:

David Burliuk and Vladimir Mayakovsky have, by the decision of the Professorial Council, been removed from the list of students at the School of
Painting, Sculpture, and Architecture . . .

"The Professorial Council," explained the school's director, V. P. Gya-
cintov, "had forbidden our students to take part in discussions, give public
lectures, etc.

"Since Messrs. Burliuk and Mayakovsky continued to take part in public discussions, the council had no choice but to dismiss them."

REMINISCENCE BY BORIS PASTERNAK:

The novices formed groups. There were groups comprising imitators and
others uniting innovators . . . As a movement, the avant garde was characterized by outward unanimity. But, as is the case of all movements at all
times, it was a unanimity of lottery tickets tossed by the wind of whirling
Fortune's wheel . . . The movement was known as futurism. The winner
and justification of the draw was Mayakovsky.

. . . In the avant-garde "Centrifuge" group, in which I soon found
myself, I learned (it was spring 1914) that Shershenyevich, Bolshakov,
and Mayakovsky were our enemies and a serious battle with them awaited
us . . . The birth of "Centrifuge" had been accompanied by unending
scandals all through the winter. Throughout the winter I did hardly anything at all except toy with group discipline at the expense of my own
taste and conscience. I was ready for another perfidy with regard to anything, if need be. But this time I overestimated my strength . . .

It was a hot day late in May and we were sitting in a coffeehouse in the
Arbat, when the three "enemies," young and loud, entered and—without
lowering their voices previously raised because of the noise made by

streetcars and carts—with a natural dignity turned to us. Their voices were pleasant . . . They were smartly dressed, while we were rather sloppy . . . The point at issue was that once they had provoked us and we replied even more rudely, and now one should put an end to this. While Bobrov had words with Shershenyevich, I had my eyes fixed on Mayakovsky . . . His companions were sitting next to him. One of them, like himself, posed as a dandy; the other was, like himself, an authentic poet. These similarities did not, however, detract at all from Mayakovsky's unique position, but rather underlined it. He seemed to play, not one game, but all games together; instead of playing a part, he played with his life. The last characteristic could be perceived from the very first glance, even without any thought of how his life was to end. It was that which fascinated one about him, but also imbued one with fear . . .

More so than the others, Mayakovsky seemed to be consistent with the phenomenon they represented . . . He sat on a chair as if it were a motorcycle saddle; he bent forward, cut and quickly consumed his cutlet, played cards . . . nasally recited, like liturgical texts, some particularly meaningful fragments of his own and other writings, frowned, grew, traveled, and appeared, while deep down under all this . . . lurked that day preceding all days, when he had begun to live at that astonishing pace . . .

Suddenly the negotiations were over. The enemies we were to rout departed unharmed. The armistice was concluded on terms which were rather humiliating for us . . .

In the meantime the street got dark. It began to rain. When the enemies had departed, the coffeehouse became dreadfully empty . . . I was mad about Mayakovsky and already longing to see him again. Must I add that I betrayed not those I wanted to?

ILYA EHRENBURG:

When Vladimir Vladimirovich was talking to women, his voice changed from his usual sharp and peremptory tone and became gentle . . . People used to joke that Mayakovsky had a different, reserve voice, especially for women. In my presence he talked in that other, very soft, affectionate voice to one man only—to Pasternak. I remember a literary evening Boris Leonidovich had . . . In the discussion that followed someone dared—as they say in our parts—"to note the negative elements." At that point Mayakovsky rose in all his splendor and with his voice raised began to extol Pasternak's poetry, defending him with truly amorous passion.

NICHOLAS ASYEYEV ALSO BELONGED TO THE "CENTRIFUGE" GROUP. HERE IS HIS ACCOUNT OF HIS FIRST MEETING WITH MAYAKOVSKY:

I recognized him, walking along Tversky Boulevard, just because he was so unlike all those surrounding him . . . guided by intuition, I went up to him.

"Are you Mayakovsky?"

"Yes, child . . ."

Having explained who I was and that I was writing and reading poetry too, and that I liked his poems very much, I was then surprised when he asked me not how I wrote but what I wrote about. I did not know what to answer. What about? About all that matters. And what does matter? Well, nature, feelings, the world. Well then—about birds and rabbits? No, not about rabbits. And whom do I like as far as poets are concerned? I was fond of Khlebnikov at that time. Exactly, that means—about birds. "Please leave out the birds and write as I do!" That was his request to me. I thought, of course, that this was an attempt to undermine my creative sovereignty. The discussion was not a success. Only much later did I realize that our talk had not concerned rhymes and rhythms but my attitude toward reality . . .

At that time I still felt a certain reserve as regarded Mayakovsky, because I was under the wing of Sergei Bobrov who was exacting and jealous in literary matters. Bobrov was rather unfriendly toward Burliuk and rejected Mayakovsky because of his "primitivism," though he recognized his talent . . .

Soon, however, my literary friendship with Bobrov grew cold and, though I was much indebted to him, I was unable to free myself from Mayakovsky's charm. I began to meet him often, at a certain time almost daily . . .

Mayakovsky was for me a human miracle, but a miracle one could see and touch every day . . . There was between us an implicit conspiracy, an identity of views. It might have been a result of our provincial origins. In our childhood we had both been free, not knowing discipline or compulsion. Hence the mutual sympathy. Before me, he had been friendly, as far as I know, with Constantin Bolshakov, a poet just as tall and outwardly self-confident as himself, but very sensitive and easily vulnerable. Besides, Bolshakov was good, which Mayakovsky could sense perfectly. But I know little about Bolshakov, at any rate less than I know about myself . . .

PASTERNAK:

Mayakovsky was seldom alone. He was usually accompanied by futurists, members of the movement . . . Not always, though, did he come in the company of the avant-garde poets. Often a poet accompanied him who went nobly through the test which proximity to Mayakovsky meant. Among the many people I saw around him, Bolshakov was the only one I could associate with Mayakovsky without any strain. Both of them could be heard at any time or place, without any strain on the ears. One could understand that friendship just as well as the later, even stronger bond with his lifelong friend, Lila Brik; it was a natural friendship. One felt that in Bolshakov's company Mayakovsky was safe; he was at peace with himself and did not waste himself . . .

❦ 9 ❦

The Critics

❦

In the years 1913–1914, futurism still meant social scandal and was an easy prey for journalists. But it was not just that. There were people who, without agreeing with the principles of the new art, tried to understand and analyze its values. Of the part played by Kornel Chukovsky we learn from his own reminiscences and from the accounts given by Shklovsky and Lyvshits. Valeri Bryusov, a poet of the preceding generation attacked by the futurists, declares—according to a journalist's note—that "he does not know a poet by the name of Mayakovsky in Russia," but six months later discusses Mayakovsky's writing in a serious article. The futurists are joined by the first representative of academic philological circles in the person of Victor Shklovsky. A particular hero of Shklovsky's and Lyvshits' reminiscences is Professor Jan Baudouin de Courtenay.

BRYUSOV'S FIRST MEETINGS WITH MAYAKOVSKY WERE CHANCE ONES. THE OBJECT OF MAYAKOVSKY'S AGGRESSION AT THE TIME

The first scandal was Bryusov's welcoming speech, in which he gave Balmont to understand that instead of being the active leader of symbolism,
he will now have to content himself with the part of master of ceremonies.
That speech marked the beginning of Balmont's lasting feud with Bryusov . . .

The second scandal was Mayakovsky's speech. Turning to Balmont, he
reminded him of how he had once proposed "to strip old idols," clearly
implying that Balmont himself is now the old idol. A toast of red wine was
proposed, which gave Mayakovsky the occasion to crack a joke to the
effect that for the first time he saw blood flowing while idols were being
slaughtered . . .

I do not remember what speeches were made and by whom, I only recall
that all of them were ceremonious and dead serious. Only Mayakovsky
made a brilliant speech "on behalf of your foes" . . . Later I saw Bryusov
scold Volodya in one of the society's rooms: "On such a festive day . . .
how could you?" But he was clearly glad that Balmont had taken a beating . . .

Brik and I enjoyed everything, but we were still outraged, particularly
myself, at the hooligans without whom no public event was possible, including broken chairs and police intervention . . .

Mr. Mayakovsky began by asking Mr. Balmont if it did not surprise him
that all the welcoming speeches had been made by persons well known to
him, or by his poetic associates. Mr. Mayakovsky then declared that he
was welcoming the poet on behalf of his foes.

"When you begin to get to know the realities of Russian life," he said, "you will encounter our naked hatred. Once upon a time your anxieties, your verses, flowing and rhythmic like rocking chairs, were close to our hearts too . . . You used to climb ancient towers, up shaking creaking steps, and look down on enamel vistas. But now the upper stories of those towers are occupied by sales offices for sewing machines, while in the enamel vistas—automobile rallies are taking place."

Mr. Mayakovsky ended his speech by reciting one of C. Balmont's charming poems: "Slowly, slowly, strip old idols of their robes . . ."

Whistles and catcalls followed Mr. Mayakovsky's speech.

C. Balmont replied to Mr. Mayakovsky with one of his poems in which he had written that a poet could not have enemies, was above enmity.

A FEW MONTHS LATER MAYAKOVSKY SPOKE AGAIN AT BALMONT'S LITERARY EVENING. THE NEWSPAPER "RANNYEYE UTRO" FOR NOVEMBER 2, 1913:

The contents of Mr. Mayakovsky's "libel" this time ran as follows:

"The Society for Emancipated Aesthetics is said to be emancipated only because only . . . its own members . . . feel emancipated in it."

Mr. Bryusov gave a suitable reply to the futurist, stressing the fact that in a hospitable house guests ought to behave decently.

Mr. Mayakovsky retorted, "If that is the case, then I am going! Good-bye."

"Who was it that said goodbye?" asked someone of those present.

"The well-known poet Mayakovsky," replied Mr. Mayakovsky on his way out.

"We don't know anyone by that name in Russia!" observed Mr. Bryusov.

That was the end of the incident.

KORNEL CHUKOVSKY:

I tried to express my ambiguous attitude to the futurists in a long article on which I worked throughout the summer of 1913. There was not much about Mayakovsky in that article, because on the basis of the few poems he had published by then I had a quite different image of him than of the entire group of his companions: through the eccentricity of his futuristic visions I felt an authentic human sadness, inconsistent with the noisy bravura of his platform declarations . . .

Setting out for Moscow I decided to meet Vladimir Vladimirovich personally and talk to him directly, because I wanted to get to the origins of his melancholy . . . I also wished to express my admiration for some of his poems which I knew by heart.

In other words, I had prepared myself for a friendly, meaningful meeting.

Things turned out quite differently, however.

On my arrival in Moscow from Petersburg I went in the evening to the Literary and Artistic Circle (at 15 Great Dmitrovka Street) on some business; I was told that Mayakovsky was in the billiards room adjoining the restaurant. Someone told him that I wanted to see him. He came out to me sullen, a billiard cue in his hand, and asked me in a rather unfriendly manner, "What is it you wish?"

I took a copy of his book from my pocket and began feverishly to tell him what I thought about it.

He listened to me for no more than a minute, without any interest of the kind shown by young authors to "influential critics," and then, to my astonishment, he said, "I am busy . . . sorry . . . they're waiting for me . . . But if you really want to praise my book, please go to that table in the corner . . . over there where the old man in a white tie is sitting . . . please go there and tell it all to him . . ."

He was polite but categorical.

"What does the old man have to do with it?" I asked.

"I'm courting his daughter. She already knows that I'm a great poet . . . But her father has doubts. So please tell him."

For a brief moment I felt offended, but then I laughed and went up to the old man.

The old man turned out to be quite charming. I talked to him for a suitable length of time and then directed my steps to the exit. Mayakovsky ran after me and got hold of me in the cloakroom. With unusual politeness he helped me put on my overcoat, but it was the politeness of a great lord. We had hardly come out into the street when he began to recite fragments of Sasha Tchorny's poems and then my translations of Walt Whitman's poetry: "Walt Whitman, a cosmos, of Manhattan the son . . ."

"Quite a good writer," he said. "But you render him too sweetly. One should do it more harshly, roughly. Your rhythms are too Balmontian, too melodious."

I replied that he knew only my youthful translations which I myself had disqualified a long time before and that now I translated Whitman in just the way he suggested, without any undue sweetness or elegance . . .

We ended up at the place where I was staying, the Lux Hotel in Tverska Street, where we wanted to read Walt Whitman, because I did not know many of my translations by heart.

It was late and the night porter did not let Mayakovsky in. So I brought my notebook out into the street. We stood in Stoleshnikov Alley in front of a photographer's lighted store window . . . and I read him my new translations. There were quite a few of them, some quite long. He listened to me carelessly, it seemed, leaning on a tall stick. But when I finished—and I must have read some five hundred lines, or more—it turned out that he had taken in every word, because he immediately repeated from memory all passages which seemed to him unsuccessful.

Of the poems of Walt Whitman which I read to him on that occasion, he singled out particularly those that were nearest to his own poetics at the time, e.g.: "The scent of these armpits, aroma finer than prayer . . ."

During one of our next meetings, Mayakovsky asked me about Whitman's life, and it looked as if he was measuring it against his own . . .

Every time I was in Moscow we used to see each other often, almost daily, but there was no harmony between us at that time . . . Mayakovsky felt solidarity with the futurists: Khlebnikov, Vassili Kamensky, Kruchenykh, David Burliuk, Kulbin. Whereas I was a stranger, and not particularly in sympathy with them. Those men, as was only natural, gauged every man by his attitude toward futurism. But futurism remained alien to me, which—I repeat—did not prevent me from being friendly with the futurists, regarding highly many of their poems and drawings, and duly recognizing their talents.

He wanted me to like his cause, whereas I only liked him. With this he was not content. During that period people interested him only as allies or enemies. And I was neither an ally nor an enemy. As soon as Mayakovsky realized this, he drifted away from me . . .

LYVSHITS:

For decency's sake, we placed Chukovsky with others who madly rushed around us, like Ismailov, Lvov-Rogachevsky, Nyevyedomsky, Osorgin, Nakatov, Adamov, Filosofov, Berendyeyev, etc. We nailed him down, called him a clown, coprophage, and goodness knows what. But none of this was very serious, no more so than his own attitude toward futurism.

Chukovsky's knowledge of futurism was only a little better than that of our other critics. He treated fairly superficially and lightheartedly even what had some value in his eyes. Even so, he was more conscientious and incomparably more talented than his professional colleagues, and what is most important, he somehow liked Mayakovsky, Khlebnikov, and Syevyeryanin. Love is the first step to understanding. For that love we forgave Chukovsky all his mistakes.

In our unending scoldings there was more humor than anger. It seemed that, once joined to him, we could not separate, and in this doglike symbiosis we rushed from platform to platform, from one auditorium to another . . .

On one point we could not agree, no matter how we tried: who is indebted to whom for money and fame. Chukovsky thought that with his lectures and articles he gave us publicity; we contended that without us he would die of starvation, because futurology became his basic interest. It was a truly vicious circle, and it seemed quite impossible to define what was cause and what effect in the closed circuit of our relations.

VICTOR SHKLOVSKY:

Kornel Ivanovich writes in the newspaper *Ryech*. But he is not liked there; rather tolerated for his talent . . .

To tell the truth, Kornel Ivanovich liked Mayakovsky's poetry, but he felt cramped by *Ryech* and by the considerable respect he had for himself. How could he put such capital—his literary reputation—on such a risky stake? So, it was better to write ambiguously, for everybody's satisfaction . . .

Chukovsky wrote about the rebel poems of young Mayakovsky in the almanac *Hawthorn* in 1914.

He had met Mayakovsky earlier . . . talked about him, lectured about him, went with his lecture around all provincial cities, trying to explain futurism. Kornel Ivanovich was a universal man, tried to understand everything . . . Unfortunately he changed all art so that it would not disturb anyone . . . Talented, knowledgeable as far as literature was concerned, he understood Mayakovsky in his own way, reduced him and gave such an account of him as not to disturb the public. In this consisted the task of criticism.

FROM CHUKOVSKY'S ARTICLE IN THE ALMANAC
"HAWTHORN," 1914, VOL. 22:

And, of course, I like Mayakovsky, his convulsions, spasms, mad drunken cries about bald cupolas, malicious roofs, a bouquet of streetwalkers, city mirages, and phantoms. But, I will whisper in secret, Mayakovsky is an illusionist, a visionary. Mayakovsky is an impressionist, and even Kruchenykh himself is occasionally ready to taunt him. Moreover, the city for him is not a wonder, or drunken joy, but the Lord's cross, a Golgotha, the wreath of thorns, and every urban vision is for him like nails driven into his very heart. He cries and shakes in an attack of hysteria.

> I warn the brick,
> I thrust the dagger of demon words
> into the swollen softness of heaven!

At such a point one would want to take him by the hand and guide him like a child out of that brick slavery, somewhere among bluebottles and camomiles. What kind of urbanist, what kind of city poet is he, if the city is for him a dungeon, a torture chamber!

SHKLOVSKY:

One day we all gathered in a room of the Tyenishevska School. Kornel Ivanovich was to give a scholarly lecture on futurism, but as he had not yet completed his research, he postponed the lecture and began to crack jokes and read quotations instead.

The audience supported him and, to make things worse, Ilya Zdanyevich came: short, stocky, dressed in ragged pants and with a drawing on his cheek. The police commissioner, in a well-cut uniform, delighted at the audience's encouragement, politely attempted to make Zdanyevich leave the room. But Zdanyevich refused to obliterate the rebel drawing and said that since the ladies paint makeup on themselves, and he regards that makeup as academic, he is not introducing new methods of makeup.

Kruchenykh spoke in a tragic vein and, for a second, shook the audience. Mayakovsky mounted the platform as an icebreaker would enter ice and proceeded to break the glaciers in the rows of the audience. Applause followed. Khlebnikov did not appear.

Kornel Ivanovich . . . liked the audience's immediate reaction. He threw dozens of quotations around the platform and danced a jolly dance above them. Thereafter, pink and energetic, he went up to Khlebnikov.

The poet, dressed in a black coat, was standing with his arms hanging loosely down. He looked at the jolly critic and, without uttering a sound, moved his lips to say one word, full of reproach and surprise.

I remembered only the poet's sad eyes and his soundless reproach.

I wanted to explain everything, because I was young. I wrote a book called *The Resurrection of the Word*—a thin brochure . . .

LYVSHITS ABOUT VICTOR SHKLOVSKY:

. . . A pink-faced youth in a student uniform, whose stiff collar forced him to hold his head high, he really gave one the impression of being a child prodigy.

Besides, Shklovsky was a man of philological culture which, with the exception of Khlebnikov, we all lacked. But the declarations made by the "king of time" were, first of all, authentic exegeses, statements made from within, as it were, instead of describing and analyzing us as a literary phenomenon, from the outside. Secondly, they had an accidental and lyrical character.

In the person of Shklovsky, an academic scholar came to us, with his university training. This was exciting: to see ourselves in a newly amalgamated glass which we would probably be reluctant to regard as the mirror of history . . .

In "The Stray God" Shklovsky gave his first lecture, entitled "The Place of Futurism in the History of Language." He talked about the word image and its petrification, about the epithet as a means of rejuvenating the word, about "market" art, about the death of objects, and about the necessity for restoring their strangeness as a means for their resurrection. On this he based his theory of transference and he looked at the main task of futurism as restoring to man his lost keenness in perceiving the world.

There was not much that was new in all this for the Hileans. Every one of us did nothing but "resurrect things" by shifting dead language strata (clichés, obsolete expressions), endeavoring to achieve this not only

through "restoring strangeness to the epithet," but also in more complicated ways: by breaking up the syntax structure, by radical destruction of
traditional composition, etc. . . .

What was new was perhaps only that Shlovsky had come to us from
outside, from the university seminar, as a philologist and theoretician.
Hitherto only contempt, mockery, and abuse had reached us from those
circles. Besides, he was a good speaker: he spoke with authentic gusto,
fervently and fluently, without using any notes. We could only congratulate ourselves on having such an ally.

SHKLOVSKY:

I have mentioned the fact of "linguistics"—words, shouts, vocal gestures
not endowed with sense, sometimes anticipating words, as it were.

The cubo-futurists were at that time fascinated by this and favored the
"word as such," the word as an aim in itself.

I collected in my brochure many statements by poets, examples of children's sound games, proverbs, ways in which nonsense sounds had been
used by religious sectarians.

Some pupils of Baudouin de Courtenay—the one-armed Eugene Polivanov, expert on the Korean language, a man of great linguistic knowledge and full of zest for life; Lev Yakubinsky—a quiet man with a lovely
forehead and Baudouin's particular favorite—became interested in my
book.

Baudouin de Courtenay threw the challenge himself, by publishing in
the supplement to issue No. 49 of the journal *Dien* in 1914, an article
entitled "Word and 'Word,' " and in No. 56 "A Contribution to the Theory
of 'Word as Such' and 'Letter as Such.' "

I went to the Professor and handed him my brochure myself . . .

Shortly afterwards a lecture, with discussion, on the subject of "The
Living Word" took place . . .

Baudouin de Courtenay got up and even before the opening of the
discussion made a speech to the effect that today, in 1914, one must not
separate word from sense, just as one must not separate literature from
life.

Baudouin used learned linguistic terms in his speech and thanks to that
the police officer present could not interrupt him when he was talking

about facts behind language politics: about the futility and despicability of attempts to destroy languages, to suppress national minorities. He also spoke about the coming revolution of the suppressed peoples.

He digressed on what is language, what is phoneme. The police officer on several occasions moved as if to rise but never quite got up to interrupt . . .

Baudouin went out, accompanied by applause. I went with the Professor into the vestibule. There he took leave of me, saying that I had my own window through which I looked at the world.

IN LYVSHITS' REMINISCENCES THE EMINENT LINGUIST APPEARS
IN A SOMEWHAT DIFFERENT LIGHT:

Whenever we organized a lecture, we had to find an agreed-upon person to chair the discussion, because the police—made wise by experience with our public evenings, almost always ending with scandal—permitted the futurists to appear publicly only when some respected professor guaranteed to maintain order and took responsibility for it.

It was not easy to find such a guarantor . . . Even Baudouin de Courtenay, at a certain period looking favorably upon our requests, finally came to the conclusion that this would not bring him glory or serve any useful purpose. Since my appearance and behavior did not betray my belonging to the Budyetlan camp, the difficult mission of tempting the old men usually fell to me.

. . . I entered Baudouin's study. He lived either in the university building or somewhere near . . .

The tidy old man, with the typical appearance of those ruined Polish landowners who before the war used to gather in Semadeni and Countess Komarowska's café in Kiev, once more convinced me by his looks that the word image has its own independent life . . .

I did not have to strain myself to touch those chords in my voice which were necessary for convincing the old scholar to chair the "Evening of the New Word" . . . Baudouin only made me promise that there would be no scandal and warned me that upon the slightest attempt at overstepping the bounds of good manners, he would leave the hall immediately. That warning did not worry me in the least: it was important for us to obtain his name for the chief of police, nothing else really counted.

Baudouin de Courtenay kept his word. As soon as he noticed on the platform next to him a futurist in a brocade blouse, made from a chasuble, and another with his tie put on in an unusual place, he got up at once and declared in a thunderous voice, "I have been duped. A quite decent young man was sent to me [here an indignant gesture directed at myself] and assured me that good manners would prevail. But I see I have come to a madhouse. I refuse to lend my name to this comedy."

At this point he left, in a shower of applause, and his place was taken by Kulbin, who brought the discussion to a successful conclusion.

FROM VALERI BRYUSOV'S ARTICLE "THE YEAR OF RUSSIAN POETRY, APRIL 1913–APRIL 1914," PUBLISHED IN THE MONTHLY "RUSSKAYA MYSL," NO. 5, 1914:

The year that has just passed will remain in the story of Russian poetry above all as a memorable year of discussion and argument about futurism. In both capitals and in the provinces public lectures and discussions on futurism have been taking place, in halls filled to capacity. Futurist plays have been performed to overflowing audiences. Futurist collections of verse and prose, both thin and fat, which have appeared one after another (the year's production has amounted to over forty), have always found critics, readers, and people to buy them. Several futurist periodicals were published which eventually merged into a fairly big *First Journal of Russian Futurists*. The futurists have been ridiculed and scorned in many different ways, but still they have been read, listened to, seen on the stage; and even the motion picture, that faithful reflection of our "day," has considered it its duty to deal with futurism and the futurists as a "topical question."

There cannot be any doubt that, since its first manifestations . . . our Russian futurism has developed considerably, and what is most important, it has attempted to define its "ideology." In their periodicals and brochures the futurists have tried to elaborate the theory of futurism. Being divided (as always happens with young literary movements) into a number of opposing factions, they have pronounced many conflicting views. But in the end, all the various directions of Russian futurism can be reduced to two definite types: moderate and extreme futurism. Both these types differ essentially from each other: the moderates recognize the leading role played by "form" in poetry and use it to reveal a certain new (from their point of view, at least) "content"; the extremists do not know and do not want to know about anything except "form" in poetry.

The moderate Russian futurism is relatively close to the Italian futurism of Marinetti and his companions . . . A contempt and slighting of all history, an extolling of the modern age, of machines and of life running at a fast pace, raising to a cult all that exists today—those are the basic tenets of Italian futurism . . . Our "moderate" futurists are reluctant to repeat all Marinetti's theses in their theories . . . But in their poems they follow the Italians fairly faithfully. The whole difference consists in the fact that Russian futurists of this orientation lack a strong temperament, so that shouts about the destruction of museums and about "wars being the world's only hygiene," are lacking or, to be more precise, are much more subdued . . .

On one point there exists a complete divergence between the Italians and our Russian futurists: in their views on love and women. As is well known, Marinetti's school proclaims a "boycott of love." Russian poets are too romantic to adopt such a view . . . They differ also from the Italians in their unsurmountable desire to "bare their souls." Italians, being Europeans, do not like to show their souls. The Russians, brought up on Dostoyevsky after all, would find it impossible to content themselves with poeticizing the external world . . .

All this changes at once when we pass on to the poems written by the "extreme" futurists. They reject Italian futurism vehemently, declaring that they created their "movement" independently and earlier . . . What strikes us first when we read the poetry and prose of the "extremists" is their "extreme" ignorance in many fields . . . In their rush after what seems new to them, they sometimes imitate the older writers in a manner which is in bad taste . . . Sometimes they search for their own "extrarational" language, categorically breaking all contact with their readers and, consequently, destroying the very existence of poetry for others . . .

All this is accompanied by a deliberate coarseness in the poems of our "extremists." They want to combat the conventional beauty of poetry through an intensive use of brutal, offensive, repulsive, or simply "rude" words.

. . . The incompetence of their theoretical formulations, and the—full of contradictions—"creative" attempts of the "extremists" lead us to the irrefutable conclusion that they are not ready in the smallest degree to clear new paths in art . . .

To be fair, however, we must repeat what we have pointed out earlier: we find most of the happy exceptions to our strictures in poems signed: V. Mayakovsky. There is much of "extreme" futurism in Mr. Mayakovsky, but there is also a vision of reality which is his own, there is imagination and a capacity for representation. It is not difficult, of course, to invent the metaphor:

> I will make myself black trousers
> of the velvet of my voice . . .
> Through the world's Nevsky Prospect . . .

But in Mr. Mayakovsky's small volume, as well as in his poems published in various almanacs, and in his tragedy, we also find successful lines and whole poems originally worked out. And then, the posthumous volume of the poetry and prose of Helena Guro contains truly artistic and emotionally satisfying pages.

To sum up the results of Russian futurism once again, we have to say that ultimately it has not brought anything positive, at least in the two or three years of its existence, so far. As before, some outlines of possible new byways are visible, but no one as yet has entered them with a sure foot, and, of course, it is not the "extremists" who will be our guides here. On this we can, it seems, part with our futurism, and part, I think, for a long time . . .

✠ 10 ✠

Maria

✠

There had been others before her, but they were nameless. David Burliuk tells about this. Maria—this was the first name of a woman to appear in Mayakovsky's poetry. Vassili Kamensky tells about the poet's first love—the girl who became the heroine of "Cloud in Pants." There is no other published material about her. Her name was Maria Denisova, she was the daughter of well-to-do parents. At the time Mayakovsky met her she was sixteen years old and a student at the Fine Arts Academy in Odessa.

FROM BURLIUK'S REMINISCENCES:

From my early meetings with Volodya Mayakovsky I had the impression that he wanted to impress people with his virility, strength, and sexual conquests. In his early youth, Vladimir Vladimirovich was not fastidious so far as the objects of his sexual pleasure were concerned.

Vladimir Vladimirovich regarded me as an "elderly" man. In the early months of our acquaintance he tried to impress me with his achievements in debauchery. He was full of young untapped, inexhaustible vigor. The same period in Pushkin's life had been marked by his dangerous participation in the "Circle of the Green Lamp." But Mayakovsky was very poor. The youth's enemies were starvation, cold, human indifference. He was separated from life's successes by a high wall which he had to break through by knocking his head against it. He had to content himself with the love of townswomen, unfaithful to their husbands while on vacation—in hammocks and on seesaws—or with the young, unbridled passion of girl students . . .

. . . Women with a name to themselves appeared in Vladimir Mayakovsky's poetry much later . . . The first of them was "Maria" in Odessa.

It is worth mentioning that Mayakovsky did not invent anything in his poetry. His poems reflected the course of his life. They were like a ship's logbook.

FROM KAMENSKY'S ACCOUNT OF THE FUTURISTS' TOUR OF
SOUTHERN RUSSIA EARLY IN 1914. ODESSA:

. . . We went out to the seaside.

Mayakovsky was looking intently at the far line of the horizon.

All around us people were promenading in the warm sun.

Suddenly I spotted an unusual girl: she was tall, graceful, with splendid shining eyes—in a word, a veritable beauty.

She was walking with a young lady very much like her. A middle-aged man accompanied them.

I said, "Volodichka, just look over there . . ."

Mayakovsky turned, looked at the girl inquiringly, and all at once seemed to become excited. He said, "You know what, you stay here, or do what you like, and I will go now . . . I shall be at the hotel in . . . well, shortly."

He quickly departed and disappeared into the crowd.

I looked at Burliuk, who smiled artfully. I took his arm and we went on.

. . . At one point I saw Mayakovsky driving by in a droshky. There was someone with him. Was it she?

"Look, Dodya, look . . . Volodya . . . He is not alone . . ."

Burliuk directed his lorgnon at the droshky and declared, "Absolutely alone."

Some two hours later we returned to the hotel.

Mayakovsky had not come back.

We waited another hour, and yet another.

Volodya did not come.

We went to the restaurant, leaving a message as to where to find us if he came back.

We went on waiting in the restaurant but finally decided to dine without Volodya.

He turned up at last.

Excited, smiling mysteriously, very absent-minded, quite unlike himself.

. . . He called the waiter at once: "Three bottles of champagne, please. I won't have any dinner."

Burliuk cleared his throat, giving him an ironic look.

. . . The next day I was called to the chief of police.

I returned to the hotel angry and irritable.

Mayakovsky and Burliuk tried to console me: "What's the chief of police, or the governor! What are trifles of this miserable earth to you, a conqueror of the skies! Forget it! Today we are invited for dinner to an excellent house. That will be a thousand times more exciting."

Mayakovsky began to blow his nose noisily and ceremoniously. He smelled of strong perfume.

From the artful expression in Burliuk's eye I knew we would be going for dinner to Gioconda's.

And so it was.

An hour later we were in the residence of the engineer whom we had seen under Richelieu's monument with his wife and Gioconda, who was, it turned out, the wife's sister.

Her name was Maria Alexandrovna.

Charming and gay, she was sincerely happy to see us.

The dinner with Gioconda turned into a poetry festival: almost throughout we talked poetry and discussed some strange festive topics.

Volodya was inspired. His jokes could even have made the Duc de Richelieu's statue laugh. He talked a lot, sensibly and amusingly.

He wanted to please all present at any price. Above all, he wanted to make a good impression on Maria. In this he succeeded easily.

In friendly jest, he invented improbable, fantastic stories concerning myself . . .

And his recital that evening was unforgettable.

On returning to our hotel we could not for a long time recover from the powerful impression Maria Alexandrovna had made on us.

Burliuk maintained a meaningful silence, watching Volodya, who strolled around the room nervously, not knowing what to do with himself or with his sudden overpowering love.

He was experiencing that powerful emotion for the first time in his life. He tossed himself around the room and repeatedly murmured, "What am I to do? Write a letter? Wouldn't that be silly? . . . 'I love you, what more is there to say?' . . . But if I say so outright, she'll get scared . . . They all will . . . They will say . . . the yellow tunic, and this. . ."

The evening of the sixteenth came.

There were three hours left before the beginning of our public appearance.

Volodya was absent, although we had decided that we would, as always, make our preparations together and enter the hall together.

Until then he had been most punctual, but apparently love changed him.

As a matter of fact we now seldom saw him.

An hour before starting time, when we were already uneasy about him, he came, with profuse apologies, blaming his watch which had stopped.

Mayakovsky began to dress hurriedly . . .

We made our way to the theater with difficulty through a dense crowd of people who could not get tickets . . .

Pyotr Pilsky, the critic, made a short, lawyer-like speech, defending us as if we were hardened criminals.

Next I gave a lecture entitled "Our Reply to Those Who Laugh at Us," in which I hit hard at our critics . . .

The evening ended with poetry readings which aroused enthusiasm among the young people present but evoked jeers and shouts of "Enough!" from the boxes and the front rows of the orchestra.

Mayakovsky was reading with an exceptional power of expression and kept looking in the direction where radiant Maria Alexandrovna was sitting.

We were showered with flowers, candy, fruit, several boxes of herring, and one stinking pike.

. . . On January 19 we gave a repeat performance at the Russian Theater, with similar resounding success.

Then we were to go to Nikolaev, Kishinev, and Kiev.

But Mayakovsky, being in love, did everything he could to delay our departure.

It was now difficult to recognize the former carefree joker, Volodya.

We wanted very much to help him somehow, but nothing could be done, because Mayakovsky was very impatient with his feelings and suffered by not wanting to accept convention.

And there were a great many social conventions in those arch-bourgeois times, particularly in the provinces, where, for instance, no young lady would risk showing herself with an artist in the street, not to speak of paying him a visit to his apartment, or, worst of all, a hotel.

I remember the complicated precautions and clever maneuvers adopted in Odessa by girls who visited us. Maria Alexandrovna was of their number. We were still very much under the influence of her charm.

Volodya, of course, was beside himself!

Burliuk kept telling him frankly, "You suffer quite unnecessarily, Vladimir, and torment us without any cause. Believe me—the first love never comes off, that's a well-known truth."

Mayakovsky was angered by this and retorted, "Maybe it doesn't come off with anyone else, but it will with me."

"When? We must be on our way."

"You go. I'll stay."

"Here? In Odessa? For good?"

"No. Without you I will not stay."

"But we're concerned with art . . ."

"So am I."

"And with matters that can't wait. In Kishinev the theater has been hired, posters stuck up. Same in Nikolaev. And then—Kiev. You've got to decide, Volodichka."

"I've decided already. But Maria . . ."

"Have a talk with her tomorrow. After all, you can come back to Odessa in a month."

"That's not how I want it. Tomorrow at four she will be here I'll tell her everything, and I'm sure Maria will agree, only . . . So, till tomorrow."

Volodya smiled bitterly at some thought of his and left us. It was late at night.

On the next day we saw him at breakfast. Volodya did not say much.

And the moment we next saw him, at noon, he said sullenly and categorically, "We're going."

He then threw his overcoat over his shoulders and disappeared.

The following morning the three of us breakfasted on board the steamer going down the Black Sea to Nikolaev.

The sea was rough.

We remained silent for a long time, being sorry for Volodya.

Burliuk tried to say something about Eastern and Western art.

But Mayakovsky was not listening.

Then in the compartment of an international train.

We are going from Nikolaev to Kishinev . . .

We talked about the need to achieve great, monumental things, good for all eternity, to earn the gratitude of future generations.

Our purpose in all that talk was to distract Volodya's attention from his thoughts.

But he looked absent-mindedly out the window at the moving panorama and kept singing the beginning of Syevyeryanin's well-known poem: "That was by the sea . . ."

He intoned that line many times, with different tunes.

Soon after, smiling dully, he began to repeat the words, stressing the rhythm of every word:

> That was,
> was in Odessa . . .

from CLOUD IN PANTS
by *Vladimir Mayakovsky*

You think—that's how raves malaria?
That was,
was in Odessa.

I'll come at four," said Maria.
Eight.

Nine.
Ten.

The evening,
cloudy,
december-like
has run from the windows
into the terrified night.

Behind
candelabra are giggling and whinnying.

In a while
will you recognize *me:*
the giant is crouching and whining—
it makes flesh creep.
What is it the lump wants?
Oh the lump has extraordinary fancies!

For oneself it does not matter
that of bronze he is made,
or that his heart—a piece of cold metal.
At night one wants to hide
the yelp of one's bell
in a tender woman's.

And so,
my gigantic hump
I bend in the window,
the pane ducked by the forehead, breaks.
Will there be love, or no?
What kind of love—
a great one, or tiny?

How can it be great with such a body:
surely a teeny weeny
modest little love.
Bristling with automobile horns.
Grateful to the bells of horse cars.

Still and still
with the rain,
face to face with its pockmarked mask,
I wait, I tremble,
splashed by the city with the lightning of flood.

Midnight thrust its knife!—
caught up,
slaughtered—
away!

The midnight hour rolled
like the condemned head from the scaffold in the sand.

The whispers on the pane
of the little gray drops of rain
made every feature into a big grimace,
as if the chimeras
of the cathedral of Notre Dame de Paris whined.

Oh you cursed one!
Even this is not enough?
Soon the shout will tear lips apart.
I hear:
a sick nerve
shyly
sliding out of bed.

Slowly at first it went—
then faster,
gathered speed,
until it ran,
galloped.
Now he, and two others too,
in mad contortions jump about.

Below the plaster peeled off the ceiling.

A string of nerves
big

and small
dances around
runs riot—
and already
the knees give way under the weight of nerves!

And the night with its eyelash fills the room;
the heavy eye will not escape the eyelash.
The door has clanked,
as if a sudden shiver
shook the hotel.

You entered
sharply, like "take it!"
crumpling your chamois gloves
you said,
"I'm getting married,
you know."

Please do.
Painful?
Oh no, this doesn't hurt me.
You see—I am calm
like a dead man's
pulse.

Remember,
you said,
"Jack London,
gold,
passion,
game."
And I knew just this:
you are Gioconda,
whom I've got to steal!

And they have stolen.
In love, again I will enter
the nightly hazards, with a flaming brow.
It happens

that even in a burned-down house
a homeless tramp finds shelter.

Are you teasing me?
"You have fewer wild dreams left
than a beggar has kopecks."
Please remember,
Pompeii fell
when they had teased Vesuvius!

Eh!
Gentlemen!
Lovers
of sacrileges,
murders and slaughters—
has anyone seen
what is most terrible of all?—
let him say—
my face,
when I am
absolutely calm and sober?

And I feel—
"I"
is for me too little.
Someone stubbornly wants to break out of me.

Hullo!
Who is it speaking?
Mama?

Oh mama!
Your son is wonderfully sick!
Mama!
It's the heart burning.
Tell sisters Olga and Ludmila,
brother doesn't know where to go.

Every word,
even that with a playful note,

which he spits out with his burned mouth,
falls to the ground as a naked prostitute
from a burning house of ill repute.
People are sniffing—
roast they have scented!
So many shining ones have gathered.
They'll bring mud!
No, you mustn't in boots!
Tell them someone:
one climbs the burning heart with caresses.

I alone.
Will roll out barrels from my tearful eyes.
Will pull myself up on the barrier of my ribs.
Will jump! Jump! Jump! Jump!
They've fallen.
You will not jump out of heart!

KAMENSKY:

. . . I went with Volodya to Presnya to visit his mama and sisters . . .

Alexandra Alexeyevna declared that during the time of his absence from Moscow he had grown stronger, stouter, gayer, more handsome and manly.

The family showered Volodya with questions about his meetings with friends in Georgia, whom he had seen in Kutais.

Volodya talked about his Georgian encounters, describing in great detail how people looked, how they were dressed, what they were doing . . . He cracked jokes endlessly and we all laughed until we cried . . . He told a great deal about our noted appearances in Tiflis and various other towns.

"But what happened in Odessa," he said slowly and quietly, lost in thought, "I can tell you only in verse . . ."

Then, obviously inspired, with immense artistry, he read a fragment of "The Thirteenth Apostle"—that was the original title of "Cloud in Pants."

When he had finished, Alexandra Alexeyevna asked quietly, through tears, after a very long pause, "And where is she now, that Maria?"

"Don't let's talk about it now, Mama," said Volodya affectionately, embracing his mother. "I just write poems" . . .

ROMAN JAKOBSON HAS PUT FORWARD A HYPOTHESIS THAT THE
LAST PART OF "CLOUD IN PANTS" DOES NOT CONCERN MARIA
DENISOVA BUT ANOTHER WOMAN:

. . . It was the Moscow heroine of the last part of the tetraptych, who was given the name of a girl written about in the first part: "Maria! Maria! Let me in, Maria!" . . . The Moscow Maria was in fact called T. G-na. All her paintings, as well as her unpublished lyrics in prose, entitled *Two in One Heart*, were connected with Mayakovsky by their subject matter. Her work, shown in the spring of 1919 at her posthumous exhibition in Moscow, soon after her suicide, are closely reminiscent in their motifs and conception, of the main part of the autobiographical scenario *How Are You*, and their hero is also the same . . . About the death of the Moscow Maria, Mayakovsky talked with an unexpected, unnaturally cruel revulsion in Pushkino in the summer of 1919 and in Paris almost ten years later . . .

FROM JAKOBSON'S LETTER TO DAVID BURLIUK, JANUARY 9, 1956:

. . . Could you answer the following question: who, according to you, is the original of the Moscow Maria in the last part of "Cloud," obviously different from the Odessa Maria of the first part? Is it the artist Gumilina, as was affirmed in Moscow artistic circles?

ELSA TRIOLET:

I knew Gumilina. Her name was Tonya, Antonina. I used to visit her in her apartment in Moscow, somewhere near Varvarca, as far as I can remember.

Gumilina was a talented painter, had her own exhibition. Mayakovsky had been with her before he got to know Lila. Tonya was obsessed by Mayakovsky. I remember her room, full of pictures, and every picture represented Mayakovsky. On one of her pictures, I remember, was a woman (a painter), sitting on the bed in her underwear, while Mayakovsky was standing by the window, quite normal, except that instead of feet he had hoofs, like a satyr . . .

Later Tonya developed a nervous depression and committed suicide. Her pictures could not be found.

FROM THE LETTER OF LILA BRIK TO THE AUTHOR OF THIS BOOK,
MARCH 24, 1966:

Tonya Gumilina? In "Cloud"? It's possible, but I doubt it. Sonka Shamardina, on the other hand, is certainly the principal heroine. Originally "Maria" appeared only at the very beginning of the poem. Later on "Sonka" was everywhere. The name "Maria" was the most feminine name for him and he used it for all women as a general term . . . Sonka is a charming woman. She is still alive. Mayakovsky loved her (before me). She left him.

CHUKOVSKY:

In 1915 Mayakovsky came to Petrograd and, I think, early in the spring, took up residence near the capital in the holiday resort of Kuokkala . . .

Kuokkala is a simple, sandy place in the pine woods on the shores of the Gulf of Finland. On the beach there are huge stones protruding from the water. Sometimes the waves cover them; at other times, when the sea recedes, they rest on the sand in a long, uneven chain.

Mayakovsky would walk on those stones, murmuring.

Sometimes he would stop and light a cigarette, sometimes he would run, jumping from stone to stone as if carried by a storm; most frequently, however, he would walk slowly, like a moon walker, widely spacing his big legs in "American" boots, without for a moment interrupting his quiet, concentrated conversation with himself.

In that way he was creating his new poem "The Thirteenth Apostle," and this lasted for some five hours every day.

The beach was nearly empty. Anyway, Mayakovsky did not mind the people. He paid attention to them only when he had to get a light for his cigarette from someone. On one occasion he rushed with a cigarette to a Finnish farmer standing not far from him on a hill. The farmer, terrified, began to run away. Mayakovsky pursued him, continuing his concentrated murmur, which very much frightened the farmer . . .

Every evening, having added new stanzas, Mayakovsky would come to me, Kulbin, or another of Kuokkala's residents and read the whole poem from the beginning, including the new stanzas written that day . . .

Sometimes a stanza would take him a day to write, but in the evening he rejected it, in order to "walk" a new one the next day. But when he had written something down, he would not change a line. He wrote mostly on cigarette boxes. At that time he did not have, it seems, any notebooks. He had such a good memory that no notebooks were necessary . . .

from *Part IV of the*
THIRTEENTH APOSTLE

Maria!

The pastures of streets are brutalized.
On the neck the rabble's fingers like a collar.

Open up!
It hurts!
You see—someone has stuck
pins from ladies' hats in my eyes!

She's let me in.

Child!
Don't be afraid
that on my bull's neck
a wet heap of sweaty-bellied women is lying still—
millions of great pure loves
I drag through my life
and billions of little dirty tiny loves.

Don't be afraid
of weather's treachery,
when it comes,
and I cling again to a thousand coral lips—
"those who love Mayakovsky!"—
an entire dynasty
of queens who trampled on the madman's heart.

Come nearer, Maria!
in trembling fear,
in undressed shamelessness,
but give me the unfaded splendor of your lips:

never have I been able to reach May with my heart,
a hundred times stumbling
over April with my life.

Maria!
The poet sings sonnets to Tyana,
and I—
all flesh,
all ordinary—
am simply asking for your body,
like Christians do:
"give us this day
our daily bread."

Maria—give!

Maria!
I fear to drop your name,
like a poet fears to drop
some
word born in the torments of night,
rivaling God in its power.
Your body
I will love and protect,
like a soldier,
stripped by war,
unwanted,
unowned,
protects his only leg.

Maria—
don't you want to?
You don't! . . .

✲ 11 ✲

The War

◤

It began on August 1, 1914, immediately altering the dimensions of everything: of everyday life and of art, the relations between people and an understanding of what had to come. Mayakovsky, whose attempt to join the army had failed, led a normal life during that period; perhaps even more "normal" than before: he published in the popular, not futurist, press, earned his keep, and—like other poets—frequented an artists' cellar. This is told by people close to him, and by himself. And yet, it seems that it was then that the intangible transformation from youth to mature man took place. At the time the war broke out Mayakovsky was twenty-one years old.

FROM MAYAKOVSKY'S AUTOBIOGRAPHY:

The war. I received the news with excitement. To start with, only because of its decorative, noisy aspects. Posters to order, fully warlike, of course . . .

The first battle. I was directly confronted with the terror of war. War is disgusting. The life behind the front even more disgusting. In order to talk about war—one must see it. I went to join up as a volunteer. They would not let me. My loyalty was questioned.

The winter. Revulsion and hatred of war. *Ah, cover, cover the eyes of newspapers,* and others.

The interest in art vanished without a trace.

LUDMILA MAYAKOVSKAYA:

That summer we remained in town. One day in August, when I went home during the lunch break, I found Mama in a nervous state. She said that Volodya had made up his mind to go to the front as a volunteer because a poet has to see the war for himself and experience everything. He wanted to go as a correspondent and said he had to buy a horse. Mama was hurriedly ironing and preparing his things. Volodya, as an only son, was at that time exempt from the draft, and his decision to go to the front was unexpected. Several days passed in great excitement. Then his departure was delayed. A number of obstacles appeared. He was told to apply to the Moscow Chief of Police. He did. But the application was refused because of his "lack of political loyalty."

APPLICATION FOR THE CERTIFICATE OF LOYALTY:

To the Chief of Police, City of Moscow,
from
Vladimir Vladimirovich Mayakovsky,
gentleman

Application

I humbly beg for the issue of a certificate of loyalty in order to enable me to enter active army service as a volunteer. Enclosed is the certificate No. 4170, issued to me at the 3rd station of the Presnya District.

Vladmir Vladimirovich Mayakovsky
October 24, 1914.

BORIS PASTERNAK:

. . . Opposite was the office of the Moscow Chief of Police. In the autumn, I came across Mayakovsky several times there and, I think, Bolshakov, in connection with formalities required for joining up as a volunteer. We kept that procedure secret from one another. I did not complete it, in spite of my father's agreement. But, if I am not mistaken, neither did my friends achieve anything at the time.

MARUSSIA BURLIUK:

. . . We lived in Michalevo, one hour from the capital . . .

At the beginning of August, Mayakovsky came to Michalevo with the poet Shengeli ("Roses from the Cemetery"). Mayakovsky was poorly dressed in faded black pants, a well-worn brown coat, and a hat which had also seen bad days. It was also evident to him that times were difficult for his friend. Burliuk, the father of Russian futurism, was now on the rocks! Mayakovsky said that he would go to Petersburg and try to earn some money there by some means . . .

Burliuk, Kamensky, and Mayakovsky continued to stay very close together. They had common aims: the want of daily bread and the fight for it under difficult circumstances, when everybody was occupied by the war. For artists and poets, these times were very precarious.

Burliuk determined to sell his pictures and to paint portraits; Kamensky, to write books and to receive payment for that. N. N. Evreinov, the noted theatrical director, ordered him to write his biography, and Burliuk and Mayakovsky were busy writing articles for the newspaper *Nov*. Mayakovsky was going the rounds and making contacts. He was full of energy.

The articles which Mayakovsky placed in *Nov* appeared on November 12, 13, 14, 15, 16, 17, 19, 20, 23, 27, and on December 19, 20, 23, 29. In the beginning they wrote them together, but soon Mayakovsky developed his own style, and more and more we see him as an outstanding original mind with his own opinions, tastes, and his own sharp (Mayakovskian) language. For some of his articles Mayakovsky brought money and gave Burliuk a part of it . . . Mayakovsky now always tried to help the Burliuks! The 21-year-young poet had a great, generous heart . . .*

FROM MAYAKOVSKY'S ARTICLES IN "NOV":

Painters, poets, artists!
Art is dead.

* The above fragment has been taken from the original English by D. and M. Burliuk, *Color and Rhyme*, No. 31, 1956.

For two months the newspapers have bewailed again and again the new wounds inflicted on the body of beauty.

The last delicate hand raised to heaven—the cathedral at Reims—has been broken; the rings from the treasures of Liége are on the fat, beer-sodden fingers of Prussian uhlans; and candy-filled bakers' wives sweep the streets of Berlin with petticoats of Brussels lace . . .

Art is dead.

It is good to be a shopkeeper!

So cheap can one now buy the loot and sell it to the mob, eager to know every rumor of today.

One can jeer at heroic peoples, condemned to death; one can mock them by staging dances of the struggling powers.

Painters can donate their stale pictures for bandages for the wounded.

Ah, how easy it is to gain the fame of a national bard, by shouting out the heroes' ambitions!

Art has been made into a field hospital, a food stall, a camp follower in the theater of war.

The Vandal enemies have robbed the art of a foreign nation.

The Vandal friends have robbed Russia.

And I am not sorry for art! . . .

To be sorry for that simple foreign cook? . . .

Art is dead, because it found itself in the backwater of life: it was soft and could not defend itself.

Life goes forward, finding new beauty . . .

I do not know whether the Germans began the war with the purpose of looting and murder. Perhaps they are guided only by that conscious thought. Woe to them who, after the war, do not know how to do anything except cut human flesh. So that there are no such men, one wishes even today to call for ordinary "civilian" heroism.

("Civilian Shrapnel")

Now, when every decent family has been involved—through a brother, a husband, or a house in ruins—in the cacophony of war, we can proclaim over the firebrand of burning libraries the notion of new beauty.

Of course, war is just a pretext. Our art must live too when the plow once more cuts through fields furrowed with trenches. Every cycle of ideas is born and strengthened through its reference to life. After all, yesterday's beauty was attached to the green skirt of villages. But is it a secret that Creuzot, Armstrong, and Krupp joyously destroy Gothic arches with the sole purpose of constructing thousand-storied skyscrapers upon their ruins! . . .

("Poets on Fougasses")

Try today to approach beauty in the bast moccasins of your truth. Even in life as it is today there is nothing real. Is it not the embodiment of our thoughts: it is called "war," people are oppressed by nightmares, legless, armless invalids come, but in reality there is nothing, except a sky, crossed every day, from Tokyo to London, with a striking geometry of missiles. Eh you, daubers, who antlike have laboriously studied nature, count how many legs a cavalry charge has, paint the egg of a darkened train, scrambled for a second of a bursting shell, paint it so it is like itself . . .

He is not a painter who, on a polished apple posed for still life, will not see those whom they hanged in Kalisz.

("To Those Who Lied with Their Brushes")

ON NOVEMBER 20, 1915, A LITERARY COLUMN EDITED BY MAYAKOVSKY APPEARED IN THE NEWSPAPER "NOV." IT WAS ENTITLED "MOURNFUL HURRAH" AND CONTAINED POEMS BY CONSTANTIN BOLSHAKOV ("BELGIUM"), BORIS PASTERNAK ("GUNNER STANDS BY THE HELM"), NICHOLAS ASYEYEV ("CUT THROUGH LIKE YOU"), DAVID BURLIUK ("TRUST IN THE HEROES"), AND VLADIMIR MAYAKOVSKY ("MOTHER AND THE EVENING KILLED BY THE GERMANS").

MOTHER AND THE EVENING KILLED BY THE GERMANS
by Vladimir Mayakovsky

On black streets the figures of white mothers
spread out like tombstones.
They cried their tears into those who roared of the defeated enemy:
"Ah, cover, cover the eyes of newspapers!"

The letter.

Mother, louder!
Smoke.
Smoke
Smoke still!
Why, mother, are you mumbling so quietly?
You see—
the air all paved
with the stone roaring with bombs!
Mo—o—o—ther!
They have just dragged the wounded evening here.
For a long time it held out—
scanty,
ragged,
and suddenly—
poor devil threw his arms around Warsaw's neck
and wept.
The stars in blue calico scarfs
sobbed:
"Killed,
my dear,
my dearest!"
And the bloodshot eye of the new moon looked
at the dead fist still holding cartridge cases.
Lithuanian towns have rushed to look
how the smart lady has been kissed by the corpse:
with tears in the golden eyes of churches
Kovno wrung the fingers of streets.
And the evening cries,
legless,
armless:
"It's not true,
I can still dance!
Beat mazurka with my feet,
jingle it with my spurs—
twirl up my flaxen moustache!"

The bell.

Mother,
what is it?
White, white, like a tombstone.
"It's about him,
telegram with news,
he's dead.
Ah, cover,
cover the eyes of newspapers!"

KAMENSKY:

The antiwar spirit of the poems compelled the editors of *Nov* to use the razor of criticism in their own paper. The literary column no longer appeared . . .
   At about that time we decided to move temporarily to Petrograd . . .

LUDMILA MAYAKOVSKAYA:

In Petrograd Volodya suffered hardships. He felt it all the more because he did not have his own room, or someone to cook for him . . . He devoted all his efforts to completing the poem "Cloud in Pants" which he had begun in 1914 in Odessa . . . Volodya began to publish in periodicals, for instance in the *New Satyricon* . . .

FROM MAYAKOVSKY'S AUTOBIOGRAPHY:

In order to eat I began to contribute to the *New Satyricon* . . .

SHKLOVSKY:

Satyricon was a strange phenomenon. Its god was the one-eyed, laugh maker Averchenko, a man without conscience, who early got used to a comfortable life, fat, fond of stuffed turkey, but a man who knew how to work. A businessman, in fact . . .
   The pale-faced, one-eyed, turkey-eating Averchenko pretended to be hampered by censorship. He even showed a drawing on which *Satyricon* itself—not unlike a fat satyr or faun—was biting the red pencils of the censor, unable to get through . . .
   In *Satyricon*, or—as it was called from 1912—the *New Satyricon*, such writers as Sasha Tchorny, Pyotr Potyomkin, and Valentin Goryansky published their work. Mayakovsky liked their poems. "Lamps burning like

cataracts," wrote Sasha Tchorny. "Pools shine like the bald heads of dead
old men . . ." Potyomkin had unexpected rhymes, changes of dimension.
    Mayakovsky knew Goryansky and many others who, perhaps, will not
be remembered. Many of them are like Mayakovsky, but the similarity
came later . . .

ASYEYEV:

"Write as you like, it does not matter if it sounds strange, ours is a humorous magazine!"—these were the words with which Averchenko greeted
Mayakovsky.

from the poem THE JUDGE
by Vladimir Mayakovsky

Galleys are going down the Red Sea,
galley slaves sweat by the rudder,
with a steel rope bound they roar and shudder,
remembering their country, Peru.

Peruvians whine about Peruvian Eden,
where there are birds, women, and dance
and where above the paradise orange grove
baobabs reach up to heaven.

Bananas, pineapples. All manner of delights!
Even old vintage wine . . .
But lo! I don't know how or why—
judges came to Peru.

They issued laws on birds,
dancing, and Peruvian girls.
The judge's eyes—cesspool-like,
two flashing tins.

The peacock pink and blue
came under his stern scrutiny—
and soon lost his splendid feathers
as if someone had bitten them off!

.   .   .

The equator, trembling, clanks its chains.
In birdless, humanless Peru . . .
only judges live there in anger and boredom,
draped in the scrolls of their laws.

And I have pity for the Peruvians' fate,
bound as they are to the helm with a rope.
The judges are in the way of birds and dancing,
in my way, and in yours, and Peru's.

KAMENSKY:

We began to frequent the literary-artistic cellar "The Stray Dog," whose manager was Boris Pronin . . .

BENEDICT LYVSHITS:

The basic assumption of the "doggy" existence was the division of mankind into two unequal categories: the representatives of art and the "pharmacists," a term used to describe all the others, no matter what their occupation or profession.

That strange view was characteristic for the caste approach to the world, with which generations of "priests of the muses" were brought up. But in "The Stray Dog" there was no pretense of a "mysterious cult" and the main objective was to rob strangers without scruple. The founder and permanent manager of "The Stray Dog," Boris Pronin, had soberly calculated the interest of the "pharmacists" in the literary-artistic Bohemia, and their desire to meet the Bohemians privately, without ceremony, and he robbed his guests to his heart's content, sometimes raising the entrance fee up to 25 rubles, as for instance at Karsavina's evening.

On so-called "extraordinary" Saturdays or Wednesdays patrons were asked to put on their heads paper hats, given them on entering the cellar. Famous lawyers, or deputies to the Duma, whose names were well known all over Russia, startled as they were, subjected themselves to that demand without any opposition . . .

Programs varied, from Kulbin's lecture "On the New Weltanschauung," or Pyast's "On the Theater of Word and Theater of Movement," to "musical Mondays," Karsavina's dancing, or a banquet in honor of the Moscow Art Theater . . . The main substance, however, was not the

planned part of the program but the unscheduled happenings which
lasted all night until morning . . .

"The Stray Dog" opened around midnight and soon filled, like an incu-
bator, with not-quite-hatched theater excitement which, in the atmosphere
heated by wine, erupted with uncontrollable applause, the signal for them
being the shout, "*Hommage! Hommage!*"

Like hot dishes, prepared in another part of the city and carried in a
thermos, newly won triumphs were brought here, when one wanted to
prolong them, taste their flavor for the second or third time, until they
acquired the sour taste of yesterday's successes.

Passing the strong smell of the lavatory next door, all who had not
taken off their top hats before crossing the threshold smashed them
against the low ceiling.

When Akhmatova sailed in, in a tight-fitting black silk dress, with a
large oval cameo on her belt, she had to pause by the entrance in order to
write her latest poems in the pigskin-bound book handed her by the insistent Pronin. They were later thoughtfully, though inconclusively, examined
by the simpleminded "pharmacists" . . .

Glistening with brilliantine, which had not yet flowed down their
faces, the Zhorzhikovs Adamoviches stealthily kissed the sweaty hands of
the Zhorzhikovs Ivanovs and squeezed each other's lustful knees under the
table.

Radiant as if he had just received Communion, Pyast appeared, having
just left Blok, and his worn shiny coat seemed to reflect some unexpected
joy.

Mayakovsky was half-lying in the position of a wounded gladiator, on
a Turkish drum which he banged every time the figure of a stray Budyetlan showed itself in the doorway . . .

SHKLOVSKY:

Going down. The ceiling painted by Sudyeykin . . . They probably
began with the idea of reforming the theater but ended by drinking wine.

At the head of all this stood Boris Pronin, a man who probably never
slept at night . . . He was really a theatrical director. He directed everything for many years: the evenings and the nights, the writers and the
painters.

Kuzmin came here sometimes, with his few hairs combed across the bald dome of his skull . . . Khlebnikov whispered his poems here. In another room, where there was no fireplace, Anna Akhmatova sat in a black dress . . . Mayakovsky liked Akhmatova the poetess.

At about that time Mayakovsky was writing his "Flute of the Spine." He used to come to "The Stray Dog." Officially they did not serve alcoholic drinks at the "Dog" at that time. They drank, say, coffee.

People for whom war meant profits were buying old collections together with the houses and wives of their owners . . . "The Stray Dog" was once hired for a woman dancer. The entire cellar was filled with flowers, the woman danced on a sheet of glass together with a little girl dressed as Cupid . . .

"The Stray Dog" was patriotic . . . Wine was prohibited and a pineapple drink was served instead.

BUNIN:

Sacrilege, blasphemy, some of the principal characteristics of revolutionary times, began with the first gusts of "wind from the desert" . . . In "The Stray Dog" in Petersburg, where Akhmatova once said, "We are all sinners, we are all whores," *The Flight of the Virgin and Child to Egypt* a pseudo "liturgical mystery," with words by Kuzmin, music by Sac, décor and costumes by Sudyeykin, was staged. It was a "mystery" in which the poet Potyomkin, who performed the donkey, walked bent at a right angle, supporting himself with two sticks and carrying Sudyeykin's wife, playing the part of the Virgin, on his shoulders. Quite a few future "Bolsheviks" frequented "The Dog": Alexei Tolstoy, then still young, big, with a full jaw, entered the place like a great nobleman, a landowner, in a raccoon fur, beaver cap or top hat, with a haircut à la moujik; Blok came with the stony impenetrable expression of a handsome man and a poet; Mayakovsky, in a yellow tunic, with very dark eyes which had an insolent and sullen provocative look, with tightly pressed, wry, toadlike lips . . .

KAMENSKY:

Soon we celebrated in "The Stray Dog" the publication of the literary almanac *The Rifleman,* where for the first time Blok, Sologub, Kuzmin, and Remizov appeared together with the futurists.

It was in *The Rifleman* that a fragment of "Cloud in Pants" was published for the first time . . .

On February 25, 1915, there was an official literary evening at "The Dog" to discuss *The Rifleman,* with the participation of invited writers and critics.

Only a short time before Mayakovsky had read in "The Stray Dog" his excellent poem "To You!" in which he lashed out at the behind-the-lines parasites and profiteers and all the wartime scum.

TO YOU!
by Vladimir Mayakovsky

To you I say, who wallow in orgies,
who have hot baths at home and warm lavatories!
Aren't you ashamed when you read
in newspapers of George Cross awards?!

Do you know, you, multiplied idiots,
who think only of things to stuff your belly—
at this very moment, perhaps, a volley
has shot off Lieutenant Pyetrov's legs? . . .

If he, who had been led off for slaughter,
wounded and shell-shocked suddenly saw
how nicely with your fat-soiled mouths
you hum Syevyeryanin's *chanson!*

For you, who only copulate, and gobble,
for your convenience—would I give my life?
I'd rather serve pineapple water
to whores in the bar.

THE NEWSPAPER "BIRZHEVIYE VEDOMOSTI," EVENING EDITION,
PETERSBURG, FEBRUARY 13, 1915:

Mayakovsky invested his dreadful poems with the highest emotions which fill us at the present time, and with our reverence for men, whose deeds evoke enthusiasm and affection. . . . A scandal followed. Men rose from their seats with shouts of indignation, ladies—with tears. The artists turned to Pronin, the owner of "The Stray Dog": "After this hideous incident we would consider coming here below our dignity."

Pronin replied, "Good riddance."

I have been called to the army; and shaved. Now I do not want to go to the front. I am pretending to be a draftsman. At night I learn from an engineer how to do drawings of automobiles. With publishing worse still. Soldiers aren't allowed . . .

Soldiering. Rotten time. I paint (still evading) portraits of the commanding officer.

Dearest Mama, Ludechka, Olenka!

Only now have my troubles with being drafted ended. I hasten to write to put your minds at rest.

I have been called to the army and sent to the Petrograd Automobile School, where I am employed in the draftsmen's office as a qualified and experienced draftsman.

There is no need at all to worry about me. After my work at the school is ended, I can do everything I was doing before. My address remains the same. Write about yourselves. How are things at home?

Affectionate kisses to you all,

Volodya

I am sending you my "military" photograph.

My dear Ludechka!

Thank you very much for your good and loving letter. I am now trying to get a decent uniform and generally to establish myself. This takes a lot of time and energy. I feel rather tired.

You ask me, dear Ludka, if I need money. Alas, I do now, and rather urgently. I have to buy a uniform, pay for it myself. I must. That's why I'm broke just now.

On this assumption, I turn to you with a big request: send me some 25 to 30 rubles. If you find it difficult to get such a sum, then send me as much as you can. I am very sorry to have to ask you for this, but there is nothing I can do. I think things will be all right in the future.

My address is the same: Palais-Royal.

Please send me the money as soon as possible, if you can.

Nothing new just now.

I am sending you my new book.

Affectionate kisses for you all,

Your Volodya

FROM INNOKENTI OKSYONOV'S ARTICLE, "THE LITERARY YEAR.
REVIEW OF LITERATURE FOR THE YEAR 1915," IN "NOVY ZHURNAL
DLA VSEKH," NO. 1, 1916:

. . . The war has brought us closer to Blok and Akhmatova, and made Bryusov and Balmont more distant.

The war as such partly inspired the writing of the futurist, Vladimir Mayakovsky . . .

Someone has said that around the names of modern writers no legend will ever grow. But it seems to me that the figure of Mayakovsky will in time be surrounded by "created legends." There is a titanic quality in Mayakovsky which raises him very high. His will be the tragic fate of a precursor. . . .

In Mayakovsky's poem "Cloud in Pants," about which (except for the futurist journals) I have nowhere as yet read a serious article—in that poem all images are as powerful as if they had been forged of iron . . .

Of course, there would be nothing easier than to brand Mayakovsky with the mark of "a displaced individualist." But his hysteria, his desperate protests—are they not the full expression of a certain aspect of the human psyche? . . .

☖ 12 ☖

Gorki

☖

When Mayakovsky met him, Gorki was already a famous and highly successful writer. Let us look at him through the eyes of his one-time friend, Ivan Bunin, and then quote from the journals of Boris Lazarevsky and Boris Yurkovsky—men who observed and commented first-hand on Gorki's interest in the young poet. The writer's wife, Maria Andreyevna, describes Mayakovsky's visit with Gorki in the fall of 1914, at the Finnish resort Mustomyaki. Vassili Kamensky describes the circumstances of Gorki's first encounter with Mayakovsky and the futurists in a somewhat different way. Gorki himself published in 1915 an article "On Futurism" which provoked a storm in the press at the time. In Gorki's archive exists a draft of an unfinished essay on Mayakovsky and a long letter to Ilya Gruzdyev. Meetings between the two writers are also recalled by Shklovsky, Vengrov, and others. After some years Mayakovsky and Gorki went in different directions and mutual sympathy gave way to irritation and dislike. This chapter de-

*scribes the beginning of their acquaintance, when the hand
extended by Gorki to the young futurist helped the latter in
his struggle for public recognition, for an understanding of
his world-shattering poetry.*

IVAN BUNIN:

. . . Every new work by Gorki immediately became an event of nationa̅
scale in Russia. He changed all the time; changed his style and his treatment of people. He now rented a house in Nizhni Novgorod, had a large
apartment in Petersburg, often came to Moscow, was in charge of a periodical . . . founded a publishing house . . .

He had already launched Andreyev, then Skitalets, and befriended
them. Sometimes he brought other writers closer to himself as well, but
more often than not, this did not last long: having charmed someone with
his attention, he suddenly deprived him of all his favor.

FROM THE JOURNAL OF BORIS LAZAREVSKY, THE WRITER, A NOTE
ON A VISIT TO KORNEL CHUKOVSKY IN KUOKKALA, JUNE 21, 1915:

. . . "Mayakuokkala" began. Quite a new phenomenon. Total derision of
beauty, feelings, God . . . Mayakovsky was in excellent spirits, showed
me a letter from Gorki, who invited him for breakfast the next day. Gorki
will be delighted, for Mayakovsky's poetry undoubtedly is the product of
a hungry enraged beast. His demonism means anger with God who did
not give him anything, though it is true that he did not ask God for anything . . . "Mayakuokkala" began with a long melodious poem. Its essence is hate and total negation . . . He finished reading and asked my
opinion; I told him I was overwhelmed—and it was true—that this was
very serious, that it was an attempt to incorporate the doctrines of anar-
chism into poetry.

FROM THE DIARY OF BORIS YURKOVSKY, A MEMBER OF GORKI'S
HOUSEHOLD:

Alexey Maximovich fusses lately about V. Mayakovsky. Regards him as a
talented, outstanding poet. Is in raptures over his poem "The Flute of the
Spine" . . . Talks about Mayakovsky's unusual verve, his individuality.
"There is really no futurism, there's just Mayakovsky. A poet of great caliber." But for all his enthusiasm, Al. Max. also points out his negative quali-

ties. "Mayakovsky is a hooligan. A hooligan due to his shyness. Just imagine. He is abnormally sensitive, ambitious, and attempts to hide all this behind his wild excesses."

A REMINISCENCE OF MARIA ANDREYEVNA:

We lived in a big wooden house, on the top floor, while almost the whole of the ground floor was taken up by one enormous room—both a living room and a dining room. In that room a very tall, young, fairly handsome man was standing. He looked familiar, I must have seen him somewhere in Moscow, but I could not remember at first who he was. I went up to him and said, "Good morning! Alexey Maximovich cannot talk to you now. Do you have some business with him?"

He turned abruptly toward me, his hands in his pockets: "I don't know what to say. Some business, I suppose . . . most probably I have some business. But I just want to see him."

"Very well. Please wait."

. . . And I turned to leave the room, but he rushed after me: "Aren't you afraid I'll steal your silver spoons?"

This seemed so odd, I remember, that I was a bit stunned, but I said finally, "No, I'm not afraid. And, frankly, our spoons are not silver anyway."

And I left the room.

Then I came back, with coffee, bread, ham, and whatever else there was . . .

Suddenly I realized: this was "the man in the yellow tunic." I turned to him and asked, "Aren't you Mayakovsky?"

"Yes. I am Mayakovsky."

He smiled broadly and lightheartedly, and I thought: so young and no teeth.

We talked for a while. I asked him, "So you came to meet Alexey Maximovich, or do you really have some business with him?"

"No, I just want to meet him."

"Well," I said, "you'll love each other."

"Why do you think we'll love each other?" he asked.

"Well, it's always like this: there are people who love him but he doesn't love them; and there are others who love him and he loves them too."

"But I'm afraid," he said.

"You do well to be afraid," I said. "But I rather think that you're not afraid of anything."

"True."

Our conversation had been exhausted.

. . . We heard the stairs creak, Alexey Maximovich came down. It was most interesting to see how nervous Mayakovsky became. His jaws were moving and he could not control them; his hands were in his pockets, out and in and out again.

FROM THE REMINISCENCES OF VASSILI KAMENSKY:

It was at just about that time that Vala Khodasyevich, a great friend of Gorki's, told us, "Tomorrow morning Alexey Maximovich returns from Finland."

And she gave us his address.

After a friendly debate we decided, at Mayakovsky's suggestion, to send me to Gorki, as our group's delegate. I was to go see him early in the morning.

. . . He opened the door himself: "Please come in."

I told him who I was.

"Yes, I've heard about you." Gorki spoke softly in a bass voice, smiling. "First come, first served. Please take your coat off and go straight into the dining room. We'll have some breakfast and talk."

. . . Alexey Maximovich prepared breakfast himself. He poured two glasses of vodka from a bulging carafe and cut two pieces of fish pie.

We clanked our glasses, drank our vodka, and began to eat the fish pie.

Gorki asked, "You say you're a flier. Are you the same Kamensky who had that terrible accident?"

"That's right."

"Interesting, very interesting. Tell me, where do you come from, who are you, and how did it come about that you became an aviator and a writer? A futurist, too! And where did you meet Mayakovsky? And that fellow Burliuk, who is he? And how about Khlebnikov? And Syevyeryanin? What do you think about the war? And about Russia? What are your ideas? Tell me all, everything. I'll give you no peace with my questions."

"By all means, Alexey Maximovich, I'll be delighted to answer all your questions. But I'm afraid it will take a lot of time."

"Are you in a hurry?"

"Oh no! I'm thinking of your time."

"Please don't pay attention to the clock. Time is at our disposal. If necessary, we can talk all through the night. Once you have found your way here, I'm not going to let you go so soon. I want to find out from you all that interests me. And I happen to be very much interested in what our younger generation is doing in art, in life, in general . . ."

We parted only the following morning.

As I was leaving, Alexey Maximovich said, "Please bring Mayakovsky and Burliuk to dinner tomorrow. I'll be waiting."

I went, of course, to the Europa Hotel where Mayakovsky was living. I woke him up, told him everything, and passed on Gorki's dinner invitation.

Volodya did not at first believe that I had only just come back from Gorki: "What, you spent a day and a night, a day and a night there?" He was astounded: "But what did you do there all day and all night? It's incredible!"

All three of us arrived punctually at seven for dinner with Gorki.

Before we mounted the front stairs, Mayakovsky asked nervously, "What if you were mistaken, Vassya, and Gorki had no intention of asking us to dinner? What then? What a shame!"

Burliuk declared categorically, "In any event, I'm going in last."

. . . We sat down at the table. Alexey Maximovich asked, "Do you drink vodka?"

"No," said Mayakovsky with a smile, "we only drink Kakhetin wine, which providently has been put here too."

"How's that?" Gorki was surprised. "Only yesterday Kamensky drank vodka . . ."

"That was because of nerves, fear . . ." I admitted.

. . . No sooner was dinner over and we went into the drawing room than Voloda stood in readiness:

"Tolstoy was right when he said, 'I cannot be silent.' Nor can I."

"Well, at least you recognize Tolstoy, that's something," smiled Gorki, rolling a cigarette.

Volodya, swaying slightly, as if he were standing on board ship, began to recite slowly in his deep bass the prologue to "Cloud in Pants:"

> Your thought,
> dreaming on softened brain . . .

At this point I noticed that Gorki received with a kind of astonishment and joy the powerful timbre of Mayakovsky's voice and the clear striking rhythm of his manly verse . . .

Gorki rose and embraced Mayakovsky with tears in his eyes . . .

Mayakovsky went on reciting poems; he recited a lot and in an excellent way.

Other guests arrived and all marveled in silence at the fact that the futurists had found their way to Gorki.

Burliuk read his poems too. And so did I.

But Gorki kept asking for more. All of us finally had to confess that we were very tired. We poked fun at ourselves. We broke up late.

The following day Alexey Maximovich invited me to come. We had breakfast, took a droshky and went to the Field of Mars . . . to see futurist paintings.

. . . At the exhibition, painters surrounded Gorki. Mayakovsky and Burliuk went up to him too . . .

A few days later, on February 25, I had dinner with Alexey Maximovich again and then we went to "The Stray Dog" for a discussion about *The Rifleman* collection.

Boris Pronin admitted so many people that the cellar was almost bursting.

It was as hot as a bathhouse on Saturday; crowds, sweat, hot, gay. Gorki was received with an ovation.

He was literally flooded with flowers.

There were correspondents from the entire Petersburg and foreign press.

Mayakovsky, Syevyeryanin, Burliuk, Kamensky, and Khlebnikov read their poems.

Gorki applauded us profusely.

After our appearance the audience began to call out, "Alexey Maximovich, please come up on the platform! Please! Please tell us something about the futurists! Should they be recognized or not? How good are they? Please tell us."

Gorki mounted the platform, stood for a minute in absolute silence, thinking, then said in a decisive manner, "They've got something."

FROM MAXIM GORKI'S ARTICLE "ON FUTURISM" IN "ZHURNAL ZHURNALOV," NO. 1, APRIL 15, 1915:

There is no Russian futurism. There are just Igor Syevyeryanin, Mayakovsky, Burliuk, V. Kamensky. There can be no doubt that there are among them men of talent, who—when the dross is thrown away—will in the future become a valuable quantity. They do not know much, they have seen little, but they will undoubtedly learn, work, and improve themselves.

They have been showered with abuse and this is certainly a mistake. One must not abuse them, one must simply approach them with warm friendliness, for even in their shouts, in their jeers, there is something good: they are young, there is no stagnation in them, they want a new, fresh word, and this is undoubtedly a good thing.

There is another good thing about them: art should be brought out into the streets, among people, among the crowd, and they are doing this —clumsily, it's true, but one can forgive them that. They are young . . . young.

Let us recall our outstanding, now meritorious poets, Bryusov and Balmont—what were they like fifteen years ago . . .

In Russia doubtless there is no genuine futurism, such as came into existence in Italy, embodied in the person of Marinetti. A rich, talented artist, he has been burning the old Italian clichés. There, as you know, museums, magnificent architecture, ancient but now dead sources of culture and thought exert an overwhelming influence. One must get out from under those massive vaults, one must break that shell . . . But here, in Russia, there is no terror of the past, we are not oppressed by antiques . . .

And all of them, that bustling group of noisy people who, for some reason, call themselves futurists, will achieve their small—or perhaps even great!—task, which will probably be fruitful.

Let there be an outcry, let there be abuse, let there be confusion; anything rather than silence, dead icy silence.

It is hard to say how they are going to turn out, but one wants to believe that theirs will be new, young, fresh voices. We are waiting for them, we want them.

They were given birth by life itself, by our contemporary conditions. They are not abortive fetuses but babies born at the right time.

Only recently did I first see them living, real—and you know, futurists are not so horrible as they make themselves out, or as the critics paint them.

Please take Mayakovsky as an example—he is young, only twenty years old, he is noisy, unbridled, but he surely does have talent. He ought to work, learn, and he will still write good, true poems. I have read a volume of his poems. One of them made an impression on me. It is written with the right words . . .

Russia is immense, infinite . . .

How many great undertakings are there in her, how many unfathomed energies. Take the Russian man. Slack, flabby within . . . He will go where a favorable wind takes him. The huge Russian crowd has no face, no characteristic traits . . .

However ridiculous and noisy our futurists might be, one must open the door wide for them; wide, because theirs are young voices calling for a new life.

FROM AN INTERVIEW WITH LEONID ANDREYEV, PUBLISHED IN THE NEWSPAPER "BIRZHEVIYE VEDOMOSTI," MAY 4, 1915:

My original attitude toward futurism was much more positive than it is now; I then nourished some vague hope . . . It was the war that became the testing time for them, as for many others. That all-embracing national cause had to reveal either their inner riches or poverty. It turned out to be not just poverty but abject misery . . . I am surprised at Gorki's statement that the futurists are achieving an important task.

FROM ARKADYI BUKHOV'S FEUILLETON ENTITLED "A BONELESS LANGUAGE" IN THE "ZHURNAL ZHURNALOV," NO. 30, NOVEMBER 11, 1915:

I do not know whether Maxim Gorki will read this note, but if so, I would like to tell him: after his published blessing of the futurists and their supporters I realized that one must not only laugh at futurism but also combat it with cruelty, anger, and firmness. When he stated that "They've got something," I thought he was scoffing at literature, but that is something one could not expect from Gorki. That is why I would like to ask him a question:

"Alexey Maximovich! All your life you have been working on human thought, translating it into images. All your life in literature you have been creating new words, without knowing it. You have remained pure even when dealing with the most sensitive subjects. You have ridiculed, without laughing at them, noisy stupidity and gaudy vulgarity. What has happened to you, since you declared about that quintessence of noisiness, gaudiness, and country-fair fraud that 'It's got something'? After all, you are a wise man, a man of talent, you have a striking gift of creative vision. Couldn't you guess that all that you have treated with such friendliness is just a boneless language? You patted a boor on the head and he spat on your favorite picture. He did not do this by accident either, but in low anger at his own nonentity . . .

"A day will come when an insolent publisher of the insolent pimply youths whom you have praised will publish a collection which he will preface with your words: 'They've got something.'

"The unscrupulous half-literary mud and creative scum will then take shelter behind your words. How sorry you will then be for your great, and not easily remedied, mistake . . ."

FROM A DRAFT OF GORKI'S UNFINISHED REMINISCENCE OF
MAYAKOVSKY:

. . . I saw him at the painter Lubavina's in the spring of '15. Poems were read by Kluyev, Yesenin, Shklovsky. V. V. was also to read his poems. Tall, clumsy, sullen, with a gray face . . . He spoke a couple of lines hastily, indistinctly, in a dull voice, then waved his hand, made a sharp about-face, and disappeared, hid in the adjoining room, closing the door behind him. The view was that he felt ashamed . . . I have heard that Mayakovsky delighted in embarrassing others and it was nice that this turned out not to be true.

In the summer he came to me in Mustomyaki. A very modest, pleasant man, who delighted in playing with words . . .

GORKI'S LETTER TO ILYA GRUZDYEV MENTIONS THE FACT THAT
AT THEIR FIRST MEETING MAYAKOVSKY GAVE THE IMPRESSION OF
A "HALF-BROKEN MAN":

. . . That impression was intensified when he came to me at Mustomyaki
in the summer of '14—or was it '15? On that occasion he read to me his
"Cloud in Pants," "The Flute of the Spine"—in fragments, and many varied lyrical poems. I liked the poems very much. He read them splendidly,
even cried like a woman, which frightened and agitated me considerably
. . . When I told him that in my opinion a great, though not easy, future
awaited him, he replied gloomily, "I want the future now," and, "I don't
need a future without joy, and I don't feel any joy." He was very nervous,
must have been in a bad psychological state . . . He spoke with two
voices, as it were: with pure lyricism, and then again—in tones of sharp
satire. One felt that he did not know himself and was afraid of something
. . . At the same time he showed an addiction to playing with words
. . . That would be good if it were gay. But he invested that far-fetched
verbal play with serious meaning, intensifying it "to the degree of mysti-
cism in phonetics," as A. Bely once put it. But one thing was clear: he was
a man in his own way sensitive, very talented, and—unhappy . . .

FROM MAYAKOVSKY'S AUTOBIOGRAPHY:

I went to Mustomyaki. M. Gorki. I read him fragments of "Cloud." Gorki,
moved, wept all over my waistcoat. I moved him with my poems. This
made me a little proud. Soon it transpired that Gorki weeps over every
poetic waistcoat.

SHKLOVSKY:

Mayakovsky read his poems one day in the apartment of the painter Lubavina in Baseynaya Street. Alexey Maximovich Gorki came, tall, a little
stooping, with a crew cut, dressed in a long coat. Behind him Alexander
Tikhonov. Mayakovsky began with a lecture, spoke slightingly about old
poets who wrote about their country manors on vellum; he referred to me.
Then he began to cry and went into another room.

He cried there, then he came back and read his poems.
Gorki liked him then . . .

FROM THE REMINISCENCES OF NATHAN VENGROV, THE WRITER:

. . . On a pillar one could still see the large poster with a suprematist drawing by Malevich advertising the futurists' evening: a huge black circle underlined by a thick black stroke . . . Above it, in big loud letters, there were the words: "They've got something. M. Gorki." . . .

I invited Gorki to the home of Lubavina, the painter, with whom I was friendly and whom he had previously visited with me. Mayakovsky was to read the manuscript of his new poem "the Flute of the Spine" there . . .

Many people had already assembled in Lubavina's studio. Mayakovsky had come with the Briks and Victor Shklovsky . . . Gorki came with Tikhonov.

By the studio's window, which occupied the length of the wall, stood Vladimir Mayakovsky, the inevitable cigarette in his mouth. He squeezed the manuscript in his hands and was perceptibly nervous. In a corner, leaning on the grand piano, stood Alexey Maximovich in a long black coat, wearing a crew cut.

Mayakovsky began on a high note: "Gracious ladies and gentlemen! . . ." And suddenly, after this first sentence, Mayakovsky grew silent. A long tiring pause ensued. The poet tried to resume his reading and was silent again. The pause again.

"I can't!" Mayakovsky said and turned toward the window.

The hostess, in order to spare the poet and the guests an embarrassing situation, invited everybody with a gesture to the adjoining room for tea. Mayakovsky was drawing something with his fingernail on the frosty window. Lubavina put a friendly arm around him and softly tried to urge him on about something.

"He's got tears in his eyes," she whispered to me in astonishment as she passed by.

After tea, back in the studio, Mayakovsky simply and clearly explained, "I am used to rotten apples and bottles being thrown onto the platform, while here it's as if one is tucked up in cotton wool. Lack of resistance."

Then he began to read his poem. This time he read it through to the end . . .

SHKLOVSKY:

Mayakovsky cried in agitation, not because of Gorki, of course, it was not he of whom he was afraid.

There was a woman involved. Besides, to oneself one does not have to pretend that one is made of bronze . . .

Then there was *Lyetopis* (*Chronicle*), with Gorki, Tikhonov, Sukhanov, Bazarov, with the lovely young Larissa Reisner and Babel, who at that time signed himself Bab-El . . .

The war was on. We were very young.

Mayakovsky was drafted. Gorki found him a place in an automobile company, as a draftsman with Captain Krit . . .

VICTOR PYERTSOV:

Maria Andreyevna's sister—Ekaterina—had married Colonel Krit, an engineer, who was attached to the command of the Automobile School . . . So, thanks to Krit's help, Alexey Maximovich arranged for Mayakovsky to be admitted there . . .

VENGROV:

. . . *Cloud in Pants.* It was said that literary-minded ladies were afraid of speaking aloud, in the bookseller's presence, the title of that little orange book, profusely spotted with the marks of the censor, a book acclaimed throughout the artistic circles of Petersburg.

Alexey Maximovich read my review of Mayakovsky's poem, written for the *Chronicle* . . . A favorable review of Mayakovsky's poem, whose author was just then active in the adventurous ranks of the futurists, was a fact of major importance. The opinion of the editorial board was divided.

Alexey Maximovich was leaning over his desk at the editorial office. He was holding the proofs of my review. Sukhanov was standing next to him. He was opposed to its publication: quietly but decisively he was talking about the impropriety of extolling futurism in the *Chronicle.*

"I've heard this already," smiled Alexey Maximovich. "I've heard this. But we will publish it. You must understand, this is necessary . . ."

THE DAILY "NOVOE VREMYA," NO. 14314, FOR
JANUARY 4, 1916:

In the spring of last year popular newspapers brought sensational news: "The Stray Dog" cellar had been visited by Maxim Gorki, who listened to the futurists' poems and made a profound statement: "They've got something."

. . . You might think it was a trifling story: well, the man wanted to be original, different. No one sees anything in the futurists except stupidity and insolence, but Maxim Gorki, if you please, sees something. A little noise, publicity—that's all! But who knows, perhaps for Mr. Gorki the story will not end well, after all. We must make this supposition on the basis of a couple of lines in the new periodical *Chronicle,* published toward the end of December in place of the deceased *Contemporary* . . . On the whole we have the old periodical with a new publisher . . . But there is something new as well. About the futurists. The periodical does not know how to treat them, sniffs around them and, though with a stammer, declares in a note about the most recent scandalously nonsensical opus of the futurist Mayakovsky that "his poems abound in authentic realism." . . .

. . . It seems that bad times have come now for Mr. Gorki, if his arch-realistic, venerably radical *Chronicle* fusses about futurism, not knowing what to do with the futurists . . . and, in spite of everything, feels compelled to discover tragic elements in . . . "Cloud in Pants."

. . . Perhaps the futurists will marry Mr. Gorki? It will be an interesting wedding. Mr. Gorki will rise at the wedding feast with a cup of grandmother's kvass and begin his speech: *"Foor boow diw"* . . .

A NOTE IN THE NEWSPAPER "DYEN" OF OCTOBER 21, 1916, ENTITLED "MOOING," IN CONNECTION WITH THE PUBLICATION BY GORKI'S PUBLISHING HOUSE OF A VOLUME OF MAYAKOVSKY'S POEMS "SIMPLE AS MOOING":

We have given up Mayakovsky and his "art," and suddenly his poems are being published by the publishing house whose motto is: "Sow what is wise, good, eternal"; the publishing house established by the *Chronicle.* Mayakovsky's publishers have taken a great sin upon their souls!

A. DEMIDOV'S REMINISCENCE OF A LITERARY EVENING IN THE EDITORIAL OFFICE OF THE "CHRONICLE" ON THE OCCASION OF THE PERIODICAL'S FIRST ANNIVERSARY:

The first to read was Mayakovsky, who stood by the grand piano and roared, "Nero!"

Then he stood silent for a while, thinking, turned around and said, "No, I am not going to read."

They kept asking him, but in vain.

♦ 13 ♦

Two Sisters

A Moscow lawyer, Yuri Alexandrovich Kagan, had two daughters. They were both petite, high-strung, very intelligent, and full of charm. They both (like their father, a lover of literature; and mother, a music lover) loved art. The elder sister—a magnificent redhead—was a painter and sculptor; the younger—a fair blonde—graduated from the Institute of Architecture and later became a well-known novelist. The first of them was Mayakovsky's great love, Lila Brik; the other became the French writer, Elsa Triolet. Mayakovsky came to know Elsa first. Lila, already married, was living in Petersburg. Mayakovsky paid attention in Moscow to the young high-school student, who early came to understand the worth of his poetry but did not treat his amorous intentions too seriously. It was thanks to Elsa that Mayakovsky came to know Lila and her husband, Osip Brik.

FROM THE REMINISCENCES OF ELSA TRIOLET:

I was still at school . . . I met him through some friends. He seemed to me big, impossible to understand, and insolent. I was fifteen and a bit afraid. Some time later he came to see me . . . I do not remember anything of that first visit except that the maid was terrified. I was not yet sixteen but I cheerfully refused to agree with my parents that my friend Mayakovsky could behave like everybody else. After a fairly long struggle they gave up and Mayakovsky was more or less recognized at our home: he was asked to stay to dinner and permitted to spread out his drawing utensils in my room. Drawing was his means of livelihood then. He came almost every day, treated my mother with elaborate and disarming courtesy, while in Father's presence he spoke only when absolutely necessary. In the end his yellow tunic was almost ignored. When he did not find me at home, he left a visiting card, big as a page from a book, on which there was only his name in big yellow letters. My mother systematically returned those cards to him, saying, "Vladimir Vladimirovich, you have left your signboard behind." . . .

Mayakovsky made passes at me, talked a bit too much, and ceaselessly murmured something, occasionally raising his voice all of a sudden, probably to check on what his verse sounded like . . . I was not interested at all in that inner creative work going on by my side and I was hardly aware of the fact that Mayakovsky was a poet. He often asked me to play the piano and paced back and forth incessantly behind me, gesticulating . . .

Usually, however, a moment came when my mother closed the lid of the piano. Clad in her dressing gown, she told Mayakovsky it was late and time to go to bed. My father was already asleep. She had to come back many times before Mayakovsky began slowly to put his overcoat on, standing in the doorway.

One also had to call the caretaker downstairs . . . and give him a tip. Mayakovsky often did not have the necessary ten or twenty kopecks. I wanted to give them to him and witnessed his silent inner struggle: should he face the anger of the old caretaker or take money from a woman? He took the coin, then put it down on a table in the hall, then took it and put it back again . . . In the end he left the coin behind and that was courageous of him.

The next day he usually came and told my mother, "Last night I just waited till you were asleep and then came back through the window using a rope ladder . . ."

Mother looked at him with an uneasy smile: perhaps he simply came back up the stairs? . . .

At about that time my sister, Lila, came to see us. She had been married and living in Petrograd. One day she asked me who that Mayakovsky was who came to us so often, and am I keen about him, because he brings Mama to the point of tears. What? This brings Mama to tears? But why didn't she tell me this earlier? When Mayakovsky telephones next time, I'll simply tell him that I can't see him because it brings Mama to tears.

A few months later, he made attempts to meet me in the country, where I was spending the summer. I came an hour or two late, hoping vaguely that Mayakovsky would be too impatient to wait. For greater security I was accompanied by one of my aunts. But Mayakovsky stood guard near the small railway station, with his head raised high, his eyes dimmed with anger, his legs wide apart . . .

It was then that for the first time the thought occurred to me that I could see him without Mother's knowledge. In that case we would have to meet in a less public place than the railway station, in the evening, if possible. Or spend a day in Moscow where I could see whom I wanted without anyone's knowing.

The empty apartment in Moscow smelled of mothballs. Steps and voices sounded strange, because the curtains and carpets had been folded up. It was a haunted house, with its white furniture covers, white sheets covering two pianos, with gauze veils hanging from the ceiling, with the windows open to the sky, with Mayakovsky's tall figure pacing the rooms.

It happened one evening that summer, in the country near Moscow, that for the first time I "heard" a poem which was recited by Mayakovsky for himself. We were walking arm in arm through the darkness, down a wide, unlighted street, a country street between two rows of little houses hidden behind fences . . .

Mayakovsky, absorbed in himself, vague, suddenly spoke aloud in verse . . .

I stood in amazement: all of a sudden I realized that Mayakovsky was writing poems and that those poems fascinated me.

"Aha!" said Mayakovsky with triumphant condescension. "You like it?"

And then Mayakovsky recited his poems for me till late at night, in front of the fence to somebody's villa . . . I was wild with emotion over the fact that I had discovered something which had been so near for so long and which I had absolutely ignored. I asked for more and more . . .

LILA BRIK:

It was my sister Elsa who introduced me to Volodya in the summer of 1915 at Malakhovka. We were sitting on a bench near the house one evening when Mayakovsky came and went for a walk with Elsa. I waited half an hour, an hour, it began to rain, but there was still no sign of them. Daddy was ill and I could not go back home without Elsa. My parents were afraid of the futurists, and to think that one of them was alone with their daughter in the woods at night . . .

Well, that dangerous futurist did take my sister into the woods. Just imagine my anxiety! When they eventually came back I scolded them and, wet and angry, took Elsa home.

The next day Mama complained to me that Mayakovsky was following Elsa, staying late, till the wee hours so that Mama had to get up every half hour to try to get rid of him, while in the morning he boasted that having left through the door he returned through the window . . .

At that time Mayakovsky was a dandy, complete with visiting cards, jacket, top hat (everything cheap though). Tragic situations occurred too, when he made a date with Elsa to go for a ride to Sokolniki but lost his money at cards during the night and in the morning, though in frock coat and top hat, took her for a ride, not in a carriage, but in a tram. Volodya was then almost twenty-two years old and Elsa was eighteen.

Before I got to know Volodya in Moscow, I had seen him once before in Petrograd, at the Nevsky Prospect. Top-hatted, surrounded by some squirts, he gave me an awfully insolent look.

About a month passed since the meeting in Malakhovka. One day, quite unexpectedly, Mayakovsky came in—just back from Kuokkala, suntanned, very handsome—and immediately began to brag that his poems were the best, that we did not understand them, we could not even read them, and that apart from his poems, those of Akhmatova are also the work of genius. I had been taught as a child that it was not nice to brag, so I told him, trying to be polite, that unfortunately I had not read his poems but would try to read them properly if he had some on him. He had "Mother and the Evening Killed by the Germans." I read it through care-

fully. Volodya was surprised at this and asked, "You don't like it?" I knew
that authors must be praised, but I was so indignant at his insolence that I
replied, "Not much" . . .

ELSA TRIOLET:

1915–16–17. I lost my father, we lived alone with mother in another house,
another district. I had new friends, new interests. On graduation from
school I joined the School of Architecture and was interested only in
mathematics and drawing. Mayakovsky, in the meantime, became "Uncle
Volodya" and was a very good friend . . .

He was then living in Petersburg. I saw him whenever he came to
Moscow for a couple of days, or when I myself went to Petersburg to my
sister Lila. In this way Mayakovsky, who first came to her in order to see
me, began his friendship with Lila . . .

The people around Lila and the Briks were highly prejudiced against
Mayakovsky's poetry—without knowing it, for that matter. Here, as in
other places, I waged many battles, shouted and argued a lot, before he
was eventually allowed to read his poems . . .

LILA BRIK:

Daddy died. I returned from the funeral in Moscow. Elsa came to Petrograd, Volodya came again from Finland. We imploringly whispered to
Elsa, "Do not ask him to read." But Elsa would not listen to us and we
heard "Cloud in Pants" for the first time. His reading was fascinating. It
was what we had been waiting for. We had not been able to read anything for some time. All poetry seemed worthless—poets were writing not
in the right way and not about the right things, and here suddenly was
both. Osya took the manuscript and held on to it for the whole evening—
reading. Elsa was triumphant, and Volodya did not go back to Kuokkala,
though he left behind there his lady love, and his laundry with the washerwoman, and all his belongings. The same evening he dedicated "Cloud"
to me . . .

FROM MAYAKOVSKY'S AUTOBIOGRAPHY:

THE MOST JOYOUS DATE. July 1915. I got to know L. J. and O. M. Brik.

LILA BRIK:

Osip Maximovich was my first husband. I met him when I was thirteen years old. It was the year 1905. In the high school which I attended, Osip was in charge of a political economics circle. We got married in 1912. When I told him that Mayakovsky and I had fallen in love with each other, all three of us decided never to part from one another.

MAYAKOVSKY'S LETTER TO HIS MOTHER, NOVEMBER 9, 1915:

Dearest Mama.

I am well as usual. Working as usual too. I moved from Palais-Royal. So now please write to me at: 7, Zhukovsky Street, Apartment 42, c/o Brik, for Mayakovsky. Dearest Mama, I have a great favor to ask of you. Redeem and send me my winter coat and send me, if possible, some warm underwear and a couple of handkerchiefs. Please do it for me, if it is not too much trouble. Do write, Mama.

Kisses for Ludechka and Olenka. Kisses for you all.

Yours,

Volodya

ASYEYEV:

Mayakovsky was not a family man in the sense most people see this . . . He regarded his mother with affectionate respect, which found its expression not through embraces and kisses but through brief inquiries about her health, food, medicines, and other necessities of life . . . In his relations with his sisters he revealed the concern of the eldest in the family, although he was younger than they were. But he did not begin, and did not like, long family debates. Their tastes must have been different. At any rate, whenever I was there, I could see that there was hardly any conversation, except on the most elementary matters. And he would take me with him when he went to see his family in order, so it seemed, to provide himself with a lightning conductor to absorb Olga's thunderous voice and the lightning in the eyes of his other sister, Ludmila, who I think disapproved of Volodya's having departed from family tradition . . .

He was estranged from domestic life, from its traditional forms, and the family was one of the principal of these. But without people who were close to him, he felt lonely. So he chose a family for himself, into which he flew like a cuckoo, without displacing and making its members unhappy, however. On the contrary, he protected that strange nest and cared for it as he would have for his own, had he been a family man. That nest was the Brik family, with whom he became friendly and lived throughout his creative life.

Osip Brik graduated from the faculty of law and had a wife, a young woman, very beautiful, with big brown eyes.

Osya Brik did not write and had a rather contemptuous attitude toward literature . . . He read much. Did not like the symbolists . . .

Osip Maximovich was called to the army and sent to the automobile company. Later it was decided that Jews were not wanted in the automobile company, so they were all assembled and sent to the front. Brik returned home.

At first he went out in uniform, then he began to wear civilian clothes. They forgot about him. Two years passed. They should have torn him to pieces. But to do that they would have had to look for him, taken an interest in him . . . Dozens of people visited him. There was only one thing he could not do: move to another apartment. If he had done that he would have become a movable object and had to register himself . . .

Brik liked Mayakovsky and so he decided to publish his work, and in general to go into publishing. It was courageous of a man who lived without any papers . . .

Mayakovsky found a place to stay . . .

Everybody spurned the poet, wounded him . . . And here, at last, home and a contract with Brik: half a ruble for every line, forever, and tomorrow he publishes . . .

Lila Brik cut Mayakovsky's hair, told him to wash himself, gave him a change of clothing. He began to carry a heavy stick . . .

Lila has brown eyes, a large head, is beautiful, redhaired, light, wants to become a dancer . . .

She likes objects, earrings in the shape of golden flies, and old Russian charms, has a string of pearls and a lot of lovely trinkets, very old and familiar. She can be sad, feminine, capricious, proud, frivolous, fickle, amorous, wise, and what you will . . .

No one wanted to publish "Cloud," although at that time Volodya had already published in the *New Satyricon*.

Osya got hold of some money . . . We knew "Cloud" by heart; we awaited the proofs as a lover does a date. We put in by hand the fragments that had been confiscated by the censor. I was in love with the orange cover, the type, the dedication, and I had my copy bound in the most expensive leather by the best binder . . .

Volodya began to introduce us to his friends. We talked about publishing a periodical . . .

SHKLOVSKY:

Later I often saw Mayakovsky at Osip Brik's on Zhukovsky Street. They had an apartment on the seventh floor. Three small rooms . . .

The lady of the house, with her large face and beautiful eyes, hunching her slender shoulders, looked at Mayakovsky as if he were a not quite tamed lightning.

ASYEYEV:

And then I was introduced by Mayakovsky into an apartment unlike any other, flowery with hand-painted fabrics, resounding with newly written or newly read poems, and the lady of the house—with expressive flaming eyes—who could convince and surprise one with her original views, her own, not borrowed from any authority or overheard in the street. We—that is to say, myself, Shklovsky, and I think Kamensky—were captivated by those eyes, by her pronouncements, never imposed on us, thrown as it were in passing, but hitting the nail of the discussion on the head. That was Lila Brik, who later became the principal heroine of Mayakovsky's poetry.

Osip Brik for his part was unexpected and disarming. He did not speak often but had very sharp judgment. He did not attract attention at first, certainly not from the first look. When, however, his voice was heard, everybody listened to him with particular respect . . .

Such were the people whom Mayakovsky befriended in 1915 . . . How were they different from other acquaintances and friends? Above all, in their extensive knowledge of both artistic and social matters. The new and unknown in poetry was just as dear to them as the new and unknown in science, in life . . . Art was for them a law of life, spiritual and material law. And if for the Briks "the relation of art to reality" was a

theory, Mayakovsky personified for them the real value of that relation . . .

LILA BRIK:

We were sometimes visited by Chukovsky, who lived in Kuokkala and was
happy now that Mayakovsky had left there. He said he could not work in
peace knowing that Mayakovsky was staying in the same place as he. But
he had a high opinion of him and liked "Cloud" immensely. One day,
when we were all sitting together and discussing the possibility of found-
ing a periodical, he said suddenly, "This is how new literary trends come
into being: while sipping tea and chatting at home." We did not believe
him just then . . .

Pasternak came from Moscow with Maria Sinyakova. He read splendid
poems splendidly, was impressive and unintelligible, and we liked
him . . .

We welcomed the new year 1916 very gaily. Our apartment was small
so we hung the Christmas tree from the ceiling in a corner. We decorated
it with a paper Yellow Tunic and Cloud in Pants. We all dressed fantastically . . . Elsa wore a tower of hair constructed by a hairdresser, and on
the top of the tower we put in a long thin quill, reaching up to the ceiling.
I had on a Scottish tartan dress and red socks, bare knees, and was wearing the white wig of a marquise.

That evening Kamensky proposed to Elsa. It was the first proposal she
had received. She was terribly surprised and rejected him. Heartbroken,
he dedicated a poem to her and went away in despair to get married
elsewhere . . .

Such big crowds began to visit us that our apartment became too
small. One floor below us in the same house, a big, six-room apartment
became vacant. We moved in there, without any furniture. We called one
room the library—Osya, as usual, had accumulated a lot of books—another, the dancing room . . . We hung up a huge sheet of paper, covering the entire wall, and everybody could write on it everything he wanted
. . . Burliuk painted skyscrapers and three-breasted women; Kamensky
cut out and stuck up paper birds of different colors; Shklovsky wrote
aphorisms, such as "Anger with humanity gathers drop by drop." . . .

The first issue of the periodical was being completed. The title was *Has
Taken.* Volodya had wished for a long time to call someone by that name,

a son, a dog, a periodical. The editorial board consisted of Mayakovsky, Khlebnikov, Brik, Pasternak, Asyeyev, Shklovsky. Osya was publishing for the first time in his life and his style became clear at once—simple and violent.

FROM OSIP BRIK'S ARTICLE ON MAYAKOVSKY'S POETRY ENTITLED "BREAD!":

We ate cake because we did not get any bread. The enterprising confectioners fed us a terrible mess! Cakes! The sweetest, fresh cake, melting in our mouths. Take your pick! Blok's sugar candy sticks, Balmont's tasty éclairs . . . And the new discovery of confectionery art—*Lilac Ice Cream.*

We were sucking, munching, going into ecstasies, swallowing those sugared specialties, honey was sticking to our lips and souls. Then we tossed in our soft beds, sick to the point of vomiting.

Rejoice, shout aloud: we have bread again!

FROM MAYAKOVSKY'S ARTICLE "A DROP OF TAR" IN THE ALMANAC "HAS TAKEN":

Futurism Has Taken *Russia in Its Mortal Grip*

Not seeing futurism before your eyes and not being able to look into yourselves, you began to shout about death. Yes! Futurism has died as a separate movement, but it has flooded over you all.

Since, however, futurism has died as an idea for the select few, we do not need it any more. The first part of our program of destruction we regard as accomplished. And for this reason do not be surprised if today you see in our hands, instead of a fool's rattle, the architect's drawing; and the voice of futurism, only yesterday soft with sentimental dreaming, will now be melted into the copper of sermon.

LILA BRIK:

Volodya and I were always together: we went to the islands, took walks, in the street. Volodya would put on a top hat, I a large black hat with feathers, and we would go to the Nevsky, for instance to buy a pencil for Osya. We would enter a store and Volodya would address the salesgirl with a mysterious expression on his face: "Mademoiselle, will you please give us a pencil so strange that it is red on one end and blue on the other!"

Mademoiselle would jump, startled, to my great delight.

At night we walked along the sea front. In the darkness it looked as if the ships did not emit smoke but sparks. Volodya said, "They don't dare emit smoke in your presence" . . .

It was sad that private soldiers did not have the right to go to the theater, or enter a restaurant, or even be seen in the streets after a certain hour. And, of course, there was no question of extravagant behavior in a public place.

There lived at that time in Petersburg a horrible squirt by the name of B. He called himself a futurist and was the editor of an almanac. He got some poems from Volodya for its second issue. Some time later we got the book and found an anti-Semitic article by Rozanov next to Volodya's poems. Volodya wrote a letter to the editor of some newspaper declaring that he should not be regarded as a contributor to that almanac . . .

LETTER TO THE EDITOR OF THE DAILY "BIRZHEVIYE VEDOMOSTI":

Dear Sir!

I would be grateful for the publication of the following letter:

In the second almanac entitled *The Rifleman,* just published under the editorship of A. Byelenson, I found myself next to the unbridled V. Rozanov. Although A. Byelenson had informed me earlier about V. Rozanov's being a contributor to the almanac, the past issue of *The Rifleman,* a strictly literary publication, and also the name of its editor, seemed to me a sufficient guarantee that it would not contain any inflammatory material or slogans. However, Rozanov's article is full of such slogans . . . Having this unpleasant material published next to mine compels me to declare that I shall have nothing more to do with *The Rifleman.*

Please accept the assurances of my highest esteem,

V. Mayakovsky
August 21, 1916

LILA BRIK:

A couple of days later Volodya met B. in the billiards room of the "Bear" restaurant. Volodya was in civilian clothes. B. approached him and said, "I have read your letter; you are a fool." Volodya was furious but was in no position to cause a scandal and had to satisfy himself with the promise of slapping him at the first chance he had to take off his uniform legally.

A few days after the February revolution I witnessed how Volodya got his own back from B. I was walking on the Nevsky with Volodya when we saw B. with a lady walking opposite us. Volodya excused himself, made a sign to B., who left his lady and immediately received such a slap that he staggered on his feet. Volodya took me by the arm and we went on, without looking back. The next day B. demanded a duel, but Volodya refused, referring to the code of honor which forbids a gentleman to have duels with a commoner.

FROM MAYAKOVSKY'S AUTOBIOGRAPHY:

Brik . . . published "The Flute of the Spine" and "Cloud." "Cloud" came out a cumulus after the censor blew into it. Six pages of dots.
Since then I have hated dots. Also commas.

LILA BRIK:

Volodya wrote "Flute" slowly; every chapter was ceremoniously read aloud. First he read the poem to me, then to me and Osya, then to all the others. It was to be like that with everything Volodya wrote.

from THE FLUTE OF THE SPINE
by Vladimir Mayakovsky

I have blasphemed.
I screamed that there was no God.
And God lowered his arm into hell's pit,
chose such a one that her sight would a mountain move,
and ordered:
love her!

. . .

It was he it was he who designed it all,
so that I would not guess who the mysterious creature was,
he endowed you with a true husband
and human notes put on the piano.
Were I to creep by the bedroom door,
make the sign of the cross on the sheet,
I know—
I would smell the burning hair,
the sulphurous smoke of devil's flesh.

Instead I rampaged till dawn
in horror that you are taken,
in order to love like wife,
and I polished my scream into stanzas,
a half-mad jeweler.
In games of cards
in wine to find the truth—
wash the throat of the heart parched with sighs.

I do not need you!
I do not want to!
It's all the same,
I know,
soon I'll die.

If it is true that you are,
my God,
God,
if you have put stars in the sky's turban,
if the pain
which daily multiplies,
is a torture sent by you, Lord,
put on a judge's chain,
wait: I'll come and visit you.
I'm punctual.
I won't be late, not even by a day.
Let the almighty inquisitor receive me!

I'll purse my lips.
I won't utter a cry
from my bitten mouth.
Bind me to comets, like to horses' tails,
let them drag me
torn
to the starry forks.
Or thus:
when my soul, turned inside out,
before your judgment stands,
it will vaguely dissolve,

you
must erect gallows out of the Milky Way
and swing me there, a criminal.

Do what you will.
You'd rather quarter me?—
I will wash myself your soiled hand.
Only let her disappear,
the cursed one,
whom you have made my love!

.   .   .

No, not for me the pink softness,
which in the throat of centuries sticks like a lump.
Today kneel, oh world, at new feet,
I extol you,
painted,
redhaired.

Perhaps, of those days,
dangerous like bayonet blades
in the white beard of ages
only you
will remain
and I
who follow you still.

You will go far across the sea,
hide in the black den of night—
I will kiss into you through London fogs
the lantern's lips bright.

In the desert heat you will go with a caravan,
where watchful lions roar—
for you
I will carpet with Sahara the flaming cheek
under the windswept storm.

You will put the smile into your lips—
the dandy toreador
jumps on the arena.

And suddenly I
will toss jealousy into your box
from the dying eyes of the bull.

You will enter a bridge with a carefree step,
over the waves
you will walk by the bank—
this is like a Seine
rising under the bridge,
calling,
baring my bad teeth.

. . .

Strong,
I shall be useful to them—
they will order:
let yourself be killed in this war!
Your name will be
the last,
incrusted on the lip crushed by agony.

LILA BRIK:

And then came the long poem "Don Juan." I did not know that Volodya
was writing it. Suddenly one day he recited the entire poem to me while
we were walking in the street. I was angry with him because it was about
love again. Doesn't he get bored with the subject?! Volodya pulled the
manuscript out of his pocket, tore it to pieces, and threw it to the winds in
Zhukovsky Street.

FROM A LETTER FROM MAYAKOVSKY TO HIS MOTHER AND SISTERS,
SEPTEMBER 1916:

Dearest Mama, Ludechka, Olenka!

Affectionate kisses for you all. I am well. I am prospering not worse
than others, and this means that it is not too bad. Thank you for the package, the food was excellent.

Do not read silly newspapers, if you can help it, and do not send cuttings. Your dumplings are much tastier and wittier . . .

I work a great deal . . .

I have moved to another room. For the time being write to me at the old address: Zhukovsky Street, Brik.

Affectionate kisses for all,

Volodya

Dear, kind Elsa!

Come here soon!

Forgive me for not writing. This is nothing. You are now, I think, the only person whom I regard with love and affection.

Most affectionate kisses.

Reply *immediately*, please, please.

Volodya

"My knees are giving way under the strain . . ."

When I received a letter from Mayakovsky with the request to come, because his "knees are giving way under the strain . . ." I did not hesitate a moment and the same evening went to Petrograd.

In Petrograd, Mayakovsky lived in a sublet room. I remember vaguely the poor, bare, badly lit room. Mayakovsky was sitting at the table; before him stood a bottle and a glass. His long, gray cheeks were even more hollow than before, his cheekbones were protruding. Under his loosely hanging coat one could almost see his ribs. He had been drinking for days, behind locked doors.

He greeted me absent-mindedly. Long moments of silence, monosyllables . . . Why did I come? The strain was unbearable. He walked up and down the room, smoked nonstop, with the cigarette stuck in his mouth; he drank, did not talk. After a few hours I was ready to howl. Why had he asked me to come?

But when, in the evening, I wanted to go, he would not let me. I told him someone was waiting for me downstairs, in front of the house. He grew angry. So did I. He raged in fury. I preferred to die rather than not leave at once. When I was slamming the door, he shouted after me, "Go to the devil, together with your sister . . ." His voice was hoarse with rage.

In a moment he caught up with me on the stairs and barred my way. He took his hat off and said, "Forgive me, madam . . ."

SHKLOVSKY:

I remember how one day Mayakovsky came with Lila Brik to the "Comedians' Inn." They went out together. Soon Mayakovsky came back in a hurry.

"She left her handbag behind," he said and found a small black handbag on the chair.

At the next table was sitting Larissa Reisner, young, beautiful. She looked at Mayakovsky sadly.

"You have now found your handbag and will carry it all your life."

"I can carry this handbag in my mouth, Larissa Mikhailovna," the poet replied.

✠ 14 ✠

February 1917

✠

History influences the course of human life—particularly a life that wishes it to. On February 27 (March 12), 1917, the tsarist rule was abolished. Mayakovsky was present where the shooting took place. In those days, and a little later, he was seen by Alexander Syerebrov-Tikhonov, Vassili Desnitsky, Olga Leshkova, Vladimir Veger (Povolzhets), and others. Anatol Lunacharsky also met him—and mentioned the fact in a letter to his wife. Proclamations, communiqués, articles, transcripts of meetings—were documents of history in the making, when the shooting ended and before new shooting began. Mayakovsky recalls with pride a couplet which he composed at that time. In the same period he completed the poem "Man."

ALEXANDER SYEREBROV-TIKHONOV:

At the first meeting of the Petrograd Soviet—on February 27, 1917—three deputies, among them myself, were asked to edit and print, before the

next morning the first issue of *Izvestya*. We requisitioned a truck on the
way and went from the Tauris Palace to Ligovka, where I had some
friends in the "Kopeck" printing works . . .

At dawn I went out into the street with a pile of wet copies.

The city was bursting with excitement.

In spite of the early hour the streets were full of people.

Somewhere near the Nevsky, Mayakovsky ran into me, bareheaded,
his overcoat unbuttoned. He lifted me from the ground, kissed my face all
over, shouted something, called out to someone, waved his arms: "Here!
Here! Newspapers!"

I was standing before him like a tree before a storm.

The sound of shooting was heard from the railway station. Mayakovsky rushed in that direction.

"Where are you going?"

"Why, they're shooting over there!" he called in ecstasy.

"But you're not armed!"

"I've been running all night to where the shooting is."

"What for?"

"I don't know! Let's run!"

He snatched a bundle of newspapers from my hands and waving it like
a flag ran in the direction of the shooting.

SHKLOVSKY:

Looking for Mayakovsky I went to the Briks'.

The smoke in the room had settled down but new waves of it were
already being added to the old ones.

Mayakovsky was not there. I do not remember seing Brik. Kuzmin was
there with many other people. They had been playing cards for two days
now.

The revolution began with bread lines, with soldiers' indignation.

It began like clouds or wind in the mountain.

I do not play cards and I went out into the street again.

In the streets the wind was blowing, spring was coming all of a sudden. Everybody was shouting, running around with guns. Nikolai Kulbin
was organizing the militia and died the first day.

Mayakovsky entered the revolution as he would his own home.

VASSILI DESNITSKY, A COLUMNIST:

In the first days of the February Revolution I moved to Petrograd and stayed with Alexey Maximovich Gorki at Kronverksky Prospect . . . In March Mayakovsky visited us frequently; not that he had any business, he came just to see us. He was very agitated. The atmosphere in the streets made him drunk. In telling us his impressions he forgot about restraint and caution. With enthusiasm he told about the arrest of General Sekretyev, the commander of his military school, and about his active participation in that joyous operation. One could feel that he had been carried away by the pathos of the street, that the atmosphere of the revolution was like air to him as a poet.

GORKI'S APPEAL OF MARCH 8, 1917:

Citizens! The old managers have departed, leaving behind them a great inheritance which now belongs to the entire people.

Citizens, protect that inheritance . . .

Art—is a beauty which men of talent were able to create even in conditions of despotic oppression, bearing witness to beauty and the might of the human soul . . .

A COMMUNIQUÉ OF THE PROVISIONAL GOVERNMENT:

The Provisional Government has fully approved the need to take measures for the protection of art treasures and has called into existence the Commissariat for the Protection of Art Treasures, consisting of the following: N. F. Nyekludov, F. I. Shalapin, M. Gorki, A. N. Benoit, K. S. Pyetrov-Vodkin, M. V. Dobushynsky, N. K. Rörich, and I. A. Fomin. In artistic circles the question is being discussed of establishing a Ministry of the Fine Arts in place of the Ministry of the Tsarist Court.

THE APPEAL OF THE FOUNDERS' MEETING OF THE "FREEDOM OF ART" ASSOCIATION, OF MARCH 12, 1917:

Taking the view that the question of normal legal conditions for artistic life in Russia can be solved only by a Constituent Assembly of all persons active in the arts and that the convening of such an assembly will be possible only after the war, the "Freedom of Art" Association categorically protests the undemocratic attempts of certain groups to obtain control of the arts through the establishment of a Ministry of the Arts and appeals to all persons active in the arts sympathetic to it to come today at two o'clock to a mass meeting of artists in the Mikhail Theater and vote for the following, who are defending the freedom of artistic art: N. I. Altman, K. I. Arabazhin, V. A. Denisov, I. M. Zdanyevich, S. K. Isakov, M. Kuzmin, V. N. Kulabko-Koretska, V. Mayakovsky, V. E. Meyerhold, N. N. Punin, S. Prokofiev, V. N. Soloviev.

FROM THE TRANSCRIPT OF THE MEETING AT THE
MIKHAIL THEATER:

Mayakovsky: Citizens, I have come here on behalf of leftist trends in Russian art. Anyone can be a leftist in the construction of life, in politics. The poet, the artist, as a citizen [here a gap in the transcript] . . . everyone has taken part. When the tsarist system [a gap in the transcript] . . . not only will be revealed the layers of reactionary spirit [a gap in the transcript] . . . it will be necessary to fight. I have come on behalf of the artists who have raised the flag of revolution—art is in danger. In the days of great upheavals art always dies down. The arm raised against the tsarist system has come down on the palaces, and the protection of palaces was a task of those who founded the commission with Gorki. This task can be easily done, just by positioning groups of soldiers. The other task is more complex and essential. Whenever a wave of social unrest surges, they say there is no room for artists, for art, that every artist has to contribute to political work, pertaining to Russia's new model. This matter we can absolutely entrust to the Provisional Government which has proclaimed freedom and is its guarantor. All these tasks we can transfer [a gap in the transcript] . . . and to the Council of Workers' and Soldiers' Delegates. Our cause—art—must mean in the future state the right of free determination for all creative artists. A Provisional Commission has now been appointed numbering 12 persons. It seems to me that this commission cannot be competent even as far as the protection of monuments is concerned, because it has not been chosen according to democratic principles. I respect all persons who are members of this commission, I have a deep respect for Gorki, who has fought for the freedom of art, but I am against its organizational defects. If there is a government, then only the familiar group of "The World of Art" will be a part of it. Benoit is a follower of a definite trend in art, to me incomplete. Palaces where Somov's works are stored will be protected [a gap in the transcript] . . . There exists an independent Russian art which is the expression of democratic tendencies. Benoit cannot deal with art realized through a broad democracy [a gap in the transcript] . . . For a broad democracy, broad representation is essential. [Applause.] You have been given a plan of an organization which seems acceptable to us on the question of a system of art. There will be an organizing committee which will prepare a provisional assembly dealing with current needs of art. In this way the Constituent Assembly will be prepared and when our friends come back from the front, it will decide how to administer Russian art. I am against a ministry, etc. I regard it as essential that art be concentrated in one definite place. My motto, and that of everybody, is—long live the political life of Russia and long live art free from politics!

Arens: Citizens, I did not know that Mr. Yermakov was going to reply to Mayakovsky who said that we had participated enough in politics and that now we must participate only in art, rejecting politics. I consider that one does not contradict the other: why can cab drivers, shoemakers, bakers participate in politics and not us? It seems to me that they unite in order to explain their needs to themselves and we must not be a separate caste. We too should be in a social organization . . .

Mayakovsky: I do not withdraw from politics, only in the sphere of art there should be no politics.

ZHEVYERZHEYEV:

. . . Every Friday my painter and theater friends began to assemble at my house.

I recall most clearly of all the "Friday" of 17/30 March, 1917 . . . Mayakovsky appeared when the evening was already in full swing. He was, I remember, in a military uniform without shoulder straps. He was gay, excited, and immediately raised the spirits of all present.

Before his arrival the conversation had centered on the Mikhail Theater meeting which had taken place a couple of days before. Mayakovsky's arrival immediately sharpened the edge of the discussion. Much was said about the stand that should be taken by "leftist" artists in the affairs of the day. It is difficult to say who was to have the first say on that occasion. I had the impression, though, that it was exactly Mayakovsky's presence which for the first time brought into the open an awareness of the necessity to unite closely the "left" of the Active Artists Association in order to counteract the power-hungry people of "The World of Art."

Such a union of the "left" was soon accomplished in the apartment of S. K. Isakov, in the so-called Leftist Bloc of the Active Artists Association. It was a bloc representing those members of the Petersburg artistic intelligentsia who half a year later, immediately after the October Revolution, overwhelmingly supported the Soviets.

NIKOLAI PUNIN:

It looked as if, in spite of everything, in spite of all our wild shouting, the right and the center—thanks to their experience in social action—organized themselves better then we did, and our hope that the Active Artists Association would in some degree be accessible to the organizations of the left was rather slight. For this reason, to counteract the meeting of March 12 . . . on Meyerhold's initiative it was decided to call . . . a mass meeting in the Troitsky Theater on March 21 . . . Mayakovsky was against it and declared that he did not recognize any left, except himself, Burliuk, and Larionov, that it was all futurist talk, while it was necessary to act. In this way he destroyed our united front of the left. It was very unpleasant at the time and we condemned him severely in our circle.

THE NEWSPAPER "RUSSKAYA VOLA," MARCH 22, 1917, ACCOUNT
OF THE MEETING OF THE "FREEDOM OF ART" FEDERATION:

Angry and intransigent, Mayakovsky rose to speak several times. Words irritated him, he demanded revolutionary action. He did not notice the inconsistency in his theses—but no matter. He, the author of "Cloud in Pants," with his followers, stood just then to the left of the "Federation of the Left." Today, tomorrow—they will publish a journal in which, firmly divided from those who were searching for a common language and agreement, for a common platform with other existing schools of art, they will openly and boldly proclaim the principle of freedom for their personal, individual creative work. What are other talents to them, not marching with them in single file? Away with them!

KAMENSKY:

. . . I proclaimed our group "the poets of all-mankind's revolution!"

On March 26 we organized in the Hermitage Theater in Moscow, "The first republican evening of art," where—besides myself (who opened the proceedings)—Mayakovsky, Asyeyev, Burliuk, Vassilisk Gnyedov, Aristarkh Lentulov, G. Yakulov, Ilya Mashkov, P. Kuznetsov, A. Osmyorkin, A. Tairov, and Valentina Khodasyevich spoke.

Everybody was in a state of festive euphoria.

PASTERNAK:

Soon after the February Revolution I returned to Moscow. Mayakovsky came from Petrograd and stayed in Stoleshnikov alley. In the morning I visited him at his hotel. He got up and, as he was getting dressed, recited his new poem "The War and the World" for me. I did not tell him my impression. He could read it in my eyes. Besides, he knew the measure of his influence on me. I began to talk about futurism and said how wonderful it would be if he now sent all this to the devil in full voice. Laughingly he almost agreed that I was right.

BUNIN:

I was last in Petersburg—for the last time in my life!—early in April, 1917, at the time Lenin came. Among other things, I attended the opening of the Finnish painting exhibition. The entire elite of Petersburg was there, headed by the ministers of the Provisional Government, well-known deputies to the Duma. Hysterically servile speeches addressed to the Finns were made. Later I took part in the banquet in honor of the Finns . . . The elite was there too, the "flower of the Russian intelligentsia"—that is to say, prominent painters, artists, writers, social workers, ministers, deputies, and one highly placed foreign representative, namely the French ambassador. However, Mayakovsky towered above them all. I was sitting at dinner with Gorki and the Finnish painter Gallen. Mayakovsky came up to us, pushed his chair between us, and started to eat from our plates and drink from our glasses . . . Gorki was convulsed with laughter. I moved away.

"Do you hate me so much?" asked Mayakovsky gaily.

I replied that this was not so: "It would be too great an honor for you!" He opened his trough-like mouth in order to say something but at this point the then foreign minister, Milyukov, rose to propose the official toast and Mayakovsky rushed toward him to the center of the table. There he jumped on a chair and began to shout so boorishly that Milyukov grew silent in consternation. A moment later he controlled himself and again spoke. He had hardly said the word "Gentlemen!" when Mayakovsky roared more loudly than before. Milyukov spread his arms in a helpless gesture and sat down. Then the French ambassador got up. He must have been sure that faced with him the Russian hooligan would give up. No such luck. Mayakovsky silenced him immediately with even louder shouting. As if this was not enough, wild and absurd madness erupted all over the hall: Mayakovsky's companions also began to shout, bang their feet on the floor and their fists on the table, laugh, howl, squeak, hawk. And suddenly, through this noise, was heard the tragic cry of a Finnish painter, who looked like a shaved walrus. Already inebriated, deathly pale, and apparently shaken to the depths of his soul by these dirty tricks, he began to shout, with tears in his eyes, for all he was worth, one of the few Russian words he knew: "Much! Much! Much! . . ."

FROM OLGA LESHKOVA'S LETTER TO MICHAEL LE DANTIEU,
APRIL 10, 1917:

At the banquet . . . Dobichina seated . . . Mayakovsky next to Gorki. A. Benoit began to declare his friendship and love to Zdanyevich, and Gorki—to Mayakovsky . . .

🐗

On April 18, 1917, the first issue of Novaya Zhizn *(New Life) was published in Petrograd. The paper was edited by Gorki; its regular contributors were Mayakovsky and Osip Brik, among others:*

DESNITSKY:

Vladimir Vladimirovich often came to the editorial offices of *Novaya Zhizn,* where Alexey Maximovich received callers who came on business with the paper's literary section. He looked in to my room too. He did not ask for "news." Sometimes he just sat in silence for a few minutes, then asked, "Busy?" and departed in silence . . .

Sometimes he would come with a sulking expression and ask outright, "Do you have any money?" When I answered in the affirmative, he took the money and went away. I do not know how he fared in those days, but

I think he was no stranger to poverty. He always returned the borrowed sum without being asked.

FROM STALIN'S ARTICLE IN THE NEWSPAPER "PROLETARIY,"
AUGUST 20, 1917, ENTITLED "TODAY'S ELECTIONS":

The group "New Life" of electoral list No. 12 is appearing before you. This group expresses the mood of intellectuals, who are alienated from life and activity. For this very reason, the group oscillates continuously between revolution and counterrevolution, war and peace, workers and capitalists, landowners and peasants . . .

To vote for that ambiguous group, to vote for list No. 12, would mean to serve the followers of the "defense of the fatherland," who in their turn are the servants of counterrevolution.

ASYEYEV:

After February, 1917, when all fences were covered with election lists of the various parties aspiring to participation in the government, the old parties, whose names were well known, came to the fore nevertheless. But apart from them there were the cadets and the renovators, the anarchists and the association of cooks, and whoever wanted to play the game. One day Mayakovsky was walking with me in Nyeglinna Street, looking at placards and lists, when suddenly he proposed that we make up our own list. What list? Well, one with the names of the futurists. Mayakovsky's name would be followed there by that of Kamensky and others. To my surprised question as to who would vote for us, Vladimir Mayakovsky replied thoughtfully, "Who knows? Times being what they are, one can even be elected president . . ."

FROM ANATOL LUNACHARSKY'S LETTER TO HIS WIFE,
JULY 1, 1917:

My Dear,

Today I am sending you a telegram to say that I'm all right.

Just think how overloaded and varied my day is. Take today's program: in the morning—writing the letter to you, preparing a speech, reading newspapers, then—early lunch (I try to have lunch at twelve, but today I don't know if there will be lunch at all due to a waiters' strike).

Later I'll go to the editorial office of *Novaya Zhizn* to attend the second meeting of the leftist-socialist satirical periodical *Wheelbarrow*, which is soon to appear. Its editor is the futurist Social Democrat Brik. Its literary contributors are the futurist Social Democrats Mayakovsky, A. M. Gorki, Pyeshkov, myself, Emil Krotki, Ol d'or, Bazarov, Levidov, and others. Among the visual artists the contributors are: A. Benoit, Pyetrov-Vodkin, Altman, Mayakovsky (the same, very talented young near-giant, bursting with energy, growing and turning left in front of one's eyes), Lebedyev, and others. The publishers are: Tikhonov, Grzhebin . . .

LETTER OF MAY 25, 1917, AND LATER REMINISCENCE OF
OLGA LESHKOVA:

A couple of days ago I happened to find myself at a meeting of the Society of Proletarian Poets and Painters at Krzhesinska's house . . . Among those attending the meeting was Mayakovsky . . .

The problem of defining the "class basis of art" was raised and it was proposed that the definition should be based on party membership . . . According to one member of the society, not to belong to the party was simply petty obstinacy. In every town district there is a district party committee and it is enough to go and join to become a member of the society as well . . . While this question was being discussed, V. V., very unhappy at what was being said at the meeting, rose to speak and, briefly, concisely, to the point, declared that he was most surprised by the talk about formal party membership which did not take into account the kind of talent and general outlook of the writers, which would be a better guarantee of their work's being useful for the proletariat . . . V. V. left the table and began to walk excitedly around the room. A few minutes later, when the meeting became very agitated, Bogdatyeva, who was in the chair, said to the perambulating V. V., "Sit down, Mayakovsky, you're interrupting our work." Mayakovsky stopped but did not sit down. He pushed open the door firmly, went out into the garden, and continued walking up and down the path . . .

FROM THE ORDER OF THE DAY OF THE FIRST RESERVE
AUTOMOBILE COMPANY, NO. 159, OF AUGUST 3, 1917:

§3. The soldier Vladimir Mayakovsky, attached to the technical division of the Command Automobile School, who is being sent to the district military commander at Petrograd in order to obtain a three-month sick leave, is to be stricken off the company register for food, tea, and tobacco supplies as of July 26, and for soap and pay as of August 1.

ZHEVYERZHEYEV:

Some time toward the end of September, 1917, Vladimir Vladimirovich, not having found me at home, left a note asking for an urgent loan of a small sum of money because, as he wrote, he "must disappear from Petrograd at once, today." From my previous meetings with him I knew that his relations with the command of his military unit had completely deteriorated and that he was threatened with serious consequences.

FROM MAYAKOVSKY'S LETTER TO LILA AND OSIP BRIK,
SEPTEMBER 25, 1917:

Dear Li, dear Oska!

Kisses for you at the start of the letter, and not at the close, as is customary: I cannot wait! How are you? The happy ones who have visited the fabulous country called "your place" only torment me with the classic expression "Lila is like Lila, as usual."

Yesterday I spoke. There were many good friends but no money.

I live in Presnya. They feed me and walk on tiptoe around me.

I like the first but not the second. A family genius—like something from Averchenko.

Whether I shall be able to go to the country, I have no idea.

Dear children, write to me!

Kisses.

Your getting-fat Volodya

FROM MAYAKOVSKY'S ARTICLE "ALL BUT THE MEMORIES":

"The Stray Dog" cellar has turned into "Comedians' Inn" . . .

At the "Inn" began to assemble the remnants of smart and rich Petersburg. To some gay tune I composed the couplet:

> Pineapples eat, hazelhens chew,
> Your last day's coming, bourgeois!

The couplet became my favorite piece with the people. In the first days of the October Revolution the Petrograd newspapers wrote that sailors storming the Winter Palace, were chanting a song beginning with: "Pine-apples eat . . ." etc.

In the same period (just before October 1917) Mayakovsky completed his poem "Man," begun in 1916. At the end of the poem his hero (author) returns after a thousand years to the city on the Neva. A passer-by, when asked about Zhukovsky Street, replies that it is now called Mayakovsky Street, "because there he shot himself at his mistress's door" and she jumped out the window—"and so two bodies lay, one on top of the other."

from the conclusion of "MAN"

Throw on me the sunray's noose!
Entangled in summer I will fly
and blazing
rattle the irons
of my thousand years' love . . .

To the sky of doom
the lament will erupt.
And he, who governs life,
over the dark of planets
the final flare
from the last suns will tear.
And only
my pain
grows high—
I stand,
embraced with fire,
on the never dying pyre
of incredible love.

12. Mayakovsky in Kiev, 1913.

13. Nikolai Kulbin's self-portrait, 1913.   14. Igor Syevyeryanin.

15. Marinetti in St. Petersburg, February 4, 1914.

3. Mayakovsky's caricature
Kornel Chukovsky, 1915.

17. Ilya Repin's drawing of
Victor Shklovsky, 1914.

18. Professor Jan Baudouin de Courtenay.

19. Valeri Briusov.

20. Maria Denisova, 1915.

21. Elsa Triolet, 1915.

22. Mayakovsky, 1915.

23. Mayakovsky and
Lila Brik, 1915.

24. Mayakovsky's drawing
of Lila Brik, 1916.

25. Osip Brik, 1915.

26. Lunacharsky, Leshchenko
and Mayakovsky, 1918.

☙ 15 ☙

October 1917

☙

History quickens its pace and—begins to speak a new language. On October 25 (November 7) the Great Socialist Revolution broke out. This chapter contains the documents of history and also the documents of poets' doubts and dreams. Mayakovsky tells in his autobiography how he accepted the revolution. The following tell about Mayakovsky in the first days and months of the revolution: Jacob Chernyak, Boris Malkin, Osip Brik, Ilya Ehrenburg, Pavel Antokolsky, and others. A hero of these accounts is also Anatol Lunacharsky, the first revolutionary People's Commissar of Education, a good and wise protector of the artists. Lunacharsky favored Mayakovsky, but the collaboration between the politician and the poet was from the start accompanied by misunderstandings.

FROM MAYAKOVSKY'S AUTOBIOGRAPHY

To accept or not to accept? There was no such problem for me (and other

Moscow futurists). It was my revolution. I went to the Smolnyi. I did everything that was necessary. Meetings began.

A REMINISCENCE BY JACOB CHERNYAK:

On October 25–26, in the days of the great uprising, I saw Mayakovsky late in the evening, or even at night, at one o'clock . . . He came agitated, with an excited expression, from the meeting of the Congress of the Soviets and said: the peasants—delegates from the Peasant Congress, which had met separately—had just come and joined the Bolsheviks. Their fraternization was moving to the point of tears . . .

Mayakovsky was deeply moved.

LETTER FROM MAYAKOVSKY TO HIS FAMILY, OCTOBER–NOVEMBER 1917:

Dear Mama, Ludechka, and Olenka!

How happy I am that you are all sound and well. Compared to that nothing else matters. I have already written to you through a friend. I am sending this letter also through a Muscovite friend. I do not trust the mails much these days.

I am quite well. I have some great and good news: I have been totally released from military service, so I am a free man again. I will stay for two to three months in Petrograd, where I shall work and have my teeth and nose treated. Then I will come to Moscow for a bit, and later still intend to go South for a final recuperation.

Hearty kisses for you all.

Your Volodya

Do write!

A BOLSHEVIK PARTY ACTIVIST, BORIS MALKIN:

A week after the October coup we attempted, on behalf of the All-Russian Central Executive Committee, to gather at the Smolnyi the entire intelligentsia of Petrograd. There had been a number of advertisements in the newspapers, posters had been put up around the city, and our call reached, thanks to the popular means of information, all circles of the Petrograd intelligentsia. The appeal from the Soviet authorities was for persons engaged in cultural and artistic work to come to the Smolnyi in order to initiate and carry through a number of activities, essential for the young, newly established authority.

At seven in the evening the entire representation of the Petrograd intelligentsia assembled: five or seven people for whom there was enough room to sit on one sofa. They were, as far as I can remember, Alexander Blok, Mayakovsky, Vsyevolod Meyerhold, Larissa Reisner . . .

All night passed in a discussion of how the intelligentsia was to be organized, what one had to do for that purpose. Mayakovsky reacted to everything warmly, somehow joyously . . .

LUNACHARSKY'S LETTER:

From the People's Commissar of Education to the Association of Art Activists.

I appeal to you, citizen members of the Association of Art Activists, because your association embraces those active in all spheres of art and all its directions.

After the first revolution of the working people, on October 25, the masses which have risen and won have taken over a number of artistic institutions. They are now the property of the nation and yours, artists of Russia.

Not only has the autocratic bureaucratic regime, which hindered art, been abolished, but so have all class and caste limitations. New, free, popular forms of artistic life should be created.

In this extremely important branch of cultural construction the working people need your help and you will give it . . .

On behalf of the people, who have now become the master of the Russian lands, I leave it to you, artists, to express the organized opinion of the entire artistic world on the subject of the most rational use of the treasures and centers of art in our Republic for the benefit of national culture . . .

FROM THE TRANSCRIPT OF THE EMERGENCY SESSION OF THE
COMMITTEE OF THE PROVISIONAL ASSOCIATION OF ART ACTIVISTS,
NOVEMBER 17, 1917:

Sologub: We do not want to take anything away from the people, as Lunacharsky thinks, because Lunacharsky is not the people but a "frock-coated gentlemen," before whom art—the national property—should be protected . . .

Mayakovsky agrees with Sologub, but how can one achieve this, how can one acquire that property—the new authorities should be approached, made welcome.

OSIP BRIK:

The "Art Activists" as a body rejected the appeal of the people's commissar . . . But some particular members reacted to the appeal positively. Among them were the "extreme" leftists and above all Mayakovsky . . . But not only the "leftists" began to collaborate with the Soviets. Among them were A. Benoit and Count V. Zubov, who saw in the Soviet authorities an "iron hand" which could protect the cultural values and monuments of the past.

The meeting with old "enemies" in the office of the revolutionary commissar astounded Mayakovsky. His passionate futurist proposals met with fierce resistance on the part of the "defenders of the old." And— wonder of wonders—Lunacharsky, the revolutionary commissar, listened more attentively to Benoit's advice on how to organize museums than to Mayakovsky's "arch-revolutionary" tirades . . .

YURI YURYEV, STAGE ACTOR:

The fall meetings at the academy took place in an atmosphere of excitement. Everybody was concerned about the future of art, whose perspectives were at that time hazy, to say the least. The most extreme and diametrically opposite conceptions were hotly discussed. Some, among whom Mayakovsky was prominent, categorically divided art into the old and the new, bourgeois and proletarian, and maintained that contemporary art was worthless, that the proletariat had to create proletarian art, totally opposed, of course, to the art of the old world . . . The discussions were quite fierce and occasionally abounded in brutal and offensive personal abuse which resulted in unpleasant incidents . . .

Lunacharsky, the newly appointed People's Commissar of Education, did much to quell the raging passions.

CHUKOVSKY:

To us, the intelligentsia of prerevolutionary background, he seemed the personification of the most attractive qualities of the Soviet authority, from the very first days of its existence. We were impressed by Anatol Vassilievich's wide reading, education, detailed knowledge of all trends and currents in world art, his proficiency regarding artistic and philosophical problems.

It would have been difficult to imagine another man so splendidly equipped for the historical role he had to play in those years. It was a difficult role, one that demanded exactly those gifts he offered so generously. His manifold talents, his temperament and tact, his erudition—all these were absolutely essential.

In Anatol Vassilievich's voice one never heard an imperative tone. He did not need it, because the source of Lunacharsky's authority was not so much the high position he held but the charm of his knowledge, his passionate love of art, his sincere, not forced, respect for people of culture and talent. How could one not admire his expert capacity for talking to Benoit and Dobuzhinsky, and Blok, even when he was engaged in fierce polemics with them and attacked the very foundations of their aesthetics . . .

The most impressive speech of his that I heard was made in the street, to an unorganized and motley crowd . . . Even on that occasion, I remember, I had the feeling that, however excellent the speech itself, the speaker was in this instance more convincing than any words he might utter—thus he stood before us, victorious, happy, talented, unshaken in the certainty of his arguments . . .

PUNIN:

Mayakovsky was in conflict with Lunacharsky . . . It would be interesting to find out if they had not quarreled at a mass meeting, or in print in a periodical or in *Novaya Zhizn.* That would explain the belated access of Mayakovsky and Brik to the October Revolution . . .

LEV NIKULIN:

I witnessed Mayakovsky's conversation with a certain writer who brutally attacked Lunacharsky. The poet sharply took him to task for it . . . Mayakovsky could speak ironically in his poems and on the platform about some of Anatol Vassilievich's foibles, but regarded him with respect, valued Lunacharsky's positive opinion of his poems, and once said with pride, "No country on earth has such a minister of education."

GORKI:

In the years '17–'18 my relations with Lenin were by no means what I would have liked them to be, but it could not be otherwise.

He was a politician . . .

And I feel an organic loathing for politics, do not believe in the common sense of the masses generally, or in the common sense of the peasant mass in particular . . .

When, on his return to Russia in '17, Lenin published his "theses," I thought that with those theses he was sacrificing to the Russian peasants the numerically insignificant but heroic legion of politically educated workers and the sincerely revolutionary intelligentsia. The only active force in Russia would be thrown, like a pinch of salt, into the muddy pool of the countryside and dissolve without a trace, disappear, without changing anything of the spirit, custom, or history of the Russian nation.

The scientific, technical—generally qualified—intelligentsia is, to my mind, revolutionary in principle and I saw in it—besides the working, socialist intelligentsia—the most valuable potential force brought together by Russia . . .

My differences with the Communists concerned their estimate of the intelligentsia's role in the Russian revolution, being prepared exactly by the intelligentsia, which includes also all the "Bolsheviks" . . . The Russian intelligentsia—working and scientific—has been, is, and will long continue to be the only draft horse, harnessed to the heavy cart of Russia's history . . .

ALEXANDER BLOK'S REPLY TO THE TELEPHONE POLL OF THE DAILY "PETROGRADSKOE ECHO," PUBLISHED IN THE EVENING EDITION, JANUARY 18, 1918:

Can the Intelligentsia Collaborate with the Bolsheviks?

Can the intelligentsia collaborate with the Bolsheviks? It can and it should . . .

Quite apart from personal reasons, the same music is sounding for the intelligentsia as for the Bolsheviks.

The intelligentsia has always been revolutionary. The Bolsheviks' decrees—are the intelligentsia's symbols. They are slogans demanding detailed development.

The intelligentsia's anger against the Bolsheviks is superficial, and it seems to be passing. A man thinks differently from the way he speaks publicly. Reconciliation, a musical reconciliation, is on the way . . .

January 14, 1918

❧

On March 3, 1918, Alexander Blok's poem "The Twelve" was published in the newspaper "Znamya Truda."

BORIS EICHENBAUM IN THE PERIODICAL "KNIZNYI UGOL,"
NO. 1, 1918:

An extraordinary phenomenon—Blok, the quiet poet of the "lyre," has written a noisy, shouting, booming poem "The Twelve," in which he appears as Mayakovsky's disciple. This is tragic, this almost brings tears to one's eyes. They say the poem is good. I do not know—I see that Blok is letting himself be crucified on the cross of the revolution, and I can only view this with pious terror.

FROM THE REMINISCENCES OF ZINAIDA GIPPIUS:

There could be no doubt: Blok was with *them*. It was also clear that Andrei Bely was with them. Both wrote for and worked at *The Scythians*, the publication of the traitor—either a leftist socialist radical, or a party member of the Bolsheviks—Ivanov-Razumnik. One heard that both work *voluntarily* also in various institutions. Blok together with Lunacharsky and Gorki. His poem "The Twelve," published in *The Scythians*, unexpectedly ending with Christ leading twelve Red Army hooligans, had a resounding reception. The idea that twelve Red Army men were like new apostles was generally liked. Even in Blok's lifetime a great body of writing existed about those "apostles." Certainly he himself was asked how he understood that unexpected Christ at the head of the twelve. And certainly he did not answer—"For this was not to be stated explicitly." The Bolsheviks, not caring about what was not to be explicitly stated, used "The Twelve" with pleasure. All over the place one could see rags with the slogan:

We'll kindle fires everywhere—
Let the bourgeoisie take care.

Even the Red Army men finally had enough of this, particularly as the fires, though kindled, did not embrace the whole world.

KAMENSKY:

In those days I pasted the "decree" all over Moscow.
About hoarding literature,
About street painting,
About balconies with music,
About carnivals of art . . .
I was convinced that every town and every settlement could be turned into an astounding vision of a picturesque holiday . . .
I even imagined that quotations from poets would be placed on the fronts of houses . . .
Incorrigible enthusiast that I was, I visualized a great many undertakings along the lines of my decree.
I even witnessed a partial realization of my proposals.
On the very next day after the proclamation of my decree, walking down the Kuznetsky I saw a huge crowd and some blocked streetcars at the corner of Neglinnaya.
What had happened? It turned out that David Burliuk, standing on a gigantic firemen's ladder placed against a rounded house front, was nailing a couple of his pictures there.
The crowd was assisting him with voices of encouragement and admiration . . .
Soon after that "happening," we continued with others: we printed the *Futurists' Journal* (editors: Burliuk, Kamensky, Mayakovsky), which we pasted on all the fences of Moscow.

VLADIMIR MAYAKOVSKY, "OPEN LETTER TO THE WORKERS"
(PUBLISHED IN THE "FUTURISTS' JOURNAL"):

Comrades!
The double conflagration of war and revolution has emptied our souls and our cities. Like burned-out skeletons stand the palaces of yesterday's

splendor. The smashed cities are awaiting new architects. The hurricane of the revolution has extirpated the crooked roots of slavery from our souls. The soul of the people is awaiting a new sowing.

To you, who have taken over Russia's heritage, to you, who (I believe!) tomorrow will become masters of the whole world, I direct the question: with what fantastic structures will you cover the site of yesterday's fires? What songs and music will flow from your windows? To what bibles will you open your souls?

I observe with astonishment how renowned theaters resound with *Aidas* and *Traviatas*, with their Spaniards and counts; how in the poems to which you listen the same noblemen's hothouse roses are flowering; how your eyes are opening wide in front of pictures showing the pomp of the past.

Will you, perhaps, when the elements let loose by revolution quiet down, go out on Sunday into the squares before your local Soviet buildings, with watch chains on your waistcoats, and stolidly play croquet?

You should know that for your necks, the necks of Goliaths of labor, there are no sizes in the bourgeois collar wardrobe that fit.

Only the outburst of the Spirit of Revolution will rid us of the rags of old art.

Let common sense restrain you from using physical force against the remnants of old art. Give them to schools and universities so that they may study geography, customs, and history, but indignantly send away whoever tries to hand you those petrified fossils instead of the bread of living beauty.

The revolution of substance—socialism-anarchism—is not to be thought of apart from the revolution of form—futurism.

Snatch greedily the big healthy chunks of young brutal art which we give you.

No one can know what immense suns will light our future lives. It may be that artists will turn the gray dust of cities into multicolored rainbows; that the never-ending thunderous music of volcanoes turned into flutes will resound from mountain ranges; that ocean waves will be forced to play on the nets of chords stretching from Europe to America. One thing is clear to us—we have opened the first page of the latest chapter in the history of art.

FROM THE "FUTURISTS' JOURNAL":

Decree No. 1 on the Democratization of Art
(*The hoarding of literature and the painting of streets*)

Comrades and citizens, we, the leaders of Russian futurism—the revolutionary art of youth—declare:

1. From this day forward, with the abolition of tsardom, *the domicile of art* in the closets and sheds of human genius—palaces, galleries, salons, libraries, theaters—*is abrogated.*

2. In the name of the great march of equality for all, as far as culture is concerned, let the *Free Word* of creative personality be written on the corners of walls, fences, roofs, the streets of our cities and villages, on the backs of automobiles, carriages, streetcars, and on the clothes of all citizens.

3. Let *pictures* (colors) be thrown, like colored rainbows, across streets and squares, from house to house, delighting, ennobling the eye (taste) of the passer-by.

Artists and writers have the immediate duty to get hold of their pots of paint and, with their masterly brushes, to illuminate, to paint all the sides, foreheads, and chests of cities, railway stations, and the ever-galloping herds of railway carriages.

From now on, let the citizen walking down the street enjoy at every moment the depths of thought of his great contemporaries, let him absorb the flowery gaudiness of this day's beautiful joy, let him listen to music— the melody, the roar, the buzz—of excellent composers everywhere.

Let the streets be a feast of art for all.

And if all this comes to pass, in accordance with our word, everyone who goes out into the street will grow to be a giant and in wisdom, contemplating beauty instead of the present-day streets with their iron books (signboards), where every page has been written on their signs by greed, the lust for mammon, calculated meanness and low obtuseness, all of which soil the soul and offend the eye. "All art—to all the people!"

The initial pasting up of the poems and hanging of pictures will take place in Moscow on the day our journal is published.

Mayakovsky, Kamensky, Burliuk

EHRENBURG:

Every morning the inhabitants carefully studied the new decrees, still wet and crumpled, pasted on the walls: they wanted to know what was permitted and what was forbidden. One day I saw a gathering of people standing in front of a small sheet of paper entitled "Decree No. 1 on the Democratization of Art." Someone was reading it aloud: "From this day forward, with the abolition of tsardom, the *domicile of art* in the closets and sheds of human genius—palaces, galleries, salons, libraries, theaters— *is abrogated.*" An old woman shrieked, "All saints have mercy, now they are taking sheds away! . . ." The man in spectacles who was reading the "decree" aloud explained, "There is nothing here about sheds, but they will close libraries and, of course, theaters . . ." The leaflet was the work of the futurists and was signed by Mayakovsky, Kamensky, Burliuk. The names did not mean anything to the passers-by, but everybody knew the magic word "decree."

I recall the day of May 1, 1918. Moscow was decorated with futurist and suprematist canvases. On the shabby house fronts, on columned empire palaces, crazy squares were in conflict with rhombs; motley faces looked out with triangles instead of eyes . . . May the first that year happened to be on Good Friday. By the Iverskaya Chapel there was a throng of praying people. Next to them trucks draped with abstract paintings were passing; actors on trucks were performing various scenes: "The Heroic Deed of Ivan Khalturin," or "The Paris Commune." An old woman, looking at a cubist painting with a huge fish eye, was lamenting, "They want us to worship satan . . ."

I laughed, but it was not a gay sort of laughter . . .

I do not remember who introduced me to Mayakovsky. To start with we sat in a café and talked about films. Then he took me to his place: a little room in the "San Remo" lodging house in Saltykov Alley. Some time before that meeting I had read his book *Simple as Mooing.* I had imagined him exactly as I now saw him: tall, with heavy-set jaws, eyes now sad now stern, ready at any moment to get mixed up in a brawl—a combination of an athlete and a dreamer, a medieval juggler who prayed walking on his head—and a relentless iconoclast.

As we were walking to the hotel, he droned François Villon's epitaph, written in the expectation of the gallows: "With a severe sentence chastened, in spite of most solemn appeal, hit straight in my very ass, the homeless eternal wanderer: God give me my rightful rest . . ." We had hardly entered the room when he said, "I'll read you something . . ." I sat down on a chair, he remained standing. He read me his newly completed poem, "Man." The room was small, we were the only people in it, but he was reading as if he were facing a crowd in Teatralnyi Square . . .

Mayakovsky astounded me: poetry and revolution, the excited Moscow streets and the new art of which the patrons of the "Rotunda" dreamed, coexisted in him peacefully . . .

It is easy to understand Mayakovsky: his poems were greeted with derision, just as the pictures of the painters who joined the futurists (Malevich, Tatlin, Rodchenko, Puni, Udaltsova, Popova, Altman) had been received with derision before the revolution. After the October Revolution, the epigones of classical poetry began to pack their suitcases. Bunin and Repin went abroad. Futurists, cubists, suprematists remained. Like the artists of the West, the prewar frequenters of the "Rotunda," they hated bourgeois society and saw their solution in the revolution.

PAVEL ANTOKOLSKY:

One has to imagine the Moscow of wartime communism, hungry and brave, badly lit, badly heated, dressed in khaki, walking in well-worn boots.

There lived in Moscow a married couple; the husband was a bit of a poet who wrote under the nom de plume "Amari," from the French "à Marie"—that is to say, "For Marie." The couple ran a "literary salon," wide open for the fraternity of poets. The salon was their calling and aim in life. Perhaps they were not unselfish and wanted to acquire fame, enter the literary world in this way.

One winter evening early in 1918 they were hosts to nearly all the poets present in Moscow: Balmont, Vyacheslav Ivanov, Andrei Bely, Pasternak, Tsvetayeva, Ehrenburg, Vera Inber, Alexey Tolstoy, Krandiyevskaya, Khodasyevich. For some reason Bryusov was not present.

About midnight, when quite a few poems had been read, the trio Mayakovsky, Kamensky, Burliuk appeared, late. Mayakovsky briefly explained to the hostess that they had been held up by some event and that they had had to walk from the other end of the city.

"Walk along the streetcar tracks, whistled at not by the audience but by the snowstorm."

While the others were reading, Mayakovsky sat in a corner, concentrating, almost gloomy. When his turn came, he got up, buttoned his coat, stretched his left arm along a bookshelf and read the penultimate chapter of "War and World," and then fragments of the poem "Man" . . .

When he had finished, Alexey Tolstoy threw himself at Mayakovsky and embraced him. Khodasyevich was angry. His small cat's face twitched in a grimace. Particularly noticeable was the exalted attention of Andrei Bely. He glued his eyes on the reader. Bely's sapphire-blue eyes shone. As soon as Mayakovsky finished, Andrei Bely began to speak. He said that even when the war was still on he had been expecting the appearance of "such a poet"—whose horizons would be open to all the world. Or something to that effect. I think he also said something about a skull raised above the brain in starry space. In a word, it was unconditional and deeply moved recognition from a man who had held himself very much apart.

"Well, Volodya, if *we* have been recognized by such a poet . . ." Burliuk began sneeringly, but Mayakovsky frowned slightly, gave him a wry look, and Burliuk immediately stopped speaking, retreated to the other end of the room, and lighted his pipe.

The hostess invited her guests to the table . . . The table was brightly lit and overflowing with excellent food, something very rare in those days: veal, ham, huge fish in glittering jelly, large chunks of yellow butter, carafes full of vodka . . .

After the first toast Balmont rose . . . In his hand he was holding a little book. He read a sonnet, written there, at the table, and dedicated to Mayakovsky: "You greeted me with abuse, Mayakovsky . . ." This first line is all I remember. Further on the author proposed that bygones be bygones, that they be reconciled, that bad things be forgotten . . .

Mayakovsky was smiling in a friendly manner; he was somewhat embarrassed and asked Balmont to give him the poem.

"Volodya, why does his lower jaw droop when he munches veal?" Burliuk began again, pointing out one of the guests with a finger on which was a very big ring . . . Again Mayakovsky compelled his Sancho Panza to be silent . . .

Mayakovsky turned with greetings, words of friendship and respect, to Pasternak, had jocularly trifling exchanges with Tsvetayeva. All pointed to the fact that he was in excellent spirits, full of energy, like a well-loaded battery. It was a triumph of life, youth, success, and strength.

PASTERNAK:

With Bely being close—which fact was a source of proud joy to me—I felt Mayakovsky's presence with double force. His essential personality was revealed to me with all the freshness of the first meeting. On that evening I experienced this for the last time.

EHRENBURG:

Vyacheslav Ivanov nodded his head from time to time. Balmont was clearly uneasy. Baltrushaytis was, as usual, impenetrable. Marina Tsvetayeva smiled, and Pasternak looked at Vladimir Vladimirovich with a loving gaze. Andrei Bely listened in no ordinary manner—he was in ecstasy, and when Mayakovsky finished, he sprang to his feet so excited that he could hardly speak. Nearly all those present shared his rapture. Mayakovsky, however, became angry at someone's cool, polite phrase. It was always like that with him: it was as if he did not notice the laurels and looked for shadows. In his poems he waged a continuous struggle with real and imaginary opponents of the new poetry. What lurked behind those accusations? Perhaps a conflict within himself?

✵ 16 ✵

The Poets' Café

✵

*Beside the history of the country and the nation there exists
—within it and without it—the history of literature. This
episode in the history of Russian literature, which took place
immediately after the great upheaval, is tied to the peculiar
institution of the "poets' café." The café made contemporary
writing known, established up-to-date hierarchies, ensured
the authors a means of livelihood. In Mayakovsky's life too
this episode had its part to play.*

VALERI BRYUSOV:

For over three years the further evolution of Russian poetry went on
underground, as it were . . . The old poetry magazines, from whose columns readers used to learn about new phenomena in poetry (on the basis
of the poems themselves, or critical utterances about them), ceased to
exist. New periodicals, which would publish poetry, were few, and most of
them ceased publication after a couple of issues. Nor were they distributed, because of transportation problems. Most publishing houses were
closed too, either temporarily or permanently, and the first to go were the

purely literary ones. In a certain period—toward the end of 1919 and in 1920—the printing of books, not only those in the category of belles-lettres, was suspended altogether because of a shortage of paper . . .

Meanwhile, poets representing all tendencies, all previously existing "schools" and those now coming into existence, went on writing, zealously too, and were joined all the time by ever-new regiments of young beginners . . .

Poets attempted to substitute for publishing to a certain extent by means of public appearances, by authors reciting their poems from the platform. Such events had originated even before the October Revolution, but they became particularly popular during the first years of the revolution when, deprived of printing presses, almost all poets turned to improvised platforms in various cafés. Hence this period of Russian poetry has been called by some the "café period" . . . Those events drew an even wider circle of listeners when the Moscow poets arranged to hold them in the big auditorium of the Polytechnic Museum, filled many a time with the public whom posters invited to the "evening of new poetry." There were even evenings when the audience awarded prizes for the best poems.

KORNEL ZYELINSKY:

It was a period of literary cafés. They originated, perhaps, in the poets' desire for the platform to replace the not always available printing press. Active too were commercial and political entrepreneurs of various kinds. The fact is that in the years of the civil war at least ten special literary cafés were functioning in Moscow. They were generally accessible platforms for poetry and for literary games. The cafés appeared and disappeared at a kaleidoscopic pace. Those that flourished, say, in the summer of 1918, declined and died away in the winter; and the literary cellars, painted in bright colors during the time the premises had to be kept warm with primus stoves, emptied in the spring. Passing through Moscow were anarchists, secretly recruited Kornilov followers, smugglers, profiteers. What improbable figures, such as Mamont Dalsky and others, so expressively described by Alexei Tolstoy in *Road Through Calvary*, filled the poetry inns in those days! The best known of them were the "Pittoresque," the "Bom," the "Futurists' Café," the "Imaginists' Café," "Pegasus' Trough," and the "Domino" or "Sopatka," so called from SOPO (Sojuz Poetov—the Poets' Union) . . . Even the followers of Proletkult had their café, called the "Forge," where among other café props, the manuscripts of V. Aleksandrovsky and other poets were exhibited.

"Pegasus' Trough" in Tverskaya Street lasted longer than others. A Red Army commander, back from the front, who stepped in there by chance, a passer-by, tempted by the light in a quiet, dark, snow-covered Moscow, patrolled by the Red Guard—both were immediately enveloped by an intoxicating poetic atmosphere. On a large sheet there was a slogan, taken from Yesenin's poem: "Spit, O wind, with an armful of leaves, I am a hooligan like you."

In the "Futurists' Café" (in Nastasyinsky Alley), against the background of a decorated canvas and livid orange walls, enlivened by the touches of Burliuk's ungovernable brush, Mayakovsky, Kamensky, Burliuk, Khlebnikov made their appearances . . . One visited the "Domino" in order to listen to disputes on the most fantastic subjects and, to the din of crockery and cutlery, behold a procession of unknown neoclassicists, biocosmists, euphuists, nichevoks, presentists, expressionists, ego-cubists, pseudo-futurists, and other poetasters, who coolly and confidently mounted the platform in turn every evening. Through the platforms of literary cafés in those years, almost all known writers passed, without exception: Mayakovsky, Bryusov, Bely, Balmont, Khlebnikov, Kamensky, Yesenin, Gorodetsky, even Lunacharsky, and many others . . .

KAMENSKY:

In the fall I returned to Moscow. Soon afterwards I found, together with Holtsshmit, a place where there used to be a laundry in Tverskaya, Nastasyinsky Alley. We decided to convert it to a "poets' café" . . .

Holtsshmit and I were selected as "directors."

Holtsshmit took care of the administration.

I—of the artistic program.

BURLIUK:

That time, in November 1917, that crucial year for Russia, the triple team of Burliuk, Kamensky, and Mayakovsky, who had worked together and helped each other since 1911, was saved from hunger and misery by dear handsome Vassili Kamensky. He became the close friend of the millionaire Filipov and his charming wife, and very soon the "Poets' Café" was opened in Nastasyinsky Alley. Mayakovsky, who at this time was trying in vain to make a living in Petersburg, came to us in Moscow and asked, "How, brothers, do you take me in?" From this evening on, all money after "closing," or the late hours, was divided into three parts. *

THE CAFÉ AND MAYAKOVSKY IN THE EYES OF THE AUTHOR OF A
NOTE IN THE MAGAZINE "VESTNIK LITIERATURI," NO. 11, 1919,
SIGNED "OLD WRITER":

. . . Behind the counter, dressed in a yellow tunic, his eyes shining from his good, well-fed life, stood Mayakovsky himself, shouting at the public, just like hired men in the bars of Parisian Montmartre . . . As a result of a few months of this fruitful futurist activity, Mayakovsky's fingers became adorned with diamond rings, his belly—with a thick gold chain, etc.

EHRENBURG:

I recall the "Poets' Café" in the winter 1917–18. It was situated in the Nastasyinsky Alley. It was a most peculiar place. The walls were covered with paintings that must have looked very strange to the public, and with sentences that were no less strange. "I like watching children die"—that line from Mayakovsky's early, prerevolutionary poem was to be seen on the wall in order to shock those who entered. The "Poets' Café" was not at all like the "Rotunda." No one talked art here, there were no discussions, no heart searchings; those present were divided into actors and spectators. The audience consisted of the remnants of the bourgeoisie—profiteers, writers, philistines in search of entertainment. It is doubtful whether Mayakovsky could entertain them: although there was much in his poetry that they could not understand, they felt that there was a clear affinity between those strange poems and the sailors walking on the Tverskaya. Everybody could understand Mayakovsky's song about the bourgeois eating pineapples toward the end of his days. There were no pineapples in Nastasyinsky Alley, but a morsel of ordinary pork stuck in some people's throats. Those who visited the place were entertained by something else. For instance, David Burliuk would mount the platform, his face heavily powdered, lorgnon in hand, and recite, "I like pregnant men . . ." Holtsshmit was also an enlivening figure. The posters called him the "futurist of

* The above fragment has been taken from the original English by D. and M. Burliuk, *Color and Rhyme*, No. 31, 1956.

life." He did not write poems, but dyed gold two locks of hair on his head, was a man of unusual strength, broke boards and threw brawlers out of the café. One day the "futurist of life" decided to erect his monument in Teatralnyi Square. It was a plaster statue, not very big; it was not futurist either—just Holtsshmit in the nude. The passers-by were indignant but did not dare to raise their hands against the mysterious monument. Only later was the statue smashed . . .

I frequented the "Poets' Café" quite often. At one time I even made a public appearance there and received a fee from Holtsshmit.

MAYAKOVSKY'S LETTER TO THE BRIKS, MID-DECEMBER 1917:

Dear, dear Lila!
Dear, dear Osya!

> Where art thou, desired one,
> Let me know, where.

Having put in this motto all the sadness of my soul, I pass on to the facts.

Moscow, as they say, is like a ripe, swelling fruit, which Dodya, Kamensky, and I are zealously picking. The main place where the picking goes on is the "Poets' Café."

The café for the time being is a pleasant gay establishment. (As far as gaiety is concerned, it is like the "Dog" in its early period!) People—thronging through the doors and through the windows. On the floor—sawdust. On the platform—us. (Now only I, because Dodya and Vasya are away till Christmas. That's bad.) We send the public to the devil. At midnight we divide the till. That's all.

Futurism is very popular.

A mass of public appearances. At Christmas we shall have a "Futurists' Christmas tree." Then an "Election of three winners of poetry." I am having talks about the possible reading of "Man" at the Polytechnic Museum . . .

A lot of fun but, alas, it's all in mime, because the characters are dumb. Imagine, for instance, how Vysotsky, Marants, and Shatilov (and the banks are closed!) listen, straining all their attention, to Dodya's "He terribly loved flies with fat abdomens."

A million new people. Crowded and senseless . . .

I will often walk behind the fence and, shielding the diagonal rays of the setting sun with my thin hand, sadly look into the distance, trying to see the familiar figure of the mailman in the cloud of dust. Don't make me do this!

Kisses for Lila.

Kisses for Osya.

Your Volodya

SERGEI SPASSKY:

. . . The public was already seated at their tables, Vladimir H. had read something, when suddenly Mayakovsky entered. He exchanged a few words with the cashier and briskly walked inside. White shirt, gray coat, cap slipped to the back of his head. He greeted those present with passing nods. His movements were decisive and elastic. I had hardly managed to say a few words when he lifted me off the ground, carried me to the platform, and threw me on the rough boards. Then he called out my name and said I would read poems.

That was how I began to work in the café. The same evening Burliuk and Mayakovsky granted me a regular salary. I came there for the next sixty-three days, not missing a single one.

The café was at first subsidized by the Moscow baker Filipov. The baker was tackled by Burliuk and made into a patron of art. The baker was most receptive. In his spare time he wrote poems in which one could trace the influence of Kamensky . . .

Later, a certain H. bought the café behind the backs of all the poets. It was only one of the clever operations of the apostle of the "sunny life." He presented everybody with a *fait accompli*, capturing all the key points at one stroke. Besides his elder sister, an opera singer, who had already been supplementing her wages by appearing at the café, his mama stood behind the counter, while his younger sister was placed at the cashier's desk. Mayakovsky was sullen that evening. He attacked profiteers in art. H. attempted to defend himself, complained that nobody understood him. The astonished public did not follow those exchanges. Burliuk tried to calm Mayakovsky down, begging him not to spoil the season.

But whoever owned the enterprise, it functioned in such a way that a few regular collaborators appeared on the platform every evening. There were poets: Mayakovsky, Kamensky, Burliuk. There was the opera singer

I have mentioned, and a "poet-singer" Aristarkh Klimov. I joined that team.

The public gathered late, usually after the theater. The program had regular features. A couple of romances by the opera singer and Klimov. My expected quota was two poems. Mayakovsky read a chapter from his newly written "Man," "Ode to the Revolution," and some other poems. Kamensky produced "Stenka Razin," Burliuk—"In Praise of Buoyancy" and "I Like Pregnant Men."

Such was the pattern of every evening. A fairly meagre pattern. But no evening was like those that proceeded or those that followed it.

Mayakovsky and Burliuk come when the public is already there in numbers, when the singers have sung their romances, and Klimov has recited his puzzling poems. One of the younger poets, encouraged by the slogan "a platform for all," shares his rhymed feelings with those present. But the evening does not gain impetus. The public is bored . . . Obviously it is time to go home.

But suddenly Mayakovsky comes in, keeps his cap on. Sometimes he has a large red knot at his neck. Mayakovsky walks across the café. He has simply come here to dine. He chooses a free table. If there are no tables, he sits at a table on the platform. They bring him his usual dish. He has come here to relax.

Sometimes Burliuk sits down next to him. At other times Burliuk and Kamensky sit apart. Mayakovsky does not notice the guests. There is no affectation in this. He really feels like that. He has come to spend the evening here. If they want to gape at him, well, he is not embarrassed. The cigarette slides to the corner of his mouth. Mayakovsky looks around, stretches himself. He feels at home wherever he is. He is surrounded by rapt attention. But Mayakovsky does not pay attention to anyone. Above everybody's heads he says something to Burliuk. Burliuk replies in such a way as to involve the audience. They go on talking. Burliuk with his ripostes incites growing interest all around. People listen to and watch that conversation near them as through an invisible barrier. Their conversation is a show in itself. But nobody is let through the barrier.

Quite a few people take offense at this. Many of those present would like to show off their wit. People seated at various tables make loud remarks. Burliuk considers whether to pass them around or not.

Most offended are people who are convinced of their right to special treatment. If, for instance, someone is an artist himself, then he thinks Mayakovsky ought to know him. Such indifference is humiliating . . .

Suddenly Mayakovsky turns his head.

He greets the artist who, flattered, bows his head. So do others, basking in Mayakovsky's favor. Burliuk gets up and, in an affectionate, respectful voice, with an expression of great joy clearly visible on his face, shares the happy news with those present: "The artist so-and-so is among us. I ask you to greet him. He will surely not refuse to appear for us."

The public applauds.

The artist mounts the three-foot rostrum as if he has been invited onto the most magnificent stage.

Nobody has ever refused. The guest is exploited to the end.

The tenor Digas has found himself here. His powerful voice is too strong for the narrow confines of the café. A pair of dancers has been dragged onto the platform. Though not properly dressed, they humbly try to prove themselves. The pale, browless Vertinsky tries to resist and excuses himself because of the absence of an accompanist. But under Mayakovsky's persistent gaze, he gives in and takes up his stance. In a guttural, almost soundless voice he declaims, presenting to the public his newest work . . .

Mayakovsky reads last. The chattering, feverish audience grows quiet and serious . . . Only in corners are some giggles still to be heard. But Mayakovsky looks around the room.

"You will be quiet," he says. "Quiet like flowers."

He stands upright, hands in his pockets, against the background of the orange wall. His cap pushed to the back of his head, cigarette moving in his mouth. He smokes nonstop. He sways on his hips, examining the public with cold flashing eyes.

"Quiet, my kittens." He keeps people under control . . .

He begins to read a stanza from "Man," the ascension scene . . .

KAMENSKY:

Not only poets, but also composers, musicians, singers, actors appeared in our café.

One day a young composer by the name of Sergei Prokofiev mounted the platform and played his new work, "Possession" . . .

While Prokofiev was playing, Volodya sketched an excellent portrait of the composer at the piano and wrote in the album, "Sergei Sergeievich is playing on the most sensitive nerves of Vladimir Vladimirovich" . . .

Volodya used to draw quite a lot in the café, on anything he had at hand. He gave all the drawings away.

With particular pleasure he drew the actresses who recited our poems.

For instance, he drew several excellent sketches of Olga Gzovskaya, who recited our work more often than anyone else.

For a long time we were amused by the fact that Mayakovsky could not listen to poetry readers, singers, or musicians without drawing them . . .

SPASSKY:

One day Syevyeryanin visited the café . . . Dressed in a military tunic, with military boots on his feet, he came proud and pompous. He was accompanied by his wife, "the thirteenth, and so the last one." Also with him was a stammering, disheveled disciple, for some reason called "Perunek," and a couple of other people. The party were seated at a table on the platform. Mayakovsky looked askance at them. He decided, however, to exploit their visit.

He made a half-jocular speech to the effect that in an apartment one needs a dining room as well as a bedroom and a study. There is no reason to quarrel here. So it is with poetry. Syevyeryanin also has his *raison d'etre*. So we will ask Syevyeryanin to read us his poems.

Syevyeryanin let "Perunek" go first. The latter took a long time to present himself to the audience . . . Unkempt, uncouth, and tipsy, he recited boringly and apathetically.

Syevyeryanin himself was drunk too. Dully gazing above the heads of those present, he chanted a tune which pierced the ears. It seemed as if he was not reacting to anything and just mechanically tossing out clever phrases. Every now and then he tottered as if he were about to fall. But no, he finished, and, without speaking one word in prose, left the café with his party.

The well-known organizer of poetry evenings, Dolidze, decided to arrange a public "song tournament." The evening was called the "election of the king of the poets." It took place in the Polytechnic Museum. The public was given voting slips. Everyone had the right to take part. Futurists were especially invited.

The presiding committee was sitting on the platform. In the chair was
a well-known clown, Vladimir Durov.

The hall was packed to overflowing. Poets in numbers read their
poems one after another. The platform too was packed like a streetcar
. . . Mayakovsky could be seen towering over the crowd. He recited his
"Revolution," scarcely able to move his hand. Trying to drown out the
chatter and background noise, he compelled the audience to listen . . .

It was not he, however, who became "king." Syevyeryanin entered the
hall toward the end of the proceedings. "I have just written a rondeau," he
drawled through his teeth to a female admirer. He mounted the platform
and read his old poems from *The Cup*.

Syevyeryanin collected more votes than Mayakovsky.

"The king of clowns," as Durov used to call himself, announced the
name of "the king of the poets" . . .

A part of the audience caused an uproar. The futurists declared the
election null and void. A few days later Syevyeryanin published a new
volume; on the cover was printed his new title. But the futurists organized
an evening with the motto: "Away with all kings."

Life in the café. Sorties to large halls invariably ended with returns to
the long painted cavern. The established program was continued, with the
public's participation. On the surface everything was gay and peaceful.
But all the discords of the period were reflected in that drop of reality.

Relentless enemies were seated at the tables. There were representatives of the youth which shortly was to join regiments of the Red Army
. . . But there were also those who would shortly prepare hasty documents proving their Ukrainian origins . . . There was the bourgeoisie,
engaged in hurried profiteering before they left Moscow. There were
young men, with traces of epaulets on their greatcoats, telling one another
news of Kornilov . . .

There was also a shady mass of people with an unmistakable appearance. They had revolvers stuck in their belts, were girdled with ammuni-
tion pouches, some in student's tunics, others in military coats. They called
themselves anarchists, shouted slogans, made a great deal of noise, invited
people to a palace they were occupying . . .

One such gang leader began to frequent the café regularly. He used a
mysterious nickname, "Hugo," was dressed in a colored silk shirt modeled
after H. Stocky, and was of dark complexion, of southern appearance,

Rumanian or Greek. Sometimes he disappeared mysteriously in a car sent for him, with switched-off lights. There were rumors that "Hugo" went for another "action." He was somehow connected with H. They used to whisper about something in the kitchen; "Hugo" used to bring something for "the futurist of life." The café was probably a convenient spot for Hugo's dubious affairs.

A similarly ambiguous and mixed company appeared on the platform. The slogan "a platform for all" made all kinds of pranks possible . . .

One of the frequenters of the café was the "poet-singer" Aristarkh Klimov, who wore nauseating makeup . . . Klimov lived in Pyotrovsky Park and was the leader of an inexplicable "commune," consisting of several girls. The girls came to the café with Klimov. They were quiet and did not attract any attention to themselves. One of them was a dance student. H. used to visit Klimov at home and the company regarded themselves as his "pupils." H. invited them to his apartment in the Lux Hotel, which was decorated with furs. It is not known what he taught them, but one could guess that the whole group was engaged in profiteering . . .

Of course, among the multilayered atmosphere of the café there were also people of a different kind: a large group of young poets, who were Mayakovsky's enthusiastic admirers. When Mayakovsky's friends from Petrograd arrived, he arranged the parade of his army. He presented every poet in turn . . .

One snow-blowing evening some newspaper vendors came into the café: a student and two girls. They turned out to be followers of the Constituent Assembly, and the paper they were selling had been published by a committee supporting the "hosts of the Russian soil," who had been removed from power. Burliuk bought all the copies.

He then mounted the platform, tore the newspapers to pieces, threw them to the ground, and trampled on them.

"We will not support the moribund."

The vendors began to shout, part of the public expressed its indignation. Mayakovsky approved of Burliuk's action, declaring himself a Bolshevik without reservations.

NIKULIN:

Moscow was starving. The food ration per head was one eighth of a loaf of half-baked bread with bran and half a pound of potatoes.

At night there were full-scale battles between the gangs and the militia. The anarchists were occupying the building of the Merchants' Club in Bolshaya Dmitrovka and the little palace in Povarskaya.

Adjacent to the Merchants' Club, in Nastasyinsky Alley, was a small house, once a laundry . . . On the wall was a sign written in crooked letters: "The Poets' Café" . . .

It is hard to say what particularly attracted the anarchists to the "Poets' Café." There were no alcoholic drinks here, no ladies of easy virtue, that is to say none of the ingredients which abounded in the anarchists' den under the black flag. But they still came to the café as if it was their home, sat comfortably on the benches and played ostentatiously with their revolvers. Their leader was a certain "Guido," a handsome dark-haired man in a black velvet tunic, with jewels shining on his bare neck and numerous rings on his fingers. All that stuff had probably once decorated the window of a jewelry store on Kuznetsky Bridge. Two automatic pistols were stuck behind his wide belt. That bandit was accompanied by bodyguards: a big fellow in a Circassian cap and a bearded man in a Russian shirt, with a bandoleer across his chest. Embroidered on the bandoleer was the slogan "Death to capital!"

. . . On that memorable evening the anarchists felt in absolute command, behaved like proprietors of the place, and even brought a cabaret singer with them and told him to appear on the platform. The singer was drunk. He mounted the platform and began to speak utter nonsense. The anarchists roared with laughter, the rest of the audience was silent. Suddenly, the powerful bass of Mayakovsky was heard: "Comrades! Don't let that type mess around here!"

Mayakovsky mounted the platform and pushed the cabaret singer aside, but the infuriated anarchists began to shout, "Get off the stage! Don't offend the *artiste!*"

Mayakovsky was standing on the platform, pale, with a cigarette in his mouth, which emphasized all the more the grimace of revulsion on his face.

"I am reciting 'Revolution!'" he announced and put out the cigarette against his heel.

"Get off the stage!" the anarchists went on roaring.

The gang leader was making his way toward the platform, waving his revolver. It is difficult to say how all this would have ended but for the intervention of a patrol of the Red Guard and armed soldiers. Rattling the butts of their rifles, they rose from their seats and advanced menacingly on the anarchists. The anarchists realized it was better to withdraw. They were reluctantly let through; one of them gave a shot in the air. Then everything was quiet . . .

BORIS LAVRENYEV:

In the spring of 1918 I met Mayakovsky in the little cellar called "The Poets' Café" in Nastasyinsky Alley. I went there with David Burliuk. The leftist socialist radical Blumkin, who later was to murder the German ambassador Mirbach, attempted to seize the role of *compère* and behaved as if he owned the place. Nearly all the tables were taken by sailors of the special regiment, who were to go to the front the next day. The sailors were sitting girdled with grenades and holding on to their guns. Poets were performing on the platform one after another: Kusikov, Shershyenyevich, Panayoti, Klark. All of a sudden, some squirt jumped onto the platform and in a goat-like voice began to sing a song then popular among reactionaries:

"Soldiers, soldiers, down the street are marching!
Soldiers, soldiers, songs are singing!"

He had hardly finished singing the first stanza when a deafening bang was heard, as if someone had fired a heavy pistol. They all leapt to their feet. The sailors raised their barkers. It turned out that Mayakovsky had simply banged his fist on the table. Towering above the cellar, he shouted with all his might: "That will do! Get off the platform! It's a shame to give such garbage to people who are going to the front to defend the revolution. Take that scoundrel away!"

Pandemonium broke loose. Some sailors supported Mayakovsky and applauded him. Others began to shout and hurl abuse. Revolvers were drawn, grenades were taken from behind the belts. The more cowardly guests rushed for the exit.

Blumkin shouted at Mayakovsky from the platform, "Do you think, Mayakovsky, that sailors understand your poems? That song is much closer to them!"

Through the din one could hear Mayakovsky's quiet reply: "We'll see."

A moment later Mayakovsky, having pushed Blumkin aside, was standing on the platform and, with his hands in his pockets and his head raised high, reading "Revolution." He did it with great passion and inspiration. When he finished, the sailors literally carried him off the platform amidst a storm of applause.

FROM A LETTER TO LILA AND OSIP BRIK, MID-JANUARY 1918:

Dear, dear, dear Lila!
Dear, dear, dear Osya!

I waited for you till the seventh (sensible boy that I am, I have not yet gone to the station). That means you won't be coming . . .

No change as far as I'm concerned. I live like a gypsy romance: sleep during the day, caress my ear at night. I am fed up with the café. A little flea house . . .

I've had plenty of public appearances. There was a "Futurist Christmas party" at the Polytechnic. People thronged like at a Soviet demonstration. At the very outset it turned out that of the four announced on the poster, Burliuk and Kamensky would not be there, and Holtsshmit refused. So I had to grind the organ by myself. I shudder to think about it. I spoke in a circus. Strange. They whistled at Chenkin, with his anecdotes, but listened to me, and how. At the end of January I am to read "Man" at the Polytechnic.

I vigorously trade with books. *Cloud in Pants*—10 rubles, *Flute*—5. *War and World* at the auction—140 rubles. If one thinks of how much alcohol costs, it will not be enough to pay for the hotel.

All women love me. All men respect me. All women are sticky and boring. All men—scoundrels . . .

To the So-o-o-u-u-th.
Do write!
How's Lila's little knee?

> A hundred kisses for you all.
> Your Volodya . . .

THE DAILY "FIGARO," APRIL 15, 1918:

A. V. Lunacharsky in "The Poets' Café"

It was a most solemn occasion—the closing of "The Poets' Café." The (official) reason—departure of the moguls of futurism for the provinces, partly with the highly cultural mission of fostering the art of the future in the hearts and minds of the provincials, who are fossilizing in "bourgeois" superstitions; and partly to fulfill their providential calling whose slogan, though vulgar, yet no less true, is "Pay up!" . . .

The proceedings began with the guests being asked to pay 10 rubles' entrance fee.

In the hope of a "gala program" the contribution was paid without any protest . . .

The introductory word was spoken by V. Mayakovsky.

"While complicating art, we also aim at its definite democratization"— this was the gist of Mayakovsky's speech.

"As far as the future is concerned, there is no doubt that it belongs to futurism, and new art can be supported by our esteemed guest—the People's Commissar for Education, Anatol Lunacharsky," the orator closed his speech.

Everybody present turned around to look. The commissar was indeed sitting at one of the tables. Compelled to reply, he mounted the platform.

With the very first words of his speech Lunacharsky captivated the audience. One felt this was a genuine, experienced speaker. The commissar's speech, delivered with great gusto, was an interesting one. He did not by any means feel obliged to flatter his hosts and relentlessly criticized the noisy and anti-aesthetic publicity tricks of the futurists, their contempt for the classics, their tendency to pretend they were anarchists at any price, the result of which was that while expressing their contempt for the bourgeoisie, they were also serving it. At the end he sweetened the pill slightly with a remark that Mayakovsky's sincerity could attract the masses and tinge futurism with an element of popular art.

Lunacharsky's brief but pointed speech was received with loud applause.

Firstly, because it was a speech. A genuine speech.

Secondly, because the commissar turned out to be a man, and not some kind of strange, frightening creature.

Thirdly, because there was hardly a word about politics.

The persons, however, who came with the commissar and also wanted to speak did not make either the guests or the hosts happy. Speeches which would be excellent at a political meeting are not proper at what was, after all, a gathering of artists.

There occurred, of course, a couple of minor scandals, and Burliuk's barking was also heard; then the café was declared closed till the fall.

EHRENBURG:

I remember the evening when the café was visited by Lunacharsky. He sat down modestly at a remote table and listened. Mayakovsky invited him to speak. Anatol Vassilievich refused. Mayakovsky insisted: "Repeat what you have told me about my poems . . ." Lunacharsky had to get up. He spoke about Mayakovsky's talent but criticized futurism and said that self-publicity was superfluous. Then Mayakovsky said that soon his monument would be raised—here, where "The Poets' Café" stood . . .

Excessive pride? Conceit? . . . Mayakovsky demanded recognition in his lifetime. This was a sign of the times, had to do with the toppling of "idols," complained of by Balmont, with the desire to attract attention to art at any price.

"I like watching children die" . . . Mayakovsky could not even look at a horse being beaten. One day in the café a friend of mine cut his finger. Vladimir Vladimirovich quickly turned his head away . . .

I remember a talk I had with him one night. It was in February or March 1918. We left "The Poets' Café" together. Mayakovsky was asking me about Paris, Picasso, Apollinaire. Then he said he liked my poem about Pugachov's execution. "You should rejoice and you are whining . . . This is no good!" I willingly agreed: "Of course it's no good." Politically he was right, I soon realized this. But we always thought and felt differently.

SPASSKY:

The café period passed under the sign of "Man." Mayakovsky read chapters of the poem every evening . . .

He managed to have "Man" published. The second edition of "Cloud" was published too, this time without the censor's interference.

Mayakovsky brought the books to the café. He checked the width of their backs and was glad the books were fat . . .

When after the café appearances we were walking through Moscow, Mayakovsky, who a little while earlier had chatted gaily with the public, fell into an impenetrable silence. He walked, wearing a woolly scarf around his neck, whose ends were hanging down his chest and back. Clutching the bundle of books under his arm, he strode the streets with long steps. It was not possible to break his silence. It seemed as if words were bouncing off him. It seemed as if there was no other man in the world so lost in himself, so hard . . .

Sometimes passers-by were stopped directly near the café, in Tverska St., by mounted patrols. The Red Guards were checking identity papers. Then we went on through the quiet Moscow streets, past doorways blocked by wooden boards . . .

A man watchfully waits for the man walking opposite to pass. Who knows what his intentions are . . .

And again the narrow groves of alleys. Sometimes they recede, giving way to little squares. All those are sites of recent battles. The walls are riddled with bullets. Bullets have bitten plaster and bricks off house fronts. There's a place from which shots were fired while people were lining up for food, and then ran away at the sound of the shots. Here's the place where the glass of a street light had been broken over my head and small splinters showered to the pavement. And battles still await us.

❦ 17 ❦

Films

❦

The poet longs for a change—and becomes a movie actor. But in the movies he plays himself too. Among people who tell about Mayakovsky's film career the softest voice is that of Lev Grinkrug. Grinkrug (Lova, Lovka) was, from 1918 until the poet's death, one of his most faithful and most disinterested friends. Throughout the period of his collaboration with the "Neptune" film studios, Mayakovsky wrote only one poem, "Good Treatment of Horses." We shall learn about the circumstances in which that important poem was written and published from reminiscences of Gorki's collaborator, Vassili Desnitsky, among others.

SERGEI SPASSKY:

"I've never envied anyone anything. But I would like to appear in films."

And he depicted with relish all the delights of such an occupation from the platform.

"It would be a good thing to become a Mozzhukhin."

Mayakovsky's sigh was overheard by the owners of the "Neptune" film studios.

They were the Antik family, once publishers of the Universal Library. The family—father, mother, and son—frequented the café. They liked Mayakovsky and showed him this by their own manner.

"With his excellent appearance he could have a great career," Antik used to say to me with conviction.

They offered Mayakovsky work in films.

He himself worked out a scenario based on Jack London's *Martin Eden*. He adapted that excellent story—which in many ways was close to Mayakovsky and which he liked a great deal—to suit Russian conditions. Martin was turned into a futurist waging war with representatives of academic art. In one episode he forced his way among them and overturned Pushkin's bust . . .

EVGENY SLAVINSKY:

At that time the success of every film studio was built on actors with well-known names. Yermolyev's studio boasted of Mozzhukhin and Lisyenko; the producer Kharitonov had Vera Kholodnaya, Maximov, Polonsky, and others.

The owners of "Neptune" dreamed of discovering their own star of the screen, whose success could become the basis for the firm's success.

In the course of these searches for a future star, many beautiful women were brought to the studio for screen tests. Devoid of acting ability, they felt embarrassed and lost their composure as soon as they were placed in front of the camera.

After a long unsuccessful search for a potential star, the owners turned to Mayakovsky. They proposed that he write a scenario and play in the film himself . . . And Mayakovsky, who had been interested in films for a long time, accepted the offer.

LEV GRINKRUG:

The Antiks took Mayakovsky on trust, realizing, of course, that his name alone was the best publicity for the film and that the money invested would bring a handsome return. He was for them that "star" all film producers dreamed about and on which the movies were then based.

For a start Mayakovsky took Jack London's novel *Martin Eden*. He adapted it to Russian conditions, introduced many changes, particularly the ending, and made the scenario about a Russian poet who overcomes all obstacles in his fight against conservative tastes and gains fame and riches. But having become famous, he is disenchanted with all that surrounds him. He looks for truth and does not find it; he strives for true, ideal love, but love turns out to be petty and unworthy of him. All this brings him to thoughts of suicide, but he is saved by faith in life. He fakes suicide, burns his rich clothes, puts on worker's clothes again, and goes off into the unknown . . .

Mayakovsky's friends—Burliuk, Kamensky, and others—took part in the filming. One episode was made in the then famous "Poets' Café." Sets representing the café were painted by Burliuk and Mayakovsky. The part of the girl was played by Marguerita Kibalchich.

I too was persuaded by Mayakovsky to take part in the film. As there was no suitable part for me, he made one up. It was the part of the brother of the hero's sweetheart.

The director of the film was Nikandr Turkin, the cameraman was Evgeny Slavinsky.

Turkin was not in sympathy with Mayakovsky's novel approach. Mayakovsky had his own view of every shot, every action, and from the outset began to interfere with the director's, cameraman's, and designer's every working move.

Turkin did not like it, of course; he was obstinate and angry. But it was not easy to get the upper hand as far as Mayakovsky was concerned, and throughout the filming there were continuous arguments and squabbles.

FROM A LETTER TO LILA BRIK, MID-MARCH 1918:

Write to me, Lila!

I feel horrible enough.

I am ill. I am bored. I am angry. My only amusement (and I would like you to see it, it will amuse you tremendously) is that I am playing in a film. I have written the scenario myself. I play the main part.

I've given parts to Burliuk and Lovka.

I'd like to see you two.

Can't write these days, lousy mood.

To be original I've begun to read in French . . .

MARIA AND DAVID BURLIUK:

Burliuk painted the sets for that film, and made all the makeup for the actors. The entire cast of "The Poet's Café" was in the film also, and Mayakovsky appeared in the picture as an already famous writer, having a "good time" . . . V. Kamensky did not participate in this activity of ours. He was busy with his great new project, "Pittoresque Café" on Kusnetsy. M and Mme Filipov gave him the money. The Café was decorated by the constructions of Tatlin and the paintings of Yakulov. By February and March we were already "working" there . . . but at the end of March the "business" was taken from the capitalists' hands, and the Filipovs were ruined.*

SHKLOVSKY:

It was a film based on Jack London; but Jack London as Mayakovsky saw him.

Ivan Nov saved a beautiful woman's brother.

Then his love for the woman began. But the woman did not love the tramp. The tramp became a great poet. He started coming to the futurists' café . . .

Ivan Nov read his poems to Burliuk . . . And Burliuk said to Ivan Nov, just as he had once said to Mayakovsky on the boulevard, "But you're a poet of genius!"

And fame began. And the woman came to the poet. The poet—in cape and top hat. He put the top hat on a skeleton's head, covered the skeleton with the cape, and put him next to an open safe.

The safe was filled *ad nauseam* with the gold he had earned. The woman came up to the skeleton with the words "What a silly joke!"

And the poet went away. He climbed the roof and wanted to jump, head first.

Then the poet played with a revolver, a small Spanish Browning.

Then Ivan Nov went away, disappearing in the distance.

Mayakovsky also acted in a film entitled *The Workers' Teacher*, in which he was a hooligan, who reformed himself, fell in love, and died under a cross.

* The above fragment has been taken from the original English by D. and M. Burliuk, *Color and Rhyme*, No. 31, 1956.

He acted without make-up and was not particularly liked by Antik. When the producer argued with him, Mayakovsky replied coolly, "You know what, I can, after all, write poems . . .

MAX POLANOVSKY:

Films were shot in Samarsky Alley, opposite the present park of the Central House of the Soviet Army. Where the stadium is now, there was a park with the film pavilion.

The owners of the building rented it to private film makers who did not have a permanent studio. The pavilion was rented for a period, either as a whole, or in part.

Sometimes a number of silent films were being shot simultaneously in different corners of the pavilion. For outdoor shooting the park was used. Many actors of the period were filmed in its alleys. In the spring of 1918 Mayakovsky was filmed there in the part of a hooligan, against the background of fresh spring leaves. Films were made by rival firms. For this reason the owners of future films kept secret from one another not only the title but also the contents of the film being made. Even the actors who appeared in it, and the cameramen, sometimes didn't know the story of the film they were working on.

The director used quickly to "go over" the scene with actors and crew, and shooting followed immediately. One could not wait. The owners did not tolerate any delays. The shooting pavilion was rented for a short period. If a film director could not complete his work on schedule he undermined his reputation. The owners preferred those directors who worked the fastest.

There was no question of retakes: that would prolong the term of hiring the pavilion. One also saved on the tape, which was not produced in Russia and imported with difficulty from abroad after the October Revolution.

SPASSKY:

Some of the action took place in the café.

We were invited to the outskirts of Moscow where the studio was located. "The Poets' Café," reproduced from plywood and suitably painted by Burliuk, awaited us.

It was early spring, the snow was melting. Slush covered the unpaved ground of the courtyard. Buchinskaya took her shoes off and ran across it.

We were all full of joy and the expectation of something out of the ordinary. Not one of us had appeared in films before.

Mayakovsky considered himself the host. The production chaos surrounding us was most congenial to him. We stumbled over wooden shields, huge spotlights with their thick cables. Workmen were nailing and shifting something. Part of a temporary roof suddenly came down, narrowly missing a certain frail poetess. Mayakovsky grabbed her and took her out in his arms as if from a burning building. Contented, agile, well disposed to everyone, he filled the pavilion with his presence.

The director arranged us sitting at the tables.

The repetition of a familiar situation transplanted into new circumstances was amusing. It was as with events recalled from the past: they are real and yet do not exist. Strong bluish rays enveloped the tables, with a hiss.

We talked, laughed, clinked our glasses. Buchinskaya danced on the table. In order not to get out of step, she recited Kamensky's poems according to the director's instructions. Mayakovsky came into the café. We greeted him, waving our hands. Our voices would not be heard from the screen, but we did not mind. We were greeting the living Mayakovsky and not an invented screen hero.

GRINKRUG:

We began filming in March 1918, and toward the end of April the picture was ready . . . Before the end of April a gala screening of the film took place in the "Modern" (now "Metropol") movie theater attended by many people, among them the People's Commissar for Education, Lunacharsky. Everyone enjoyed the movie, except Mayakovsky himself, who said that he did not fully succeed in showing Turkin as he wanted to.

Mayakovsky's performance must really have been successful because he was immediately offered parts in other films . . . Later in the same period, Mayakovsky appeared in two more movies: *The Lady and the Hooligan,* based on the story *The Workers' Teacher* by Amicis, and *In the Fetters of Film,* from his own original scenario.

FROM LETTERS TO LILA BRIK, MARCH–APRIL 1918:

Dear, beloved, very dear Lila!

From now on no one will be able to accuse me of reading too little: I read your letter all the time.

I don't know whether this will increase my education, but I am happy already.

If I am to be regarded as your puppy, I will tell you honestly, I don't envy you, because the puppy is not worth much: the ribs are sticking out, the coat is in shreds, and next to the red eye, especially to shed a tear, a long bald ear.

Zoologists say that puppies always get like that when given to strange, unloving hands.

I don't go anywhere.

I stay three, four chairs away from women—so that they don't blow something awful on me . . .

More than anything in the world I want to be with you. If you go away anywhere without seeing me, you will be unkind . . .

Dear and only Lila!

Don't be ill, for God's sake! If Osya does not see to you and take your lungs (here I had to stop and get inside your letter to check the spelling of "lungs") to the right places, I will bring a pine wood to your apartment and arrange a sea in Osya's study just as I please. And if your thermometer pushes higher than thirty-six degrees, I will knock all its paws off.

Well, my fantasies about coming to see you can be explained by my general capacity for dreaming. If my business, nerves, and health continue as before, your puppy will fall under a fence, paws up, and give up to God his calm little soul.

If, however, a *miracle* happens, I will be with you in two weeks or so!

I am just completing a film . . . I'm not writing any poems, though I very much want to write something impressive about a horse.

In the summer I would like to be with you in a film. I would work out a scenario for you.

I will develop this plan in more detail when I come. I don't know why, I am sure you will agree. Do not be ill. Write. I love you, my kind and warm little sun.

Kisses for Osya.

I embrace you so strongly that bones creak.

Your Volodya

P.S. . . . Forgive me for writing on such exquisite paper. It's from "Pittoresque," and they simply can't do anything without being exquisite.

It's a good thing that at least in their lavatory there is no cubism, for this would be hard to bear.

Dear, but to me not very kind, Lila!

Why aren't you writing to me? Not a word. I sent three letters to you and not a line in reply.

Are six hundred versts so impassable?

Don't do it, baby. It doesn't become you!

Write, please! I get up every day with nostalgia and ask, "How's Lila?"

Don't forget that I don't want anything and am not concerned about anything, except you. I love you.

I try to save myself through the movies. Too much so.

Eyes ache terribly.

Next Monday I go for an operation. They will cut my nose and throat.

When (if!) I see you, I am going to be all clean and renovated. A locomotive straight from the workshop!

The film people say I'm an unheard-of artist for them. They tempt me with speeches, fame, and money.

If you do not write now, it will be clear I have died as far as you are concerned and I'll have to provide myself with a little grave with little worms. So, write!

Kisses.

Your Volodya

Kisses for Osya!

"RAMPA AND ZHIZN," NO. 22, 1918:

In the "Neptune" film studio shooting takes place for a picture based on the novel by Amicis, *The Workers' Teacher*, with Alexandra Rebikova and the poet-futurist Vladimir Mayakovsky taking part. The picture is being made by the cameraman Slavinsky.

SLAVINSKY:

As an actor, Mayakovsky did not invent any special gestures. He behaved in front of the camera with that victorious and charming naturalness which characterized him in life.

Whoever knew Mayakovsky well, his gestures and habits, would recognize them at once when watching the poet on the screen.

In the scene with the hooligan at an inn there was an episode in which the waiter gave the hooligan a mug of beer and put it in front of him. Mayakovsky, in the part of the hooligan, took the mug and looked at it closely, inside as well as outside. It was a typical gesture for Mayakovsky who was very concerned about cleanliness and had an aversion to objects and vessels which were not his.

"MIR EKRANA," NO. 3, 1918:

The poet Mayakovsky has written the history of the cinema entitled *In the Fetters of Film*. This original scenario has been bought by the "Neptune" film studio. Within the next few days the director Turkin will begin work on the film. In the principal parts the following ladies will appear: Lila Brik, Marguerita Kibalchich, Alexandra Rebikova. The author of the scenario, Vladimir Mayakovsky, will also play one of the leading parts.

THE SYNOPSIS OF THE SCENARIO "IN THE FETTERS OF FILM," WRITTEN DOWN BY MAX POLANOVSKY AS RELATED BY LILA BRIK:

The painter is bored. He walks the streets. At a boulevard he sits down next to a woman, begins to talk to her, but the woman suddenly becomes transparent and in place of her heart only her hat, necklace, and pins can be seen. The painter returns home. His wife is transparent too: she has saucepans where her heart ought to be. The painter meets a friend, and he has a bottle and a pack of cards in place of his heart.

A gypsy on the boulevard wants to divine the painter's future. He likes her, takes her to his studio and begins to paint her portrait with gusto, but his brush moves more and more slowly. The gypsy girl becomes transparent: she has coins instead of a heart. The painter pays her and throws her out of his studio. The wife tries unsuccessfully to console the worried painter. He leaves the house.

A big film rental office. Business is slack: no best sellers there. A smartly dressed man with a beard enters. He looks like a character from Hoffmann, or like Mephistopheles. The bearded gentleman has brought a cassette with the film called *The Heart of the Screen*. The proprietors of the office are enthralled. They buy the film.

Feverish publicity. Posters of *The Heart of the Screen* (a ballet dancer holding a heart in her hands) are pasted all over the city. Sandwich men are walking around, handing leaflets to passers-by. *The Heart of the Screen* is being shown in all movie theaters.

The bored painter enters a movie theater to watch *The Heart of the Screen*. The content of the film includes the entire world of the movies: the ballet dancer (Heart of the Screen) is surrounded by Max Linder, Asta Nielsen, and other film celebrities, as well as cowboys, detectives, and other characters, mainly from American popular movies. The show is over, the spectators go out. The painter walks toward the screen and claps his hands enthusiastically. He keeps applauding even when he is alone in the darkened theater. The screen lights again, the ballet dancer appears on it, steps out and approaches the painter. He puts his arm around her and leads her to the exit. The street is dark, rainy, noisy. The ballet dancer looks out disapprovingly, takes a step back and disappears through the locked door. The painter, in despair, bangs on the door, but in vain—the door remains closed.

The painter goes home. He falls on his bed, ill. The doctor examines him, writes out prescriptions, leaves. Near the house he meets the gypsy girl, who has fallen in love with the painter. They are standing by the poster of *The Heart of the Screen*. The gypsy girl is asking about the painter's health. The eyes of the ballet dancer on the poster turn toward them: the ballet dancer listens to their conversation.

The painter's housekeeper is buying medicines at a drug store. On her way back she gapes at the sandwich men. The paper in which medicines are wrapped is torn, the medicines fall out. The housekeeper wraps the medicines in a poster picked up from the ground and takes them to the painter. He manages to send his wife out of the room, unwraps the package and sees the poster. He smoothes it out and stands it against the bedside table. The ballet dancer on the poster comes to life, sits on the table and approaches the painter. The painter, overjoyed, gets well at once.

At the very moment when the ballet dancer comes to life, she disappears from all the posters on the walls and from the leaflets in the hands of the people reading them. She also disappears from the film itself. At the film rental office there is a panic. The bearded gentleman flies into a rage.

The painter invites the ballet dancer to his suburban villa. He puts her on a divan, rolls her up like a poster, ties a ribbon around her, takes her carefully in his arms, gets into the car with the "poster" and moves off.

They arrive at the suburban villa. He gives her a dress to put on, lays a table for lunch, tries to entertain her. But she already longs for the screen, throws herself at everything white which reminds her of the screen, strokes the tile stove and the tablecloth. In the end she pulls the tablecloth off the table with the crockery, hangs it on the wall and strikes a dancing pose against its background. She asks the painter to find her a genuine screen. The painter takes leave of her and drives at night to the deserted movie theater, where he cuts out the screen with a knife.

While the painter is stealing the screen, the ballet dancer takes a walk in the garden. The gypsy girl, jealous, has got into the villa and is lying in wait for the ballet dancer: she makes a scene and eventually stabs the ballet dancer. On the tree against which the ballet dancer leaned hangs a poster, pierced with a knife. The terrified gypsy girl rushes to the bearded gentleman and tells him where the ballet dancer is. The girl has hardly left the garden when the ballet dancer is again standing on the path.

The ballet dancer is waiting for the painter in a room of the suburban villa. The bearded gentleman comes in and with him are the characters from the film *The Heart of the Screen,* as well as the gypsy girl who has shown them the way. The ballet dancer is glad to see them—she was beginning to miss her own kind. The bearded gentleman wraps the celluloid film tape around her, the ballet dancer dissolves in the tape. All go out, except the gypsy girl, who has fainted.

The painter returns with the screen. He does not find the ballet dancer, runs around the room trying to find her. He revives the gypsy girl, who tells him what has happened. He pushes her aside, studies the poster of *The Heart of the Screen* as if trying to understand the secret there. He notices the name of the film land printed at the bottom in tiny, barely legible letters.

The painter by the window of a railway compartment—is on his way to find the film land.

LILA BRIK:

Mayakovsky wrote the scenario with the seriousness and passion that he usually reserved for his best poems.

It is a great pity the scenario has not been preserved. The film, from which it could be reproduced, has not been preserved either. I rack my brains in vain, trying to remember the name of the country which the "painter," the film's hero, goes in search of.

As far as I can remember, the "painter" sees in the street a poster from which "she"—the "heart of the screen"—has disappeared after she was again imprisoned on the film tape by the "man of the movies." Looking intensely at the poster, the "painter" with difficulty reads the name of the film land, printed in small type at the bottom of the poster, and then sets out in search of that country. It is a word like "Lublandia," some wonderful name of a film land. We liked it so much then! We talked about it a great deal. I cannot recall it now.

ALEXANDRA REBIKOVA:

Having been drawn by Mayakovsky into the new "movie game," like most of those who worked in our pavilion I wished to take part in this film. Even though as a rule I had leading parts as an actress in films, I agreed to take the small part of a gypsy girl who fell in love with a painter and was jealous of a phantom ballet dancer . . . I found the new atmosphere of work and play, created by the poet, both fascinating and amusing . . .

The work in Samarsky Alley drew many film people closer to Mayakovsky. We used to go to the movies, dinners, with the Antiks, the "Pittoresque Café" on Kuznetsky Bridge, where the poet occasionally recited his poems in the evenings.

One day Vladimir Vladimirovich presented me with his poem "Cloud in Pants." We were in a droshky, I think, when I told him that there were many places in the poem I did not understand. I opened the book, read some of them and laughed. "You don't understand anything," said Mayakovsky with a grim smile. "I am the greatest modern poet. One day you will realize this." He then snatched the book from my hands and tore it to shreds, which he threw away on the Kuznetsky Bridge.

SLAVINSKY:

I once asked Mayakovsky when he found time to write his poems. He used to spend days filming, evenings—in cafés, or with the Antiks, or somewhere else . . . Mayakovsky replied that when he felt like writing he would find time and nothing could stop him.

It soon happened that at a crucial moment in the filming, which was going on all the time, day after day, Mayakovsky did not appear at the Samarsky Alley.

They looked for him in his apartment, in the apartments of all his friends, asked for him in all the places he used to frequent, or where he might be. But they did not succeed in finding Vladimir Mayakovsky in Moscow.

The actors gathered in the morning at the studio, the proprietors were flustered, all work stopped, people wandered around with nothing to do . . .

But the poet soon appeared at the studio, ready to continue filming.

"Where have you been, Vladimir Vladimirovich? Where did you get to?"

"I worked. I had the need to write a poem, so I found the time. I warned you, remember?"

During the period spent at the "Neptune," Mayakovsky wrote one poem, "Good Treatment of Horses." Perhaps it was the work on that poem which made the poet disappear from the studio . . .

It is possible that the theme of the poem was born on the way from Samarsky Alley to the "Pittoresque Café" on the Kuznetsky Bridge . . .

For some time after his disappearance from the studio, Mayakovsky was the object of kindhearted jokes:

"In one respect you're like your ballet dancer, Vladimir Vladimirovich!"

"How's that?"

"Just like your heroine you disappear from the picture . . ."

VASSILI DESNITSKY:

In the spring of 1918, unexpectedly for myself, I suggested to both Gorki and Mayakovsky the theme for a kind of creative rivalry.

I do not remember whether I described the following street scene to them together or individually: in the street, close to the sidewalk, a horse is lying on his side, without a harness. There are no visible bruises. His bulging belly heaves heavily. The horse lifts its head from the pavement with a great effort. It seems as if it is looking at the passers-by with astonishment and reproach. People walk by, stop for a little while, look at the horse and walk on. A boy, perhaps ten years old, plucks some dusty grass and, bending over, gives it to the horse. The horse sighs deeply and does not touch the grass . . .

Alexey Maximovich wrote his sketch directly under the influence of my story. Mayakovsky could also have tackled the theme independently from my account. It is worth noting, however, that the poet used my story, with its possible social and moral conclusions, though without concrete details (summer, period of acute food shortage just beginning, etc.).

Both their works on the same subject appeared at the same time in the newspaper *Novaya Zhizn.*

FROM GORKI'S STORY "IN THE SICK CITY," "NOVAYA ZHIZN," MOSCOW EDITION, JUNE 9, 1918:

A horse, emaciated from work and starvation, falls on a heap of paving stones. The sharp end of a broken wooden pole is jabbing at his swollen belly. The horse is crying: big, dirt-stained tears are flowing from under the thin, convulsively moving eyelids.

He is surrounded by a crowd of grim-faced people, who obviously are not in a hurry to go anywhere. They talk about the horse being old, the cart being overloaded. The driver, seated by the cart, talks about the high cost of fodder and adds: "We will all soon die for lack of food. People too."

Someone tosses the remark: "The rats have already begun."

Children are running around, with tufts of grass, pulled from somewhere with their roots. Squatting in front of the elongated horse's mouth, they put the grass and flowers in his flabby lips, withdrawing their frightened little hands from the broad gray teeth.

It is as moving as if tender lyric poems were being read to a man dying in an agony of suffering.

The horse munches mechanically, continuing his powerless and ineffective efforts to tear himself away from the sharp pavement stones . . .

GOOD TREATMENT OF HORSES
by Vladimir Mayakovsky

Bouncing were the hoofs.
Playing as if:
—Humps.
Mumps.

Tombs.
Nubs.—

Wind-drunk,
in ice stocks
bound streets.
The old horse
has thumped on the ice—
and soon
the gaping crowd gathered
to parade in the Kuznetsky their pants:
"The old horse has fallen!"
"Look at the old horse!"
The crowd is overjoyed.
The Kuznetsky laughed.
Only I
did not mix my voice with the crowd's howl.
The old horse
I approached:
I saw the street flowing from his eyes . . .

I came nearer—
from the horse's eyelash
drop after drop
flows down the hair . . .
And here a common
animal sadness
splashed out of me
and whispered:
"Horse, let it be.
Horse, do not think,
you are worse than they—control yourself!
Oh kid,
we all of us pull something,
each of us is something of a horse."
Maybe
the sense of my consolation
seemed meager to the old horse,

maybe my compassion
did not move him at all,
but
the old horse
sprang
to his feet,
and whined
and went on.
He is now in his stable
and paws at the ground
and wags his tail
gaily.
The old horse thinks
he is a young colt again,
and will go on living
still, will carry on.

SPASSKY:

In the spring Mayakovsky had his farewell appearance in the "Pittoresque Café," that last venture of Filipov . . .

Mayakovsky mounted the platform—strong, stocky. In the winter he had grown as it were, felt mature and sure of himself . . .

He recited with confidence and joy, walking around the big platform. The poems, heard many times before, were often familiar in all the details of their intonation. Many a poem recited there I heard then for the last time . . .

He also read his latest work. About the horse that slipped in the Kuznetsky and was surrounded by a gaping crowd. And about Mayakovsky himself approaching and addressing the horse . . .

YURI OLESHA:

I have seen the early films in which Mayakovsky acted. Not films really— only a few fragments have been preserved. It is strange to see them: fluttering, pale like water, images almost absent. On them—the face of young Mayakovsky—sad, passionate, evoking immense compassion, the face of a strong and suffering man . . .

♛ 18 ♛

Utopia

♛

The great director Vsyevolod Meyerhold speaks about the need for a utopia, felt in those days by himself as well as by Lunacharsky and other men of the theater. The playwright whose work came to be connected with those longings was Mayakovsky. The circumstances under which Mystery-Bouffe *was written are mentioned by Lila Brik and Vassili Kamensky; the facts regarding the production of the play are described by the director, Vladimir Solovyov, by the well-known actor-to-be Golubyentsev, and by the poet himself. In his second stage appearance, Mayakovsky is not the futurist Hamlet— "Vladimir Mayakovsky"—but the revolutionary Messiah— "Simply a Man."*

KAMENSKY:

In this period Mayakovsky conceived the idea of *Mystery-Bouffe* and dreamed about the play's being produced in the theater.

I did my best to add fuel to the fire by drawing up the most monumental production plans, designed for the stage of a nonexistent colosseum, with thousands of spectators.

Our imaginations were fired to such a degree that ordinary theaters seemed to us futile, good-for-nothing matchboxes.

We were dreaming of a revolutionary mass theater of the future, where thousands of people, as well as hundreds of cars and airplanes, would fill a gigantic arena, creating for millions the vision of, say, the heroic epic of the October Revolution.

Mayakovsky thought that the project could be realized in the Vorobyov Hills.

We sincerely believed that all this was fully practicable, and we even wanted to present our plan to Lenin . . .

For that matter, new creative projects of a cosmic scale were born in our circle every day.

We wanted, for instance, to build a "café-merry-go-round" in the Kuznetsky, all glazed windows, so that the entire premises, in the middle of which a real merry-go-round was to whirl, could be seen from the street . . .

Volodya was then thinking of building a Palace of the Poets, a place where we could have a printing press to publish a journal and books, establish a poets' club, and have our apartments there as well . . .

MEYERHOLD:

For many years not only I, but also Lunacharsky and other comrades occupying leading places in the Soviet theater wished to see the so-called utopian art on the stage—the art which would not only pose problems of today but would project decades into the future. We never had to ask Vladimir Mayakovsky to write such plays for us: he brought them to us himself. One must note that in all his plays, from *Mystery-Bouffe* onward, one can discern an urgent need to look into that marvelous future . . .

The art of the stage requires the solution not only of present-day problems but also of those present-day problems that are thoroughly imbued with the future . . . Take *Hamlet,* for example. *Hamlet* is so constructed that we feel its hero to be standing on the edge of a future life . . .

Therein lies the nature of the theater and Mayakovsky's importance as a writer for the theater.

FROM MAYAKOVSKY'S LETTER TO THE CENTRAL COMMITTEE
FOR THE OCTOBER CELEBRATIONS, OCTOBER 10–12, 1918:

. . . in accordance wich your wish, comrades, I give you a concise summary of *Mystery.*

Act I. The whole world flooded by the deluge of revolution. Seven frightened "pure" couples are climbing to reach the only area that is still dry—the pole. There is a Turkish pasha, a Russian merchant, a Chinese emperor, a priest, and other "white" representatives of the five continents. Climbing behind these frightened and moaning creatures are seven "impure" couples: the proletarians, who do not drown in this upheaval . . . When the bloody stream erupts through the pole in the footsteps of the fugitives, the pure ones, as a last resort, exclaim, "Let's build an ark! . . ."

Act II. To the accompaniment of the tears of the pure and the laughter of the impure, the earth is submerged in waves . . . As they rave about Mount Ararat, exhausted and starving as they are . . . a radiant mountain appears before them. Walking on the waves as if on dry land, toward the ark is not Christ—who has experience in such practices—but the simplest of men. Standing on top of workbenches and furnaces, he delivers a great sermon on the mount, the promise of a future paradise on earth . . . The man disappears. They soon realize that he was their own will embodied in the shape of man . . .

Act III, scenes 1, 2, and 3. Through paradise, whose inhabitants tempt them with their austere heaven, through hell, in which the worker has enough spirit to mock its cauldrons, which seem so insignificant compared to the fires of big furnaces, the pure ones, having overcome all obstacles, and driven by their unbreakable will, reach the promised land, which turns out to be the world they have left . . . They see, though, that they had been wrong to condemn the earth: washed by revolution and dried with the heat of new suns, it appears to them in a dazzling brightness, in which only we can see life, we, who beyond all the terrors of the day can clearly sense another, marvelous existence . . .

Monologue of
"SIMPLY A MAN"
by Vladimir Mayakovsky

. . . All the thunderbolts have not yet crawled out of the caves,
the echo of the latest storms has not yet exploded.

Woe to the sluggards who have clutched
with their earthly ark at the washed-out rot!
You're looking for Ararats?
They are not there,
oh no!
Swamped in their sleep they dream about Ararats.
But since the mountain
won't come to Mahomet,
to the devil with it!
I am not divining you Christ's paradise,
where prudes are sipping their Lenten tea—
I shout about the real one, you must believe in the one
which is on earth, here, nearer to us.

       .   .   .

There you don't tire your hands in vain toil,
work blossoms like a rose in your hand.
Sun is doing such wonders
that every step sinks in the sea of flowers.
Here you toil for centuries in your garden—
vegetables in hot beds, compost heaps,
but in my garden
on dill stalks
pineapples grow six times a year.

       .   .   .

My paradise is for everyone
except for the poor in spirit,
whose bodies are swollen like a moon from fast.
It's easier for a camel to slip through the eye of a needle
than for such an elephantine apostle to me.
Let him come to me—
who could stab with a dagger
and leave the foe's body without a sigh!
You, who have not forgiven,
come first
into my heavenly kingdom.
Come, adulterer, torn by passions,
whose veins the bogy cuts with anxious heat—

for you, with never sated lips,
is my heavenly kingdom.
Come all to whom foul humility is hateful.
All who are cramped and uncomfortable know:
for you—
is my heavenly kingdom.

ZHEVYERZHEYEV:

Early in August Vladimir Vladimirovich read his *Mystery-Bouffe* in the
Briks' apartment to a small gathering, among whom were Lunacharsky,
Leshchenko, Solovyov, and many other men of the theater . . .

The very next day, I believe, Lunacharsky gave the order for the play
to be read and then produced at the Alexandrinsky Theater . . .

Pashkovsky, the actor who at that time headed the "autonomous"
troupe of the theater, proposed that the play by the young poet, which
had been recommended for production by Lunacharsky, the People's
Commissar for Education, be read to the company.

The reading began in dead silence. The actors, who filled the foyer,
received the commissar's recommendation and Pashkovsky's introduction
with unfriendly reserve . . . When the reading was over, a long silence
ensued, and some voices were eventually heard complaining about the
short time for preparation and the difficulties of mastering a text in
verse . . .

After a few brief statements from the floor, Pashkovsky, who presided
at that meeting, summed up the views of the company, which he knew
very well. Very cleverly, with numerous compliments addressed to the
ironically smiling Mayakovsky, he declared that, in his opinion, the old-
fashioned theater company would not be able to cope with such an interesting modern play and that young and modern actors, contemporaries of
the author, would have to be found for its production . . .

MAYAKOVSKY:

We could not find a theater, because they were all crowded with *Macbeths*. We were given a dilapidated circus, which had been run down by
the mass meetings held there.

The director of the theater department, Maria Andreyeva, however,
ordered that even the circus be taken away from us.

I had never seen Anatol Vassilievich shout, but on this occasion even he was furious.

A little while later on I went away with a sealed piece of paper . . . We had been given the Music Drama Theater.

Actors were recruited, of course, wherever we could find them.

"SYEVYERNAYA KOMMUNA," OCTOBER 12, 1918:

Appeal to Actors

Comrade actors! It is your duty to celebrate the great day of the revolution with a revolutionary show. You should perform *Mystery-Bouffe*—the heroic, epic, and satiric picture of our era, written by Vladimir Mayakovsky. Let all come on Sunday, October 13, to the concert hall at the Tenishevskaya School (33 Mokhovaya). The author will read *Mystery*; the director will present his production ideas; the designer will show the sketches; and those of you who are attracted to this work will act in it . . . Time is precious! We ask only those comrades who would wish to take part in the production to come. Seating is limited.

V. Meyerhold, V. Mayakovsky, P. Lebyedyev,
C. Malevich, L. Zhevyerzheyev, O. Brik.

FROM THE REMINISCENCES OF NIKOLAI GOLUBYENTSEV:

It was early fall 1918. My brother Alexander and myself, students that we were then, decided to improve our material situation somewhat by enrolling as extras at a theater. We were not accepted by Maryinsky and Mikhailovsky, and when we came to the Music Drama Theater, someone—I cannot now recall whom—suggested that we take part in the production of Mayakovsky's play *Mystery-Bouffe* . . . Most of the participants in the production were students at the university, the music conservatory, and the academy of fine arts. Only the principal roles were played by professionals . . .

For most of those taking part it was the first encounter with Mayakovsky's work. As for myself, I seem to remember vaguely, I had as a boy read some strange poems in the *Satyricon*. The text, which we began to read at rehearsals, astounded us at first, made us laugh and sometimes joke. None of us understood anything at all . . . Mayakovsky worked with us like a dog, explaining the meaning and reading the text with us over and over again . . . In the course of daily rehearsals we young people imperceptibly and gradually became familiar with the unusual verse form in which the play had been written. The day suddenly came—it was, I think, the tenth or eleventh rehearsal—when we felt not only that we understood what the play was all about but that we liked it and were won over by it as well. We came to like the verse. We knew not only our own parts but whole fragments, scenes, and monologues by heart . . . We began to quote from *Mystery* in our conversations . . .

FROM THE REMINISCENCES OF VLADIMIR SOLOVYOV:

In his conversations with actors and in his detailed remarks on the nature of individual parts, Mayakovsky adopted, as it were, the formula of the Romantic theater, with its clear division of all characters into two levels: the sublime and the grotesquely ridiculous. From the actors playing the "seven impure couples" he demanded strong will, heroic pathos, and grandeur. With the "seven pure couples" he was willing to tolerate exaggerated parody, including the somewhat coarse elements of satiric buffoonery and popular farce . . .

Mayakovsky also took part in the production of *Mystery-Bouffe* as an actor. In the course of the rehearsals one part always remained vacant—the part of "Simply a Man," who appears at the end of Act II before the impure ones and delivers a new "sermon on the mount," an appeal to take up revolutionary action. The part consists of a monologue, which, although it is not long, demands a great temperament and tragic pathos from the actor. All attempts to cast the part remained unsuccessful. Some of the prospective candidates gave up; others were clearly unsuited . . . And so it happened that the text of "Simply a Man" was spoken by Mayakovsky. It became obvious to everyone that a better performer would not be found. Mayakovsky accepted the part and took up his actor's duties with great zeal . . . The first appearance of "Simply a Man" was to be a visually monumental, signifying the coming of a new Messiah, walking on the waves toward liberated mankind . . .

MAYAKOVSKY:

The theater's administration sabotaged the production in every way. Entrance doors were locked, even nails were kept under lock and key . . .

Posters were brought on the day of the opening—with painted contours only—and a declaration was immediately issued that no one be allowed to paste them up.

I painted the posters myself.

Our maid Tonya went to the Nevsky with the posters and nails and put them up wherever she could. They were immediately torn down by the wind.

And then, when evening approached, actors began to disappear, one after the other.

I had to assume, on the spot, the parts of "Simply a Man" as well as Methuselah and one of the devils.

On the next day *Mystery* was scrapped and to the joy of the academics, *Macbeths* again began to bore us. How could it be otherwise? Lady Macbeth was played by Andreyeva herself . . .

GOLUBYENTSEV:

I remember the first performance. The darkened house was full, Commissar Lunacharsky in the official box. I suppose we did not act well, voices did not carry, sets were unwieldy and hastily put together. The audience listened in amazement to the text, which sounded quite unlike what they were used to hearing, and looked at the fantastically painted drops. But we, the participants of the show—I think I can say this on behalf of us all—felt a great satisfaction. The audacity and novelty of all this enchanted us . . .

FROM THE NOTEBOOK OF ALEXANDER BLOK:

Celebrating the October anniversary with Lyuba. In the evening—went to Mayakovsky's *Mystery-Bouffe* . . .

Historic day—for me with Lyuba—complete.

In the day time—the two of us in town—decorations, procession, rain over the graves. Festive day.

In the evening—a hoarse and sad speech by Lunacharsky, then Mayakovsky—plenty.

I will never forget that day.

SHKLOVSKY:

I later saw Blok with Mayakovsky on a few other occasions.

At the Miniature Theater on Lityeyna Street Mayakovsky read *Mystery-Bouffe* . . .

Blok said, "We are very talented, but we are not geniuses. You cancel us out. I understand this, but do not feel joy because of it."

FROM NIKOLAI PUNIN'S REVIEWS IN "ISKUSSTVO KOMMUNY,"
NO. 2, DECEMBER 15, 1918:

New theater has been talked about for dozens of years—without success . . . New theater can exist; judging by many signs, it is near. It is symptomatic that, instead of directors' theories, plays appear; instead of productions we get dramatic works which dictate how they are to be produced. Such a dictating play is Mayakovsky's revue. One simply must not produce it in the way it was done at the Music Drama Theater on the October anniversary. I did not expect and do not expect anything from Meyerhold; he is a kind of "friend-of-the-house, mummy's-lover" director. But in spite of this production I expected and still expect things from Malevich . . .

The play is a classic one. Mayakovsky the rebel, Mayakovsky the Apache, street-corner poet, etc.; yes, we know, we know. But when his rebellion was elemental there was nothing to be said . . . Mayakovsky has become quiet, bright, and gay. *Mystery* is the gayest work in Russian literature since Griboyedov's *Wit Works Woe* . . . The most interesting thing about *Mystery-Bouffe* is that Mayakovsky, after all his street rhetoric, has now placed himself in a square like a monument and, as the first among futurist poets, has clearly said "we." At that moment he ceased to be a romantic and became a classic. In the future, no matter how much he would like to, Mayakovsky will not be able to bring himself to such ungovernable rebellion as before . . .

Neither Meyerhold nor Malevich felt this classicism-in-the-making of Mayakovsky's verse. Their approach had no connection with Mayakovsky's play. If his early pieces could not be staged, *Mystery-Bouffe* can be, because the poet's own hand checked his unbridled dynamism, and the poet himself brought his harridan muse down to earth. Stand and admire, O passer-by, how thunders roll and continents topple, but stand nevertheless . . .

There has not been another artistic movement so rich in classicist potential as futurism.

On Olga Kameneva's initiative I took *Mystery* to Moscow . . . Meyerhold decided to produce it again.

I made the text more topical.

In the unheated corridors and lobby of the First Theater of the Russian Socialist Federal Soviet Republic, interminable rehearsals went on.

When the rehearsals were nearing an end, a paper came with the following declaration: "In view of the enormous cost and the harmful content of the play, production must cease."

I hung up a placard, which invited comrades from the Central and City Committees and from the Worker and Peasant Inspection to come to the cold theater.

I read *Mystery* with the enthusiasm essential for a man who has to warm up not only the audience but also himself to keep from freezing.

It had its effect.

Toward the end of the reading one of the Moscow Council activists (I do not know why he was sitting with a violin) played the *Internationale*— and the freezing audience sang though there was no official occasion.

Mystery-Bouffe ran a hundred performances at the Meyerhold's theater.

FROM THE ANONYMOUS REPLIES OF SPECTATORS TO THE
QUESTIONNAIRE OF THE FIRST THEATER OF THE RUSSIAN SOCIALIST
FEDERAL SOVIET REPUBLIC:

"These are all Jewish tricks."

"Shame on the author."

"A fighting play. Take it to the square, to the streets."

"I liked the play very much. This is life itself, although I don't understand futurism."

"Pity the miserable actors."

"Coarse, vulgar, insipid."

"Marvelous, astonishing. It is the first time I have seen such a performance and the first time since the revolution that I have felt satisfied, though I've been to the Bolshoi, the Moscow Art, the Kamerny, and other theaters."

✳ 19 ✳

"The Art of the Commune"

✦

The futurists, in their combat against old aesthetic canons, desire to join communism. The debate over the image of revolutionary culture is carried on within the new institutions of Soviet authority and in the columns of the press. Their attitude toward Pushkin and Raphael enflames passions. The struggle for principles is accompanied by the struggle to occupy the leading positions. Mayakovsky attacks and is attacked. Press documentation from this period is both more ample and more telling than memoirs.

"IZVESTYA," SEPTEMBER 10, 1918:

Maxim Gorki and the Commissariat for Education.
On the eve of his departure from Petrograd Comrade Lunacharsky, the People's Commissar for Education, signed an important agreement with Maxim Gorki. Maxim Gorki will organize a publishing establishment, "World Literature," attached to the Commissariat for People's Education.

Gorki plans the publication of a large series of translations (260 volumes), which will include the greatest works of eminent writers of all nations from the last decade of the eighteenth century and the entire nineteenth century . . .

At a meeting with the People's Commissar, M. Gorki stated that terrorist acts directed against the leaders of the Soviet Republic have made him decide to cooperate as closely as possible with them.

Gorki has proposed the establishment, by the Commissariat for People's Education, of a bi-weekly journal—to be edited by himself and Lunacharsky—to inform the mass public in Russia and abroad of the results of the constructive and cultural activities of the Soviets, which, in Gorki's opinion, are developing ever more widely and consistently, in spite of appalling living conditions.

APPEAL OF THE RED ARMY MEN OF THE REVOLUTIONARY MOSCOW
RESERVE INFANTRY REGIMENT TO MAXIM GORKI, "IZVESTYA,"
SEPTEMBER 25, 1918:

To the Author of The Harbinger of Storm

We are very happy. Gorki is with us again. He is ours! We love him . . . we welcome from the depths of our hearts his return to our ranks.

Let his capable pen serve us again, for his cooperation will speed us on our thorny road to the kingdom of socialism.

Long live the world revolution!

Long live Comrade Maxim Gorki!

FROM AN ACCOUNT BY OSIP BRIK:

The concern for creating new artistic values and preserving the monuments of old art and taking over the artistic heritage found its external expression in the establishment of two departments at the People's Commissariat for Education: the Department of Visual Arts and the Department of Museums and the Protection of Monuments.

The head of the Department of Visual Arts was the painter David Shterenberg, who returned from Paris in the middle of 1918. Around him were grouped those avant-garde artists who saw in the making of the new department a possibility of renewing the fight for their principles within the Commissariat for Education . . .

There immediately ensued a conflict with the Department of the Protection of Monuments. Any reason was good enough to spark off a flare-up: a proposed exhibition site, the purchase of works of art, the composition of a competition jury, etc.

In the fall of 1918, Mayakovsky joined the committee of the Department of Visual Arts. He had realized by then that the struggle for new art could be waged only from within the Soviet institutional framework.

Mayakovsky obtained Lunacharsky's agreement for the publication of a small chrestomathy [anthology] of futurism. It was published under the title *The Unsifted Word*.

THE PREFACE OF THE PEOPLE'S COMMISSAR FOR EDUCATION TO
"THE UNSIFTED WORD":

In the present, difficult period, writers are often deprived of the possibility to publish their work.

In the old days such difficulties were most frequently encountered by revolutionary writers; not only those who expressed revolutionary ideas but those who aimed at revolutionizing form and declared themselves against accepted conventions.

Our nation of workers and peasants must now undertake, on an ever-increasing scale, to publish literary works either directly through state publishing houses, or those under the aegis of the Soviets, or by subsidy alone.

One thing is clear: the principle of state activity must be to give the mass reader access to all that is new and fresh. It is better to make a mistake by giving the people something which will never gain their sympathy than to hide a work that may bear fruit in the future under a bush on the grounds that it does not suit somebody's taste just now.

For this reason the Commissariat for Education has gladly helped with the publication of *The Unsifted Word*. The book has been written by futurists. Attitudes toward them vary and one may justly criticize them. But they are young, and youth is revolutionary. No wonder then that their defiant, glaring, though sometimes odd, art is imbued with an atmosphere of bravery, audacity, and grandeur close to our hearts. In Mayakovsky's poems many tones resound to which no revolutionary, young in body or soul, will remain indifferent.

Let the proletarian know and appreciate everything: the old and the new. We will not impose anything on him, but we will show him everything.

A. Lunacharsky

FROM THE STENOGRAPHIC TRANSCRIPT OF THE MEETING OF THE COMMITTEE FOR VISUAL ARTS, DECEMBER 5, 1918:

Chairman [Nikolai Punin]: . . . Let's pass on to publishing matters. The first issue of our journal *Iskusstvo Kommuny* [*The Art of the Commune*] has been prepared and printed. The issue has been prepared within a week. I request that the committee members have a look at it and voice their views.

[Nathan Altman says that a permanent editorial committee is required and declares his surprise at some articles in the first issue.]

Mayakovsky: Comrade Altman is absolutely right when he says that the committee must be responsible for the journal they are editing. The publication of the first issue without all committee members' having been informed in detail about the material to be included can be explained by the urgent need to move the whole machine forward without collaborators being available. Neither Comrade Rudnyev nor Altman nor Shterenberg, whom I troubled many times, saying, "Be so kind as to have a look at the material"—I am not inventing this, it was really like that—nobody wanted to be the first to deal with it. I think that these matters will regulate themselves with the second issue. One just can't avoid responsibility for what one has done. There is a simpler way out: not to publish the journal at all. Ten thousand copies have been printed. One does not have to distribute them but may simply take them home as a souvenir. The literary and publishing department, on whose behalf I am unofficially speaking, decided today to face the committee with the accomplished fact of the journal's having been printed, with the object of involving the entire committee in editorial work from now on.

Chairman: . . . I know how much time Comrade Mayakovsky devoted to the publication of this issue. It had to be published as a matter of urgency.

Mayakovsky: At present it is the literary section that took the initiative and is responsible for the publication. The first editorial meeting was attended by Brik, Punin, Shtalberg, and myself, as a kind of advisory horse who trotted about on the journal's business.

🖋

On December 7, 1918, the first issue of the weekly Iskusstvo Kommuny *was published with articles by Osip Brik, Casimir Malevich, Nikolai Punin, Mayakovsky's poem "Orders for the Army of Art" and an account from the mass meeting on the subject "Temple of Factory."*

FROM MAYAKOVSKY'S STATEMENT QUOTED IN THE ACCOUNT:

What we need is not a dead temple where dead works of art can fossilize but a live factory of human spirit. We need raw art, raw words, raw deeds . . . Art ought to assemble not in lifeless temple-museums but everywhere—in the streets, in streetcars, factories, laboratories, and in workers' districts . . .

KORNEL ZYELINSKY:

I have managed to preserve all nineteen issues of this periodical, published in winter 1918–1919. Its format was small, its contents astonishing. If comets, which get to the earth from unknown spaces of the universe, move according to mathematically confirmed laws, then such comets as *Iskusstvo Kommuny*, edited by the futurists at the Department of Literature and Art of the People's Commissariat for Education, were subjected only to the laws of fantasy. One had to "hunt" for every issue. The journal found itself in the hands of the so-called avant-garde writers and painters who leaned toward futurism. The mood of the all-destroying revolutionary storm, of unusual possibilities opening for everyone, the pathos inherent in the abolition of the entire aged social system, hovered visibly over that periodical. The strangest slogans cut across its pages. For instance, "Let the Milky Way split into the Milky Way of the conquerors and the Milky Way of the purchasers" (from Khlebnikov's "Martian Trumpet"); "Our beauty is in the unbending betrayal of our own past"; and, "There is no beauty without struggle; there are no masterpieces without violence." This is the background against which Mayakovsky's "Orders for the Army of Art" were first published. Their verses were repeated as slogans: "Streets are our brushes; squares—our palettes."

Brik edited the journal *Iskusstvo Kommuny*. He worked in the Commissariat of Art. The Department of Visual Arts was situated in Isaakevsky Square, in the lovely Myatlev house . . .

David Shterenberg and flat-faced Nathan Altman are here. Often seen are Vladimir Kozlinsky and Vladimir Mayakovsky. They play billiards together.

Brik is the commissar of the Academy of Fine Arts and calls himself the Revolution's doorman. The Briks still live at Zhukovsky Street No. 7, the same stairway as before but in a larger apartment. The apartment is very cold in the winter.

All except Mayakovsky sit in overcoats.

Nikolai Punin comes here. He used to work in the "Apollon" and is a futurist now. He tells drawing teachers about cubism with a snobbish and academic calm . . .

The Art of the Commune proclaims slogans of modern art; futurism wants to conquer the country.

I stand apart . . . am against *The Heart of the Commune* and, politically, occupy the right wing of the futurists.

On the square opposite the Cinizelli Circus, is a bookshop called "Book Corner," which deals in old books and also in new hand-written books by Kuzmin and Sologub.

In the same house, upstairs on the fifth floor—no elevator—futurist paintings are hanging in the empty rooms. There are stools but nobody sits on them. It is IMO.

IMO means the art of the young [*iskusstvo molodykh*]. Mayakovsky, Brik, and myself—we publish books . . . Mayakovsky published his *Mystery-Bouffe* here.

The book was set overnight, but the compositor had not been told otherwise and began every line with a capital letter. Mayakovsky took it calmly and said it was his own fault. A fat book entitled *Everything Composed by Mayakovsky* and the collection *Poetics* were also set and published here.

Poetics had 165 pages of very small print, with wide lines.

Brik's, Yakubinsky's, and my own works were printed here . . .

In the Winter Palace a huge exhibition is taking place—all the rooms are filled up. There is Repin, as well as Chagall with a dead man on the roof and candles burning in all directions; also a still life of a herring on a table by that picturesque ascetic David Shterenberg; and a relief by Lila Brik . . .

FROM "DO NOT REJOICE," BY MAYAKOVSKY, PUBLISHED IN "ISKUSSTVO KOMMUNY," DECEMBER 15, 1918:

A white army officer when you catch
you beat him!
And what about Raphael?
Have you forgotten Rastrelli?
It's time to make
museum walls
a target.
Let the mouths of big guns shoot the old rags!

. . . With deaf ears
to the whispers and gossip of the whites,
we have positioned our artillery by the wood.
And why
does Pushkin still hold?
When do we attack
the generals' classics?

FROM THE DIARIES OF ALEXANDER BLOK, AN UNSENT LETTER TO MAYAKOVSKY, DECEMBER 17–30, 1918:

Not like this, comrade!

The Winter Palace and museums are no less hateful to me than to you. But destruction is as old as construction, and just as "traditional." Destroying what we hate, we are bored and yawn no less than when we look at the process of building. The tooth of history is far more venomous than you think; we can never get away from the condemnation of time. Your cry still remains a cry of pain not of joy. Destroying, we still remain slaves of the old world: to break tradition is also a tradition. We are cursed by an even greater evil: we cannot avoid the necessities of sleeping and eating. Some will build, others will destroy, because "there is time for everything under the sun"; but everybody will remain a slave until a third force appears, something unlike construction and destruction.

LUNACHARSKY'S ARTICLE "A SPOON OF ANTIDOTE," PUBLISHED
IN "ISKUSSTVO KOMMUNY," DECEMBER 29, 1918:

Some of my collaborators were greatly embarrassed by the early issues of *Iskusstvo Kommuny*. One must not hide the fact that in this connection a slight conflict arose between the Committee of the Commissariat for Education of the Northern District and the Department of Visual Arts of the Commissariat.

I must confess that I am embarrassed too.

They tell me that the commissariat's policy in the sphere of art is clearly defined. Not for nothing, they tell me, has so much effort, sometimes heroic effort, been devoted to protect all artistic monuments; we were even open to the criticism that we were guarding "noblemen's treasure." After all this we cannot permit the official organ of our commissariat to represent all artistic heritage from Adam to Mayakovsky as a heap of trash meriting destruction.

The problem also has another aspect. I have declared dozens of times that the Commissariat for Education must be impartial in its attitude toward the various trends of artistic life. As for the question of form in art, the taste of the People's Commissar and of all the representatives of the authorities does not count. One must make possible a free development of all creative groups and individuals. One must not allow one trend, armed either with acquired traditional fame or with fashionable success, to destroy the others . . .

I see nothing wrong with the fact that the worker-peasant authority has given serious support to modern art: they were really cruelly refused recognition on the part of the "elders." Not to mention the fact that the futurists were the first to support the revolution, that among all intellectuals they most sided and sympathized with it. They also revealed their ability to organize themselves in many respects in practical activity, and I expect the best results from the free visual arts studios and many district and provincial schools organized according to a far-reaching plan.

It would not be good, however, for modern artists, even though they are revolutionary, to regard themselves as a state artistic school, as activists of the official art dictated to from above.

Two tendencies of the young periodical in whose columns I am printing this letter therefore give rise to certain fears: the destructive tendency in relation to the past and the tendency to speak in the name of authority when speaking on behalf of a particular artistic school.

I do not wish, however, that those concerned about the journal attribute too much importance to all this. Not for nothing does the fighting futurist Punin sweat for all he is worth in order to save the traditions of icon painting in Mster and is concerned about the prohibition of local authorities to export icons from Mster—and all this on the back pages of the same periodical whose façade is adorned by Mayakovsky's passionate compositions.

I can assure one and all that genuine talents among the innovators sense, or even consciously realize, how much beauty and charm there are in old monuments and, like the augurs, smile at each other and wink when they deride everything old, knowing perfectly well that all this is just a young pose and, unfortunately, imagining that it becomes them.

FROM THE UNPUBLISHED ROUGH DRAFT OF
"A SPOON OF ANTIDOTE":

Vladimir Mayakovsky causes me serious concern.

He is a man of great talent. It is true that in the new characteristic form of his writing—fairly brutal, but strong and interesting—very old thoughts and very old tastes are in fact hidden. Of what does Mayakovsky's lyric poetry consist? Apart from youthful conceit we find lyrical whining on the theme of unfulfilled love and lack of recognition on the part of the cruel crowd for a young genius . . . I welcomed as great progress his passing from the oh-so-nice romantic routine to the revolutionary-collectivist routine . . .

But in spite of everything he is a man of talent. In time we can expect a greater maturity of mind and heart from him, and even now he has made outstanding achievements as far as the mastery of form is concerned.

His prolonged boyishness causes concern too. Vladimir Mayakovsky is an adolescent.

And, indeed, an adolescent can be forgiven when he beats his chest every ten minutes and declares in a cocky voice, "I am a genius; look at me: a genius is here."

Such an adolescent, I suppose, can be forgiven when he is envious of his elder brethren in the Parnassus and cannot talk about them without hate; when it seems to him that the great dead, with their eternal masterpieces, seriously hinder the success of his own little work . . .

But such an attitude is unforgivable in the case of the man that Mayakovsky ought to be by now.

Genius is congenial to genius. Genius is moved by *all* beauty, genius is magnanimous to other geniuses and feels fraternal love for them; genius could not utter those arrogant and unsavory words about Pushkin with which Mayakovsky has soiled his mouth.

I realize that the faults of boasting and spitting on high altars, the desire to impale the giants—all this can be the result of young talent having been too long thwarted. But one must know the measure in everything . . .

I am sincerely impressed with his great talent. I am very glad that talent has turned to revolutionary aims. I am painfully shocked, however, and blush for Mayakovsky when I hear the noise of self-publicity and when the song of envy for the fame of the famous begins—the kind of envy that is not a sign of talent but, on the contrary, is more suitable for those who do not possess it.

I have told many people who are equally tormented and irritated by this sad characteristic in so promising a man, "Just wait; he now has his share of fame, he has grown up; the yellow tunic, the tunic of envy and publicity, is no longer necessary for him."

And I feel embittered when I find on the first page of *Iskusstvo Kommuny* dear Vladimir Vladimirovich again dressed in his ridiculous and soiled costume.

FROM PAVEL BESSALKO'S ARTICLE "FUTURISM AND PROLETARIAN CULTURE" IN THE PERIODICAL "GRYADUSHCHEYE," NO. 10, 1918:

Futurism and proletarian culture are two sphinxes looking one at the other and asking, "Who are you?" The fate of these two literary trends depends on the replies they give. One trend must annihilate the other. The opponents sense this and for that reason delay their answer. One of those trends in particular clearly avoids giving an answer. Futurism employs subterfuges: like a chameleon, it tries to assume the coloring of the proletariat's revolutionary culture, which is alien to futurism.

. . . We assume that proletarian culture is made by workers them-selves, not by the intelligentsia, who by chance, or even deliberately, have come around to the ideas of the proletariat.

No one thinks of calling Cooper's novels and Longfellow's poems about Red Indians the literature of Red Indians. Why then do the intelli-gentsia chameleons writing about workers call their literature the litera-ture of the workers? Does a caterpillar which, for reasons of self-preserva-tion, assumes the appearance of a knot on the tree, cease to be a greedy caterpillar? Simulating though it may, does it not reveal its nature when the first reaction of fear is over?

Hence the conclusion that one cannot seriously consider the literature made by the intelligentsia as literature of the workers and that it should be seen merely as an attempt of one class to brainwash another class in its own interest . . .

How should the makers of proletarian literature treat the work of the futurists? Very simply—as a carpenter treats a growth on a walnut tree: when cut and sawn into thin slats, it can be useful for making various little pieces of furniture . . .

CASIMIR MALEVICH, "OUR TASKS," 1919:

1. War with academism.
2. Directorate of innovators.
3. Establish a world collective for art.
4. Set up embassies for the arts in all countries.
5. Found permanent museums of modern art throughout the country.
6. Build a connecting railroad through the Russian Republic for the movement of mobile exhibitions of creative art.
7. Set up a Central Museum of Modern Creative Arts in Moscow.
8. Appoint commissars for art in Russian provincial capitals.
9. Publicize Russian creative arts throughout other nations.
10. Publish a journal devoted to problems of art for the masses.

FROM THE JOURNALS OF ALEXANDER BLOK:

. . . all this is *terrible*. Who will win this time? Total anarchy [apropos the provinces' showering the commissariat with complaints that classics instead of political brochures are being published] or a new "cultural order"?

I do not know . . .

All cultures—scientific and artistic—have something of a demon in them. And the more scientific, the more artistic, the more demonic it is as well. The bearers of the science now mobilizing itself to combat chaos are not the silly little professors but a science more subtle than theirs.

But demonism is a force. And to be forceful means to overcome weakness, to *harm the weak* . . .

The poor ones *knew* all this. They knew better than I, the initiated. They knew that the young master—with his handsome horse, his pleasant smile, his pretty fiancée—is still a master. And they thought, "pleasant, or not pleasant, just wait, master, we will show you."

And they did show.

And they are showing. And even if they scrap the book of a writer who is only "a little" meritorious for the revolution (namely, A. Blok) from the printing press with their hands, which are even more soiled than mine—I don't know that either and I'm not a judge, O Lord—*I do not dare judge* . . .

Demon is the master.

The master will dodge any difficulty. And will remain master . . .

Coming back to "politics." Meyerhold has a similar "social sense." In a different way but in the same direction politically—Mayakovsky (otherwise, nothing in common, except "politics"!) . . .

Another "camp"—Gorki. Hence the struggle between two departments and two ladies. Anatol Vassilievich conciliates and is not a "Bolshevik by temperament."

And I ought to renounce at last my vaudeville function of chairman . . .

KORNEL ZYELINSKY:

. . . Mayakovsky's appearance before sailors in the ex-Guards Barracks has clearly remained in my memory. In addition to sailors' caps with ribbons one saw cyclist's caps, women's wraps, and even a few hats. Sailors from the ships stationed on the Neva were crowding a small bar almost all day long, from early evening at any rate. Red Army men and ordinary people came here. Girls were brought here too. Someone always brought an accordion and dances were started. Everyone danced fully-clothed—overcoats, warm jackets, girls in fitted sheepskins. The most popular dances were the polka and the "sailor dance." The building was not heated, but one did not feel the cold too much in those days . . .

I learned about the literary evening at the Guards Barracks from a sailor I knew and went there with him. We came quite early and were deafened by the noise from several accordions: each of them had its own circle of dancers. I must say I did not believe that the evening of the poet-futurist—as the poster described it—would take place. The atmosphere clearly favored dancing. When Mayakovsky's tall figure appeared on the platform, however, and the poet declared in a loud voice, "Sailors! I wrote a poem especially for you," their interest was aroused. All went inside.

In spite of the terrible cold, Mayakovsky took off his overcoat and cap but left a wide scarf around his neck. He began to recite a poem which was soon to become famous—"Left march." When he spoke the words, "Marching column, rise! Time will blot out vain words," while at the same time unfolding his scarf with one hand and making a wide gesture with the other, and then the words, "Now you, Comrade Mauser," applause broke out. The audience warmed up at once, grew silent, and gazed attentively at the speaker. "We've lived long enough by the law given by Adam and Eve"—at these words a man close to me, his head leaning on a girl's arm, laughed but was hushed up by others and stopped.

> Who there moved his right?
> Left!
> Left!
> Left!

This stanza was spoken by Mayakovsky in a particularly inspired way, while lightly stamping his foot. The unusual rhetorical structure of the poem, slapping one in the face as it were, the aggressive delivery, the gesture of his hand cutting through the air, the all-pervading voice of the poet—all this captured the mixed audience at once and resulted in thundering applause . . . On that occasion I sensed the strange new bond which joined Mayakovsky with that audience . . .

FROM A. YEVGENEV'S ARTICLE "THE FUTURIST HECUBA AND THE PROLETARIAT" IN THE PERIODICAL "VYESTNIK LITIERATURI," NO. 10, 1919:

All those futurists, ego-futurists, budyetlan-story-tellers, imaginists, and whatever else they are called—they are all poisonous berries from one field . . . And a strange thing has happened! Those who call themselves ego-futurists and imaginists were earlier apologists of extreme individualism and egoism . . . And suddenly the winged individualists, in the post-October days, declared themselves the authentic "collectivists," heralds of the proletarian revolution, of new proletarian literature and art.

What is there in common between futurist tricks and . . . the real worker-peasant masses, their needs, ideas, and tastes? Absolutely nothing . . .

And what would happen to Russian literature if the futurists, who in a certain period were availing themselves of a certain influential protection, managed to "throw out of the steamer of modern times," the old Russian literature and in its place enthrone their own "extra-rational" writing?

But God does not give horns to a cow that butts. The futurist dictatorship and supremacy in the sphere of literature has been a fiasco. In painting, the makers of monstrous daubery have totally compromised themselves. The nation has not understood, appreciated, or accepted them . . .

One often hears complaints about doubtful allies who have glued themselves to the authorities. Outcasts from police stations apart, such "glued on" allies have been the futurists. They have been told unequivocally that they are not suited to be the makers of the new proletarian art and literature . . .

The imaginists, who have appeared as an alternative to the futurists, feeling the ground slipping from under their feet, began to cut themselves off from their spiritual brethren. In their Moscow café "Domino," they ceremoniously buried futurism, having made a sepulchral plaque for it, with a cross and the names of Mayakovsky and others . . .

FROM BORIS KUSHNER'S ARTICLE "LEAP TO SOCIALISM," "ISKUSSTVO KOMMUNY," NO. 8, JANUARY 26, 1919:

We must quell completely the rotten seed of the bourgeoisie—and its dirty culture—and create an absolutely new civilization of work.

This revolutionary task has been undertaken by a group of Communist comrades from the Viborg district . . .

The revolutionary negation of bourgeois culture was born in its inner depths. It first exploded—passionate, angry, and unbridled—in the sphere of art.

This negation is called futurism.

It was born almost simultaneously with the world's first Soviet of Workers' Delegates.

In Russian it appeared as a "Slap to the Public's Taste."

The bourgeoisie fought futurism just as desperately and relentlessly as it fought the Bolsheviks at a later period.

Both names are equally hateful to the bourgeoisie; both mean a death sentence for her.

The Viborg comrades have rightly understood the situation. Their task is to destroy the old culture and create a new one, and to fulfill it they joined with the futurist movement.

In the Viborg district of the Communist party, the Collective of Communists-Futurists has been established.

This collective ought to achieve a great revolutionary task.

Above all, the comrades from the Com-Fut Collective ought to remember that fifteen months of the revolution have been lost and it is up to them to make up for the lost time . . .

FROM THE DECLARATION OF THE IMAGINISTS, PUBLISHED IN THE BI-WEEKLY "SIREN" ("VORONEZH"), JANUARY 30, 1919:

The youth is dead, the noisy ten-year-old boy (born in 1909, died in 1919). Futurism is dead. Let us cry in unison: death to futurism and futurizing. The academism of futurist dogmas blocks the ears like absorbant cotton to all that is young. Futurism means death of life.

Do not rejoice, you bald symbolists and you, pathetic passéists. We do not call for a retreat back from futurism but a move forward and forward, through its corpse, and ever more to the left . . .

Let some diligent person create the philosophy of imaginism and explain with a fitting depth of intellect the fact of our appearance. We do not know why we came. Maybe because yesterday it rained in Mexico, maybe because last year your soul had pups, there may be yet another reason—but imaginism had to come and we are proud that we are its servants and that through us it speaks to you as if through posters.

The first line of the imaginists.

Poets: Sergei Yesenin, Rurik Ivnyev, Anatol Marienhof, Vadim Shershenyevich.

Painters: Boris Erdman, Georgi Yakulov.
Musicians, sculptors, and the rest: ?

"ISKUSSTVO KOMMUNY," NO. 9, FEBRUARY 2, 1919:

On January 28, the Viborg District Committee of the Russian Communist party considered the question of registration of the Organization of Communists-Futurists as a party collective.

Notwithstanding the spokesman's declaration that the tasks and activities of Com-Fut have a strictly political and not educational character, that its constitution and program are totally in accord with the spirit and resolutions of the party, that is to say the organization ought to be registered as a party cell, the District Committee refused to register the Com-Fut Collective.

The refusal has been motivated by the statement that "the constitution of our party does not envisage collectives of this kind" and that "through accepting such a collective we could create an undesirable precedent for the future . . ."

One can doubt whether the Viborg Committee will be able to maintain an attitude so out of keeping with the spirit of communism and the best traditions of the party.

"ISKUSSTVO KOMMUNY," NO. 17, MARCH 30, 1919:

The Vitebsk Sub-Committee for the Visual Arts is organizing the first State Exhibition of Painting in the city of Vitebsk and Vitebsk Province and requests comrade painters to give notice of their participation to the following address: Vitebsk, Bukharinska No. 10, Sub-Committee for the Visual Arts . . .

There is to be no adjudication at this exhibition . . .

The opening is scheduled for the end of next April.

The Provincial Plenipotentiary for Art and Director of the Sub-Committee,

Marc Chagall

AS ABOVE:

"Guillaume Apollinaire":

According to the information received by us from private sources, Guillaume Apollinaire, one of the most outstanding leaders and promoters of new art, died a year ago in Paris from influenza.

Apollinaire published a number of essays on modern art, in which he characterized the artistic trends of cubism and futurism in France with particular insight and precision. He was the first to point out the masters whose work was noteworthy in the intense and complex development of modern European art.

Apollinaire was perhaps the first to write about such artists as Picasso, Gleizes, Braque, and Metzinger.

As soon as possible we hope to publish Apollinaire's book *On Cubism*, which has already been translated.

AS ABOVE: THE SHKLOVSKY-PUNIN DISCUSSION,
"On Art and Revolution"

. . . Art has always been free from life and its color never reflected the colors of the flag over the citadel . . .

But we futurists are binding our art with the Third Internationale.

Comrades, this means giving up all our assets.

Futurism was one of the purest achievements of human genius. It was a sign of how high the understanding of the laws of creative freedom could be raised. Is not this rustling tail clipped from a newspaper editorial, now attached to futurism, offensive?

V. Shklovsky

. . . We were persecuted and will be persecuted, not because we are anti-bourgeois, or the other way around, but because we possess the gift of creative art. This is the reason we cannot be tolerated by mediocrity, even by communist mediocrity. And as for our "proofs," they belong to another order and result from the whole system of our outlook on the world . . .

Art is form (being), just as socialist theory and Communist revolution is form. Besides, art is the most synthetic and, through this, perhaps the strongest form. Speaking about futurism, we always spoke about power. Moreover, we pointed out that futurism is a correction to communism because futurism is not only an artistic movement but a whole system of forms . . . And now we are even ready to declare that communism as a theory of culture cannot exist without futurism . . .

Comrade Shklovsky writes, "But we futurists are binding our art with the Third Internationale," and he considers this a crime . . . The Internationale is just as much a *futurist form* as any other creative form . . . I ask what difference is there between the Third Internationale and Tatlin's bas-relief of Khlebnikov's "Martian Trumpet"? To me there is none. The first, the second, and the third are new forms which mankind enjoys, employs, and plays with. The future belongs to them; the future belongs to all who are with them—and that is futurism . . .

Nikolai Punin

The literary studio of the Moscow Proletkult would not have to devote even these few words to Messrs Futurists, but for the fact that the protection of the People's Commissariat for Education and the insolent self-publicity of Messrs Futurists create the false impression that the futurist chaos is revolutionary and proletarian art . . . We are convinced that the Great Revolution, while destroying the foundations of the bourgeois system, would have eliminated futurism, which is an act of the ultimate decomposition of that system, but for the fact that the People's Commissar for Education gathered the rotten straws of futurist imposition in the first days of the October Revolution and tried to weave from them a life belt of revolutionary art.

The futurists, with a practical sense characteristic of them, used that false step of the commissar to their advantage and flocked to occupy all responsible positions in the art departments . . . Directing the Department for the Visual Arts like Punin and Tatlin, defining the line of literary tastes like Mayakovsky, Ivnyev, and Marienhof, heading the literary publishing department for the military like the "excellent" Vassili Kamensky, swelling their ranks with obviously talentless people and not so obvious cheats, Messrs Futurists exploit the organs of Soviet authority to recommend their rotten bourgeois art as proletarian art.

There is no room here for ideological discussion. The futurists, who are mechanically attached to the proletarian revolution, must just as mechanically be driven away from the warm places they now occupy . . .

OSIP BRIK:

In spring 1919 Mayakovsky moved to Moscow and severed contact with the Department for the Visual Arts. The journal *Iskusstvo Kommuny* ceased publication shortly afterward. The personal composition of the departmental committee underwent changes too, and the circle grouped around it dispersed.

⚜ 20 ⚜

"One Hundred Fifty Million"

⚜

Mayakovsky makes further attempts to identify with the masses: he gives up lyric poetry in favor of drawing and writing propaganda texts for ROSTA (Russian Telegraph Agency). Next he publishes an epic poem and, instead of signing it, declares himself the spokesman for the collective "Ivan." Some years later he will confess, with an equal amount of bitterness and pride, that he "trampled on the throat" of his song in the name of service to the revolution. Now, however, in the years 1919, 1920, and 1921, his intentions rarely meet with understanding. Among the representatives of established authority, only Lunacharsky and a handful of young people favor him. Lenin does not like futurism but his praise of one of Mayakovsky's satires opens the columns of a large daily paper to the poet.

FROM MAYAKOVSKY'S AUTOBIOGRAPHY:

The year 1919. My mind is occupied with "150 Million." I joined the ROSTA propaganda work.

The year 1920. I completed "150 Million." I am printing it without my name. I want everyone to add to it and improve on it . . .

Days and nights at ROSTA. All kinds of Denikins attack us. I write and draw. I have done about 3,000 posters and 6,000 captions.

LILA BRIK:

In 1919 Mayakovsky saw the "Exhibition of ROSTA Satire" in the Kuznetsky and went to ROSTA's director, Kyerzhentsev.

The painter, Mikhail Tcheremnikh worked here. Kyerzhentsev sent Mayakovsky to Tcheremnikh. They came to an agreement. In place of one satiric article or illustrated poem, they began to produce several posters with captions for every exhibition.

The production grew. Tcheremnikh was put in charge of a department. In two and a half years about fifty branches were opened in the provinces. Almost all painters with any inclination toward Soviet authority began to work there.

They worked joyously. Kyerzhentsev was very happy about every successful "exhibition" and liked us.

We drew on newspaper cuttings, then stuck rough edges together. If something was not quite right, instead of rubbing it out we simply stuck something else on top.

We followed this technique: Mayakovsky drew in charcoal; I colored the drawing; then he finished it and polished it off.

We worked in an unheated place. The only source of heat to warm freezing paints and glue was burning newspapers in an old stove.

Mayakovsky composed up to eighty captions in verse daily.

We worked almost without sleep. Tcheremnikh did fifty posters per night. Sometimes he would doze off in the course of working from sheer fatigue. He maintained that upon waking up he found that the work had been completed by inertia.

There was an inspection in our department. They decided that Tcheremnikh was a futurist and had to be removed. Mayakovsky was not accused of futurism. He ardently defended Tcheremnikh and managed to save him . . .

AMSHEY NYURENBERG:

Wages were paid in ROSTA twice a month. We came to the cashier with bags because sometimes we used to get quite a sizeable and heavy heap of paper money.

With the money we used to go to the Sukharevsky Market, where one could buy flour and Ukrainian salt pork from traders.

In the evenings we used to gather frequently at Osmyorkin's place. To his large and bright room came Konchalovsky, Lentulov, Malutin. Mayakovsky did not come often. His presence would have transformed a social evening into a stormy discussion.

The poet seated himself majestically in a rocking chair and, swinging rhythmically, began to speak calmly and condescendingly: "Still lifes and landscapes all the time . . . all right, all right . . ."

We pricked up our ears.

"Everything for the Polish front and the Donbas, of course . . . The soldiers and workers will be overjoyed . . . They will thank you. The Moscovites have seen to it already, God preserve them . . ."

Osmyorkin's face went red. "You want to forbid painting?" he asked, hardly able to contain his irritation.

"Yes, yes, I forbid it, Comrade Osmyorkin."

"You would send everybody to ROSTA . . ."

"And I will!"

"That will be unfortunate."

"Oh yes, those who specialize in still lifes and landscapes will be in no mood for a laugh."

The discussion was clearly turning into a quarrel. In order to turn the attention of those present to something else, Osmyorkin's wife brought a big pot of pale tea brewed from carrots and a dish of thin gray cakes. Munching a cake, Mayakovsky made a wry face and uttered a biting remark: "Very tasty, like your painting."

SHKLOVSKY:

The Briks lived in Polyuektovyi Alley and shared their apartment with David Shterenberg. The entrance was in the courtyard; a white backhouse, if I remember. Three steps, staircase, and by the stairs, on the snow, a lively dog called Shchen . . .

It was from this place that Mayakovsky used to go to ROSTA in Sretyenka . . .

In ROSTA there is a stove with a flue. The smoke has settled and is standing still at the level of my cap.

Mayakovsky, in the smoke, can hardly lift himself up.

The work is done on the floor. Mayakovsky draws a poster; others prepare stencil plates and cut out contours from cardboard. Still others duplicate posters from the stencil. Lila, in a green dress of velvet portiere lined with squirrel, is painting too.

Lila knows how to work, when she is working.

Work at ROSTA is hard . . .

Mayakovsky worked days and nights and slept there with a log of wood under his head in order to wake up more easily . . .

Life was hard. Lila did not avoid scurvy at that time . . .

Blok was wrong when, after *Mystery-Bouffe*, he accused Mayakovsky of happiness, meaning the good life.

Volodya ought to have worked at ROSTA, but not so hard.

KORNEL ZYELINSKY:

Some people today—partly in imitation of Mayakovsky's polemical fervor —attribute exceptional importance to Mayakovsky's work at ROSTA, his posters and captions. For us, who worked in newspapers and at ROSTA, all those different propaganda endeavors, such as trains full of literature, propaganda through sculpture, posters in railway stations, in squares, etc., seemed quite natural in those years. And in this sense, Mayakovsky's work at ROSTA (excepting, of course, his talent), was not essentially different from many similar enterprises at that time. For that matter, the very idea of ROSTA exhibitions was not Mayakovsky's but originated in a collective grouped around Platon Kyerzhentsev.

For this reason, in the fall of 1919 and during 1920, when Mayakovsky's propaganda captions began to appear under his drawings at ROSTA, I must confess that it did not make a particularly great impression on me . . . But the poem "150 Million," published by Mayakovsky in 1920 at the height of his work at ROSTA, is quite another story. This poem has captured my heart forever.

MAYAKOVSKY:

The ROSTA exhibitions were something fantastic. It meant a nation of 150 million people being served by hand by a small group of painters.

It meant news sent by telegraph, immediately translated into posters, decrees into couplets . . .

It meant Red Army men looking at posters before a battle and going to fight not with a prayer but a slogan on their lips.

I remember that work dying out.

One of our billstickers, the fat Mikhailov, came and said, "They won't let us stick them on at Yeliseev. There's to be a shop there."

THE LETTER OF THE PEOPLE'S COMMISSAR FOR EDUCATION TO THE DEPARTMENT OF EDUCATION AND PROPAGANDA OF THE WORKER-PEASANT INSPECTION, IN CONNECTION WITH THE BAN ON THE PERFORMANCE OF MAYAKOVSKY'S THREE SHORT PROPAGANDA PLAYS:

Enclosed you will find the order issued by your department, signed by Comrade Kitaevsky, and the petition I have received from the Theater of Satire. I categorically protest against the ban issued by Comrade Kitaevsky.

I have personally read Mayakovsky's plays and, should you want to read them, will send them to you. Comrade Kitaevsky apparently does not like anything which even slightly smells of futurism.

Everyone can make mistakes, everyone can applaud or boo when sitting in the theater as a member of the audience, but the fact that a particular cockade is stuck on his head does not mean that his personal preferences have suddenly acquired an unusual purity and clarity. One must be able to separate in oneself the state functionary, who as such must not have any literary preferences, from the man with personal preferences.

Mayakovsky is not just anybody. He is one of Russia's greatest talents, with a wide circle of followers among the intelligentsia as well as among the proletariat (a number of proletarian poets are his disciples and imitators). He is a man, most of whose work has been translated into all European languages, a poet valued highly by such writers as Gorki and Bryusov, who are not futurists at all.

Mayakovsky has written three quite pleasant playlets for the Theater of Satire. They are not masterpieces but quite well-done caricatures with a good tempo. Because the tragedy *Mystery-Bouffe* was produced by the Petrograd Executive Committee, I do not understand at all why these deeply Soviet playlets may not be done by the Theater of Satire.

I wish to draw attention to the fact that for a year and a half Mayakovsky served at ROSTA, flooding all Soviet Russia with his caricatures and
jokes, and the Inspection did not object. The Theater of Satire, with Soviet
people in charge, has already spent up to 80,000 rubles on costumes and
sets for these first satirical studies. Comrade Kitaevsky's taste has not only
put a stop to all the artistic work that went into them, but is also the cause
of considerable material loss to the nation . . .

> The People's Commissar for Education, A. Lunacharsky
> Secretary A. Flakserman

July 7, 1920

FROM SERGEI SYENKIN'S REMINISCENCES ABOUT LENIN'S AND
KRUPSKAYA'S VISIT TO THE WCHUTEMAS STUDENT HOSTEL
(FORMERLY THE STROGANOV SCHOOL):

"Well, what are you doing now at your school, fighting the futurists, I
suppose?"

Again they answered in unison, "But no, Vladimir Ilyich, we are all of
us futurists."

"Really! It would be interesting to have a discussion with you. But I
won't have it now—you would have me defeated. I have not read enough
on the subject as yet, but I will, I will. I really must have a discussion with
you."

"We will supply you with literature, Vladimir Ilyich. We are sure you
will become a futurist too. You can't be on the side of the old rotten trash,
especially since the futurists are at the moment the only group on our side;
all the others have gone over to Denikin . . ."

He asked us how we found Mayakovsky. We were for him to a man, of
course, and in our turn we asked Vladimir Ilyich whether he knew Mayakovsky's poems. Lenin jocularly replied that he would read them when he
found the time.

Krupskaya, sitting next to him, remarked, "You did promise before,
Volodya. I showed you those poems before and you always put off reading
them."

Lenin, laughing, said he would find the time to read them. He then
added, "I learned about the futurists only a short time ago, and only because of some polemics in the press, and it turns out that Mayakovsky has
been working at ROSTA for about a year now . . ."

FROM THE ARTICLE BY VLADIMIR FRITCHE "OCTOBER IN POETRY,"
IN THE PERIODICAL "KHUDOZHESTVENNOE SLOVO," NO. 2, 1920:

. . . according to most, if not all our most recent tendencies, a poet's task is to express his personal moods and experiences. Of course, there are no fully personal experiences. Behind the poet there is a definite social group. Our most recent poetry expresses, for the most part, the experiences of social groups which are remnants of the past and not the only collective that deserves to exist in the future—the collective of the working people. From now on the only experiences that are to be regarded as necessary and valuable are expressions of the working collective, and only those moods that favor its existence and development and can make its fight for survival easier . . . Such moods and ideas, which, on the one hand, express the technical substance of the collective and, on the other, are valuable from the point of view of its fight for existence, are: the pathos of fighting, the sublimity of collective work, awareness that the individual is only a part of a more powerful entity—social and cosmic . . . readiness of the individual to subordinate himself to the interests of the collective, etc.

The beginning of *"150 MILLION"* by Vladimir Mayakovsky

150,000,000 is the name of the master of this poem.
The missile—rhythm.
Rhyme—from building to building fire.
150,000,000 speak with my lips.
The rotary machine of steps
prints the text
on the gray cobblestones of city squares.

VLADIMIR TRENIN

"150 Million" differs from Mayakovsky's earlier poems in its plot structure above all.

Mayakovsky's first long poem, "Cloud in Pants," is a lyrical poem with a monologue structure . . . The monologue principle also characterizes the structure of his other poems—"War and World" and "Man" . . . Unlike those, "150 Million" is, in both intention and execution, a fairy-tale epic poem . . .

In the first two parts, the Russian Revolution, which is growing into a world revolution, is treated symbolically. Lofty pathos is the tone of these two parts. The mythological figure of Ivan, the embodiment of the revolutionary energy of the Russian people, appears here for the first time . . .

The figure of Wilson—the embodiment of capitalism—appears in the third part of the poem in a grotesque vision of bourgeois America. That hyperbolic figure is taken from posters in the most literal sense: revolutionary posters that represented the capitalist with a fat belly in a shiny top hat . . .

The succeeding stanzas depict the mythical struggle between Ivan and Wilson. This description also maintains the tradition of duels waged by strong heroes with monsters in old Russian tales. The two streaks of the poem—the pathetic and the satiric—cut and weave across each other.

BORIS PASTERNAK:

Mayakovsky read "150 Million" in a small circle. And for the first time I had nothing to say to him. Many years passed; I saw him at home and abroad; we tried to be friends; but I understood him less and less . . . In those years I reached the frontiers of my understanding, apparently impossible to cross.

BRYUSOV'S LETTER TO THE STATE PUBLISHING HOUSE, AUGUST 31, 1920:

The Committee of the Literary Department of the People's Commissariat for Education, on recognizing the manuscript "150 Million" by Comrade Mayakovsky, submitted to the State Publishing House, as a work of exceptional propaganda importance, requests the publication of said manuscript as a matter of urgency.

The Literary Department requests speedy notification of your decision.

Deputy Director of the Department,
Bryusov

FROM MAYAKOVSKY'S LETTERS TO THE COMMITTEE OF THE STATE PUBLISHING HOUSE (GOSIZDAT), OCTOBER–NOVEMBER 1920:

Comrades!

Half a year ago I submitted to the Literary Department my book "150 Million."

The Literary Department reviewed the book and gave it an exceptional opinion as a propagandistic, revolutionary work. Since then, for six months, I have been standing at the threshold of your office, and every time I always get the standard reply, "Tomorrow we'll go into print."

Comrade Veys called today and assured me that the book had already gone to the printer, and that only technical formalities remained. In the technical department, the secretary altered the mark "first turn" into "third turn" with red ink in my presence and told me that with "third turn" one cannot say anything about the printing date.

Comrades! If from your point of view the book is unintelligible and unnecessary, return it to me.

If, however, it is necessary, stamp out sabotage, for how else can one explain its being withheld from print, if trash issued by speculators can be printed within two weeks? . . .

Comrades!

About two weeks ago I asked you either to publish or return "150 Million" to me and blatantly described your attitude to the book as sabotage. Never mind the word. This can all be called mockery with regard to the author . . .

Today, on the fifth, I asked the secretary, "Is it with the printer?"— "No, it's in the technical department." "When is it going to the printer, then?"—"Impossible to tell; it isn't marked. You see, this is the list of books which are marked. These will go to the printer first."

Comrades! Maybe at the price of another six months' walking around I could finally get that "mark," but I don't fancy the idea of being a messenger boy to Comrade Veys.

It took me a year and a half to write that book. I renounced the profit I would get by selling it to a private publisher; I renounced my authorship, submitting it for anonymous publication; and I have the right, having obtained the unanimous decision of the Literary Department to the effect that it is an "exceptional" book and suitable for propaganda, to demand from you the proper attitude toward the book.

I am not a petitioner in Russian literature, but rather its benefactor. . . . "150 Million" is being copied by hand. I don't give a hoot, let the book appear not in the original but in a plagiarized version. Is there no one, among you, however, who does not realize that this is a scandal?

I demand categorically: return my book. I am sorry for the sharp tone —I have been forced to use it.

Vlad. Mayakovsky

Copies for the Lit. Dept. and A. V. Lunacharsky.

FROM THE JOURNALS OF KORNEL CHUKOVSKY, DECEMBER 5, 1920:

Mayakovsky arrived in Petrograd yesterday in a mail train at my invitation . . . He came (with L. J. Brik) to the Arts House around 2:00 P.M. They were allotted the unheated library next to the dining room . . . We [members of the Arts House] had a meeting . . . Then a procession began: people came swarming in for Mayakovsky. Dmitri Tsenzor, Zamyatin, Zin, Vengerova, S. P. Remizova, Gumilev, Zhorzhik Ivanov, Kiselyeva, Konukhes, Altman, Victor Khovin, Grebyenshchikov, Punin, Mandelshtam, the painter Lebyedyev, etc. A most moving and amusing corner was occupied by children: pupils of the Tyenishev School. At their head: Dreiden in spectacles. God, how they applauded!

Mayakovsky appeared—very young (looked twenty-four), his shoulders unnaturally broad, nonchalant, but not too much. His introductory speech was very bad: "So many of you have come here because you thought that '150 Million' meant rubles. No, it's not rubles. I gave that work to the State Publishing House and then demanded its return: they began to say that Mayakovsky asks for the return of 150 Million rubles, etc."

Then poems began—about Ivan . . . I noticed that everyone enjoyed those places where Mayakovsky exploited the inflections of the colloquial speech of our period, the year 1920. It seemed new and fresh and bold . . . When Krilov and Griboyedov reproduced the natural inflections of their period it must have caused the same effect. The third part was tiring, but the applause was terrific . . . And then the Tyenishev pupils under the leadership of Lila burst into his room and asked for "Cloud in Pants." He read them his "Horse . . ."

SHKLOVSKY:

The Arts House was situated in a large building overlooking the Moyka, Nevsky, and Morska. There was a two-story apartment there, which was previously occupied by Yelisyeyev, his wife, and fourteen servants . . .

For the most part it was now occupied by acmeists. But at the end of the corridor, behind the bathroom, The Serapionovy Brethren had already settled . . . Nikolai Tikhonov was just starting here, writing ballads.

In Leningrad they were attracted to narrative poetry and to Kipling.

Mayakovsky used to come here and stay in the big library. There were red bookcases with green glass and very few books.

They brought him a tray with a battery of tea glasses and another tray with pastries.

People gathered. Eichenbaum, Tynyanov, Lev Yakubinsky, and many others came.

It was here that Mayakovsky read his "150 Million" . . .

The butler, who had been in service with the Yelisyeyevs, brought the tea. Mayakovsky approached him and, taking the tray from him, asked, "Well, they can't write like that here, can they?"

Yefim had been profoundly and intimately trained by poets, so he replied with unexpected coolness, "Personally, I prefer the acmeists, Vladimir Vladimirovich."

And he departed with great dignity.

Mayakovsky did not reply. In the evening he heard the ballads and liked them.

And he remembered the ballads, as indicated in his poem "About This."

FROM KORNEL CHUKOVSKY'S LECTURE "AKHMATOVA AND MAYAKOVSKY," GIVEN AT THE ARTS HOUSE AND PUBLISHED IN THE PERIODICAL "DOM ISKUSSTVO," NO. 1, 1921:

. . . But of what does the essence of his writing consist?

He is a poet of catastrophes and convulsions . . . Everything broke its bondage, moved forward, whirled in a catastrophic twister. The most apathetic, heavy objects, immobile for centuries, are jumping like mad in those verses . . . Mayakovsky is a poet of movement, dynamics, wind storms. From 1910 onward, from his very first poems, everything rushes and gallops somewhere . . . As if the war and then the revolution began especially for him. Without war and revolution he simply could not get along. How is a catastrophic poet to live without catastrophes? . . . It is interesting to note that before the revolution occurred he had already foreseen it, lived with it, and raved about it. In June 1915, when the war was already in full swing, I read the following line of his with amazement:

In revolution's wreath of thorns the year sixteen will come . . .

It is true that, in his impatience, he was a bit wrong: the revolution occurred a year later, but his was an immense impatience . . .

Old writers had their readers, but Mayakovsky, when composing his poems, imagines himself standing before large, listening crowds. In their very structure his poems appeal to a mass audience. He dreams of himself standing alone—like a wild, inspired giant—on a high platform, facing a raging or admiring crowd and carrying them away with his inspired cries . . . Sometimes he throws invectives at the crowd, calls them a "centi-headed louse," a "multi-boorish mug," a "mass-fleshy mob"; sometimes he spits in their faces . . . But all of the poet's writings are related to the masses only. He gratifies their desires, and that is the most important fact about the poet. In his best, most inspired works, one can hear a mass-meeting speaker. I do not mean this disparagingly. He is a cheeky poet, a shouting poet, a street, public poet, and this is what I like about him most of all. There would be no sense in calling him a writer: his calling is not writing but shouting his head off. He needs not paper but larynx. He is what a poet of the revolution ought to be. He is Isaiah in the guise of an Apache. Through his throat the revolutionary street is shouting, and who is there to blame if he is sometimes as vulgar as a street brawler and as elementary as a shot? . . .

Occasionally it seems that Mayakovsky's poems, in spite of the pictur-esque flamboyancy of his images, depict a poor and monotonous pattern of poor and monotonous thinking, always the same, repeating itself like a pattern on wallpaper. Does not the scarcity of literary effect testify to the author's psychological poverty? Does not the simplicity of style hide the simplicity of soul? . . .

It is hard to be a Mayakovsky. To write something new every day, something peculiar, amazing, eccentric, sensational—there is no sufficient strength for that in any man. Of course, a street poet cannot do otherwise, but is it easy to amaze, move, shatter day after day? No. Not only is it not easy but it is also risky. In art it is a most dangerous thing. At first it seems all right, but let this become a constant occupation, and the greatest of talents will not survive it . . .

It looks as if all Russia has now divided herself into the Akhmatovas and the Mayakovskys. There is a gap of thousands of years between these people. And they hate one another.

Akhmatova and Mayakovsky are as hostile to each other as the times that made them. Akhmatova is an assiduous inheritor of all the most valuable prerevolutionary treasures of Russian literary culture. She has many ancestors: Pushkin, Boratynsky, and Annyensky among them. She has that elegance of spirit and the charm that one acquires through centuries of cultural tradition. Mayakovsky, on the other hand, in every line, in every letter, is a product of the present revolutionary era, focuses in himself its beliefs, shouts, and falls into ecstasies. He has no ancestors. He is his own ancestor, and if there is a strength in him, it will belong to his descendants. Before him is the glorious future of many centuries. Akhmatova has kept the old Russian faith in God. Mayakovsky, like a true bard of the revolution, is a sacrilegious blasphemer. For her, the most sacred value is Russia, the motherland, "our soil." He, like a true bard of the revolution, is an internationalist, a citizen of the world, who treats with indifference the "snowy monster," the motherland, and loves the whole man-made planet, the world. She is a silent recluse, always in a hermitage, in stillness . . . He is in the street, at a mass meeting, in a crowd; he is himself a crowd . . .

In other words, the difference between these two—good or bad—poets is not a chance one; they are as different as two elements, two incarnations of gigantic historic forces, and let each man decide for himself which of these two poles he is to join, which to reject, and which to love.

I can say of myself only that . . . to my surprise, I love both of them: Akhmatova and Mayakovsky; they are both close to me. The question: Akhmatova or Mayakovsky? does not exist for me. I love both the cultural, quiet, old Russia impersonated by Akhmatova and the plebeian, violent, bravura-thundering Russia of the street impersonated by Mayakovsky. For me those elements are not mutually exclusive but complement each other; they are both equally necessary.

I think the time has come for a synthesis of both these elements . . .

FROM A REVIEW OF THE PRECEDING ARTICLE
BY ANATOL LUNACHARSKY, PUBLISHED IN
"PYECHAT' I REVOLUTSYIA," NO. 2, 1921:

This is excellently written and, in many respects, very true, but not in the most important way. The hermit Akhmatova can, I suppose, be regarded as a typical representative of the old world . . . Mayakovsky, however, does not represent new Russia; it is simply ridiculous to say this. Mayakovsky is recognized (and rightly so) by some of our youth and our proletariat. He is, of course, a very outstanding phenomenon, but not a model figure. A great many proletarian writers, whom Mayakovsky looks down upon—without any objective reasons—do not recognize him, and only some of them have borrowed certain formal innovations from him. The party as such, the Communist party, which is the main builder of the new life, treats coolly, and even in a hostile manner, not only Mayakovsky's early works but even those in which he presents himself as a herald of communism. Not to mention the fact that to christen all new Russia as "Mayakovshchina" means to narrow the dimensions considerably. Chukovsky, trying to find an objective approach to Mayakovsky, as he alleges, narrows himself too much . . .

Mayakovsky as a thinker is not an eagle, and he is all for effect, though he goes about it in a different way from Igor Syevyeryanin. Can we say, however, that Mayakovsky finds it difficult to be Mayakovsky? Is it not clear to any objective observer that Mayakovsky has immense resources of images and words? Writing flows out of him as water from a fountain or a hot spring. He finds it very easy to be himself. He is elemental. If Chukovsky did not sense this, then he sensed nothing about Mayakovsky . . . I object to his idea of old Russia, with the quiet and elegant Akhmatova as her symbolic representative, being opposed by a new Russia under the name of Mayakovshchina. One must not, however (to devalue the flag by denigrating its bearer), treat Mayakovsky simply as a not very talented boor with a strong throat . . .

LENIN'S NOTE TO LUNACHARSKY, MAY 6, 1921:

Aren't you ashamed to vote for the publication of 5,000 copies of Mayakovsky's "150 Million"?

This is absurd, stupid, monstrously stupid, and pretentious.

In my opinion only one in ten of such pieces should be printed and *not more than* 1,500 copies for libraries and eccentrics.

And Lunacharsky should be whipped for futurism.

Lenin

ON THE REVERSE SIDE—LUNACHARSKY'S REPLY:

I did not particularly like that piece, but (1) such an eminent poet as Bryusov was enthusiastic and asked for 20,000 copies to be printed; (2) when read by the author himself, the piece was clearly successful, and with workers at that.

LETTER FROM LENIN TO MIKHAIL POKROVSKY, WHO DEALT WITH
GOSIZDAT ON THE PARTY'S BEHALF:

Comrade Pokrovsky! Again and again I ask your help against futurism, etc.

(1) Lunacharsky (alas!) got the committee to approve the publication of Mayakovsky's "150 Million."

Can this be prevented? This must be prevented. Let us say we will publish those futurists not more often than twice a year and *not more than* 1,500 copies.

(2) Kisyelis, who they say is a "realist" painter, has again been thrown out by Lunacharsky, who favored a futurist, directly and *indirectly*.

Could not *anti*-futurists be found on whom one might rely?

Lenin

NIKOLAI MYESHCHERYAKOV, CHIEF EDITOR OF GOSIZDAT:

I recall a very interesting fact. When Mayakovsky's poem "150 Million" was published, the author took a copy, inscribed it, "To Comrade Lenin. With Com-Fut greetings. Vladimir Mayakovsky," and sent it to him. Lenin was a very agile man, interested in everything, bold. He read the poem and said, "You know, this is a most interesting piece of work. A peculiar brand of communism. It is hooligan communism."

ANCHAR'S REVIEW OF "150 MILLION" IN THE MONTHLY
"KRASNAYA NOV," NO. 2, 1921:

The reader who is little versed in poetry will not know who the author of this book is. Let us reveal the secret. The book was written by the well-known Vladimir Mayakovsky.

"One hundred fifty million speak through my lips." (That is why Mayakovsky did not print his name in the book.)

Let us begin by saying that . . . we have serious doubts on this subject.

The 150 million people of Soviet Russia have enough lips of their own with which to speak about themselves; they also have more thoughts, more freshness, more political substance, and—most important of all—a stricter, simpler, and clearer, approach to life, even although it varies from the point of view of class . . .

This is Mayakovsky the individualist, who for his own justification wants to drag 150 million "Ivans" by the hair, because (as Mayakovsky knows very well) such a support is advantageous . . . And it is easy to understand why Mayakovsky says that it is not supposed to be *his* poem, but through him 150 million are speaking.

We, on the other hand, consider the author and speaker of the poem to be Vladimir Mayakovsky, an individual not connected with the 150 million, because . . . Mayakovsky does not and cannot understand revolution. And this is the only thing he can astound us by.

Let Mayakovsky shout the most revolutionary words, let him show his contempt for the world's bourgeoisie, let him ridicule it, because he does it with gusto and wit. But in spite of all this, he will remain a typical product of narrow, individualistic reception and elucidation of the revolution . . . The poet of the revolution should sound in unison with the revolution, and this is possible only when he is organically connected with it, instead of being joined to it as a fringe witness of its achievements. Such a witness is Mayakovsky . . .

FROM A. HORNFELD'S ARTICLE "CULTURE AND LITTLE CULTURE"
IN THE PERIODICAL "LYETOPIS DOMA LITIERATOROV,"
NO. 1, 1921:

There is no modesty in this kind of anonymity. Everyone would be flattered by saying, "I have not invented this; 150 million Russian citizens speak through my lips" . . .

No matter how Mayakovsky strains himself shouting, how he strives for street-corner brutality and aims at amazing us with hooliganism, he is not brutal but peaceful, cultured, and well-behaved. His audience is not that of mass meetings but of connoisseurs; he is appreciated not by Ivans but by the intelligentsia. With all his abuses shouted at the "little culture," he is not to be thought of, and indeed, unnecessarily, outside its context and its general line of development . . .

FROM MARINA TSVYETAYEVA'S LETTER TO ANNA AKHMATOVA, IN CONNECTION WITH A RUMOR ABOUT AKHMATOVA'S SUICIDE, AUGUST 31, 1921 (PUBLISHED IN THE MONTHLY "NOVY MIR," NO. 4, 1969):

. . . For days dismal rumors concerning you have been circulated, ever more persistent and seemingly irrefutable. I am writing about this, because I know the news would reach you anyway, and I want it to reach you in the right way. I will tell you that among poets, as far as I know, your only friend ("friend" means action!) turns out to be Mayakovsky, who, looking like a slaughtered bull, walked around the cardboard "Poets' Café." *Killed with despair*—really, that is what he looked like. He also sent, through friends, a cable asking about you, and it is *to him* that I am indebted for the joy of receiving news about you . . .

FROM MAYAKOVSKY'S LETTER TO THE LEGAL DEPARTMENT OF THE MOSCOW TRADE UNION COUNCIL (MGSPS), AUGUST 6, 1921:

. . . A year ago the Central Arts Committee, chaired by the People's Commissar, discussed the theater program for the October celebrations and considered *Mystery-Bouffe* as one of the best and leading plays of the communist repertoire . . . The Theater Department of the Central Committee for Political Education . . . sent instructions for a speedy publication of the play to Gosizdat. On April 2, I received an extract from the protocol, with the decision, "Put aside for reasons of paper shortage," and with the note, "The book has not been reviewed." I told Citizen Veys that to use the shortage of paper as an argument is irrelevant, because, firstly, Gosizdat finds enough paper to print the most awful trash . . . secondly, 100,000 copies of that trash are published. *Mystery*, on the other hand, could be published in a limited edition—solely for the requirements of the theaters . . . Citizen Veys replied that "of course, for a particularly important piece paper could be scraped together somewhere, but we do not take such a view about *Mystery* and we are generally opposed to this kind of writing." "But," I asked him, "how do you know that my play is unimportant if you didn't have it reviewed, and if an opinion about the play has been formed before reading it, why the comedy with the commission?" I was not honored with a reply.

. . . The editor of *Vyestnik Teatra*, Comrade Zagorsky, offered to publish the play in his periodical, which on a number of occasions printed revolutionary plays . . . Comrades Myeshcheryakov and Veys told me that we should all be put before the Revolutionary Tribunal for unlawful publication of *Mystery* and that the matter would be considered by the Gosizdat committee . . . When I went to Gosizdat for some information one week later, a new surprise awaited me: Having come to the conclusion that it is difficult to prosecute for the publication of a revolutionary play, printed quite legally on paper given to the periodical, which published a double issue for the purpose, the committee tried a new way to discourage me from writing and trying to have my work published. On the pay list the following was written: "The Administrative Committee, 15/7: Instruct the Finance Department to check the list against normal rates and to pay for all but Mayakovsky's play *Mystery-Bouffe*, 18/7" [signatures].

. . . Comrade Bogomolov telephoned Citizen Veys to give his reasons for refusing payment. Citizen Veys (I repeat, after Comrade Bogomolov) replied in a most irritated tone that the publication of the play had been forbidden [postponed for shortage of paper—could it be a ban?!—V. M.], that it had been published by a trick, and that no payment was due . . . Comrade Bogomolov stated that, none the less, work done had to be paid for, and one could possibly prosecute for illegal publishing. It is the duty of a trade union to protect the interests of workers. Citizen Veys replied, "As far as *Mystery-Bouffe* is concerned, Mayakovsky does not deserve to be called a worker in the least," and threw down the receiver . . .

Having wasted one and a half months on inquiries about the publication of the play and two and a half months on going after my fee, I must give up this occupation, since I have other things to do. In view of the fact that the Gosizdat directors, firstly, do not want to recognize the existing laws about pay for work done; secondly, are following their private inclinations in this matter, which is intolerable in the republic's institutions; thirdly, such private inclinations are harmful to the development of literature in the republic; fourthly, the persons administrating Gosizdat show in their choice of literary works for publication a total professional illiteracy, not to be reconciled with their responsible positions; fifthly, Gosizdat is adamant in its illiteracy, sabotaging the publication of high quality literature, ignoring even the demands of the working masses; sixthly, the form of their replies to justified questions is clearly offensive both for the inquiring trade union and for myself, a working man protected by the union—I ask you to examine this matter, to compel the State Publishing House to pay me for my work, and to take legal steps against the Gosizdat directors, in accordance with the six points I have mentioned . . .

FROM MAYAKOVSKY'S LETTER TO NIKOLAI CHUZHAK-NASIMOVICH, EDITOR OF THE PERIODICAL "TVORCHESTVO" IN CHIT, SECOND HALF OF AUGUST 1921:

Dear Comrade Chuzhak!

To your jocular question, "How does Mayakovsky fare and work," I reply as follows: The thing here is to fight one another so hard that slaps resound in the air. There can hardly be any work done: these struggles, propaganda work, etc., take everything out of me, including my liver. To illustrate this I enclose a copy of my letter to MGSPS concerning Gosizdat. Twenty-fifth Disciplinary Tribunal. The accused—Gosizdat (Veys, Mye-shcheryakov, and Skvortsov). The accuser—myself . . . Do not think that what I have said in my statement is an exceptional case; there are thousands of such cases. It was like that, or worse, with "150 Million." I was on a wild goose chase for about nine or ten months . . . But all these are trifles. The most important thing is that we are winning. The number of our followers grows. Everyone who is opposed to us, is so shallow and stupid that everyone who does not have a vested interest in annihilating us comes over to our side . . .

A NOTE IN THE JOURNAL "KOMMUNISTICHESKYI TRUD," AUGUST 31, 1921:

No Mystery at All

Mayakovsky was extremely lucky: *Mystery-Bouffe* made quite a lot of noise. To tell the truth, it was a rather scandalous noise . . . But there are people to whom noise and scandal are useful as good publicity.

Mayakovsky wanted to have his *Mystery* published at any price. . . .

Gosizdat, as was to be expected, refused. Gosizdat has many sins on its conscience, but much will be forgiven, because on this occasion it paused in time and avoided making a mistake.

The energetic author, however, did not restrain himself and, finding the front door locked, knocked at the back door of the reformed, re-shuffled editorial board of *Vyestnik Teatra,* an organ of the same Gosiz-dat. The watchful eyes of Gosizdat's workers do not reach as far as the periodical's editorial board . . . and *Vyestnik* published *Mystery* as its special issue.

Having pushed his manuscript through the back door, the author went to Gosizdat through the front entrance to claim his fee, but was again shown the door.

"So much the better! Gosizdat's fees are small, but this incident can be used for big publicity!" And he did use it. He turned to the disciplinary tribunal of the relevant union.

The union accepted the case for consideration and, overstepping its bounds, gave a verdict in which Mayakovsky's property rights and his talent were defended.

What publicity for a fashionable play! If he managed to write *Mystery-Bouffe* for the theater, why not try to bring buffoonery into life?

                                                                            N.O.

L. SOSNOVSKY'S ARTICLE "ENOUGH OF MAYAKOVSHCHINA" "PRAVDA," SEPTEMBER 8, 1921:

It was difficult to believe one's eyes when reading about this event in the newspapers.

In the dock were seated Communists from Gosizdat, our aged Com-rade Skvortsov-Styepanov among them. Posing as accuser was the futurist Mayakovsky.

Mayakovsky charged Skvortsov with having refused payment at Gosiz-dat for some futurist nonsense published in a theater magazine.

And the judges . . . sentenced Styepanov to six months' suspension from membership in the union.

Thus a revolutionary of old standing cannot be a member of a proletar-ian union, but futurist Mayakovsky can. He can do everything he wants.

In my opinion this episode has gone too far. We are good-hearted and patient people. But we will not let anyone smear our gates with tar.

Mr. Mayakovsky is indignant that he has not been paid for the publication of his play. Let a commission composed of workers examine real fees of our nonchalant poets and futurist painters to find out with whom they really deal.

Have you seen at the ROSTA exhibition in Tverskaya the colored posters, supposedly revolutionary, which were exhibited there? Fortunately they are not there any more. But until recently they offended our eyes daily. Whom did they please?

They pleased the futurist gentlemen. For it was they who received fantastic fees for them . . .

The provinces got infected too. Too clever fellows were found there, imitators of Mayakovsky, overgrown oafs, without any knowledge of painting and without any desire to paint, but with a great desire to "consume" at the highest rate.

Having received a slice of Mayakovshchina from Moscow, they decide to snatch their bread and butter the same way.

Dabble, dabble paint on paper. The poster is said to be finished.

It is terrible to think how much money has been squandered through the youthfulness and stupidity of our Mayakovshchina.

And now those comrades, who are not inclined to lightheaded squandering of the meager funds of a poor country, are put in the dock and an attempt is made to discredit them by having them expelled from the union.

You must be joking, futurist gentlemen.

We will endeavor to compel you to stop these improper jokes, which are too expensive for the republic. We hope that soon Mayakovshchina will be sitting in the dock . . .

FROM LETTERS TO LILA BRIK, OCTOBER–NOVEMBER 1921:

My dear, my dearest, my beloved, my adored Lila!

. . . Do not forget me, by the love of God, I love you a million times more than all the others put together. I do not want to see anyone, talk to anyone, only you. The most joyful day in my life will be the day of your return. Love me, child . . .

Dear Lila! Kind Lila! Marvelous Lila!

I received your loving letters at last and a load was lifted from my heart at once. (In the past days I went about so sullen that everyone kept asking what was happening to me. I hung around bars, saw some acquaintances, and returned even more sullen. Now I am more quiet.) I was particularly anxious because you did not write anything about yourself. I was convinced *that you had reasons not to write about yourself.*

I spent the day of your birthday magnificently. All day long I thought about Pussy . . . Then I walked for a long time around the boulevards; there was a telescope on the Tversky and I looked at the old moon for a long time—I don't know why. I asked them to direct it at Riga—they told me they couldn't . . .

I am writing badly—can't be helped . . .

My kind, dear and beloved Lila!

I am your puppy, still the same, I only live thinking about you, I am waiting for you and adore you.

Every morning I come to Osya and say, "It's sad, brother, without Lila," and Osya says, "It's sad, brother Puppy, without Pussy."

We have received your parcel with tea, chocolate, and oats. Thank you, child . . .

150 million kisses . . .

On March 5, 1922, Mayakovsky's satire on "meeting addicts," bursting with apparent activity appeared in Izvestya. *The poem was approved for publication by the editorial secretary Osaf Litovsky in the absence of the chief editor Styeklov, who was opposed to Mayakovsky and to his writings.*

FROM LENIN'S SPEECH AT THE METAL WORKERS' CONGRESS, MARCH 6, 1922:

Yesterday I came across a poem by Mayakovsky by chance in the *Izvestya* on a political theme. I do not count myself among the admirers of his poetic talent, though I fully admit my lack of competence in that sphere. But it is a long time since I have felt so satisfied from a political and administrative point of view. In that poem, the poet utterly derides meetings and mocks the Communists because they confer and debate all the time. I do not know whether it is good poetry, but I promise you he is absolutely right from a political point of view . . .

As always, I received from the secretariat all the ROSTA stencils which, according to their content, I sent to the various departments for study. Unexpectedly—it was in the evening and Styeklov was about to leave—Mayakovsky's name on one of the stencils . . . drew my attention. I turned the page and saw the title, "Lenin's speech to the Metal Workers' Congress Committee." I marked the stencil: "for Union Department." But what did this have to do with Mayakovsky? I then read through the bulletin . . . and marked with red pencil the passage where Vladimir Ilyich praised the poem "Meeting Addicts," then sent it to the editor through a messenger.

Styeklov left the editorial office without a word. And we, Mayakovsky admirers, mostly young people full of excitement, discussed the incident, telephoned Mayakovsky, made all sorts of plans . . .

On the following day, as if nothing had happened, I went into the editor's room to plan the next issue of the journal. When we had finished, I got up and made my way to the door. There Styeklov stopped me. Looking not at me but through the window, Styeklov said, "It would be a good idea to publish some other poem on the struggle against bureaucracy."

"So it would," I replied, "But whom should we ask for it?"

"Well, what do *you* think?" asked the editor.

"I don't know . . ." I began to mention all sorts of poets, those who did and those who did not publish in *Izvestya*, but carefully omitted Mayakovsky's name.

Styeklov was silent but his eyes were white with rage: he realized I was poking fun at him.

Mayakovsky's name was finally uttered. Neither during our conversation nor at any later time, however, did Styeklov define with a single word his relation to Mayakovsky's published poems . . .

🦋

In the years 1922–1923 Mayakovsky published over thirty pieces of poetry and prose in Izvestya.

⚜ 21 ⚜

Leave-Takings

⚑

*In the period of stabilization critics speak about the end of
futurism. Mayakovsky becomes ever more isolated. David
Burliuk has gone abroad. Now—after Boris Pasternak—Sergei Spassky no longer understands his friends; Katarina Nizen,
a former participant of the futurist almanacs, confesses her
disappointment with "the public's poet"; Gorki no longer sym-
pathizes with Mayakovsky. Khlebnikov dies. Dead too is a
great poet whom Mayakovsky was never able to befriend but
whose presence he clearly felt just as the other, thirteen years
his senior, felt his presence—Alexander Blok. Mayakovsky
writes articles about the dead poets and gives expression to his
longing for a world which will overcome human pettiness and
death.*

VICTOR SHKLOVSKY:

It is difficult to say how the year 1921 was different from 1919 and 1918. In the early years of the revolution there was no existence, or rather, the storm itself was existence. There was no man of caliber who did not go through a period of faith in the revolution. One believed in the Bolsheviks. Germany and England would fall—and the frontiers that no one needed any more would be ploughed up. And heaven would be rolled up like a scroll of parchment . . .

We, many of us, were glad to have noticed that in the new Russia one could live without money . . .

But the gravity of worldly customs pulled the stone of life to the earth, thrown horizontally by the revolution . . .

KORNEL ZYELINSKY:

A utopian understanding of revolution, a romantic view of the inde-structible in order to change everything at once, as Blok wanted it, and an "unreal," existence of being constantly on the move—all this was rolled into one. Perhaps only the "chairman of the world," Velimir Khlebnikov, who was entirely immersed in it, wished for nothing else. All the others began to organize their existence as they could . . .

SPASSKY:

Burliuk was preparing himself to go on his way. Spring. Time to pick up a paintbrush. He carefully filled a heavy trunk with the books he had bought for his family. Cuttings from newspapers, posters, and all kinds of mementos of the season which had just passed also disappeared into the trunk. And huge stocks of paints as well, with which Burliuk would gener-ously cover his canvases . . .

He did not guess then that he would never return to the city which was so close to him. The war cut Russia into segments. Burliuk found himself on White territory. Unable to cross into RSFSR, fearing persecutions from the Whites for futurism, Burliuk went with his family to Japan . . .

BURLIUK:

. . . with my sister Marianna and the writer Chetverikov, I was earning money by lecturing on futurist poetry and modern art, and with art exhibi-tions in the towns of Siberia . . . In 1920 I came to Japan as a famous poet-artist . . . on the Japanese gunboat *Chikusen Maru* . . . In August

1922, Marussia and I with our two sons left Kobe via Canada for the United States (New York City).*

FROM IVANOV-RAZUMNIK'S BOOK "VLADIMIR MAYAKOVSKY:
MYSTERY OR BOUFFE?," PUBLISHED IN BERLIN (1922):

The heroic period over, the bourgeois public has been dazzled enough; before us—futurism tamed, domesticated, eating out of hand . . . "The word has meaning!"—This is the measure of treason against itself that has been reached by futurism, which once meant a revolution of form; external revolution came and futurism buttoned up its officially recognized uniform.

A tiny detail: it is worth comparing Mayakovsky's poems published in individual futurist collections in the years 1912 to 1915 . . . with the same poems collected in his book *Simple as Mooing.* How he has tidied himself up with punctuation marks, assumed an everyday appearance, given up those innocent puzzles (so irritating for some reason to Lady Public), drawn out the lines in proper rows . . .

Futurism does not wish to cover up its meanings anymore with the unnecessary shell of tricks. "No one who has lighted a candle will cover it up with a jar"—this is an old truism; and futurists are convinced that they have lighted a candle . . .

KATARINA GURO (NIZEN) IN THE PERIODICAL "SIEGODNIA,"
NO. 7, 1922:

A fat book is lying on my table, but I have no wish to cut its pages. The weary cover is bored with itself . . .

And why so fat? There are only about 160–200 pages of Mayakovsky in it. And the rest? So many Australians, Abyssinians, Neguses, Wilsons. And a strange thing—one can clearly sense the public in them. The same public about whom Mayakovsky used to say:

> In an hour your bursting ex-man's fat
> will flow from here into the clean alley.

"And if today, I, the brutal Hun, will not play the clown for you?" But now the Hun will not spit. Now one waits for the public. All those

---

* The above fragment was taken from the original English version, by D. & M. Burliuk, *Color and Rhyme*, No. 31, 1956.

Australians—all that journalistic sensationalism gets in the way and fiddles in order to direct attention to itself.

It is bad that after thirteen years of work a book of weariness has been published . . . Is it the revolution come into its own or *Mystery-Bouffe?* . . . Well then? Is he finished? I do not think so. One wet night, while waiting for a train on a chance station . . . he will again be embraced by the infinite. And again he will desire to be nobody in the line of success, nobody except himself.

OSIP MANDELSHTAM IN THE MONTHLY "ROSSIYA,"
NO. 2, 1922:

Mayakovsky is solving here the fundamental and great problem of "poetry for all, not for the chosen." Extensive widening of the field of poetry takes place, of course, at the expense of poetic culture, its intensity and substance. Intimately familiar with the richness and complexities of world poetry, Mayakovsky, when embarking on his "poetry for all," had to send all that was obscure to the devil, that is, all that presupposed a minimum of poetic knowledge on the part of the listener. But to address in poetry an audience altogether unprepared for it is just as ungrateful a task as to have oneself impaled. A totally unprepared listener will not understand anything at all, or, alternatively, a poetry liberated from all culture will cease to be poetry, and only then, through a strange peculiarity of human nature, will become accessible to countless numbers of listeners. Mayakovsky, however, writes poems, mostly cultural poems at that . . . It is a pity, therefore, that he so impoverishes himself . . .

FROM IVAN AXYONOV'S ARTICLE "REGARDING THE ABOLITION OF
FUTURISM," IN THE BI-MONTHLY "PYECHAT' I REVOLUTSYIA,"
NOVEMBER–DECEMBER 1921:

Technically and formally, poetry has become futuristic.

The situation of futurism nonetheless recalls the situation of its enemy symbolism, after 1906 or 1907, to the point of being ridiculous. Futurism has been recognized by all but the very same people who, at that time, did not recognize futurism's predecessor; futurism has been made popular to the same degree that symbolism was then; but like symbolism, it is factionally splintered away; within its own circle emerge groups of poets who are superficially identical with it in technique, pretending to the title of new schools . . . and clearly showing that futurism has ceased to exist, as a literary sect and is in the process of decomposing as a literary movement.

FROM VASSILI BRYUSOV'S ACCOUNT OF LITERATURE IN THE HALF-DECADE 1917–1922, ENTITLED "YESTERDAY, TODAY AND TOMORROW," IN THE PERIODICAL "PYECHAT' I REVOLUTSYIA," SEPTEMBER–OCTOBER 1922:

Within five years, the poetic tendencies of the right have revealed their total impotence. The symbolists gradually disappeared from the stage: some of the principal exponents of that school died . . . others became almost silent . . . still others lost all importance as poets. The acmeists, who had evolved from the symbolists, found themselves outside the mainstream of literature as fringe priests of "pure art" (O. Mandelshtam and others).

The main representatives of the past five years are the futurists and the followers of trends which evolved from futurism. Among those, all whose ideology had been based on extreme individualism (ego-futurists, etc.) have perished. Those who survived and developed were able to accept the spirit of revolution to some degree (Mayakovsky, Khlebnikov, Asyeyev, Tretyakov, Pasternak, and others). On the other hand, the imaginists (Shershenyevich and others), less sensitive on that score, originally came to the fore and then were pushed to the background. The basic task of futurism was to realize in practice the principle that language, as the material of poetry, is subject to treatment by the poet. Futurism has realized this principle in theory and in practice and with this achievement one can also regard its role in Russian literature as complete.

SPASSKY:

In 1921 I came to Moscow in a rather vague mood. It would have been natural to go at once to see Mayakovsky. But now I could not unreservedly accept all his ideas. Shortly before he had called for museums to be shelled, Pushkins to be toppled, and Raphael and Rastrelli to be shot. It is easy now to pass over the extremities of futurism . . . In those days one reacted differently to many things.

I also made the mistake of not taking into consideration the fact that in the time I had spent away from Moscow, the circle of poets had become sharply divided. My literary evening took place at the café "Bom," the headquarters of the imaginists. I appeared there by chance, on the basis of my personal acquaintance with some members of that group. Soon even these relations were decisively broken. Mayakovsky, however, learned about my evening there. I met him in the Arbat.

"Greetings, Mr. Imaginist Spassky."

I could feel he was displeased.

Even so he gave me his address. I went to the Briks' apartment in Vodopyanyi Alley.

Mayakovsky, walking around the room, looked at me askance. I talked to Brik and told him what I was doing. I explained my involved theories to him: that futurism had had its day and that the period of polemics with the past was over. I proposed a synthesis of futurism with the classics. Mayakovsky stretched out on the divan. He was tired and sullen. "That means we are going to have something like academic futurism," he roared without looking at me.

And that was that. Kamensky arrived and recited his poem "Juggler," which consists of irrational fireworks of sound. I took leave of the company and went out to the street. From that time on I observed Mayakovsky from outside only.

SHKLOVSKY:

Gorki is seated at the table. Presiding over the table is Maria Fyodorovna Andreyeva, very beautiful, though no longer young. A samovar is standing in front of her.

. . . I used to come here quite often. Larissa Reisner came with her exciting stories . . . Later Maria Budberg—a wise and also beautiful woman—made her appearance. The painter Mme Khodasyevich was there. And Gorki's son, Maxim Pyeshkov, used to come . . .

Only a short time ago Volodya was very friendly with Gorki. Gorki played cards with the Briks . . .

And then we learned that Gorki had been told that Volodya had harmed a woman.

I went to Alexei Maximovich with Lila Brik.

The conversation, naturally, was unpleasant for Gorki; he thumped his fingers at the table, saying, "I don't know, I don't know, it was a very respectable comrade who told me that. I will give you his name when it is given to me."

Lila Brik looked at Gorki with a frantic smile.

The comrade's name was not given to Alexei Maximovich, and Gorki wrote a few words on the reverse side of Lila Brik's letter to the effect that he would find out who had said that.

Everyone thought an explanation would be possible, that we would find the contact.

It did not come to an understanding.

A new man will come, the huge rooms will fill with warmth, flags will be put out, a new life will come for mankind, battles will be excused and forgiven . . .

If that man comes into Alexei Maximovich's study, the writer will rise, move his hand over his not yet gray crewcut, smile with his blue eyes, make room for the new newcomer, and make a fire so that the guest can warm himself.

Alexei Maximovich is waiting. He has already seen the young, red-bearded Vsyevolod Ivanov, the stooping Izaak Babel; corresponded with Fyedin; befriended Zoshchenko (who had a dark complexion, soft voice, and attentive look); he knew Blok and had discussions with him.

He had liked and ceased to like and quarreled with, had recognized and ceased to recognize Mayakovsky. For even the most avid expectation of something can fail one.

CHUKOVSKY:

. . . Early in 1920 a mysterious, incurable infirmity began to consume Blok, a disease which soon took him to his grave. We saw his deep sadness and did not realize it was the sadness of a dying man. The last time he was with me in Moscow, he read a cycle of poems at the Press House, and was followed on the platform by some wild "bard," who began to argue that Blok was already dead as a poet: "I ask you, where is the dynamics here? They are a dead man's poems, written by a corpse."

Blok leaned toward me and said, "It's true."

And though I could not see him, I could sense that behind my back he was smiling: "That man is right: I have died . . ."

I asked Blok why he did not write any more poetry. He always gave me the same answer: "All sounds have stopped. Can't you hear that there are no longer any sounds? . . ."

The speech about Pushkin, which he made in 1921, was a total condemnation of the mob. I heard that dying speech of his and remember the
angry melancholy with which he spoke about his old enemy, the mob
which had destroyed Pushkin . . .

"I close my eyes so as not to see those apes," he told me once in a
streetcar.

"Are they apes?"

"As if you didn't know," he said wearily and reproachfully.

SHKLOVSKY:

A woman Mayakovsky was in love with asked him to bring her an autographed book by Blok . . . Blok willingly autographed a book entitled
Gray Morning. Mayakovsky took the book from Blok and was about to go
out. They were standing there, facing each other, knowing each other very
well, ready for mutual sacrifices.

"Since you have come, we could have a chat," said Blok.

Mayakovsky's reply was typical of a very young man: "Haven't got
time; she's waiting for the autograph."

"It's good when love won't let a man have time, forces him to hurry.
But it is a pity we have no time for each other."

This story was told to me with sadness by Vladimir Vladimirovich himself . . .

NIKULIN:

In the spring of 1921 Blok came to Moscow and read his "Retaliation" in
the big auditorium of the Polytechnic Museum.

On the following day I met Vladimir Vladimirovich at lunch in a restaurant at Velikaya Dmitrovka.

"Did you go there last night? What did he read?" asked Mayakovsky.
He said this in such a way that the question could only concern Blok.

" 'Retaliation' and other pieces."

"A success, of course. Though there is no other poet who reads so
badly . . ."

After a short silence he took a pencil, wrote two rows of figures on a
paper napkin, then divided them with a vertical line. Pointing to the figures, he said, "I have five good poems, three so-so, and two bad ones, out

of ten. Blok has eight bad poems and two good ones out of ten, but those two are better than I could ever write."

And, lost in thought, he crumpled the napkin.

BORIS PASTERNAK:

On that day Blok recited his poems in three places: the Polytechnic Museum, the Press House, and the Dante Alighieri Society, where his most ardent followers gathered and where he read his *Italian Poems.*

Mayakovsky was present at the Polytechnic Museum. In the course of the evening, he told me that an anti-Blok demonstration, booing, etc., was in the offing at the Press House, under the pretext of critical incorruptibility. He suggested that the two of us go there and prevent that villainy.

We left at once, but we walked, while Blok was taken to the place of his next appointment by car. By the time we reached Nikitsky Boulevard, where the Press House was situated, the event was over, and Blok went on to the Society of Lovers of Italian Literature. The scandal we had feared had taken place. After Blok had recited at the Press House, a lot of monstrous things were said to him. They did not shrink from telling him to his face that he had outlived his time and that he was inwardly dead. He quietly accepted all this. That incident occurred just a few months before his death.

SHKLOVSKY:

Blok was growing weaker all the time. Gorki tried to obtain permission for the poet to go to Germany, where he could not only undergo treatment but also eat properly. Alexei Maximovich already had the beginnings of scurvy himself . . .

Blok spent his days in bed . . .

He died in the fall . . . The funeral was attended by few people. Emaciated horses slowly pulled the coffin through the city . . . There were no speeches over the grave. Andrey Bely stood holding onto a birch tree, looking with his large, wide, almost square eyes at the open grave . . . On the way people often asked us, "Whose funeral?"

"Blok's," we replied.

Inevitably, the next question uttered, as if they wanted to be reassured beyond doubt about something they knew, was, "Henry Blok's?"

Henry Blok was a banker of moderate means, who was widely publicized in old Petersburg, then went bankrupt and hanged himself. He died a fairly long time ago, but Henry Blok's name could still be seen on enamel signposts and remained in people's memories.

MAYAKOVSKY'S ARTICLE IN THE NEWSPAPER "AGIT-ROSTA," NO. 14, AUGUST 10, 1921:

Alexander Blok Is Dead

The writings of Alexander Blok cover a whole era in poetry, the era of the recent past.

An excellent master-symbolist, Blok greatly influenced modern poetry.

Some still cannot free themselves from the spell of his poetry. They take some word from Blok and develop it for pages and pages, constructing all their poetic wealth upon it. Others, who had passed beyond his early Romanticism, declared poetic war on him and, having swept the remnants of symbolism from their souls, lay the foundations of new rhythms, piled up the stones of new images, fastened their stanzas with new rhymes; they have undertaken the heroic effort of creating the poetry of the future. But all remember Blok with equal affection.

Blok approached our great revolution honestly and enthusiastically; it was not possible, however, for the subtle, refined words of a symbolist to carry its most real and brutal images. In his famous poem "The Twelve," which has been translated into many languages, Blok overstrained himself.

I remember how, in the early days of the revolution, I passed a thin, stooping figure in a soldier's coat, warming himself by the fire near the Winter Palace. He called after me. It was Blok . . . I asked him, "Do you like it?" "It's pretty," Blok replied, and then added, "They've burnt my library in the country."

I listened to him this May in Moscow. In the half-empty auditorium, which was as silent as a cemetery, Blok was softly and sadly reading old poems about gypsy songs, about love, about a lovely lady—there was no way forward. There was only death. And it came.

SPASSKY:

When spring came, the disturbed aura around Khlebnikov began to get worse.

I did not deal with his affairs at that time, but it was clear they were not good. There were some obstacles; he could not get his book published, though he felt a great need to publish it.

I remember walking once through the dark, winding alleys of the Myasnitskaya to the Wchutemas house, where Khlebnikov was living. Just then I remarked, I do not know why, that it was time to put Khlebnikov's work in order. I said that it was all scattered, a number of brochures, lost in space. Where is it all? There is no book to speak of.

He reacted to this with unexpected passion. There was anxiety and excitement in what he was saying. He did not complain about any particular person. But he spoke about careless treatment of his manuscripts, about unrealized projects. He was reproachful of friends who did not support him in something or other.

In this period the people around Khlebnikov were trying to prejudice him against Mayakovsky.

In the spring Khlebnikov suddenly felt extremely tired. He would sit sulking in his brother's room. He would rush to the table, spread his manuscripts, panic, and sigh over them. He would rush to the Briks, full of anxious decisiveness. On one occasion he took me with him. He was in a hurry, as if anxious to explain something. In answer to the question from behind the door, he frantically shouted his name. The Briks were not in; Khlebnikov rushed on. It was as if he were looking for someone with whom he wanted to share some urgent reflections.

Sometime in May he moved out of his brother's apartment and left Moscow.

In the summer news came of his death.

MAYAKOVSKY'S ARTICLE IN THE MONTHLY "KRASNAYA NOV,"
NO. 4, JULY–AUGUST 1922:

V. V. Khlebnikov

Victor Vladimirovich Khlebnikov has died.

Khlebnikov's poetic fame is infinitely smaller than his worth.

Fifty readers out of a hundred called him a scribbler, forty read him for pleasure and wondered why he failed them, and only ten (poet-futurists, philologists of "Opoyaz") knew and loved that Columbus of new lands of poetry, which we now populate and cultivate.

Khlebnikov is not a poet for consumers. He cannot just be read. Khlebnikov is a poet for producers.

Khlebnikov didn't write any long poems. Only his published pieces seem finished. The appearance of completeness was more often than not the work of his friends. From the heap of rough drafts, we chose what seemed to us the most valuable and took it to the printer. The tail of one sketch would quite often be attached to a strange head, to Khlebnikov's hilarious amazement. He could not be permitted to read proofs: he would cross everything out and replace it with an entirely new text . . .

Khlebnikov's life is identified with his dazzling verbal constructions. His life story is an example for poets and a reproach for poetic business-men.

Khlebnikov and the word.

For so-called modern poetry . . . particularly for the symbolists, the word is the material with which poems are written (the expression of feelings and of thoughts, material whose structure, resistance, and treat-ment are unknown.) The material was handled unconsciously in each par-ticular case . . . The shape of a word, as one found it, was regarded as permanent; one attempted to stretch it to embrace things which had out-grown the word.

For Khlebnikov the word is an independent force which shapes the material of emotions and thoughts. Hence his preoccupation with roots, with the time when the name corresponded with the thing . . .

I knew Khlebnikov for twelve years. He often came to Moscow and, except in the last days, we saw each other daily.

I was astounded with Khlebnikov's laboriousness. His otherwise empty room was always full of notebooks and loose sheets, large and small, filled with his small handwriting. Unless by some chance an almanac was being published and someone would snatch a sheet from the printer's pile, Khlebnikov, when setting out on a journey, would fill a pillowcase with his manuscripts and, on the way, sleep on that pillow, which he then lost.

Khlebnikov was very often on the move. It was impossible to foresee the reasons for or the dates of his trips. About three years ago I managed, with great difficulty, to arrange for the publication of his manuscripts, for which he was to be paid. . . . On the eve of the day he was to receive both the publication permit and the money, I met Khlebnikov carrying a small suitcase in Theater Square:

"Where?"—"To the south, spring has come! . . ." And he went.

He sat on the roof of a railway carriage. He traveled for two years, retreated and attacked with our army in Persia, caught typhoid again and again. He came back last winter in a carriage full of epileptics, emaciated and in rags, dressed in a hospital gown only.

He did not bring back a single line with him . . .

Khlebnikov was loved by all who knew him. It was, however, a love of healthy people for a healthy, highly-educated, and ingenious poet. He did not have any relatives capable of devoted attention. The illness made Khlebnikov demanding. He began to be suspicious of people who would not give him all their attention. He would interpret a chance opinion, which might not even refer to him, as a lack of recognition for his poetry, as a poetic slight of his person.

For the sake of preserving the proper literary perspective, I consider it my duty to state in black and white, on my own behalf and, this I do not doubt, on behalf of my friends Asyeyev, Burliuk, Kruchenykh, Kamensky, and Pasternak, that we regarded Khlebnikov, and we regard him still, as one of the masters in poetry and a splendid knight without blemish in our struggle for poetry.

After Khlebnikov's death, compassionate articles about him appeared in various newspapers and periodicals. I read them with revulsion. When at last is the comedy of posthumous serving of medicines going to end?! Where were the writers of those articles when the living Khlebnikov was treading about Russia and insulted by critics? I know some living men who are not so great as Khlebnikov, perhaps, but will meet with a similar fate.

It is time to put an end at last to the ceremonious centenary jubilees, to the veneration of posthumous editions. Write your articles for the living! Give bread for the living! Give paper for the living!

ROMAN JAKOBSON:

In the spring of 1920 I returned to the blockaded Moscow. I brought with me new European books and scientific news from the West. Mayakovsky asked me several times to repeat the complicated account of the general theory of relativity and the discussion raging about it at the time. The liberation of energy, problems of time, the question whether speed faster than light is not reverse movement in time—all this enthralled Mayakovsky. I seldom saw him so attentive and impressed. "Don't you think," he asked suddenly, "that in this way we will achieve immortality?" I looked at him with amazement and mumbled something incredulously. To this, Mayakovsky moved his jaws with hypnotic obstinacy, a trait which was familiar to all who knew him well. "I am quite convinced that there will be no death. The dead will be resurrected. I will find a physicist who will explain to me Einstein's book, paragraph-by-paragraph. It is impossible that I should not understand. I would pay that physicist the salary of an academician." At this moment I discovered a quite new Mayakovsky, one who was dominated by the desire for victory over death. He soon told me that he was writing a poem, "The Fourth Internationale" (he later changed it to the "Fifth") and that all this would be in it. "Einstein will be a member of that internationale. This will be far more important than '150 Million.' " At that time Mayakovsky wanted to send Einstein a cable with greetings: for the science of the future from the art of the future. We never returned in our conversations to this subject. "The Fifth Internationale" was never completed.

⚜ 22 ⚜

"To Her and Myself"

⚜

At the turn of the years 1922 and 1923, Mayakovsky writes his greatest lyric poem. His letters and a footnote to them speak about the personal situation and spiritual state of the poet. Nikolai Asyeyev recalls the more general situation, connected with, among others, the New Economic Policy (NEP). The lyric hero of "About This" is besieged by doubles—one of them has come "from beyond the seven years," from the poem "Man." Near the end of the new poem the triumphant bourgeoisie shoots the hero. In the Epilogue the dream of immortality returns.

FROM FOOTNOTES TO MAYAKOVSKY'S LETTERS, PUBLISHED IN "LITERARY HERITAGE":

At the end of December 1922 . . . there occurred a disagreement between Lila Brik and Mayakovsky. They therefore decided, by mutual consent, to part for two months. At the root of the conflict were moral problems and questions regarding their personal relations, both of which were very painful and difficult to solve at that time. Mayakovsky spent exactly two months—from December 28, 1922, to February 28, 1923—in a "voluntary prison," in his room in Lubyansky Alley, seeing almost no one and leaving his house on business only. During those two months the poem "About This" . . . was written.

FROM NIKOLAI ASYEYEV'S COMMENTARY ON THE POEM
"ABOUT THIS":

. . . The waves of NEP were already rolling overboard in the revolutionary ship . . . It was very difficult to remain on board; one had to clench one's teeth and hold onto the balustrades in order not to be swept into the sea of obscurantism and philistinism. Many people with revolutionary pasts found themselves overboard. Many lives were broken by the pressure of growing contradictions. For Mayakovsky, as a revolutionary and as a poet who grasped the world with his senses, who strove to control his sensory reaction through intellectual purposefulness, it was doubly difficult to experience and think all this through . . .

At that time, all the leading exponents of avant-garde art, who were active in different parts of the union, gathered in the center but were not utilized to full advantage in practical revolutionary work, except in a fragmentary way, according to their personal understanding and capabilities . . . The honesty of those people, who were the first artists to have reacted positively to the appeal for the participation of the intelligentsia in the October Revolution, was considered suspect and their value was constantly questioned . . .

Excessive fatigue resulting from barren efforts, from all those side effects of an artist's existence . . . weakened the alertness of Mayakovsky's temperament. It was then that his need for a self-critical estimation of his strength, of his potential and sense of purpose, grew and resulted in the poem "About This" . . .

Its roots reached well into the past, went "from beyond the seven years," from the prerevolutionary year 1916, when the poem "Man" was written . . .

The dynamite with which Mayakovsky exploded the bastions of petty bourgeois existence was love, the relations between "him" and "her." But the force of the explosion went far beyond the reach of the rays of its visible radiation . . .

Lilek!

I see you have irrevocably decided. I know that my insistence is painful to you. Still, what happened with me today is too terrible not to make me try to grasp at a straw—this letter.

I have never felt so bad . . . Once, when you chased me away, I believed in our meeting again. Now I feel I have been entirely separated from life, that nothing more will ever be. Without you there is no life. I have always said so, always known. Now I feel this, I feel this with all my being. Everything, everything I thought about with pleasure is now worthless, loathsome.

I am not threatening, I do not ask forgiveness. I will not, will not do anything to myself—I am too afraid for mother and Ludmila. Grown up but sentimental, that's me. I cannot promise you anything. I know there is no promise you would believe in. I know there is no way of seeing you, of getting reconciled, which would not become a torment to you.

But in spite of everything, I am unable not to write, not to ask your forgiveness for everything.

If you made your decision with difficulty, with a struggle, if you want to try for one last time—you will forgive, you will reply.

But even if you do not reply—*You* are my only thought. I love you now, this second, just as I loved you seven years ago. I will do at once whatever you desire, whatever you ask, will do it with delight. How awful it is to part knowing that one loves and that parting is one's own fault.

I sit in the café and weep. The waitresses laugh at me. How terrible to think that my whole life will now be like that.

I am writing only about myself, not about you. Awful to think that you are self-possessed and with every second are drifting farther and farther away from me. A few more seconds and I shall be quite forgotten.

If, as a result of this letter, you feel something other than pain and revulsion, reply, for God's sake reply at once. I am rushing home to wait. But if not—it will be a terrible, terrible misfortune.

Kisses. All yours,

I

It is now ten o'clock. If you do not reply by eleven, I shall know there is nothing to wait for.

Lila!

I am writing now, for you could not reply when Kolya was around. I must write to you right now lest my joy prevent me from thinking and understanding anything at all later on.

Your letter rouses my hopes, which I dare not and will not count on in any event, for all calculations based on your prior relationship to me are groundless. And your new relationship to me can come into existence only when you get to know me as I am now.

You must not and cannot take my little letters into consideration, for whatever decision about our life (if there is one) I ought to and can make must not be made until the 28th. This must be so, for if I had the right and the chance to make some final decisions about my life just now, if I could vouch for them in your eyes, you would ask me today and give me your reply today. And in an instant I would be a happy man. If that thought is destroyed in me, I shall lose all strength and all faith in the necessity to bear the terrible experience I am undergoing.

I have clutched at your letter with a boyish, lyric passion.

But you should realize that *you will come to know an altogether new man, as far as you are concerned. Everything that will take place between you and him will begin to be based not on past theories, but on deeds from February 28 onward, your deeds and his.*

It is a great chore to write this letter to you, for at this very moment I am going through a nervous shock, such as I have not known since the moment of our parting.

You can realize what love for you, what feelings, are dictating this letter . . .

You allowed me to write when it would be "very necessary" for me. The "very" has just come.

You may ask, "Why is he writing all this? This is all obvious." If that is what you think, it is well. Forgive me for writing now, when you have guests—I do not want to sound nervous or to play the wise guy in this letter. And if I wrote tomorrow it would be like that. This is the most important letter in my life. It is not even a letter, it is my "being."

I embrace your little finger with all of me.

Pup

Moscow. Reading Gaol, 19/1/23

My beloved, kind, dearest little sun, Lili!

Perhaps (it is well, if so!) the silly Lovka got you worried yesterday with my little nerves. Be joyful! I will be. It's nothing, a trifle. Today I learned that you are sulking a bit. Don't, my little Sunshine!

You realize, of course, that without you an educated man cannot live. But if that man has a tiny little hope of seeing you, then he is very, very happy. I would be glad to give you a ten times bigger toy, if only you smiled. I have five little scraps of yours, and love them terribly; one of them saddens me, for it says only "Thank you, Volodya," but others have something more—those are the ones I love.

Surely, you are not very angry with me for my stupid letters. If you are, stop it; they are the cause of all my joy.

I go with you, write with you, sleep with your cat namesake, etc.

I kiss you, that is, if you are not afraid to be torn apart by a mad doggie.

> Your Pup
> alias Oscar Wilde,
> alias the prisoner of Chillon

. . . It's February 1. Thirty-five days have passed. That means at least 500 hours of constant thinking . . .

Could I be different?

It's incomprehensible that I have become like this.

I, who for a year would throw even a mattress or a stool out of my room, I, who was leading three times the "not quite normal" life I lead today—how could I, how dared I let myself be eaten so by moths? . . .

People talking about my poem think, I suppose, that "he has found a way to intrigue his readers. An old little trick . . ."

I have been sitting scrupulously, honestly until today, I knew I would be sitting exactly like this until 3 o'clock on February 28 . . .

I am sitting only because I myself want to; I want to think about myself and about my life . . .

Does love mean everything for me? Everything, but in a different way. Love is life, the essential life. It is the motor that moves the poetry, the work, all the rest. Love is at the heart of everything. If it stops, the rest will die, will be superfluous, unnecessary. But when the heart is working, it cannot but manifest itself in everything . . . But when there is no "activity" I am dead . . .

Love can be won not by "I must," or "I mustn't"—but only by a free competition with the whole world . . .

I have worked literally for sixteen and twenty hours at a time; I have done more than I ever did in half a year . . .

> My dear little child!
> I am sending you the ticket.
> The train leaves exactly at eight.
> We will meet in the carriage.
> The dismal days are over,
> The time of redemption has come.
> Boldly, comrades, fall in step, etc.
>
> Kisses yours

03.01 hours. 28/2/23

from the second part of ABOUT THIS
by Vladimir Mayakovsky

. . . Admirers are crawling from under the wardrobes,
Readers. A faceless, countless parade.
A procession abounding in unalloyed cheer.
Moss from their houses got into their beards . . .
But what is most terrible:
                    from his height, his skin,
his clothes—
          from his step even!—
I recognized in one—
              who are you, double?—
myself—
      I
          myself.
From the mattresses,
              swelling the sheets,
bedbugs have raised their legs in salute.
The samovar's radiant shape
is opening its arms in greeting.

The wallpaper pattern

                   stained by flies

of itself

        is crowning

                the shining foreheads.

The angels are blowing hard their trumpets,

pink above the bed.

Christ,

        having raised his crown

                of thorns,

makes a polite bow.

Even Marx, in his lobster-purple frame—

is also imprisoned in Philistine routine.

           .   .   .

I am standing by the wall

              in my misery,

overgrown with the absurd of days.

Don't let her, don't let her

voice resound just now!

I have sold

        a day, a year of commonplace,

the absurd would not let me breathe.

Life

      it consumed with dwelling smoke.

From upstairs—

        I dare you!—

              called me down.

I was hiding from the yell of open windows,

loving I ran away—

           in corners too narrow

let only verse,

        let only wander by night.

You are making a poem—

            and they measure souls by the fee.

You love with poems,

        but in prose—dumb,

you cannot,

you don't know how,
you have no words.
But where, dearest,
where, my loveliest,
did I prove faithless—
to my love—
in song?!

. . .

Horror has come.
Filled the brain,
is straining the nerves of strings.
It is roaring with the roar of seas,
pinned down,
erupted:
Stop!
I have come from beyond the seven years,
I have come from beyond six hundred miles,
to give you the order:
Not like this!
to stop you:
Enough!
Enough!
What do entreaties,
what do reproaches mean,
if
you alone succeed?
To be together,
with the whole loveless world,
together,
with the human,
worldly swarm—
seven years I have been waiting for this
and can
wait two hundred,
this is why I here stand.
Exposed to laughter
and to contempt,

                                              on the bridge of years,
I mark the redemption of worldly love,
for all I stand,

                    here stand I must,
    for all I pay,
    for all I cry.

                              .   .   .

They have found.

                    Signals go in all directions.
From everywhere

                    in groups and individually,
signals have brought them

                              to settle accounts with me:
the masters of insults and duels.
Bristling,

          lurking,

                    unrelenting . . .
They spit in their fists.

                    And soon
with their hands,

          winds,

                    countlessly,

                              totally
my mug

          to a sponge have wrecked.
The ladies,
unfolding their perfumed sweetness,
in the corridors of glovers' shops,
were throwing in my face

                    armfuls

                              of gloves
and the shops

          whipped my face too.
Newspapers,

          time to amuse yourselves as well!
To support those that attack me,
let the rag

shower the bucket of abuse,
let them thresh out
        slander
           and gossip!
Well, I am a naked and sore
invalid of love.
        Let a washed-out stream of lies flow—
but why am I in your way so?
           Why the insults?
I'm only poetry,
        only a soul.
And from below:
        You've been our enemy for ages!
Once we managed to get such a one—
           a hussar!
So until the pistol has bullets,
you will not get away!
        Get him, get him!
More violent than rain-storm,
        faster than thunder,
brow to brow,
        in a straight line,
from every rifle,
        every battery,
from all mausers,
        brownings,
from a hundred steps,
        ten,
           two,
between the eyes—
        bullet after bullet.
They will pause,
        to get a breath—
           and again
with lead
        to the death,
           to the kill . . .

The slaughter is over.

                      In their blunt joy
they are dragging their weary feet step by step.
And only in the Kremlin

                           a shred of the poet
flutters like a red flag.

                    .   .   .

from the Epilogue

. . . Here

                over an experiment

                          the future chemist
sweats—

           he must not rush.
Before him spread out the Book of Earth.
Twentieth Century.

                  Whom to resurrect?
—Mayakovsky, eh . . .

                Is it worth it?
There are more beautiful men.

              No, not he,

                   too early . . .
I will shout:

           —Don't hesitate over this page!
And do not turn pages in the book!

               Resurrect me!
Pour blood into my heart,

            into all veins.
Let the smooth skin

           tighten with movement.
I lived too short on this earth,
loved too short and not to the end.
In life

        I was

           quite a fellow—
what good was it

           that I steadfastly

scratching with my pen, spent my days
in the little room, narrow box?
I'll do
      for a pickax
              or wheelbarrow—
I'll do all you will ask me to do.
I can be a street sweeper.
Have you got sweepers in your world?
I was joyful—
          what's this to anyone?
A load of misery is hard to hide.
In our world
        teeth are bared
to gnash
      or bite.
Little happens—
        hardship
            or misery . . .
I know clownish tricks—
           ask me, please!
A pun is useful,
        or a hyperbole,
with a funny poem
           I will cheer you up.
My love . . .
        What good will it do to revive
old pains . . .
        There is no sense any more . . .
I like animals too . . .
          have you got
zoos?
      I can be a keeper in the zoo.
I like them.
        A dog will stop in my way—
here at the baker's—
          starved, with shabby coat—
I am ready

          to tear my own liver for him—
without regret—
              here, my little one, eat!
Maybe,
        sometime, perhaps,
                it will happen so—
for she liked animals too—
              down the green path in the zoo
she will pass smiling
          just as she is
              on this photo.
She is beautiful—
          it is certain she will be revived.
Your
      thirtieth century
          will abolish
the trifles that tore our
        hearts.
Will return
      what we
        had no time
           to love properly,
of future nights
        countless
          stars.
Because
      I rejected
        the heap of everyday trash,
waited,
      believed,
        saw you
          bodily,
because I was a poet—
        revive me for this!
I want to live what is mine—
        revive me!
            Revive me!

27. Maxim Gorki.

28. Mayakovsky the actor, 1918.

29. The poster of
Not for Money Born.

30. Scene from *Not for Money Born;*
Burliuk and Mayakovsky in the center.

31. Mayakovsky in *Not for Money Born.*

32. A poster for
In the Fetters of Film.

33. Mayakovsky's sketch
for *Mystery-Bouffe*.

34. Kasimir Malevich.

35. Lila and Osip Brik,
Roman Jakobson and
Mayakovsky, 1923.

36. Aleksandr Blok.

37. Cover of an issue of *LEF*.

38. Fragment of a ROSTA poster.

39. A Rodchenko montage for
the first edition of *About This*.

✙ 23 ✙

Left Front

✙

Mayakovsky seeks support in a new group of avant-garde enthusiasts, with whom he founds the magazine LEF (Left Front). In addition to the futurists of yesterday, such as Osip Brik, Asyeyev, and Shklovsky, among the members of LEF we find, Nikolai Chuzhak, Sergei Tretyakov, and Pyotr Nyeznamov. The seven issues of LEF reflect the history of a successive attempt to shape revolutionary art—art not conceived in the same way by all the fellow fighters. Other publications of the period also say something about the various conceptions, misunderstandings, and struggles. The later accounts by the participants and outsiders speak of this, too, as well as about the life and writings outside the scope of LEF theory.

OSIP BRIK'S ACCOUNT:

Only toward the end of 1921 did Mayakovsky begin to think again about the possibility of some kind of organizational grouping of avant-garde art-

ists. The problem had to do mainly with the chance of publishing books
by the group's members . . .

Toward the end of 1922 Mayakovsky presented a memorial to the
Propaganda Department of the Central Committee of the Russian Communist (Bolshevik) party, with a request for permission to publish the
magazine *LEF* . . .

VICTOR SHKLOVSKY:

There was a Society for the Study of Poetic Language Theory, which we
called "Opoyaz" . . . It grouped people connected with Mayakovsky's
and Khlebnikov's poetry, that is to say, futurists and young philologists
who were well acquainted with modern poetry. What was it that could
attract the academically minded pupils of Baudouin de Courtenay to the
futurists, people often oddly dressed and invariably odd in the way they
spoke? Verbal analysis and untraditional ways of thinking . . . "Opoyaz"
had been founded during the war, before the outbreak of the revolution.
Two collections were published by its members in the years 1916 to 1918
. . . As for their political views in the early years of the revolution, the
"Opoyazists" were, in principle, for October. Boris Kushner was a Communist; Evgeny Polivanov, Lev Yakubinsky, Osip Brik became Communists; Yuri Tynyanov worked as an interpreter for Komintern at a time
when most Russian intelligentsia were on strike; Boris Eichenbaum
worked at Goslit and was engaged in making a new textual criticism . . .

After the October Revolution, "Opoyaz" was given an official seal and
was registered as a learned society. Publishing activities were entrusted to
Osip Brik and myself . . . We now worked more in an academic manner,
without administrative barriers, and continually argued about the principle of creative literary writing . . . This period ended after a few years
with the leaders of "Opoyaz" joining the LEF group, that is to say, mainly
Mayakovsky.

The great passion of LEF was a desire to participate in the making of
a new life.

What was strange about them was that their periodical, with Mayakovsky in charge, attempted to negate the importance of art, particularly
of poetry.

Mayakovsky, Asyeyev, Pasternak, Tretyakov, Kirsanov, and other recognized poets published their work there, but the magazine had a nega-

tive attitude toward poetry and painting, while favoring journalism and textile pattern in the first instance.

The magazine, which negated poetry, published not only poems but also articles about poetry and had connections with Meyerhold, Eisenstein, and new architecture.

LEF also collaborated with "Opoyaz," all of whose writings were devoted to art . . .

EHRENBURG:

Mayakovsky liked Léger; they had something in common as far as their conception of the role of art in modern society was concerned. Léger was fascinated by machines and town planning, wished for art in everyday life, did not go to museums . . . Mayakovsky fought for a number of years against poetry not only in manifestoes and articles—he wanted to annihilate poetry through his poems. A death sentence on art was published in *LEF* . . . Painters were advised to deal with the aesthetics of machines, textiles, and objects of domestic use in place of easel painting; theatrical producers were told to arrange popular fetes and demonstrations and to say goodbye to footlights; poets were told to abandon lyric poetry and to compose inscriptions on posters and slogans instead.

To renounce poetry was not an easy thing to do. Mayakovsky was a strong and brave man. Occasionally, however, even he departed from his program. In 1923, when *LEF* was still opposed to lyric poetry, Mayakovsky wrote the poem "About This." Even those close to him did not understand that . . .

PYOTR NYEZNAMOV:

The first two meetings of the editorial board of the newly founded *LEF* took place early in 1923. Although I was the editorial secretary, I was not invited to these two meetings. I learned from those who attended that at the first meeting the magazine's policy line had finally been shaped. At the second meeting there were fierce arguments with Chuzhak, who was opposed to the publication of Brik's short story in the first issue . . .

VICTOR PYERTSOV:

Chuzhak-Nasimovich was not a representative figure of the group of writers who surrounded Mayakovsky in 1923, though he was regarded as one

of the chief theoreticians of *LEF*. Throughout his life he was connected
with editorial work and was an old party journalist. After Kolchak had
been defeated in the Far East, Chuzhak was in charge of an important
Far Eastern newspaper *Krasnoye Znamya*. He then organized there the
journal *Tvorchestvo*, which was devoted to the question of shaping communist culture. Chuzhak attracted many young writers with revolutionary
tendencies, Nikolai Asyeyev among them. Under Chuzhak's editorship,
Tvorchestvo propagated Mayakovsky's work and futurism in the Far East
. . . On their arrival in Moscow, Asyeyev and Chuzhak joined the editorial board of *LEF* . . . But Chuzhak, an enthusiast of Mayakovsky,
wanted Mayakovsky in turn to be enthusiastic about his own theoretical
dogmas. Mayakovsky did not fulfill his hopes . . . Within *LEF*, Chuzhak
stood in opposition to Mayakovsky and . . . to *LEF* itself . . . In his
aesthetic views, Chuzhak was an extreme dogmatist and scholastic . . .
He naïvely believed that his holy *LEF* dogma could create, out of noth-
ingness, uniform ranks of revolutionary poets, whom he would lead . . .
and that Mayakovsky would be one of many . . .

NYEZNAMOV:

Chuzhak was a dull and gloomy man . . . In his Vladivostok period, he
was first an opponent then a defender of futurism, but his defense was so
exaggerated that it could be explained only by his lack of tact and knowledge . . . He was a slow thinker but was forced to make quick decisions.
The mixture of ill-understood futurism with intellectual indolence was
paradoxical in him . . .

MAYAKOVSKY'S LETTER TO CHUZHAK, AFTER AN EDITORIAL
MEETING OF "LEF," JANUARY 22, 1923:

Dear Chuzhak!

I am writing this letter immediately after your departure and will send
it to you at the earliest opportunity . . .

I regard as absolutely horrible the fact that we have come to an understanding with the Central Committee and with Gosizdat (often with
people aesthetically-wise quite hostile to us) but are unable to come to an
agreement with you, *our tried friend and comrade.*

I will try once again today, in all friendliness, to find within our board
a way to come to an understanding with you.

I am at a total loss, however, as to your wishes; I am unable to get to the bottom of your arguments . . .

Please arrange your arguments in some order and formulate them directly—as concrete demands. But remember that the purpose for which we have unified our efforts—*communist art* (as part of com-culture and communism in general!)—is still a vague concept, evading exact classification and theory, a field in which practice and intuition is often still in advance of the most experienced theoreticians . . .

Whatever your reaction to my letter is going to be, I hasten to "impose" myself on you—disregarding all possible replies—in declaring that I still regard (and we all regard) you as a friend and companion in our work.

Do not widen the gap in our views by external impressions. Do not give a hoot about all this and *come*—even if we cannot agree, we can at least talk.

I shake your hand, and even embrace you,

Mayakovsky

In the last days of March 1923, the first issue of LEF appeared, numbering over 250 pages. Mayakovsky's name was given as the responsible editor; Gosizdat figured as publisher; 5,000 copies were printed. The first issue contained, among other things, Mayakovsky's poem "About This," poems by Asyeyev, Kamensky, Kruchenykh, Pasternak, Tretyakov, and Khlebnikov, prose by Osip Brik and Asyeyev, theoretical and polemical articles by Chuzhak, Tretyakov, Brik, Vinokur, Arvatov, and Levidov, plastic structures by Lavinsky and Rodchenko, Dmitri Pyetrovsky's reminiscence of Khlebnikov, reviews and a chronicle of events.

THE ISSUE WAS INAUGURATED BY THREE ARTICLES: "WHAT IS 'LEF' FIGHTING FOR," "WHOM DOES 'LEF' BITE INTO," "WHOM DOES 'LEF' WARN."

"What Is LEF Fighting For"

. . . *October has purified*, shaped, reorganized. Futurism has become the left front of art. "We" have become . . .

Apart from organizational activities, *we* created the first *art objects in the October era* (Tatlin—the monument to the Third Internationale, *Mystery-Bouffe* in Meyerhold's production, Kamensky's "Stenka Razin") . . .

Gradually losing their belief that the Soviets would not last more than two weeks, the academicians began, individually and in groups, to knock at the doors of people's commissariats.

Without the risk involved in giving them responsible functions, the Soviet authority put at their disposal—in deference to their European fame—the cultural and educational activities.

There entrenched, they began to set dogs on avant-garde art, an activity gloriously crowned with the closure of the *Iskusstvo Kommuny*.

The authorities, occupied by the war fronts and economic disorder, did not intervene in aesthetic conflicts, content with seeing that there was not too much noise in the cultural background, and with mitigating us out of respect for the "venerable" seniors.

A moment of respite has now come after the war and the hunger. *It is LEF's duty to demonstrate* the panorama of *arts* in the RSFSR, to establish the proper perspective and to take our rightful place . . .

LEF *must rally avant-garde forces.* LEF *must survey its ranks* and prevent the past from dragging on. LEF *must close the ranks in its front* in order to explode old trash, in order to commence the struggle for the domination of new culture . . .

N. Asyeyev
B. Arvatov
O. Brik
B. Kushner
V. Mayakovsky
S. Tretyakov
N. Chuzhak

ON APRIL 1, 1923, A LITERARY OLYMPICS TOOK PLACE IN THE POLYTECHNIC MUSEUM. FROM THE JOURNAL OF A SENIOR HIGH-SCHOOL PUPIL, TATYANA LESHCHENKO:

Bryusov himself inaugurated the evening, then Mayakovsky—mighty, beautiful, great!—read and talked to the public. Someone shouted, "I don't want to listen to you!" He just smiled and said, "You've paid for the ticket, so please listen!" The public roared and the applause was like thunder. He recited many poems, and the way he did it! His voice, and his sincerity! It was such that the obscurest expressions became clear. "And you, could you plan a nocturne on a flute with gutter pipes?" And it was a mighty nocturne, *our* Revolutionary Nocturne. I had not been thinking about revolution as revolution lately . . . But now I begin to love revolution again and realize something I had not understood before. Mayakovsky and his poems did this . . . There was also much applause for Kamensky, who read: "Forty Year Olds—We Are Still Boys." But he is a little boy too, beside Mayakovsky. Ilya Selvinsky, also a new poet, recited his poems . . .

Please God, let Mayakovsky be happy, let him live longest of all! Let all poets be happy! Not like Pushkin and Lermontov!

FROM MAYAKOVSKY'S STATEMENT IN THE DISCUSSION ON
"FUTURISM TODAY" AT PROLETKULT, FOLLOWING THE READING
OF FRAGMENTS FROM "ABOUT THIS," APRIL 3, 1923:

The first thing to which I want to draw your attention, comrades, is your odd slogan, "I don't understand." You wouldn't try to approach any other field with this slogan. The only reply I can give you is, "Learn" . . . It has been said that the keynote of my poem cannot be grasped. First of all, I have only been reading fragments, but even those fragments contain the essential theme: our way of life. The way of life which has not been altered in almost any respect—the way of life which is now our worst enemy, which makes us bourgeois . . . You say we lack substance and yet out of one of our poems you make fifty of yours. The proletarian writers come over to us. Both they and we are learning from life . . .

FROM LUNACHARSKY'S ARTICLE "ON, AND IN RELATION TO,
ALEXANDER OSTROVSKY," "IZVESTYA," APRIL 11–12, 1923:

We need a "serious" art, *capable of embracing our contemporary morals,* an art that would proclaim modern ethical values, which are just being born . . . We can already proudly mention some work of that kind: Mayakovsky's ("About This"), some poems by Asyeyev, many of the best proletarian poets, and the brightest star now rising in our literary firmament: Nikolai Tikhonov . . .

FROM RESOLUTIONS OF THE XII CONGRESS OF THE RUSSIAN
COMMUNIST (BOLSHEVIK) PARTY, APRIL 17–25, 1923:
In view of the fact that literature in Soviet Russia has become a powerful
social force in the course of the past two years, spreading its influence
above all among the masses of workers and peasant youth, it is imperative to bear in mind the problem of control over that form of social activity in day-to-day practical party work.

FROM NIKOLAI CHUZHAK'S ARTICLE "LEF," NO. 2, APRIL–MAY 1923:
Let us take the recent long poem "About This"!
    "I dedicate it to her and myself" . . .
    A sentimental romance . . . Schoolgirls will shed tears over it . . .
But we, who know other things as far as Mayakovsky is concerned, and
know many other things besides, are not moved in the least, in 1923 . . .
    "There's nowhere he can go!" . . .
    In 1914 the poet was more shrewd and his "hero" knew what to do
with himself . . .
    When Mayakovsky's enraged, lyric hero talked with God on familiar
terms in 1914, it sounded impudent and even proud . . . Even if he was
an individualist then, he was a heroic individualist. Much has changed
since then and—most important of all—the "heroes" and the "crowd" have
changed places . . .
    One last thing: in the finale of the poem there is said to be a "way out."
It consists in the belief that *in the future everything will be different*;
there will come an "astonishing new life" . . .
    In my opinion, it is a belief that originates in *desperation*, resulting
from the "there's nowhere he can go," a belief very far removed from the
vision of 1914. It is *not a way out, but the absence of one.*

🦋

In the third issue of LEF *(June–July 1923) more than a dozen
articles, feuilletons, and letters appeared, answering the attacks with which a large part of the press had greeted the two
earlier issues of the magazine; also published here was Dzhiga
Vertov's film manifesto* Kinoki *and Sergei Eisenstein's pro-*

gram article "Montage of Attraction." 3,000 copies were printed.

FROM NIKOLAI CHUZHAK'S ARTICLE "LITERATURE AND ART. STRUGGLING FOR ART. (A DIFFERENT APPROACH TO 'LEF')," PRAVDA, JULY 21, 1923:

As a man close to *LEF*, not only by a formal attachment but in a most definite way, on the principle of common past . . . I declare: the left front of art is undergoing a deep inner crisis. There is almost a struggle between two fractions in *LEF*: between (1) the old futurism, which has reached productivity art with the mind, and under external pressures, but gives to production only its left-hand technique, while it is clearly swayed between production and bourgeois lyricism; and (2) the productivity fraction of *LEF*, which attempts—still rather roughly and shyly—to draw topical and practical conclusions out of theory, and—what is most important—stakes its future not on the individualist and the inevitably egotistic art of the experts but on the art of the masses, which comes from below and has to be shaped only.

VICTOR SHKLOVSKY:

The headquarters of *LEF* was situated on the first floor of the house where the bakery was, at the corner of Vodopyany Alley and Myesnitskaya (now Kirov) Street, opposite the General Post Office.

It was the Moscow apartment of Osip and Lila Brik. Two rooms in a larger apartment: one, I think, had three windows, the other two.

There was one telephone in the apartment, with extensions for the remaining lodgers. Lila's telephone conversations with Mayakovsky were often interesting from a literary point of view, but were also tragically true of life. No wonder then that, when calling the Briks, one heard not only the voice of the person one was talking to, but the breathing of someone avidly listening . . .

One man who worked in the editorial office of *LEF* was Pyotr Lezhankin, a poet (he used the nom de plume Nyeznamov) and ex-officer in the army, who had some difficulties for this reason . . .

Mayakovsky was there all the time, except the two months when he was writing "About This" and talked to Lila Brik only by telephone . . .

I feel guilty with regard to many persons. I am guilty of having rarely mentioned Osip Brik with gratitude.

He was a man who disliked empty phrases, who could immediately sense insincerity in a conversation.

His own sincerity, Osip Maximovich hid within himself.

He was still young, black-eyed, broad-headed. He was a man of great knowledge, ascetic, devoted to Mayakovsky, and a good colleague of the other members of *LEF*.

RITA RAYT:

. . . Lunacharsky used to say half in jest that Mayakovsky assembled the futurists like Robin Hood his band of robbers, while Brik was the monk who accompanied the robbers and absolved them of their sins . . .

SHKLOVSKY:

If we are to say that the very concept of art is different in various periods, that there are epochs when a poem is not art but a letter is, that architecture can sometimes be expressed with greater clarity and precision in a bridge than in a colonnaded house, then *LEF*'s position at that time will seem less strange to us. But the discussion about love, which was carried on at Vodopyany Alley—the passionate discussion described in the poem "About This," which reminded one of a winter earthquake, the discussion about a new quality of man—could have been easier, if we had understood then that communism inherits all of mankind's culture and that one must not argue with Shakespeare . . .

The different arts, as I have said, were developing and met in one common stream. It is impossible, however, to understand Eisenstein and Vertov—the documentary film maker whose methods have been taken over by the entire world—without Mayakovsky. Neither can the poem "About This"—whose hero passes from one circle to another and undergoes various metamorphoses—be understood without a knowledge of the cinematography of the time, without the awareness of what it meant then for artists to be violently confronted with fragments endowed with a unified overall sense, revealed in a number of conflicts . . .

PYOTR NYEZNAMOV:

We used to go there every evening . . . Mayakovsky talked, played cards, cracked jokes, gave his characteristic replies to questions raised . . .

When told, in a somewhat humorous way, how the one-eyed Burliuk was crawling about from town to town, loaded like a truck, Mayakovsky said, unsmiling, "Poor Dodya, to cross the whole of Siberia—with one lamp, too!" . . .

LEF did not keep strictly to its policy line: many writers of talent who were not at all close to the magazine's avowed line were published here; Babel is one example . . .

Various expressions taken from Babel were then used by the LEFists for a long time. Mayakovsky, with many trumps in his hand, would say to his partner at cards, "And now, little father, we will finish you."

To which he would receive the reply, "Keep cool, Manya, you're not on a job now . . ."

ASYEYEV:

One of the most devoted and disinterested friends of the poet was Pyotr Nyeznamov (Lezhankin) . . . There was no one more absorbed in the question of every issue's publication, no man who could be more depended on for proofreading and in relations with the printers. When a printing error was found in the magazine, a most rare occurrence, Nyeznamov experienced it as a tragedy. A poet of great verbal precision himself, with a dislike of unnecessary prettiness, he treated the reading of a text as a Muslim would treat the Namaz. Nothing could distract him from proofreading or revising the columns. Though he received an extremely modest salary, he did not care about any other literary income and devoted all his time to the magazine.

He was a talented poet, devoted as a matter of principle to the then prevailing theory amongst us of "factography," or the duty to reflect reality, as opposed to work of the imagination, to the use of fiction . . . Mayakovsky, and I in turn, did not really follow this theory in practice—whose principal apostle was Sergei Tretyakov . . . Mayakovsky did, however, "renounce" the poetic genres; and to Pyotr Nyeznamov this meant a total confirmation of the new theory of poetry, to which he gave himself totally, with all his soul. This strongly curbed his vivid imagination . . .

No, Mayakovsky's relations with people close to him could not be described either as "team spirit," or as a patriarchate in art, but rather as a form of companionship, a kind of cooperative. It was also a kind of "ministry" of art, an unofficial one, but no less influential than the one headed by

Lunacharsky, who paid frequent friendly visits to the Briks' and Mayakovsky's apartment . . .

NATALYA ROZENEL-LUNACHARSKAYA:

In the summer of 1923 a literary discussion took place in the great hall of
the conservatory, with Lunacharsky as a participant. I do not remember
exactly what it was called, but I think the posters described it as a discussion about *LEF*.

The discussion began after a long delay. The impatient public stamped
their feet and chanted: "It is time! It is time!"—just as they do in cheap
suburban cinemas. Osip Brik finally stepped onto the platform, perplexed
and upset. He begged the audience's forgiveness for the delay and explained that Arvatov, who was to be the main speaker on behalf of LEF,
would not appear, because he had just suffered a nervous breakdown. The
audience reacted with deafening stamping, whistles, and shouts.

This episode set the tone of the entire discussion. Many people spoke. I
remember Nikolai Myeshcheryakov and Alexander Bogdanov, probably
because they rarely took part in discussions of this sort. Both brutally attacked LEF . . . The public waited for Mayakovsky to appear, but he
did not come. (I think he was away from Moscow at the time.)

The discussion was summed up by Lunacharsky. Anatol Vassilievich's
speech was full of verve, exact in its wording, and quite sharp in places.
Its gist was something like this: Mayakovsky is a new literary phenomenon created by Soviet life, and no one has the right to "tread down and
suppress" this new phenomenon . . . At the same time, Lunacharsky
called the attempt to create a special "LEFist" theory of literature something like "turning somersaults," and clearly separated Mayakovsky from
this literary group . . . The mood of the public changed in no time.
Anatol Vassilievich's speech, severe on occasion, but tactful and wise, was
interrupted many times by applause, and the public gave him an ovation
at the end . . . Downstairs in the vestibule, he said to me, tired but
obviously pleased, "Pity Mayakovsky is not here! How he would have listened!"

FROM THE REMINISCENCES OF SERGEI EISENSTEIN:

"So this is how you look," a huge fellow says to me, his legs wide apart.

My hand disappears in his big claw. "Just imagine, all last evening I was very polite to F., the director, mistaking him for you!"

. . . Before me stands the editor of *LEF*, Vladimir Mayakovsky. I am just about to join their fighting community. My first show has not yet seen the light of day, but the baby is so noisy in its cradle and has such clearly defined characteristics that it has been accepted by *LEF* wihout an examination . . .

FROM THE REMINISCENCES OF YURI LIBYEDINSKY:

I was introduced to Mayakovsky early in 1923, in the editorial office of the periodical *Molodaya Gvardya* . . . Mayakovsky was dressed a bit differently from us: we had not yet taken off our war-time and civil-war communist clothes: military tunics, high boots . . . Mayakovsky was the only one among us dressed like a European, though without ostentation . . . We were rugged, he was clean-shaven . . .

In the period about which I am writing, the LEF group had already come into existence and the early issues of its magazine had appeared . . . The journal *Na Postu*, like *LEF*, stressed the mission of serving the cause of communist education with the artistic word . . .

One of the meetings with the LEFists, perhaps decisive for our rapprochement, took place in Osip Brik's apartment in Vodopyany Alley.

I set out for that meeting with the "futurists," interested and excited. I had expected the apartment to be furnished in an unusual manner and was astonished at first when I did not notice anything "futuristic" about it: in the hall, an ordinary coat hanger; the dining room modestly furnished and set for tea. Lila Yuryevna at the table, friendly but restrained, dressed in good taste without ostentation, again nothing futuristic about her. If there was something unusual about her, it was her eyes—brown, expressive, shining with a vivid and wise radiance.

Mayakovsky, too, who was also in this small room, seemed disproportionately big and behaved quite unlike a futurist. I noticed his bow when he accepted a glass of tea from Lila Yuryevna's hands: he behaved as they do in "polite society."

Alexei Kruchenykh was also seated at the table. I saw him there for the very first time and, at first glance, he too seemed to me not at all futuristic, with his youthful, very Russian face, dressed in a provincial tunic, with, I think, Ukrainian embroidery. But when I listened to his speeches, I felt a deep satisfaction: this was true futurism . . . some pedantic deliberations about vowels and their division into "pure" and "impure."

His eccentricity was something new for me. Mayakovsky was sipping his tea in silence, and Lila Yuryevna, whom Kruchenykh seemed to be addressing, reacted with a polite smile but remained silent—one could look at her indefinitely.

Syemyon Rodov, who came with me, went at once in to the next room, from where we could hear his loud conversation with Osip Brik. The colleague for whom we were waiting came—I do not remember now who he was—and we went into the next room. Kruchenykh did not join us . . .

Rodov, our leader at the time, was demanding that *LEF* stop publishing Pasternak and Shklovsky. I had already read Pasternak's poems and I must confess that I did not understand them. I had no idea about Shklovsky, though, but I believed my senior colleague and fellow-believer, who used to scare us with Shklovsky as if he were the devil himself.

The room was now filled with the resounding voice of Mayakovsky defending his colleagues: it seemed as if the resonance made the window panes quiver . . .

This is how our alliance came into being. The joint declaration was signed by Brik and Mayakovsky on behalf of LEF, and by Rodov and myself on behalf of MAPP.

The alliance was a real one: Brik and Shklovsky began to hold seminars on prose in the "Young Guard" group. Mayakovsky, in the course of his numerous trips around Russia, invariably got in touch with local organizations of proletarian writers . . .

FROM THE AGREEMENT CONCLUDED BETWEEN THE MOSCOW ASSOCIATION OF PROLETARIAN WRITERS (MAPP) AND THE LEF GROUP, PUBLISHED IN "LEF," NO. 4, AUGUST–DECEMBER 1923:

The parties to the agreement:

(1) Without ceasing their laboratory work, will concentrate all their creative activity on organizing the psychological conditions and awareness of the readers for the Communist tasks of the proletariat.

(2) By means of personal appearances, and in print, will steadfastly

unmask the bourgeois-gentry and pseudo-sympathetic literary groups and promulgate their own principles of class artistic policy . . .

Will avoid mutual polemics, without abandoning discussion and objective comradely criticism . . .

MAPP:	LEF:
Y. Libyedinsky	V. Mayakovsky
S. Rodov	O. Brik
Leopold Averbakh	

In the same issue of LEF were published, among others, eight short stories by Izaak Babel, Mayakovsky's poem "To the Workers of Kursk," Asyeyev's poem "The Black Prince," Tretyakov's play "Gas Masks," articles by Arvatov, Shklovsky, and Grossman-Roschin, and Chuzhak's statement that "for reasons of essential and organizational differences" he is leaving the editorial board.

FROM VADIM SHERSHENYEVICH'S FEUILLETON IN THE JOURNAL "GOSTINNITSA DLA PUTYESHESTVUYUSHCHIKH V PRYEKRASNOM," NO. 3, 1924:

How wonderful that both groups (each numbering, certainly, one and a half persons) have united *at last*. There now exists *a united association to produce a nonexisting product*. It reminds one of those immigrant groups in Paris which divide a subsidy they have not yet received. Are the future priorities of "proletarian culture" not being divided in the same way by those two groups, now resting next to each other in the pose of a wolf and a sheep? Who will eat whom? No one can tell, if only because neither group has anything to be eaten, as far as its opponent is concerned. Fictitious "opponents" have been transformed into fictitious "friends" . . .

True, in the ranks of the parties to the agreement, a certain lack of coordination can be noticed. Yes, they throw insults at each other in spite of the agreement, but this is because one cannot somehow abolish at one stroke all those buckets of dishwater that they threw on one another in previous issues. But this does not matter. Those who like each other are not terrified by such trifles. Throw mud over him, he will wipe himself off and call it a "friendly dew." All the more so because this lack of coordination can happen even within one periodical. For instance, Comrade Volin in *Na Postu* complains about informers, and on the last page, without any scruples, publishes a slight denunciation of LEFists himself . . .

OSIP BRIK:

LEF, or rather Mayakovsky, had a great attraction for people. But sometimes it took such incongruous and sickly forms that Mayakovsky had to reject, in a most categorical manner, the people who asked him to stand at the head of some fantastic front of avant-garde art.

As an example of such an aberration I will quote a preserved letter from one of the self-styled organizers of "South-LEF":

". . . Having organized a division, I intended to march on Berlin. But everything was quiet. It was impossible for me to sit in the petty bourgeois quagmire in Podolya. So I went to Kharkov and asked the Central Committee to release me from the army. I bickered for a month and finally left the army in a flurry. Of course, if there were a war, I'd be the first to join. But for the time being I have decided to study publishing and journalism and to give my serious attention to art . . .

I do not know what you will think of my decision to introduce strict discipline from the start. I shall not tolerate any quarrels . . . The slightest attempt to cause dissension in our ranks will be punished by eviction without the right to apply for membership again. One cannot do otherwise. We are faced with a great struggle against the "white" front in the arts. We have to create a mighty army of "red" art. And might can only be created by discipline, solidarity, and serious work . . .

Greetings to all!
Your L.

Odessa, 27/5/24

I have declared myself LEF's plenipotentiary—this is essential for the cause! Formally confirm the appointment!"

Mayakovsky received many such letters and verbal requests to create at any price and stand at the head of "a unified front of avant-garde art" . . . It all ended in January 1925, with the most enterprising group of "organizers" calling the "First Moscow Conference of the Left Front in Art." Willy-nilly Mayakovsky had to take part in it . . .

At the conference, Mayakovsky protested categorically against all "inflexible" programs and "stiff" organizational forms . . . Mayakovsky persisted in his conception of LEF as a free association of individual creative artists, united not by external forms, but by a common activity . . .

The conference had no practical results. It did not succeed in organizing the "Left Front." Soon the *LEF* magazine ceased publication too. The magazine's financial deficit was given as the official reason. There were deeper reasons, however. Internal divisions within the magazine grew; some elements were more and more at variance with others. The vital and noisy, though in many respects false, artistic programs moved to the fore, together with exaggerated polemics on purely artistic issues, pushing all that was most valuable in the magazine to the background: the works of writers, above all of Mayakovsky himself . . .

1,500 copies of the seventh and last issue were published in the spring of 1925. It contained the first part of Mayakovsky's poem "Vladimir Ilyich Lenin."

✵ 24 ✵

A Russian in Paris

✵

In 1922 Mayakovsky, for the first time in his life, takes a trip abroad. Other journeys will soon follow. The city he will visit most often and most readily is Paris. Lev Nikulin tells about the circumstances of Mayakovsky's departure for Paris; Shklovsky, about Mayakovsky in Germany; Elsa Triolet, about Mayakovsky in Paris. The poet makes a "seven-day review of French painting." In addition to the sketches of his journey, he writes letters and poems.

LEV NIKULIN:

The French senator de Monzie, having heard Mayakovsky one day in the Hall of Columns, said, "This mug must be seen in Paris."

This remark of the senator opened the way to Paris for Mayakovsky even before diplomatic relations between the Soviet Union and France were established. Mayakovsky went there six or seven times and came to love the city, in which he would have liked to live and die "if he did not know the land called Moscow" . . .

Eh, Rita, Rita,
    You taught me German, but I am to talk in French.

Schüler

SHKLOVSKY:

Mayakovsky came to Berlin with the Briks. When they left, Mayakovsky remained there by himself.

A very modest room, with a lot of wine in it: every bottle just started. With regards to wine, he was only curious . . .

Norderney, as its name shows, is an island in the North Sea.

Traces of many sand-carrying waves. Traces of wind, which carries sand from the shore . . . Hotels in a row, music in the hotels . . .

Here I happened to meet Mayakovsky.

He was young and gave the impression of being a sixteen-year-old boy—happy, cloaked in the wind.

I was dressed in a light suit, because I was in love. Mayakovsky's attitude to this ailment was compassionately ironic.

We did not know how to dance.

They danced in the hotel with others.

Beyond us stood other hotels, just like the one we were staying in.

Except that big chopped crabs were served there.

We, too, were trying to catch crabs in the waves, but crabs with no commercial value, ordinary citizens of the sea.

Crabs were escaping sideways.

We were playing with the waves, running long distances, and arranging stones in the water . . .

Mayakovsky played with the sea as a little boy.

Then we left. We were late for the train and Volodya ran after it, followed by me.

We were trying to stop the train, almost catching it in our nostrils. We stopped it.

FROM MAYAKOVSKY'S TRAVEL SKETCHES:

The French frontier. Passport control. A special police commissioner. He looks at a passport and hands it back. Looks at another and hands it back.

My document obviously delighted the "special" gentleman.

He looks enthralled at my document and at me: "Your nationality?"
"Russian."
"Where did you come from?"
"Berlin."
"And to Berlin?"
"From Stettin."
"And to Stettin?"
. "From Revel."
"And to Revel?"
"From Narva."
"And to Narva?"

There were no more foreign cities to be mentioned. What will be will be. I shoot: "From Moscow."

In reply I receive a slip of paper with the high-sounding name—"sanitary passport"—and the order to report to the Prefect of the Police in Paris within twenty-four hours.

Paris. I leave my luggage in a random hotel. Go by car to the prefecture . . .

I stand in a long line. My turn comes at last: "I have a 'sanitary passport.' What am I to do?"

"Take your picture. Four photographs, to be authenticated at your local police station and left there, four others to be authenticated and brought to us . . ."

Instead of going to the photographer I went back to my hotel. I told my story and added, "If I have to go through this rigmarole, please buy me a ticket to Berlin for tomorrow."

"Snap your fingers and stay here for ten days or so!"

I snapped my fingers with pleasure.

EHRENBURG:

Elsa Yuryevna . . . married the Frenchman André Triolet in the early days of the revolution . . . She was very young, attractive—pink like some Renoir canvases—and sad . . . Elsa Yuryevna lived in Paris then; I used to see her nearly every evening at Montparnasse. She met Aragon there in 1928 and soon began to write in French.

ELSA TRIOLET:

How I liked to go to meet him at the station! How big he seemed when he emerged from the train! One can really notice someone's appearance after a period of absence, even a short one. And the voice, how strange it sounds to a close friend after an absence!

Monumental, he made his way down the platform and passers-by were already turning to look at him. He stopped every now and then to look at me and say, Let me see how you look! We have been spreading rumors in Moscow that you are pretty; I must find out if the rumors have not been false . . ."

He only liked "his own" people . . . Travels were a servitude he imposed on himself, thinking of them as essential for his work. He did not have an aversion to Paris, if only because he met me there, someone from the "family," someone he liked, someone who shared his likes and dislikes for the same things and the same people, who regarded the aversions and sympathies of the other person as natural. He needed to feel secure. He valued loyalty, demanded it from others, and was loyal himself in life and in death . . .

With regard to his friends, he could be suspicious, jealous, reserved, impetuous—and altogether unbearable! When he wanted to, he could make life difficult for himself and give a tinge of drama to trifles. He was a demanding friend, and any incident could be proof to him that he was being neglected and treated indifferently by his friends . . . During one of his visits to Paris, an incident involving a bar of soap cost us three days of not talking to each other and was the cause of unpleasant insinuations, etc. Mayakovsky was a maniac for cleanliness and felt an almost pathological fear of infection. He washed his hands an unusual number of times a day, and whenever he was away from home, he used the soap he carried in his pocket. When passing through Berlin, he bought a bar of soap in a white soap holder . . . Now he wanted to acquire another soap holder, a Parisian one. It was my duty, of course, to purchase it, because Mayakovsky did not speak French. But, unlike the Germans, the French are not "practical," and I could not find a soap with a suitably small holder. There were soaps and there were holders, but they were not especially fitted to one other.

"You're doing it on purpose," Mayakovsky declared. "You simply don't want to do anything for me . . . Maybe I ask too much of you . . . No soap anywhere? You can't buy soap for me? Unbelievable! . . . Well, if this amuses the esteemed lady, I will tread the streets myself in search of it . . ."

And after three days of sulking, "Goodbye, I will manage without you, madame . . ."

I cried with rage. Mayakovsky left and came back with a nice, small, round aluminium box. I found it difficult to hide my feeling of triumph and let him wash his hands with Gibbs' tooth soap! It was quite clear he had noticed the soap in a window a long time ago, but instead of buying it, wanted me to serve him, to test my friendship . . .

In 1922, when Mayakovsky came to Paris for the first time, I happened to be in Berlin . . . When I came back to Paris, he came to stay in the same little hotel where I was living. Because he could speak only Russian (and Georgian), he would not let me out of his sight, convinced that without me he would be lost, sold, betrayed. To turn into a deaf mute and make himself understood only in "triolet" language, as he called it, made him lose his patience. Not to be able to prove that the Soviet Union is the only country fit for living, not to understand what the French are saying and thinking, not to be able to dominate those around him with the power of language, as he was used to doing—this struck him with horror . . .

So Mayakovsky began to help himself with exaggerated gestures . . . At the tailor's he sketched a whole lot of tiny drawings, showing the defects in his physique and pointing out how those defects were to be corrected by the cut of the suit. Wherever we went, we caused a peculiar kind of astonishment. That giant moved among men as a big dog among children: he nudged them delicately and bit lightly, without harming anyone . . .

Suddenly, a few days after his arrival, Mayakovsky received an order to leave Paris from the prefecture. He quietly went about the kinds of activities that are common among all foreigners in Paris. He visited the Louvre and night clubs, bought shirts and ties, and now they tell him to leave! Why? It occurred to me they must have mistaken Mayakovsky for Yesenin, because they were both poets. And Yesenin had left the police rather bad memories for reasons that had nothing to do with politics, but with drinking. Mayakovsky, however, had a good head for drinks. What could they want of him?

So we went to the prefecture. We wandered around the long, dirty corridors, and were sent from office to office; I went first, Mayakovsky followed, stamping heavily in his hobnailed shoes, his stick banging accidentally against walls, doors, and chairs. Finally, we came into the office of some important person. He was a very ill-tempered man, who got up from his chair in order to tell us more categorically, in a loud and resonant voice, that Monsieur Mayakovsky must leave Paris within twenty-four hours! I mumbled something not very convincing while the horrid Mayakovsky interrupted me all the time, asking, "What are you saying to him? . . . What is he telling you? . . ."

"I told him that you were not very dangerous because you didn't know a single word of French . . ."

Mayakovsky's face beamed; he gave the ill-tempered gentleman a trusting look and said innocently in his low voice, "*Jambon* . . ."

The gentleman stopped shouting, looked at Mayakovsky, smiled and asked, "For how long do you wish to have your visa?"

In a large room Mayakovsky handed his passport through the window, to be stamped finally in the required manner. The official looked at his passport and said in Russian, "You come from the village of Bagdadi in Kutais Province? I lived there for many years. I had a vineyard . . ." Both of them were delighted at their encounter! One more proof of the smallness of the world, where people tread on one another's toes . . .

FROM MAYAKOVSKY'S TRAVEL SKETCHES:

After the misery of Berlin, Paris dazzles one.

Thousands of cafés and restaurants. Each of them full of lobsters and bananas, even exhibited outside. Innumerable perfume shops are daily devastated by brilliant lady customers. Countless cars are whirling in a waltz around the fountains of the Place de la Concorde . . . In the "Maillols" and "Alhambras"—even while the lights are out during the performance—it is bright with sparkling diamonds. Lamps in the bars of Montmartre alone would suffice to light all the schools in Russia . . .

Show me a writer! I asked my guides to introduce me to the most respected, the most fascinating writer in Paris. Of course, I mentioned two names at once: France and Barbusse. My guide, an "expert," decorated with the ribbon of the Légion d'honneur, made a wry face, "This is what interests you 'Communists, Soviet politicians.' Paris likes style, likes pure—well, psychological—literature. Marcel Proust—the French Dostoyevsky —he is the man who fulfills these requirements."

This was said on the eve of Proust's death. Three days later I could see only the funeral, which was attended by all artistic and official Paris—the last earthly journey of this really great writer.

My chances of seeing Anatole France and Barbusse improved. Having been given a note to France (a strange combination: to see France, a Communist, Mayakovsky had a note from some ultra-right deputy), I rushed to see him, but France was in Tours, and Barbusse, according to the newspapers, in Petrograd.

So, instead of whom I had asked for, I saw Jean Cocteau, the most fashionable writer in Paris just now . . .

Cocteau is an ex-dadaist, prose writer, theoretician, contributor to *Esprit Nouveau*, critic, playwright, the wittiest man in Paris, the most popular—even a fashionable restaurant has been named after the title of his play—*Le Boeuf sur le toit*. Provincial as I was, I asked him outright about literary groups and schools in Paris. Cocteau explained to me in simple terms that there were no such phenomena in Paris "A free individual," improvisation—these are the moving forces of "France in general and literature in particular" . . . "Schools, classes," observed Cocteau slightingly, "mean barbarity, backwardness." Having persisted further, I managed to get from him, though, certain descriptions from which I learned that there is, indeed, a "little Cocteau school" . . .

A Seven-Day Review of French Painting. A review—there can be no other name for my seven-days' acquaintance in 1922 with French art.

In that time I could only roughly see the countless rows of canvases, books, theaters.

From this review I have singled out my impressions about French painting . . .

Before the war . . . schools and art trends came into being, lived, and died to the orders from artistic Paris.

Paris gave the orders: "Propagate expressionism! Introduce pointilism! And in Russia one began at once to paint in colored dots only.

Paris recommended: "Regard Picasso as the patriarch of cubism! And the Russian Shchukins spent all their energy and money on buying the biggest, the most improbable Picassos.

Paris gave the sentence: "Futurism is dead!" And Russian critics began to give requiem masses at once, and then went on to proclaiming the newest Parisian "dada," which, incidentally, was called "Paris fashion."

Revolutions and discoveries made by artists in Russia were condemned to death *in absentia:* They've had it in Paris for a long time and they do it better. . . .

I went to Paris trembling. I saw everything with a schoolboy's diligence. What if we turn out to be provincial again?

Painting. The external elements (called "form" by the vulgar critics) always dominated in French art.

The inventiveness of the Parisians therefore turns to fashion in real life, and that's how the "chic Parisian" was created.

In art this assured the domination of painting over all other arts, since painting is the most impressive, the most decorative art . . .

France gave the world thousands of the best-known names in painting.

For every famous painter there are a thousand good ones. For every good one, thousands whose names are the concern of no one but their *concièrges.*

One must plug one's ears to the humming of ten mutually destructive theories, and one must have a good knowledge of earlier painting to get the total view and not fall under the influence of the picture-bacteria of some quite uninfluential artistic school.

I take the prewar pattern: at the head, cubism, attacked by a group of colorists (simultaneists); on the side, a neutral group of fauvists without party allegiance, and on all sides, the ocean of canvases of countless academicians and salon painters; occasionally, some "latest shout" from somewhere gets everybody to their feet.

Armed with this pattern I pass on from trend to trend, from exhibition to exhibition, from canvas to canvas. I think that the pattern is only a kind of guide. One must discover the artistic visage of today's Paris by oneself. I make desperate sorties outside the pattern. I look for some discovery in painting. I expect some new artistic task to be posed. I look at the corners of the pictures, trying to find at least one new name. In vain.

Everything in its place . . . Eight years of the same persistent lethargy . . .

How enviously, avidly, and with what interest they ask about Russia's tendencies and possibilities . . .

For the first time, not from France but from Russia, a new word in art has come: constructivism. How strange to find this word in a French encyclopedia.

Not the kind of constructivism that constructs unnecessary little instruments out of good and necessary wires and sheet metal. But the constructivism which conceives of the artist's formal work as engineering only, essential for the shaping of our practical lives.

Here French artists have something to learn from us . . .

I do not wish to say that I do not like French painting. To the contrary.

I had liked it already. I am not renouncing my old love, but it has changed into friendship and soon, if things stand still, I may end as a simple acquaintance . . .

Of course, the Russian production of pictures cannot be compared with the French . . . That is not the point.

The point is that time has put a question mark on the existence of the pictures, and on their makers. It has put a question mark on the existence of a society content with the little artistic culture of the picture-decorated salon. This culture has had its day. I gladly yield the first place in picture painting to the French.

I also say: our *peintres* must give up painting pictures, because the French do it better. But the French have to give up painting too, for they will not paint any better . . .

Picasso. The first studio which must be visited in Paris is, of course, Picasso's. He is the greatest artist, both through his impetus and the role he plays in world painting. In the center of the apartment, whose walls are covered with paintings that are well known to us from photographs, a stocky, sullen, energetic Spaniard. Characteristic of him, and of other painters I have visited, is a passionate love for Rousseau. The walls are covered with his paintings. The eye of a blasé Frenchman apparently wants to rest on those absolutely naïve, absolutely simple things.

One thing interests me greatly: the question of Picasso's return to classicism. I remember that Picasso's latest drawings have been reproduced in some Russian periodicals with the title "Return to Classicism." In the articles it has been asked why, if an innovator such as Picasso has abandoned his "oddities," some outlaws in Russia are still interested in levels, forms, and colors, instead of going on to copy nature, simply and conscientiously.

Picasso shows me his studio. My fears are dispelled. There is no return to classicism here . . . His big, so-called real canvases, those women with huge arms—all this, of course, is not a return to classicism, but, if you must use the word, the confirmation of a new classicism. He is not copying nature but transforming all of his previous cubistic analyses. In those leaps from method to method one can see not a departure but a search, in all directions, of an artist who has already reached the limits of formal achievement in a definite manner and is looking for a way of employing his knowledge in practice, and cannot find it in the stale atmosphere of present-day French reality.

Delaunay. Delaunay is an absolute contrast to Picasso. He is a simultaneist. He is looking for a chance to paint pictures whose form would consist not in striving after mass and volume but of color only . . . He is obstinate. Cubism, which has covered the canvases of all other French painters, will not let him rest. Buyers are not after him. He has no reason to turn to classicism. The whole of Delaunay—even his shoulders, even his arms, not to mention his paintings—signifies a feverish search. He knows that no speeches will pierce the wall of tastes of the French salons, and by some roundabout route he too approaches revolution . . .

He listens with envy to the stories about our holidays, when a painter gets a house, an art school, a district, and can paint the walls to his heart's content. The idea is close to his heart. Even in the studio his paintings look not like canvases but like entire walls, so much space there is in them. His colored illuminations are so superfluous, so out of place against the gray walls of his studio, but he cannot take them out into the street: opposite, there stands, not only a police sergeant but also the gray building of the Academy of Fine Arts, from where, Delaunay says, fists are raised against him when he passes by . . .

Léger. This artist, whom famous experts of French art treat somewhat patronizingly, has made the greatest and nicest impression on me. Stocky, he looks like an authentic painter-worker, who regards his work not as a divine calling but as an interesting, necessary craft, equal to other crafts in life. I have seen his outstanding work. I am glad about the aesthetics of industrial forms, about his lack of fear as far as the most brutal realism is concerned. I am struck by his matter-of-fact treatment of paint—so unlike other French painters: he treats the paint not as a means of transmitting some sort of space, etc., but as the material which colors objects. His attitude toward the Russian Revolution, too, is not an aesthetic but a practical one . . . He is most interested not in the problem of where and how he could exhibit his work upon his arrival in Russia, but in the technical problem of what route he should take and what use his knowledge could be in general building practice . . .

Conclusions . . . Naked formalism has given all it could give . . . What remains is either to die repeating oneself, or . . .

There are two "or's."

The first "or" of Europe: To employ the achieved results to satisfy the needs of European taste. It is not a very complicated taste. The taste of the bourgeoisie . . . There is no chance of any development here. The artist can meet only with degrading demands to produce work that is not more revolutionary, in the purely artistic sense, than that of the salon. And we see how Braque is giving way, how he begins to produce pictures in which there is more prudery than painting.

No, the greatest men in the world did not study the methods of coloring and illuminating life in order to make pictures. One's discoveries should be measured not against the salons but against life, production, work of the masses, which makes the life of millions more beautiful.

But here we come to the second "or"—RSFSR. "Or" of every country washed by the workers' revolution. Only in our country can all this formal work find its use, its content (visual not moral, of course). Not in a bourgeois country . . . where one cannot shape but must be subservient to the tastes of the consumer . . .

But the second "or" is not for France, for the time being . . .

For the time being, in spite of all our technical, backwardness, we, the workers of art in Soviet Russia, are the leaders of the world's art, the carriers of avant-garde ideas.

But . . . all this has to be transformed from theory into practice, and we still have to learn from the French in the former.

NIKULIN:

On his return from foreign travels, Mayakovsky often spoke about technical progress, about all that we did not yet have in those days; he wanted to transfer not only the métro, the Eiffel Tower, and good automobiles, but also well-cut suits and shoes to our country. Politeness in public places, good treatment of horses by Parisian drivers, good food, clean tables, and good service in restaurants—for him, all this meant an essential level of external culture toward which one should strive . . .

Dear Dodya!
    I avail myself of the chance to send you greetings.
    I am sending you books.
    If you send me the visa, I will be in New York in two or three months.
    My address: Berlin, Kürfürstenstrasse 105, Kürfürsten Hotel, or Moscow, *Izvestya,*
    or: Lubyansky Alley 3, Apt. 12, Moscow
    or: Vodopyany Alley 3, Apt. 4, Moscow.
    Regards for yourself and all your clan.
    Kisses for you.

Yours,
V. Mayakovsky

Berlin, 15/10/23

Dear-dear, kind-kind,
dearest-dearest Lila!
    I have been in Paris for a week but did not write, because I do not know anything, as far as I am concerned. I am not going to Canada and Canada is not coming to me. I have been allowed to stay in Paris for two weeks (I am trying to get an extension), and I do not know whether to go to Mexico—that may not be worth anything. I am trying to contact America again with the prospect of going to New York.
    How I have been living through this time, I do not know myself. My basic feeling now is anxiety, anxiety to the point of tears, and a total lack of interest in anything here. (Fatigue?)
    I badly want to go to Moscow. If I were not ashamed before you and the editors, I would go today.
    I am staying in Elsa's hotel (29, rue Campagne-Première, Istria Hotel); I did not cable the new address, because Elsa says letters reach her at the old address. They will reach me too—*if you write.* I am very anxious about you.
    What about the books and contracts? . . .

In Paris nobody waited for me at the station because the cable came ten minutes before the arrival of the train, so I looked for Elsa on my own, using my knowledge of French. I stayed in Elsa's hotel, after all, for it is the cheapest and the cleanest little hotel, and I am trying to save, and not to walk about too much, if I can.

I am very friendly with Elsa and André. Fur from you and me for her has been managed; we breakfast and lunch together always.

I spend a lot of time with Léger; I went to see Larionov but did not find him in. I did not go anywhere else, otherwise, except to the theater . . . Zdanyevich came to see me once, but he is in love and is normally under a lady's wing.

I gradually get clothes for myself under André's supervision and even got marks from fittings. But this occupation does not rouse much enthusiasm in me.

We spent the first day of my arrival going shopping for you. We have ordered a splendid little suitcase for you and have bought hats. We will send them as soon as the pigskin suitcase is ready. I have sent off the perfumes; if they reach you intact, I am going to send more . . .

Very bad without the language! . . .

I am afraid; I fear I shall be taken for a provincial, I hate traveling and I so much want to come back and read my poems.

I am weary, weary, weary, weary without you.

Without Osya it's no good either. I love you both awfully!

With Elsa's every intonation that is similar I fall into melancholic, sentimental lyricism . . .

I kiss you, my child, I kiss Osya, all yours, Vol.

I kiss Lovka, Kolka, Xanusya, Maltsyo, and Levin. They are all of them a hundred times wiser than all those Picassos.

V. Mayakovsky

Paris (Paris does not mean me!)

9/11/24

⚜ 25 ⚜

The Great Ode

⚑

Shocked by the death of the leader of the Russian Revolution, Mayakovsky writes his poem "Vladimir Ilyich Lenin." Having read the poem to the Communists gathered at the Press House, he publishes the first part in the last issue of LEF. A little earlier LEF has protested against the "trafficking in Lenin" by literary opportunists and superficial hagiographers.

THE GOVERNMENT COMMUNIQUÉ, SPECIAL ISSUE OF "PRAVDA" AND "IZVESTYA," JANUARY 22, 1924:

Yesterday, January 21, at 6:50 P.M., Vladimir Ilyich Ulyanov (Lenin) died suddenly in Gorki near Moscow. The end was unexpected. Lately a considerable improvement was observed in the state of health of Vladimir Ilyich. All signs pointed to the supposition that the improvement would last. Quite unexpectedly, the state of health of Vladimir Ilyich worsened yesterday. A few hours later Vladimir Ilyich left us.

The All-Russian Congress of the Soviets now in session in Moscow and the All-Union Congress, which will open in the next few days, will make the necessary decisions to guarantee the further uninterrupted work of the Soviet government. The heaviest blow to the working people of the Soviet Union and the whole world, since the workers and peasants of Russia assumed power, will mean a deep shock for every worker and peasant, not only in our republic, but in all countries. The working masses of the whole world will bewail the loss of their greatest leader. He is no longer with us, but his work will continue uninterrupted. The Soviet government, which expresses the will of the working masses, will continue Vladimir Ilyich's work and follow the path he has charted. Soviet authority is steadfast on guard, watching over the achievements of the proletarian revolution.

LEV NIKULIN:

An ordinary house on Okhotnyi Ryad Street . . . the office of *Rabochaya Gazieta*. On one of those very cold nights, when Moscow was paying its last respects to Lenin, when an unending stream of people, their breath steaming out of their mouths, was slowly moving toward the House of Unions, Mayakovsky came into the editorial room, numb with cold. He took off his gloves, blew on his frozen fingers, and looked out the frost-covered window. After several minutes he went out, again crossed the street, and again—who knows for which time!—joined the end of the line, somewhere beyond the Strastnyi Monastery, in order to walk past Lenin's coffin in the Hall of Columns, together with them all, arm-in-arm with the working people of Moscow and Russia.

ASYEYEV:

Always so lively and reacting directly to everything, Mayakovsky hardly spoke a word in those days. He contracted, as it were, into a single knot of muscles and nerves, so as not to let his genuine, immense sadness erupt and dissipate in external manifestations.

🙚

In January and in early February, the National Press published poems dedicated to Lenin, written by Bryusov "On Lenin's Death" and "Era," Bezimyensky, Vera Inber, Asyeyev, Zharov, Tretyakov, Kamensky, Gerasimov, Dorogoychenko,

Kirillov, Golodny, Alexandrovsky, Gorodetsky, Obradovich, Poletayev, Rukavishnikov, and many others. Mayakovsky's poem (with the refrain "Lenin lived, Lenin lives, Lenin will live"), dated March 31, 1924, was published in the monthly Molodaya Gvardya.

LETTER FROM LENINGRAD TO LILA BRIK, MAY 20, 1924:

My Dear Foxy!

I am unpopular everywhere, because they all expected you. When I phone, they first say, "Ah!" and then "Eh . . ." Yesterday I made a public appearance and will make others today, tomorrow, Thursday, and Friday. It means I'll be coming on Saturday or Sunday. No business, for all directors have gone to Moscow. Tomorrow at five Rita will be coming to tea, and at seven, all the linguists . . .

FROM BORIS EICHENBAUM'S NOTEBOOK:

May 21. Saw Mayakovsky at the European Hotel, Room 26. Also present were Yakubinsky, Tynyanov, Tikhonov, Punin, Vinokur. We talked about LEF.

In the fifth issue of LEF (*Summer 1924*) *a series of articles on Lenin's language, written by Shklovsky, Eichenbaum, Yakubinsky, Tynyanov, Kazansky, and Tomashevsky, was published. The same issue contained, fragments of Tretyakov's play* Roar, China!, *Boris Pasternak's poem "Lofty Disease," prose pieces by Babel and Vyesoly. The editorial article entitled "Do Not Traffic in Lenin!" had been removed by the censor.*

FROM YURI TYNYANOV'S ARTICLE "THE TRANSITIONAL PERIOD," IN THE JOURNAL "RUSSKI SOVREMENNIK," NO. 4, 1924:

Writing about poems is almost as difficult now as writing poems. And writing poems is almost as difficult as reading them. Such is the vicious circle of our times. There are fewer and fewer poems, and we have to deal not so much with poems as with poets. And that is not so small a task as one might think . . .

Schools have disappeared; literary trends have ceased to exist simultaneously, as if to order. They had been growing in geometric progression,
have undergone polarization, have broken up; then the self-determination
of small poetic nationalities started taking place in spaces as enclosed as
apartments; in the end everyone was left to himself . . . This substitution
of poetic schools by individuals is characteristic of literature in general,
but the suddenness of the changes, the relentlessness of the struggle, and
the rapidity of the downfalls reflect the tempo of our age . . . Only individuals are still alive.

The poetry game is now played for high stakes. Verse is a speech
undergoing transformation—human speech which has outgrown itself.
The word in a poem has a thousand unexpected shades of meaning; verse
gives the word new dimensions. A new poem means a new vision. The
accumulation of these new phenomena occurs only in those traditional
periods when the law of inertia ceases to operate. We really know only the
impact of inertia: a period when there is no inertia, according to the perspective of history, seems a blind alley to us. (In the final analysis every
innovator works for inertia, every revolution takes place to establish a new
canon.) In history, however, there are no blind alleys. There are only transitional periods . . . It is difficult to talk about the objects, ready-made
poems, and even more so about the books, of a transitional period. It is
easier to talk about the poets who are passing through this transitional
period . . .

The theme overwhelms Mayakovsky, too, and overflows the brim of
his work. Russian futurism sprang from the tame culture of nineteenth-
century verse. In its relentless struggle, in its achievements, it is more akin
to the eighteenth century, with which it shakes hands over the head of the
nineteenth. Khlebnikov is akin to Lomonosov; Mayakovsky, to Derzhavin . . .

Mayakovsky renewed the gigantic vision, lost somewhere since Derzhavin. Like Derzhavin, he knows that the secret of a gigantic image does
not consist in its "loftiness" but in the extreme contrast of associated levels
—the high and the low; what the eighteenth century called "the bringing
together of words unequally high," and also "the connection of ideas remote from one another" . . .

Soon this hyperbolic image will pop its head from the poems, cut
through them, and take their place. In "About This" Mayakovsky again

stresses the fact that the element of his word is hostile to epic storytelling, that the uniqueness of his form lies in the fact that it is not an "epic" but a "great ode" . . .

IN OCTOBER 1924, AFTER ALMOST A YEAR'S WORK, MAYAKOVSKY COMPLETED HIS POEM "VLADIMIR ILYICH LENIN." FROM MAYAKOVSKY'S AUTOBIOGRAPHY:

I have completed the poem, "Lenin" . . . I had been afraid of this poem, for it would have been so easy to reduce it to an ordinary political summary . . .

KORNEL ZYELINSKY:

On October 18, 1924, Mayakovsky read his poem at a crowded literary gathering . . .

I went up the wide stairs of the Press House, in the company of Boris Agapov and Ilya Selvinsky . . .

The great hall of the Press House can be called big only in the sense that the home in which they are growing up seems big to children. A hundred people filled the hall to capacity; a hundred and fifty made it impossible to breathe, and then the door was opened to the adjoining room and to the terrace.

When Mayakovsky mounted the platform, Selvinsky and I managed to push our way into the hall through a side entrance with great difficulty and listened to the entire poem, standing. Agapov had more luck: he managed to get himself a chair . . .

Most of the people present were Communists, and there were many people engaged in everyday party work, some of whom had come here from the far corners of Russia. Most of them were seeing Mayakovsky for the first time, though, of course, everybody had heard about him. But the style and atmosphere of Moscow literary evenings—always adorned in those days by the presence of artistic Bohemia—were alien to those people. Moreover, some who had heard of Mayakovsky came here with reserve, even, perhaps, with considerable reluctance or, at any rate, with the desire to criticize sharply what the Moscow personality had written about—what to all those sitting in the hall was dearest and holiest—Lenin . . .

As soon as there was silence in the hall, Mayakovsky, without any introduction, clearly and quietly read the title: " 'Vladimir Ilyich Lenin.' A poem."

Then, after a short pause, he added, emphatically and boldly, "I dedicate it to the Russian Communist party."

The opening stanzas of the poem were read by Mayakovsky in the style of a tale from epic chronicles: "It is time—I begin my tale of Lenin."

Later, however, the epic intonation was substituted by a personal, lyrical one, revealing deeply-felt experience. It is a story about how he, a poet, felt about Lenin, how he understood him and what Lenin meant in Mayakovsky's life. And here I noticed that the personal confession, almost a page from a diary, absorbed the attention of his audience . . .

The middle part of the poem, in which Mayakovsky depicts the figure of Lenin against the background of history, could be listened to only with the greatest difficulty. Some asked that he read it more slowly. I tried to listen carefully to every single line. I felt that Mayakovsky had invested the maximum of work, inventiveness, and wit in order to describe, let us say, the history of capitalism in Russia, the role of capital, the struggle of the workers, in such a way as to make it not boring but convincing and clear. Mayakovsky would put in a *chastushka,* or the use of the poetics of the feuilleton and pamphlet. If the first part of the poem was read in a serious and matter-of-fact manner, the second part was treated in the way that was characteristic of Mayakovsky: a lyrical intonation would be followed by thunder of irony, delivered in a roaring bass . . .

Mayakovsky read the last scenes of the poem, which depict Lenin's funeral in the Red Square, with particular force . . . The last part of the poem—lofty, forceful, and containing slogans—was read by Mayakovsky in one breath, as it were. There was no trace left of his former restraint. He turned himself—with voice and gesture—into what the phrases of the poem were proclaiming:

> Slaves,
>   straighten
>   your backs and knees!
> Let Revolution live,
>   joyful and swift!

The closing stanzas were drowned in the warm, sincere applause of the listeners. Mayakovsky stood there, serious again, but happy now . . .

Slips of paper with questions began to reach the platform before the reading was finished. They asked how long it had taken him to write the poem, whether he was a party member, why he would not join the party, etc. Mayakovsky approached the table and began to sort out the heap of questions, which were as numerous as ever. Unlike his usual custom, he did not reply to all of them but fished out one, which must have hurt him most, and said in a loud voice, "A comrade is asking here why I have written a course of political education in verse. To this I reply: for the education of those who have not yet been politically educated."

Voices of protest and indignation could be heard in the audience. But Mayakovsky stopped his emotional defenders and said that the question was quite in order. When writing the poem, he had been anxious all the time about not falling into sheer political journalism. Poetry is poetry.

"I remained a poet while writing this poem. It was very difficult, comrades," said Mayakovsky, as if explaining his present state.

FROM THE REMINISCENCES OF ILYA SELVINSKY, A CONVERSATION
WITH MAYAKOVSKY:

"If you want to know, the work of art of a highest order today is political propaganda!"

"Highest for you, because you cannot succeed in epic or in tragedy."

"My poem 'Lenin' is a genuine epic indeed!"

"As far as the volume of voice is concerned, but not in essence. Your poem is really 'I and Lenin,' while I want Lenin without your 'I.' "

"What you really want is poetry without my 'I' . . ."

♛ 26 ♛

Fame

♛

The thirty-year-old Mayakovsky, watching Bryusov celebrating his jubilee, realizes the bitterness of fame—Lila Brik tells about this. In 1925—as other observers assert—he is at the height of his fame. Though still opposed by dull officials and disloyal literary opponents, Mayakovsky gains the admiration and friendship of his younger colleagues. What he was like, how they saw him—this is told by Yuri Olesha, Mikhail Svyetlov, Vissaryon Sayanov, among others. In his "Message to Proletarian Poets" Mayakovsky offers to share his fame with them.

LILA BRIK:

I can only remember vaguely the occasion of Bryusov's half-centenary jubilee at the Bolshoi Theater in 1923. I recall I was sitting in a box with Mayakovsky.

There must have been a presiding committee and the like, but in my memory there is just the lonely Bryusov on the huge stage. Not one of his

old fellow writers was there—neither Balmont, nor Bely, nor Blok—no
one. Some died, others left Soviet Russia . . .

At one point Mayakovsky leaned toward me and whispered hastily,
"Let's go and see Bryusov; he must feel very bad just now." I remember
we had to walk a long way, probably around the entire theater. We found
Bryusov; he was standing alone, and Vladimir Vladimirovich spoke to him
in a particularly warm tone: "I congratulate you on your jubilee, Valeri
Yakovlevich!" Bryusov replied, "Thank you, but I don't wish you such a
jubilee." On the surface everything went on as it should have, but Mayakovsky sensed instinctively the state Bryusov was in.

ELSA TRIOLET:

I visited Moscow again in 1925 . . .

I had not witnessed Mayakovsky's climb to fame. But when I came to
Moscow in 1925, it was an accomplished fact. Cabmen, passers-by would
recognize him. One heard whispers, "Mayakovsky . . . look, Mayakovsky . . ."

Autographs, expressions of esteem . . . Soviet youth was with him
and on his side . . .

YURI OLESHA:

Soon after my arrival in Moscow, I was walking one fall evening with
Valentin Katayev. We were just going up Rozhdyestvensky Boulevard by
the monastery, when opposite us we saw a tall man in a short coat and fur
cap walking briskly and carrying a stick.

"Mayakovsky," Katayev whispered, "Look, look, Mayakovsky!"

I agreed at once that it must be Mayakovsky. He passed by—a man in
the dim yellow light of a misty day—passed by the lamp post, and it
seemed to us he had not two legs, but ten, as things usually look in the
fog.

I was not convinced it was Mayakovsky; Katayev was not quite convinced either, but later we came to be sure it must have been Mayakovsky.
We would tell our friends how on Rozhdyestvensky Boulevard we had
met Mayakovsky, how he had walked in the fog, and how it had seemed
to us in the fog that his legs had flashed like the spokes of a bicycle . . .
So much did we want to make contact with him, so great was our interest
in the poet! . . .

It is important that the reader understand the nature of Mayakovsky's fame. Even now we have well-known writers, artists, people active in all walks of life. But Mayakovsky's fame was legendary. What do I mean by such a description? The name of the man was constantly uttered; everyone would want to say something about him . . . Not even about his work, but about himself!

"I saw Mayakovsky yesterday and he . . ."

"And you know, Mayakovsky . . ."

"They say Mayakovsky . . ."

Such was his legendary fame. Yesenin had it too. It is most probable, if contemporary witnesses are to be believed, that Shalapin had been a legend to the same degree. And it is beyond any doubt that the whole country, and even the whole world, surrounded Maxim Gorki with such an aura.

That legendary fame was peculiar to the man himself. It may have originated in his very appearance. But it is born most surely when something particularly fascinating had occurred in the hero's past. Thus Gorki had been a tramp, Shalapin, a peasant, Mayakovsky, a futurist.

Gorki tried to ward off fame ("What do you take me for—a ballet dancer?") . . . Well, others whom I mentioned had not striven for it either; it followed them of its own accord. Mayakovsky, since we are speaking about him, never made faces, never struck poses. I remember once, having noticed someone's admiring eyes gaping at him, he said, not without humor but with some irritation, "He's looking at me and whispering something . . ."

His appearance, no matter where, always caused sensation and joy, was met with great interest, like the curtain going up in some exciting theater.

When I met Mayakovsky I was young, but I would forget any date with a girl, give it up, if I knew I could spend that hour with Mayakovsky.

To be with Mayakovsky was very flattering to one's self-esteem.

He probably knew this but used his influence on people—or rather, the force of the impression he produced—with great subtlety, carefully, delicately, always in good humor, so that, if the need arose, he could reduce his own importance for the sake of his partner's good frame of mind. He was, like all great personalities, a good man . . .

. . . He has just entered the crowded foyer of the "Chat Noir" Theater at Strastny Square. I am standing at the other end of the hall talking to the girl with me. I had just seen Mayakovsky for lunch in his apartment. Suddenly I see Vladimir Vladimirovich pushing his way through the crowd toward me, from one end of the hall to the other. He approaches us, takes off his hat respectfully and, bowing slowly, gives me a hearty handshake. I look at him with surprise. I do not understand what this means. But Mayakovsky turns around sharply, obscuring the view of half the hall with his broad shoulders, and goes away, again pushing his way through the crowd.

The next day I asked him, "Did you want to tell me something in the movie theater yesterday, Vladimir Vladimirovich? You greeted me so ceremoniously . . ."

"I had nothing to tell you," Mayakovsky replied seriously in his bass voice, "I just wanted to please your girlfriend by the fact that Mayakovsky himself greeted you so."

NATALYA BRIUKHANENKO

I seemed to have the impression that wherever Mayakovsky appeared, something interesting happened.

One day Mayakovsky and I went to the movies. There was a lottery in the foyer. One had to tear slips of paper with numbers on them from a big sheet. Mayakovsky got bored with the slow procedure, so he bought all the lottery numbers and won everything. We were handed pieces of soap, notebooks, some dishes, and carried away all those objects with us.

He was recognized everywhere: friends greeted him; enemies stopped him; everyone received a witty reply.

"Last night—and it was an audience of workers coming straight from work—someone recites, 'Work, work, work—there will be time to rest later!' What a dirty trick! This boorish tone. This is the way bourgeois owners speak to workers: 'Work, you will get your rest later, on Sunday.' He pats tired men on the shoulder. I hate the primitive accumulation of 'proletarian poets.' Tresses down to their shoulders, shining mugs, fame for the sake of girls. How they rush about, whisper in one's ear, introduce themselves, shake hands, envy one another, thinking, 'He has managed to get himself nicely settled with his poems.' 'Get nicely settled with poems' —just think! To be a working man's poet means hard work, day and night. I strain myself so over a line that I want to cry; I wake up at night, searching for the right word; I weep for joy when the line is finally completed . . . Do eat this sausage. You must eat sausage; butter too is good for you. Not for you, Bulka, butter is not for you. What a dog! Nice dog. The best dog under the sun."

Bulka—a French female bulldog—is fawning, her eyes protruding from their sockets. Mayakovsky looks at her seriously and affectionately and rubs her wet nose.

"A very handsome bulldog, the most handsome bulldog will be Bulka's husband. The doggie will be pregnant, no question about it, that doggie will be pregnant. Bulka, take your paws away, I must not be made nervous. Men are so nervous today. Do you fall in love sometimes? You don't? Maybe your love is not reciprocated. There will be wars, revolutions, then she will come to love you. Have you read Chernishevsky's *What to Do?* I am reading it now. The book interests me from a special angle. The problem then consisted of how to get out of the family; now it is how to get into it, how to create a family. This is very difficult. In the aspect of time— it is easier to build socialist cities . . ."

ILYA SELVINSKY:

"Please come and see me," Mayakovsky said to me one day.

"I will take you by the hand and lead you to Gosizdat."

"But they are not very keen on publishing you either."

"I don't give a damn. We'll go."

We did go.

Mayakovsky was carrying a bundle of books tied together with string. The secretary looked askance at the books and told us the director was in conference and no one was allowed in.

"You will go in and say 'good morning,' " Mayakovsky told me and went into the director's study.

I went in after him, stopped by the door and greeted them. Nobody reacted to me, because all of them, surprised, were looking at Mayakovsky, who, without paying attention to anyone, went up to the window sill, broke the string, and began to arrange his books, as if on parade. "Unfolding in parade the armies of his pages," he pointed them out to the people in conference with a wide gesture.

"There you are! See for yourselves! I've ripened for collected works! If you don't publish Mayakovsky, then whom do you publish?"

The chairman looked at Mayakovsky from above his spectacles and said dryly, "Comrade Mayakovsky, you are hindering us in our work."

"I? I hinder you?"

Mayakovsky could not contain himself for amazement: "I hinder you? It's you who hinder *me*! And that young man here! and all literature! You! You hinder us!"

VISSARION SAYANOV:

In January 1925, a numerous delegation of poets from Leningrad went to the first conference of proletarian writers . . .

We made our way into the crowded hall. An autograph collector, who happened to be sitting next to me, mentioned with a significant smile the eminent writers at the presidium table. At the far end of the platform one could see a man, cleanly-shaven head, an unlit cigarette butt in the corner of his mouth. He walked slowly between the empty chairs, lost in thought, concentrating, on something and not looking at the auditorium, not listening to the conversation of the people sitting near him.

"Mayakovsky," my neighbor said to me, and I felt excited almost in spite of myself. I was looking at the great poet for the first time. I always carried with me his book *Everything Composed by Vladimir Mayakovsky*, and I had to tolerate many disparaging words from the poet's enemies because of the affection I felt for him.

Mayakovsky . . . I find it difficult to describe how moved I was when my neighbor mentioned his name indifferently. Frozen with joy, I rushed to the front of the hall, sat down in the first row and began to look closely at Mayakovsky. He seemed to me young and beautiful. In the meantime the session had started and it was difficult to go on observing Mayakovsky: the first rows of the presidium were packed by now and he still remained at the back of the stage . . .

There was silence in the hall; members of the presidium talked in whispers; women stenographers were writing quickly in fat notebooks.

Mayakovsky was given the right to speak and greeted those present, but this did not disturb the order of the meeting . . . Demyan Byedny was to speak after him. But Demyan Byedny refused to speak immediately after Mayakovsky, from whom, according to him, proletarian writers had nothing to learn. Sosnovsky, a well-known journalist in those days, who was sitting next to Demyan Byedny, asked Mayakovsky, "Why did you make Lenin a general?"

The speaker who had taken the platform after Mayakovsky did not want to move away, and the poet had to reply from his seat: "I do not understand your question . . ."

"You will soon," Sosnovsky shouted, "You will soon . . ."

People began to shuffle in their seats; there were shouts and general noises . . .

The next speaker was not listened to very attentively. Everyone was waiting for Sosnovsky to explain his allegation that Mayakovsky had compared Lenin to a general. At that time, in the twenties, one could hardly think of a more insulting word.

Sosnovsky mounted the platform at last and cast a heavy scrutinizing look around the tensely expectant audience. The newspaper Sosnovsky was clutching in his hand was, as it turned out, a copy of *Izvestya*. He unfolded it and, in a very loud voice, read the following fragment from the poem *Vladimir Ilyich Lenin* . . .

> And from there
>   when the sight
>   reaches our days,
>   It will see
>   Lenin's
>   enormous trace.
>   It is
>   from the slavery
>   of ten thousand years
>   to the commune of ages
>   a sparkling general.

After the last line the audience uttered a groan.

"You see what liberties Mayakovsky allows himself in the columns of the Soviet press! He makes Lenin a general, and a sparkling one too . . .

Mayakovsky, agitated, rushed to the platform but was pushed back. He grew pale, and from a distance it looked as if he was biting his lip.

He wanted to reply, but the chairman closed the meeting. There was an uproar in the hall and no one could hear what Mayakovsky was saying . . .

An incredibly old beginner poet from the "Workers' Spring" group approached Demyan Byedny and said in a loud whisper, "I'll give you more examples from his poem . . . I've put them down . . . It's incredible . . .

Demyan Byedny pushed the pestering poet aside and left the hall with Sosnovsky, whose speech had made such a powerful impact.

Mayakovsky passed through the hall on his way out without looking around, his head raised high, not wishing to talk to anyone just then.

At the evening session that followed, the hall was packed full. Many young poets took their places on the platform. I was there too. I could see the people sitting on the stage very well. Mayakovsky was composed, a cigarette in the corner of his mouth and a faint smile on his face. He leafed through the pages of his notebook, into which someone sitting next to him was insolently trying to peep. Mayakovsky shrugged his shoulders and changed his place with some irritation.

At last the meeting was commenced. The chairman gave Mayakovsky the right to speak, to make his explanation. The poet walked to the rostrum with a slow, steady step. There was not much applause, but people listened carefully, trying to catch every word. An unusual silence fell as Mayakovsky began his speech. He spoke in a loud, clear voice and did not smile, or crack jokes, as he was accustomed to doing. It was a short, matter-of-fact, informative speech: facts, dates—no excitement in his voice, no polemics with the people who had bullied him about his poem.

Yes, the word "general" was printed in the *Izvestya,* but it was an error: not the poet but the typist who had copied the poem was to blame. Mayakovsky had not read the proofs—he had been in Paris at the time, a very long way from the editorial office. Is it convincing? Is it clear? So, those who attacked him were wrong. It is strange that they should have come forward with such a charge. Everyone who knows something about rhyming would know that one could not rhyme in this way. This is just illiteracy. In fact, the stanza runs differently:

And from there
                    when the sight
                                        reaches our days,
    It will see
            Lenin's
                    enormous   trace.
    It is
            from the slavery
                                of ten thousand years
        to the commune of ages
                            a sparkling trail.*

Sosnovsky made an involuntary grimace and shouted something from
his seat, but his words were drowned by applause. Mayakovsky was standing on the rostrum, big and strong, but it was apparent that he was taking
it hard: the wrinkles in the corners of his mouth were sharply out-
lined . . .

FROM ALEXANDER VORONSKY'S ARTICLE "VLADIMIR MAYAKOVSKY"
    IN THE MONTHLY "KRASNAYA NOV," NO. 2, 1925:

Mayakovsky's poetry is the cry of a "great physical" man, whose hands and
feet have been tied with the gigantic tentacles of a stony octopus, which is
sucking his marrow and blood. Mayakovsky has reflected the tragedy of
what is Peruvian in us, innate but perishing in the embraces of stony
snakes . . . Mayakovsky has shouted his SOS with an unusual force, because his hero—unfortunately, maybe—is unlike other people—with his
great height, large hands, with all his piled up emotions and instincts. . . .
    Mayakovsky is very lonely and remote from people. He does not like the
masses, the collective. The tribune and orator of his poems is isolated from
the crowd. He is an extreme individualist and an egocentric. He rightly
calls himself a demon in American shoes: there lies on him the brand of
rejection, exile, separation, and isolation . . .
    He is characterized by an unusual egocentrism. Mayakovsky, Mayakov-
sky, Mayakovsky, I, I, I, to me, with me, of me—the head spins with all
that. With such an egotism it is difficult to stand on equal footing with the

* In the original, instead of the word "pyeryeval," the newspaper printed the word
"gyenyeral," differing from the right one by a couple of letters only, and with a
similar sound, but making havoc with the sense of the stanza.

masses, even with the working masses, to feel equal, to grasp the same pulse of life, to take human needs to one's heart . . .

Mayakovsky has yet another constant and enduring theme—love . . . Mayakovsky has devoted his best, most inspired, and most forceful pages to that theme. He has created passionate, burning, and forceful words and images. Dealing with this theme, he has never put on the yellow tunic, never slid into grimace and falsehood. Who knows if in all our poetry we shall find other poems abounding in such passion and torment, in such fully revealed feeling. This, indeed, is heart and nothing but heart . . . It is not only physical. Love has been transformed into a deity, has become a religious emotion. From his beloved, the poet has made a phantom, a mirage . . . It is in fact a kind of escape from life. The poet's dreams and emotions have focused on the person of his beloved. She illuminates everything pagan and earthly—hate for the "ruler" and for everyday exist-ence, loneliness, longing, depression, and "the soul's forget-me-not"—and runs the gamut of his spiritual tremors . . .

In our Communist circles there are sceptics (Sosnovsky and others) who take the view that Mayakovsky only pretends to be a revolutionary and a Communist. This is a sad misunderstanding. Mayakovsky is sincere . . . But Mayakovsky does not view the revolution as an organized process of struggle and a victory over all difficulties and obstacles . . . Hence the schematic and abstract character of Mayakovsky's revolutionary poetry . . . His "Lenin" is a poster figure . . . Mayakovsky lacks an instinctive understanding of Lenin . . .

The sentiments "there is nowhere to go" and "I can't do anything about it," can be felt in much of Mayakovsky's recent work. But he stubbornly looks for ways to reach the new mass reader. Some chapters of the poem such as Lenin's funeral, prove that his search is not barren. At any rate, there is no ground for celebrating requiem masses for the soul of his tal-ent. New times demand new songs. It is not so easy to compose them, not at once. It is our custom to bury writers before their time. It would be better to think of how they could be helped. One must not forget that writers, both proletarian and others, are apt to go through quite heavy crises in our time, though talent is not lacking.

LUNACHARSKY'S LETTER TO THE DIRECTOR OF THE STATE
PUBLISHING HOUSE (KNOWN IN SHORT AS GIZ OR GOSIZDAT),
MARCH 16, 1925:

Dear Comrade!

Strange misunderstandings have occurred with Mayakovsky's collected works. Everyone agrees that he is a most outstanding poet, and no one, of course, has any doubt about his total unanimity with Soviet authority and the Communist party. But Giz publishes hardly any of his books. I know that the leading party circles think very highly of him. Why this blockage? Talk to Comrade Mayakovsky personally. I am convinced you will find a proper solution to this situation.

🦋

On March 26, Mayakovsky concluded an agreement with Gosizdat for the publication of his collected works in four volumes.

NATALYA KALMA, IN HER CHILDHOOD, WAS MAYAKOVSKY'S
NEIGHBOR IN A CRIMEAN RESORT:

The landlady felt a particular respect for Mayakovsky. It originated when he was staying at the little white house and tried, half in jest, and maybe half in earnest, to persuade Anna Ivanovna to order a commemorative plaque for the house in advance.

"Yes, babushka should order a plaque with an inscription to the effect that in such and such a year the well-known poet Mayakovsky lived here. He died in such and such a year. After my death they will certainly put a plaque on the wall of your house."

Anna Ivanovna spat and crossed herself: "What are you saying! You'll live a hundred years, Vladimir Vladimirovich."

But Mayakovsky insisted; "Seriously, you should order a plaque. After my death the state will buy this house from you."

This final argument was effective: "Where does one order such a plaque?" asked Anna Ivanovna.

from "THE MESSAGE TO PROLETARIAN POETS"
by Vladimir Mayakovsky

It is not my intention
              to boast
                      of the latest slogan,
but communism—
            is a place
                 in which for sure
for ever
        we shall say goodbye
                    to the bureaucrat
and find
        songs
            poems
               in plenty . . .
One thing I only fear,
             I must confess—
lest our souls
          be   flattened,
lest we lift up
          to communism's heights
some shallow sketches
             some trifling *chastushkas* . . .
Comrades,
        let us not bicker
              like shopkeepers:
are we to be afraid
        of poetry's
           little shop?
All I have ever done—
        is yours—
rhymes,
     themes,
        diction,
          bass!
What is there

that turns to ashes
faster
than fame?
Shall I take it
to the grave after death?
Comrades,
I don't give a damn
for money,
fame
and all the other rubbish! . . .

♯ 27 ♯

The Discovery of America

♯

The poet of the new era visits the New World. In Mexico he looks at "the first communist frescoes in the world" of Diego Rivera; in the United States he is satisfied that the original "futurism of naked technology" has been realized and formulates his revised program for civilization. On the way back he reveals his homesickness in the poem "Homeward Bound!"

FROM THE REMINISCENCES OF ELSA TRIOLET:

Mayakovsky was about to set out on a world trip and, as a result of persistent saving, had a sum of 25,000 francs, which he cashed at a bank one day in a lump sum, I do not know for what reason. On the next day a disaster occurred. I came to fetch him from his room in the morning. He was in his shirt sleeves, eating breakfast—his *jambon*. Before leaving the room he reached for his jacket, which was hanging on the back of the chair, and, with an automatic gesture, checked if there was everything he might need in the pockets. Suddenly I saw him turn pale! I have never seen anyone turn the color of ash just like that: all his money, all 25,000 francs had been stolen.

At the very start of his trip around-the-world, which was to last a year, he found himself without a sou in his pocket . . .

Anyone else in his place would have tried to find the money for a return trip to Moscow and leave, somewhat ashamed and very angry. But not Mayakovsky. His depression did not last more than an hour. On the way to the police station, though forgetting to adjust his step to mine this time, he was already saying, "Above all, we must not change anything in our way of life. We will have lunch at the "Grande Chaumière," and then I'll do some shopping . . ." It was not his custom to give way to life's pressures . . .

He now went about getting money so that he could collect the sum he had lost. Lila managed to obtain a fairly large loan for him from a Moscow publisher, which he was to repay in a year or two. He tried to get the balance wherever he could. He asked everywhere for loans. From the start it turned into a game: "What do you think, how much will so-and-so give me? Two hundred? I say, one hundred and fifty. The balance is for you. And so-and-so? Nothing? And I say, a thousand. If he gives me anything, you will owe me twenty francs." This was in 1925, while the Exhibition of Decorative Art was on; there were quite a few Soviet Russians in Paris. From then on we judged people by how much money they would give and in what manner, if they gave anything at all. Friends who had money and refused a loan, ceased to exist for Mayakovsky . . .

On the other hand, someone who gave Mayakovsky more than he had counted on, gained his sympathy at once. Thus Ilya Ehrenburg, whom he had until now treated fairly indifferently, captured his heart with fifty Belgian francs. Ehrenburg had just come from Belgium and his financial situation was not good. Those fifty francs were the object of the constant affectionate remarks on the part of Mayakovsky: "Belgian, he would say, just think, they're Belgian!" He would then roar with laughter. He began to call Ehrenburg by his first name and to discover all kinds of good qualities in him . . .

TELEGRAM FROM PARIS, JUNE 10, 1925:

I kiss dear Pussy. Do not worry and do not send me money. Just press Gosizdat. Ticket has not been stolen. Kisses. All yours Pup

LETTERS FROM THE BOAT "ESPAGNE":

Dear Lila!

Since we have sighted Spain, I am availing myself of the opportunity to let you know I am now successfully going around her and even entering a little port—look it up on the map—Santander.

My *Espagne* is quite a good boat. Have not found any Russians as yet. There are men wearing both belts and suspenders (they are Spaniards) and women with huge earrings (they are Spanish women). Two little dogs are running about. Japanese, but carrots, and both identical.

I kiss you, darling, and rush to look up in French how to send this letter off.

I kiss you and Osya.

All yours,
Pup

Dear-dear, kind, kind, kind
and my most beloved Lila!

Did you get my two letters from the trip? We are now approaching the island of Cuba—its port, Havana (the one that gives its name to cigars). We shall stay here a day or two. I avail myself of the opportunity once more to post a letter, hopelessly.

Unbearable heat!

Just now we are making our way through the tropic.

I have not yet seen the Capricorn in whose honor the tropic has been named.

To the right, the first genuine land, Florida, is to be seen (if we discount trifles like the Azores). It would be the right thing to do to write a poem about Christopher Columbus, but this is very difficult: It is impossible to find out the diminutive for Christopher. And to find rhymes for Columbus (difficult enough as it is) haphazardly—would be something heroic under the tropic.

I can't say I find the boat trip very pleasant. Twelve days of water is good for fishes and professional explorers, but for landsmen it is too much. I have not learned to speak French and Spanish, but I have improved my facial expressions, because this happens to be the way I communicate with people . . .

My Dear, only, beloved little Pussy!

I posted a letter in the daytime, and now it is evening and I am already missing you, already and awfully, awfully.

I walked on the upper deck where there are only machines and no people and suddenly I saw a gray and very young kitten I had not seen before.

I went up and caressed him instead of you, but he ran away from me behind the lifeboats.

But you, Pussy, will not run away from me behind the lifeboats, will you?

You mustn't run behind the boats, darling!

I love you awfully, awfully!

Two little yellow Japanese dogs and one Spanish grayhound bitch send you their regards. They understand everything and talk to me in Russian.

The dinner bell has just rung.

It is terribly boring to have to go to dinner.

Everyday when I get up I think about why everything is so awful and why you do not get up from the empty berth No. 104.

I want to see you badly.

I kiss you, my dearest, and love you.

All yours,
Pup

TELEGRAM TO LILA BRIK FROM MEXICO, JULY 10, 1925:

Well Have arrived Stop Address Whin 37 Mexico Kisses Pup

FROM AN INTERVIEW WITH MAYAKOVSKY, PUBLISHED IN THE MEXICAN NEWSPAPER "EXCELSIOR," JULY 10, 1925:

The poet was talking through an interpreter with the Mexican painter Diego Rivera, when we called at the embassy for an interview . . .

The embassy's secretary, Mr. Volynsky, warned us that Mayakovsky spoke only Russian. When we expressed surprise at the fact that he had managed to cross the ocean and so many countries without an interpreter, Mayakovsky replied that he had passed the time on board ship playing poker . . .

We asked Mayakovsky whether he was on a mission from the government of his country and whether he was a party member. The gist of his answer was that he had renounced official activity a long time ago and the only purpose of his journey was to fulfill a very strong desire to get to know our country . . .

Mayakovsky led us to understand that Russian literature dealt solely with social themes and was favorably disposed to the system of government in Russia . . .

FROM MAYAKOVSKY'S "MY DISCOVERY OF AMERICA":

Diego Rivera greeted me at the railway station. That is why the first thing I came to know in Mexico was painting.

I had heard earlier only that Diego was one of the founders of the Communist party in Mexico, that he was the greatest Mexican painter, and that he could hit a coin thrown in the air with his revolver. I knew also that Julio Jurenito was meant by Ehrenburg to be Diego's portrait.

Diego turned out to be a formidable man, with quite a paunch, and with a broad, ever-smiling face . . .

From the station we went to the hotel to leave the luggage, then to the museum. On the way Diego acknowledged hundreds of greetings, shaking hands with those closest to him and exchanging shouts with people walking on the opposite side of the street. In the museum we looked at the ancient, round Aztec calendars engraved in stone from Mexican pyramids and at two-faced wind deities whose one face was chasing the other. They were not shown to me for nothing. The Mexican ambassador in Paris, Mr. Reyes, a well-known Mexican novelist, had already informed me that modern art in that country had its origins in the ancient, colorful, unsophisticated folk art of the Indians, not in the decadent eclectic forms imported from Europe, and that the idea of art is part—perhaps not yet quite consciously so—of the idea of the struggle and liberation of colonial slaves.

In his as yet uncompleted work—the frescoes on the building of the Mexican Ministry of Education—Diego wants to combine the simple characteristic ancient art with the latest novelties of modern French painting.

On dozens of walls, the past, present, and future history of Mexico is represented . . .

On that day I had dinner at Diego's residence . . .

Afterward we went into the drawing room. In the middle of the divan his one-year-old son was lying; at the head—on a cushion—a big Colt revolver.

LETTER FROM THE NEW YORK ART STUDIO OF WILLY POGANY, JULY 15, 1925:

Dear Mr. Mayakovsky:

·Your friends have informed us of your desire to visit the United States and organize here an exhibition of your posters and other publicity material. Our studio will gladly offer you this chance and is also ready to give you all necessary assistance. We are writing about this to the State Department, informing them that we will be happy to help you, that you are coming at our invitation, for a limited time only, that you wish to acquaint yourself with American art and the American way of life, and also to exhibit some of your work. We expect to have the pleasure of seeing you soon and wish you a pleasant journey.

DECLARATION OF A NON-IMMIGRANT ALIEN
ARRIVING IN USA

American Consular Service

American Consulate. Mexico City, *July 24, 1925.*

I, *Vladimir Mayakovsky,* citizen of *Russia,* holder of passport no. *36258,* issued *January 12, 1925* in *Moscow, Russia,* intend to visit United States of America accompanied by ————.

I was born on *July 7, 1893* in *Bagdadi, Russia.* Occupation practiced in the last two years—*artist-painter.* At present—*likewise.*

I want to go to the United States in order to *exhibit my work there* and I intend to stay for the period of *up to 5 months.* My address in USA will be: *Willy Pogany, 152 West 46 Street, New York.*

. . . I understand that in view of the fact that I do not belong to the category of persons who are excluded from the application of USA immigration laws, whose purpose is to limit the influx of foreigners to USA, it may so happen that my classification as a non-immigrant alien will be revised on arrival in the United States and that in such a case the USA immigration authorities can hold or expel me, and I take upon myself all the risk of expulsion or compulsory return, which this entails.

I solemnly swear and declare that all my answers given above are absolutely true in the sense I understand them.

Vladimir Mayakovsky

Signed and sworn on July 24, 1925.
Vice-Consul USA /signature/
Visa issued as a non-immigrant, according to 3/2/ of the Act of 1924. Purpose of journey: temporary stay. The validity of this visa expires exactly 6 months after the day of issue. /N.b. the italic text has been filled in on a typewriter, the rest is printed./

FROM THE NEW YORK RUSSIAN LANGUAGE COMMUNIST
NEWSPAPER "NOVY MIR," JULY 30, 1925:

Vladimir Mayakovsky in New York

After a brief stay in Mexico, Vladimir Mayakovsky arrives today in New York.

ELSA TRIOLET:

An old friend of Mayakovsky's, David Burliuk . . . has lived in America for some years . . . Mayakovsky telephoned him on arrival: "Mayakovsky speaking."

"Hello, Volodya. How are you?" Burliuk's voice replied.

"Thank you. In the last ten years I had a cold once . . ."

THE NEW YORK PAPER "RUSSKI GOLOS," AUGUST 1, 1925:

. . . In our Sunday edition, read David Burliuk's feuilleton "With Mayakovsky," in which Mayakovsky describes his trip to Mexico.

"RUSSKI GOLOS," AUGUST 2, 1925, DAVID BURLIUK:

I had not seen Vladimir Mayakovsky, poet and painter, the most outstanding bard of contemporary new Russia, since April, 1918 . . .

It was then that I parted with him in Moscow.

I was greatly moved when I heard his sonorous, manly, basso profundo voice on the telephone.

I recognized his voice at once—the same voice! The voice had not changed!

I rushed to the subway and hurried to Fifth Avenue, where Mayakovsky was staying.

From the distance I already noticed the big "Russian" foot on the doorstep and a couple of heavy suitcases in the doorway.

I recognized that foot at once: it could only belong to Mayakovsky . . .

We looked at each other for a long time, first in the dark hall. Then I
watched Mayakovsky take a bath; he washed the dust of tropical Mexico
and hot Texas from his lion's mane and powerful body.

. . . As the poet said, more than seven years have flown by like swift
birds. So much has changed . . .

And Vladimir Vladimirovich is just as young, throws the bricks of his
jokes around just as before. There is nothing strange in this. After all, he is
only thirty. And who will be weighed down by fame, even if world fame,
at the happy age of thirty?!

INTERVIEW WITH MICHAEL GOLD, "NEW YORK WORLD,"
AUGUST 9, 1925:

Russia's Dynamic Poet Finds New York Tame; We're Old-Fashioned,
Unorganized, to Mayakovsky; "Manhattan is an Accident
Stumbled On By Children," He Declares

Mayakovsky is in New York; Vladimir Mayakovsky! Boom, bang, boom!

Tear the subway out of the ground. Wrap it around the neck of the
Woolworth Tower, and let it wave like a modern scarf in the wind.

Sharpshoot the meaningless sun out of the sky and turn it to modern
uses. Paint it with futurist advertisements for culture and release it back
into the vacant heavens.

Church bells for cymbals, huge cannons for drums, and a thousand
wild brass cornets and trombones and tubas to serenade Mayakovsky!

Let the elevated roar twice as loud as ever, the street cars clang, the
taxis rattle and squeal and honk, the riveters spatter and punch, the city is
too quiet for Mayakovsky! Get up a parade to impress him; with floats
holding derricks, steam-shovels, garment factory dynamos, and sewing
machines and a procession of giant proletarians juggling skyscrapers and
steel foundries coming last in triumph . . .

The Industrial Age, this is what Mayakovsky arrived in New York a
few days ago to see, Mayakovsky, who for the past ten years has been the
best-known poet in Soviet Russia, the voice of its new storm and chaos
and construction, the laureate of its new machinery, the apostle of indus-
trialism to a nation still half Asiatic and medieval . . .

"No, New York is not modern," he said, in his room near Washington

Square, as he restlessly paced the floor. "New York is unorganized. Mere machinery, subways, skyscrapers and the like do not make a real industrial civilization. These are only the externals.

"America has gone through a tremendous material development which has changed the face of the world. But the people have not yet caught up to their new world . . . Intellectually, New Yorkers are still provincials. Their minds have not accepted the full implications of the industrial age.

"That is why I say New York is unorganized—it is a gigantic accident stumbled upon by children, not the full-grown, mature product of men who understood what they wanted and planned it like artists. When our industrial age comes in Russia it will be different—it will be planned—it will be conscious . . .

"Or take these self-same skyscrapers of yours. They are glorious achievements of the modern engineer. The past knew nothing like them. The plodding hand-workers of the Renaissance never dreamed of these great structures that sway in the wind and defy the laws of gravity. Fifty stories upward they march into the sky; and they should be clean, swift, complete, and modern as a dynamo. But the American builder, only half-aware of the miracle he has produced, scatters obsolete and silly Gothic and Byzantine ornaments over the skyscrapers. It is like tying pink ribbons on a steam dredge, or like putting Kewpie figures on a locomotive . . .

I interrupted the torrent of futurist energy and asked him a question which he did not like: "These liberal intellectual mystics you mentioned run away, in America, from the machine. They think it is destroying the soul of man. Don't you Russians have the same fear of becoming too mechanical?"

"No," said the poet positively. "We are the masters of the machine and therefore do not fear it. The old mystic, emotional life is dying, yes, but a new one will take its place. Why should one fear history? Or fear that men will become machines? It is impossible."

. . . he was raging up and down, puffing cigarettes like a smokestack. But he wanted to say these things to the Russians, on paper, in a futurist poem. And so the interview closed abruptly and he was left to himself, to stand by the window and contemplate lower Fifth Avenue.

The modern Russians have a great respect for this young giant . . . Not an insignificant achievement for a young man of thirty, living in a nation of 150 million. And now the young man is living near Washington

Square and at night he goes to Negro cabarets in Harlem or shoots pool on Fourteenth Street. Occasionally he talks to a friend and complains about the peculiar provincialism and smalltownishness of New York.

FROM MAYAKOVSKY'S "MY DISCOVERY OF AMERICA":

I LIKE NEW YORK in the fall, on ordinary working days.

Six in the morning. Stormy and rainy. It is dark and will be dark till noon.

A man gets dressed by electric light, in the streets electric lights, houses with electric lights, evenly cut by windows like the pattern of a publicity poster. Houses spread endlessly, traffic lights flash with colored signals, movements double, triple, multiply on the asphalt, on the rain-licked mirror. In the narrow groves of buildings some adventurous wind roars, tears, rattles the signboards, tries to sweep people off their feet and escapes unpunished, unarrested by anyone, down the many miles of dozens of avenues cutting through Manhattan Island—from the ocean to the Hudson. On both sides the storm is accompanied by the countless little voices of narrow streets, also even, to measure, cutting across Manhattan, water to water. Under cover—or on fine days just on the pavement—big bunches of newspapers are lying, brought earlier by trucks and thrown down here by newsboys . . .

Down below, a mass of human flesh is flowing: first the black mass of Negroes, who do the hardest and least pleasant work. Then—at about seven—a sea of whites. They go in one direction, hundreds of thousands of them, to their places of work. Only the yellow impregnated raincoats are shining in the electric light, wet through but unextinguished even under that rain.

There are almost no cars or taxis yet.

The crowd flows, filling the entrance holes to the subway and the covered passages of the elevated railway, going up in the air on two levels and three parallel tracks in fast trains, seldom stopping, and local trains stopping every five blocks . . .

I like New York best in the mornings and in the storm: there are no gaping passers-by, not one superfluous person, only members of the huge working army of a city of 10 million inhabitants.

Masses of workers disappear into clothing factories, into the new, not yet completed subway tunnels, go to the innumerable occupations in the

port. At eight the streets are filled with slender, cleaner, and more cultivated young ladies, most of them with short hair, bare knees, rolled stock-
ings—they work in banks, offices, and shops. This crowd will disperse
throughout the many storys of the downtown skyscrapers, on both sides of
the corridors reached by the main entrance with dozens of elevators . . .

If you need an office, you do not have to think about how you are going
to arrange for one.

You just telephone someone on the thirtieth floor: "Hallo! Get a six-
room office ready for tomorrow. Twelve typists. Signpost: 'The Great and
Reputable Business for the Provision of Pressed Air for Pacific Subma-
rines.' Two office boys in brown livery—caps with star ribbons and 12,000
letterheads, headlined as above. Goodbye."

On the next day you can just go to your office and will be greeted by
your enthralled messengers: "How do you do, Mr. Mayakovsky."

At one—a break: an hour for the office staff and fifteen minutes for the
workers.

Lunch.

Everyone consumes lunch according to the weekly pay he gets. The
fifteen-dollar earners buy a packed lunch for a nickel and munch it with
youthful diligence.

The thirty-five-dollar earners go to a large automat, deposit 5 cents,
press a button, and an exact measure of coffee pours into a cup; two or
three more coins open a glass compartment with sandwiches on large,
food-filled shelves.

The sixty-dollar earners eat pancakes with syrup and scrambled eggs in
bathroom-white Childs' Rockefeller restaurants.

Those who earn more than a hundred dollars go to restaurants of all
nationalities—Chinese, Russian, Assyrian, French, Indian—all but American, because those serve bad food and guarantee indigestion caused by
Armour's canned meat, which almost reminds one of the War of Independence . . .

You would try in vain in New York to find grotesque organizational
methods, speed, cold bloodedness—all those qualities made famous
through literature.

You will find many people walking about without any particular purpose. Everyone will stop and talk to you on any subject. If you raise your
eyes and stop for a while, you will soon be surrounded by a crowd, con-

trolled with difficulty by a policeman. I am, for the most part, reconciled to the New York crowd thanks to their ability to find other entertainment besides the stock exchange.

Work again till five, six, seven in the evening.

The hours from five to seven are the noisiest and most crowded.

Those who are on their way home from work are joined by shoppers and people just taking a walk.

On the very crowded Fifth Avenue, which divides the city in two, from the heights of the upper decks of hundreds of buses, you will see, washed down by a recent rain and now shining, tens of thousands of cars, rushing in both directions in rows of six to eight . . .

At six or seven, Broadway lights are up. This is my favorite street, which, among streets and avenues that are as straight as prison bars, is the only one that cuts, capriciously and insolently, across the others. To lose one's way in New York is more difficult than in Tula. Avenues run from south to north; streets, from east to west. That is all. I am at the corner of Eighth Street and Fifth Avenue, and I am looking for the corner of Fifty-third Street and Second Avenue; that means I have to walk uptown, pass forty-five side streets, and turn right to the corner of Second Avenue.

Lights do not go on all along the entire, twenty-five-mile-long Broadway (here a man is not going to say, "Please drop in; we're neighbors; we both live on Broadway") but only from Twenty-fifth to Fiftieth Street, particularly at Times Square—this is, as the Americans say, the Great White Way.

It really is white and one really has the impression that it is brighter there at night than in the daytime, because there is light everywhere in the daytime, but this White Way, against the background of the black night, is bright as day. The lights of street lamps, the jumping lights of advertisements, the glow of shop windows and windows of the never-closing shops, the lights illuminating huge posters, lights from the opening doors of cinemas and theaters, the rushing lights of automobiles and trolley cars, the lights of the subway trains glittering under one's feet through the glass pavements, the lights of inscriptions in the sky.

Brightness, brightness, brightness.

One can read a newspaper, the newspaper of the person next to one and in a foreign language.

There is light in the restaurants and in the theater district.

The main streets, where owners and those who are grooming themselves for the part live, are clean.

But in the poor Jewish, Negro, Italian quarters—where most of the workers and office staff live—on Second and Third Avenues, between First and Thirtieth Streets, it is dirtier than in Minsk. And it is very dirty in Minsk.

Garbage cans stand there with all kinds of refuse, from which beggars pick out bones and other scraps. Stinking pools of yesterday's and the day before yesterday's rain, are still around.

One walks ankle-deep in all kinds of rubbish, not metaphorically but literally ankle-deep.

All this at a distance of only fifteen minutes' walk, or five minutes by car, from the dazzling Fifth Avenue and Broadway.

The closer to the port, the darker, dirtier, and more dangerous it is.

In the daytime it is a most interesting quarter. There is a constant roar here—work, shots, shouts. The ground is shaken by cranes which unload ships, and are almost capable of lifting up a whole house at once.

When there is a strike, picket lines are set up and no strikebreakers are allowed to pass through.

The avenues next to the port, are called the "Avenues of Death," because of the freight trains, which drive right onto the street, and because of the little bars full of gangsters.

They provide bandits for the whole of New York . . .

A bandit who gets caught risks the electric chair in Sing Sing. But he can get out of it, too. When setting out on a robbery, he goes to his solicitor and declares, "Give me a ring, sir, at such and such a time, such and such a number. If I am not there, it means you have to stand bail for me and get me out of the jug."

Bail is always large, but bandits are not poor and they are well organized . . .

Newspapers have written about a certain bandit who left the prison forty-two times on bail. The Irish are active here on the Avenue of Death; in other quarters there are other nationalities.

Negroes, Chinese, Germans, Jews, Russians—all have their own quarters, with their own customs and languages, keeping their identity intact through the decades.

In New York, not counting the suburbs, there are approximately:

1,700,000 Jews
1,000,000 Italians
500,000 Germans
300,000 Irishmen
300,000 Russians
250,000 Negroes
150,000 Poles
300,000 Spaniards, Chinese, Finns

A puzzling picture: who are the Americans, and who among them is 100 percent American? . . .

At midnight those who come out of the theaters drink one last soda, eat one last ice-cream cone, and are at home by one or by three, if they have spent about two hours rubbing against each other in a foxtrot, or in the latest fashion—the Charleston. But life does not end even then. Shops of all kinds are open as usual, elevated and subway trains run as usual, one can find an all-night movie house and sleep there to one's heart's content for the 25 cents he has paid for admission.

Having come home, if this is spring or summer, shut the windows to keep out the mosquitoes; wash your ears and nose and cough out the coal dust . . . If you have scratched yourself, put iodine on it: the New York air is full of all kinds of bacteria, from which you can get sties (all scratches are apt to swell), and which millions who have nothing and cannot get away anywhere, have to breathe . . .

SHAKHNO EPSTEIN: "WITH VLADIMIR MAYAKOVSKY THROUGH
FIFTH AVENUE," IN THE NEW YORK YIDDISH COMMUNIST
NEWSPAPER "FREIHEIT," AUGUST 14, 1925:

"Well, Vladimir Vladimirovich, how do you like America?"

Mayakovsky throws away the stub of a Russian cigarette, lights another cigarette, and begins to walk across the big furnished room on Fifth Avenue. His tall, strong figure, with energetic suntanned face and strong muscles is as deft as if he had been marching . . . It is very difficult to recognize the Russian in him. He looks more like a Mexican cowboy. He stops, glances through the window at Fifth Avenue and says in his deep, thundering voice, which fills the entire room with its reverberation, "Eh, it's boring here . . ."

We walked down into the street . . . Around us a merry-go-round of

cars, a deafening noise of advertisers . . . The poet says, "So we are supposed to be a 'backward,' 'barbarian' nation. We are only just starting.
Every new tractor is an event for us. Every new threshing machine, a very
important thing. And if a new power plant is opened, this is something
sensational. We still come here for these things. But, in spite of everything,
it is dull here, while in our parts it is gay. Here everything smells of decay,
is dying, rotting, while our life is boiling over, the future is ours . . .

"We are walking now through one of the richest streets in the world—
skyscrapers, palaces, hotels, shops, and crowds. But I have a feeling I am
walking among ruins, and I am depressed. Why am I not depressed in
Moscow, where the pavements are really dilapidated and still not re-
paired, where there are many ruined houses, where streetcars are over-
crowded and worn out past repair? The answer is simple: because there is
life there, thriving, seething; the energy of an entire nation-collective has
been liberated and is overflowing . . .

"Let us take our films and yours. Our technical equipment (lights etc.)
is still very bad. You have all the latest technical inventions, a sea of lights.
But with us, all the old trash is being swept away, everything reaches for
the light. And here? You don't have those aspirations; you have only dirty
little "moralizing," sentimental sniveling, as if one suddenly found oneself
in the deepest provinces, in the Middle Ages. How can this kind of "moralizing" coexist with the highest technical achievement—I mean radio?"

We had been so engrossed in our conversation that we hardly noticed
that we had arrived at Central Park. We sat down on a bench in a path
leading to Fifth Avenue. It was dusk. A mad whirlpool of cars, buses,
streetcars, ever-growing crowds of people, never beginning, never ending.
All this rattles and roars, rings and crackles. Mayakovsky withdrew into
himself. I could see what an effect the peculiar language of the street had
on him. It was as if he were taking in all those sounds. He took out a
black, leather notebook and began to write something in it, very fast, as if
to the rhythm of the din surrounding us. His figure gradually attracted
general attention. Some people began to gape at him with a surprised
look. But he did not notice anyone, not even me sitting next to him.

Suddenly Mayakovsky got up and said, "Let's go."

When we were back in his room, Mayakovsky said, "I have caught the
tempo of New York, the dull, suppressed tempo. It will be a new poem:
"Mayakovsky on Fifth Avenue" . . .

from "BROOKLYN BRIDGE"
by Vladimir Mayakovsky

. . . If the world topples,
                              cataclysm comes,
chaos
        strikes the planet
                              the final blow,
and only the one
                the last
                              will remain
the bridge bristling
                    over the rock of extermination—
as from excavated bones
                          from little fragments
an ancient reptile
                  is in museums reborn,
from this bridge,
              a future
                              geologist of ages
our days
        will recreate
                      all our world.
He will say:
            —This here
                          steel paw
prairies and seas
                had joined,
from here
          Europe
                      crawled to the West,
having set,
            with the wind,
                              Indian feathers on fire . . .
Electric yarn
              had supplanted steam—
from it I see

what at that time they could do:
send a winged machine
                    up to the skies,
in a big voice
            to each other
                        roar on the radio.
Here
        some
                carefree
                        led their lives,
others howled from hunger,
                        cursed their vale of tears.
From here—
            to the Hudson's roaring mane,
the unemployed
            threw themselves
                        headlong.
And other details—
                just trifles—
are from the former
                an obvious conclusion:
it was right here
            that Mayakovsky stood,
standing here
            he composed his poems.—
. . . Like a child
            with his nose glued to the shop window,
like an Eskimo at a train,
                like magpie at a bone,
I
    am looking
            at Brooklyn Bridge—
yes . . .
            That is something indeed!

"FREIHEIT," AUGUST 13, 1925:
Who does not avail himself tomorrow of the chance to meet Mayakovsky

personally will not forgive himself for a long time. Get your tickets today, so that tomorrow you are not one of the crowd of those unable to get in.

"NOVY MIR," SEPTEMBER 17, 1925:

In unity, strength. Who will stay at home on Saturday? Nobody! Who will go to the movies? Nobody! Who will be asleep at 8:30? Nobody! Everybody will go to Unity Cooperative Camp at a poetry reading by the poet Vladimir Mayakovsky.

"NOVY MIR," SEPTEMBER 26, 1925:

Listen, Clevelander! Theater will not run away, movies will not run away; friends will not run away; but Vladimir Mayakovsky is leaving for the Soviet Union. But before he leaves, he will visit Cleveland. That is why we will all go to Carpenter Hall, 2226 East 55 Street, on September 29 to see Mayakovsky and listen to a poetry reading by him.

DAVID BURLIUK:

In the course of all his public appearances, Mayakovsky sold his books to the public. First he published a collection *To the Americans,* printed in the printing house of the newspaper *Novy Mir,* with the author's portrait facing the title page. But soon 10,000 copies of the book were sold and his public still asked for the book as a souvenir, and with the autograph of the popular poet.

It was then that Mayakovsky suggested that I undertake to publish two books: *Sun* and *The Discovery of America* . . . I made drawings for them; I set the type and read the proofs myself . . . Instead of *Sun* I put on the cover: *Sun Visits Mayakovsky.* Volodya was angry, but it was too late to do anything about it. I did not feel any remorse because of my "mistake." I did what I thought was best . . .

MAYAKOVSKY:

I suppose that foreigners respect me, but it is not impossible either that they think I am an idiot . . . Put yourselves in the Americans' position: they have invited a poet, who they have been told is a genius. Genius is something more than a personality. I come and the first thing I say is, "Give me please some tea!"

Very well. They give me tea. I wait—and then, "Give me please . . ."

They serve tea again.

And I go on and on, changing my inflection and facial expression, "Give me" and "some tea," "some tea" and "give me" I say. And so the evening passes . . .

"Translate them this," I roar to Burliuk. "If they knew Russian, I could —without touching their undershirts—nail them with my tongue to their own suspenders, I would turn on the spit all that insect collection . . ."

And Burliuk translates conscientiously, "My eminent friend, Vladimir Mayakovsky, asks for another glass of tea."

FROM ALEXEI KRUCHENYKH'S STATEMENT, ENTITLED "HAS LEF DIED?" IN THE DAILY "VECHERNAYA MOSKVA," OCTOBER 9, 1925:

One often hears questions: Why does not LEF (Left Art Front) organize literary evenings any more? Why does it not publish its periodical and, in general? Why does it not roar and make noise as it used to do in the years 1913–1914, or 1922–1923? Is it not exhaustion? Is it not decline?

Nothing like that.

In the years 1913–1914, we LEFists concentrated our forces . . . now we devote our attention not to the concentration of forces in one place but to the widening and deepening of our activity.

Mayakovsky is now engaged in LEFist agitation abroad, particularly in America. In the organizing of meetings he is being helped by David Burliuk, who has been living in New York for two years now and has founded the "American LEF" there. He is editing a periodical with that title . . .

On the way to America Mayakovsky stopped for a time in Paris, where he met the leader of Italian futurists, Marinetti. Their conversation will be published.

Ilya Zdanyevich carries on LEF activities in Paris. Rodchenko's and Lavinsky's posters, which received awards at the Paris exhibition, greatly helped LEF's propaganda.

Sergei Tretyakov has just returned from Peking, where he lectured in Russian literature at the university.

All this means a broad LEF front.

LEF is becoming international . . .

The futurism of naked technology, of superficial impressionism of smoke and cables, whose great mission was to revolutionize the set, village-ridden mentality—that original futurism has been finally confirmed by America . . .

The following task of LEF is standing before art workers, not to extol technology but to curb it in the name of humanity's interests; not to look for aesthetic delight in iron fire escapes of skyscrapers but to arrange living quarters.

What is there in automobiles? . . . There are many cars; it is time to think how not to let them poison the cities' air.

It is not a skyscraper—a place where it is impossible to live, and yet one lives.

The wheels of the rushing subway spit out dust and it seems the train is running through our ears.

Not to extol noise but to put up sound absorbers we poets must talk in the cars.

Flight without an engine, wireless telegraph, radio, buses which push streetcars out of the way, the subway which drives underground everything that could be seen above.

Perhaps the technology of tomorrow, multiplying man's strength a millionfold, will find a way to abolish scaffoldings, booms, and other technological surfaces.

"HOMEWARD BOUND"
by Vladimir Mayakovsky

Sail away, thoughts, go your way.
Let soul's depths
                    unite
                            with depths of sea.
He who is cheerful all the time—
is
    in my view
                a common fool.
I am stuck
            in the worst of all cabins,

till the morning
        over my ceiling
                they shuffle their feet.
Till the morning
        stubbornly
              constantly
the tune is whining
          they toss about dancing:
"Markita, Markita,
about you I dream,
why oh, Markita,
don't you love me . . ."
And why should
        Markita love me?
I have not got
        a bent sou.
Give her a hundred francs—
           that's all—
just wink—
        Markita's yours.
It's not much, you know—
          why not live smartly once?
Oh no,
      you intellectual,
           frowning your poet's brow,
will force on her
        the poetic machine,
stitch by stitch
        backstitching poems.
Below
      the proletarian
           to communism strides,
through the murmur of fields
          and the noise of factories—
I
    from the skies of poetry
         throw myself into communism,

for without it
                there is for me
                                no love.
I deported myself,
                have been deported—
                                what's the difference—
the steel of words rusts
                and copper of bass blackens.
Why
        in rainy foreign parts
am I to soak and rot—
                I really do not know.
I am lying
        somewhere beyond the seas,
parts of my mechanism
                are hardly vibrating.
I feel I am
        a Soviet factory,
producing happiness.
I do not want
                like a flower on the clearing
to be plucked,
                when they take their rest.
Let a state commission
                make plans,
over a task for me
                sweating.
I want
        the commissar of time
                        over a thought
To hover with a demand.
I want
        the expert according to a list
To issue
        love
                for the heart.
I want

the plant's director
                    after working hours
to put a padlock on my lips.
I want
            pen to be equaled with bayonet.
I want
        a report
                on making poetry
to be delivered
                on Polit-Bureau's behalf
                                by Stalin,
as much as those
                on cast iron and steel.
"Thus
        and thus . . .
                    to the highest achievements
we have come
                from a monstrous past.
In the Union of Republics
                    the understanding of poems
has exceeded
                prewar standards . . ."
I want my native country
                    to understand me—
and if it doesn't—
                I will bear this too:
I will pass
        sideways
                    over my country,
like a sidelong
            rain
                does pass.

On his return to Russia, Mayakovsky published the poem
"Homeward Bound!" twice in the above version, but printing
it for the third time, omitted the last stanza.

✵ 28 ✵

Yesenin

✧

On December 27, 1925 Sergei Yesenin hanged himself in the Angleterre Hotel in Leningrad at the age of thirty. Vladimir Mayakovsky shot himself four and a half years later. But it was not then that their fate first coincided; not even when, on the publication of the poem Yesenin had written just before he died, Mayakovsky engaged in a unique poetic polemics with him. They had been brought together much earlier by what had both joined and divided them: both Yesenin and Mayakovsky reached for supremacy over their countrymen's souls. In this era other excellent poets were also active. But these two overstepped the boundaries of poetry and threw their personalities, their entire lives, on the scales. Everything about them was different: their origins, views, way of life, and style of writing. One was a bard of organized city life, the other a bard of idyllic landscapes; one was a scoffing chatterer, the other a sentimental poet; one wanted to be the voice of the revolutionary era, the other was nostalgic for the world that

*was passing . . . Ignoring each other, they became partici-
pants in each other's biographies.*

BORIS PASTERNAK:

Mayakovsky had neighbors . . . On the prerevolutionary platform Igor Syevyeryanin was his rival, on the revolutionary arena and in human hearts—Sergei Yesenin . . .

The Russian soil had not produced since Koltsov a phenomenon more native, natural, proper, and genuine than Sergei Yesenin, who endowed an era that was uncommonly free . . . Yesenin was a living, throbbing example of the kind of art which, following Pushkin, we call the higher Mozartian element.

Yesenin treated his life like a fairy tale . . . He also wrote his poems in a fairy-tale manner: he would either play the game of patience with words or write with his heart's blood. His most valuable asset was the vision of nature from his native land—woody, middle-Russian Ryazan—rendered with dazzling freshness, as he experienced it as a child.

Compared to Yesenin's, Mayakovsky's talent may seem heavier and more brutal but, perhaps, deeper and more comprehensive. The place of Yesenin's nature is occupied, as far as he is concerned, by the labyrinth of today's big city, where the lonely modern soul has strayed and become morally entangled. The poet depicts its dramatic, passionate, and inhuman experiences . . .

VASSILI KAMENSKY SPEAKS ABOUT YESENIN'S ENTRY INTO THE
LITERARY SALONS OF PREWAR PETERSBURG:

One evening at dinner with Fyodor Sologub, after Mayakovsky's appearance, the host asked a fair-haired boy, said to have just arrived from the country, to read his poems.

A curly-haired young farm hand, looking like a shepherd from Nestyerov's pictures in his tarred boots and tunic with patterned embroidered designs, came forward.

It was Sergei Yesenin.

In a melodious peasant's voice he recited a few short poems about fields and birch trees.

He recited them nicely, with a modest smile.

When asked for more, he declared, "How can we rustics compete with townsmen like Mayakovsky? They have nice suits and fashionable shoes and loud voices, while we are quiet and humble."

"Don't fuss, boy," Mayakovsky roared. "Don't fuss, dear, and you too will have fashionable shoes, a nice tie, and pomade in your pocket."

Alexander Blok told me he saw Yesenin last year at Merezhkovsky's, in the same dress, and talking in the same theatrical fashion.

On the whole, however, everybody liked Yesenin's picturesque appearance and his clever game of playing a country bumpkin.

His poems were pretty, fresh, and tender, like early grass in a meadow.

Watching Yesenin, Burliuk asked, "Why do you come to these salons?"

"Maybe they will like me and make a man of me," Yesenin replied, with a sly smile.

MAYAKOVSKY:

The first time I saw him he was dressed in a shirt embroidered with some crosses and had bast moccasins on his feet . . . Knowing how eagerly a genuine—as opposed to a theatrical—peasant changes his attire to town jackets and shoes, I did not believe Yesenin. He seemed to me put-on and showy. All the more so because he was already writing successful poetry and could certainly afford shoes.

Having worn a yellow tunic myself, and having ceased to do so, I asked him a matter-of-fact question: "Is this for publicity, or what?"

Yesenin answered with the kind of voice oil would speak in if it became alive in the lamp.

He said something like this: "We country people, we don't understand your stuff . . . we somehow . . . in our own way . . . simply, roughly . . ."

His talented, and most idyllic poetry was, of course, unacceptable to us futurists.

But he himself impressed us as an amusing and nice boy.

On my way out I said to him, just in case; "I bet you will give up all those bast moccasins and embroidered shirts."

Yesenin denied this with great conviction. He was dragged away by Kluyev, who behaved like a mother dragging away her daughter for fear she would not be able to resist temptation.

Yesenin kept appearing and disappearing. I came to know him better at Gorki's after the revolution. With my usual lack of tact I roared; "I've won the bet, Yesenin. You have a jacket and a tie on!"

FROM YESENIN'S LETTER TO ALEXANDER SHIRAYEVETS;
JUNE 1917:

God be with them, those Petrograd writers . . . We are the Scythians . . . and they are the Gauls, brother, Westerners all. They need America and we . . . need the song and heart of Stenka Razin.

There is no question of trying to "please"; one must simply pull one's boots up as high as possible and wade into the pond as deep as one can, and stir, stir, until the fishes pop their noses up and notice you, notice that you are "you" . . .

Yes, brother, our getting together with them is impossible . . . What one must do is not get close to them but trim them like some flat wooden board and carve the patterns one desires. Such is Blok, such is Gorodetsky, and others . . . their name is legion . . . It is most amusing to taunt them, particularly when they catch the bait, disregarding its metallic sound . . .

FROM EHRENBURG'S REMINISCENCES:

In the fall of 1917, in Petrograd, I was invited to Maria Shkapskaya's, a young poetess whom I had known from Paris. Kluyev was also at the table, dressed in a peasant's tunic and loudly lapping tea from a saucer. He seemed to me to be an actor playing a studied part for the thousandth time. The conversation was dying when a new guest appeared: a young, pretty boy, looking like an operatic hero. Smiling, he introduced himself: "Yesenin, Sergei, Seryozha . . ." He had bright and naïve eyes. Maria Mikhailovna asked him to read some poems. I realized this was a great poet; I wanted to talk to him, but he smiled and left.

I met him several times after that in Moscow: we talked about poetry, about events. Unlike Kluyev, Yesenin changed roles . . . but he did not know how, or did not want, to play them. I often saw him, looking with his blue eyes at the person he was talking to, reply with slight irony, "I don't know how it is in your parts, but with us, in Ryazan Province . . ." In May, 1918, he told me one must pull everything down, change the structure of the world, that the peasants would set everything on fire and that the world would burn down . . .

AT ANOTHER MEETING, A FEW YEARS LATER:

. . . Yesenin surprised me when he began to speak about painting. He had recently seen Shchukin's collection and had become interested in Picasso. It turned out that he had read Verlaine, and even Rimbaud, in translation . . . He suddenly began to attack Mayakovsky! His words did not surprise me: recently I had been present at an evening in the Polytechnic Museum, where Mayakovsky and Yesenin had hurled abuses at each other throughout the evening. Even so, I asked Yesenin why he was so indignant about Mayakovsky. "He is a poet striving for something, and I am just a poet . . . I don't know myself what I am driving at . . . He will live to eighty, and they will erect a statute of him . . . But I shall die under some fence on which his poems are pasted. And yet I would not change places with him." I tried to contradict him. Yesenin was in a good mood and admitted reluctantly that Mayakovsky was a poet, but an "uninteresting" one. He began to argue about futurism. Art inspires life, it must not be dissipated in life . . . People? Was not Shakespeare a popular writer? He did not scorn a country fair booth; yet he created Hamlet. That was not a Titus and Vlas (he quoted a Mayakovsky propaganda piece in which Titus and Vlas appeared). He recited Pushkin again and said, "When one has written one poem like this, it will not be terrible to die . . . And I shall certainly die soon . . ."

That long conversation in Kislovka enabled me to see the true Yesenin. How many people had been taken in! Ivanov-Razumnik, having heard his "Transfiguration," exclaimed, enraptured, "Here is authentic revolutionary subjectivism . . ." Various "Scythians" regarded Yesenin as an exponent of their ideology. I remember A. A. Shreyder in Berlin, arguing that the poet's call, "Calve, o Lord!" would shake bourgeois Europe. Young poets saw in Yesenin the maker of a new poetry: "imaginism" declared itself to be not one of many poetic trends but the tablets of Mount Sinai.

It would be wrong to think that Yesenin deceived or, if you like, mystified others; he often mystified himself; his differing emotions demanded expression, and when that happened, he would construct a program of melancholia, a literary school out of his perturbed spirit.

He was lucky in a way that few other poets were . . . Mayakovsky had to contend with lack of understanding, with the taunts of some and the coldness of others, while Yesenin was understood and loved; loved *in* his life time. There was a sincerity in his poems, an unusual tone which captured even those who were not well disposed toward him; those who had heard about his preposterous and vulgar adventures. He dreamed of fame and acquired it in excess . . . The great artist Isadora Duncan came to love him . . . Her affection delighted him as much as world recognition. He wanted to see the world and was one of the first to flash through Europe; he also saw America. Women loved him . . . He did everything he wanted to and even the austere guardians of Soviet morality turned a ·blind eye to his excesses.

At the same time, it is difficult to imagine a more unhappy man. He could not stay in one place. Love bored him; he suspected his friends of intrigues, was a hypochrondriac, thought constantly that he would die soon . . . Why did he take to drink? Why did he break down even at the start of his life and of his poetic course? Why was there so much bitterness even in his early poems, at a time when he did not drink or brawl? They say that his "Pothouse Moscow" was written when scum crawled out of their dens at the time of NEP. But "Hooligan's Confession" had been written before NEP, the winter that Moscow reminded one of a phalanstery, or monastery, with a strict rule . . .

LIDIA SEYFULINA WRITES ABOUT ONE OF MAYAKOVSKY'S PUBLIC SKIRMISHES WITH YESENIN, IN 1920:

It was a terrible winter . . . In the capital of a big and rich country there was not enough bread and fuel . . . We educational workers had been brought to the capital from the various outskirts of the great republic for advanced training courses . . . Our hostel was situated . . . in Usachovka. We lived in an old and decrepit one-story wooden house . . . We heated it at nights, dismantling the rotting wooden fences of Usachovka for that purpose.

One frosty evening—I cannot recall the day and month—we saw, on a fence which had survived our activities, a poster announcing that "today there will take place in the Polytechnic Museum, a disputation of the futurists with the imaginists. Sergei Yesenin will appear on behalf of the imaginists, Vladimir Mayakovsky on behalf of the futurists. In the chair— Valeri Bryusov." . . . The very awareness of the fact that we would see the makers of Russian poetry "live," that we would hear their living, human voices, warmed us with an unforgettable enthusiasm. It did not matter that the streetcars were not running, that the distance from Usachovka to Lubyanka was six kilometres or more, that we had poor shoes . . .

He appeared not on the platform but in the auditorium, in the passage between the back rows; he came in suddenly and absolutely noiselessly. But such was Mayakovsky's peculiarity—that wherever he appeared, he would not remain unnoticed. Among the crowded audience there was a stir, a din of an undefinable excitement . . . Mayakovsky was dressed in an unostentatious, gray winter coat down to his knees and was holding a fur-lined cap of the type that was popular then. He stood quietly and did nothing to distract our attention from what was happening on the platform. But once Mayakovsky had arrived, for me personally, as for most people in the hall, the other people disappeared, I ceased to hear their speeches on the platform and the din in the auditorium . . . The din grew into a noise . . . At one point a youthful voice, sincere and resounding, shouted; "Mayakovsky is here! We want Mayakovsky!"

And soon a chorus of voices, shouted out of tune, but convincingly loud and passionate; "Mayakovsky to the platform! We want to listen to Mayakovsky! Mayakovsky! Mayakovsky! To the platform!"

Mayakovsky's strong voice drowned and stopped the general voice at once. The poet walked quickly down the passage toward the platform and began to speak while still walking: "Comrades! I have just come back from court. An unusual case has been tried, some children have murdered their mother."

. . . Frightened whispers began in the auditorium. But Mayakovsky was already standing on the platform: tall, "twenty-year-old" as ever, visible from the most distant row, and audible by all. He went on: "The murderers justified themselves by saying that their mother had been an awful swine. But the fact of the matter is that the mother had been poetry herself, and the children were the imaginists."

The audience laughed, clearly relieved. The imaginists on the platform literally hurled themselves at Mayakovsky. The poet shook them off with a slight gesture of the arm and began to parody the imaginists' poems. The audience roared with laughter. Replies could be heard throughout the auditorium; the imaginists hurled loud insults.

Valeri Bryuosov made several attempts to ring the chairman's bell, but gave up, threw the bell on the table, and sat with his hands crossed on his chest.

But Mayakovsky, cutting short the laughter, the shouts of the enemies, and the hearty noise of friends, spoke ominous and grave words about the terrible sin of contemporary Russian poetry, said that Soviet poetry had no right, could not and should not be apolitical.

The thin, small Yesenin jumped on top of the chairman's table. Like an angry child, he tore off his tie, ruffled his golden, wavy hair and shouted in his sonorous, fine, and strong voice, "It's not we but you who kill poetry. You don't write poems but propaganda."

. . . When Mayakovsky retorted, Yesenin, in order to silence him, began to recite his poems.

Mayakovsky stood and listened to them for a while, then continued to argue.

The audience went simply wild.

IN THE REMINISCENCES OF THE CO-FOUNDER OF IMAGINISM, FRIEND AND ALLEGED "EVIL SPIRIT" OF YESENIN, ANATOL MARIENHOF, MAYAKOVSKY'S NAME IS MENTIONED ONLY ONCE. YESENIN AND MARIENHOF SHARED THE OWNERSHIP OF A BOOK-SHOP ON NIKITSKAYA STREET. THIS IS HOW THEY SOMETIMES SERVED THEIR CUSTOMERS:

. . . someone would enter the shop and ask, "Have you got Mayakovsky's 'Cloud in Pants'?"

Then Yesenin would take two steps back, his eyes would narrow into slits with which he scanned the questioner from head to foot, then from ear to ear, and, after a scornful pause (in the course of which the confounded customer began to shift restlessly), address his victim icily: "Perhaps, sir, you would like a . . . Nadson . . . we have a luxury edition in brocade with gold edge."

The customer would feel offended: "Why should I need a Nadson, comrade?"

"Because to my mind it is the same kind of trash! . . . To substitute one for the other will neither add nor detract anything of poetic value . . . while Nadson's cover is incomparably better."

The customer would blush . . . and retreat from the shop.

NIKOLAI POLETAYEV:

Yesenin argued with Mayakovsky and, almost crying, shouted at him,

"Russia is mine, understand, mine, and you . . . you're American! Russia is mine!"

To this the restrained Mayakovsky, I think, replied ironically, "Take her, please! Butter your bread with her!"

FROM THE REMINISCENCES OF LILA BRIK:

In Yesenin's lifetime Mayakovsky argued with him, but they had, in fact, a mutual high regard for one another, but for reasons of principle did not voice their good opinion about one another.

Yesenin transferred his respect for Mayakovsky to me, and when we met he called me "little Beatrice," which was tantamount to comparing Mayakovsky with Dante.

ASYEYEV:

I remember how Mayakovsky attempted to secure Sergei Yesenin's cooperation. We were sitting in a café on Tverskaya Street when Yesenin came in. They had, I think, made the appointment by telephone. Yesenin was proud and conceited. It seemed to him they wanted to force an unfavorable transaction upon him. At that time he was still siding with ego-futurists on the one hand and peasant-idealizers on the other. It was a somewhat absurd combination in itself: Shershyenyevich and Kluyev, Marienhof and Oryeshin. Yesenin kept his reserve, though he was clearly more interested in Mayakovsky than in all his companions put together. The conversation concerned Yesenin's participation in LEF. He immediately demanded that the whole group be accepted. Mayakovsky, half-laughing and half-angry, replied that "it is all right to take group pictures at school graduations." It did not satisfy Yesenin. "But you have a group," Yesenin persisted. "We don't have a group, we have a whole planet!" . . .

Mayakovsky tried to persuade Yesenin: "Leave your Oryeshins and Klichkovs. Why are you dragging with you that clay on legs?"

"I drag clay, and you—cast iron! Man has been made of clay, and of cast iron—what?"

"Monuments!"

. . . The conversation took place shortly before Yesenin's death.

And so Yesenin's union with Mayakovsky did not take place.

One more episode has remained in my memory from the same period. One evening Vladimir Vladimirovich came to me agitated, worried about something. "I have seen Sergei Yesenin," he said bitterly, then fever-ishly, "drunk. I hardly recognized him. Kolya, we must do something about Yesenin. He's stuck and will perish. Such a devilishly talented man."

MAYAKOVSKY:

My last meeting with him made a depressing but great impression on me. By the Gosizdat cashier's office a man with a swollen face, twisted tie, and cap only by a miracle holding onto his head, caught by a fair lock of hair, threw himself at me. He and his two horrid (to me at least) companions smelled from alcohol. With the greatest difficulty I recognized Yesenin. With difficulty, too, I rejected his persistent demands that we go for a drink, demands accompanied by the waving of a fat bunch of banknotes. All day long I had his depressing image before me, and in the evening, of course, I discussed with my colleagues what could be done about Yesenin. (Unfortunately, in such a situation everyone always limits oneself to talk.) We cursed the "environment" and parted convinced that Yesenin was be-ing taken care of by his friends—the "Yeseninists."

EHRENBURG:

He was always surrounded by satellites: the imaginists, Kusikov with a guitar, and the "peasant poets." Poets were pushed aside by simple drunk-ards, glad that they had been admitted to the table of an eminent man.

If futurism, in spite of the yellow tunic and Burliuk's lorgnette, was a great artistic phenomenon, imaginism always seemed to me a haphazardly concocted description for a chance group of writers. Yesenin liked brawls and gladly joined the imaginists to fight the futurists . . .

The saddest thing of all was to see, next to Yesenin, a random group of men who had nothing to do with literature, but simply liked (as they still do) to drink somebody else's vodka, bask in someone else's fame, and hide behind someone else's authority. It was not through this black swarm, however, that Yesenin perished, he drew them to himself. He knew what they were worth; but in his state he found it easier to be with people he despised . . .

THE LAST POEM (untitled)
by Yesenin

Good-by, my dear, good-by.
Friend, you are sticking in my breast.
The promised destinies are weaving
the thread from parting to a meeting.

Good-by, my dear, no hand or word,
Do not be sad, don't cloud your brow,
To die—in life is nothing new,
But nor is new, of course—to live.

NIKOLAI ASYEYEV, "WEEP AFTER YESENIN":

He had plenty of weepers and mourners. Well? I suppose it is well.

It is well that one of us, a man of our profession, has been so universally mourned. That thousands of hearts have been made sad because of him. That many sad eyes accompanied him to his grave. And many more, having read accounts of his death and funeral, grew dim with sorrow and pain for the song interrupted on a high note.

It is well that in our austere, revolutionary days, when . . . their romantic aspects, in worn shoes, are being pushed out of institutions which are filled with plans, it is well that on that day a song, in spite of everything, was able to unite so many people, who, so it would have seemed, had forgotten about it.

It is well that Yesenin has turned people toward poetry. Is it necessary, however, for all the good to be revealed, raised above the din of office typewriters, over the coldness of official slogans, over the astonishment and inattention of shrugged shoulders—is it necessary for all this to destroy oneself, to tie oneself in a knot, break, and injure oneself, and then to tie a noose around one's neck?

Is this the only price at which attention can be bought for a poet? The attention and interest not only of individual admirers and worshipers but the universal attention, the great human sigh, which no one hides, no one is ashamed of? . . . He put his own biography at the root of his popularity. His biography was opposed to the waves of time, at variance with what was going on around him.

. . . Through his biography he appealed to the reader, pointing to the divergence between his fate and the general course of events.

. . . His material was cheap and lacking in solidity: easily getting into one's ears, passing outside awareness.

But he put himself at the inflexible point facing the reader's awareness.

Consolidating that awareness, thrusting himself deeply into it, and remaining there for a long time, he became a victor.

He captured that awareness and introduced in it his authentic, exquisite poems.

He cultivated that awareness with authentic song, only on rare occasions cutting through the ballast of temporary, transient, and chance material, which he himself regarded as preliminary action with regard to his reader.

We discussed this at our last meeting, about two weeks before he died.

Yesenin—swollen, injured through his biography, shaken by its irresistible urge to extermination—leaning toward me, with his burning blue eyes, said in a hoarse, terrible whisper, "You think I am not a master? Yes? You think it's easy to write all this rubbish? . . . Then I'll tell you: one can't do otherwise! Otherwise no one will know you. One needs a ton of manure to get a pound of crops. That's what we need . . .

From behind his disheveled mask traits of a stubborn and heavy will were emerging, a will that sentenced itself to annihilation in order to fulfill the plans which he could no longer abandon, even if he had wanted to.

That evening he read "The Black Man," a work which he valued highly and on which, he said, he had worked for more than two years.

From behind that work emerged another face of Yesenin; not the one generally known, with a calm smile, the same for everyone; not the face of a dashing boy with fair, wavy hair; but the living, sincere, creative face of a poet, the face washed with cold despair, suddenly revived with the pain and fear of its own reflection.

Gone was the insipid color of nationalism. Gone was the convulsive balancing on a rope of ambiguous success. Before me stood a man, colleague, poet, seeing his annihilation, clutching at my hand only to feel human warmth. This was the Yesenin I am weeping for.

MAYAKOVSKY:

Yesenin's end distressed me, saddened me in a human way. But from the very first moment his end seemed to me quite natural and logical. I learned about it at night . . . the next morning, the newspapers printed the lines he wrote just before his death:

> To die—in life is nothing new,
> But nor is new, of course—to live.

After this poem Yesenin's death became a literary fact.

It became clear at once that many people who hesitate—this strong poem, exactly, a "poem"—would drive to the noose or to the revolver.

And no, I repeat, no journalistic analyses and articles will annul this poem.

One can and should fight this poem through poetry and *through poetry only.*

. . . Considering this death from all points of view, and going through the material of others, I formulated and set myself a task:

Aim: in a thoughtful manner, to neutralize the impact of Yesenin's last poem, to make Yesenin's end seem uninspiring; to put forward another kind of beauty in place of the easy beauty of death, because much energy is needed by the working humanity for the revolution that has now begun, and no matter how hard the road, what striking contrasts there are in NEP, it demands that we praise the joy of life, the fascination of the arduous march toward communism.

Now that I have my poem in hand, it is easy to formulate statements, but how difficult it was to begin it then!

The work coincided with my lecture tours in the provinces. For about three months I returned to the subject every day and could not think of anything sensible . . . For three months I did not have a single line worked out . . . Only when I had almost reached Moscow did I realize that the difficulty and delay in the writing had to do with it's being too much in accord with my personal situation.

The same hotel rooms, the same pipes, and the same compulsory loneliness.

The conditions absorbed me, did not allow me to escape, gave me neither the impressions nor the words required for condemning and denying, did not give me material for raising spirits . . .

FROM THE DAILY "VYECHERNYEYE RADIO," KHARKOV,
JANUARY 26, 1926:

The gay, vigorous, witty poet captured his audience. There was much laughter; we learned much. Only once did silence ensue, when, replying to a question concerning Yesenin, Mayakovsky said, "I don't give a hoot about monuments and wreaths after death . . . Protect the poets!"

The conclusion of "TO SERGEI YESENIN" (1926)
by Vladimir Mayakovsky

. . . Riff-raff
            till now
                        have bred in plenty.
It's no joke—
            to get rid of old trash.
First
      we have
                  to change our lives,
once changed—
                  can be dressed in song.
This epoch
            resists the pen—
but tell me,
            you,
                        invalids   and cripples,
who of the great ones,
                        when,
                                    did choose
a smoother
            and lighter
                        path?
The word—
            is the leader
                        of human might.
March!
            Through the crackle

　　　　　　　　　　of exploding
　　　　　　　　　　　　　days—
So that only wind
　　　　　　　　tangled hair
　　　　　　　　　　　with a flutter
at one's back
　　　　　　rushes
　　　　　　　　　in the time that's past.
Of fears and sadness
　　　　　　　　　　our earth knows in plenty.
We must discover
　　　　　　　joy
　　　　　　　　　in future days.
To die—
　　　　　in life
　　　　　　　is not so hard.
To make life—
　　　　　harder by far.

🙤 29 🙤

Salesman of Poetry

🙤

Mayakovsky is more and more eager to face his readers and convince them that he is a good poet. Mayakovsky's impressario, Lavut, and some other people recall the poet, reading his poems from the platform and talking to the audience. The provincial tours which Mayakovsky now undertakes will continue—with some intervals—almost to the end of his life.

FROM MAYAKOVSKY'S AUTOBIOGRAPHY:

The year 1926. In my work I deliberately switch over to journalism . . . I write for daily newspapers: *Izvestya, Trud, Rabochaya Moskva, Zarya Vostoka, Bakinsky Rabochi,* and others.

My other occupation—I continue the interrupted tradition of troubadours and minstrels. I tour cities and read. Novocherkask, Vinnitsa, Kharkov, Paris, Rostov, Tiflis, Berlin, Kazan, Sverdlovsk, Tula, Prague, Leningrad, Moscow, Voronezh, Yalta, Eupatoria, Vyatka, etc., etc.

FROM MAYAKOVSKY'S LETTERS TO LILA BRIK, 1924–1926:

Dear, dazzling

and my only little sun Foxy!

I long for you very terribly!!

Yesterday I came to Kharkov and in half an hour I go back to Kiev.

I wouldn't say it was a very comfortable journey. And yesterday I
found on my neck an animal that was eating me. I killed the animal, but I
am sitting and counting the days. Please do not leave me; what if the beast
was a venomous one!

I am finishing this letter in the railway carriage. I do not think I am
going to be able to manage Rostov—all places there are occupied by Soviet
congresses.

The hall was full in Kharkov, though there were fewer people in the
boxes. But in Kiev there was such a Tower of Babel that two people even
got injured. With books nothing comes off, for I do not spend more than
half a day in any one city.

There's my life in a nutshell . . .

My dear and only Foxypuss!

. . . I am staying in Baku now where I have seen (as on the way
here) many interesting things . . .

My life is gay: if there's something—I recite "Left March" and fault-
lessly answer questions—what futurism is and where David Burliuk lives
at present . . .

On Tuesday or Wednesday I shall be going to Tiflis and, after performing there, to Moscow with all speed. I have had enough—such a muddle.
The organizers are young. There are long gaps between appearances, and
not one reading had been timed to coincide with comfortable trains. For
this reason I travel with my head resting on the banal "huge ear of stars,"
instead of in pullman cars . . .

Spring is here. They sell mimosas in the streets. One can walk around
without an overcoat, but it is very cold. To my left is a little street and on
it a barber shop called Aelita. All in all, everything here is Turkestan but
looks foreign, because they have introduced the Latin alphabet: a phar-
macist in their language is called an "aptiq," and instead of Sunday they
have Friday. To the right of me is the Caspian Sea, into which the Volga
runs every day, but has nowhere to go out, because it is a lake-sea and
there is no way out from it . . .

I long to see you very much, my dearest. Everyone has to have a human being for keeps, and for me you are such a human being. I mean it . . .

Dear-dear, only, beloved and kind Puss!

Strange though it may seem, I am writing from Simferopol.

Today I am going to Eupatoria and back to Yalta tomorrow, (where I am going to wait for your cables and letters).

All the money from Odessa has been spent and I must go and earn some more with readings.

Unfortunately, this too brings in almost nothing. For instance, in Sebastopol the organizers—who said they were MOPR people—not only refused the agreed-upon payment, but canceled the event and insulted me publicly in what I thought was not a nice language. As it was, I wasted all day on that racket, had to call the meeting of the CP secretariat, and the CP secretary rebuked the insolent little tyrant. I had total moral satisfaction but my pocket remained empty. On top of that, instead of poems, I have nothing to write but letters to the editor . . .

What grieves me most, though, is the fact that you are certainly without a cent, everyone bothers you, and Osya has no money to go to the Volga. If this situation does not change, I will come back to Moscow in a week or two . . .

My kind and beloved Child!

I am living like Robinson after the shipwreck: I am saving myself on a fragment (of ten rubles), around me is the uninhabited (by you and Osya) Eupatoria; one Friday has passed and another one will come tomorrow.

The main similarity is that you do not write either to Robinson or to me, and you have not written at all . . . Possibly it is all my fault, and a bunch of letters and cables may be waiting in Yalta. But it is not really my fault, because I have been stuck here for a week with an awful flu. I got out of bed only today, and tomorrow I must get back from this dirty place to Yalta.

Three readings, which had been organized in Sebastopol and in Eupatoria with such difficulty, had to be canceled again . . .

What news about Osya's vacation?

Why doesn't he come to Yalta?

For my reading given to patients in a sanatorium I got room and board in Yalta for two weeks. We could arrange the same thing for Osya.

The sight of Puss on the balcony in Yalta would, of course, be dazzling! . . . But the fragment of a banknote is crumbling, and there are no other fragments, and who knows when they will come?

In my view, I have become a terribly proletarian poet: I have no money and do not write any poems . . .

FROM THE REMINISCENCES OF MAYAKOVSKY'S IMPRESSARIO IN THE YEARS 1926–1930, EX-ACTOR PAUL LAVUT:

. . . We met in Odessa.

I was then at a loss: I had left one theater and did not join another. I was about to go from Odessa to relatives in the Crimea . . .

Mayakovsky had a reading in the Sailor's Home.

The audience was sluggishly assembling. The tall, broad-shouldered man was pacing up and down the empty platform with a big stick in his hand. He was agitated, a cigarette dangling from the corner of his mouth. He smoked one cigarette after another and, not being able to find an ash-tray, threw the stubs on the corner of the stage and stamped them out with his foot.

He was alone. I took advantage of that fact: "There are rumors here in Odessa that you are going to the Crimea?"

"Just imagine: the rumors are true."

"Don't you want to give readings there?"

"Who would want to come, if even in Odessa I do not have an audience?"

I was convinced that the empty hall was the result of faulty organization. I said so to Vladimir Vladimirovich: "I am convinced that people in resorts will be very interested in your appearance. If you do not object, I could try to arrange it, particularly since I am just about to go to Sebastopol . . ."

We concluded the details of our agreement in the London Hotel in a couple of minutes . . . I suggested that our collaboration be sealed with a document which could be useful in travels.

"I wouldn't advise it," he said. "And I warn you for the future: if I sign an agreement I may not keep to it. But with verbal agreements I will never fail."

I devoted myself entirely to the difficult but fascinating work of organizing Mayakovsky's appearances, having given up the theater altogether. The relations we had were very firm and lasted to the end of his life . . .

Throughout those years Mayakovsky visited more than fifty towns of the union and made more than two hundred appearances there. He went to many towns—such as Kharkov, Leningrad, Odessa, Kiev, Rostov, Minsk, and the Crimea—several times . . .

PAVEL MAXIMOV, A JOURNALIST AND CONTRIBUTOR TO THE NEWSPAPER "SOVETSKY YUG" IN ROSTOV ON THE DON, RECALLS MAYAKOVSKY'S VISIT TO THE PAPER'S OFFICE, ON FEBRUARY 8, 1926:

The editor of our daily was a sullen, not very pleasant man. He was not interested in literature and he used to say about poetry that he'd "be damned if he could make it out." . . . The editor did not think it necessary to insert even a small note about and a picture of Mayakovsky on the day preceding his appearance, as I had suggested . . .

Sitting in the chair in front of the editor's desk, Mayakovsky was smoking a cigarette and telling, in a quiet voice, with obvious reluctance, about literary life in Moscow. The editor was listening, sulking, breathing heavily, saying nothing. The conversation flagged. The bookkeeper came in with a pile of papers, and, after an indifferent glance at the visitor, began to show the papers to his superior.

The editor concentrated on the papers and looked as if he had forgotten about his visitor. Mayakovsky stepped aside, sat down on the window sill and stared for a long time at the street below . . . It was hard to believe from his strong, massive shoulders, short-hair, and rough-edged, square face with protruding jaw, that he was a poet. He looked rather like a boxer or a sports trainer.

It seemed to me, though, that the massive stooping shoulders and the eyes showed signs of fatigue.

Mayakovsky's face was apathetic, his eyes were heavy and cloudy—he must have been very tired from travel and frequent public appearances. I learned later on that he was simply not well, that he had a cold.

DURING HIS STAY IN ROSTOV MAYAKOVSKY MET THE LOCAL POETS. MAXIMOV NOTED DOWN THE FOLLOWING:

The new woman poet Maria Yershova came from a village across the Don and, blushing, gave him a notebook with her poems. Mayakovsky, seated at the table, immediately perused some of Yershova's poems and, when the meeting ended, while putting on his coat, said to the girl, encouraging her, "Your poems are, on the whole, not bad. I will write to you in more detail from Moscow . . . Please write and send me all your work."

He put Yershova's notebooks in the side pocket of his jacket and jotted down his Moscow address for her on a slip of paper.

SHKLOVSKY TELLS ABOUT MAYAKOVSKY'S NEXT MEETING WITH
YERSHOVA:

. . . in the local RAPP there was a poetess; they often photographed her with a head scarf to make her look like a peasant woman; they told her she looked well in it.

In print they called her "poet kolkhoz-worker."

And then they stopped printing her poems. That is how people were often treated at RAPP.

The girl somehow got a revolver and shot herself in the breast.

Mayakovsky read her poems in Rostov. They were not bad. He went to the hospital and told her, "This is not the way to settle things. You must have friends. They will do something. Or I will."

He made arrangements for treatment and vacation for her. He asked, "How are things? Bad?"

She replied, "You know, the wound isn't painful. One has a feeling that somebody suddenly called one. Pain comes later . . ."

TO LILA BRIK FROM KRASNODAR, NOVEMBER 29, 1926:

Dear-dear, kind,

my beloved

pussy baby Foxy! (so-called little sun) . . .

I go places like mad.

I have already appeared in: Voronezh, Rostov, Taganrog, again in Rostov, Novocherkask, and twice again in Rostov. I am now stuck in Krasnodar. In the evening I am going not so much to read as to gurgle. I implore the organizers not to take me to Novorossyisk, but they implore me to go to Stavropol as well.

It is hard to make all these appearances. I make them everyday; on

Saturday, for instance, I spoke in Novocherkask from half-past eight in the evening to quarter to midnight. They asked me to appear again at eight in the morning at the university and at ten in the cavalry regiment, but I had to refuse, the reason being that at ten I went to Rostov, where from half-past one to ten to five I gave a reading at RAPP and again at half-past five in the Lenin Works, where I could not refuse: this was for the workers, and gratis!

Rostov is not a bed of roses either.

A local chronicler told me while we were taking a walk, "They say genius and evil do not go together, but here in Rostov they flowed into one." Translated into prose it means that a few months ago their water and sewer pipes burst and got mixed up together! Now they do not drink unboiled water, and they advise that even boiled water should be drunk within four hours after boiling, or else, they say, there is a "deposit."

You can imagine what I did in Rostov!

I drank mineral water and washed myself in mineral water, and I can still feel gas evaporating from me.

I did not touch soup and tea for three days.

Such is intellectual life.

With the spiritual and romantic life things are bad too.

Only one romantic event happened, quite strange though. After my reading at Novocherkask, a local professor of chemistry invited me to his laboratory and eagerly filled me with home-made, or rather lab-made, and home-grown wine. He also used the occasion to read me his own sixty-three-year-old poems. Considering that the wine was excellent, and there was nothing to eat, except "manganese and anhydrite," there was nothing left for me to do except quickly raise my spirits and kiss heartily the poetry loving chemist.

The distilling flasks are very thin and if one puts them on the table they break. I realized this before long and reached for my flat glass, but found only the case: the glass itself had been stolen by students as a souvenir, so the university did not suffer any loss, but it made me even more afraid of Rostov and I am quite defenseless.

I shall have to boil the mineral water and wash the crockery with it. But how do I know whether the mineral water has been boiled, since it is always gassy?!

Life is dangerous, as the writer Elsa Triolet says . . .

In Krasnodar his voice refused to obey him—influenza and over-fatigue. Mayakovsky was nervous. He went to play billiards to relax.

"One doesn't need a voice to play billiards."

In the evening he felt even worse. From the stage of the Grand Winter Theater he apologized for his hoarse voice; "I don't want to fail you and I'll try to stay and win . . ."

He decided to lie down till evening in the hotel.

But he could not get any rest. Although the receptionist assured visitors that Mayakovsky was not in his room, people went there and knocked on the door, insisting to be let in. Mayakovsky did not answer, but even this did not always work. Some people kept knocking for such a long time that I had to go out and explain that Mayakovsky was ill.

He had to receive the most insistent visitor—the manager of a bookshop. He came in leading a boy by the hand: "This is my son. He did not want to come with me, but I told him, 'You will tell everybody that you have seen Mayakovsky in the flesh, silly.' I so looked forward to your coming here, and I have even decorated my shop window with your books."

"Are there many of my books in your bookshop?"

"Plenty."

"Please bring them to the theater tonight, I will buy them all."

During the break in the reading, the sale of his books was arranged. People crowded around the table where Mayakovsky was autographing books . . .

At first they were distrustful and shy, but later on the crowd of customers grew dangerously large. The bookshop manager clearly became anxious: "Just see how they are interested in poetry all of a sudden! Who's going to pay, though, I wonder!" The table was creaking with people pushing from all sides. The manager was more and more anxious: "We have to make sure that the books are not stolen."

Mayakovsky put his mind at rest at once by paying a substantial sum on account. The bookseller cheered up: "If it were not for you, these books would stand on the shelves for years; some of them are not easily sold, old editions . . ."

In Tiflis Vladimir Vladimirovich felt at home. He was cheerful and energetic. Everything here gave him pleasure; he was happy about every-thing . . .

I remember some questions and Mayakovsky's replies . . .

"Comrade Mayakovsky, who will read your poems when you are dead?"

Mayakovsky replied angrily and brutally, "The questioner has relatives in Homel, I suppose. I seem to recognize the writing. There, too, a wise-guy asked me this question . . ."

"How do you like Tiflis girls?"

Mayakovsky did not reply, only spread his arms and, smiling, made a courtly bow.

"*Tu icit kartuli?*" (Do you speak Georgian?)

"I try not to forget it . . ."

In the course of another reading at the university, two students came to blows near the platform, as a result of their differing views on Maya-kovsky's writing. Mayakovsky tried to pacify them. The opponents insul-ted each other in Georgian. Mayakovsky addressed them in Georgian.

The audience was thrilled. With some difficulty the brawling students were parted and seated in opposite corners of the hall.

When the young people heard some Georgian words uttered by Maya-kovsky, they insisted that he say something in Georgian. He recited a frag-ment from "Left March." An ovation followed . . .

Dnyepropyetrovsk. No taxis or droshkys at the railway station. We barely managed to reach the hotel. Mayakovsky was so weak that I had to help him walk up to the second floor.

The doctor categorically forbade him to appear in public: high fever, influenza, sore throat. He promised to send a nurse. Mayakovsky wanted to pay for the visit, but the doctor refused: "I don't take money from someone like you. I am honored to meet you . . ."

Mayakovsky's meeting with the students of the Mining Institute and, another tentative meeting at a certain club were scheduled for that day. I notified both institutions that Mayakovsky was ill.

A few hours later, without any warning, another doctor came unin-vited into the room. One only had to take a look at Mayakovsky to know he was ill. But the doctor took his temperature and auscultated him for a long time. It was clear that the purpose of this visit was to check that Mayakovsky was not evading public appearances.

Mayakovsky did not show that he realized the purpose of the visit. To the contrary, he was extremely polite to the doctor and thanked him at the end, but when the doctor had gone, Mayakovsky said, "That's what calumny means . . ."

In order to drag him away from unpleasant thoughts I began to sing the aria about slander from *The Barber of Seville* . . .

Mayakovsky stayed in bed for a whole week . . . Two hours before leaving Dnyepropyetrovsk, not wishing to break his promise, he gave a reading for the mining students.

BECAUSE OF VARIOUS COMPLICATIONS ON THE WAY, MAYAKOVSKY
REACHED BIERDICHEV FOUR HOURS LATE:

Could one count on a miracle: that the audience would not leave but wait from eight in the evening until almost midnight? The miracle happened!

Mayakovsky first of all asked the theater manager, "How many people have left?"

"About thirty or forty."

"They are those who are least interested in poetry . . . Those who have stayed are the true audience. To appear before them is both a pleasure and an honor."

For an hour and a half he held the audience in a state of joyous excitement, having canceled the break by general consent. Judging from the audience's reaction, they felt fully rewarded for the torments of waiting. Mayakovsky was satisfied too . . .

The next morning his first question was: "Do you know what there is of interest in Bierdichev?"

"Balzac was married in the church here."

"Let's not waste time; let's go and see the church." . . .

Again we went by a "milk train" to Penza; the trip lasted for more than twenty-four hours. We returned late that evening . . . Mayakovsky asked whether I knew where Meyerhold had lived or where he was born . . .

Everything here had been planned up to the minute: we had to take the luggage to the People's House, begin the reading punctually at eight, shorten the break, and end at exactly twenty past ten—otherwise we would have been late for the train to Samara. We agreed that if Mayakovsky lost track of the time, I would go into the box and signal him by raising my hand that it was time to finish. This is what we had to do.

It is worth noting that the Political Education Department at Penza had refused permission for Mayakovsky's public appearance on the grounds that it was not known who he was. The Municipal Party Committee intervened and permission was granted . . .

In Saratov . . . another obstacle. The Political Education Department did not give permission for Mayakovsky's appearance and demanded that the poems be submitted with a detailed resumé of his talk. I managed to persuade the committee not to harass a sick man, and the matter was settled later on as in Penza.

. . . I came to Sverdlovsk on January 7 and negotiated with the club manager for the rental of the hall so that Mayakovsky's appearance there could take place on January 26.

He received me with cold indifference and put forward conditions I could not agree to. I went out quite angry. The next day, Sunday, I went to the club again, hoping I could manage, after all, to persuade the manager somehow.

While walking down the badly-lighted corridor, suddenly I came across a group of people. Among them, Lunacharsky.

I wanted to pass unobserved, but Anatol Vassilievich extended his hand: "Good morning! What are you doing here?"

"I am here on Mayakovsky's business."

"What, Vladimir Vladimirovich is here as well? I am very glad."

"Mayakovsky isn't here yet." I was more precise. "I am arranging some appearances for him for late-January."

"Please come with us." Anatol Vassilievich showed me the open door and led me into a room where a table was laid with some food.

In the doorway I saw the figure of the club manager. He must have recognized me. On that day we reached an agreement.

When I told Mayakovsky this story, he laughed: "Fortunately, we happened to be dealing with a yes-man!" . . .

IN VYATKA (FAMOUS FOR ITS BUTTER):

During the break between two readings Vladimir Vladimirovich proposed a "final" billiards game with me. I wanted to step into a shop on the way to buy some Vyatka butter.

"What an idea! Don't do it . . ."

Nevertheless, I bought the butter.

Mayakovsky was against accumulating "provisions." But within an hour of our return to Moscow, his housekeeper, Pasha, brought me his visiting card on which was written, "Please make me happy with some butter." Pasha explained: "When at home they made him see the light, it worked . . ."

FROM MAYAKOVSKY'S REPLIES TO HIS AUDIENCES' QUESTIONS,
WRITTEN AND ASKED, AS NOTED DOWN BY VARIOUS AUTHORS:

Q. Mayakovsky, what is your real name?

A. Shall I tell you? Pushkin!!!

Q. Your poems are too topical. Tomorrow they will be dead. You will be forgotten. You will not be immortal . . .

A. Please drop in a thousand years from now, we'll talk then!

Q. Mayakovsky, you regard yourself as a proletarian poet, a collectivist, but everywhere you write, "I, I, I."

A. Do you think that Czar Nicholas was a collectivist? He used to write, "We, Nicholas the Second . . ." Can you say "we" in every situation? Will you propose to your sweetheart, by saying, "We love you?" If you do, she will ask, "How many of you are there?"

From the audience: You are a profiteer . . . I mean, a literary profiteer.

Mayakovsky: And you are a fool.

From the audience: This is an insult.

Mayakovsky: A literary fool.

Q. Why don't the workers understand you?

A. You must not think so poorly of the workers.

Q. I, for instance, do not understand you.

A. That is your fault and misfortune.

Q. Why don't other poets write publicity slogans?

A. I've asked them about it too.

Q. Comrade Mayakovsky! Barbara Bisyevich recites your poems splendidly. You're not nearly so good!

A. My congratulations to Barbara Bisyevich. On my part I will endeavor to keep up with her.

Q. What do you think about poetic inspiration?

A. I've already said, inspiration is not important. Inspiration can be organized. One must have ability and be conscientious. The first quality does not wholly depend on oneself.

Q. Comrade Mayakovsky, do not worry that some people say that you are brutal and your poems cannot be understood. If one reads them carefully, everything can be understood, and the poems make a better impression when read in the book; you are more human and closer to us then.

A. One must read slowly, in an ordinary way, understand what one is reading, and then it does not matter whether one reads aloud or to oneself . . . And with regards to brutality, it mostly is the answer to a similar brutality.

The woman librarian of the Putilovskaya Library in Leningrad: Nobody asks for your books in the library and nobody reads them, because they are not interesting!

Mayakovsky: Do you recommend my books to the readers?

Librarian: What for? He who likes them will take them himself.

Mayakovsky: Then you do not read them yourself and do not fulfill your duty which is to propagate books . . . With such librarians we won't go very far.

FROM CARDS PRESERVED AT THE MAYAKOVSKY MUSEUM:

"Is it true that in 1910–1912 you smashed Pushkin's bust and went around Moscow in yellow swimming trunks?"

"Is it true that when you feel a wave of inspiration, you ask to be tied up with your legs to the ceiling and in this position you compose your best poems?"

"Have you ever loved a girl, and how was it? I am sorry."

"At every reading you are asked why the proletariat does not understand your poems. This is nonsense. During every break workers ask me to read your poems to them."

"We live, it seems, in the Soviet Republic, but judging by the mentality of the asses in this hall, we must be living in Zulu country. They are ready to laugh at you, as if you were a clown, though your word means the birth of something new; every word is intelligible and is a joy . . ."

"They do not understand you not because they do not understand but because they do not want to understand; they are too lazy and won't spend time on it."

FROM A NOTE ABOUT MAYAKOVSKY'S LITERARY EVENING IN THE
NEWSPAPER "BAKINSKY RABOCHI," DECEMBER 7, 1927:

"What is futurism?" someone asks.

"Why do you take money for your appearances?"

"How does one become a poet?"

And many other factual questions to which Comrade Mayakovsky
gave sharp, accurate answers. Somebody said, "Comrade Mayakovsky,
tomorrow at seven we have to get up for work, hurry."

And the poet hurriedly ended his performance.

40. Nikolai Asyeyev.

41. Mayakovsky and
Boris Pasternak, 1924.

42. Mayakovsky and Lila Brik, 1924.

43. Mayakovsky in Mexico.

Добро пожаловать, Тов. Маяковскнй

OUT of far away Red Russia, thru the cordons of misrepresentations, lies and columnies, comes to us a ray of the new world that is being built under the leadership of the Communist Party, in the Union of Socialist Soviet Republics.

Comrade Vladimir Mayakovsky, the revolutionary poet of the new Russia is coming to Chicago today.

The intellectual bankrupts, the "socialist" lackeys of the bourgeoisie, all the enemies of the revolution united in the attack against the Soviet Union. All of them claim that the revolution brought only destruction. Nothing new is being created, they claim. But in spite of these claims, a new world is growing under our very eyes. Not only in material improvements, but also in science, literature and poetry, the NEW is being created and the OLD discarded. The cultural level of the masses is being raised. New artists, scientists, writers and poets are appearing. Comrade Mayakovsky is one of them. They are responding to the masses and not crawling on their bellies before the bourgeoisie as their brethren in the bourgeois world. Never before has the Russian Academy of Science had such possibilities as under the Soviet government. There is nothing new in Europe in music worth while, says Stock of the Chicago Symphony Orchestra, except in Soviet Russia.

Things are created there in spite of the handicaps to which the capitalist world contributed liberally.

Things are created for the wide masses of the producers instead of the small class of parasites as in all other countries.

Comrade Mayakovsky is one of the these new creators. He is a singer of the masses, a singer of the revolution.

Welcome to our city, Comrade Mayakovsky!

* * *

We are printing here, one of his poems, "Our March," in the original Russian language. We hope to be able in the near future to print some of his poems translated into English. Most of his work has been translated into many languages, but we have been unable to secure a translation in English.

НАШ МАРШ

Бейте в площади бунтов топот!
Выше горьых голов гряда!
Мы разливом второго потопа
Перемоем миров города.

Дней бык пег.
Медленна бег арба.
Наш бог — бег.
Серце — наш барабан.

Есть ли наших золот небесней
Нас ли сжалит пуля — оса?
Наше оружие — наши песни.
Наше золото — звенящие голоса.

Зеленью ляг луг,
Выстрелы дно дням.
Радуга дай дуг,
Лет быстролетный коням.

Видите скушно звезд небу!
Без него наши песни вьем.
Эй, Большая Медведица! требуя,
Чтоб на небо нас взяли живьем.

Радости пей! Пой!
В жилах весна разлита.
Серце бей бой!
Грудь наша медь литавр.

В. В. Маяковский

Welcome, Comrade Mayakovsky!

44. Mayakovsky welcomed to America, 1925.

45. Mayakovsky and David Burliuk in New York, 1925.

46. Mayakovsky with Burliuk's two sons, 1925.

47. Sergei Yesenin, 1924.

48. Mayakovsky at writers' meeting, 1929.

49. Mayakovsky with Meyerhold and Shostakovich during rehearsals of *The Bed Bug*.

50. Mayakovsky's literary evening at the Polytechnic Museum.

51. Mayakovsky's funeral.

꩜ 30 ꩜

"LEF or Bluff?"

꩜

This chapter contains the records of a press campaign against Mayakovsky and his group, conducted by the well-known critic, columnist, and editor Vyacheslav Polonsky. In 1927 Mayakovsky was also bitterly attacked in the press by A. Lezhnyev "In the Matter of a Corpse," I. Grossman-Roshchin, M. Olshevets, among others, while Georgi Shengeli published as a brochure his pamphlet Mayakovsky in All His Splendor. *In that year, after a fairly long break, LEF resumed publication of their periodical and demanded equal rights with other literary groups.*

FROM THE REMINISCENCES OF PYOTR NYEZNAMOV:

When the periodical *LEF* ceased publication, Mayakovsky thought constantly about continuing it in some other form. He wanted to make it more effective and cohesive. At the same time the magazine was planned in such a way that others, the constructivists in particular, were to join it as well . . .

This was not realized . . . About eighteen months later *LEF* was to be resumed, also as a bi-weekly publication, with the participation of Nikolai Tikhonov and the Leningrad literary scholars Tynyanov, Eichenbaum, Yakubinsky, and others. This, too, did not materialize. Seven months later, when *New LEF* finally came into being, it was a homogeneous periodical with a definite program.

In the period preceding the magazine's appearance, Mayakovsky and the Briks spent the summer at Sokolniki . . . On Osip Brik's birthday, dinner was given in a large dining room for about thirty people. Even Chuzhak was present; he had been reconciled to the others. Pyetrov, a photoreporter from *Izvyestya* and *Krasnaya Niva,* came to take pictures . . .

Mayakovsky read his poems for children. Someone told how a little boy, upon seeing Mayakovsky, asked naïvely, "Mama, is he a giant?"

And the great Mayakovsky smiled.

It was here, too, that Mayakovsky mumbled Pasternak's stanzas . . .

New LEF was mainly edited in Briks' apartment. There were no paid positions; the authors, that is to say, the editors themselves, had to cut their fees to get money for office and other expenses. Mayakovsky, of course, had to pay more than anyone, . . .

SHKLOVSKY:

New LEF is thinner than the old *LEF.*

They begrudged us paper.

But *New LEF* is published winter and summer . . .

In *New LEF* not articles but trunks of articles are published.

Half-finished products.

Thoughts which ought to take roots in the reader . . .

A newspaper is still being proclaimed.

"Art is vanity and nothing more," Brik says . . .

A great writer cannot be contained exclusively in his writing. He transcends it. Great writers often turn out to be great editors. Pushkin dreamed all his life about a periodical, a newspaper.

Nyekrasov, Saltykov-Shchedrin, Gorki, and Mayakovsky were great editors.

Mayakovsky needed *LEF* . . .

🏴

In January 1927, the first issue of the monthly New LEF *appeared, subtitled:* Journal of the Left Front of Art. *Editor:* Vladimir Mayakovsky. *In this issue, poetry, columnist and information texts by Mayakovsky, Pasternak, Asyeyev, Brik, Shklovsky, Arvatov, Kushner, Kirsanov, Pyertsov, Tretyakov, Nyeznamov, and Zhemchuzhny were published; as well as plastic works by Styepanova, Lavinsky, and Rodchenko; and stills from films by Eisenstein and Dzhiga Vertov.*

FROM MAYAKOVSKY'S UNSIGNED EDITORIAL ENTITLED "READER!":
We have published the first issue of *New LEF*.

Why have we published it? What is there in it that is new? Why *LEF*?

We have published it because the situation of culture in the sphere of art has been completely messed up.

Market demand has become for many people the measure of value as far as cultural phenomena are concerned.

. . . *LEF*—the periodical—is the stone which we are throwing into the quagmire of existence and art . . .

What is there in it that is new?

New in LEF's situation is the fact that, in spite of LEF workers having been dispersed, in spite of the lack of their unified voice expressing itself in a periodical, LEF has won and is winning in many sectors of culture.

. . . LEF is a free union of all workers of avant-garde revolutionary art.

LEF sees its allies in the ranks of workers of revolutionary art only.

LEF is a union based exclusively on work, on action.

LEF does not caress the ear or the eye, and substitutes the art of representing life with the work of constructing life.

New LEF is the continuation of the struggle for communist culture which we have always waged.

🏴

Early in January the Federation of Associations of Soviet Writers was established, incorporating: The All-Russian Asso-

ciation of Proletarian Writers (WAPP), The All-Russian Union of Writers, and the All-Russian Association of Peasant Writers.

The writers in the LEF group request the admission of LEF to the Federation of Associations of Soviet Writers on the same principle as three other associations have already been admitted . . . LEF unites the best qualified elements in new Soviet literature . . . We consider the fact that LEF has not been given a chance to participate in the initial organizational phase of the Federation's activities a sad misunderstanding . . .

◆

In February LEF was admitted to the federation and Mayakovsky was put on the council and executive committee.

The second issue of New LEF contained, among others, Tretyakov's article "We Sound the Alarm," a poem, article, and fragment of a scenario by Mayakovsky, articles by Brik, Chuzhak, and Pushas, and Rodchenko's letter from Paris.

I have leafed through the monthly's pages. I looked at the column entitled "Current Affairs" . . . Those "current affairs" are, of course, important to the members of *New LEF*. But we assume that in our country a periodical is published not only for its contributors but also for its so-called readers. Is it in the interest of the latter that the thin magzine should be filled not with the "practice" of new innovators but with communiqués about that "practice"? These are worse than proclamations. The trouble is that there is no, or almost no, "practice" of *New LEF*. This circumstance alone explains why Rodchenko's correspondence with his wife, which is of interest

to no one, is offered to the reader as something worthy of attention: half a
loaf is better than no bread at all.

I go through the pages: Vladimir Mayakovsky's article "Help." Why is
our celebrated poet shouting for help? Apparently, he has written a scenario, about which Victor Shklovsky himself has said, "I have read thousands of scenarios but never one like this. It is a breath of fresh air. A
window has been opened." But Sovkino's management has rejected the
scenario. That is why Mayakovsky cries for help in a periodical which he
himself edits. Following his cry "help" is a fragment of the disqualified
scenario . . . If the complete scenario is like the published part, I am on
Sovkino's side! Let Mayakovsky shout "help" himself. He has lots of time
and, apparently, nothing to do . . .

What strange people they are! When they had no publication of their
own, the LEFists boasted, "If we had a periodical, we would show what
we can do!" Now the periodical lies in front of us. And what do we see?
LEFists go on boasting, "We'll show you!" Show us, dear comrades, we
beg you, do not hide the excellent examples of your true "fighting, class-
active art" in your desks. Where is it? We wipe our eyes, we seek—but do
not find. True, in the "Current Affairs" column we read that O. Brik is
writing (writing!) a short story entitled "The Jew and the Blonde," but he
is still writing it. The scenario which Mayakovsky has written is weak, and
LEF has no reason to be proud of it. The trouble is that when we turn
from LEFist proclamations and promises to their practical achievements,
we see that LEF has nothing new to offer. LEF *is frozen, arrested in its
development.*

[The author quotes fragments of the editorial from the first issue of
New LEF.]

Well, isn't this boastful talk? It seems there are not and never have
been any fighters for communist culture, except LEFists. All the others are
quagmire . . . True, there is the Communist party and there are Communist agencies in which cultural workers are active. But Communist cultural workers are not members of LEF. It is clear then that they are the
quagmire at which the light stones of their heavy wit are thrown by our
New LEFists.

. . . In the dawn of their misty youth, the young futurists, pushing
through the literary cafés to the center of bourgeois attention, dazzled the

bourgeoisie with their extravagant vocabulary and wide, sweeping gestures. But everything in its proper time and place. Those methods were
good in the past, but there is no need to resurrect them. And we will not
let them be resurrected . . .

In the present situation of that particular literary group, one feels there
is a separation from the stream of Soviet literature, and even from the
building of Soviet society. The boundless pretensions of its leaders, their
overblown ambitions, the poor quality of their creative work, all this signifies the decline of the group. Some people change their signposts; the
LEFists change their name: they were futurists; they attempted to become Com-Futs; they transformed themselves into simply LEFists; and
now we have the New LEFists, though the "new" LEFists resemble the
old LEFists, just as one portrait of Mayakovsky resembles another portrait
of Mayakovsky.

The tragedy of this literary trend consists of its being rejected by new
groups of young people, in spite of its insistent pretensions, expressed for
so many years now.

. . . Futurism is dead! And you, turned into epigones, still resist; you
do not want to go "into the basket" . . . and try to put into it those young
people who, "jumping on the light cadence of their first stanzas," send you
into a rage . . . LEFists have not even noticed that they have long since
turned into dry and unfeeling academics, drunk with fame, set on self-
glorification, guarding their comfortable seats in literature, and resisting
the attacks of new pretenders . . . LEF has been left behind by life. LEF
is the enemy of youth. Being the epigone of futurism, it has outlived itself.
That is why it has nothing to say, and that is why it insults, gets angry,
jostles, shouts "help" . . .

. . . This article is not directed against individual poets—Mayakovsky, Asyeyev, Tretyakov. It is not even directed against Shklovsky and
others. Each poet, considered alone, merits the closest attention . . .

But when those talented writers, who really represent *different ideas*,
form a conspiracy,

single themselves out from Soviet art, which they proclaim to be an
academic quagmire,

usurp for themselves the monopoly of supplying "the best, first-rate,
leading, authentic," etc., revolutionary art, without having anything new to
say . . .

then an urgent need arises to raise one's voice in the interest of literary youth, of new creative forces making their way from the worker and peasant masses, and those who sympathize with them, and to say to one and all that the aggressiveness of LEF signifies an attempt to capture the living by the dead, that LEF, when looked at closely, is simply a bluff.

FROM THE NEWSPAPER "VYECHERNYAYA MOSKVA," MARCH 24, 1927:

LEF or Bluff?
Discussion at the Polytechnic Museum

. . . The discussion concerning LEF went the worst possible way: the exchange of personal invectives.

What is Polonsky? Mayakovsky asks. . . . Why has Polonsky attacked LEF? . . . Apparently only because LEF dared publish a periodical of its own . . . And Polonsky is an editor himself. In his person an editor—a wholesaler of literary material—has spoken.

Mayakovsky attacked; Polonsky defended himself. And because attack is the best defense, they both attacked.

. . . Mayakovshchina is Khlestakovshchina. "You with a P, and I with an M," Mayakovsky says to Pushkin, assuring him that he is his equal. But one hundred years ago this was the way Khlestakov was addressing Pushkin: "What, Pushkin, brother?" Polonsky, however, does not attack LEF in general, nor does he dream of belittling the LEF poets' immense merits. He attacks LEF's other aspects: Khlestakovshchina and self-publicity . . .

Others, both defenders and opponents of LEF, had little time at their disposal. Shklovsky defined the Voronsky-Polonsky line as "reactionary in the literary sense." Beskin (from GIZ) managed to declare that LEF does not have sufficiently well-defined principles, that it embraces different tendencies, including Shklovsky's and his reactionary arguments. Levidov accused Polonsky of attacking LEF at the time when literature was threatened by the bourgeoisie. Asyeyev vehemently protested against the accusation that LEF was rejecting the young. Only L. Averbakh, in his short speech, was able to produce a point of view based on firm principles. Averbakh shares Polonsky's view that LEF is a group with a harmful, muddled ideology. But Polonsky's attack is untimely. Polonsky is silent about the neo-bourgeois threat and attacks LEF at the same time. In spite

of LEF's errors, Averbakh thinks it proper, rather than attacking LEF, to
fight hand-in-hand with LEF, the neo-bourgeois threat to literature.

9 P.M. The hall is full. Mayakovsky and his friends from LEF are on the
platform. The chairman is there too, but Polonsky is missing.

The audience is restless.

"It is time . . ."

"Mayakovsky, begin . . ."

Mayakovsky shrugs his shoulders.

"It's not my fault . . . Everyone from LEF is here, only no one from
"bluff" has turned up . . ."

On this occasion, Mayakovsky used quotations to attack Polonsky,—
characteristic of the critic's style: "Polonsky writes about someone: 'sharp
like spirits and flowery like a precious stone.' At which liquor store, at
which jeweler's did he find those meaningless words? Can one say 'sharp
like spirits'? Strong perhaps? It is hard to think that Polonsky does not
know what spirits are, so I assume he does not know what 'strong' is . . ."

FROM VYACHESLAV POLONSKY'S ARTICLE ENTITLED "BLUFF
CONTINUES," PUBLISHED IN THE MONTHLY "NOVY MIR" NO. 5,
MAY 1927:

The bohemian has always and everywhere been a reservoir of unusual
conceit. Forgotten geniuses, rejected innovators, ill-starred writers, expelled reviewers, poet-scamps, rhymesters and poetasters constantly looking at themselves in mirrors, drunk with the might of their voices, often
semi-illiterates, ignoramuses and boors, shouters and bullies—from the
depths of the literary rock bottom, spat with coxcomb contempt on everything they could get hold of: on the Atlantic Ocean, on Shakespeare and
Pushkin, on the *Venus de Milo*. This basic trait of the bohemian's psyche
was laconically expressed in its time by Mayakovsky:

> On everything that has been done,
> I put—*nihil*
>   "Cloud in Pants"

This, perhaps its most characteristic trait, has reflected, of course, the
worries and unpleasantries, and to the highest degree, the ambition and

admiration of one's own person. Hence the pose of genius, the self-glorification . . . the sickly desire to direct attention to oneself, mostly through scandalous means, the shamelessness, the forced Titanism, the pomposity, the desire to get on the neighbors' heads and trample them with one's boots.

All this has found an unusually powerful expression in the writings of *New LEF's* leader. In front of me lies a book entitled *Everything Composed by Mayakovsky*—a literary monument erected by the bohemian. Our literature knows no other example of such a splendid reflection of a bohemian, shouter, and nihilist posing as a genius. The 1912 cycle is opened by the poem "I!" followed by "A Few Words About My Wife," "A Few Words About My Mama," and "A Few Words About Myself." How much "I" is there? Not too much for one man? But this is only a beginning! Further on we find a tragedy (tragedy!) entitled *Vladimir Mayakovsky*— its protagonist is the poet Vladimir Mayakovsky. This is followed by an ode entitled "I and Napoleon" . . .

These poems were written in the period of Mayakovsky's revolt against the bourgeoisie. But it was, at the same time, a bourgeois kind of revolt— the revolt of a bohemian, who was himself a refined, subtle, sharpened bourgeois. For that reason the revolt had a grotesque, farcical character; the tragedy *Vladimir Mayakovsky* is more like a "farce-delusion," and the "tragic hero" is very much like a circus performer entertaining the gay public . . . The bourgeoisie, even the revolted bourgeoisie, would cease to be themselves, if they could only find a really great impetus. For this reason, too, Mayakovsky's leitmotif turned out to be an irritated "I," whose toes had been tread on by someone; his absolutely drunken egocentrism, improbable self-adulation, is repulsive even in the case of authentic talents and quite out of keeping with genuine geniuses . . .

The reader could observe, "Well, all these were the sins of youth—they are a thing of the past. Let bygones be bygones."

But the reader would be wrong. Not all "sins of youth" pass without a trace . . . One of the sins which remains is egocentrism . . . The heavy man close to forty, with "graying temples," has kept his old habits: in 1927 we have before us the same noisy fellow, who could very well repeat his former words:

I shout, but am able to prove nothing.

The "egocentric" is being transformed before our eyes into an eccentric, into "Mister Buffo," into "the champion of our streets," into "the favorite of these parts"—he who used to be ready to shake politely Nero's and Napoleon's hand. As in the old days, long since gone, he looks at himself in his pocket-mirror and peeps all around himself trying to find out an ocean to spit into and a way to climb Ivan the Great's belfry—with the help of Rodchenko and trick-photography . . . Times have changed but the style is the same: Narcissus courting eternity . . .

This nonchalance, this desire to impress with his "free manner," to "dazzle" the admiring gallery—all this once meant audacity, poetic hyperbole, revolt, even if bourgeois revolt, against authority and established fame, etc. All this sounded most amusing in its time but has now turned into a "set pattern," and it is difficult to understand why Mayakovsky's friends will not direct his attention to that fact, will not explain . . .

I am not saying that Mayakovsky is the Khlestakov of Russian poetry. If I did, it would mean I did not appreciate Mayakovsky's role in poetry. I am not diminishing it—it was great. "Cloud in Pants" has left a clear and permanent mark on the development of Russian poetry. If a whole generation of Russian artists at the end of the nineteenth century was produced by Gogol's *The Overcoat*, then a whole generation of Russian poets of the period 1915–1922 was produced by Mayakovsky's "Cloud in Pants." As the reader can see, I am not minimizing our poet's merits. I am only suggesting that what is best and authentic in Mayakovsky's poetry should be separated from "Mayakovshchina," that is, from all those repulsive and ridiculous qualities of the bohemian mentioned earlier. They were repugnant in Igor Syevyeryanin and are no less repugant in Mayakovsky, perhaps even more so, because Syevyeryanin, a bourgeois snob, individualist, and aesthete, did not play the role of an ideologist of the proletariat, did not undertake to defend communist culture against the Communists, did not attach to himself a following of nonentities who, without any right, usurp for themselves the honor of developing the history of literature . . .

Mayakovsky's misfortune consists not only in that he is unable to take off the rotten bohemian attire but that he becomes a promotor of bad literary habits in our young literary circles, willingly or unwillingly.

The misfortune consists also in the fact that his fixed pose of "genius" is accompanied by a lowering of standards as far as his poetry is concerned

. . . What do we get as a result of sloppy poetic work? A low-quality product. This is bad in itself. But worse still is the fact that the public's attention is impudently drawn to that low-quality product: that was one of the charges I made against *New LEF*. How is one to judge all this?

FROM A. LEZHNYEV'S ARTICLE "IN THE MATTER OF A CORPSE," "KRASNAYA NOV," MAY 1927:

LEF is lying across the road and blocking traffic. It pulls literature backward—to ode writing, to propaganda, and to simplified and schematic art, which in its time was unavoidable but rings false under present circumstances. In theory—and, for that matter, in practice—it objectively favors conformism and officialdom. That is why we are fighting it. What if it is condemned by history: we cannot coolly contemplate a natural process, for we ourselves are the participants of a literary process and struggle. To move the corpse out of the way is indispensable, though, as it turns out, sometimes not so easy.

THE ENDING OF THE BOOK "MAYAKOVSKY IN ALL HIS SPLENDOR" BY SHENGELI:

. . . I hope that in this concise work I have succeeded in proving quite conclusively that Mayakovsky's pretensions to poetic leadership are groundless and immodest; his assurance about his total kinship with our time is unjustified; his role in our poetry is a negative one. From his poems one can learn how not to write poetry.

Weak in ideas, with a limited horizon, a hypochondriac, neurasthenic, poor craftsman—beyond any doubt he is not worthy of his era, and his era will turn away from him.

FROM BORIS PASTERNAK'S LETTER TO VYACHESLAV POLONSKY, JUNE 1, 1927:

I am leaving LEF definitely this time. I probably will formulate this in a letter to V. V. You know how much I like and still value him . . . Here is part of the letter, concerning yourself and your article: "The nonsense pervading a considerable part of V. Polonsky's article *cannot be unconscious* . . . The way you turned out to appear in Polonsky's eyes is the only way a poet can appear when one takes as the basis LEFist aesthetics, LEFists' role in disputes concerning Yesenin, LEF's polemical tricks, and above all LEFist artistic perspectives and ideals. Glory to you as a poet, since the foolishness of LEFist premises has been shown up by your example . . . I consider LEF's existence, now as before, to be a logical puzzle. The key to it has ceased to interest me."

This break is not easy for me. They do not want to understand me, and many others do not want to understand. I shall remain even more lonely than before . . .

FROM THE REMINISCENCES OF NATALYA
ROZENEL-LUNACHARSKAYA:

After a film premiere, S., an old acquaintance, invited me to his place. With us were: the film actress Kira Andronikova, the choreographer Shakhovskaya, the directors Shengelaya and Barnet, Mayakovsky, the pianist Makarov . . . One of those present, apparently unfamiliar with both film and poetry, said "Shengeli" instead of "Shengelaya" by mistake. Mayakovsky, with a sudden grimace, interrupted the speaker: "Why are you calling him so? Kola Shengelaya is a good fellow."—He lightly put his arm around him. "Shengeli is quite a different matter. He is a sin of Anatol Vassilievich!"—He said this in an irritated tone, turning directly to me.

We went away from the remaining guests gathered around the piano. No one could overhear us.

"I want to tell you that Anatol Vassilievich commits a great and unforgivable mistake! He has taken under his wing an absolutely hopeless case of lack of talent!"

I interrupted him: "Why are you telling me this, Vladimir Vladimirovich? I suppose you want me to repeat this to my husband? But why? Would it not be better and simpler if you told him all this yourself? . . ."

When I repeated this conversation with Mayakovsky to Anatol Vassilievich, it depressed him. He said that LEF is behaving aggressively, provocatively. All the worse for the LEFists, if they do not understand that it was Lunacharsky who tried to prevent their total annihilation . . .

FROM GORKI'S ARTICLE "ON THE NEED FOR EDUCATION" IN THE
PERIODICAL "CHITATYEL I PISATYEL," NO. 11, MARCH 17, 1928:

Talking to writers and reading magazines, one can clearly sense the stuffy atmosphere of vicious small "circles," the harmful seclusion of group interests in narrow little squares, the tendency to get into the limelight at any price. This is particularly characteristic of an institution such as LEF, where a few braggarts do their best to confuse young writers by proclaiming that literature is superfluous . . .

POLONSKY'S "LEAVES FROM A NOTEBOOK" IN THE JOURNAL "PYECHAT' I REVOLUTSYIA," APRIL 1928:

Gorki, who observes all that happens in Soviet literature with the closest attention, has reacted to my polemics with LEF and the "napostovtsy" as follows: "Let me tell you that your polemics with LEF and the 'napostovtsy' is your great merit. Of course, you are absolutely right: LEF is nihilistic roguery; its prose is incompetent."

☙ 31 ☙

"Good!"

☙

Mayakovsky undertakes to write a play for the tenth anniversary of the October Revolution and—writes the poem "Good!" instead. It is the poet's second "great ode" in honor of his native land, in honor of socialism. New LEF proclaims the slogans of topical and functional art. Mayakovsky, in accordance with the theories of his group, compares his poem to a telegram that informs about facts; but a few months later he publicly reveals his longing for the permanence of a work of art, which has more than immediate value.

ZHEVYERZHEYEV'S REMINISCENCES:

In 1927 the management of Leningrad Academic Theaters commissioned Mayakovsky to write a play for the tenth anniversary of the Great Socialist Revolution. Toward the end of the 1926/27 season, sometime early in June, Mayakovsky read his work in the conference room of the Leningrad Theater Museum. The board of management of the academic theaters and the managers of all three of its theaters were present.

Mayakovsky read what a few months later became his well-known poem "Good!" But at that time he called it "The Twenty-fifth."

The general impression of the reading reminded me closely of *Mystery-Bouffe*. The same irresistible charm of the master-reciter and a similar coolness on the part of the "official" listeners. After an enthusiastic applause and praise for the poet, the theater managers began to put forward their statements and reservations. The representatives of the Dramatic Theater declared that they were preparing for the premiere of *The Armored Train* for November 7; the Opera and Ballet Theater informed about its production of *The Storming of Perekop*. The question was also raised that the piece was in fact a poem, whose production would be very difficult if not impossible. Smolich, however, who at that time was in charge of the Little Opera Theater said his theater would be very happy to produce this excellent poem.

FROM PYOTR KOGAN'S BOOK "LITERATURE OF THE
GREAT DECADE," 1927:

We ask ourselves why Mayakovsky did not become the herald of an era, why he did not succeed in uttering the most important and greatest words about revolution, though he had every chance to do so. Audacious, swept by the winds of revolution, sensitive to the voices of the street, instinctively strange and hostile to the bourgeois spirit of modern Europe, he, who had raised his voice against war at a time when all poets were singing patriotic hymns, he, who had forecast the coming of the revolution three years before its storms broke loose and courageously joined it when it came, he, who more boldly than others liberated himself from the power of all traditions of the bourgeois world—literary as well as moral—he, who demolished its idols, unafraid of sacrilege, nevertheless did not become a revolutionary poet in the fullest sense, the exponent of its deepest aspirations. Mayakovsky's fate is perhaps the best proof of the fact that to be a great poet means above all: to have a world view, a new content, and, last of all, craftsmanship. Mayakovsky did not accept entirely the proletarian outlook; occasionally he approached proletarian class consciousness, but more often he remained an anarchist-individualist . . .

. . . Tuesday, September 20—the first LEFist Tuesday after the summer vacation and Mayakovsky's return to Moscow.

It was an ordinary LEFist meeting—Lunacharsky, Averbakh, and Fadyeyev were there too. About thirty people. I have no idea how they all managed to fit into that small room. The telephone was disconnected and Bulka was seated on someone's knees . . .

Mayakovsky stood in the corner by the door leading to his room.

. . . Really, to write something was for him a task only half-done. He had to read it too!

Reading was for him a direct continuation of the creative process . . .

A few days later Lunacharsky read a paper about the cultural development of the decade at the jubilee session of the Central Executive Committee of the USSR . . . He said, "Mayakovsky composed, in honor of the tenth anniversary of October, a poem which we ought to acclaim as a splendid fanfare in praise of our festive occasion, a fanfare in which there is not one false note . . ."

Lunacharsky said more or less the same thing on that occasion in the small dining room in Gendrikovy Alley. He spoke first. His speech was lofty, maybe even a bit old-fashioned, but well composed and emphatic . . . He turned not to Mayakovsky but to all those present, and when he finished, he almost bowed—a habit he had when speaking to large audiences.

He spoke with sincerity and with genuine devotion to Mayakovsky, recalled *Mystery*, which he had twice supported. "About This," a poem to which he was particularly attached, and many other things besides . . .

"This is the October Revolution cast in bronze."

Fanfares, bronze . . . this sounded, perhaps, too pretty for LEFist taste, but such was the manner in which he was used to expressing himself.

Lunacharsky sat down.

A samovar appeared on the table and a general conversation ensued. People recalled the poem they had just heard, passed glasses to one another, asked Vladimir Vladimirovich to repeat some stanzas. And—little by little—a vehement conflict arose.

It was started, I think, by Averbakh . . . Averbakh was speaking and flashing his spectacles with the speed of a machine gun (no stenographer could stand his pace). He was a great diplomat and, proclaiming his point of view, declared reservations all around . . . He realized it was better not to make a frontal attack on Mayakovsky. For that matter, the ratio of their powers was not advantageous to him.

The same line was continued by Fadyeyev. He was a new man in Moscow literary circles, his poetic inclinations were unknown, and he could be judged only by articles in *Na Litieraturnom Postu*. He spoke directly and fiercely. LEFists had already managed to say some disparaging things about him in their periodical, and a part of his fierceness was, perhaps, the result of a desire to clarify their mutual relations and to dot the *i*'s. The rest resulted, of course, from the fact that Fadyeyev was defending the RAPP slogans concerning psychology and the so-called living man in literature (just about eighteen months later this slogan would be declared invalid!). From this point of view many aspects of the poem struck him as wrong . . .

Of course, he met with opposition . . . They shouted, argued, interrupted each other. People tried to convince one another. Poets, critics . . . Fadyeyev on his part, attacked and repulsed attacks, and as he shouted, the color of his face changed from pink to purple. The atmosphere of the discussion became more and more heated; the temperature rose.

Averbakh began to "dance pirouettes" and tried to open some safety valves in particularly sharp moments. He tried to change the subject by telling jokes. He even referred to the people's commissar.

The commissar, however, made only short replies from time to time but observed everything with great interest and enthusiasm.

When the discussion had almost reached its culmination, Natalya Rozenel turned to him behind my back (I was sitting between them): "Anatol, it's time we left. I have a rehearsal at nine. The car is waiting . . ."

But Anatol Vassilievich whispered in reply, "Let's wait a bit longer, Natashenka. Let's see how this is going to end . . . It's interesting"

How could it end? There were many LEFists, but it was not just a question of numbers: they knew how to argue and did not suffer from a shortage of arguments. Fadyeyev's situation was bad . . .

Even so, he wanted to have the last say. He said emphatically, "When in Vladivostok we used to come from the underground, in disguise, so to say, to the cabaret; we saw poets there . . . Today those poets are writing revolutionary poems . . ."

NATALYA ROZENEL-LUNACHARSKAYA:

Anatol Vassilievich came back from Leningrad in the morning, worked hard all day long, and felt tired and not well in the evening. But a few days before leaving for Leningrad he had promised Mayakovsky to attend the reading of "Good!" and he was determined to keep his word, even though he was not feeling well. While Mayakovsky was reading I saw Anatol Vassilievich taking nitroglycerin, which meant he was having heart failure. I wrote on a slip of paper that we should quietly leave. Anatol Vassilievich shook his head to signify refusal . . .

Mayakovsky's place was particularly crowded on that evening. There were not enough chairs, people were sitting on window sills and on arms of chairs.

Among those present was Alexander Fadyeyev—young, tall, in a navy-blue Caucasian shirt with lots of straps and buttons. He had light chestnut hair and seemed to have the roughness of youth. He was obviously not in his own territory. On that evening they mauled him and he did not succeed in paring off all the blows . . . There was a vehement argument with Asyeyev. Mayakovsky kept walking around the room smoking and from time to time would make short, accurate replies, although Fadyeyev mostly addressed him. Anatol Vassilievich did not take part in the discussion, but listened with close, slightly ironical attention.

On our way back we gave Fadyeyev a lift home. Only in the car did he begin gradually to recover: "I came to listen to poetry; they invited me so politely, and yet they attacked me so."

Anatol Vassilievich replied, laughing, "Aleksandr Aleksandrovich, you took the floor alone against them all. That is to your credit."

FROM ALEXANDER FADYEYEV'S PAPER AT THE CONGRESS OF
PROLETARIAN WRITERS, MAY 1928:

. . . An *artist* would never be able to analyze with sufficient truth and force the manifold processes taking place in the country without looking into the peasant's psyche and showing all the conflicting tendencies struggling inside it . . . Mayakovsky, for instance, who together with the LEFists combats psychology, was unable in his poem "Good!" to show those tendencies, because he had not looked into the mentality of the peasants, and his Red Army men, throwing Wrangel into the sea with bravura, are false Red Army men, pompous poster figures, in whom no one will believe . . .

What is the objective sense of LEFist revolt against psychology, against the living man? Apparently we have to deal with a social group which must *hide* its real nature . . . No matter how many revolutionary words LEFists might use, how many subjectively good intentions they might have, such a theory is objectively advantageous now only for the new, aggressive Soviet bourgeoisie . . .

THE DAILY "RABOCHAYA MOSKVA," OCTOBER 20, 1927:

Yesterday at the meeting of party activists, organized by the press sub-department of the City Committee of the Soviet Communist party, Vladimir Mayakovsky read his new poem "Good!" devoted to the tenth anniversary of October.

For an hour and a half the audience listened with unflagging attention to the new work by that talented poet.

The reading was occasionally interrupted by shouts of approval and applause.

It must be noted that the poet came not just to read his poem but to obtain from middle-party activists—agitprop workers, etc.—a reply to the question whether, and to what extent, the poem is clear, whether on the whole it gives the masses of readers what they need at present . . .

The gist of critical remarks about the poem could be summarized as follows: "The poet did not succeed in giving an exhaustive review of the events connected with the October Revolution. The poem is steeped in individualism, depicts individual heroes, but does not present the masses. The past seven years of socialist construction are poorly reflected in the poem."

The majority admitted, however, that the poem is good, as far as its contents as well as its form are concerned. One cannot say that such a poem contains the history of the October Revolution. It gives a good image of October and of all stages of the revolution. The heroism of armed struggle and the "every day of reconstruction" have been artistically rendered in the poem . . .

Comrade Mayakovsky, who spoke after this exchange of views, declared that none of the comrades had replied negatively to the fundamental question posed to those assembled. No one said the poem is unintelligible—and that was the main thing he had expected from the meeting.

Comrade Lazyan, chairman of the press sub-department of the City Committee of the Soviet Communist party, declared that the poem is unquestionably an achievement in our literature.

LETTER OF THE GREAT ACTOR VASSILI KACHALOV TO
MAYAKOVSKY:

Dear Vladimir Vladimirovich!

I have tried in vain to reach you on the telephone. I wanted so much to thank you for "Good!" At the Kuznetsky we met face-to-face, I almost came forward to shake your hand, but I am shy and did not dare. Still, I cannot remain silent; I want to thank you. Even though this might be indifferent to you, even though you don't care a hoot, I must express somehow my joy and gratitude.

Perhaps you do not live at your old address, but I suppose this letter will reach you.

I will learn your poem—I have begun work on it already—and will read fragments at least, if you have no objection.

With greetings and deep respect,

Vassili Kachalov

ACCOUNT OF MAYAKOVSKY'S READING GIVEN ON OCTOBER 20,
1927 AT THE MOSCOW POLYTECHNIC MUSEUM, IN THE JOURNAL
"SOVYETSKAYA SIBIR," OCTOBER 30, 1927:

Mayakovsky received a note: "What I liked most in the poem was the line 'with Lenin in the head and a Nagan revolver in hand.' In a calm voice, not like the one he normally used at his readings, the poet said, quite ordinarily and seriously, turning toward the gallery, "I wish, comrade, that you always have Lenin in your head and a Nagan revolver in your hand . . ."

And he added jokingly ". . . and sometimes also my poem in your heart."

THE ACCOUNT OF MAYAKOVSKY'S EVENING AT THE LENINGRAD
PRESS HOUSE, EVENING EDITION OF THE DAILY "KRASNAYA
GAZIETA," OCTOBER 30, 1927:

. . . The day before yesterday we witnessed at the Press House a most shameful event. The literary philistines, who once masked themselves in Mayakovsky's fashion, have now turned about-face and have coldly received the eminent poet, who came to the city of revolution with his poem about the great anniversary. But coldness was not the worst part of it. Toward the end of the evening, the literary philistines went very far in their public effrontery. Mayakovsky was given notes asking questions about his fees, about his poems being "insincere," and one note was simply a hooligan's exploit. Mayakovsky was handed a note on which was written: "Tell us, you beast, how much they pay you for a day?" A philistine will always remain a philistine; nothing can be done about it. It is amazing, though, that the Press House has become the arena for philistines.

ON NOVEMBER 6 THE FIRST NIGHT OF "THE TWENTY-FIFTH" TOOK
PLACE. ZHEVYERZHEYEV RECALLS:

I have to confess I was very worried by what I saw on the stage of the Little Opera Theater. The stage version of the poem corresponded very little to the impression left after the first reading by the author in the spring!

What was the reason? Let us even assume that Vladimir Vladimirovich, when accepting the commission for a play from the academic theaters in 1927, consciously rejected the principle of writing a "play" and wrote an excellent "poem."

It is possible that it was really very difficult to "stage" that "poem" and that only a director as brilliant as the poet could have solved that problem. But even so, it seems to me now that the error had been committed of making obsolete tricks, worn out by their use at innumerable club theaters, the basis of the production. There was collective verse-reading and a living newspaper, a narrator, and masks (a procession of kings), and gymnastics (sailors sliding down the ropes from the fourth balcony onto the stage), etc.

. . . Box-office sales amounted to 50 rubles at the third performance of *The Twenty-fifth* and . . . 14 rubles 50 kopecks at the fourth.

REMINISCENCES OF ILYA SELVINSKY:

When my poem "Pushtorg" was published, Mayakovsky said:

"Well, well. I greeted the tenth anniversary of October with the poem

"Good" and you with "Pushtorg." I sing about revolution and you put holes in it."

"I find fault not with the revolution but with those who, pretending to be Communists, are dragging the revolution through bourgeois mud."

"Forgive me, Ilya, but you are a political dullard. To write such a poem in the jubilee year is the supreme example of lack of tact."

"And I regard your 'Good!' as the supreme example of lack of tact. 'Cheeses not stained by flies,' 'lamps glisten,' 'reduced prices,' 'we beat with money—very good!' Quiet and peaceful. And meanwhile the party is torn asunder by internal struggles. And without Lenin! My 'Pushtorg,' if you want to know, is much more topical than your 'Good!': you are fighting Milukov and Kerensky, political corpses, and I am fighting the rot that is eating the party from inside. 'Kroll or communism'—that is 'Pushtorg's' slogan."

"But you have opposed a non-party expert to Kroll, not a Communist."

Yuri Libyedinsky, one of RAPP's leaders, was present at our discussion . . .

"You want to educate Selvinsky like a hen educating a duckling," Libyedinsky said. "But he must swim! There is nothing to be done about it. We have already thought about it in RAPP."

"And what have you decided?" Mayakovsky asked viciously. "To clip Selvinsky's wings? So that he can swim?"

LAVUT:

Reading after reading: Rostov, Novocherkask, sometimes two, three times a day. Mayakovsky grew very tired and came down with influenza. And just then he read a review of the poem "Good!" in the daily *Sovetsky Yug*, under the insultingly malicious title: "A Cardboard Poem." The reviewer said that Mayakovsky had "not reflected the revolution" and that under his cry of "Good!" "every philistine" could sign himself.

The review ended with the words:

> For the tenth anniversary, the working people of the Soviet Union have offered the republic valuable gifts: power stations, factories, railways.
> Mayakovsky's poem is not one of those gifts.
> It is rather like gaudily painted jubilee triumphal gates and pavilions made of plywood and cardboard for the feast day.

Such a gate, as one knows, is not durable. A month or two will pass, the gate will get wet, the paint will peel off, the passers-by will look at it with indifference.

. . . Vladimir Vladimirovich looked depressed. "Perhaps the poem is really good for nothing?" he said to me as we were leaving Rostov.

KATANYAN:

Some people found the Rostov review to their tastes. They made it their business not to let the review pass by unnoticed by having been printed in a provincial paper . . . They took it up, reprinted it, and jabbed Mayakovsky with it once more.

Such people were to be found on the editorial board of Averbakh's periodical *Na Litieraturnom Postu.*

The gangsters from Averbakh's band loved it when someone insulted Mayakovsky. They behaved slyly and cautiously and were a little afraid of him, did not risk open combat with him, but could not, of course, give up an opportunity to kick him with somebody else's boot. Seven months later —in July, 1928—the review from the Rostov daily was reprinted in Nos. 13–14 of *Na Litieraturnom Postu* under the hypocritical title "A Reader's Statement About Mayakovsky's Poem 'Good!'" The original source was not even given! Just to denote that *we* have nothing to do with it, that this is not our judgment, nor that of the professional critics, *but of the readers themselves!*

FROM A NOTE IN THE KIEV DAILY "PROLETARSKAYA PRAVDA," MARCH 18, 1928:

All seats taken, people are standing in the passageway, in the exits, are sitting all around the platform, leaning on the piano, have crawled under the piano . . .

On the platform Mayakovsky, the poet.

"The publication of my poem 'Good!'" says Mayakovsky, "has been attached as it were to the celebration of our tenth anniversary. But I would not like it to adorn this decade only. It will be necessary, and will play its part, in twenty and forty years from now. Yes, this is what I think. I am sure of it . . ."

♖ 32 ♖

"Bad!"

♞

*After "Good!" Mayakovsky announces a poem entitled "Bad!,"
but writes the plays* The Bedbug *and* The Bathhouse *instead.
Work on the production of* The Bedbug *is recalled by: Vsevolod Meyerhold, Dmitri Shostakovich, Igor Ilyinsky, and
others.*

FROM MAYAKOVSKY'S AUTOBIOGRAPHY:

This year 1927 . . . Basic work at the *Komsomolskaya Pravda,* and, in
addition, I compose "Good!"

I regard "Good!" as a program piece . . . *The year 1928.* I am writing
the poem "Bad!"

FROM A PAPER BY ALEXANDER MYETCHENKO:

"Good!" is the last poem that Mayakovsky completed. The poet wanted to
write a poem called "Bad!" afterward but the intention was not realized.
Instead, he wrote an excellent cycle of satiric poems and his two best
dramatic works, also satiric in character.

FROM MAYAKOVSKY'S SPEECH AT THE JUBILEE MEETING IN
HONOR OF THE MEYERHOLD THEATER, APRIL 25, 1926:

Comrades! It is with pleasure that I offer congratulations to the Vsevolod Meyerhold Theater and to Vsevolod Meyerhold himself. I find it all the easier to do so because we are almost congratulating ourselves—not personally but the entire left front in art, which wholeheartedly—with their arms, front and rear—supported this theater at a time when there was no question of either speeches or even a simple "good morning" . . .

All of you comrades who are sitting here in the Meyerhold Theater remember that this theater was born and created by revolution, that it was officially created by the left front in art—by LEF [Applause]. . .

Usually a speech is followed by an address. I can hand comrade Meyerhold only one address—mine: Gendrikov Alley No. 15, Apartment 5 [Applause]. At this address he will always find support in the form of plays and in the form of action—the kind of support that LEF has given him during all of his activities.

MEYERHOLD ON MAYAKOVSKY:

Meetings with Mayakovsky always excited me. I regarded him as a very great man, not only a great poet, but a great man in general, a man who overwhelmed one with his greatness. He was so out of the ordinary, so witty, so wise that even a man of the world, like myself, felt a bit ill at ease in his presence.

MEYERHOLD'S LETTER TO MAYAKOVSKY, MARCH 23, 1926:

Dear friend Mayakovsky,

You told me yesterday I was getting younger and younger. This is to inform you that since yesterday I knocked off another ten years, the reason being that the production of your play awaits me. I will produce it myself but will ask for your help. Whom would you propose as a stage designer? Do not answer by letter, or by Butorin; you will tell me personally. We must meet. Could you and the Briks, perhaps, come to us in the next few days? A propos: Zinaida Nikolayevna asks for your poem devoted to Yesenin's memory. The children were delighted by the book. They have already learned it by heart.

Kisses,
Your loving Vsevolod

For the last time I appeal to your common sense. The theater is dying. There are no plays. They force me to give up classics. I do not want to lower the standard of the repertoire. Please tell me seriously: can we count on getting your play this summer. Cable urgent: Sverdlovsk, Hotel Central, Meyerhold.

. . . Yesterday Vladimir Mayakovsky read to us a play he has just completed, entitled *The Bedbug*. With this play Mayakovsky gives a new utterance in the field of playwriting, and at the same time, the work dazzles with its virtuosity of language . . .

We are happy that our theater has been enriched in the year 1927 with four plays by four outstanding, talented modern poets: Mayakovsky, Selvinsky, Erdman (*A Suicide*), and Tretyakov. These authors offered their plays to our theater in a period of acute repertoire crisis . . .

I have produced plays for many years but can never afford the luxury of allowing the playwright to take part in the production. I always try to keep the author away when directing his play, to keep him as far away from the theater as possible, because a serious director-artist is always hampered by a playwright who interferes with his work. But as far as Mayakovsky is concerned, I not only let him work with me but could not even begin to work on the play without him. Such was the case with *Mystery-Bouffe, The Bedbug*, and *The Bathhouse*. I could not begin my work until Mayakovsky set things going. Whenever I happened to begin work by myself, I invariably ran to the telephone and begged him to come. Mayakovsky was always present in my theater at all early rehearsals . . . He always realized whether a particular scenic conception was right or wrong from a director's point of view. He had an excellent sense of composition (and our theater always worked out its scenic constructions not only according to theatrical laws but also according to the laws of plastic arts) and was invariably right when pointing out my every mistake in this sphere.

NOTE IN THE WEEKLY "RABIS," JANUARY 29, 1929:

"In the Playwrights' Workshops."

by V. V. Mayakovsky:

The Meyerhold Theater in Moscow has begun preparatory work on the production of my new play *The Bedbug*—a fairy comedy in five acts and nine scenes.

The problem of the play: unmasking the bourgeoisie of today.

The first four scenes take place in our time. The action concerns an ex-worker, ex-party member Prysipkin, who celebrates a "Red wedding" with the barber's daughter, manicurist Elzevira Renaissance.

This part of the play ends with a fire which breaks out during the drunken wedding orgy. All the characters perish, but Prysipkin's corpse is not found.

The second part takes the spectators ten Soviet five-year plans forward.

The future generation finds Prysipkin's frozen corpse and decides to resurrect him. In this way a flamboyant specimen of a bourgeois finds itself in the new world. All attempts to make a man of the future of him are thwarted. After many kinds of adventures he finds himself at the end in a zoological garden, where he is exhibited as an exceptional specimen of *filistra vulgaris*.

In the finale the hero addresses the zoo visitors—and above their heads, the audience, and invites them to take their places beside him in the cage . . .

FROM THE FINALE OF "THE BEDBUG"—PRYSIPKIN'S MONOLOGUE:

Citizens! Brothers! Countrymen! Beloved! Where have you come from? How many of you are there? When did they manage to defrost you all? Why am I alone in the cage? Dearest brethren, please, come to me! What am I suffering for?! Citizens! . . .

IGOR ILYINSKY:

I do not remember why I was late for the first readings and rehearsals of *The Bedbug*.

"You must listen to Mayakovsky himself reading the play," said Meyerhold to me after our first meeting at the table, apparently dissatisfied with my performance.

I asked Vladimir Vladimirovich to read to me a number of fragments from the play in which Prysipkin appears.

In his author's interpretation Mayakovsky did not endow Prysipkin with any characteristic traits or moral attributes. He read the part in his usual manner of monumental authoritativeness and with a solemn, even noble (yes, also in this part!) pathos, peculiar to himself.

. . . I began to build Prysipkin's part as a "monumental" flunkey and boor. This monumentalism made for a larger scale of that character. Though it may seem paradoxical, I adopted for Prysipkin, even externally . . . Mayakovsky's manner. But to his manner, in itself impeccable, and even perfect, I added certain compromising shades: I enlarged the brisk-ness of his movements, I imbued the majestically fixed expression on his face with dull cretinism, I stood pigeon-toed. The characteristic contours, for the moment external, of a pathetically triumphant philistine began to take shape. External characteristics then had to be enriched by more and more living traits. Decisive convictions turned into self-complacency; self-confidence and glibness, into hopeless insolence . . . Mayakovsky and Meyerhold ceaselessly watched my work, myself, our common child, Pry-sipkin, being born in me.

MEYERHOLD:

The characters in Mayakovsky's plays are always a part of Mayakovsky himself, just as a part of Shakespeare is in all of Shakespeare's heroes. If we want to imagine the legendary figure of Shakespeare, we do not have to dig in old church registers, in genealogies, but ought to examine the characters in his plays. I can even imagine his voice, just as I always hear Mayakovsky's voice in his comic characters.

DMITRI SHOSTAKOVICH:

Early in 1929, Vsevolod Meyerhold, who was producing *The Bedbug*, suggested that I compose music for the production. I undertook this work with pleasure.

In my naïveté I supposed that Mayakovsky remained a tribune, a brilliant and witty speaker in everyday life. When I met him at one of the rehearsals, I was surprised at his softness, politeness, and simple good manners. He turned out to be a nice, attentive man, who would rather listen than speak. It seemed right that he should have talked and I should have listened, but it turned out the other way around.

I had several conversations with Mayakovsky on the subject of my music for *The Bedbug*. The first of them I found rather strange. Mayakovsky asked, "Do you like firemen's bands?" I replied that sometimes I liked them and sometimes not. To this Mayakovsky said that he liked firemen's music most and that such music was required for *The Bedbug*.

. . . I cannot judge whether Mayakovsky liked my music or not. He listened to it and just said, "It will do." I took this to mean approval, since Mayakovsky was a very sincere man and never paid hypocritical compliments.

I have to say about *The Bedbug* that it is not one of my favorites among Mayakovsky's works. I think there are excellent parts in it, but the final scenes are, to my mind, inferior to the first half of the play. There could be irony in it: future seen through Prysipkin's eyes.

KUKRINIKSY (THIS PSEUDONYM WAS USED IN COLLABORATION BY THREE YOUNG PAINTERS: KUPRYANOV, KRILOV, AND SOKOLOV):

One day toward the end of 1928, we were sitting in the canteen of the Herzen House. Mayakovsky, who had just returned from Paris, came in . . . He usually sat down at a free table and was soon surrounded by acquaintances. On this occasion he unexpectedly came to our table, and, sitting down, said, "I need you. I've written a play called *The Bedbug*. It will be produced by Meyerhold. Will you do the designs?"

We had heard of the play and we liked the first sentence, which ran, "Because of a button it's not worth getting married; because of a button it's not worth getting a divorce . . ." But to do the stage design? We, who had never worked in the theater! We told Mayakovsky as much. He replied, "That's why I need you."

"Yes, but we . . ."

Our doubts did not move him. He had already made the decision and we had to try. On the next day we met in the theater and read the play. We were overjoyed; we were terrified. We agreed, though . . .

"You will do the first four scenes—'the present'; and 'the future' will be done by Rodchenko. 'The present' will have to be decorated with today's objects. You will buy all the real things in shops; let the audience see the same tasteless objects they buy in shops on the stage. You do not have to invent anything, no props, everything will be real . . .”

Mayakovsky himself looked at every sketch for the costumes and sets, made his remarks . . . One day he sat for a long time, smoking, and . . . carefully drew a mirror in a fanciful frame and flowers of the kind with which mirrors were embellished in cheap barbershops . . . He advised us to visit barbershops, particularly in the area of Trubny Square, and to examine their interiors. So we began going there to get a shave and a haircut and to draw . . .

ILYINSKY:

Shortly before opening night Mayakovsky told the Kukriniksy that I did not need a costume: “Take him to the tailor’s and put the first suit you find there on him. It will be just right.”

The Kukriniksy cheerfully agreed. I had my doubts, because I already had some experience in “dressing the character.” It was difficult, however, to oppose the author and the stage designers.

I went with the Kukriniksy to the tailor’s.

I tried on dozens of suits. Not one of them was right. The result was not Prysipkin but a bookkeeper, a dentist, or simply an uninteresting young man.

“Now you see,” I told the stage designers. “A suit from the present-day tailor is just a poetic image given to you and me by Mayakovsky.”

We told Meyerhold and Mayakovsky himself about it. Meyerhold believed us, Mayakovsky did not. He went with us to the tailor’s and realized that his “poetic image” had no suitable naturalistic embodiment.

Together with the Kukriniksy, I had to look around in theatrical costume stores and try on old coats made in different styles. At last we found one, narrow in the waist, with slightly protruding tails and baggy sleeves. That was the present-day coat which fully satisfied all of us, the audience included.

The first night of *The Bedbug* was a great success. Mayakovsky was very pleased with the audience’s reception of the play and did not miss a single performance in the first part of the run. He was enthusiastically called out, so whenever he was present at a performance, he came out and took a bow with Meyerhold.

KUKRINIKSY:

February 13, 1929, was the first night of *The Bedbug*. We often went into the wings to see Mayakovsky. He was nervous, walked in the corridor of the manager's office during intermission, and smoked. For a long time he did not come forward to the clapping and shouting audience. Pushed by the actors, who took him by the arms, he appeared for a few seconds, with an embarrassed smile, and disappeared again into the wings.

Someone sitting next to us confessed he had never thought Mayakovsky could be embarrassed.

MARIA SUKHANOVA, ACTRESS:

There were many successful things in the production. Particularly good were Igor Ilyinsky as Prysipkin. The press both praised and condemned the performance. Those who condemned it demanded that the characters be psychologically deepened, that life in the student hostel be more realistically portrayed. They charged the author with being primitive. In the second part of the play they wanted to see an exact image of socialistic life. And the performance was: satiric, poster-like, conventional.

FROM THE REMINISCENCES OF NATALYA
ROZENEL-LUNACHARSKAYA:

In February, 1929, Anatol Vassilievich saw Mayakovsky's play *The Bedbug* at the Meyerhold Theater.

During the intermission, we were invited backstage, and, while sipping the traditional tea in Vsevolod Emilievich's study, the critics and the people of the theater who were present exchanged their impressions of the performance. The author, of course, was there too. It seemed to me that he was nervous. He did not want any tea, hardly took part in the conversation, smoked one cigarette after another, and occasionally threw in a reluctant word.

Anatol Vassilievich was of the opinion that *The Bedbug* was undoubtedly a success of both author and director, that it was an absolutely deadly satire on the bourgeoisie and on philistinism, that our language would be enriched by a number of excellent words and expressions borrowed from the play, but at the same time took the view that this was only a beginning for Mayakovsky the playwright, that he could have much more to offer if he were seriously set on the theater. Neither was Anatol Vassilievich fully satisfied with the way the director treated the "future" scenes, and told Meyerhold about this directly, adding, "If it is any consolation to you, Vsevolod Emilievich, I must say that such scenes have never come off yet: those fantastically utopian people of the future are always too conventional, abstract, and . . . boring. Please observe that in utopian plays and novels 'men of the future' always busy themselves with talking only about 'men of the past.' "

Meyerhold replied that he himself felt the audience's attention falter in these scenes, that something was not quite right there, and that he had already worked out some changes to be introduced.

FROM THE REVIEW BY N. OSINSKY, "IZVESTYA," FEBRUARY
26, 1929:

Mayakovsky's play is the first of four plays by contemporary authors on contemporary subjects to be produced at the Meyerhold Theater this season. It seems to us the play has not been helped but harmed by the publicity, the noise that preceded the opening. One should not have made all that noise. The audience begins to expect too much and is then disappointed. Mayakovsky's play is not bad in general but has a number of essential defects and does not fulfill the tasks which it sets for itself. Mayakovsky set a praiseworthy goal for himself: to ridicule the bourgeois and philistine elements which also exist within the working class, and to help the struggle for a new morality, for a cultural revolution. Did he, however, draw the basic background—the life of the working classes in our time—on a sufficiently wide scale, in a sufficiently precise form? Did he, against this background, clearly present the characteristics of these bourgeois elements? To both questions, one must, unfortunately, reply in the negative.

. . . When the action, in turn, is transferred to the year 1979, the play's line remains too primitive, unprofound. Reluctantly we come to the conclusion that life in 1979, under socialism, is fairly dull . . . Besides, Mayakovsky's socialists are too easily infected with bourgeois germs. The author needs all this to construct a number of scenes; but socialism, as a result, also turns out to be superficial (and with specific LEFist deviations, the abolition of "feelings," art, etc.).

As a result of all these circumstances, as we have said before, the play does not fulfill the tasks it has set for itself. In addition, it is also some-what diffuse in the middle part. But in spite of all this, it does contain several successful and quite amusing scenes; there are many witty words and remarks, a number of original and amusing situations, and one sees the hand of a good writer in this material.

The production must, on the whole, be considered quite successful, particularly its first part (year 1929).

GOLOS TEKSTILEY, FEBRUARY 19, 1929:
"After Such a Performance Drinking Is Repulsive"
"The Voice of the Textile Workers" organized a collective performance of *The Bedbug* for the social activists of the "Krasnaya Zarya" factory. All workers unanimously state that that the play made a great impression on them. At the same time, the audience points out to the theater certain faults which in future can certainly be corrected.

Let the members of the audience speak.

Comrade Grinevich: "It is a good thing that the performance aims at drunkenness. A repulsive sight! We too are like that, when we drink . . ."

Comrade Savin: "The play moves to the core. It is doubtful, though, if life will change so much in fifty years' time. The action should have been advanced by at least one hundred years. And then, where, in 1979, did they find vodka for Prysipkin? They should have given him pure spirits in a chemist's flask with a prescription, not a bottle with spirit monopoly's label . . ."

Comrade Kutirev thought the play heavy: "After a day's work, and after such a play, one can get a headache."

Comrade Brayer does not agree with Kutirev: "If it is not pleasant to watch Prysipkin wallowing in his cage, it means that the performance has been effective. This play spits in the face of everybody who is like Prysipkin."

QUOTING A POEM, DISTRIBUTED AFTER THE OPENING OF "THE BEDBUG," MYETCHENKO EXPLAINS THAT "THERE" MEANS "ABROAD":

You know what Mayakovsky's like:
Didn't take long *Bedbug* to write,

Less time by half to opening night . . .
Maybe they'll scold him like a hack,
But if not honest, he's got a knack.
They'll scold him here. They'll thank him—there.

✹ 33 ✹

"To the Left of LEF"

✹

In the period that Mayakovsky writes and stages The Bedbug, *the literary group he is the leader of declines and dies. Mayakovsky breaks with* New LEF *and "grants amnesty to Rembrandt." Old enemies and those who shortly before were friends attack the poet.*

FROM KORNEL ZYELINSKY'S ARTICLE "ARE WE TO GO WITH
MAYAKOVSKY?" IN THE PERIODICAL "NA LITIERATURNOM
POSTU," NO. 5, 1928:

Yes, Mayakovsky and LEF are going through a crisis again. This second crisis is not so much a continuation of the first as the result of a new verification in the light of new demands, posed by the revolution to the old nihilistic intelligentsia, which in October had passed on its hopes to the futurists . . .

The tragedy of Mayakovsky and his colleagues in LEF is the tragedy of the nihilist intelligentsia, which is also dragging its heritage in the period of revolution. Thus Mayakovsky's fate is taking on the proportion of a great social problem, a basic problem of the new culture . . .

The new crisis Mayakovsky is going through marks the end of his historic role . . .

Where is Mayakovsky rushing? What passionate desire tells him to get lost in facts, dates, the language of an era, in order to find himself a place there, to raise his voice to a thunder? One can feel in all this the Russian intellectual—orphaned and homeless.

One parts from Mayakovsky not readily, but after a kind of inner struggle. After all, for many Mayakovsky was a "first love." *But one can arrive at the new understanding of revolution only by stepping across Mayakovsky.*

SERGEI EISENSTEIN:

. . . agony of New LEF, this frail posthumous child of the once bravely fighting LEF. Belief in yesterday's LEFist slogans has evaporated. New slogans have not been put forward. Whims and airs . . . And at its center, no longer the spirit of Mayakovsky but the "editorial apparatus." Long disputes on the subject of LEFist orthodoxy. I am already on the list of deserters . . .

Not entering New LEF, I turn my back on it. I am not going its way. Nor is Mayakovsky, for that matter. New LEF will soon break up . . .

SHKLOVSKY:

LEF was slowing down its pace.

We began to quarrel easily and to make peace with difficulty. I quarreled with Lila Brik in Gendrikovy Alley about some trifles.

When a man is weak, or when movement stops, a slight pretext is enough to cause death.

The literary salons were outdated. We were not aware of this and were angry at one another.

The LEF home was falling to pieces.

Then there was REF. Here everyone could sit at the table and sip tea without quarreling. But this was not needed any more.

LEF—the last Soviet literary group—was at an end.

NYEZNAMOV:

. . . LEFists did not invent "literature of fact," but learned it instinctively. But when some of them made of it "a closed, new aesthetic enterprise," Vladimir Vladimirovich Mayakovsky left *New LEF* . . .

The periodical existed until the end of the year, but it was really a different *LEF* . . .

Mayakovsky had "opened" *LEF;* Mayakovsky "closed" it. On that occasion Brik recalled the story of *Vyesy,* twenty years earlier: it had been founded by Bryusov, who "killed" the periodical when it turned to be contrary to his practice.

MAYAKOVSKY'S LETTER TO THE CHAIRMAN OF THE BOARD OF
CINEMATOGRAPHY (WUFKU), VOROBYOV, JULY 25, 1928:

Dear Comrade!

In April I received from WUFKU a notification of the "ban" imposed by the Repertory Committee on my scenarios *History of One Revolver* and *Away with Fat,* and in relation to that, a demand for the return of 2000 paid in advance.

To invoke a "ban" by the Central Repertory Committee is astoundingly simple and quite unacceptable. When? Why? How? It seems to me that such an act is inadmissible with regard to a Soviet writer . . . Please send me an extract giving reasons for the ban . . .

Over all my relations with the Scenario Department of WUFKU there always hovered something unsaid: I was sent from editor to editor; editors invented principles nonexistent in film, new every day, and clearly believed in their own abilities as far as scenario writing was concerned.

If we cannot agree on the subject of the submitted scenarios, I will, of course, return the advance . . . but would rather return it with work—a new scenario for WUFKU . . .

🦋

In July the seventh issue of New LEF *appeared—the last under Mayakovsky's editorship.*

FROM D. TALNIKOV'S ARTICLE "OUR PEOPLE ABROAD," IN THE
AUGUST ISSUE OF THE MONTHLY "KRASNAYA NOV":

Mayakovsky's entire story about his trip is kept in the usual vulgar and nonchalant tone of a "newsboy" . . . Thoughtlessness, superficiality, and rashness spout like a fountain from every page of these "discoveries" of America . . .

Though the author admits that . . . "he who is always cheerful is, in my opinion (!), a common fool," all his doggerel verses, in which he wants to demonstrate his radicalism, are distinguished by a peculiar "cheerfulness."

> Below the proletarian to communism strides,
> through the murmur of fields and the noise of factories—
> I from the skies of poetry throw myself into communism,
> for without it there is for me no love.

But the reader does not believe in this phraseology, which reverberates like an empty barrel rolling down the street, devoid of authentic poetic emotion, authentic ardor of spirit . . .

Let us, however, return to America, in order to sum up its new "discovery." Of what does this "discovery" consist? Of trivial nonsense.

LETTER TO THE EDITOR OF "KRASNAYA NOV":

Will you, please, kindly publish the following: I am astonished at the nonchalant tone of ignoramuses writing in the monthly *Krasnaya Nov* under the pseudonym Talnikov.

I regard my continued collaboration as unadvisable.

Vladimir Mayakovsky

16/8/28

NO. 8, 1928, OF "NEW LEF" WAS SIGNED BY SERGEI TRETYAKOV
AS EDITOR. IN THE SAME ISSUE, THE CHRONICLE COLUMN BEGINS
WITH THE NOTE:

In view of his departure for a long trip abroad, V. Mayakovsky has handed over the editorship of the periodical *New LEF* to S. Tretyakov.

IN "NEW LEF," NO. 9, TEXTS BY S. TRETYAKOV, P. NYEZNAMOV,
I. TERENTYEV, V. SHKLOVSKY, A. RODCHENKO, L. VOLKOV-LANNIT,
AND OTHERS WERE PUBLISHED. IN THE CHRONICLE COLUMN THERE
WAS A NOTE BY I. TERENTYEV ENTITLED "MAYAKOVSKY TO THE
LEFT OF LEF":

Mayakovsky's appearance with the reading of "journalist" poems and his talk "To the Left of LEF" has aroused a great deal of interest.

Mayakovsky himself has described this interest as follows: "Critical bulldogs and mongrels have come here to hear me insult my comrades. I will not do this. To the contrary, I confirm that LEFists have been and still are the best qualified force on the cultural front."

Offering a description of the general state of "fronts" and "groups," Mayakovsky declared that all literary and artistic groups, including WAPP and LEF have lost their significance, because "there is no one to fight with any more."

Mayakovsky's generally negative attitude toward literary factions apparently did not call for further justification. He was satisfied with an appeal to work "together with the country's economic institutions and on production."

Mayakovsky proclaimed this LEFist slogan in connection with the fact that he regarded other LEFist slogans of a negative character as outdated: "I grant amnesty to Rembrandt"; "I say that not only a newspaper, but a song and a poem are also necessary"; "Not every boy pushing a camera button is a LEFist," etc.

In conclusion, one must add that LEF has never regarded such things as rejecting classics and giving predominance to journalism and photography as dogma, but has considered them dialectically. It is therefore possible that the members of the audience did not understand in detail the theoretical part of his lecture and took away with them a number of bare statements, which they interpreted in a way Mayakovsky had not intended.

FROM A NOTE ENTITLED "AROUND LEF; MEYERHOLD . . . MAYAKOVSKY . . ." IN THE PERIODICAL "SHKVAL," NO. 41, 1928:

LEF's father and founder has repudiated LEFists . . .

This public penance took place during Mayakovsky's evening at the Moscow Polytechnic Museum.

Mayakovsky was scoffing, malicious, and relentless as always . . .

He declared that from now on he did not regard a daily newspaper as the poet's basic tribune: "Long live poetry, long live verse."

Painting, the same painting to which LEFists have always been op-

posed, accusing it of mawkishness and aestheticism, does not repel Mayakovsky anymore.

He no longer regards photography as the principal branch of the plastic arts. "Well, I am ready to grant amnesty to Rembrandt . . ."

FROM GROSSMAN-ROSHCHIN'S ARTICLE "CRIME AND PUNISHMENT
(THE SUPPRESSION OF THE SUPPRESSORS),"
"NA LITIERATURATURNOM POSTU," NO. 22, 1928:

Was it not Proudhon, who said that the institution of concubinage cannot
be reformed, that it must be suppressed? LEF cannot be reformed; it must
be suppressed . . .

We warn the readers against the light-hearted belief that LEF has
already been annihilated; against light-hearted hopes that Mayakovsky
has straightened himself out and his line. Nothing like it. We welcome
with joy any real renunciation of errors. *We are ready to help in any way*
all those who are searching for the proper path. But the expression of our
help is a decisive line, a watchful look, a strong will . . .

Reflect seriously on the road you have tread, define your line clearly,
and then, perhaps, you will deserve a more durable place than a chance
bunk in the *Komsomolskaya Pravda*, whose patience is not without limits,
either. We are ready to help you even through revealing the social sense of
your failure.

"KOMSOMOLSKAYA PRAVDA" ON A FILM BASED ON MAYAKOVSKY'S
SCENARIO ENTITLED "OKTYABRYUKHOV AND DYEKABRYUKHOV,"
OCTOBER 4, 1928:

Withdraw a Philistine Film

In the last few days the City Committee plenum organized a showing of
one of the new films produced by Sovkino entitled *Oktyabryukhov and
Dyekabryukhov.* In the plenum's opinion, the film is another manifestation
of the most impudent and small bourgeois and philistine ideology. The
City Committee plenum regards as essential that Sovkino consider the
question of withdrawing the film from public exhibition.

FROM SERGEI TRETYAKOV'S ARTICLE "TO BE CONTINUED,"
IN THE LAST (TWELFTH) ISSUE OF "NEW LEF":

We regard the factovist movement as the most essential in today's art.

We are absolutely opposed to the disdainful statements of some LEFist comrades, such as, "Is every little reporter, every boy who pushes a camera button, to be a LEFist?" This is an aesthetically aristocratic approach . . . Every boy with a camera is a soldier engaged in combat with easel painters, and every reporter carries, objectively, at the tip of his pen, death to belles-lettres . . .

Let our enemies shout joyously that LEF is dead. Your joy is premature! The continuation will follow: through LEF to the factovists.

CHUZHAK'S ARTICLE "TO THE LEFT OF LEF,"
ALSO IN NO. 12, OF "NEW LEF":

A misfortune has occurred at the LEFist home. Admittedly, not the misfortune of literature in general . . . only our little, domestic, but still authentic, undoubted, misfortune. The pseudo-left plague, which has now affected some of the superstructures, a "LEFtist" disease of not at all childish rightist deviationism, has not spared our little "left front of art." It has torn from our ranks several artists, not at all new to art, who suddenly have found themselves . . . to the left of LEF . . .

Some comrades, appeased by rightist courtesies, are departing, not for the first time, from the leftist "dogma" under the cover of some arch-leftist smoke screen. The only difference is that some do it quietly and unobtrusively, while others hire the hall of the Polytechnic Museum for that purpose and publicly cater to what they had no less publicly condemned the day before. Have they become heroically "wise"?

About those of our comrades who have lately become "wise," however, we cannot even say that they have been generously "endowed" by it. What kind of endowment could it be, if they, like us, are left with an empty till! We are left disorganized and without a periodical; they are left platonically waiting for a transfer of penal categories. Poor bastard children of our time, who have achieved an authentic revolution in art and are now humbly waiting for . . . its adoption! Was it worth it to "grant amnesty to Rembrandt" so noisily, provoking only dirty smiles on the faces of enemies? . . .

Heroic . . . renunciation of oneself! . . .

FROM MAYAKOVSKY'S STATEMENT AT THE MEETING OF THE
FEDERATION OF ASSOCIATIONS OF SOVIET WRITERS, DURING THE

DISCUSSION ON PLATONOV KYERZHENTSEV'S PAPER,
DECEMBER 22, 1928:

We are very happy that Comrade Kyerzhentsev, and all comrades who are
to speak here, will discuss the problems of literary policy with us . . . because we want to join our literary activity with the work of the masses,
with their representative—the party, the trade unions, etc. But it is not the
unemployed architects from *Na Postu,* rushing from one literary anteroom
to another, who ought to straighten out LEF's Communist ideology. I
cannot understand this at all. To me it is clear that, in this instance, the
literary names do not correspond to the literary substance. We must,
therefore, throw off the rotten rags of literary groups, throw them off with
the utmost decisiveness of which we are capable . . .

I accepted full responsibility for my words three days ago at an evening at the Press House: I regard myself as a proletarian poet, and the
proletarian poets in WAPP—as "poputchiki"—who follow in my footsteps.
And I insist on repeating this formula today . . .

Platon Mikhailovich has just called to step up the activities of the Federation of Soviet Writers. It must be clearly stated that the problem of
creating a federation of writers, as opposed to a trade federation, with
various titles of literary groups, has now ripened . . .

A writer chained to a literary group becomes not a worker of the
Soviet Union and of socialist construction, but an intriguer for his own
group . . .

Now the last question, comrades, the question of the masses. I do not
know about others, but I am obsessed by this question.

I am, in principle, a follower of the masses—body, soul, and spirit. But
in all my encounters at editorial offices, with no matter how many people
with conflicting points of view, not once did somebody approach me on his
own behalf; everyone praises or reproaches me on behalf of the masses.
And any little intriguer pronounces any arbitrary verdict on me in the
name of the masses . . .

🚩

In mid-January 1929, while rehearsals of The Bedbug *were
still under way, Mayakovsky went to Kharkov for a few days,
where he gave his lecture "To the Left of LEF" and a reading
of poems and fragments of the play.*

Always cheerful and full of confidence, on this occasion he was, for some unknown reason, nervous. It was apparent that he had appeared by a great effort of will. I was most startled, however, by one small episode: someone in the audience shouted to Mayakovsky, "Louder!" That innocent call had a deadly effect on Vladimir Vladimirovich: he jolted, as if frightened by something, then tried to crack a joke, "Well, if you ask *me* to speak louder, comrades, you must be out of your minds!"

The next morning I went to see him on the top floor of the "Red." Our talk was mainly concerned with the dissolution of LEF and the new slogans of revolutionary art promulgated just then by Mayakovsky.

. . . The telephone rang. Vladimir Vladimirovich had a long conversation. From his words one could guess he was talking to a doctor, who was communicating something very serious to him. Vladimir Vladimirovich returned from the telephone a different man. He was greatly disturbed . . . "What's to be done now?" he asked. "Three more readings."

. . . Then he went to the mirror and looked at his throat. He asked me to have a look. Indeed, his throat was red, his tonsils swollen.

"The doctor says there is nothing to be done. I have strained my vocal cords from frequent readings. He says I should have trained my voice twenty years ago, as actors do. And now it is too late. What shall I do?"

⚜ *34* ⚜

Tatyana

⚜

Still the period of The Bedbug *and "To the Left of LEF." In the fall of 1928 Mayakovsky spent two months abroad. He wrote, gave readings, negotiated with publishers and film directors, tried to buy a car. In Paris he met Tatyana Yakovleva —a woman about whom diarists still argue.*

SHKLOVSKY:

Vladimir Vladimirovich went abroad. There was a woman there whom, perhaps, he loved. I was told they were so like each other, so well matched, that people in cafés used to smile with satisfaction on seeing them . . .

EHRENBURG, QUOTING THE ABOVE PASSAGE, GOES ON TO SAY:

Mayakovsky's poem, addressed to T. A. Yakovleva, was published recently. She was the woman mentioned by Shklovsky. I have the manuscript of *The Bedbug*, given by Mayakovsky to Tata (T. A. Yakovleva) and thrown away by her as unwanted. No, she was not like Mayakovsky, though she too was, tall, beautiful . . .

from "*LETTER TO TATYANA YAKOVLEVA*"
by Vladimir Mayakovsky

You
  alone
        are my height—
brow to brow
        by me
              to stand,
allow me
        this important evening
to tell you
        in a human word.
Five.
        Silent is the chorus of streets,
empty
        the forest of people,
dead
        the peopled Paris,
I only hear
        the argument of whistles,
tracks are trembling
              to Barcelona.
In the lightnings
        sky is black,
the drama of skies
        thunders through clouds.
No, not thunder,
        but simply—
jealousy is moving
        mountains.

LETTERS AND TELEGRAMS FROM PARIS TO LILA BRIK,
OCTOBER–NOVEMBER 1928:

. . . I am negotiating with René Clair about a scenario. If successfully,
then I hope there will be a car. Kisses.

Your Pup

I am buying a Renault. Handsome gray 6 horsepower 4 cylinders *conduite intérieure*. On December 12 it will go to Moscow. I will arrive about the eighth. Cable me. Kisses. Love.

Your Pup

Dear and beloved Pussy!

I am late with this letter, for I cabled you saying I'm "buying" and have still not changed it into past tense "bought." But now, it seems, nothing will be in the way and, with the help of good souls in this world, I am going to scrape and earn. The car is nice . . .

I asked for a gray one, they said yes, if there is time, and if not—navy blue.

I will stay in Paris for a bit in order to collect the car personally from the factory, pack it and send it off, otherwise this will drag on for months. For the time being I sit and sweat over play and the scenario. This is the first gasoline the Renault is attempting to devour . . .

Puss, please telephone Kostrov that I am writing poems, with profit and pleasure, but for good reasons will send or bring them a little later.

Foxy, please send thirty rubles by cable—Penza, 52 Krasnaya Street, Apt. 3, Ludmila Alexseyevna Yakovleva . . .

My life is strange, nothing happens, but there are some details, though not suitable for a letter . . .

FROM THE PARIS PERIODICAL "YEVRAZYA,"
NO. 1, NOVEMBER 28, 1928:

V. V. Mayakovsky in Paris

Visiting Paris just now is V. V. Mayakovsky. The poet has appeared here more than once with public readings of his poems. The editor of *Yevrazya* prints below the statement of Marina Tsvetayeva, dedicated to Mayakovsky.

To Mayakovsky

On April 28, 1922, on the eve of my departure from Russia, I met Mayakovsky early in the morning at the quite empty Kuznetsky.

"Well, Mayakovsky, what am I to tell Europe of you?"

"That we here are right."

On November 7, late evening, on the way out of the Café Voltaire, to the question, "What will you say about Russia after Mayakovsky's public appearance?" I replied without hesitation, "That there is the might."

EHRENBURG:

I remember how in the fall of 1928 he spent over a month in Paris. We used to meet often. I can see him sulking in the "Coupole" bar. He ordered White Horse whisky: he drank little, but he composed a song: "Good horse, white horse, white skin, white hair . . ." One day he said, "You think this is easy? . . . I could write better poems than any of them."

At the Paris cafés, in order not to touch the glass with his lips, he used to drink hot coffee through straws they served with ice-cold drinks. He laughed at superstitions, but constantly wondered: is it or is it not going to come off? He adored gambling: heads and tails, odd and even. In the Paris cafés there were automatic roulette machines; one could put five sous on red, green, or yellow and win a chip to pay for a cup of coffee or a tankard of beer. Mayakovsky would spent hours at these machines. When about to go away he left Elsa Yuryevna hundreds of chips; he did not need the chips, but felt the need to foresee what color would win.

ELSA TRIOLET:

Mayakovsky played all games, cards, and billiards, and played them very well. Maybe he liked games because they made him relax, think about something different from the bothersome work. He liked risk too—in games and in life.

Then there were women. In the first place—that woman, his woman, to whom he dedicated all his books, the passion for whom filled his love poems . . .

But there were others. Mostly very young and very beautiful. He treated them with a grace that was astonishing in such a giant. Especially when they bestowed their favors on him. His constant worry then was not to show a woman too little respect, not to hurt her somehow . . . In the presence of women he became outspoken. The attention with which Mayakovsky would surround a woman, the concern to make her life easy, particularly if she was a working woman, to give her gifts, flowers . . . When a woman resisted him, he pursued her with the energy of a persistent railway engine. There were some women who, without resisting him

on principle, out of habit preferred their husbands and most common lovers. Over Mayakovsky's height they were breathless, they were afraid. He
did not score a tenor's successes among women; there was nothing about
him of the spicy, impure, seductive, and ambiguous qualities that women
like so much.

One must say he was stubborn not only with regard to the women he
wanted to win. He had in life a certain perseverance, courage, will characteristic of someone sure of being right, certain to witness the triumph of a
truth he knows and desires . . .

ROMAN JAKOBSON:

Toward the end of October (1928) Mayakovsky meets, in the drawing
room of a Parisian doctor, an eighteen-year-old Russian girl; fur coat and
pearls—fashions of the day—were most becoming to her.

ELSA TRIOLET:

It was I who introduced Mayakovsky to Tatyana. I had met her shortly
before at a friend's apartment. Tatyana occupied herself just then with the
making of hats. She was young and pretty; it was a short-lived beauty, but
in the period of its flowering she made a great impression. She was very
tall, had long legs and arms. When I saw her, I said, "You and Mayakovsky would make a good couple."

She was lively, gay, sociable. Her attitude was very anti-Soviet.

When Mayakovsky came to Paris, I took him to my friend. Tatyana
was there too. Mayakovsky fell in love with her on the spot. He took her
home by taxi and in the taxi fell on his knees before her.

Tatyana was not made of stone. There was only one thing she did not
agree to: to go with Mayakovsky to Russia as he wanted her to. Volodya
took it very hard and made me the confidante of all his love worries. It
was not an easy role.

LETTER FROM PARIS TO COMRADE KOSTROV
ON THE ESSENCE OF LOVE
by Vladimir Mayakovsky

. . . Just imagine:

                            into the room sails

    a beauty

in fur and pearls.
And I to her
speak thus—
I come,
comrade,
from Russia,
in my country
I am famous.
I know
quite a few girls more beautiful,
quite a few, who are nice and graceful.
. . . No,
not for me
cheap conquests
and shallow fleeting adventures.
I am
forever
hurt by love,
love
owns in me
all.
. . . Love is not gardens of paradise,
for us
love
shouts
that the cold
engine of the heart
is again
fit for work.
. . . Myself
to the last whisper in my breast
like a doctor I take under fire,
I listen:
it resounds, it is here—
human
and the simplest there is.
The roar

of elements

is rising:

the wind,

the fire,

the sea.

Who can

resist them?

Try, if you can . . .

from "LETTER TO TATYANA YAKOVLEVA"

. . . The feet,

which through hunger and snow

had waded

in those not easy years—

you dare expose

to the caresses

of an oil man

for a supper?

From under your straightened brows

stop

blinking your eyes at me.

Without vain fears

and hesitations

come out

into the crossing

of my helpless

arms.

You don't want to?

Then stay, if you like it here.

I will add to my bills

this insult

and in any case

one day

will take you—

alone

or together with Paris.

JAKOBSON:

The "Letter to Tatyana" is full of jealous allusions to her drawing-room meetings with oil men, or to the possibility of her going to Barcelona where Chaliapin was giving concerts at that time; he too aroused Mayakovsky's jealousy. Tatyana was noncommittal about Mayakovsky's efforts to get her to go with him—as his wife—to Moscow. On the next day, while they were having lunch at the "Petite Chaumière," he read her the poem he had written the night before . . .

On December 3, 1928, Mayakovsky went to Moscow to complete his fantastic comedy *The Bedbug*, arrange for its production on the stage, and return to Paris. He sent letters from there and, even more often, cables.

FROM LETTERS TO TATYANA, DECEMBER 1928–JANUARY 1929:
What about me? We have written (your Waterman and I) a new play. We read it to Meyerhold. We wrote it 20 hours a day, without breaks for meals. My head has swollen with all this work (I cannot even put my cap on). I cannot say as yet how this has come off, and I am not sending other opinions so as to avoid accusations of self-publicity, and also out of my immense modesty. (I think I have just praised myself nonetheless. It does not matter. I deserve it.) I work like a bull, lowering my muzzle with its red eyes over the desk. Even my eyes have failed me and I am wearing glasses! I put some awful cold stuff to my eyes as well. This is nothing . . . I can work with glasses on. And the eyes I need only to look at you, for there is no one for me to look at, except you. There are mountains and tundras of work. I will make some money and rush off to see you. If we fail through some super-unhappy accident . . . you will come to me. Yes? Yes? . . . What are you writing about the New Year? You are crazy! What vacation can I have without you? I am working. This is my *onliest* pleasure.

I work until my eyes go hazy and my back breaks. Besides writing I now have daily readings and rehearsals of the play. I hope to complete my work here in a month. I will rest then. When I am altogether tired, I say to myself, "Tatyana," and again, animal-like, bite into the paper . . . I do not write to you much (professional hatred of writing), but if all my conversations with myself concerning you were put together, all those unwritten letters, unsaid affectionate things, then my collected works would be three times as fat with sheer lyric stuff.

🙬

*In mid-January Mayakovsky began another series of readings
in the Ukraine, but after the first two he canceled the seven
that were to follow, because of his sore throat, and returned
to Moscow.*

FROM THE LETTERS:

I have canceled my tours and now stay put for fear that my reading of
your letters will be delayed by as much as an hour. Work and waiting for
you is my *only* joy.

Reflect and collect your thoughts (and then things) and measure your
heart to my hope that I shall take you on my paws and bring you to us, to
ourselves, to Moscow. Let us think about that and then talk. Let our parting be a test. If we love—is it worth spending our hearts and time on a
tiring march along telegraph poles? "Right or perhaps wrong?"

🙬

On the day after the first night of The Bedbug, *February 14,
1929, Mayakovsky again went to Paris.*

JAKOBSON:

In Paris they were together all the time . . . Whoever met the two of
them would remember how attentive and shy he was, how careful to
avoid all roughness and ambiguity. He was delighted by her, as he called
it, "absolute hearing" for poetry and willingly recited out of memory Pasternak, sometimes Yesenin, most often his own poems, for her . . .
Through Tatyana he came to like Paris again. Mayakovsky was impressed by the fact that Tatyana was not a genuine Parisian, but a Russian
with Parisian polish—smart, well bred, and resolute, full of strength and
courage, so unlike the female frailty he knew. He avoided talking politics
with Tatyana . . .

LEV NIKULIN:

. . . On the day of his departure I came to the farewell lunch at the
"Grande Chaumière" restaurant . . . Present were Louis Aragon, Elsa
Triolet, a certain Parisian acquaintance of the poet—a fervent motorist—,

and a young beautiful woman, whom we had often seen in Paris in the company of Vladimir Vladimirovich . . . In the evening we went to the Gare du Nord. We went there very quickly, driven by the fervent motorist. Soon we were at the dirty station, which smelled of coal smoke. On the platform—the train, with the direct car Paris-Nyegoryeloye . . . We assembled by the car, while Vladimir Vladimirovich and his lady companion walked hand in hand on the platform until it was time to go into the car. Last handshakes, parting jokes, laughter, and the train moved; the carriage platform, with the tall figure, hat in hand, slowly disappearing from view . . .

FROM LETTERS AND CABLES TO TATYANA, MAY—JULY, 1929:

I am only now beginning to work: I shall be writing *The Bathhouse* . . . Please do not grumble and do not reproach me—I've experienced so much unpleasantness—both great and small—that you must not be angry with me.

I am trying to get to see you as soon as possible.

I have begun to write *The Bathhouse* (with a hellish delay!). So far I have not even invented all the names of the characters . . . I have not written a single line of verse. After your verses all others seem insipid . . . It must not happen that we are not together for all time . . .

I long for you, will try to see you as soon as possible.

I cannot imagine life without you after October (the date fixed by us). From September I will begin constructing wings so that I can fly to you . . . I am so tall, bear-pawed, loathsome. Today also sulking . . . I write very little. My head does not work. I must have a rest . . . Come here, eh?

🖋

In September the poet was refused a passport for foreign travel. In October he learned that Tatyana Yakovleva had married.

ELSA TRIOLET:

Tatyana had a fiancé, I think a Count Duplessis, a French diplomat. She was very impressed with his title. When Mayakovsky went to Russia, she soon married her count. I then wrote to Lila, "Tatyana got married. Do not tell Volodya about this." Lila was reading my letter aloud and in her stride read those two sentences as well.

NIKULIN:

Toward the end of January 1930, I came back to Moscow and telephoned Vladimir Vladimirovich . . . He sounded as if my call pleased him. We arranged to meet at the writers' house at 52 Vorovsky Street.

"You can have a look at my exhibition at the same time."

. . . In a small, cozy room, painted for some reason a livid blue, Victor Shklovsky, who had also arranged to meet Mayakovsky, waited for him. He soon came, asked me about his Parisian friends, about almost everybody; he only did not ask about the young woman who had seen him off at the railroad station.

35

The Law of Inertia

⚜

Mayakovsky makes his last attempt to organize a literary group. Nyeznamov, who tells about it, uses the word "inertia." Lila Brik, Olesha, and others tell about the last toy he both enjoyed and worried about: the car brought from Paris. Lavut tells about Veronica Polonskaya, the last woman to enter Mayakovsky's life. On December 30, 1929, his friends gather for the last time at the poet's home in Gendrikovyi Alley to celebrate his jubilee.

FROM THE CHRONICLE OF LITERARY LIFE:

February, 1929,—the Constructivist Literary Center published a collection of texts entitled *Business*, edited by Selvinsky and Zyelinsky.

April, 1929,—the first issue of *Litieraturnaya Gazieta*—organ of the Federation of Associations of Soviet Writers—was published.

The programmatic collection of LEFist material, entitled *The Literature of Fact*, was published, edited by Nicholas Chuzhak.

June, 1929,—the decision to organize a higher educational establishment for literature was announced.

July, 1929,—Maxim Gorki, who some weeks earlier had returned to Russia after years spent abroad, became the chief editor of the periodical *Litieraturnaya Uchoba,* destined for beginning writers.

OSIP BRIK:

It would have seemed that Mayakovsky had given up for good the idea of organizing his own group and the thought would never again enter his head, if the writers' community had drawn the right conclusions from Mayakovsky's attitude. But things turned out otherwise . . . For the last time Mayakovsky attempted to get together a small group of friends, turning LEF into REF.

NYEZNAMOV:

In my opinion, REF as a group existed through sheer inertia. It might not have existed at all, for that matter.

Toward the end of 1928 Mayakovsky already had a negative attitude to all literary and artistic groups. Their "devaluation" (as V. Pyertsov called it) was obvious to him. And if, in spite of everything, REF came into being within a year, it was only because Mayakovsky lacked the nerve to pass in silence over the sneers of little fools . . .

LETTER TO THE STATE PUBLISHING HOUSE:

. . . The basic core of REF consists of: Mayakovsky, Asyeyev, Osip Brik, Rodchenko, Styepanova, Nyeznamov, Lomov, Lila Brik, Zhemchuzhny, Kirsanov, Kassil.

REF requests facilities for the publication of its periodic almanacs . . .

REF's almanacs are meant to appeal to the activists of the worker-peasant youth. For this reason the required number of copies would be no less than seven to eight thousand.

On behalf of the REF group: V. Mayakovsky, O. Brik, 14/5/1929.

LILA BRIK:

Mayakovsky brought a car from Paris, so small that he could hardly get into it, bending double . . .

Mayakovsky expected all kinds of gossip because of his new car and replied to it in advance with the poem "Reply to Future Gossip."

Even so, after the car had arrived in Moscow, Demyan Byedny met Mayakovsky and asked, "You seem to have turned bourgeois—driving your own car."

Mayakovsky: "As far as I know, you've been using a car for years."

Demyan: "Yes, but it's not a private car, it's a state car."

OLESHA:

I remember one morning a group of people standing at a crossing. The day was hot, the sun reflected from the surface of the car, Mayakovsky's car . . .

"Where are you going, Vladimir Vladimirovich?" I asked.

"To Mother," he replied willingly, with obvious pleasure . . .

In those days to have a private car was unusual and the fact that Mayakovsky had one was a topic for conversation in our circles. In the purchase of a car was revealed his enthusiasm for all that was modern, industrial, technical, journalistic; an enthusiasm expressed also by the fountain pens sticking out of his pocket and by his thick, supermodern shoe soles . . .

On July 15, 1929, Mayakovsky went to the Caucasus.

FROM THE REMINISCENCES OF PAVEL LAVUT:

Having arrived at Sochi and installed himself in a modest room at the "Riviera," Mayakovsky immediately took a rubber bath out of his suitcase and asked the chambermaid for some hot water. She clapped her hands in amazement: "Extraordinary! They want to have a bath in their room! With all the sea around they're making their own bath! . . ."

After his ablutions he dressed with meticulous care.

"I want to be smart," he said and added playfully, "After all, that's what I came to Sochi for."

"But you do not like dandyism," I remarked.

"There are exceptions in one's life. I am going to see a girl. And then, once in a lifetime one can be smart."

And he asked my advice as to what tie he should wear . . .

. . . At that time a number of Moscow artists were resting at Khosta . . . An actress Mayakovsky knew, Veronica Polonskaya, was also expected there. It was to her that Vladimir Vladimirovich went directly upon his arrival in Sochi, but she was not there; she came a couple of days later . . .

From Sochi Mayakovsky went to the Crimea in a boat powered by an internal combustion engine.

"What a boat! That's something. And we already have a few of these. It's a joy!"

Polonskaya was to have come from Khosta. She promised she would come to Yalta in a day or two, but she still was not there. Mayakovsky became nervous.

He sent an urgent cable. No reply. Then another, and another—still no reply. He went to the harbor several times every day, asked questions, watched the arrival of all boats. He went onto the pier even when no boats were expected.

Vladimir Vladimirovich asked me to help him compose an official cable to the postmaster in Khosta asking him to "find the addressee, pass on, and reply."

I recall the embarrassment with which the woman assistant accepted that long, private, peculiar cable.

No reply came.

Mayakovsky's low spirits were reflected in everything he did; even in his public readings: he kept to the full schedule, but he was less jocular and spoke the poems with less enthusiasm. For a long time I could not distract or entertain him.

The first reading in the Crimea took place in Miskhor. The reading of fragments from *The Bedbug* was followed by a heated discussion among the audience. One critic was particularly outspoken. Mayakovsky turned his attention to him: "Eh, you 'activist'! Why are you hiding in the dark and flapping your hands so much? Please come out here, we shall talk in the full light!"

The "activist" turned out to be brave and went onto the platform where he made a rather venomous speech. He argued that the play was odd, that Mayakovsky had misrepresented socialism, etc. Mayakovsky contained himself with difficulty. When he began his reply and someone tried to interrupt him, he protested categorically, "I kept quiet! Now you will sit quietly and listen to me!"

Some noisy men tried to shout him down. Hardly pausing at all, in the same sharp tone, Mayakovsky turned on them fiercely: "An athlete who could shout me down has not yet been born!"

He sweated profusely . . .

The next day he saw me in the hall of the Marino Hotel. I was having an acute attack of hepatitis. I could hardly move. He helped me to the stairs, took me in his arms, carried me to bed, and mumbled, as if excusing himself, "Now it's my turn to take care of you."

He called a doctor, gave me a hot water bottle, ordered drugs, brought me fruit and flowers . . .

At last the cable from Khosta came . . . Polonskaya was down with malaria . . .

KATANYAN:

By some chance I have kept the ticket to the closing session of the First All-Union Pioneer Rally . . .

August 25, 1929. Dynamo stadium . . .

I remember—the same morning the telephone rang: Mayakovsky had returned from the Crimea.

"How are you? What's new?"

There was some news, which I passed on to him.

". . . Pioneer Rally. Closing today at six. Let's go! Have you seen the stadium?

"No, I haven't. In that case, come see me earlier. I'll give you something to eat and we'll go there . . ."

On the way we dropped in at the Herzen House for a cold drink. The bar, which was situated in the cellar, spread its odors onto the asphalt of the street in summer.

"At least the gonococci are not crawling up the walls," Mayakovsky remarked, sulking, and ordered three bottles of lemonade.

I suggested I'd call the driver.

"No," Mayakovsky said, "you mustn't. They're looking at us all around . . . You know what they'll be saying tomorrow? That we broke into the bar with the car, drunk, broke all the glasses, pulled the cloakroom attendant's beard, and escaped without paying the bill . . ."

He did not say another word. His anger did not leave him even on the way to the stadium.

At the Leningrad road we passed a droshky in which there were squeezed on top of one another three half-writers we half-knew. They waved their hands, Vladimir Vladimirovich did not even turn around.

"Droshky full of dung . . ."

But in the stadium, dazed by the impressive view of mile-long amphitheaters, red handkerchiefs, happy faces, the green oval of the field, he calmed down at once and fell into a mood of elated friendliness.

"What's happening here! This is socialism already! To think that fifty thousand people have come to look at some children . . .

He then undertook to read pioneer poems from the tribune and his voice resounded in dozens of loudspeakers.

And when he scrambled out of the small radio booth, he said, "To write an excellent poem and read it here—then one can die" . . .

MAYAKOVSKY'S OPENING OF REF'S FIRST EVENING,
FROM THE "LITIERATURNAYA GAZIETA," OCTOBER 14, 1929:

A year ago we closed LEF here. Tonight we are inaugurating REF. What changes have occurred in that year, as far as the situation in literature is concerned, and what are REFists proclaiming on the literary front? First of all we must declare that we are not renouncing our past activity as futurists, Com-Futs, and LEFists. Our attitude today is wholly a result of our past struggle. All our arguments, with enemies, and with friends, on the subject of what is more important: "how to do things" or "what to do," we now replace with our main literary slogan: *"what to do things for,"* thus establishing the *supremacy of purpose over content and over form.* Regarding art as a weapon of the class struggle, we must, in our literary work, see clearly above all our common purpose and the concrete combat tasks of socialist construction standing before us . . .

NYEZNAMOV:

That evening Mayakovsky was in excellent form and cracked jokes . . . Meyerhold, who was present, said, "Mayakovsky's genius is astounding: how he leads the discussion!"

Mayakovsky's polemics really reminded one of fencing. He struck blows at dullards. But in general he wanted to live in peace with others. "Whose method is better—we will find out in competition." Interpenetration, yes, but not devouring one another.

The evening had quite an echo. It was talked about for a long time. It was the first and last evening of "REF."

"LITIERATURNAYA GAZIETA," DECEMBER 2, 1929:

Neither LEF nor REF

We have been asked the question: Why are you not in REF? We want to explain.

REF does not differ in its organization from LEF, within which we were forced a year ago to wage a decisive struggle with the present leaders of REF: Brik and Mayakovsky.

REF has inherited LEFist errors. It continues to be a salon, a social gathering of a few well-known literary figures. This salon does not recognize group discipline, does not have any set of rules, one can join it not so much on one's own initiative as by invitation.

We are living in a period of mass organizations. Associations of the LEF-REF type are doomed to the role of specialist corporations for the chosen few and are unfit for organized activity . . .

When the earth is on the move like broken ice, how small-minded seems the argument concerning literary-group interests and slogans. One cannot aim indefinitely, one must finally fire.

It is time for writers to regard themselves as being mobilized to occupy all positions of the front, where their work could be of use. It is time for writers to understand that what matters now is not the problem of style, of expressing their individual creative peculiarities, but the problem of maximum communicativeness and usefulness for the five-year plan . . .

We propose to REF socialist competition . . .

We suggest that *Litieraturnaya Gazieta* be the arbiter in our competition.

S. Tretyakov, V. Pyertsov, N. Chuzhak

LEV KASSIL:

Two days before the New Year, on December 30, friends of the poet—writers, actors, producers, poets, Cheka men, artists—came to his apartment in Gendrikovyi Alley. Mayakovsky was sent to his study in the Lubyansky Alley, with the request that he not come back until everything was ready.

The table was carried out of the small dining room so that there would be more room. Old posters, collected through the years, adorned the walls of the apartment. Glued to the ceiling was a big, long poster, with red letters running from wall to wall: "M-a-y-a-k-o-v-s-k-y." The apartment was more and more crowded. Costumes were brought from the theater. The guests searched through piles of gaudy fabrics, put on shawls, cloaks, capes, rehearsed a funny jubilee cantata . . .

NYEZNAMOV:

All the friends were there; Zinaida Reich with Meyerhold, Veronica Polonskaya, Janshin.

The celebration had a playful character. Meyerhold let us have various theater props. Zinaida Nikolayevna put the make-up on us, Kirsanov composed a cantata . . .

KASSIL:

Asyeyev impersonated one of those dull critics, who for a long time now had beset Mayakovsky with their silly writings. He made a long congratulatory speech, toward the end of which it turned out that the critic had mixed Mayakovsky up with someone else and had come to celebrate quite a different poet.

FROM THE "GROSSMAN-ROSHCHIN MONOLOGUE" SPOKEN BY ASYEYEV:

Esteemed Comrade Mayakovsky!

However unpleasant this might be, I must greet you on behalf of the philosophers' masses: Spinoza, Schopenhauer, and A. V. Lunacharsky. The crux of the matter is that the creative forces of the developing class have to find their Shakespeare, their Dante, and their Goethe. His appearance is determined by the class consciousness of the proletariat. Yes, well. If this does not happen, art may indeed sing its swan song.

However, we are not in the least pessimistic. The genius of your poetry may serve as an example: your poetry is, subjectively, absolutely solipsistic, but objectively can turn out to be collectivistic in the altered situation of our socialist economic reconstruction.

In particular, what do we observe in this example? Here, as everywhere, and in all things, it is evident that the anarcho-individualistic Bohemia is melting into the steel ranks of the life-giving class forces, stipulating the necessity of the fight against formalist destruction of the LEFist purse . . . Whither goes the resurrected Lazarus of art? To the frail LEFist-REFist flower beds, in order to delight in the refined aroma of its formalist inclinations? No, he absconds from there, stopping his nostrils before the vulgar smell of activist manure. Where does he go then? He goes in the direction of the mighty oak forest of management over proletarian art. He goes to the editorial office of *Na Litieraturnom Postu,* to find there a friendly bludgeon . . . So, we welcome you, Comrade Mayakovsky, and, from the bottom of our hearts, congratulate you on the recent, irrefutably important, certain, and recognized by all—nomination of Anatol Vassilievich Lunacharsky to the post of director of a publishing house. Also in the future we are going to note in a friendly fashion everything that, somehow or other, will influence your writing, steadfastly standing on the leading positions of RAPP, MAPP, and LAPP.

LAVUT:

The hero of the jubilee sat astride a chair, put on the mask of a he-goat and replied with a serious bleating to all "congratulations" . . .

Kamensky played a loud flourish on the accordion.

We laughed until we cried.

The daughter of David Shterenberg, the painter, came unexpectedly into the room, extravagantly dressed and with a hairdo à la schoolgirl, and read "greetings from schoolchildren." It ended with the words:

> We are all your children now
> Since we are your—pupils!

KASSIL:

Later we played living charades and Mayakovsky had to guess which lines from his poems we had in mind . . .

One of us sat behind the desk, another, with an angry look, took his fountain pen from his pocket, put it vigorously on the desk and walked away.

"I've got it, I've got it!" Mayakovsky shouted. " 'The Conversation with the Tax Inspector': 'Here, comrade, you have my pen and write yourself, if you please!' "

Late at night we asked Mayakovsky to recite some of his old poems for us. He refused for a long time, complained he had no voice, that none of his old poems were interesting any more. We asked him in unison, begged, persuaded him. At last, with a loud sigh, he gave up. First he recited "Good Treatment of Horses." He got up and, having put his hand on the edge of a wardrobe, gave us a look we will never forget, and spoke, not loud, suddenly sad:

> Bouncing were the hoofs.
> Playing as if:
> —Humps.
> Mumps.
> Tombs.
> Nubs.

NYEZNAMOV:

Then we had supper and drank champagne. We were exceptionally gay and carefree . . .

In January, 1930, a closed plenum of REF took place (in the Federation Club), but Mayakovsky spoke there only on the question of the theater. He did not say anything about literature, about poetry. I think he was bored at that plenum.

36

"Whom Does the Bathhouse Wash?"

Enter the overwhelming and sinister Nachdirdups Pobyedo-nosikov, accompanied by the servile journalist Momentalni-kov, whose name recalls the poet's personal enemy—Talnikov, the critic—but who represents something more: an entire phenomenon now spreading in literary life. Mayakovsky set his heart to this play even more than to the former, but it brought him more trouble than the previous one had.

FROM THE NOTEBOOK OF LILA BRIK:

5/9/29. V. read us a fragment from *The Bathhouse*. It seems to be strong stuff.

10/9/29. V. gave the play out for copying.

15/9/29. V. read *The Bathhouse* to me. Osya came—he read it once again to both of us. We liked it very much, but it's still a bit rough.

22/9/29. In the evening V. read *The Bathhouse* at home. Some thirty persons were present.

23/9/29. V. read *The Bathhouse* at the theater. Immediate success. They mentioned Molière, Shakespeare, Pushkin, Gogol.

26/9/29. In the evening V. talked to us about *The Bathhouse*. He wants to do the stage designs for it himself.

FROM LAVUT'S REMINISCENCES:

The guests, crowded in a small room, received the play very warmly. There was much applause, enthusiastic shouts. Everyone waited for Meyerhold's statement. After all, he was to produce it, so the play's fate depended to a large degree on him.

Meyerhold gave a deep sigh and said one word: "Molière!" He was very serious and genuinely moved.

FROM THE TRANSCRIPT OF A MEETING OF THE ARTISTIC-POLITICAL COUNCIL OF THE STATE MEYERHOLD THEATER, SEPTEMBER 23, 1929:

Mayakovsky: Comrades, it is more difficult to write one's second play. I found it more difficult to write because there is not much time for thinking it out and there is always the danger that a new play will be made out of the remnants of an old one, and also because just as the appetite comes with the eating, so it is with the passion for work in the theater. A man learns by his own work, by his mistakes, and I too am trying to get rid of sheer journalism.

[After a speech from one of the participants in the discussion] . . . Comrade did not understand me. I am not saying I am giving up the tradition of *The Bedbug*. On the contrary, I hold on to it all the time.

Question: Comrade Mayakovsky, why did you call the play *The Bathhouse*?

Mayakovsky: Because it's the one thing the play doesn't have.

MIKHAIL ZOSHCHENKO, WHO WAS PRESENT AT THE MEETING, RECALLS:

Actors and writers split their sides laughing and applauded the poet. Every statement was approved without reservation . . . I did not like the play, I thought it was theatrically clumsy. On that occasion I was, for the first time in my life, insincere, thinking that perhaps I did not understand something in it. When Mayakovsky asked me whether the play was good, I said it was.

🖋

In that period Mayakovsky went several times to Leningrad,
also in connection with the productions of The Bedbug *and*
The Bathhouse, *which were being mounted there.*

IGOR ILYINSKY:

. . . I also found myself in Leningrad. Vladimir Vladimirovich invited me
to his room at the Europe Hotel, where he read his play to me and to
Erdman, who did not know it either . . .

Whether Mayakovsky read badly—accustomed as he was to appearing
in front of large audiences, always reacting with loud laughter, whereas
here he had to deal with a couple of "dull comedians"—or because I had
heard too much about the play, there was none of the enthusiasm which
the author had expected from Erdman and myself . . .

When I returned to Moscow, I commented drily on *The Bathhouse* in
a conversation with Meyerhold . . .

FROM THE TRANSCRIPT OF A DISCUSSION ON THE TEXT OF
"THE BATHHOUSE" AT THE FIRST MODEL TYPOGRAPHY CLUB,
OCTOBER 30, 1929:

Question: Why do you call your play a drama?

Reply: To make it funnier, and secondly—don't we have a lot of bureaucrats, and is it not a drama of our country?

. . . Comrade Rogozinskaya has just said that *The Bathhouse* is better
than *The Bedbug* . . . When I am dead, you will say what an excellent
poet died . . . The fact that you regard *The Bathhouse* as better than
The Bedbug proves that with *The Bedbug* I raised your interest in dramatic works somewhat.

FROM THE REMINISCENCES OF MARIA SUKHANOVA:

It was in January-February 1930. We had reading rehearsals for *The
Bathhouse* with Meyerhold and Mayakovsky. We sat crowded together,
Mayakovsky was close by, we saw him smoking, a cigarette in the corner
of his mouth, tousling his hair, we watched his eyes, hands. He was
radiant and gay in those days. Every day he came in a fresh shirt and a
new tie. One day we felt like kidding him about it: we began to whisper,

giggle, point at the tie. Mayakovsky could not contain himself: "Well, what are you neighing about?" Someone said shyly, "Because you've got on a new tie again." "So what—I liked it, so I got it," he said and blushed deeply. We burst out laughing.

I also remember something concerning me personally. About six actresses were considered for the part of Pola, Pobyedonosikov's wife. The part was open to competition, as it were. The difficulty, as far as this part was concerned, consisted in the fact that in the text there frequently occurred the words "funny" and "not funny." How were they to be spoken? Mayakovsky insisted that they be spoken casually, as one often uses certain conventional phrases in conversation, without meaning them. For instance, someone might put in the words "I understand" everywhere—where they are needed and where they are not. But I risked a "meaningful" reading of "funny" and "not funny," fitting them to the basic text of the part. To oppose Mayakovsky was something awe-inspiring, but I took the risk, having thought everything out at home. When I did this, the text came to life, all the "funny's" and the "not funny's" found themselves in their right places. Mayakovsky admitted that the text was enlivened, interestingly punctuated, and that he had been persuaded by the actress that this was the right thing to do. The next day, passing me during a break, he gave me an orange. I squeaked for joy and exclaimed, "Oh, what am I to do? Eat it, or keep it as a souvenir?" "What nonsense! You got an orange, it means you've got to eat it, not keep it!" And added, "Funny!" We both laughed.

FROM MAYAKOVSKY'S STATEMENT, PUBLISHED IN THE "OGONYOK"
WEEKLY, TOGETHER WITH A FRAGMENT FROM THE LAST ACT
OF THE PLAY, NOVEMBER 30, 1929:

The Bathhouse—is a "drama in six acts with circus and fireworks."

The Bathhouse—washes bureaucrats.

The Bathhouse—has journalistic objectives, and for this reason not so-called "living men" appear in it but "tendencies come to life."

. . . Theater has forgotten that it is a show, a spectacle.

. . . The point of my work in the theater is an attempt to restore spectacle to the theater, an attempt to transform the boards of the stage into a platform.

The action of the "drama" is roughly as follows:

1. Tsudakov, the inventor, invents a time machine, which can carry people into the future and back.

2. The invention just cannot be pushed through the bureaucratic channels and barriers, the most important of which is Comrade Pobyedonosikov, Nachdirdups—the chief director for the coordination of certain matters.

3. Comrade Pobyedonosikov comes to the theater, watches himself, and maintains that in real life such things do not happen.

4. The phosphoric woman arrives from the future in the time machine in order to select the best people for transfer into the next century.

5. Pobyedonosikov, overjoyed, has prepared and written out orders of allocation and allowances for himself for a period of one hundred years.

6. The time machine rushes forth in five ten-year stages, taking the workers and spitting out Pobyedonosikov and others like him.

FROM THE THIRD ACT OF "THE BATHHOUSE":

Pobyedonosikov: All this seems to be so condensed; it does not happen this way in life . . . That Pobyedonosikov, for instance. It's not right somehow . . . All in all, he seems to be a responsible comrade, and here he is represented in a dubious light and called "Nachdirdups," or something. There are no such people among us, it is unnatural, not lifelike, unlike anything! This must be altered, softened, poeticized, rounded off . . .

Ivan Ivanovich: Quite so, quite so, it's not right! Have you got a telephone here? I will call Fyodor Fyodorovich, he will, of course, be sympathetic . . . Ah, it's not proper while the performance is on? Well, I'll do it later. Comrade Momentalnikov, we must initiate a campaign on a wide front.

Momentalnikov:

> Excellency, I am yours!
> With my modest appetite.
> No need to repeat it twice—
> Whom you wish, him I will bite.

Producer: But comrades! A negative literary character has been introduced here as something exceptional, with the purpose of self-criticism and by the censor's permission.

Pobyedonosikov: What did you say? "Character"? Is that the way to describe a responsible state official? In this way one can talk only about some nonparty loafer. Character indeed! After all, he is not a character but a Nachdirdups, appointed by higher authority, and you call him—a character! If in his actions any illegal misdemeanors occur, one has to inform the appropriate authority so that the case can be considered, and then the information checked by the prosecutor's office and revealed by the Board of Supervision should be transformed into symbolic scenes. Yes, that's the way to do it, but to expose to public ridicule in a theater . . .

Producer: You are absolutely right, comrade, but this results from the course of action.

Pobyedonosikov: Action? What action? There can be no question of any actions here. Your duty is to perform, and action will be taken care of by the appropriate party and Soviet authorities, never fear. Besides, one should also show the bright sides of our present reality. Take a model example, the institution in which I work, for instance, or myself for that matter . . .

Ivan Ivanovich: Yes, yes, yes! Go to his institution. There directives are given, circulars are passed around, rational thinking introduced, papers lie in absolute order for years. There is a conveyer for applications, complaints, and appeals. It is a true corner of socialism. Most interesting!

Producer: But comrade, let us . . .

Pobyedonosikov: I won't let you!!! I cannot let you and I wonder that you have been allowed to do this! This discredits us even in the eyes of Europe . . .

FROM THE FINALE OF "THE BATHHOUSE":

Explosions of Bengal lights. "The march of time." Darkness. On the stage Pobyedonosikov, Optimistenko, Belvedonsky, Mezaliansova, Pont Kitch, Ivan Ivanovich, thrown off and scattered by the hellish time machine . . .

Pobyedonosikov: What did she, and you, and the author—want to say through this? Is it that I, and others like me, are not needed for communism?!?

FROM THE NOTEBOOK OF LILA BRIK:

8/11/29. He read *The Bathhouse* to Kyerzhentsev.

14/12/29. Complications about permission for the production of *The Bathhouse*.

20/12/29. He read *The Bathhouse* to the Repertory Committee. He just managed to pull it through.

✒

The Bathhouse *was produced in Leningrad earlier than in Moscow, on January 30, 1930, directed by V. Lutse (a pupil of Meyerhold).*

ZOSHCHENKO:

The audience received the play with a murderous coldness. I do not recall a single burst of laughter. After the first two acts there was not the slightest applause. I have never seen a more terrible flop.

FROM THE NOTEBOOK OF LILA BRIK:

2/2/30. They say *The Bathhouse* is to be forbidden in Leningrad. V. became upset.

3/2/30. There is no question of the play's being forbidden, but it is performed to poor houses and the newspapers hurl abuse . . .

FROM VLADIMIR YERMILOV'S ARTICLE "ON THE MOODS OF PETIT BOURGEOIS 'LEFTISHNESS' IN LITERATURE," "PRAVDA," MARCH 9, 1930:

The petit bourgeois revolutionary intelligentsia, who joined the proletariat when its victory had been firmly established, the intelligentsia whose self-awareness developed in the conditions of Soviet reality and who participated in Soviet construction, occasionally begins to feel itself "the salt of the earth," as it were. Unconnected with the proletariat's past, with the traditions of its struggle, the intelligentsia is prone to regard itself as more "leftist," more revolutionary than the proletariat itself. Unable to take part organically in the working out of proletarian strategy and tactics, the intelligentsia shows a quality typical of petit bourgeois revolutionaries—i.e., the tendency to revolutionary slogans, based on the misunderstanding of all revolutionary tenets, on simplifying schematism. The peculiar, most precious qualities of the proletarian revolutionary, developed by the old

guard through decades of struggle, the participation in offensives and re-
treats, attacks and celebrations, sometimes seem to representatives of the
petit bourgeois revolutionary intelligentsia narrow, limiting, primitive.
The orthodox constancy, the revulsion for sluggishness, for a lack of precision in thinking and action, for the notorious "broadmindedness," for the
so-called "right to doubt"—seem to them "party obscurantism" . . .
Here the author analyzes the negative heroes of Selvinsky's poem "Pushtorg"—Krol and Mek] . . . Mek reminds one of another "representative"
of the old Bolshevik guard in literature—Pobyedonosikov in Mayakovsky's
play *The Bathhouse,* of whom one of the characters says, "He simply overwhelms us with his merits and long party standing. You know his life
story. Once, they say, he escaped from prison, having thrown tobacco in
the guard's eyes. And now, twenty-five years later, time has thrown a
thousand trifles and minutes in his eyes, which run with contented satisfaction and unconcern." . . . The danger of exaggerating "krolovshchina"
and "pobyedonosikovshchina" beyond the limits where they express anything concrete faces Comrade Mayakovsky too, as one can judge from the
published excerpt of his new play *The Bathhouse.* When, for instance, the
degenerated and brutal bureaucrat Pobyedonosikov, reciting his merits,
says, "I . . . do not drink, do not smoke, do not give tips, do not deviate
to the left, am never late," there is no doubt that we hear a false "leftist"
note in Mayakovsky, a note which we know not only from literature . . .

FROM THE POLEMICAL STATEMENT OF VSYEVOLOD MEYERHOLD
IN THE NEWSPAPER "VYECHERNYAYA MOSKVA," MARCH 13, 1930:

V. Yermilov in *Pravda* . . . by way of digression (and most inappropri-
ately), in attacking Mayakovsky declares that in his play *The Bathhouse*
there rings a false "leftist" note. Yermilov puts forward this quite serious
charge having read *not the whole* play but a published fragment.

One should never give an opinion on the basis of a fragment, even if,
as sometimes happens, a play is not intended for the stage but for reading
only . . . But to pass judgment, on the basis of a fragment, on a play
composed for the theater is tantamount to a total lack of understanding as
to what happens with a play when it receives a theatrical form.

V. Yermilov, on careful consideration, declares that Mayakovsky is
threatened with "some danger" because in *The Bathhouse* he exaggerates

the "pobyedonosikovshchina" to the limits beyond which it ceases to express anything concrete.

However, the stage arrangement shows quite clearly that by "exaggerating 'pobyedonosikovshchina'" Mayakovsky was not and is not threatened with any danger, but on the contrary: Mayakovsky's strength consists in his having magnified, and—what is most important—condemned "pobyedonosikovshchina."

. . . In *The Bathhouse* Mayakovsky ridicules the Pobyedonosikovs. But where did Yermilov get the idea that in the guise of Pobyedonosikov Mayakovsky showed a degenerate party member? . . . In Mayakovsky's play the tragic conflict of a worker-inventor with bureaucracy, official waste, a narrow practical approach, has been shown in a masterly way. This is one aspect of the play. In another aspect Mayakovsky, having constructed a number of theatrical situations, shows his enthusiasm for the proletariat's will to surmount all obstacles on its way to socialism . . .

FROM YERMILOV'S REPLY, "VYECHERNYAYA MOSKVA,"
MARCH 17, 1930:

In his note . . . Comrade Meyerhold attempts to argue with my observation on one of the characters in *The Bathhouse*—Pobyedonosikov . . . However, Comrade Meyerhold does not succeed in his argument for the simple reason that Comrade Meyerhold substitutes one problem for another. In my article I was discussing a literary fact: the play *The Bathhouse*, fragments of which were published in one of our periodicals; while Comrade Meyerhold speaks about a future theatrical production . . .

Now a few words on the character of Pobyedonosikov himself. Judging by Comrade Meyerhold's note, in the theatrical performance he will not represent the phenomenon we call party degeneracy. This is both good and bad. It is good because Pobyedonosikov, as presented in the published excerpt, is distinguished by elements which are false and do not let him be a fully convincing representative of the said phenomenon. It is bad—because self-criticism, "with no regard to persons," demands great courage from the theater and only some theater officials . . . could question the necessity of exposing such a character to public ridicule. The theater, however, must not be aimlessly "courageous": it must be able to present concrete social phenomena, it ought not to be led astray to fight windmills, it should not substitute abstract criteria for social ones . . .

On March 16, 1930, The Bathhouse *had its opening perform-*
ance at the Meyerhold Theater, directed by Meyerhold, with
stage designs by S. Vakhtangov and A. Deyneka, music by
V. Shebalin, with Maxim Shtraukh in the part of Pobyedono-
sikov.

FROM THE REMINISCENCES OF MAYAKOVSKY'S DRIVER,
VASSILI GAMAZIN:

Preparations for the production of *The Bathhouse* were nearing an end.
The date of the public rehearsal had already been fixed. Several days before the opening night Vladimir Vladimirovich distributed invitations. He
was in good spirits. One morning he gave me an invitation too. "Please
come see *The Bathhouse,* Comrade Gamazin; this is for two persons, so
bring your wife too."

On the day of the public rehearsal Vladimir Vladimirovich went to the
theater in the morning. But on our way back I noticed that something was
wrong. Vladimir Vladimirovich was breathing heavily and sighing deeply,
one could feel he had had some very unpleasant experience . . . I tried to
ask him about it: "Vladimir Vladimirovich, is there something wrong?"
Vladimir Vladimirovich sighed again. "It's nothing," he said and added
after a while, "Don't come to the theater tonight, Comrade Gamazin, there
won't be any performance. I'll tell you when there is one."

Soon came the opening night of *The Bathhouse,* after which Vladimir
Vladimirovich waited impatiently for the reactions of the press. A few
days later the first note about *The Bathhouse* appeared, in *Vyechernyaya*
Moskva, I think. It said that *The Bathhouse* must be rewritten.

ILYINSKY:

I saw Vladimir Mayakovsky for the last time at the first night of *The*
Bathhouse at the Meyerhold Theater. After the performance, received not
very warmly by the audience (at any rate, Mayakovsky painfully felt that
this was so), he stood alone in the lobby, letting everybody pass, looking
straight in people's eyes. Such he has remained in my memory.

SERGEI YUTKEVICH:

I saw Mayakovsky for the last time at the first night of *The Bathhouse* at the Meyerhold Theater, from a distance. He seemed sulking and nervous. The performance was not a success.

SUKHANOVA:

The performance got bad reviews. The audience received it most oddly: some spectators sat as if made of stone, others reacted well . . .

During the first ten days of April, Mayakovsky used to come to the theater for performances of *The Bathhouse*. He said that the performance was a flop; he was restless, sullen, and his eyes, which had been able to see right through people, now did not look at anyone. Sometimes he would not even answer questions he was asked and just go away . . .

I have omitted in my recollections all that concerns the production— Meyerhold's work on the play. One thing I must say, though: the play was produced by a master of the stage, a man of genius, who had the gift of enchanting his actors, making them fall in love with him and taking from them all that was best, most valuable for the performance; a master who knew how to use all the component parts of the theater to the best advantage: light, music of the best composers, excellent production ideas, the then technically best equipped stage.

To work with Meyerhold and Mayakovsky was happiness. That happiness we were lucky to experience.

REVIEW BY N. GONCHAROVA, "RABOCHAYA GAZIETA," MARCH 21, 1930:

It is very pleasant to dream about such a time machine, which can remove Pobyedonosikov *et consortes* and take us directly into the age of communism. But it is not possible to believe Mayakovsky's dream, because the poet himself does not believe in it. His "time machine" and "phosphoric woman" are just cold noisy babbling. And his scoffing at our present, in which he does not see anyone except garrulous ignoramuses, conceited bureaucrats, and licksplittles—is most characteristic. In the whole play there is not one man on whom the eye can rest. The workers painted by Mayakovsky are quite unreal figures, talking the heavy involved language of the author himself. To sum up: it is a tiring, confused show, which can be of interest only to a small group of literary fans. It is doubtful whether such a bathhouse will be to the worker audience's liking.

REVIEW BY A. CHAROV, "KOMSOMOLSKAYA PRAVDA," MARCH 22:

It seems to us that this *Bathhouse* will not be to the liking either of the worker audience or the "literary fans." One must admit openly that the play turned out to be bad and there was no need for Meyerhold to produce it.

FROM THE TRANSCRIPT OF MAYAKOVSKY'S STATEMENT IN THE
DISCUSSION ON "THE BATHHOUSE" AT THE PRESS HOUSE,
MARCH 27, 1930:

Comrades, I have been existing physically for thirty-five years, and for twenty years as a so-called creative writer. Through all this time I have defended my views with the strength of my lungs, with the force and vigor of my voice. And I am not afraid that what I am doing will be declared null and void. Lately an opinion has circulated that I was a widely recognized talent and I am glad that *The Bathhouse* is shattering this opinion. Leaving the theater I wipe the spittle from my massive forehead, metaphorically, of course.

. . . It would be very easy to say that I have written an excellent piece but the theater messed it up. It would be too easy a way out, which I won't take. I assume full responsibility for the defects and for the good qualities of this piece . . .

Someone has said: *The Bathhouse* has failed, it is a flop. Why failed, why flop? Because a little man in *Komsomolskaya Pravda* peeped that he was not amused, or because someone did not like my poster? Have these been my aims through the twenty years of my work? No. I have aimed at filling my works with literary and dramatic material of real value . . . I know that every word of this play, from the first to the last, has been composed with the same diligence with which I worked on my best poetic works . . .

REVIEW BY M. ZAGORSKY, IN THE FORM OF A DIALOGUE BETWEEN
THE "WRITER" AND THE "CRITIC," "LITIERATURNAYA GAZIETA,"
MARCH 31:

Critic: . . . If you recall *The Bedbug* by the same Mayakovsky, there was a character called Prysipkin, a warm, living man, who can be played and in whom many spectators recognized themselves, their friends and relatives. And in *The Bathhouse?* Who will recognize our sly, dissembling, practical bureaucrat in the smart, talkative Pobyedonosikov? . . . And what kind of argument is it that does not aim at something concrete, does not yield results? What would Mikhail Koltsov look like if none of his heroes were brought to trial? No, dear comrade, art without action is dead. And what action is there in *The Bathhouse?*

Writer: What action is there in the philosophic novels of Voltaire, in Heine's poems, in ironic reflections of Anatole France? Are not thought, anger, generalization, the sharp word, the biting aphorism, more important than criminal adventures in plays of Fayka, Romashov, Zavalishin, Nikulin? Ivan Ivanovich has degenerated! Catch him! Pyotr Syemyonovich steals! Arrest him! This is not a theater but a court of inquiry. In *The Bathhouse,* however, no one is caught and put to prison, but there is loud laughter, a gay smile, a sharp word, and a witty gibe . . .

ACCOUNT OF AN EDITORIAL CONFERENCE, WITH THE PARTICIPA-
TION OF WORKERS OF THE "BURYEVYESTNIK" WORKS, THEATER
CRITICS, AND THE AUTHOR OF THE PLAY, "VYECHERNYAYA
MOSKVA," MARCH 31:

Advice to Meyerhold Theater and Comrade Mayakovsky
Polish up The Bathhouse
Mass Audiences do not Understand the Play

Debatable characters: where are the communists, where are the workers?

. . . *The Bathhouse is unintelligible for mass audiences*—this was an almost unanimous statement of the workers participating in the conference. Not only particular moments in the play, but also some of the basic ideas and characters (the "time machine," the "phosphoric woman") remained unclear for a substantial part of the audience . . . As Comrade Voytse-khovich said, the spectator does not get any idea of the main theme of the play. According to comrades Sazonova and Mosyelkova, the "Buryevyest-nik" workers came out of the performance of *The Bathhouse* completely disappointed . . . Why is the bureaucrat not countered with the worker masses, or party members? Comrade Zuyev asked. Why is it not they who gave the bureaucrat the bath, as happens in reality?

. . . In reply to things said, the play's author, Comrade Mayakovsky, first of all declared he did not regard *The Bathhouse* as a failure; on the contrary, he considered that production as a big success of the Meyerhold

Theater . . . Mayakovsky rejected the imputations concerning the absence on stage of the worker masses, party, trade unions, pointing out that the play had been written and produced from the viewpoint of the workers and party members . . . sitting in the auditorium. In conclusion Mayakovsky admitted the need for further work on the play.

⚜ 37 ⚜

The Jubilee

This chapter directly precedes the finale. It describes the events that filled the last months of the poet's life. Mayakovsky wants to sum up "twenty years of his work" and arranges his exhibition. Not wanting to remain any longer on the suspect fringe of official literary life, he dissolves REF and joins RAPP —the Russian Association of Proletarian Writers. Friends turn away from Mayakovsky; his loneliness grows. Mayakovsky writes the poem "At the Top of My Voice," in which—over the heads of contemporaries—he addresses posterity. He also writes the scenario of a big circus show—Moscow in Flames. He speaks from many platforms but complains that he finds it more and more difficult—the throat disease grows worse. Young enthusiasts of the poet organize the "Mayakovsky brigade."

FROM THE NOTEBOOK OF LILA BRIK:

6/12/29. V. collects material for his exhibition and is excited at the thought that he has done so much.

9/12/29. V. and Natasha compile a book from texts for posters.

11/12/29. I am in Leningrad. I have requested Pushkin House and Zhevyerzheyev to supply material for V.'s exhibition.

29/12/29. V. is on the move from early morning till late at night. He spends half the night sticking up exhibition albums with Zina Svyeshnikova.

8/1/30. V. appeared at the evening of satire. The speaker maintained that in our conditions satire was unnecessary, that it was simpler to report things to the proper authority. V. said that new ranks of satiric writers were needed.

21/1/30. Kassil came: he had listened on the radio to V. reciting "Lenin" at the Bolshoi Theater. He said V. recited in an astonishing way and there was applause for five minutes. In the morning they came to commission a circus pantomime from V. The theme: the year 1905.

BORIS MALKIN:

Firmly entrenched in my memory is one of Mayakovsky's last public appearances: the reading of the poem "Lenin" at the solemn meeting in the Bolshoi Theater on January 21, 1930, in commemoration of Lenin's death. All those present, deeply moved, listened to that splendid poem and applauded Mayakovsky enthusiastically . . . The entire Political Bureau clapped. Mayakovsky was greatly impressed by the ovation.

LILA BRIK:

26/1/30. V. read "At the Top of My Voice" to us.

from the poem "AT THE TOP OF MY VOICE"
by Vladimir Mayakovsky

. . . I, garbage collector and water carrier,
        through revolution
                        drafted and called,
        set out for the front
                        from the gardens
        of poetry—
                a capricious miss.

                        .   .   .

. . . Not much of an honor from rose beds
to reveal one's bust
among squares,
　　　　　where the whore and the scoundrel
　　　　　　　　　　　are rut-

　　　ting,
where T.B.
　　　　　and syphilis.
And I
　　　am fed up
　　　　　　with agitprop,
And I would
　　　　　sing the praises
　　　　　　　　　of lofty feelings—
I would have income
　　　　　　and recognition.
But year after year
　　　　　　I suppressed my song,
I trampled
　　　　its throat
　　　　　　　for all I was worth.
Listen,
　　　comrades descendants,
to the tub-thumper,
　　　　　　the mass meeting leader!
Drowning
　　　　the semitones of lyric poetry
I will leap
　　　　through its stream,
　　　　　　　　volume after volume,
speaking
　　　living
　　　　　to the living.
I will come to you
　　　　　in the communist faraway
not like
　　　Yesenin

       bard of the lands of song.
My poem will reach
       over the backs of ages,
over the heads
      of poets and governments.
My poem will reach,
      but reach in a different way—
not like Amor's arrow
      from lyric dreams,
not as a worn shilling
      reaches a collector,
not like the ray
     of dead stars.
My poem
   with effort
      will break through mountains of years—
will appear,
    tangible
      and visible,
as into our days
     the aqueduct has broken,
hewn
   by the slaves of Rome.

        .   .   .
. . . The enemy of the working class—
        is also
my inveterate foe
    forever
      for a long time.
We were ordered
    to go and serve
       under this flag
by years of labor
    days of starvation.
We
   opened
    Marx's

                    every volume,
like window shutters
                    in the morning
                              at home,
but even without reading
                    one knew
                              this,
whom to fight against
                    whom to be friendly with.

                         .   .   .

. . . Let genius
                    be followed with a sad widow's step
by fame
          dragging her feet
                              in a cortege—
fall, my verse,
                    perish like a common soldier,
as so many of our men
                    have fallen
                              in the attack.
I don't give a damn
                    for the noble bronze of heavy armor,
I don't give a damn
                    for the slippery marble rock.
Let us share fame—
                    we are all comrades,
let
     our common monument
                              stand:
socialism
          raised
               in battles.
Posterity,
          check floats in dictionaries:
from Leta
          will flow
                    remnants of such words

as "prostitution,"
            "tuberculosis,"
                        "blockade."
For you, who are
            well and strong,
    the poet
            licked consumptive spittle
on the rough posters of streets.
With the tail of years
            from day to day
                        more like

excavated
            monsters
                  I am.
What if we
            went faster
                  through life
through the five year plan
                  of written days
                              the rest?
I have not
            saved on poems
                        a ruble,
the antique dealer
                  has not cajoled me.
And frankly—
            to be happy I do not need
anything
            except a newly washed shirt.
In the Control Commission
                  of the bright years to come,
over the gang
            of poetic
                        sly foxes and frauds
I will raise
            like a Bolshevik party card

all the hundred volumes

of my

party booklets.

FROM THE NOTEBOOK OF LILA BRIK:

28/1/30. The literary editor of *Pravda* apparently learned about Volodya's success at the Bolshoi. He telephoned and asked him for poems to publish in *Pravda*. Volodya was very glad and said it would be a good idea to have a general talk about his collaboration with *Pravda*. But there was no question of that, only of publishing poems, just as had been the case with Demyan Byedny. V. said that in that case he would not supply the poems—he was not interested.

29/1/30. The invitations printed for the exhibition are sadly lacking in taste . . . V. is worried—he wanted everything that had to do with the exhibition to be perfect.

30/1/30. The boys want to place the following inscription above the newspaper exhibit: "The masses do not understand Mayakovsky."

31/1/30. The exhibition committee did not assemble for a single meeting and the exhibition which, in V.'s dreams, was to have been a dazzling example of how such exhibitions should be arranged, turned out to be interesting only thanks to the material gathered there.

A RECOLLECTION OF ARTEMI BROMBERG, A YOUNG WORKER ON
THE STAFF OF THE LITERARY MUSEUM, WHO VOLUNTEERED TO
HELP ARRANGE THE MAYAKOVSKY EXHIBITION:

The FOSP [Federation of Associations of Soviet Writers] Club was situated at 52 Vorovsky Street, where now the offices of the Writers' Union Executive are. The club management gave the so-called conference hall for purposes of the exhibition . . .

Hardly anyone on the exhibition committee gave Mayakovsky any help. One could sense resistance in the atmosphere of this enterprise. Mayakovsky arranged every detail of the exhibition himself, from start to finish. The poet Lugovskoy, who was then in charge of the Writers' Club, went away and there was no one to take over from him. Mayakovsky encountered a number of unexpected difficulties and obstacles . . .

The exhibition came out very well. There was clearly too much material for the space allotted to it . . . Not one inch remained. At the entrance were placed the futurist collections of 1912–1914 in which Mayakovsky published his work *Slap to the Public's Taste* and others. The first editions of his prerevolutionary poems, massacred by tsarist censorship, were also placed here. Over this stand was the inscription, "And what did you do before 1917?" . . .

On the table, in thick brown covers, were albums of clippings containing critical reviews concerning Mayakovsky, and dozens of thin notebooks with questions the poet had been asked in the course of his numerous readings during the years 1926–1929 . . .

The critical material was assembled in the albums with sharp polemical contrast. Next to favorable articles and notes on Mayakovsky's work were also extremely adverse statements. For instance, glued to the first pages of one of the albums was Shengeli's shameful booklet *Mayakovsky in All His Splendor,* published in 1927 . . . Mayakovsky devoted much attention to the ROSTA "exhibitions of satire" and gave them an entire room . . .

LAVUT:

At first friends used to come, but to look rather than to work. Then many of them disappeared: they had quarreled with Mayakovsky. (At about that time he had left REF and joined RAPP. It was one of the main reasons for the conflict.)

NATALYA ROZENEL-LUNACHARSKAYA:

Unfortunately I could not go to Mayakovsky's "Twenty Years' Work" exhibition at the Writers' Club: I was busy at the theater and could not accompany Anatol Vassilievich.

I had imagined that on his return from the exhibition, Anatol Vassilievich would share his impressions with me . . . But he came back in a silent and sulking mood. When I began asking him, he replied reluctantly, "Doubtless it is interesting. Twenty years of colossal work, poems, plays, posters, tours all around the Soviet Union, Europe, America . . . But—I find it difficult to formulate the reasons—this exhibition failed to satisfy me."

After a while, he added, "I think I know why today's exhibition left me with an unpleasant feeling: this may be strange, but the culprit is Mayakovsky himself. He was quite unlike himself, sick, with hollow eyes, exhausted, voiceless, dejected. He was very polite to me, took me around, explained, but all this was forced. It is hard to imagine Mayakovsky so indifferent and tired. I have often seen him angry, enraged, mad, hurling blows right and left . . . I'd rather see him that way than in his present mood. This had a depressing influence on me."

LILA BRIK:

1/2/30. At 6:00 P.M. we went to the opening of the exhibition. The place was packed with young people. The exhibition was not polished in details, but even so very interesting.

V. is terribly exhausted. He spoke with a very tired voice. Someone made a speech, then V. read the introduction to a new poem and made a very great impression, though he was reading from a script and in a rather forced way.

BROMBERG:

In the hall there were some two hundred and fifty seats. Some three hundred persons were present, mostly young. Of the writers I knew, only Byezimensky and Shklovsky came to the opening. There was not one representative of literary organizations . . .

Mayakovsky mounted the platform.

"Comrades!" the poet began. "I am very glad that all those first-class, spit-soiled aesthetes are not here, the kind of people who don't care where they go or whom they congratulate, as long as it is a jubilee. There are no writers? Excellent! But one must remember this. I am happy that Moscow's youth is here. I am happy that you are reading me! I welcome you here!"

He was answered by a storm of applause . . .

Mayakovsky gave thanks for help in the preparation of the exhibition to Osip and Lila Brik, to the plastic artists, to Lavut and, I think, Natalya Briukhanenko . . . and many others: he thanked all those who helped him in even the smallest way. He mentioned me too . . .

S. KOVALENKO:

The list of persons invited also contained, besides the poet's friends and those close to him, the party and government leaders, activists on the cultural front, such as Khalatov, Kyerzhentsev, Gandurin, Raskolnikov, Lebyedyev-Polansky, Fadyeyev, Demyan Byedny, as well as literary associations and newspaper editors.

As early as the middle of January a letter, containing information about the exhibition, signed by "REF," had been sent to newspaper editors. However, only in *Komsomolskaya Pravda* did a short note appear, on January 31, that is to say on the eve of the opening. The opening itself was not attended by representatives of the press or any other official persons . . .

It would be wrong to say that the exhibition was ignored in an organized manner. But those who "boycotted" the exhibition included, for one reason or another, a varied collection of people. Apart from RAPP, whose members were engaged in personal politics, and the REFists, whose absence was to be explained by a quarrel on the eve of the opening, enough people were offended by the poet's "contrary" character. . . . On the invitation list compiled by Mayakovsky there were, for instance, the names of Ilya Selvinsky and Pyotr Kogan, relations with whom were complicated by the polemics that dragged on through the years . . .

LAVUT:

The first day was over. From then on, hundreds of people came here every day.

Vladimir Vladimirovich's mother and sisters came to the exhibition several times. One day Alexandra Alexeyevna (the poet's mother) went around the exhibition with Ludmila Vladimirovna. Mayakovsky took them around, with moving care.

"You must be tired," he said, showing his concern for his mother.

He kissed her goodbye and to those who witnessed this he said, as if explaining, "Well, it's all right to kiss my Mother."

ALEXANDER SYEREBROV-TIKHONOV:

We met by chance at Nyeglinna.

"It's been years . . . Why don't you come to see me?"

We went through Moscow together and kept walking until dawn: he would see me off to Prechistyenka, then I would see him off to Lubyanka.

Moscow was asleep. In the entire city only the two of us, and railway engines at the stations, were talking.

"The devil take it!" he roared, treading on the street with his American soles. "I've had enough of this Pushkin stuff . . . I'm fed up . . . Fame, like the beard on a dead man, will grow on me after death. While I am alive, I shave it . . .

"Pushkin has a long one. They've been combing it for a hundred years . . . And where is my Belinsky? Where is Vyazemsky? Friends? . . . I have no friends. Sometimes I have such nostalgia I could get married! Yes, I'm joining RAPP! . . . We'll see who will beat whom! It's ridiculous to be a fellow-traveler when one feels like a revolutionary . . . Have you been to my exhibition? Well, you see, even you did not come . . . And I suppose you booed *The Bathhouse,* didn't you?"

LIBYEDINSKY:

In February, 1930, I came to the inauguration of the MAPP conference. In the doorway I met Sutirin, member of RAPP's secretariat, a well-known literary critic. He had a somewhat embarrassed look.

"I must consult you on a certain matter," he said. "You know, Mayakovsky came and said he would speak directly and declare that he was joining MAPP. I told him I would have to consult one of my colleagues— Fadyeyev or Libyedinsky . . ."

"What is there to consult about?" I asked, though I was somewhat taken aback myself. Mayakovsky's entry into MAPP made me glad but was a total surprise.

Mayakovsky was sitting on a window sill. I went up to him and shook his hand. Not without embarrassment, but from the depths of my heart I spoke some not very coherent sentences, expressing my satisfaction that we would work together. He replied something in his usual style, very briefly, with a quiet friendliness, with which he always treated me.

Mayakovsky mounted the platform; I followed him but did not go up on the platform: I sat in the first row of the auditorium. Mayakovsky was already towering above the hall, "At the Top of My Voice" was roaring over the audience.

There were about a hundred delegates at the conference, most of them members of workers' circles, young poets—an auditorium which always understood and valued Mayakovsky. The reading of the poem was followed by a thunder of applause.

Mayakovsky's entry into the ranks of the proletarian writers' organization was greeted by the then leaders of MAPP and RAPP with a certain embarrassment; it was as if we were afraid that our fragile little boat would not carry such an elephant. He was not even put on the presidium of RAPP, as he should have been at that very conference.

"VYECHERNYAYA MOSKVA," FEBRUARY 8, 1930:

For the Consolidation of Proletarian Literature

. . . Yesterday's report of Comrade A. Fadyeyev was devoted to RAPP's tasks in the period of reconstruction.

"*The struggle against bourgeois tendencies,*" Comrade Fadyeyev said, "*continues to remain one of the basic tasks of RAPP.* One should complete the unmasking of Pilnyak and Zamyatin. This is all the more urgent since a number of writers (V. Ivanov and others) show serious leanings in a bourgeois direction.

"One must continue to combat the not yet fully unmasked Voronsky theory and its application to concrete literary questions, such as we find in the work of D. Gorbov. One must combat the servile attitude toward the old culture, which has its roots in the Trotsky-Bukharin literary theory . . . Finally, one must unmask the attempts to hide behind Marxist phraseology on the part of such writers as Sakulin, Eichenbaum, Shklovsky, etc., not to mention such double-faced people as Fatov. One must also unmask to the end such a man as Pyeryevyerzev, who acts within Marxism and at the same time criticizes the present stand of his disciples, who turn away from their master much too slowly . . ."

Comrade Fadyeyev takes the view that *proletarian literature lags behind the processes now happening in the country.* One cannot speak about the help given to the revolution by proletarian literature if that literature does not reflect the processes connected with the industrialization of the country, the collectivization of agriculture, etc.

Comrade Fadyeyev takes the view that in the ranks of RAPP there were and are many writers who cannot be regarded as proletarian in the full sense of the word (Sholokhov and others) . . .

RAPP has lately admitted into its ranks Artem Vyesyoly, Svetlov, M. Golodnyi, M. Gyerasimov, and others . . .

Comrade Mayakovsky declared at the conference his intention of joining RAPP. After the statements of individual constructivists, K. Zyelinsky read a statement recognizing a number of constructivism's errors, which objectively reflected the ideology of social classes alien to the proletariat, and put forward to RAPP the question of admitting the constructivists into RAPP.

. . . Comrade V. Mayakovsky was admitted as a member of RAPP.

In this connection Comrade A. Fadyeyev said yesterday at the MAPP conference, "Mayakovsky is suitable material for RAPP. As regards his political views, he has proved his affinity with the proletariat. This does not mean, however, that we are admitting Mayakovsky with all his theoretical background. We will admit him to the degree to which he gets rid of that background. We will help him in this."

SELVINSKY:

Thus then Mayakovsky joined RAPP. That step of his caused a sharp protest on the part of his friends. Kirsanov published a poem in which he wrote that he would wipe the traces of his handshakes with a pumice stone. This caused a split in my group too: two well-known constructivists —Edward Bagritsky and Vladimir Lugovskoy—left me for RAPP. What Mayakovsky could not make us do, while consolidating his group, he achieved easily by leaving it.

ZYELINSKY:

On the previous day the constructivists had their public evening . . . We decided that Bagritsky and Lugovskoy would join RAPP. Lugovskoy prepared himself ceremoniously and eloquently, and Bagritsky rather nonchalantly, as if he were keeping away from something unpleasant.

Thus all three of them, including Mayakovsky, joined RAPP; on the same evening, having put in similarly worded applications. In the presidium, his head shaven, sat Leopold Averbakh, glad, not hiding his satisfaction, flashing his thick spectacles. Mayakovsky was reading—his fingers banging at the green cloth; sometimes he would look at the sheet of paper (clearly he had not yet memorized the poem). He was inspired and angry and his voice boomed over the hall.

> I don't give a damn
> > for the noble bronze of heavy armor,
> I don't give a damn
> > for the slippery marble rock.

Let us share fame—

we are all comrades,

let

our common monument

stand:

socialism

raised

in battles.

. . . Anger and irritation, love and farewell, and hope—all this resounded in his voice. It really shook me . . .

KATANYAN:

When, after his appearance, Mayakovsky was leaving the hall by a semi-
circular gangway, Korneli Zyelinsky approached him and said the hair on
his back had stood on end when he was listening to the poem. Mayakovsky was gloomy and not in the mood for conversation. He gave Zyelinsky
and absent-minded look and said, "I didn't know you were so hairy . . ."

LILA BRIK:

8/2/30. V. terribly tired at the end of the day—tired, I think, of RAPP
stupidity. V. intends to be in charge of a large poetry circle for the workers
of three factories—he will teach them how to write poems.

ASYEYEV:

. . . We had the first and only conflict; caused by his going over to RAPP
from REF without previous consultation with other members of the
group. This seemed to us undemocratic, arbitrary: to tell the truth we felt
abandoned, as it were in a forest of contradictions. Where to go? What to
do? Mayakovsky's responsibility for the fact that we were unable to solve
these problems for ourselves worried and angered us. Should we join
RAPP too? But they are prejudiced and suspicious with regard to nonpro-
letarian origins. Even Mayakovsky himself, when being admitted, had to
listen to very boring clichés about "the necessity to break with the past,"
"with the ballast of habits and false views" on poetry, the proper understanding of which, according to the RAPP members, was the privilege of
people of their own proletarian origin. I remember how Mayakovsky,

leaning against the balustrade on the platform, moving a cigarette from one corner of his mouth to the other, looked sullenly at the man who expounded to him the conditions for admission into RAPP.

So, all former members of LEF, selected by him later for REF, rebelled against Mayakovsky's individual action and decided to make him understand that they did not approve of his dissolution of REF and joining of RAPP without his colleagues.

. . . Only Brik, Katanyan, and Nyeznamov remained at his side. The Briks soon went to England for two months, I longed for Mayakovsky very much, but we decided not to condone his arbitrary actions and not see him until he stretched out his hand to us himself. People close to him did not understand his state of mind. Not one of the LEFists helped him arrange his exhibition. An unbearable state of isolation ensued.

SELVINSKY:

Mayakovsky's accession to RAPP was not received there with enthusiasm . . .

By joining RAPP, Mayakovsky posed a hard problem to its members: he was too gigantic a figure to play a subordinate part. It had been assumed he would stand at the head of poets in RAPP, but the original RAPP members did not consent to this . . . A solution was found by establishing within RAPP a poetry group called "October," which consisted of all RAPP poets plus Bagritsky and Lugovskoy but minus Mayakovsky. In this way the poets' cadre in RAPP consisted of two parts: on the one hand there was the "October" group, on the other—Mayakovsky himself.

Vladimir Vladimirovich, for whom the entry into RAPP had been a desperate step, and who had counted on some friendly warmth on the part of his new comrades, was now condemned to total loneliness, and he organically hated loneliness.

In that period Mayakovsky and myself mutually avoided each other, but I realized he was going through the most difficult period in his life. Meeting Fadyeyev once in Tversky Street, I asked him, "Well, what are you going to do now with Mayakovsky?"

"Why should we do anything with him?" Fadyeyev wondered.

"After all, by joining RAPP he broke with his best friends—with Brik, Asyeyev, Kirsanov! And now what? The "October" group has been organized, and he is not there . . . He is lonely now."

"Well, it cannot be helped at first!" Fadyeyev said. "Nothing will happen to Mayakovsky. He's got broad shoulders."

LIBYEDINSKY:

I was away from Moscow in the period from February to April 1930, but I know that Mayakovsky was being "mauled" then at the RAPP secretariat, and that this was done in a small-minded, schoolmasterly way—Mayakovsky's plays clearly did not fit within the framework of RAPP dogmas.

SHKLOVSKY:

The road to RAPP seemed to Mayakovsky the right one for a man who served communism . . .

But RAPP had already become a blind alley . . .

He was looking for friends, did not find friends in RAPP.

He longed for recognition by the country . . .

Mayakovsky had been tired with LEF. LEF either old or new, was not needed any more . . . But in LEF there had been literary life, considerable knowledge, and ability to understand poetry.

But in RAPP in those years there was boredom.

Mayakovsky had joined RAPP in order to be closer to his workers' audience.

He found himself in still water, surrounded by prohibitions and quotations . . .

I went to the exhibition, learned that poets did not go to it. I gave a lecture about Mayakovsky, about new versification born out of his newspaper poems.

There was only one person I knew in the hall: the quiet Lavut.

Then Vladimir arrived. Still, heavy, he stood there, his legs slightly apart, in good quality shoes.

His lips were large, clearly defined, tired. His hair was gray at the temples.

He stood there quietly, then asked sadly, "Well, have I done much?"

BROMBERG:

The exhibition was to be closed on February 15. There were so many people attending it on that day that the movie theater was filled to overflowing.

A student of the courses for workers by the name of Anisimov was elected chairman, M. Koltsova was chosen secretary.

. . . A letter was read, composed by Byezimensky on behalf of a group of readers . . . a protest against the "conspiracy of silence" surrounding Mayakovsky's "Twenty Years' Work" exhibition. The letter was sent to *Komsomolskaya Pravda* . . .

The club management agreed to prolong the exhibition for another week.

On February 22 the "second closing of the exhibition" took place . . . After the meeting, enrollment for the "Mayakovsky storm youth brigade" was opened . . . The brigade's core became the poets' circle at *Komsomolskaya Pravda* . . .

Mayakovsky looked at every one of us searchingly, calmly, without haste, as if giving us to understand that he was accepting the brigade's friendship seriously and lastingly; he also put down the names and addresses of the most active comrades.

Victor Slavinsky was the most active in the brigade . . .

In the middle of March the brigade set out to organize a Mayakovsky exhibition at the Komsomol House in the Krasnaya Presnya district.

🖅

Early in March, 1930, Mayakovsky went to Leningrad in connection with the transfer there of the "Twenty Years' Work" exhibition.

VISSARION SAYANOV:

In 1930 the Leningrad writers did not have their own club, and the many meetings and conferences of LAPP (the Leningrad Association of Proletarian Writers) took place at the Press House . . .

One day I was told that my term of duty fell on the day of the opening of Mayakovsky's "Twenty Years' Work" exhibition.

On the day I came to the Press House long before my normal hours.

There were few people . . . Time passed, but people still would not turn up. I saw Mayakovsky in front of one of the stands. He was explaining something to a pretty young woman, who looked at him attentively with her dark eyes.

The most annoying fact was that there were no Leningrad writers in the exhibition rooms. Unexpectedly the director of the Press House, Shalit, came up to me and asked me to chair the evening. I tried to refuse, but there was no way out: someone had to open the proceedings, and none of the well-known writers were on the premises.

At last I went up to Mayakovsky and told him I had been asked to chair his evening and welcome him on behalf of Leningrad writers.

Mayakovsky leaned toward me: "Well, you can welcome me on behalf of Brockhaus and Efron . . ."

All of a sudden I made the confession: "You know, this will be the first time that I am going to chair a jubilee evening . . ."

"You're embarrassed to mount the platform first?" Mayakovsky asked, understanding the reason for my embarrassment. "It's nothing! We'll mount the platform together."

Before I could say anything, he moved toward the platform, giving me a slight push with his elbow . . .

Mayakovsky mounted the platform amid applause. I remained behind. Mayakovsky turned around and, in a confident tone he used to adopt with unfamiliar audiences, said, "I declare the evening open. Now I am going to be greeted by Vissarion Sayanov . . ."

I went forward and began my welcoming speech . . .

Mayakovsky began his reply with the following words: "I listened to the words of greeting with some surprise . . . Lately one has talked of me more and more often as if I were a beginner . . . My billiard partners know me better than poets do . . ."

I was standing in a side passage. Beside me emerged two gentlemen, known on the fringe of literature and at that time respected in literary circles. I could hear their loud whispering:

"An old tune!"

"Indulging in self-publicity again . . ."

The next day I went to the Press House again to have another look at the exhibition. The first person I met there was Mayakovsky. I greeted him and sensed at once that he had greatly changed since the previous night. He was irritated about something. . . .

In an irritated tone Mayakovsky spoke about RAPP's attitude to poetry. He had been left out of the poet's commune, just organized by RAPP, because they feared lest he be offended by being put on a level with younger and lesser known poets.

"I don't like it," Mayakovsky said, and I noticed that his left hand was helplessly pressed against his side, as if he had had it in a sling for a long time and was now afraid to put it down. Had he banged it against something? Or did he simply feel pain, like someone with a sick heart?

That helpless hand, in spite of me, attracted all my attention and I could hardly follow the things he said . . .

OLGA BERGHOLTZ:

I will never forget how, in the Press House, at Vladimir Mayakovsky's "Twenty Years' Work" exhibition, almost boycotted for some reason by "adult" writers, we—a handful of people from the young writers' group "Relay"—were on duty literally for days by the stands, physically suffering at the sight of the tall man: with a sad and austere face, arms folded behind him, he paced the empty rooms, as if waiting for someone very dear to him and becoming more and more convinced that person would not come. We did not dare approach him, and only Boris audaciously suggested a billiards game to him. Vladimir Vladimirovich willingly accepted the proposition and we all felt better somehow; of course, we all went into the billiards room to look at "our Kornilov playing with Mayakovsky" . . .

FROM A LETTER TO LILA BRIK, MARCH 19, 1930:

My dear, nice, and beloved Puss!

Thanks for the photographs and the letter. Bulka looked at Schneid with interest and was offended by the other pictures. "So now," she said, "Pussy carries carpet-knights in her lap and has forgotten about us." I managed to pursuade her that you remember, will come and carry her too. She calmed herself and promised to wait . . .

The Bathhouse opened last night. I liked it, except for certain details. In my opinion, it is the first piece of mine well produced. Shtraukh excellent. The audience is ridiculously divided. Some say they have never been so bored, others—they have never enjoyed themselves so. What they are going to say and write—nobody knows.

Here the same people come all the time. No new faces . . .

Everybody writes to you and loves you as always, and some (we) even more, for we yearn for you. Early in April the Meyerholds will probably be in Berlin. They are not taking *The Bedbug* with them, but I do not really object; my principle is: let it rather be enjoyed at Saratov . . .

Write to me, my dears, and come back as soon as possible . . .

FROM MAYAKOVSKY'S SPEECH IN THE KOMSOMOL HOUSE, KRASNAYA
PRESNYA DISTRICT, AT THE EVENING DEVOTED TO HIS TWENTY
YEARS' WORK, MARCH 25, 1930:

. . . Twenty years—it is very easy to celebrate a jubilee, collect one's books, elect a bearded committee, tell five or ten people about one's merits, ask one's good acquaintances to stop chiding one in the newspapers and write sympathetic articles. Well, all this could be nice . . . However, this is not the point, comrades. The point is that the old reader, the old drawing-room listener . . . is dead once and for all and only worker audiences, only proletarian and peasant masses, who are now building our new life, are building socialism and want to spread it to the world, only they must become the genuine readers, and I ought to be the poet of those people.

There are two difficulties here. It is very easy to write poems that would not irritate you. They will be very popular today and forgotten tomorrow. All my life I have worked, not to produce nice trifles and cajole the ear, but somehow managed to cause unpleasantness to everybody. My main occupation is to chastise, to scoff at what I consider wrong, things that have to be fought against. And the twenty years of my literary work have mainly been a literary bashing of heads, not literally, but in the best sense of the word, that is to say, at every given point one had to defend revolutionary literary views, fight for them and fight against the fossilization which does occur in our thirteen-year-old republic . . .

I have been handed the following note: "Comrade Mayakovsky put the stress in your speech, not on the commentary to your poems, but on their direct reading." I have come to you tonight quite ill, I do not know what is happening with my throat, maybe I shall have to stop my readings for a long time. This may be one of my last evenings, but nonetheless I agree that it would be better to read a few pieces for the comrades who have not heard them.

It is very hard to do the work I want to do. The work of bringing worker audiences closer to great poetry, to poetry created seriously, without hack writing and without a deliberate lowering of standards . . .

The fact that I have joined RAPP, the organization of proletarian writers, proves my serious and urgent desire to go over, in many respects, to the work for the masses . . .

Now, after this general introduction, I will pass on, for five minutes, to my exhibition. Why did I arrange it? I did it because, as a result of my quarrelsome character, I had been . . . accused of so many sins, real and imaginary, that I sometimes thought: how I would like to go somewhere and stay there for a year or two, just so I wouldn't hear those abuses.

But on the next day, of course, I got rid of that pessimism, cheered up and set about to prove the reason for my being as a revolutionary writer, as a writer for revolution, not a renegade. This is the purpose of the exhibition: to show that a writer-revolutionary . . . is a man, who participates in everyday common life and socialist construction . . .

The exhibition requires long and serious commentaries . . . But I did not even manage to have a catalogue printed, because one has to prove at every point that the activity and work of a poet is essential in our Soviet Union . . .

Very often lately, people who are irritated by my literary and polemical work have said that I have forgotten how to write poems and that posterity will damn me for it. My view is this: A certain communist said: "What does posterity matter! You will have to explain things to posterity, but I have to make excuses to the district committee. And this is much worse." I am a resolute man. I want to converse with posterity myself, instead of waiting for what my critics are going to tell it in the future. For this reason I address posterity directly in the poem called "At the Top of My Voice." [He reads the poem.]

. . . Comrades, there are many notes here, but relatively few questions. Many questions repeat themselves. Some notes ask me to read particular poems. There are also questions like: why do I use coarse words. Here, for example, a comrade has said that of the words I use in my poems, though I do not use them in speech, socialism will not be built. It is a naïve thought that I should want to build anything out of such words. That comrade was right. Socialism will not be built out of any words . . . Often people say I use the word "scum." I use it because it exists in life. As long as the concept exists, it will also appear in poetry . . .

"Comrade Mayakovsky, why were you imprisoned?"—"For being a party member, but this was long ago."

"And now are you a party member?"—"No, I am a nonparty man." [A voice from the floor: "Pity."] "I do not think it a pity." [Voice from the floor: "Why not?"] "Because I have acquired a lot of habits that cannot be reconciled with organized activity. It may be a superstition, but I have waged so many battles, I have been attacked so much. Today you called me your poet, but nine years ago publishers did not want to publish *Mystery-Bouffe* and the director of Gosizdat said, "I am proud of the fact that we are not publishing such garbage. One must sweep this garbage out of the publishing house with an iron broom . . ."

"Mayakovsky, what is your life story, how old are you?"—"I am thirty-five years old, I was born a gentleman, have no property . . . [gap in the transcript] never did any trading, have never exploited anyone, but have been exploited up to my neck." [Laughter] . . .

There is also a question: "Why don't you go to a kolkhoz?"—"Well, not everyone can go to kolkhozes, leave the cities empty as if there was a plague . . . Instead of plowing the soil, I will read you some of my poems." [He reads his poems.]

NATALYA BRIUKHANENKO

In 1930 I worked as a secretary in the "Klubnyi Repertuar" publishing house. Three weeks before Mayakovsky's death we signed a contract with him to publish his play *Moscow in Flames,* written to celebrate the twenty-fifth anniversary of the 1905 Revolution . . . The play had really been written on commission from a circus. All the possibilities of the circus were to be exploited: trapezes, water, etc., . . .

Mayakovsky liked the idea. The circus technique, stadium, mass show, all this encouraged him to work. He said he would write another piece of that kind for the party congress, to be performed in the Park of Culture and Recreation.

I asked him whether he would take part in the production of the show. He replied, "Absolutely. If they don't let me in, I will climb through the fence and poke my nose in."

VICTOR SHKLOVSKY:

The Briks are abroad. At night in the apartment in Gendrikovyi Alley there is only the nice dog Bulka.

In the little boat room in the Lubyansky—no one at all . . .

I saw him for the last time in the Writers' House on Vorovsky Street. The room was lit by spotlights placed in the corners in such a way that the light got in one's eyes.

A man passed, then another. They carried briefcases. They were on their way to talk about organization matters. A short man passed, bald, his skull covered with pale skin.

He was carrying a large, shiny case.

He was in great hurry: he was going to re-educate Mayakovsky.

Vladimir went by, stopped for a while.

He talked.

He began to praise the living communes, which he formerly had not trusted.

They must have convinced him, obviously.

38

The Finale

The last days of Mayakovsky's life are recalled by: Pavel
Lavut, Victor Slavinsky, Lev Nikulin, Alexander Dovzhenko,
Nikolai Asyeyev, and others. In their accounts there are, of
course, gaps, and occasionally contradictions. But we still hear
the poet's voice in them, we learn about at least some of the
matters which preceded the revolver shot on April 14, 1930.

On April 8, Katanyan met Mayakovsky at the showing of
Alexander Dovzhenko's film Earth at the writers' club. The
film was sharply criticized, by Demyan Byedny among others;
the critics demanded extensive changes; the director had a
very bad time.

On April 9, in the morning, Artemi Bromberg took Mayakovsky around the literary museum attached to the Lenin
Library.

ON APRIL 9, IN THE EVENING, MAYAKOVSKY HAD A MEETING
WITH STUDENTS OF THE PLEKHANOV NATIONAL ECONOMICS

Mayakovsky: "I will read the first introduction to the poem about the five-year plan, 'At the Top of My Voice.' "

When Mayakovsky reads the stanza: "Not much of an honor from rose beds to reveal one's bust among squares, where the whore and the scoundrel are rutting, where T.B. and syphilis"—voices of protest against the vulgar words are heard in different parts of the hall.

Mayakovsky interrupts the reading. He says he wanted to read to the end but he cannot. "Mutual relations with the audience have not turned out well."

Makarov, a student, speaks and declares that the poems published in the collection, *Literature of the Twentieth Century,* are unintelligible.

. . . The poet: "Which poems are unintelligible?"

" 'Cloud in Pants,' " they shout.

Mayakovsky reads a note, handed up from the audience: "Is it true that Khlebnikov is a poet of genius and you, Mayakovsky, are nothing by comparison?" There is noise in the hall; some people laugh, others are indignant.

Mayakovsky: "I do not compete with poets, do not measure poets against myself. This would be stupid . . . Unfortunately we have too few poets. Among a hundred and fifty million people there should be at least a hundred and fifty poets, and there are only two, or three."

Shouts: "Who are they? Tell us! Names!"

Mayakovsky: "Svyetlov, a good poet; Selvinsky, not bad; Asyeyev, a good poet."

Voices: "Is that all? You exclude yourself?"

Mayakovsky ironically: "I do . . ."

Zaytsev rises to speak.

Mayakovsky warns, "We will talk like this: you have your say, and I will reply directly."

Mayakovsky descends, sits down on a platform step; he sits with his eyes closed, leaning against the boards, can hardly be seen by part of the audience. I feel terrible. Vladimir Vladimirovich cannot stand on his feet but will not ask for a chair. I want to bring a chair but cannot leave the transcript. I think, "A Golgotha of an auditorium."

Zaytsev: "Comrades! Workers do not understand Mayakovsky, because of the Mayakovsky manner of splitting the verses."

On the platform the poet replies: "In fifteen or twenty years' time the cultural level of the working masses will be higher and all my poems will be intelligible to everybody."

Another student, Mikhyeyev: "Let Mayakovsky prove that in twenty years' time they are going to read him. [Laughter.] If Comrade Mayakovsky cannot prove this, it is not worth writing."

The chairman hands the poet a note. Mayakovsky reads: "What is the main theme of the poem about the sun?"

The reply: "It is a jocose poem. Its basic thought is: one must shine, disregarding the dismal reality!"

Mikhyeyev, standing on the platform steps: "What do you mean: dismal?"

. . . Chestnoy, another student, speaks: "Many reject Mayakovsky because he is unintelligible. I do not find him unintelligible, but I find him inadmissible. [Laughter.] I think that Mayakovsky is right, that he will be understood some time later, several decades from now."

Kirkun, another student, speaks (he is drunk): "How do backward workers accept the reconstruction of the national economy and, above all, of the particular industrial unit in which they are employed? With reluctance and a certain inertia. The reconstruction of literature, carried on by Mayakovsky, they receive reluctantly, conservatively. A writer must orient himself to the proletariat. Mayakovsky is going in the right direction. But Mayakovsky exaggerates in his work, just as party men exaggerate in their political work. Mayakovsky has written a poem in which the expression tic-tock tic-tock is repeated for nearly two pages."

The poet hastily mounts the platform and angrily protests: "Comrades! He is lying! I have not written such a poem! I have not!"

Both speakers are on the platform. The drunken student manages to shout, "Mayakovsky is little read, because he exaggerates."

The poet speaks very loudly, with rage: "I want to learn from you, but protect me from lies . . . I don't want them to hang all those 'poems' on me that I have not written. I have no such poems as the one that has just been quoted here! Do you understand? I have no such poems!!! [Applause.] I say that all my poetry is just as intelligible as the poem "Vladimir Ilyich Lenin!"

Makarov asks for the right to speak again. He quotes examples of unintelligible poems:

1. "To the Plaques . . ."
2. "But Could You?"
3. "And Still . . ."
4. "The War Declared . . ."

"Does all this have anything to do with revolution? All about himself. All unintelligible."

The poet is on the platform again: "That was written in 1909 and 1910. To pull fragments, lines out of context and argue that they are unintelligible—that is being a demagogue . . ."

The poet reads the poem "But Could You?" and says that "every proletarian should be able to understand this. If a proletarian does not understand it, he is simply semiliterate. One must learn. I want you to understand my work."

The poet is waiting for new replies, statements. The listeners are silent.

The poet: "Why don't you say anything?"

No one replies, no one wants to speak.

The poet: "If you are silent, it means you understand my poems now. I will read you a fragment from "Good!"

The poem is very well received.

. . . In the back rows a female shout is heard.

"What does this high voice mean?" [Laughter.]

A woman student jumps to her feet and rattles away . . . The poet's bass drowns the din. I find it difficult to take notes . . . I look up at the speaker, then at the audience. I ask Bessonov what to do, how to calm Vladimir Vladimirovich down.

The general temper rises. Someone tries to shout something. The woman student waves her hands in protest.

Mayakovsky: "Please don't wave your hands, the pears will not fall from the tree, and here on the platform a man is standing."

Quoting the students' statements, he shows up their poetic illiteracy and says, deeply hurt, "I am astonished at the audience's ignorance. I did not expect such a low cultural level among students of a respectable institution."

A man with glasses in the first row (behind my back) shouts, "A demagogue!"

Mayakovsky, turning in the direction of the shout: "Demagogue?!"
Then, turning to the audience: "Comrades! Am I a demagogue?!"

The man with the glasses does not calm down, he jumps to his feet and
goes on shouting: "Yes, demagogue."

In desperation, I snatch an empty carafe from the table and make for
the exit. Lavut stops me. I am persuaded that such events are not unusual
at Mayakovsky's public appearances but Mayakovsky always wins.

Mayakovsky, leaning from the platform, looks with hatred at the
shouting fool and orders him with his mighty voice, "Sit down!!!"

The fool does not sit down and goes on shouting.

Pandemonium in the hall. Everybody jumps to their feet.

"Sit down! I will make you listen!!!"

They quiet down and take their seats. Vladimir Vladimirovich is very
tired. Tottering, he descends from the platform and sits on the steps.
There is complete silence.

He has won.

The chairman: "I suggest that the talking stop and poems be read."

He asks for "Left March."

Mayakovsky reads . . .

Well received. A storm of applause.

"This march warmed the sailors when they were storming the capitalists."

He also mentions his favorite couplet, sung by the Red Guards on
their way to storming the Winter Palace.

> Pineapples eat, hazelhens chew,
> Your last day's coming, bourgeois!

"Comrades! This is our first acquaintance. In a few months we will
meet again. We have shouted and abused each other a bit. But boorishness was unnecessary. You must not be angry with me. And now, comrades, we will let Comrade Bessonov speak. Listen to him."

Vladimir Vladimirovich puts on his coat in the doorway.

Bessonov talks about the exhibition, about the storm brigade. Mayakovsky attempts to leave unobserved. With him leave about a quarter of
those present.

LAVUT:

When we were in the car, Mayakovsky realized he had left his stick behind. He never forgot anything—either in hotels or in trains. And he never parted with his stick.

In the car he suggested we go to the theater, and insisted for a long time that I not leave him alone. But I felt too tired and Mayakovsky drove me home.

🐾

In the course of the same public reading, just before it began or during the intermission, a peculiar incident took place, connected with an event, known to the poet, which had occurred a couple of days earlier. The magazine Pyechat' i Revolutsyia *prepared an insert with Mayakovsky's portrait and congratulations on the occasion of his "Twenty Years' Work" Jubilee.*

RUDOLF BYERSHADSKY, OF THE EDITORIAL STAFF, RECALLS:

As soon as we received the rough copy of the February issue (it was very late: came out early in April), I called Vladimir Vladimirovich on the telephone and promised to send him the first of the checking copies, as soon as they arrived. Vladimir Vladimirovich answered he would rather call and thank the editors in person.

The checking copies arrived a few days later. However, there was no insert with Mayakovsky's portrait and congratulations. On the same day, however, the editors received a letter from the then director of GIZ . . . He hurled thunder and lightning: By what right did *Pyechat' i Revolutsyia* dare to call the "fellow-traveler" Mayakovsky a great revolutionary poet?! He also demanded that the name of the contributor who authorized this "outrageous text" for printing be given him immediately. At the same time the editorial board was notified that the director had ordered Mayakovsky's portrait to be torn out of the magazine (already bound) and destroyed . . . Vladimir Vladimirovich learned at once about the destruction of his portrait.

LAVUT'S ACCOUNT OF THE EVENING AT THE
PLEKHANOV INSTITUTE:

A member of the brigade showed Vladimir Vladimirovich the insert from the magazine *Pyechat' i Revolutsyia*—Mayakovsky's portrait, which upon the order of a man who disliked the poet, had been torn out of the finished issue. The brigade member described with indignation where he had found the insert . . .

Vladimir Vladimirovich listened, looked, and said something softly . . . Mayakovsky had already known about the torn-out portrait, but that evening the insult became a visible fact.

ON APRIL 10 ALEXANDER FEVRALSKY MEETS MAYAKOVSKY IN THE
MEYERHOLD THEATER AT A PERFORMANCE OF "THE BATHHOUSE."
FEVRALSKY:

He was very gloomy . . . I tried to say that an objective article about *The Bathhouse* (by Popov-Dubovsky) had at last been published in *Pravda*. Mayakovsky replied, "It doesn't matter, it's too late now." . . . He said goodbye to me and went away.

ﬂ

April 11: Mayakovsky does not turn up at a prearranged public reading.

LAVUT:

On April 11, as usual, I telephoned him after 10:00 A.M. But, to my surprise, he was not at home. Pasha, the housekeeper took the call (Mayakovsky had been living alone for the last two months: the Briks were abroad) and to the question as to whether Vladimir Vladimirovich had remembered about his engagement today, she said yes. I asked her to remind him again on his return and I gave her the address of the Second University.

Mayakovsky had never before failed to turn up at a reading. But on this occasion the audience waited for about an hour. Many people came. A comrade went to get him by car, first to Lubyansky, then to Taganka, to Gendrikovyi Alley. There was little traffic. The comrade saw a car very much like Mayakovsky's Renault in front of him. Finding himself even with it, he realized that this indeed was the car. He asked the driver to cross the car's path and stopped it in Tagansky square.

A stormy dialogue followed. Mayakovsky declared that he did not know anything about tonight's reading. He banged shut the door of his car, in which Veronica Polonskaya was sitting, and the car moved on.

We had to apologize to the audience and explain that Mayakovsky had been taken ill and a new date for his reading would be announced later.

THAT EVENING MAYAKOVSKY HAD GUESTS. PRESENT WERE VERONICA POLONSKAYA, HER HUSBAND—THE WELL-KNOWN ACTOR YANSHIN—ALSO ASYEYEV. ASYEYEV:

Mayakovsky kept walking around the apartment. He had a cold and was apathetic. Usually he was noisy, aggressive, crushed people with his wit. On this occasion he did not crack jokes; it was as if he had been exhausted by some great physical effort. We played cards. All those present defeated him, but he made no attempt to get his own back. During the game he was apathetic and humble. That was unusual too: when losing, he made a lot of noise and pretended that everything was all right.

When everyone was on the way out, he asked in the hall in an indifferent tone, "Well, who's going to lend me a ruble?"

I took my money out, did not find a ruble, so I laid three rubles on the basket, saying, "Here you are, Volodya."

He covered the coin with spread-out fingers. We fixed the date for a return game.

When I returned home, I remembered that Mayakovsky had been very depressed. I said to Xenia, "Damn it, when one doesn't see Volodya for a long time one forgets what eyes he's got. And when one sees him again—they seem so big and full of expression, like no other eyes in the world."

🖤

April 12: Lavut visits Mayakovsky in his apartment; Nikulin and Dovzhenko meet him in the Writers' Federation House (so-called Herzen House, 25 Tversky Boulevard), Asyeyev twice talks to him on the telephone. On the same day Mayakovsky writes his last letter, "To all."

LAVUT:

In the morning I came to Vladimir Vladimirovich to fix a new date for his public reading.

Mayakovsky was in bed. Beside him, on the chair—a sheet of paper.

He was writing something. I stood in the doorway, and when I wanted to approach him, he stopped me sullenly: "Don't come near me, or you can get infected."

I was surprised: he had been taken ill so many times in my company on our travels and he had never said anything like that. Later I realized he had something else on his mind. Beside him must have been lying his unfinished farewell letter. He did not want me to notice it.

"I am not going to appear. I don't feel well," Mayakovsky said and added, "Please give me a ring tomorrow."

I was surprised by this unusual reception. In the passage Pasha once again confirmed that Mayakovsky had remembered about his public reading the night before.

NIKULIN:

I saw him for the last time at Herzen House, two days before his death. He was sitting at a table by the door, in the lower, semicellar room. Next to him was a young playwright, author of a play just being produced on the smaller stage of the Moscow Arts Theater. Mayakovsky asked the author if he was satisfied with the production and whether the play was successful with the audience. He seemed to me gloomy, and he really was just that, but no more than on other occasions when he was in a bad mood, after some unpleasant experience, for instance after a vulgar, unjust article in the newspaper. The conversation with the playwright livened him up a little. Silence followed. To break it, I asked Vladimir Vladimirovich whether he was satisfied with his small Renault car, brought from Paris. I remembered how he had praised that car, primitive though it was from today's viewpoint, for its comfort and durability. I thought Mayakovsky would react to it, that the conversation would interest and cheer him up; he always liked to talk about technical things. He gave me a slightly surprised look, did not reply, then said goodbye and left. Through the window I saw him walking away, with big, heavy steps.

ALEXANDER DOVZHENKO:

We were sitting in the garden of Herzen House, both in a depressed state of mind: I because of the savageries done to my *Earth*, he—tortured by the RAPP-cannibal scoundrels and hacks.

"Come to me tomorrow, we will see if we cannot bring together a small group for the defense of art, because what is happening around us is unbearable, impossible."

I promised to come and shook his huge hand for the last time.

ASYEYEV:

. . . Mayakovsky telephoned me in the evening and expressed the wish that I invite Yanshin and Polonskaya . . . They never visited me and I did not know how to receive them: there was nothing to eat at my place, and it was too late to shop. Mayakovsky said nothing was needed, except, perhaps, a pretzel to go with tea. I agreed and telephoned Polonskaya, though I was not close to those people, but I did it because Volodya asked me to. They were not at home, however, they had just left. I telephoned Mayakovsky immediately. I could feel he was very disappointed. He was silent for a while, as if thinking about something, then said, "Well, we must put it off to some other day."

VERONICA POLONSKAYA:

On April 12 he asked me to come see him after the theater. He said things were bad with him. He also said, "By the way, Nora, I have mentioned you in the letter to the government, I said I considered you my family. You are not going to object?"

"I do not understand what you mean. But please mention me wherever you think necessary." I felt he was not himself. On the same evening I asked him to give me his word that he would go see a doctor; I asked him to go away to some rest home, if only for a couple of days.

🜲

These are all the accounts of the day marked on Mayakovsky's farewell letter. To the letter the poet attached a stanza from an unfinished poem, written at an unknown date: perhaps on the same day, perhaps a few days, weeks, or even months earlier. Even if the poem had been written earlier, however, the poet returned to it on that day.

HERE ARE FRAGMENTS OF THE TEXT, REGARDED AS THE "SECOND PRELUDE TO THE POEM," FOUND IN MAYAKOVSKY'S LAST NOTEBOOK:

1

She loves—she loves not.
                    I twist my hands,
I wring my fingers
                    furtively.
Thus,
        in fortune telling,
                        from corolla to stamen,
camomile
            petals
                    are   plucked.
Let the silver of years
                    ring profusely.
The gray-haired
            barber
                    will trace the rim.
I hope,
        I believe:
                    never will come
to me
        shameful common sense.

2

It is after one.
                    You must be fast asleep.
In the night
            the Milky Way
                        with the silvery Oka
                                        is flowing.
I am not in a hurry,
                    lightnings of cables
                                in space
to send,
        will not rouse you from sleep.
As they say,
            a bungled story.

Love's boat
            smashed
                        against existence.
And we are quits
            with life.
                        So why should we
idly reproach each other
            with pains and harms?
Just look,
            what stillness around.
The sky
            is paying a starry tribute
                        to the night.
In such moments
                        I want to rise
                                    and call out
to the ages,
            to history,
                        to the universe.

IN ANOTHER NOTEBOOK, A VARIANT OF ONE OF THE STANZAS:
It is after one.
                        You must be fast asleep.
Or maybe
            you too
                        are going through the bad hour.
I am not in a hurry,
            lightnings of cables
                                    in space
to send,
            will not rouse you from sleep.

            ALSO FURTHER NOTES FOR THE POEM:
to what dog
            under the tail
for all my outgrown vastness

                              I am to find

                                        he was not

                                                        alone

    alone between heaven and earth
    a more terrible insult I do not know.

                    THE LAST LETTER:

To all!

    Do not charge anyone with the responsibility for my death and, please,
do not gossip. The deceased very much disliked gossip.

    Mother, sisters, friends, forgive me—this is not the way (I do not rec-
ommend it to others), but there is no other way out for me.

    Lila—love me.

    Comrade Government—my family is: Lila Brik, mother, sisters, and
Veronica Vitoldovna Polonskaya.

    If you care to assure them a decent existence—I thank you.

    Please give the unfinished poems to the Briks, they will get the hang of
them.

            As they say,

                        a bungled story.

            Love's boat

                    smashed

                            against existence.

            And we are quits

                    with life.

                            So why should we

            idly reproach each other

                            with pains and harms?

To those who remain—I wish happiness.

                                        Vladimir Mayakovsky

                                        12/4/30

Comrades RAPPists, do not charge me with lack of character. Seriously,
there is nothing to be done.

    Goodbye.

Tell Yermilov: . . . we should have completed the argument.

V.M.

There are 2000 rubles left in the desk—pay the tax.
The rest is to be collected from GIZ.

V.M.

LAVUT:

On the thirteenth I telephoned, but Mayakovsky was out. I left Pasha the number of Herzen House and during the day Mayakovsky telephoned me. We agreed that I would come to him on the next day, at the usual time—half past ten in the morning.

VALENTINA KHODASYEVICH, PAINTER, AN OLD ACQUAINTANCE OF THE POET, WAS THE STAGE DESIGNER FOR THE CIRCUS SHOW, COMPOSED BY MAYAKOVSKY, "MOSCOW IN FLAMES." ON APRIL 13, AT FOUR IN THE AFTERNOON, ACCORDING TO HER RECOLLECTIONS, SHE WAS PUTTING TOGETHER FRAGMENTS OF STAGE DESIGNS ON THE EMPTY ARENA:

All of a sudden, in the total silence of the empty circus, I hear an awful, piercing, unpleasant, nerve-shattering clatter, fast approaching the part of the arena where I am arguing with the head carpenter. I turn around and see Mayakovsky, walking briskly between the first row of chairs and the arena barrier. He has a stick in his hand, raised to the height of the first row chair-backs. The stick rattles, jumping from one wooden back to another.

Mayakovsky is in a dark overcoat and black hat, his face is very pale and angry.

He walks toward me. I greet him from the arena. From a distance he shouts loudly and gloomily, "Come here, please!"

I climb through the barrier, approach him. We greet each other. He is very serious and sulking. He says, "I've come to find out the time of rehearsal, I want to be present, and there is no one at the manager's office and I couldn't find out anything at all. You know what, let's go for a drive, I have my car here . . ."

I reply outright, "No, I can't, I have a technical rehearsal, which I mustn't skip . . ."

"No?! You can't?! You refuse?" Mayakovsky roars.

His face is quite white, twisted, his eyes inflamed, the whites brown, like those of icon martyrs. Again he bangs his rhythm unbearably against the chair next to which we are standing and again asks, "No?"

I say, "No."

Suddenly, there is almost a whining, or a sob. "No? . . . Everyone answers me 'no'! Only 'no'! Everywhere 'no'!"

He shouts this while walking, or rather rushing, out of the circus. The stick bangs again and rattles even more wildly against the backs of chairs . . .

I rush into the street and catch up with Mayakovsky by the car . . .

We are driving. Unpleasant silence at first. Then he turns his face toward me, watches me and speaks, kindly, with a guilty half-smile (and I can see he is thinking about something else): "I will sleep tonight in Lubyansky Alley—I'm afraid of oversleeping and missing the rehearsal. Please give me a ring there at about ten in the morning."

He speaks, but his eyes are vacant . . .

Suddenly Mayakovsky speaks to the driver: "Please stop!"

. . . The car has hardly stopped before Vladimir Vladimirovich opens the door and jumps onto the pavement, wildly spinning his stick in the air, so that people scatter in the street. He almost shouts at me, "The driver will take you where you want to go! And I will take a walk! . . ."

ASYEYEV:

On the thirteenth, unfortunately, I was not at home from the morning on. In the apartment was my wife's sister, Vera, who had known Mayakovsky for a long time. At four the telephone rang. Vera took it: it was Mayakovsky. She thought it strange that he did not greet her, though he was fond of her, but at once asked, with anxiety in his voice, it seemed to her, "Kolya at home?" She said he was not and thought that having recognized her voice he would say something to her. She waited an unusually long time, over a minute. Mayakovsky did not put the receiver down, nor did she. He then sighed and having said, "Well, it means that nothing can be done," he hung up. Vera was surprised and immediately told my wife, "What's the matter with this Mayakovsky, he didn't say hello, asked about Kolya, kept silent for a while and put the receiver down." My wife told me about all this when I came back home late at night. I had to finish some work on a deadline, I sat up late, till about 5:00 A.M. . . .

VERONICA POLONSKAYA:

On the evening of the thirteenth . . . Mayakovsky visited Valentin Katayev. Vladimir Vladimirovich was very glum, irritable . . .

KATAYEV:

My memory has not retained almost anything of the—so important—details of that evening, except Mayakovsky's big hand, his nervously moving fingers; I had them all the time before my eyes, next to me: they dipped mechanically into a bearskin, tore at it, nibbled at it, while his eyes strained across the table to Nora Polonskaya . . . very young, charming, fair-haired, with little dimples in her pink cheeks . . .

With a slightly frightened smile she was scribbling—on little bits of cardboard torn out of a chocolate box—her replies to Mayakovsky's notes which he threw her from time to time across the table, with the gesture of a roulette player . . . The cardboard squares flew across the table, over a dish of meatballs, and back again, until the chocolate box was completely destroyed. Then Mayakovsky and Nora went into my room. Tearing shreds of paper from anything they could lay their hands on, they continued their hurried correspondence, reminding one of a silent mortal duel . . .

At three in the morning the guests . . . began to disperse . . .

Livanov, in Moscow fashion, kissed me goodbye, as Mayakovsky was handing Nora her coat. On seeing Livanov and me kissing, he crept between us, jealously pushed Livanov away and, leaning, brought his long face, with protruding cheekbones, which in the semidarkness of the hall seemed huge and dark like iron, close to me . . . He looked into my eyes, as if through magnifying glasses, with a hurried affection and desperation —and I felt the touch of his unshaven cheek on my face. Then he kissed me with his large public speaker's lips, not fit for kisses, and said—for the first time using the familiar second person form we had never used before —which seemed to me terribly strange, "Don't be sad. Goodbye, old man."

And all at once—big, clumsy, the hat pulled over his eyes, his neck wrapped in a scarf—he went out, following Nora Polonskaya down the dark, unlit staircase . . .

ON APRIL 14, IN THE MORNING, THE LAST CONVERSATION BE-
TWEEN MAYAKOVSKY AND VERONICA POLONSKAYA TOOK PLACE
IN THE POET'S ROOM IN LUBYANSKY ALLEY. VICTOR PYERTSOV'S
ACCOUNT, BASED ON POLONSKAYA'S RECOLLECTIONS:

Mayakovsky was in a very bad way, demanded of Polonskaya that she
remain with him, not leave the room, but she was in a hurry for a rehearsal of the new play *Our Youth,* in which for the first time she had a
big part . . . At the Moscow Arts Theater there was strict discipline, an
actress could not be late. Mayakovsky was angry, insisted on her not going
to the rehearsal. She tried to explain why she considered it impossible to
give up work in the theater.

When one has learned in life such an interesting work as that of the Arts
Theater, it is impossible to become just one's husband's wife, even if he
should be as great a man as Mayakovsky . . .

. . . I went out, walked a few steps to the front door. I heard a shot.
My legs gave way under me, I began to shout and rave about the corridor;
I could not make myself open the door to the room . . .

*On April 14, 1930, at 10:15 a.m., Mayakovsky shot himself in
his room in Lubyansky Alley, with the revolver which twelve
years before had served him as a prop in the film* Not for
Money Born.

He was lying on his side, face to the wall, stern, big, under the sheet reaching up to his chin, with his mouth half-open, as if asleep. Proudly turned
away from everyone, even lying here, even asleep thus, he was stubbornly
tearing himself away and going somewhere. His face restored the time
when he called himself the beautiful twenty-two-year-old, because death
had stiffened the facial expression, which hardly ever gets into its clutches.
It was the expression with which one begins life, not the one to end it . . .

♟ Notes ♟

1. CHILDHOOD. The recollections of the poet's mother—from A. A. Mayakov-skaya, *The Childhood and Youth of Vladimir Mayakovsky* (Moscow-Leningrad, 1953).

2. POLITICS. Fragments of Vladimir Mayakovsky's autobiography, *I Myself*—according to the latest Russian edition of collected works (Moscow, 1955–1961). Others texts by Mayakovsky are also quoted from this edition, un-less another source is specified.

Recollections of the poet's sister and the letters to her which are quoted have been taken from L. V. Mayakovskaya, *Lived Through* (Tbilisi, 1957). The reminiscences of Sergei Medvyedev and Isidore Morchadze, as well as the transcript of Ivan Karakhan's reminiscences have been published in the collection, *Mayakovsky in the Reminiscences of His Contemporaries* (Mos-cow, 1963).

Reports and police protocols, interrogation depositions, correspondence of the Security Department and other material of this kind, taken from state archives of the USSR, were published by Vladimir Zyemskov in *Litieratur-noye Nasliedstvo*, Vol. 65 entitled "New About Mayakovsky" (Moscow, 1958).

Also included in that edition is the note from *Moskovskye Vedomosti*. The date of Mayakovsky's admission into the Stroganov School is given by N. Khardzhiyev in an article entitled "Mayakovsky and Painting" in the collection *Mayakovsky* (Moscow, 1940) on the basis of the School's archive.

3. THE DILEMMA. Ludmila Mayakovskaya's and Sergei Medvyedev's recollec-tions—as in the preceding chapter.

David Burliuk's account—in the periodical *Color and Rhyme*, New York, No. 31, 1956.
Pyotr Kyelin's, Lidia Yevreinova's, and Lev Zhegin's recollections from the collection *Mayakovsky in the Reminiscences of His Contemporaries*. Nikolai Asyeyev's reminiscence from the monthly *Krasnaya Nov*, No. 6, 1930.

4. DAVID BURLIUK. Ludmila Mayakovskaya's and Pyotr Kyelin's recollections —as above.
Fragments of Benedict Lyvshits' reminiscences from *One-and-a-half-Eyed Hunter* (Leningrad, 1933).
The fragments by Victor Shklovsky from his diary, *There Were Once*, published in the monthly *Znamya*, Nos. 8–11, 1961; No. 12, 1962, and Nos. 1–2, 1963, and from the book *About Mayakovsky* (Moscow, 1940).
In 1964 a new edition of *There Were Once*, published in Moscow also included *About Mayakovsky;* both cycles, however, appeared there in shortened versions and the original editions proved more useful for the purposes of this biography.
Velimir Khlebnikov's poem, written probably in the fall of 1921, was published in the poet's collected works, Vol. 3 (Leningrad, 1931).
Burliuk's first recollection appeared in the journal *Tvorchestvo*, Vladivostok, No. 1, 1920. The others, written with Maria Burliuk, and Maria Burliuk's own account have been taken from the almanac *The Red Arrow* (New York, 1932) (Three chapters from the book *Mayakovsky and His Contemporaries*, in Russian). In these recollections, written by both Burliuks in turn, just as in the more extensive English version of 1956, it is not always possible to distinguish one of the two authors from the other.
Vassili Kamensky's reminiscence from the book *Life with Mayakovsky* (Moscow, 1940).

5. FUTURISM. Marinetti's manifestoes—according to the Russian version by Vadim Shershyenevich, *Manifestoes of Italian Futurism* (Moscow, 1914).
Lyvshits' recollection—as above.
Slap to the Public's Taste manifesto, and the introduction to *Sadz sudei II* —according to the collection *Literary Manifestoes* (Moscow, 1929).
Kruchenykh's recollection—from the book V. Khlebnikov, *Zoo* (Moscow, 1930).
Shklovsky—from the diary *There Were Once*.
Lev Zhegin's reminiscence—as above, with a completing sentence, quoted by Katanyan in *Mayakovsky: Literary Chronicle* (Moscow, 1961) on the basis of the manuscript in the Mayakovsky Library-Museum.

6. THE YELLOW TUNIC. Kamensky's recollections (with David Burliuk's undated letter), as well as those by Lyvshits, Ludmila Mayakovskaya, and Alexandra Mayakovskaya—as above.
Shklovsky—from the book *About Mayakovsky*.

Laryonov's and Zdanyevich's manifesto was quoted by N. Khardzhiyev in the essay "Mayakovsky and Painting," published in the collection *Mayakovsky: Material and Studies* (Moscow, 1940). Also included there—in the essay "The Cubo-Futurists' Tournée 1913–1914"—is the information about the prototype of the yellow tunic.

Alexander Blok's diaries—according to his collected works, Vol. 7 (Moscow-Leningrad, 1963).

Chukovsky's recollections—from the book *The Contemporaries* (Moscow, 1962).

Boris Pasternak's reflections—from *Safe Conduct* (Leningrad, 1931).

Other material—from the Russian Press, 1913.

7. THE NAME OF TRAGEDY. Reminiscences of Ludmila Mayakovskaya, Lyvshits, Chukovsky, and Pasternak—as above.

Shklovsky—the first paragraph from *There Were Once*, the rest from the book *About Mayakovsky*.

Maria Burliuk—from *Color and Rhyme*, No. 31, 1956.

Kruchenykh—from the almanac *The Trio* (Petersburg, 1913).

Malevich's letter to Matyushin—quoted by Trenin and Khardzhiyev in the footnotes to Mayakovsky's collected works, Vol. 1 (1935).

Zhevyerzheyev's recollection—from the collection *To Mayakovsky* (1940).

Matyushina published her recollection entitled "Unextinguished Sparks" in the monthly *Zvyezda*, No. 10, 1959.

Mgyebrov's recollections were included in the collection *Mayakovsky in the Reminiscences of His Contemporaries*.

Khardzhiyev's information and remarks from the work *Mayakovsky and Painting*.

8. ALLIANCES AND SKIRMISHES. Lyvshits' and Pasternak's reminiscences—as above.

Lavrenyev's account—from the monthly *Novy Mir*, No. 7, 1963.

Both letters to the editor—from the periodical *Nov*—from Mayakovsky's collected edition of 1935, Vol. 1 (the second, also in the latest edition).

Khardzhiyev's account has been taken from the work "The Cubo-Futurists' Tournée 1913–1914." Also Khardzhiyev quotes Mikhail Matyushin's unpublished recollection. Burliuk's letter to Lyvshits—partly from Khardzhiyev, partly from the addressee.

David and Maria Burliuk's recollections—from *Color and Rhyme*.

When writing about financial problems, the authors convert all sums to dollars at an unknown rate, and the reconversion to Russian rubles is difficult. The account of the Poltava adventure was published by Burliuk in *Nov*, No. 40, March 1, 1941.

Sergei Spassky's recollections, *Mayakovsky and His Fellow Travelers* (Leningrad, 1940).

Khlebnikov's and Lyvshits' appeal is given, in addition, by Lyvshits and Ka-
mensky, who also quotes the undated note in *Moskovskaya Gazyeta.*
Ehrenburg's account—from his book *People, Years, Life,* Vol. 2 (Moscow,
1961).
Asyeyev's reminiscence—from the book *Who and Why Needs Poetry*
(Moscow, 1961).

9. THE CRITICS. Lyvshits' and Chukovsky's recollections—as above.
Shershyenyevich's recollection—according to a transcript in the Mayakovsky
Library-Museum, has been quoted by Victor Pyertsov in *Mayakovsky: Life
and Work (Before the Great Socialist Revolution)* (Moscow-Leningrad,
1950).
Lila Brik's account—from *Almanac with Mayakovsky* (Moscow, 1934).
Shklovsky's first fragment—from *About Mayakovsky;* the remaining ones—
from *There Were Once.*
Other material—from the Russian Press, 1913–1914.

10. MARIA. The heroine of "Cloud in Pants," who was never to see Mayakovsky again, married the later well-known Red Army commander, General
Shchadyenko. After the civil war she lived in Taganrog, where she was in
charge of a nursery school and worked in a welfare committee for the poor.
She died in 1944. The details about Maria Denisova-Shchadyenko, as well
as her hitherto unpublished photograph, have been obtained from her
daughter.
Burliuk's recollection—from *The Red Arrow;* Kamensky's—as above.
Jakobson's hypothesis—from his "Commentary on Mayakovsky's Late Lyric
Poetry," *Russki Litieraturnyi Arkhiv,* No. 1, 1956 (Harvard College Library
and Department of Slavic Language and Literature of Harvard University);
Jakobson's letter to Burliuk—in *Color and Rhyme,* No. 31, 1956.
Elsa Triolet gave her account of A. Gumilin in a conversation with the
author of the present book in Paris on April 3, 1965.

11. THE WAR. Kamensky's, Pasternak's, Lyvshits', Ludmila Mayakovskaya's ac-
counts—as above.
Shklovsky—from *About Mayakovsky;* Maria Burliuk—from *Color and
Rhyme.*
Averchenko's opinion has been quoted by Asyeyev in the introduction to
the earlier edition of the collected works, Vol. 1.
Ivan Bunin's book *Autobiographical Recollections* (Paris, 1950).
Other material—from the Russian Press, 1915–1916.

12. GORKI. Bunin's recollection of Gorki, dated 1936, is taken from the book
mentioned in the note to the preceding chapter. Vassili Kamensky's account
—as above.

Pyertsov's information—from *Mayakovsky: Life and Work* (1950).

Maria Andreyeva's recollection has been published in the collection *Mayakovsky in the Reminiscences of His Contemporaries*. Scholars question the date of Mayakovsky's visit to Mustamyaki given by Andreyeva (Fall, 1914), as well as the suggestion that it was then that his acquaintance with Gorki began. It is thought rather that their first meeting took place in February, 1915, in Petrograd (this agrees with Kamensky's account) and that in the summer of 1915 Mayakovsky, then staying in the nearby Kuokkala, was invited by Gorki to Mustamyaki.

The manuscripts of Yurkovsky's and Lazarevsky's diaries are preserved, the former in the Gorki Archive, the latter in the Leningrad Institute of Russian Literature at the Academy of Sciences of the USSR. Their fragments are quoted by Katanyan (*Mayakovsky: Literary Chronicle*) and by Boris Byalik in *On Gorki* (Moscow, 1947).

From Byalik's book—Gorki's letter to the student of literature Ilya Gruzdyev (written April, 1930) and the rough draft of Gorki's unfinished recollection of Mayakovsky. According to scholars, Gorki did not remember the exact dates and the succession of meetings: the literary evening at Lubavina's took place in December, 1915, that is, after their first meeting, described by Kamensky, and after the visit in Mustamyaki.

Khlebnikov's article—according to his collected works, Vol. 5 (Leningrad, 1933).

Shklovsky's recollections—the first fragment, from *About Mayakovsky;* the second, from the article "Accident at Work," in the periodical *Stroyka*, No. 11, 1931.

Natan Vengrov's recollection—in the monthly *Novy Mir*, Nos. 7–8, 1943.

A. Demidov's recollection—in the collection *Gorki* (1928).

Other material—from the Russian Press, 1915–1916.

13. TWO SISTERS. The recollections of Elsa Triolet—from *Mayakovsky: Vers et Proses de 1913 à 1930: Traduits du russe et présentés par Elsa Triolet et précedés de ses souvenirs sur Mayakovsky* (Paris, 1957).

Lila Brik's account—from *Almanac with Mayakovsky*; fragment on her marriage to Osip Brik—from *Literary Heritage*, Vol. 65.

Letter to Elsa Triolet—as above.

Asyeyev's and Kamensky's account—as above.

Shklovsky—the first fragment from *About Mayakovsky*, the others from *There Were Once*.

Mayakovsky's letter to the editor of the magazine *Birzheviye Vedomosti*—from his collected works, Vol. 1 (1935).

The fragment of Brik's article in the inaccessible almanac *Has Taken*, has been quoted by V. Pyertsov in the book quoted above.

14. FEBRUARY 1917. Syerebrov-Tikhonov's recollections have been published in the collection *Mayakovsky in the Reminiscences of His Contemporaries* [the latter in the footnotes].

Asyeyev's, Pasternak's, Zhevyerzheyev's, Kamensky's recollections—as above. In the book *The Enthusiast's Way* (Moscow, 1931) Kamensky gives a somewhat different list of the participants of "The First Republican Evening of Art," namely: Burliuk, Mayakovsky, Gnyedov, Roslavets, Lentulov, Yakulov, Tatlin, Malevich.

Vassili Desnitsky's account—in the collection *For Mayakovsky* (1940).

The documents of the period, such as appeals, communiqués, transcripts of the mass meeting, the order of the day, and Nikolai Punin's account, were published by Yefim Dinershtein in *Literary Heritage*, Vol. 65. There, too, Vladimir Zeldovich published Lunacharsky's letter to his wife. In that publication the names of the editorial board of *Zvezda* are not listed, except for those of Lenin and Lunacharsky.

Ivan Bunin's recollection was included in his *Autobiographical Notes*.

Letters and unpublished recollections of Olga Leshkova have been quoted by Katanyan.

Stalin's article—from the periodical *Proletaryi,* according to his collected works, Vol. 3 (Moscow, 1950).

The date of the completion of work on the poem "Man" shortly before October, 1917) has been established by R. Jakobson in the work already quoted. Also Y. Dinershtein and other students agree with him and are inclined to the view that Mayakovsky himself gives the wrong date in his autobiography (1916).

15. OCTOBER 1917. Jacob Chernyak's recollection—from the monthly *Novy Mir,* No. 7, 1963.

Malkin's and Punin's accounts, Lunacharsky's letter, protocol of the meeting of the Association of Art Activists—published by Y. Dinershtein in *Literary Heritage.*

Osip Brik's recollection—in the article "Mayakovsky—Editor and Organizer," in the monthly *Litieraturnyi Kritik,* No. 4, 1936.

Gorki's account—from reminiscences about Lenin, written in the years 1924–1930—according to the collected works, Vol. 17 (Moscow, 1952).

Kamensky's recollection—in *The Enthusiast's Way* (Moscow, 1931).

Chukovsky, Ehrenburg, and Pasternak—as above.

Alexander Blok's reply to the poll—according to the collected works, Vol. 6.

Pavel Antokolsky's recollection—from the collection *Mayakovsky in the Reminiscences of His Contemporaries.*

The fragment of Nikulin's unpublished recollections has been quoted by Pyertsov in *Mayakovsky: Life and Work.*

The recollection of the actor Yuryev—according to his *Notes*, Vol. 2 (1963). The recollections of Zinaida Gippius, *Living Faces*, appeared as an emigré publication in 1925 by the "Flame" publishers in Prague.
Other material—from Russian Press, 1917–1918.

16. THE POETS' CAFE. Reminiscences of Sergei Spassky, Ilya Ehrenburg, Yakub Chernyak, Lev Nikulin, Boris Lavrenyev—as above.
Vassili Kamensky—*Life with Mayakovsky;* David Burliuk—from *Color and Rhyme.*
Valeri Bryusov's article "Yesterday, Today and Tomorrow of Russian Poetry," in the magazine *Pyechat' i Revolutsyia*, No. 7, September–October 1922.
Kornel Zyelinsky's account has been taken from his *On the Frontier of Two Epochs* (Moscow, 1959).

17. THE CINEMA. Recollections of Sergei Spassky and Vassili Desnitsky—as above.
Lev Grinkrug's account—from the collection *Mayakovsky in the Reminiscences of His Contemporaries.*
Shklovsky—*About Mayakovsky;* the Burliuks—*Color and Rhyme.*
Lila Brik: "From the Recollections of Mayakovsky's Poems," in the monthly *Znamya*, No. 4, 1941.
From Max Polanovsky, *Poet on the Screen (Mayakovsky the Film Actor)* (1958)—the author's own writing, the accounts of cameraman Evgeny Slavinsky, and the actress Alexandra Rebikova, the summary of the movie *In the Fetters of Film*, and notes of the film press.
Gorki's sketch, published in *In the Sick City*, and not republished since in any collected editions, or in any selections, has been given in its entirety by V. Katanyan, *Stories about Mayakovsky* (Moscow, 1940).
Yuri Olesha's notes, "From Literary Diaries," appeared in the second almanac, *Literary Moscow* (1956).

18. UTOPIA. Vassili Kamensky's, Victor Shklovsky's, Levki Zhevyerzheyev's recollections—as above.
Vsevolod Meyerhold's remarks have been published in the collection *Mayakovsky in the Reminiscences of His Contemporaries;* Solovyov's and Golubyentsev's accounts, in the collection *For Mayakovsky* (1940).
The fragment from the notebook of Alexander Blok was published in the two-volume collection of his works, Vol. 2 (Moscow, 1955).
The results of the poll of The First Theater of RSFSR have been quoted by M. Zagorsky, *Theater and the Audience of the Era of Revolution*, in the collection *On the Theater* (Tver, 1922). Dmitri Furmanov, *From the Writer's Notebook*, (Moscow, 1934).

Mayakovsky's notes—from the article "All But the Memories" (1927), reprinted here, as other texts by the poet, on the basis of the latest collected edition.

Other material—from the Russian Press, 1918–1921.

19. "THE ART OF THE COMMUNE." The imaginists' manifesto—according to the anthology *Literary Manifestoes* (Moscow, 1929).

Anatol Lunacharsky's preface—from *The Unsifted Word: The Futurists' Revolutionary Chrestomathy* (Petrograd, 1918).

Transcripts of the meetings of the Committee for Visual Arts Department were published by A. Fevralsky in *Literary Heritage*, Vol. 65. There, too, V. Zeldovich published the rough draft of "A Spoon of Antidote" from Lunacharsky's posthumous papers, made accessible by the author's widow.

Fragments from the diaries of Alexander Blok—according to the collected works, Vol. 7. The "two fighting ladies" mentioned by Blok in the note of January 6, 1919, are Maria Andreyeva and Olga Kameneva, whom Mayakovsky also mentions in his reminiscences.

Shklovsky's, Zyelinsky's, and Osip Brik's accounts—as above. Casimir Malevich's program—from the periodical *Izobrazitielnoye Iskusstvo*.

Mayakovsky's recollections—from the article "All But Reminiscences" and from his statement at the meeting with Komsomol members on March 25, 1930.

Other material—from "The Art of the Commune" and from other Russian newspapers and periodicals, 1918–1919.

20. "ONE HUNDRED FIFTY MILLION." Nyurenberg's and Syenkin's recollections—from the collection *Mayakovsky in the Reminiscences of His Contemporaries.*

The recollections of Lila Brik, Shklovsky, Zyelinsky, Pasternak—as above.

Mayakovsky's recollections—from the article "All But Reminiscences."

Lunacharsky's letter to the Worker-Peasant Control Commission, published by A. Fevralsky in *Almanac with Mayakovsky.*

Vladimir Trenin's remarks—from the dissertation "Contribution to the History of the Poem '150 Million,'" in the collection *Mayakovsky* (Moscow, 1940). Also included is Bryusov's letter to the State Publishing House.

The fragment of the unpublished journals of Kornel Chukovsky was published by Katanyan in his *Chronicle.*

Lenin's notes and Myeshcheryakov's recollection—given by Evgeny Naumov in *Literary Heritage*, Vol. 65.

Lenin's speech at the Metal Workers' Congress—according to the Russian edition of collected works, Vol. 33.

Letters to Lila Brik were connected with the addressee's foreign travels. Lila intended to go to England, where her mother was employed at the

Soviet Commercial Mission, but was stopped in Latvia and, after a few months, returned to Moscow.

Litovsky's unpublished recollections, preserved at the Mayakovsky Library-Museum, are quoted by Pyertsov in *Mayakovsky: Life and Work.* Other material—from the Russian Press of the period.

21. LEAVE-TAKINGS. Shklovsky's first fragment—from *The Sentimental Journey* (1924); others—from *About Mayakovsky* and *There Were Once.*

Zyelinsky's, Spassky's, Burliuk's, Chukovsky's, Nikulin's recollections—as above.

Roman Jakobson's recollection—from the dissertation "About the Generation Which Has Wasted Its Poets," (Berlin, 1930).

Pasternak's fragment—from *Autobiographical Sketch* (1956), according to the four-volume, collected edition (The University of Michigan Press, 1961).

22. "FOR HER AND MYSELF." Mayakovsky's letters to Lila Brik, as usual, according to *Literary Heritage,* except the sixth, whose fragments have been quoted by the addressee in her reminiscences, *Znamya,* No. 4, 1941. This letter, said to be a very long one and having the character of a diary, has not yet been published in its entirety.

Nikolai Asyeyev wrote an introduction to Mayakovsky's poem "About This" in the collected edition, Vol. 5 (1934).

23. LEFT FRONT. Osip Brik's, Victor Shklovsky's, Ilya Ehrenburg's, Nikolai Asyeyev's recollections—as above.

Rita Rayt's recollections from the collection *Mayakovsky in the Reminiscences of His Contemporaries.*

Notes of Sergei Eisenstein have been published in the collection *Mayakovsky in the Reminiscences of His Contemporaries.* There too—Pyotr Nyeznamov's recollection, except for the first fragment, which is taken from the text published in the collection *Mayakovsky and Soviet Literature* (Moscow, 1964).

The resolution of the Twelfth Congress of the Soviet Bolshevik Party—according to the *History of Russian Soviet Literature,* Vol. 1, The Academy of Sciences of USSR (Moscow, 1958). Also in that collection, the constructivists' manifesto.

The diary of the schoolgirl T. Leshchenko is quoted by Katanyan in his chronicle. Sergei Yutkevich's recollection of Mayakovsky—in *Director's Counterpoint* (Moscow, 1960).

The reminiscences of Natalya Rozenel-Lunacharskaya, actress, widow of the People's Commissar for Education—from her *Memories of the Heart* (Moscow, 1962).

The reminiscences of Yuri Libyedinsky—from his *Contemporaries* (Moscow, 1958).

Other material—from *LEF* and other Russian periodicals and newspapers of the period.

24. A RUSSIAN IN PARIS. Mayakovsky undertook nine foreign travels in the years 1922–1929. He visited France and Germany six times. His travel sketches were published in the newspaper *Izvestya* in 1923. His extensive essay *A Seven-Day Review of French Painting*, illustrated with many reproductions, was intended as a separate book but was not published; after Mayakovsky's death, V. Katanyan succeeded in obtaining the manuscript from the archives of the State Publishing House.
Nikulin's, Shklovsky's, Elsa Triolet's recollections—as above Ehrenburg—from *People, Years, Life*, Vol. 3 (Moscow, 1963).

25. THE GREAT ODE. Nikulin's recollection—as above.
Asyeyev's recollection—*Smyena* No. 2, 1939; Zyelinsky's—from *Znamya*, No. 4, 1963; Selvinsky's—from *Oktiabr*, No. 9, 1963.
Boris Eichenbaum's note has been quoted by Katanyan in his *Chronicle*.
Other material—from the Russian Press, 1924.

26. FAME. Elsa Triolet, Ilya Selvinsky, Yuri Olesha—as above.
Lila Brik—from the notes "Poems of Others," included in the collection *Mayakovsky in the Reminiscences of His Contemporaries*. In the same collection—the reminiscence of Vissarion Sayanov.
Lev Kassil's recollection—from *Mayakovsky—Alone* (Moscow, Leningrad, 1940).
Natalia Briukhanenko's *Meetings with Mayakovsky* were published in the magazine *Litieraturnyi Sovremennik*, No. 4, 1940; the reminiscences of N. Kalma—in the collection *Our Mayakovsky* (Moscow, 1960).
Mikhail Svetlov's autobiography was included in the collection of lives of Soviet writers, Vol. 2 (Moscow, 1959).
Lev Elbert's recollection was one of the first to appear after Mayakovsky's death—in the weekly *Ogonyok*, No. 12, April 30, 1930.
Lunacharsky's letter and the information about the conclusion of the agreement with Gosizdat—from Katanyan's *Chronicle*.

27. THE DISCOVERY OF AMERICA. Most of the material concerning Mayakovsky's trip to America (interviews and notes in the Mexican and US Press, letters of Willy Pogany, Consular Document) were published by Salomon Kemrad in the periodical *Druzhba Narodov*, No. 7, 1958, and No. 10, 1959.
Some press notes—according to Katanyan's *Chronicle*. Burliuk's article from the Khabarovsk newspaper and his recollection about Mayakovsky's books published in New York has been quoted by Katanyan in *Stories About Mayakovsky*.
Recollections of Elsa Triolet—as above.

28. YESENIN. Mayakovsky's recollections—from the essay "How to Make Poems" (1926).

Pasternak's fragment—from *Autobiographical Sketch*.

Kamensky, Ehrenburg, Lila Brik, Asyeyev—as above.

Asyeyev, "Weep After Yesenin"—according to the book *The Poet's Diary* (Leningrad, 1929).

Seyfulina's recollections—from the collection *Mayakovsky in the Reminiscences of His Contemporaries*.

Anatol.Marienhof's recollections, *Story Without Lies* (1928).

Yesenin's letter to Shirayevets—according to the poet's collected works, Vol. 5 (Moscow, 1962).

Nikolai Poletayev's recollection, published in the not easily accessible collection *Sergei Alexandrovich Yesenin* (Moscow, 1926), is quoted by V. Zemskoy in *Mayakovsky's Meetings with Yesenin* (*Mayakovsky and Soviet Literature*) (Moscow, 1964).

29. SALESMAN OF POETRY. Pavel Lavut's recollections, "Mayakovsky Travels Around the Union" appeared in the monthly *Znamya*, Nos. 6, 7, 1940, and —in somewhat altered form—published as a book by Sovetskaya Rossyia (Moscow, 1963). Both versions have been used for my purposes.

Pavel Maximov's *Reminiscences of Writers* (Mayakovsky, Fadyeyev, and Stavsky) were published in Rostov on the Don, 1958.

Shklovsky's fragment—from the book *About Mayakovsky*.

Replies quoted here are taken from Lavut's book, from Lev Kassil's *Mayakovsky—Alone*, and from the notes of Alexei Kruchenykh in a stenciled collection, "Mayakovsky Living," Issue 3 (Moscow, 1930) published by "A Group of Mayakovsky's Friends." Cards from the archives of the Mayakovsky Museum are quoted by Lavut and L. Shilov in the book *Mayakovsky Lived Here* (Moscow, 1959).

The quotation in the letter to Lila Brik—from "Cloud in Pants," whose new edition of 20,000 copies was published shortly before.

30. "LEF OR BLUFF?" Reminiscences of Rozenel-Lunacharskaya, Nyeznamov, and Shklovsky—as above.

Katanyan's recollection—from *Stories About Mayakovsky*. Information concerning the Federation of Associations of Soviet Writers—based on *History of Russian Soviet Literature*, Vol. 1.

Georgi Shengeli's *Mayakovsky in All His Splendor* (All-Russian Poets' Association: Moscow, 1927).

Boris Pasternak's letter to Polonsky—in the monthly *Novy Mir*, No. 10, 1964.

Gorki's article—according to the collected works, Vol. 24 (Moscow, 1953),

Lezhnyev's fragment—according to his *The Everyday of Literature* (Moscow, 1929).
Other material—from the Soviet Press of the period.

31. "GOOD!" Zhevyerzheyev's, Lavut's, Nyeznamov's, Rozenel-Lunacharskaya's, Selvinsky's recollections—as above.
Katanyan's recollections—from the collection *Mayakovsky in the Reminiscences of His Contemporaries.* Kachalov's letter—also from that collection.
Fadyeyev's paper "The Main Trend of Proletarian Literature" was also published as a book (Priboy Publishers: Leningrad, 1929).
Other material—from Soviet Press of the period.

32. "BAD!" Ilyinsky's and Rozenel-Lunacharskaya's recollections—as above.
Shostakovich's and Sukhanova's recollections—from the collection *Mayakovsky in the Reminiscences of His Contemporaries.*
Alexander Myetchenko's book *The Writings of Mayakovsky, 1925–1930* (Moscow, 1961). The author does not give the source of the libelous poem he quotes.
Meyerhold's letter was published in *Litieraturnaya Gazieta,* No. 18, February 11, 1964, Meyerhold's cable is quoted by Katanyan in his *Chronicle.*
Meyerhold's first statement relating to Mayakovsky was made in his Leningrad lecture on May 22, 1936, published in the almanac *Poetry Day, 1936;* the recollection—from the collection *Mayakovsky in the Reminiscences of His Contemporaries;* and the last statement—from A. Gladkov's publication *Meyerhold Speaks,* in the periodical *Novyi Mir,* No. 8, 1961.
The Kukriniksy recollections—from the monthly *Yunost,* No. 6, 1963.
Other material—from the Soviet Press of the period.

33. "TO THE LEFT OF LEF." Eisenstein's, Shklovsky's, Nyeznamov's recollections —as above.
Poltoratsky's recollection—according to Katanyan's *Chronicle.*
Other material—from the Soviet Press of the period.

34. TATYANA. Shklovsky's, Ehrenburg's, Nikulin's recollections—as above.
Elsa Triolet's recollections—as above, except for two fragments referring directly to Tatyana Yakovleva, which were made in conversation with the author of this book in Paris on April 3, 1965.
Recollections and remarks of Roman Jakobson—in the periodical *Russki Litieraturnyi Arkhiv,* Harvard College Library and Department of Slavic Language and Literature at Harvard University, No. 1, 1956—in the footnote to the poem "Letter to Tatyana Yakovleva" published there, and in the dissertation "Commentary on Mayakovsky's Late Lyric Poetry." Jakob-

son also quotes fragments of Mayakovsky's letters to Yakovleva, made accessible to him by the addressee.

N. Reformatskaya, author of notes to the collection *Mayakovsky in the Reminiscences of His Contemporaries,* gives Yakovleva a different age than that given by Jakobson, namely 22 years. She also says that Yakovleva left Russia in 1925 to join her father in Paris.

The information about the refusal of a foreign passport is given by Jakobson. The text from the periodical *Eurasia*—from Katanyan's chronicle.

Mayakovsky probably offered *The Bedbug* for publication to the German publishers Malik-Verlag, and for production to Erwin Piscator. Neither these negotiations nor any others mentioned in letters to Lila Brik proved successful.

Taras Kostrov, mentioned in one of the letters and in the title of the poem was an editor of *Komsomolskaya Pravda* and *Molodaya Gwardiya.*

Ludmila Yakovleva was Tatyana's mother.

35. THE LAW OF INERTIA. The chronicle of literary life—according to *History of Russian Soviet Literature,* Vol. 1.

Osip Brik's, Lila Brik's, Nyeznamov's, Olesha's, Lavut's, Katanyan's, Kassil's recollections—as above.

The Monologue of Grossman-Roshchin—based on the typescript preserved at the Mayakovsky Museum—is given in the notes to the collection *Mayakovsky in the Reminiscences of His Contemporaries."*

36. "WHOM DOES THE BATHHOUSE WASH?" Fragments of Lila Brik's notebook—from her quoted recollections.

Lavut's, Ilyinsky's, Sukhanova's, Yutkevich's recollections—as above.

Gamazin's recollections are quoted from the manuscript by Katanyan in his *Chronicle.* Also from that edition—fragments of reminiscences published in not easily accessible publications: Chumandrin's Occasional Sheet of FOSP (Leningrad, April 24, 1930) and Zoshchenko's Introduction to *Platform Almanac* (Leningrad, 1933).

Other material—from the Soviet Press of the period.

37. JUBILEE. Fragments of Lila Brik's notebook and Lavut's, Rozenel-Lunacharskaya's, Syerebrov-Tikhonov's, Libyedinsky's, Asyeyev's, Shklovsky's, Sayanov's, Natalya Briukhanenko's recollections—as above.

Accounts by Boris Malkin and Artemius Bromberg—according to the collection *Mayakovsky in the Reminiscences of His Contemporaries.*

S. Kovalenko's work *Twenty Years of Mayakovsky's Work (History of the Exhibition),* in the monthly *Voprosy Litieratury,* No. 4, April, 1963. The author used, in addition, material from the Soviet literary archives, such as the list of persons invited to the opening of the exhibition, etc.

Selvinsky's recollections—as above, with the additional sentence (in the first fragment), quoted from the manuscript of S. Kovalenko.

Zyelinsky—according to *Ogonyok* weekly, No. 47, November 17, 1963.

Katanyan—in the monthly *Novy Mir*, May 1964.

Olga Bergholtz's recollection—from her introduction to the selection of Boris Kornilov's poems (Leningrad, 1960).

Victor Kin's recollection is quoted by Katanyan in his *Chronicle*.

Mayakovsky's letter of March 19, 1930, is the last of the known letters of the poet to Lila Brik. It was sent to Berlin, where the Briks stopped on their way to England. "The new people, Syomka i Klavka," mentioned in this letter are Syemon Kirsanov and his wife, who, as it appears from the letter, attempted to be reconciled with the poet. In Asyeyev's similar attempts, Lev Grinkrug (Lova) acted as mediator.

The abbreviations used in this chapter—MAPP, WOAPP—are the names of territorial units and hierarchical grades in the complex organizational structure of the Russian Association of Proletarian Writers—RAPP.

Brockhaus and Efron—a well-known encyclopedia before World War I.

38. THE FINALE. Pavel Lavut's and Lev Nikulin's recollections—as above. Katanyan's information—from his *Chronicle*; Bromberg's—from the recollection quoted above.

Victor Slavinsky, activist of the "Mayakovsky Brigade," transcribed the meeting with students on April 9, 1930. The minutes were first printed in the collection *Mayakovsky in the Reminiscences of His Contemporaries*.

Byershadsky's recollection—from the collection *Mayakovsky* (Leningrad, 1940); Fevralsky's—from the monthly *Zvezda*, 1945; Valentina Khodasyevich's—from the monthly *Moskva*, No. 4, 1965.

Asyeyev's recollections from the *Almanac with Mayakovsky* (1934)—with the additional names (Yanshin and Polonskaya) from the later published book *Who and Why Needs Poetry* (1961).

Alexander Dovzhenko's recollections are take from his journals, published posthumously in the Ukrainian periodical *Dnipro*, Nos. 7–12, 1962. We rely here on fragments reprinted by the Moscow *Litieraturnaya Gazieta*, No. 134, November 16, 1962. Dovzhenko states that his conversation with Mayakovsky took place on the eve of the poet's suicide, that is, on April 13, but says that the next day was Sunday and that the meeting took place in the garden of the Hertzen House. This means that the meeting in fact took place on Saturday, April 12. Unpublished recollections of Veronica (Nora) Polonskaya are quoted by Victor Pyertsov in the book *Mayakovsky: Life and Work in the Last Years (1925–1930)* (Moscow, 1965). Pyertsov's own accounts, also included, are clearly based on Polonskaya's recollections.

Boris Pasternak's fragment—from *Safe Conduct*.

⚜ Index ⚜

The symbol (q) *placed before a page number or group of page numbers indicates quoted material.*

Manifestoes, *see* "Go to the Devil!", *Hatchery of the Judges*, Marinetti, *Slap to the Public's Taste*, "Why Do We Paint Ourselves?"

MAPP (Moscow Association of Proletarian Writers), 501, 502; agreement with LEF, (q) 324–325

Marienhof, Anatol, 256, 259, 392; (q) 391

Marinetti, F. T., 38, 44, 84, 93, 112, 149, 379; his lecture in Moscow, 94–96; his manifestoes, 39–41

"Martian Trumpet," 246, 259

Martin Eden, the novel, 217–218, 219; filming of scenario of, by Mayakovsky, 218, 219; *see* Scenarios *under* MAYAKOVSKY

Mashkov, Ilya, 24, 43, 179

Matisse, Henri, 43, 93

Matyushin, Mikhail, 44, 71, 73, 76, 95; (q) 94

Matyushin, (q) 75–76

Maximov, Pavel, (q) 403–404

"Mayakovshchina," 274, 281, 419, 422

Mayakovskaya, Alexandra Alexeyevna, 12, 15, 17, 18, 56, 60, 71, 124, 500; (q) 1–7, 67, 130, 135

Mayakovskaya, Ludmila, 2, 3, 4, 5, 6, 8, 15, 25, 56, 161; (q) 17, 18, 24, 31–32, 59–60, 66–67, 70–71, 130, 135

Mayakovskaya, Olga, 2, 3, 4, 6, 15, 56, 71, 161

Mayakovsky, Mikhail Konstantinovich, 5

Mayakovsky, Vladimir Konstantinovich, 1, 2, 3; death of, 5

MAYAKOVSKY, VLADIMIR ("VOLODYA") VLADIMIROVICH

Chief events of his life—1893, birth, 2; 1899, self-education, 2–3; 1902, enters school, 4; 1906, death of his father, 5; family moves to Moscow, 5; 1908, leaves school, 10; joins Bolshevik party, 11; watched by police, 11–13; enters Stroganov School, 13; 1909, arrests and imprisonment, 14–18; 1910, gives up politics for art, 21; 1911, admitted to School of Painting, 22; joins "Hilea," 29; meets Burliuk and writes his first published poems, 29–32; 1912, co-operates in *Slap to the Public's Taste*, 37, 49–50; 1913, cooperates in *Hatchery of the Judges*, 51; becomes fighter for futurism, 55; episode on Kuznetsky

Bridge, 56–57; the yellow tunic, 59–66; production of *Vladimir Mayakovsky*, 70–71, 73–78; 1914, growth of "Russian futurism," 84–85; cooperation in "Go to the Devil!", 89; lecture and reading tours of southern Russia, 90–91, 115–118; dismissal from School of Painting, 97; begins "Cloud in Pants," 119; love for Maria Denisova, 115–118; writes for *Nov*, 131–133; meets Gorki, 146; 1915, military service, 141, 154; meets Elsa Yuryevna (Triolet), 157; meets Lila Brik, 159; falls in love with Lila Brik, 161; 1917, February Revolution, 173; political activities for art and literature, 175–176; October Revolution, 186; advocates new proletarian art, 188, 192–194; 1917–1918, literary café period, 201–202; 1918, writes and acts in films, 216–226; production of *Mystery-Bouffe*, 238–239; struggles of the futurists, 244, 245; publication of *The Art of the Commune*, 245, 246; 1919, works for ROSTA, 261–265; writes "150 Million," 267–268; 1920, struggles with GIZ, 268–270; 1921, "150 Million" published, 274; Lenin's disapproval, 275; Lenin's approval of "Meeting Addicts," 282–283; 1922, 1923, 1924, trips to Berlin and Paris, 328–329; 1923, completes "About This," 299; edits *LEF*, 315; 1924, writes "Vladimir Ilyich Lenin," 341; 1925, reaches height of his fame, 348; travels to Mexico and New York, 361–380; 1926, switches to journalism, 399; reading tour of many Russian cities, 400–412; 1927, *New LEF* appears, 414; hostility of the press, 416–423; writes "Good!," 426–427; 1928, writes *The Bedbug*, 438; breaks with *New LEF*, 447–454; visits Paris, 458–460; love for Tatyana Yakovleva, 456, 457, 460, 461–464; 1929, production by Meyerhold of *The Bedbug*, 439–443; visits Paris, 464; writes *The Bathhouse*, 465; organizes REF, 468, 472; reading tour of the Caucasus, 469–471; 1930, reading of "At the Top of My Voice," 492; productions of *The Bathhouse*, 483, 486–487; exhibition of "Twenty Years' Work," 499–500, 507–509; leaves REF, joins MAPP, 501–503; loses friends,

About the Author

Wiktor Woroszylski was born on June 8, 1927, the son of a doctor, in Gordno, then in Poland. In September, 1939, his native town was taken by the Russians; in June, 1941, by the Germans; in June, 1944, again by the Russians, this time for good. His youthful war-time encounters with his neighbors had a lasting, though varying, impact on his life. Having come to hate fascism, he regarded communism as its radical opposition. He cannot say now, though, whether it was communism that originated his emotional attachment to Russian literature (particularly poetry), or whether it was the Russian literature he studied (including Mayakovsky's revolutionary poetry) that brought him close to communism.

In March, 1945, he went to Poland with his family, and settled in Lodz. That same year, he was graduated from high school and entered the university; he gave up medical studies after a year for Polish philology. That year, too, his first poems were published in the press, and he began to work as a reporter. He joined the Party at the age of eighteen; he was forty when they struck him from the membership roll.

In 1948, Woroszylski moved to Szczecin, where he worked for a local daily and married. (He is now the father of two children.) In 1949, he published his first book, a volume of poems, entitled *There is No Death*.

In 1950, he moved to Warsaw, where he now lives. He soon joined the editorial board of the new daily "Sztandar Mlodych" (Flag of Youth), then the weekly "Nowa Kultura" (New Culture).

From 1952 through 1956 he studied Russian philology in Moscow and was awarded the degree of Candidate of Sciences, the Russian equivalent of Ph.D. His dissertation was on Mayakovsky's lyric poetry as seen against the background of Russian poetry of the twenties. Working on it he began to collect material for this book. His life in Russia during this period—the time of the Doctors' trial, Stalin's death, the liquidation of Beria, the return of thousands from prison camps, the XXth Party Congress with Khrushchev's denunciation of Stalin's crimes—profoundly influenced him. He emerged a changed man.

He returned to Poland at a time when things there, too, were in turmoil. For the first time, hope arose for "socialism with a human face." Through his work on the editorial board of "Nowa Kultura" and his own writings, he actively supported the movement which resulted in the peaceful Polish revolution of October, 1956. On the outbreak of the Hungarian uprising, he flew to Hungary with a medical supplies team. On his return, he published his "Hungarian Journal" in "Nowa Kultura" and "France-Observateur." Throughout 1957, he was editor-in-chief of "Nowa Kultura," having been elected by his friends on the board. With them, he left the weekly in May, 1958, and since then has remained outside public life, devoting his time to writing.

Woroszylski has published over a dozen volumes of poetry, two volumes of short stories, two novels, and several books for children. He co-edited an anthology of modern Russian poetry.

The Life of Mayakovsky was originally published in 1966. The author calls it "a factographic story, constructed on the lines of a documentary film." A stage version, entitled *Mayakovsky is Dead,* was produced at Warsaw in 1967.

About the Translator

Boleslaw Taborski was born in 1927 in Torun, Poland. He took part in the Polish Resistance, notably the Warsaw Rising of 1944, and was a P.O.W., in Germany, liberated by the Welsh Guards. After obtaining an M.A. from Bristol University, he settled in London. He frequently visits Poland, where he has published a book on modern English drama and five volumes of poetry. In addition, he has written poetry in English. His translations into English include three books by Jan Kott.

This book was set on the linotype in Caledonia.
The display type is Bulmer.
The composition is by H. Wolff Book Manufacturing Co., Inc.
The printing and binding by Halliday Lithograph Corp.
Designed by Jacqueline Schuman.